Published in the United Kingdom 1980 by
George Prior Publishers
37–41 Bedford Row
London WC1R 4JH

British Library Cataloguing in Publication Data
Shaw, Bernard
  The collected screenplays of Bernard Shaw.
  1. Moving-picture plays
  I. Dukore, Bernard Frank
  791.43'7   PN1997.A1

ISBN 0-86043-405-2

Typeset by Computacomp (UK) Ltd, Fort William, Scotland
and Printed by Biddles Ltd, Guildford, Surrey

THE COLLECTED
SCREENPLAYS OF
BERNARD SHAW

EDITED WITH AN INTRODUCTION

BY

BERNARD F. DUKORE

GEORGE PRIOR PUBLISHERS

LONDON · ENGLAND

TO MARGI

Contents

List of Plates

G.B.S. in the U.S.A. Luncheon party in Marion Davies' bungalow on the M.G.M. lot in Culver City. Charlie Chaplin, Bernard Shaw, Marion Davies, Louis B. Mayer, Clark Gable, George Hearst

How He Lied to Her Husband. She tries to prevent fight between He and Her Husband. Edmund Gwenn, Vera Lennox, Robert Harris (*E.M.I.*)

British *Pygmalion*. Photograph taken at press showing at Leicester Square Theatre (London), 4 October 1938. Bernard Shaw, Anthony Asquith, Wendy Hiller, Leslie Howard, Gabriel Pascal (*Humanities Research Centre, University of Texas*)

British *Pygmalion*. The ball. Violet Vanbrugh, Iris Hoey, Esme Percy, Leslie Howard, Viola Tree (*Janus Films Production*)

British *Pygmalion*. At the ball, Liza is about to dance with her prince charming. Wendy Hiller and Leo Genn (centre); Violet Vanbrugh, Iris Hoey, Esme Percy, Leslie Howard, Viola Tree (group left) (*Janus Films Production*)

British *Pygmalion*. Liza receives beauty treatment. Anthony Quayle (holding wig), Jean Cadell, Scott Sunderland, Wendy Hiller, Leslie Howard (*Janus Films Production*)

British *Pygmalion*. Liza meets Mrs Eynsford Hill at Mrs Higgins's at-home. Leueen MacGrath, O. B. Clarence, Everley Gregg, Leslie Howard, Wendy Hiller, Marie Lohr, David Tree (*Janus Films Production*)

British *Pygmalion*. A terrified Liza brazens it out as she meets Mrs Higgins. Marie Lohr, Wendy Hiller (*Janus Films Production*)

British *Pygmalion*. Liza at home, before a mirror. On the wall are pictures of Robert Montgomery and Johnny Downs. Wendy Hiller (*Janus Films Production*)

British *Pygmalion*. Higgins and a cowering Liza, surrounded by the crowd, including Pickering and Mrs Eynsford Hill (upper right). Leslie Howard, Wendy Hiller, Scott Sunderland, Everley Gregg. (*Janus Films Production*)

British *Pygmalion*. Liza and Higgins argue after the ball. Wendy Hiller, Leslie Howard (*Janus Films Production*)

Dutch *Pygmalion*. Higgins and Liza after they argue. Johan de Meester, Lily Bouwmeester

German *Pygmalion*. Comic strip story of film, with captions in rhymed couplets

German *Pygmalion*. Higgins reads phonetics transcript to Liza while bystanders observe. Jenny Jugo, Gustaf Gründgens

British *Pygmalion*. Higgins about to pop a marble in Liza's mouth. Wendy Hiller, Leslie Howard (*Janus Films Production*)

Cæsar and Cleopatra. Cleopatra's music room. Jean Simmons (playing harp), Vivien Leigh (fanned by slaves) (*Rank Organisation Ltd.*)

Cæsar and Cleopatra. Apollodorus on the crane with Cleopatra rolled inside the carpet. Stewart Granger (aloft) and Cecil Parker, Basil Sydney, Claude Rains (*Rank Organisation Ltd.*)

Cæsar and Cleopatra. Cæsar and an exultant Cleopatra in her palace. Vivien Leigh, Claude Rains (*Rank Organisation Ltd.*)

Cæsar and Cleopatra. A centurion and Ftatateeta observe as Apollodorus puts a pilum out of harm's way. Michael Rennie, Stewart Granger, Flora Robson (*Rank Organisation Ltd.*)

Cæsar and Cleopatra. On the set at Denham Studios. Gabriel Pascal, Cecil Parker, Bernard Shaw (*Wisconsin Centre for Film & Theatre Research, University of Wisconsin*)

Cæsar and Cleopatra. Advertisement in unidentified American magazine (*Humanities Research Centre, University of Texas*)

Cæsar and Cleopatra. The men rise when they hear Pothinus's death cry. Stewart Granger, Vivien Leigh, Basil Sydney, Claude Rains (*Rank Organisation Ltd.*)

Arms and the Man. Petkoff and Catherine respond to Sergius embracing Louka. Frederick Lloyd, Margaret Scudamore, Angela Baddeley, Maurice Colbourne (*E.M.I.*)

Major Barbara. Cusin pours vodka into the fire. Robert Morley, Rex Harrison (*Janus Films Production*)

Major Barbara. Shaw meets the actor cast as Cusins before Rex Harrison was engaged (on the wall are a poster, by Aubrey Beardsley, of the 1894 production of *Arms and the Man*, directed by Shaw, and a photograph of William Morris). Bernard Shaw, Gabriel Pascal, Andrew Osborn

Major Barbara. Todger Fairmile makes Bill Walker pray while Mog prays. Robert Newton, Cathleen Cordell, Torin Thatcher (*Janus Films Production*)

Major Barbara. Bill Walker pulls Jenny Hill's hair while she prays. Deborah Kerr, Robert Newton (*Janus Films Production*)

Major Barbara. Barbara gives a sermon. Wendy Hiller, Deborah Kerr (*Janus Films Production*)

Major Barbara. On the set, at Denham Studios, when Shaw filmed what was originally intended to be a separate short subject, an address to American audiences, but which became a preface to the American print of *Major Barbara*. Wendy Hiller, Rex Harrison, Bernard Shaw, Gabriel Pascal (*Wisconsin Centre for Film & Theatre Research, University of Wisconsin*)

Major Barbara. Bill Walker flaunts his victory before a despairing Barbara. Wendy Hiller, Robert Newton (*Janus Films Production*)

Major Barbara. On location at the Albert Hall, London. Rex Harrison, Robert Morley, Bernard Shaw, Gabriel Pascal (*Wisconsin Centre for Film & Theatre Research, University of Wisconsin*)

A Note on Notes

Someone—John Barrymore, I think—compared a narrative interrupted by a footnote to a bridegroom who on his wedding night has to go downstairs to answer the doorbell. One might also compare footnotes to *Time* magazine's boxes, which though useful tend to interrupt stories that surround them. Too frequently, when one returns to the stories, one has forgotten where one left off. True, the bridegroom can let the doorbell ring and not answer it. The reader of *Time* can ignore the boxes until he has finished the story. But both doorbell and boxes are persistent. Their sound and frames demand attention. So do notes at the foot of a page.

Yet a scholar, or anyone else who happens to be interested, has a legitimate right to know the source of a statement. He may want to check its accuracy; he may want to explore the material further; he may simply be curious. To accomodate him, I have placed footnotes that document sources not at the bottom of the page but at the end of the introduction. The reader who is uninterested in learning the source of a statement should ignore the numerals which key those statements to the notes, for they would interrupt the narrative. Notes that expand points in the narrative are at the foot of appropriate pages when such notes might be of more than passing interest.

Another kind of note—required by some, unnecessary for others—concerns the sources of the screenplays, Shaw's idiosyncratic spelling and punctuation, and related matters. These are discussed in A Note on the Texts.

Acknowledgements

In one respect, cinema research has been unlike any other research I have conducted. It resembles a meeting of old friends with new friends who, surprisingly, also know them. Again and again, a stranger who helped me seemed to be renewing a movie experience he had long ago shared with me, whether that stranger was a generation older or younger, a European or American or Asian, a film actor or scene designer, a script editor or motion picture industry administrator, an archivist or shop owner who sold old movie stills. Although most research, including this, is often and perhaps inevitably a solitary activity, this research was also the friendliest and most gregarious I have ever engaged in.

These Acknowledgements are therefore a pleasure as well as an obligation. Several individuals warrant recognition at the outset: Dan H. Laurence, Literary Advisor of the Shaw Estate, who has been more generous than anyone would have a right to expect; Roma Woodnutt and Elizabeth Barber, of the Society of Authors, whose assistance exceeded the line of duty; Valerie Pascal, who unhesitatingly made available to me almost a hundred letters and postcards from Bernard Shaw to her late husband Gabriel; Marjorie Deans, Pascal's Script Editor for *Major Barbara* and *Cæsar and Cleopatra*, who graciously showed me letters and typescripts, and (equally important) gave me her time, even though she was preparing a book on the two Shaw films she had made with Pascal; and Margaret Mitchell Dukore, whose criticism of the first draft of the Introduction was enormously helpful.

For the time that made it possible to prepare this book, I am deeply indebted to the National Endowment for the Humanities for its Fellowship for Independent Study and Research in 1976-77. I am also very grateful to the University of Hawaii Office of Research Administration, whose research award in 1975-76 marked the start of this project.

I owe a debt of gratitude to so many other people and institutions that I must, only for the sake of convenience, list them according to place and alphabet. Some have written to me, some permitted me to interview them, some provided me and granted me permission to use documents in personal or institutional archives; and some have helped in a variety of ways. I hope I have not accidentally omitted a name.

England: The Association of Cinematographic, Television, and Allied Artists; Elisabeth Bergner; The British Film Institute and National Film Archive (and Jeremy Boulton); The British Library; Martin Esslin; Sir John Gielgud; Robert Harris; Jack Hildyard; Wendy Hiller and Ronald Gow; Vincent Korda; Vera Lennox; The London School of Economics and Political Science, British Library of Political and Economic Science; Raymond Mander and Joe Mitchenson; Robert Morley; Andrew Osborn; Julian Peach; Sir Ralph Richardson; Dame Flora Robson; The Royal Academy of Dramatic Art; Mr and Mrs Charles Sharp; *Spotlight*; David Tree; Penelope Dudley Ward (Lady Carol Reed); and Frederick Young.

The United States: Sidney P. Albert; The American Society of Cinematographers; The Bancroft Library of the University of California, Berkeley; The Henry W. and Albert A. Berg Collection, The New York Public Library, Astor, Lenox and Tilden Foundations; Charles A. Berst; Saraleigh Carney; Wallace Chappel; Bernice Coe, Coe Film Associates; Cornell University Library, Department of Rare Books; Donald P. Costello; The Gotham Book Mart; The Walter Hampden-Edwin Booth Theatre Collection and Library; Fred Henderson; The Margaret Herrick Library of the Academy of Motion Picture Arts and Sciences; Sylvia Hormann-Alper; Humanities Research Centre, The University of Texas at Austin; Janus Films; Harold Levitt; The Library and Museum of the Performing Arts, New York Public Library at Lincoln Centre; The Library of Congress; Joseph Maltby; Metro-Goldwyn-Mayer, Inc.; Donald D. Mitchell; The Motion Picture Association of America; Michael Mueller-Ali; The Mugar Memorial Library, Boston University; The Museum of Modern Art; *The New Yorker*; Public Broadcasting System; R.K.O. General Pictures; Gene Tunney, John Tunney, and K. M. Skallon; The University of California, Los Angeles, Film Archive; The Library of The University of Colorado at Boulder; The Wisconsin Centre for Film and Theatre Research; and, to break the alphabetical arrangement, Hamilton Library of the University of Hawaii (and Ellen Chapman and Rachel Liang), as well as Dennis Carroll and Edward Langhans, of the Department of Drama and Theatre, who shared Shaw with me and enabled me to link plays and films.

Elsewhere: A.B. Europa Film (Sweden); Frances Frazer (Canada); S. I. Hsiung (Hong Kong); John Hu (Taiwan); Cecil Lewis (Greece); and Staatliches Filmarchiv der D.D.R. (German Democratic Republic).

THE COLLECTED SCREENPLAYS OF BERNARD SHAW

Introduction

PROLOGUE

In an interview published on 1 Jan. 1946, half a year before his ninetieth birthday, Bernard Shaw was asked, 'If you had your time over again would you write for the screen rather than the stage?' His reply was succinct and unambiguous: 'Yes.'[1] By 1946, Shaw had a dozen years' experience as a screenwriter and had won an Academy Award for the best screenplay of 1938, *Pygmalion*. In 1939, the octogenarian writer evidently saw a future for himself in cinema, for that year he joined The Screenwriters' Association and paid ten years' dues.[2] In 1947, then a nonagenarian, he gave grandfatherly advice on how the American Screen Writers' Guild might help its members.[3]

Between 1892, when he completed his first play, and 1950, the year of his death, a year or two occasionally passed when he did not begin or complete a new play. Longer periods of dramatic inactivity occurred only twice. Between the completion of *Saint Joan* in 1923 and the start of *The Apple Cart* in 1928, Shaw's dramatic impulse lay fallow and he wrote an important non-dramatic work, *The Intelligent Woman's Guide to Socialism and Capitalism*, later revised to include Sovietism and Fascism. The only other such gap in his playwriting activities was longer and his dramatic impulse, far from lying fallow, expressed itself in the medium of cinema. In 1937 he not only did not begin or complete a new play, he abandoned a play begun the previous year, *Buoyant Billions*. During the next eight years, he extensively revised *Geneva*, completed in 1936, but his only new play, "*In Good King Charles's Golden Days*" (c. 23 Nov. 1938?–?2 May 1939), he originally intended to be 'an educational history film'.[4] Until he took up and completed the abandoned play in 1945, Shaw—with an exception that reveals his preoccupation with cinema—wrote plays not for the stage but for the screen.

His screenplays are noteworthy not only because of his age, not only because they fill a gap in the dramatic activities of one of the major playwrights in the English language, they are also important intrinsically. Unlike William Faulkner, Shaw did not write for the movies because he was in financial straits. By 1934, when he began to write screenplays, he

1

had been a millionaire for quite some time. For over two decades he had turned down film offers, and when he took them up, they were entirely on his own terms.

Shaw's interest in motion pictures may derive from his interest in the drama and, as Donald P. Costello asserts, from his fascination with still photography,[5] which lasted from the 1880s until a few months before his death in 1950, when he took photographs with his 35 mm. camera.[6] Yet his absorption in movies may be less a matter of derivation as such than of interrelated interests and developments. In point of time, early Shavian drama and theatre, Shaw's attraction to still photography, and the beginnings of motion pictures interweave. Might not these related areas have mutually sustained and influenced his interest?

In the 1880s, when photography began to occupy his attention, inventors in the United States, England, and France tried to make and project motion pictures. In 1892, Shaw completed his first play, *Widowers' Houses*, produced the same year. In 1894—when he first directed a play, *Arms and the Man*—New York, London, and Paris saw the first commercial appearance of the kinetoscope, a cabinet with a peephole through which a single person at a time could watch photographs that revolved on spools. On 1 Nov. 1895, Max and Emil Skladanowsky, in Berlin, gave the first public demonstration of motion pictures projected on a screen. In December, Shaw began his seventh play, *You Never Can Tell*, and Louis and Auguste Lumière, in Paris, publicly projected moving pictures on a screen. In October 1898, seven months after he published *Plays: Pleasant and Unpleasant*, he published his first photograph.[7] By 1900, motion pictures had become popular in amusement arcades, travelling fairs, music halls, and vaudeville theatres. In 1901, after he had begun *Man and Superman*, he published his first article on photography.[8] During the next three years, his letters, including some to professional photographers, reveal knowledgeable references to lenses, time exposures, and film, and they indicate the large amount of photographic and developing equipment he owned.[9]

Was Shaw aware of advances in motion pictures during this period? Considering his understanding of still photography and drama, it would have been surprising if he were not. Coincidentally, the earliest Shavian movie reference I have discovered is 12 Dec. 1908, two months after he refused to make a distinction between literature and art because literature is a form of art and 'all art is one'.[10]

He found movies irresistible, he confided to fellow-playwright Arthur Wing Pinero in the December 1908 reference just mentioned, and he displayed his familiarity with one-reelers, the activities of the Pathé Brothers, and an experiment in which music-hall entertainer Harry

Lauder made a short movie with a synchronized record.[11] Excited about
the new medium, he told Mrs Patrick Campbell in 1912 that whereas he
goes to an ordinary theatre only with reluctance, he 'cannot keep away
from the cinema.'[12] By 1915, he had seen Sarah Bernhardt's *Queen
Elizabeth* (1912), films of the French comedian Max Linder, and
American cowboy movies.[13] 'I am very fond of the movies,' he
announced in 1927. 'I am what they call in America a "movie fan." '[14]
Shaw praised Charlie Chaplin and Harold Lloyd; admired Adolph
Menjou, Buster Keaton, Douglas Fairbanks, and Mary Pickford;
applauded the American film *The Big Parade* and the French film
Carnival in Flanders.[15] Eisenstein's *Potemkin*, he asserted, 'is, artistically,
one of the very best films in existence.'[16] When Ivor Montagu and others
organized The Film Society in 1925 for the purpose of showing
intrinsically meritorious new and old films unavailable to spectators in
commercial movie houses, Shaw was among its first guarantors.
According to Montagu, 'he used to drop into the cutting rooms, and we
ran films specially in the projection theatre for him.'[17] During the 1930s
and 1940s he continued to see movies, and his Engagement Diary for
1947 carries an entry for July 26, his ninety-first birthday, 'Films at
Rectory Cottage'.[18]

SHAW AND SILENT
MOVIES

As with still photography, Shaw was not a passive spectator. To say, as
film historian Rachel Low does, that Shaw 'refused to have anything to do
with the cinema until the sound film arrived,'[1] is to mislead. In 1908, he
told Pinero that if the gramophone could be successfully synchronized
with motion pictures, a fresh career might open for both of them.[2] By
1912, he had discussed synchronized records and movies with producer-
exhibitor Leon Gaumont, who could produce eight-minute records and
hoped soon to do forty-minute records. Shaw recognized that this
development was momentous, and he predicted that screenwriters who
do not direct their work will be at a disadvantage since the director will be

3

the most powerful person in motion picture production.[3] For a playwright who by then had considerable experience directing his own plays,[4] the next step was obvious. In June 1913, he accepted an invitation to attend a movie rehearsal at Gaumont Studios, which wanted him 'to do plays for them; and I said I wanted to see how the thing had to be done—how fast they could move—what space the lens confined them to.'[5] A month later, Shaw negotiated with the Gaumont Co. to direct both a film version of one of his plays and an original screenplay.[6] Negotiations came to nothing. In February 1915, he announced that *Great Catherine*, which was first published in English that month, 'ought to do excellently on the movies. It is a scenario almost as it stands.'[7] The following year, he declared that if he does 'meddle with the cinema theatre,' he will not sell adaptation rights but rather write expressly for the new medium.[8]

Shaw recognized the profound potential importance of cinema to politics and society in general and to theatrical art in particular. 'I shall not be at all surprised,' he said in 1915, 'if the cinematograph and phonograph turn out to be the most revolutionary inventions since writing and printing, and, indeed, far more revolutionary than either; for the number of people who can read is small, the number of those who can read to any purpose much smaller, and the number of those who are too tired after a day's work to read without falling asleep enormous.'[9] Because it appeals to the illiterate as well as to the literate, he observed the previous year, 'the cinema is going to produce effects that all the cheap books in the world could never produce.' With considerable accuracy, he predicted that movies will 'form the mind of England. The national conscience, the national ideals and tests of conduct will be those of the film.'[10] Though concerned with the immoral effects of continuous illegal violence in movies, where virtuous individuals rather than the law administer justice with fist or gun,[11] he nevertheless recognized, 'No art can have power for good without having power for evil also. If you teach a child to write, you thereby teach it to forge cheques as much as to write poems.'[12] Essentially, Shaw was optimistic. 'Think ... of Democracy when all the great political speeches are filmed,' he prophesied in 1915.[13] But even then, silent cinema had political consequences, as did still photography. In 1913, he observed that newspaper photographs were in the process of destroying the idolatry and glamour 'on which the whole social structure is based. So long as you have a peer or millionaire who is known only by name and by reputation, people may believe him to be a great man, quite unlike themselves; but the moment you put his portrait into the papers, it is all up: the shew is given away.'[14] How much more destructive than newspaper pictures were moving pictures that showed the idols, people like ourselves, in ordinary activities, even if such activities related to extraordinary ones, for entering

No. 10 Downing Street is the same as walking into any house. With significant social impact, as Shaw perceived in June 1914, movies exhibited 'to masses of poor children ... the habits, dress, manners and surroundings of people who can afford to live decently.' By showing a better and more desirable way of life, it made them aware of the squalor and ugliness of their own.[15] Such awareness, he noted four months later, creates social discontent, which carries revolutionary potential.[16]

What will cinema do to the theatre? It 'will kill the theatres which are doing what the film does better, and bring to life the dying theatre which does what the film cannot do at all.'[17] The spoken drama of the stage will lose the well-made play to the silent, subtitled drama of the cinema. Such drama, with ingenious plots but worthless dialogue, can be shorn of the latter. With its scenes rearranged to show on screen those offstage actions reported by exposition, it can become more effective. In the art of scenic illusion, the theatre will be beaten by the movies, which can change scenery instantly and frequently, and show the very locale rather than imitate it with paint, canvas, and wood. Since the greatest drama of the past, ancient Greece and Elizabethan England, employed no illusionistic scenery or costume, silent movies can liberate the theatre by restoring the drama to those conditions under which it reached its highest ground, the path of wit and poetic speech. With the perfection of synchronized cinema and records, Shaw predicted in 1915, theatre managers could bring great actors in well-mounted productions of great plays to remote villages and thereby raise the level of popular culture.[18] Moreover, he observed years later, by selecting the best scenes from various takes and editing them together, motion pictures 'can reach a point of excellence unattainable by the stage. Only, you must know which are the best bits. If, like many American producers, you prefer the worst, and piece them together, the result is a sustained atrocity beyond the possibilities of a penny gaff.'[19]

More often than not, Shaw declared, such atrocities dominated the screen. Capable producers, with a sense of art, beauty, and good fun 'are more wanted than anything else at present.'[20] Among his chief complaints against American movies is that their producers, who 'are presumably all business men', consider that 'as long as [a film] costs money, it must be good.'[21] Hollywood and 'film-factories' manufacture movies filled with 'the stupidest errors of judgment,' including 'overdone and foolishly repeated strokes of expression, hideous make-ups, [and] close-ups that an angel's face would not bear.' They over-expose faces, under-expose backgrounds, and lacking dramatic imagination they waste hundreds of thousands of dollars 'spoiling effects that I or any competent producer could secure quickly and certainly at a cost of ten cents.'[22]

Furthermore, the cinema's 'colossal proportions make mediocrity compulsory.' Because films must go everywhere and please everyone, producers 'aim at the average of an American millionaire and a Chinese coolie, a cathedral-town governess and a mining-village barmaid.'[23] To secure maximum profit, movies have to go unchallenged by charges of immorality. As a result, they reek with 'desolating romantic morality.' Movie melodramas are more platitudinous than stage melodramas, movie farces cruder than stage farces. Movies of all genres contain 'no comedy, no wit, no criticism of morals by ridicule or otherwise,' and 'nothing that could give a disagreeable shock to the stupid or shake the self-complacency of the smug.'[24]

Infrequently, Shaw appeared in silent movies. In 1914, he, G. K. Chesterton, and William Archer played cowboys in a comic skit directed by playwright J. M. Barrie. In 1917, he was one of several dozen theatrical celebrities in *Masks and Faces*, a short film made for the benefit of the Royal Academy of Dramatic Art.[25] In 1926, he appeared in a movie about the handwriting of eminent people.[26] On one occasion, according to a newspaper report thirty-four years later, he acted the role of a chronic gambler in Rex Ingram's *The Three Passions*, made in 1928.[27] Although I have found no account or list of credits of *The Three Passions* which mentions Shaw or even refers to a chronic gambler, a 1928 photograph taken at Ingram's studio at Nice during its filming shows him, star Alice Terry, and Shaw.[28] But one should not jump to conclusions. In 1928, Shaw visited Ingram there to discuss the possibility of his filming *Arms and the Man*.[29]

It was Shaw the playwright, however, not Shaw the personality or actor, whose services silent movie producers sought. In 1908, Shaw and Pinero were each offered £120 to compose a short one-reeler. Since they did not have to provide witty or thoughtful dialogue, the offer implied, their job would not be difficult. 'Now, to you and me,' Shaw told his colleague, 'this is very much as if they assured Paderewski that he would find it quite easy to give a particular sort of concert at which there would be no piano.' What all such offers amounted to, Shaw recognized, was a desire for their names to attract audiences.[30] During the following years, film offers multiplied, and as early as 1913 Shaw declared, 'I am up to my neck in cinematic proposals!'[31] When such offers, instead of naming a specific play and a specific amount of money, merely referred to 'some of your plays', 'one of your plays', or 'any of your plays',[32] Shaw usually did not bother to respond. By late 1915, when Louis Calvert offered a thousand pounds each for film rights to *John Bull's Other Island* and *You Never Can Tell*—on stage, he had played Broadbent in the former play, the Waiter in the latter—Shaw was so blasé about movie offers, he jokingly replied that if the price per play were $5,000 net, if the producers would accept a time limit of three years from date of release, if the actresses were both satisfactory and beautiful, if Calvert repeated his stage roles and Arnold Daly did not repeat his, then he probably would leap at the opportunity.[33] Before the end of the year, Shaw had received so many film offers that at the foot of one, he instructed his secretary to create a separate file for film proposals if she had not already done so.[34]

The figures rose. In 1919, the sum was $25,000 to $30,000 per play, with the rate of exchange $4.20 to the pound.[35] Early in 1920, Shaw was offered a million dollars for film rights to all his plays; later that year, $50,000 for one play, and by then that figure was the standard amount.[36] A few years later, Harry Warner made Shaw 'an unheard of offer,' a statement which may or may not have been hyperbolic, for it was undisclosed.[37] For an original screenplay, Samuel Goldwyn tried a different approach in 1919: £1,000 in advance of either 15 per cent of the gross or one-third of the profits.[38] In 1926, Cecil B. DeMille tried to persuade him to write an original scenario. Rather than argue or haggle, he ended the discussion by calling himself 'too old a dog to learn new tricks.'[39] His numerous statements to the effect that American and European movie makers were continuously badgering him and offering him enormous sums to write for the movies were not exaggerated.[40]

Such stupendous offers were to no avail. One reason Shaw refused the million dollars was that he would be subject to the highest scale of taxation in both the United States and England. But as he recognized, he could avoid this problem if he sold his plays separately and gradually.[41] Money was not his only reason: 'Filming kills a play stone dead, and should therefore be applied to the corpses of plays that have had their run. Mine are immortal.'[42] To put the matter less controversially, theatre attendance slackens, Shaw felt, when audiences believe that having seen the movie version of a play there is no point in seeing the play. Whereas most plays have a run in New York or London, then perhaps a tour, and are thereafter for all practical purposes dead, Shaw's plays are continually revived in the major theatrical cities and also remain alive in repertory companies.

But a film licence for a limited period of time, after a successful revival of a play in a major city, might circumvent this objection. In 1926, the Theatre Guild revived *Pygmalion* in New York with Lynn Fontanne as Liza. After the 1926–27 season ended, Jack Leo, Vice President of Fox Films, proposing a silent film version, made an offer whose terms included a five year time limit and a promise to collect and destroy all copies and negatives within three months after the time limit expired.[43] Shaw still refused. 'A play with the words left out is a play spoiled.' Silent movie versions of plays are inevitably dreadful except when the original dialogue is so bad that its omission is an improvement.[44] To transfer a classic like *King Lear* to the silent screen would be to deprive it of the only feature that distinguishes it from a play like *The Murder in the Red Barn*.[45] In this sense, his own plays are classical; and, 'depending so much as they do on dialogue, and so little on the sort of action that the pictures can give, are not very suitable for the cinema.'[46] In order for *Pygmalion* to be intelligible, it must be heard.[47] How could one possibly film 'Not bloody likely'? he once inquired rhetorically.[48] 'Subtitles,' a film maker might have replied. Shaw derided these as a 'vulgar and silly' feature of movies: 'one of the joys of the cinema would be gone without such gems as "Christian: Allah didst make thee wondrous strong and fair"'[49] To Shaw, subtitles were an inadequate substitute for any dialogue save bad dialogue. Undoubtedly, this attitude toward subtitles underlies Shotover's command, in *Heartbreak House* (written during the silent era) that Mangan talk like a human being rather than like a movie.

Although Shaw ultimately refused all propositions to make silent movies of his plays, he frequently flirted. With one play, *The Devil's Disciple*, flirtation became serious, but it stopped short of consummation. By 18 March 1914, said Shaw, without giving details, he had an offer of a large advance against royalties for a movie adaptation of *The Devil's Disciple*. In May, another proposal came, and a year later still another, which he declined: £500 to £750 in advance of royalties of $17\frac{1}{2}$ per cent in the United States and 15 per cent in the United Kingdom. In August 1915, he reconsidered and felt half inclined to permit the Hepworth Manufacturing Co. to do its worst, as he put it.[50] The worst would be to use his name but rewrite the play entirely.* Such fears were well grounded, for movie makers were capable of carrying adaptation to heights—or depths—undreamed of even by Nahum Tate.

---

* In a 1921 parody of such a worst, Robert A. Simon announced a forthcoming Hollywood film: 'TOOTSIE MINERVA in the Screen Classic Beautiful *A Woman's Embrace*,' followed in parentheses and very small type, 'Based on Bernard Shaw's famous drama of piety and passion, *Arms and the Man*.' In larger type and capital letters for appropriately larger billing came the producer, followed by the uncapitalized but large credit for the author of the film's subtitles: 'A ROLLO B. SLUDGESMITH SUPER-PRODUCTION Titles by Clinton H. Goldsmith.' Among the film's changes, the Swiss Captain becomes an American naval lieutenant, Raina a princess and 'the passion lilly of the rugged Balkans,' and the Byronic Sergius 'Karl von Donner, the notorious German spy, disguised as a Balkan officer.' Improving upon 'blundering Bernard Shaw', the bedroom scene moves from the beginning to the more appropriate climactic end, where Raina removes a $100,000 fur coat, but not before a close-up advertises the manufacturer's label.[51]

To prevent Hepworth's Nahum Tate from doing his worst, Shaw began to write his own scenario of *The Devil's Disciple*. 'After I had written a practically complete history of the causes leading up to the American Revolution,' he said later, 'together with vivid scenes from the Boston tea party, a close-up of Indians, and so forth, I found that the amount I'd written already needed almost 50,000 feet of film and I hadn't got to the beginning of *The Devil's Disciple* itself.'[52] As he told the Hepworth Co. in 1915, his scenario had not yet reached the beginning of the play but was going to cost them £50,000. With the prospect of a screenplay by Shaw, their response was delight, not dismay. So wonderful were cinematographers, they replied, the £50,000 would look much smaller, and they invited Shaw to visit Cecil M. Hepworth to discuss the technical aspects of scenario-writing.[53] Nothing came of the project. What became of the scenario, I do not know, though Shaw may have incorporated some sequences in his 1939 scenario, also uncompleted, to be discussed below.

Since American producers wanted to film Shaw's works, they considered adapting his novel about boxing, *Cashel Byron's Profession*, which was not copyrighted in the United States and several European countries. According to Shaw, there was no such danger, since if the film were successful, a rival could quickly bring out a competing movie.[54] While his assessment was correct in terms of major film-producing countries, he neglected to consider smaller countries, with unfashionable languages, whose film industries were too small to have the problem of competing movies with the same story. In 1921, Czechoslovakia filmed *Cashel Byron's Profession* under the title *Roman Boxera*.[55]

But the novel still interested American producers, who sought protection via the author's authorization. According to a 1926 newspaper report, Jesse Lasky offered Shaw $75,000 for permission to film it, and he proposed that new heavyweight champion Gene Tunney play the hero, dethroned champion Jack Dempsey the villain; Shaw demanded $100,000; Lasky refused. Gene Tunney's different account is no doubt more reliable. When Lasky, Adolph Zukor, and Walter Wanger approached Tunney, who had read the novel, he pointed out that despite its brilliant prose, the book might be unsuitable for silent movies since it had a great deal of talk and little plot; besides, the story was shallow, the people sentimentalized, and the title character 'a soap-box orator bore.' Reporters in search of good copy picked up Tunney's remarks and anticipating a blisteringly witty response conveyed them to Shaw, who surprised everyone, the boxer included: 'Did Tunney actually say those things? If he did the young man must have some literary taste. I'd like to meet him.'[56] He did, and they became friendly. According to Tunney in 1964, Shaw advised him to have nothing to do with the movie companies, which merely wanted to exploit the publicity of their names, and said he opposed filming the novel.[57]

With works that were protected by copyright, Shaw's attitude was different. When French, English, and American film companies used titles Shaw had employed, he or his attorneys responded vigorously. When a Budapest firm, The Hungarian Film Factory, went so far as to use his name, he had the Society of Authors take action.[58]

A far more serious copyright infringement was a musical based on *Arms and the Man*. Shortly after Shaw's play opened in London in 1894, an announcement appeared that the German composer Oscar Straus was preparing a comic opera version, with libretto by Rudolf Bernauer and Leopold Jacobson. Immediately, Shaw warned them against infringement of his copyright. Jacobson pleaded that denial of this professional opportunity would ruin him. Feeling sorry for him, Shaw asked to see what he had written. Jacobson sent him a manuscript copy of *Der tapfere Soldat*, which translates as The Bold, Brave, or Gallant Soldier, a musical burlesque of Shaw's play. 'I did not object to it as such,' said Shaw, 'but I took exception to certain passages which had been translated verbatim from my play. I struck these out and told Herr Jacobson that if they were omitted and no attempt made to connect my name with the production I thought he might venture to rely on the customary privilege of burlesque.' Jacobson agreed to the omissions but argued that if Shaw did not permit him to say that his work was suggested by *Arms and the Man* he would be called a plagiarist. Shaw told him to do as he liked provided he did not implicate Shaw in his musical, which Shaw disliked. Published in 1908, *Der tapfere Soldat* was produced in 1909. In 1910, in a translation by Stanislaus Stange entitled *The Chocolate Soldier*, it was staged in London. Although the title change tended to identify the work with Shaw's play, Shaw assumed that the musical was a faithful translation with the promised omissions. He took no action.[59]

In July 1925, Jesse Arnold Levinson, an American attorney, visited Shaw's Adelphi Terrace flat to discuss his plan to purchase an option on exclusive world film rights to *Der tapfere Soldat*. Blanche Patch, Shaw's secretary, outlined Shaw's point of view and on July 14, at Shaw's instruction, reiterated it in a letter to Levinson: *The Chocolate Soldier* and *Arms and the Man* are two distinct plays; if *The Chocolate Soldier* were filmed, nothing must be quoted from *Arms and the Man* and Shaw's name must not be used in connection with it, or he would prosecute. On the basis of these statements, Levinson bought the option in August. In September, the Theatre Guild launched a successful revival of *Arms and the Man*. In October, Levinson exercised his option.[60]

In January 1926, Shaw read *The Chocolate Soldier* for the first time, to discover that Stange, whose English title makes no sense except in reference to the contents of *Arms and the Man*, reinserted the very plagiarisms whose omission Shaw had stipulated for Jacobson. To make a silent movie of this comic opera, Shaw recognized, would be impossible without reproducing substantial portions of his play.[61] He therefore cabled his American attorneys, Stern & Reubens, that any film entitled *The Chocolate Soldier* or based on the libretto of *Der tapfere Soldat* would infringe his copyright and should be prosecuted.[62] When Levinson attempted to negotiate a movie version of *The Chocolate Soldier* with First National Pictures, Stern & Reubens, on 18 Feb. 1926, relayed Shaw's message to them. Levinson then returned to England and sued Shaw to prevent him from claiming that a film called *The Chocolate Soldier* would infringe his copyright on *Arms and the Man*, to declare that Levinson was entitled to produce such a film with the stipulations mentioned in Blanche Patch's letter, and to restrain Shaw from interfering with any such production or planned production.[63] In defence, Shaw pointed out that his secretary had no authority to deal with his literary property but her statement that *Arms and the Man* and *The Chocolate Soldier* were

> two distinct plays refers to my habitual insistence that 'Arms and the Man' is technically a classical comedy and the 'Chocolate Soldier' an opera bouffe for which I am in no way responsible. Such a statement could not be taken by a qualified dealer in copyright to exclude the possibility of infringement. Mozart's opera Le Nozze di Figaro is a musical setting of Beaumarchais' comedy Le Mariage de Figaro, and would be a gross infringement of its copyright if the two works were modern; but they are widely different works. Thomas Lodge's novel 'Rosalynde' and Shakespeare's play 'As You Like It' are equally distinct works *but Shakespeare's story is lifted incident by incident from Lodge's novel*, and would be quite illegal to-day.[64]

In March 1927, the judge decided in Shaw's favour. Although Shaw's authorized biographer maintains that the judge awarded £800 to Shaw, who made no effort to collect it, Shaw himself said that his legal victory cost him £1,000 and concluded, 'It is cheaper to buy off plaintiffs than to contest their actions.'[65]

THE ARRIVAL OF SOUND

As Hollywood attempted to capture *Cashel Byron's Profession* and Gene Tunney, and as the courts ruled against Levinson and for Shaw, the era of silent movies was drawing to a close. Before the first world war, as we have seen, Shaw was familiar with experiments in synchronizing records and movies. With the development of radio broadcasting, such experiments accelerated. 1920 saw the beginning of commercial broadcasting in the United States, 1922 the founding of the BBC. Also in 1922, Günther Vogt, Josef Masolle, and Erich Engel, who would later direct Shaw's *Pygmalion* for German cinema, patented a system of talking films. In 1926 came demonstrations of several inventions that synchronized sound and pictures, such as Warner Brothers' Vitaphone Corporation in America and the DeForest Phonofilm Company in England.[1]

In October 1926, in Italy, Shaw participated in a short film interview, with synchronized film and phonograph.[2] In December, back in England, he saw a demonstration of Phonofilms and seriously considered permitting the DeForest company to film a scene from *Saint Joan*. But he proceeded cautiously.[3] During the week of 18 July 1927, he, Sybil Thorndike, and her husband Lewis Casson, made a five-minute phonofilm in which they discussed a film version of *Saint Joan*[4] (three years earlier, she had played the title role in its London premiere, codirected by Shaw and Casson). Because Shaw was wleased with this phonofilm, he permitted the DeForest company to film the cathedral scene of *Saint Joan*. If he considered it successful, he would permit the filming of more scenes from the play. On 27 July, in a small studio located under a railway arch in South London, Sybil Thorndike played in the first movie version of a Shaw play.* The scene was produced by Vivian Van Dam and directed by Widgey Newman.[5] It was the only scene to be filmed.

On 6 Oct. 1927, America saw the premiere of what is commonly regarded—Vitaphone, Phonofilms, and other experiments notwithstanding—as the first talking movie, Warner Brothers' *The Jazz Singer*, starring Al Jolson. Shaw was undoubtedly aware of this momentous development. On 28 Nov. he told Augustin Hamon, his French translator, that he had seen and heard the Italian dictator Benito Mussolini in a Movietone News talkie. Repeating his prophecy of a dozen years before, he insisted that the political ramifications of talkies were enormous.[6]

* For credits of movies based on screenplays written or supervised by Shaw, see Appendix A.

In June 1928, he made the first of many appearances in a Movietone newsreel.[7] Casually walking in his garden, he pretended to catch sight of the audience: 'Oh, ladies! Well, this is a surprise! Have you all come to see me, ladies and gentlemen? Well, I should never have expected this.' Disarmingly, he told them he was really a harmless, kindly person, though sometimes he could appear ferocious, whereupon his face changed from genial to fierce. This, said he, perhaps recalling the Movietone he told Hamon about, was his 'Mussolini stunt.' Concluding his performance with a 'good night', he paused to consider that since the audience might see him at a matinee, 'call it good afternoon, good day, and anyhow, goodbye and good luck.'[8] Soon after, he told an interviewer he would probably appear in lots of movies—taking roles away not only from Ramon Navarro and Ronald Colman, but also from Clara Bow and Greta Garbo.[9]

With the advent of sound, Shaw reconsidered his refusals to have his plays turned into movies. The screen's silence, he announced, 'was the only reason I did not permit the filming of my plays, because their greatest strength was in their dialogue.'[10] As he asserted on many occasions, 'I have no objection on earth to have my plays filmed.'[11]

Talking pictures have not only come to stay, Shaw shrewdly perceived in 1930, they are already superseding the theatre.[12] The relationship between a talkie and a stage play is that of a Rolls Royce and a Victorian four-wheeler: 'It just plays it off the stage when it is well handled.'[13] Provincial audiences will not be satisfied with a low-budget touring company of a play when they can see a high-budget talkie, and they 'won't accept third-rate actors when they can see and hear "stars" on the screen.' The theatre will remain as a training ground for actors and for the public, who would learn to appreciate the experiments of dramatic pioneers.[14]

Among the first stars to visit Shaw after the advent of sound was Pola Negri, who in 1928 was looking for an appropriate vehicle for her British film debut. 'It seemed perfectly reasonable,' says she, 'that if one wanted the best drama, one went to the best dramatist.' When she did, Shaw invited her to lunch, where another guest, Sir Almroth Wright, the model for Ridgeon in *The Doctor's Dilemma*, wagged his finger at her and said her place was in the home. When Miss Negri looked up at him and with mock naïveté asked in whose home he would suggest, Shaw was delighted. According to her, he immediately proposed to let her film *Cæsar and Cleopatra*.[15] Going further, the press reported he might alter the play to suit the film medium.[16] Blanch Patch, however, attests that the affair was a crude trial balloon intended by Shaw 'to attract Hollywood's attention to the film possibilities of *Cæsar and Cleopatra*.'[17] In either case, nothing came of it. As Shaw cautioned Siegfried Trebitsch, who seized the opportunity to ask Shaw to interest the star in his own play, *Jitta's Atonement*, which Shaw had translated into English, one should not believe everything one reads in the newspapers.[18]

Celebrities and non-celebrities visited Shaw. Mary Pickford tried to acquire film rights to *Cæsar and Cleopatra*—in vain, for Shaw feared she would alter his play significantly.[19] Widgey Newman, Phonofilms' director of the cathedral scene of *Saint Joan*, sought permission to film the entire play.[20] Directors and studio executives badgered Shaw. Anthony Asquith, who in 1938 would codirect *Pygmalion* in England, approached Shaw in 1929 about directing it for Paramount in America, but while Shaw encouraged him, nothing developed.[21] Nor did anything come of proposals that G. W. Pabst direct *Mrs. Warren's Profession*, that Carl Laemmle of Universal produce *Cashel Byron's Profession*, or that Warner Brothers produce it.[22]

Although sound movies could accomodate Shavian drama, they did not immediately do so. What stood in the way were movie makers, who had not yet discovered that 'talkies are not movies with spoken sub-titles and that dramas are not children's picture books.'[23] In the typical Hollywood product, said Shaw, 'The photography is good, the acting is good, the expenditure is extravagant; but the attempt to tell a story is pitiable: the people expend tons of energy jumping in and out of automobiles, knocking at doors, running up and downstairs, opening and shutting doors, drawing automatics, being arrested and tried for inexplicable crimes, with intervals of passionate kissing'—all to no dramatic purpose.[24]

According to him, the only use that film studios had for a play was to cut it and rearrange its scenes so that actors could mainly be seen and occasionally be heard. What was necessary was 'a race of artistic producers who understand the new technique ... and who know good work from bad when they see and hear it, *and who don't prefer the bad*.'[25] As for Hollywood, 'When it gets a good bit of stuff, it takes infinite pains to drag it down to its own level, firmly believing, of course, that it is improving it all the time.'[26]

As Shaw told an interviewer in 1929, he would not permit his plays to be filmed unless he were satisfied that their producer knew his job.[27] Knowing his job meant agreeing with Shaw, whose theories of cinema differ from those of most film theorists and practitioners. In the conventional view of cinema, the function of dialogue is minimal: the sparser the better. Once dialogue has conveyed the necessary information, it can stop, for it has fulfilled its function. The camera, not language, is primary. In 1936, in a discussion that followed a Shavian lecture on motion pictures, an unidentified speaker articulated this notion: 'The main function of the screen is to relate the stories in terms of moving images. Strictly speaking, speech should be secondary, whereas on the stage speech is primary. Otherwise the film may tend to become a photographic replica of a stage play. The screen should tend to sever its connection with the stage.' To the contrary, replied Shaw, one need not change the setting with every other speech. By means of camera and editing, one can obtain all the variety one wishes within a single room. To regard talking movies in terms of losing the movement once you emphasize the talk is to miss the point. Drama on film 'must hold the audience as drama.' In Shaw's heretical view, one must 'keep the camera in its place' and not permit the photographer to 'get the upper hand'. When you film the work of a writer who has mastered the art of dramatic dialogue, 'You have to remember ... that you are ... not giving an exhibition of photography.'[28] To put Shaw's heterodox idea in somewhat different terms:

> There is an enormous amount of nonsense talked about what is or is not 'cinematic,' and when a film is an adaptation of a play, there are some who jump to the conclusion that it cannot be true 'cinema', that it must be 'just a photographed play' ... unless the scenes in the play are given visual movement which extends beyond the limits imposed by the stage set. Such people believe that if you have a scene in a play where two people are sitting talking to each other, the only escape from the theatrical medium is to start the dialogue in the room, get them to move out, dissolve to them on top of a bus, dissolve to them on ... the Underground and finish them in a punt on the river. By doing this they believe they have translated a theatrical scene into film terms by giving it the kind of movement which is impossible in the theatre.
>
> This, of course, is a complete misunderstanding, both of the nature of dramatic movement and the fundamental difference between the theatre and the cinema. It is true that sometimes such movement is appropriate ... but more often, the dramatic movement is in the growing tension between the two characters and depends on the ebb and flow of the dialogue. If you impose visual movement which neither accompanies the dialogue nor adds point to it by its very incongruity, especially movement which involves dissolving from one setting to another, you will find you have slowed down the real movement of the scene if not destroyed it altogether. It is perfectly possible to film a scenario out of a play without altering one comma, or adding one movement, and yet have achieved the necessary translation from one medium to another.

The author of these words is not Shaw but a major British film director, Anthony Asquith, who published them twenty-three years after Shaw's discussion of talkies.[29]

Shaw did not issue blanket objections to changes of locale or additional scenes. He recognized they were sometimes necessary. He objected only when they were useless or irrelevant, and he rejected what seemed to be a rule of Hollywood movies, 'that ninety-five per cent of a film must consist of going up and down stairs and getting in and out of motor cars. Not even the success of Chaplin has taught them that staircases are not interesting unless the hero falls down them. My plays do not depend on staircases for their interest. I am therefore told that I do not understand the art of the screen.'[30] What they do depend on is dramatic dialogue: 'not ... occasional remarks to illustrate pictures, but ... verbal fencing matches between protagonists and antagonists, whose thrusts and ripostes, parries and passados, follow one another much more closely than thunder follows lightning.' The notion of cutting half his dialogue and filling the gaps with changes of scenery seemed to Hollywood indispensable, to Shaw ridiculous.[31]

Common sense would seem to dictate that if one were to film a Shaw play, one would make the most rather than the least of Shavian assets, such as language. Such common sense, however, was uncommon among movie makers who wanted to film Shavian plays. Among those directors who understood Shavian drama was Anthony Asquith (his responsibility for the success of the British *Pygmalion* will be discussed later):

> The heart of a Shaw scene is nearly always a verbal one. ... It is almost impossible to break up such scenes into small sections without destroying the general rhythm and also making it far harder for the actors. ...
>
> Generally speaking, with Shaw I try to make the visual flow and emphasis correspond to the rhythm and sense of the dialogue ... to concentrate the attention [of] the audience on what is being said. This does not, of course, mean that I never use individual silent reactions from characters who are not speaking.[32]

The typical view is Robert C. Roman's, that 'Shaw's plays, in their original form, are unsuited to the screen.' To make them suitable, the adapter must invent action, which is minimal in Shaw's plays. Equally important, the adapter must himself supply 'brilliant dialogue ... for the "bridges" he constructs to connect action and other scenes in the film. Shaw's forte of course, was writing dialogue for situations that were essentially intellectual, and all of his plays deal with *ideas*. Which is the cause of the primary difficulty all who try to film Shaw, must overcome.'[33] Whereas Asquith talks in terms of making the most of distinctively Shavian features, Roman talks of overcoming them. Curiously, Roman's statement bears a remarkable resemblance to what theatre critics once said of Shaw's plays: too talky, too intellectual for the stage.

In the 1980s, it is Asquith's observation rather than Roman's which seems sensible, perhaps obvious. But this was not the case previously. To generations of movie makers and movie critics whose cinematic experience began with silent films, and to generations influenced by those generations, dialogue is an appendage to the camera, which is paramount. Nowadays, however—one recalls Eric Rohmer's *My Night at Maude's*, with long and excitingly intelligent discussions, and Peter Hall's film version of Harold Pinter's *The Homecoming*, which except for two or three minutes exists, as on stage, in a single setting—movies successfully challenge the received wisdom of earlier generations.

Shaw was well in advance of his time. Do the arts of stage and screen differ? Said Shaw in 1937: 'Dramatically, not in the least. The resources of the screen are enormously larger than those of the stage ... but the art of employing these larger resources dramatically is the same as that of keeping within the small ones. You have to tell a story and make its characters live and seize and hold and guide the attention exactly as Shakespeare and Molière did.' Does he suggest that movies have no unique dramatic technique, different from the theatre's? 'I don't suggest. I tell you flatly and violently that there is no difference whatever. The dramatic technique is precisely the same.' But should not cinematic devices like the close-up, the fade, and instantaneous changes of scene and distance, none of which is a feature of a stage play, be employed in a screen version of one of his plays? 'Why not?'[34] As Shaw put it as early as 1 Jan. 1930, 'Drama is a method of re-arranging the higgledy-piggledy happenings of actual life in such a way as to make them intelligible and thinkable. Its forms, processes and instruments include the stage, the screen, the camera, the microphone, the actor,' and cinema is new only in the sense that 'a new instrument added to the orchestra or a new verse form' is new.[35] Time has caught up to Shaw. Half a century later, critic and BBC producer-director Martin Esslin observes, 'one point of fundamental importance ... continues to be persistently overlooked,' that mechanically reproduced drama (movies, television and radio) 'different though it may be in some of its techniques, is also fundamentally drama and obeys the same basic principles of the psychology of perception and understanding from which all the techniques of dramatic communication derive.'[36]

Insisting a work of art must undergo some sort of adaptation in its transfer to a different medium, Samuel Goldwyn argued by analogy that a train and an airplane both travel between Hollywood and New York, but the train cannot fly and the plane cannot move on rails.[37] Despite the proliferation of inaccurate statements on the subject, Shaw agreed. It is simply untrue, as Blanche Patch, Cecil Lewis (director of *Arms and the Man*), Walter Mycroft (Scenario Editor of British International Pictures, its producer), critic Robert C. Roman, and Valerie Pascal assert, that until her husband Gabriel Pascal arrived, Shaw refused to permit a word of his plays to be cut or changed for the screen.[38] To the contrary. When an interviewer asked if there were any truth to Shaw's alleged statement that should anyone want to film one of his plays 'they jolly well had to do it as if they were photographing the play on the stage and not go fooling with camera tricks,' Shaw retorted, 'That's absurd.'[39] As Shaw urged a BBC drama producer, his plays 'must always be adapted intelligently to the studio, the screen, the stage, or whatever the physical conditions of performance may be.' Peter Noble is accurate when he states that Shaw really insists that the adaptation 'must be by himself, not ... by the office boy or the nearest bar tender or studio loafer as (he alleges) the Hollywood habit is.'[40]

Shaw made similar statements well before 1946, the year of the last two. Would he have written his plays in a different form if he had written them for the screen in the first place? 'Yes, of course,' he replied in 1937. Would not such a form have approximated that which a movie adapter might give his plays? 'No: it would have approximated to the form that I myself would give my plays for the screen ... but that is not the same thing.'[41] What Shaw did not want, he said the following year, was the distortion of his plays by movie makers, who 'can't tell my story for me the way I want to have it told.'[42] In the matter of dialogue, he resolutely maintained, the appropriate person to make any necessary cuts and changes is the original writer.[43] It is certainly not the movie director, whom Shaw would ruthlessly make stick to his own job and not meddle with the writer's, which he believes he understands but does not.[44]

Shaw practiced what he preached. In 1930 he refused to permit a movie of *Major Barbara* because it was 'too long—*as yet*, for the screen.'[45] Since he did not want to mutilate his play, he preferred to wait until moviegoers and movie makers became accustomed to longer films. As for movie versions he did permit to be filmed, later analysis will show he helped Cecil Lewis cut and change *Arms and the Man*; when he wrote scenarios for *Pygmalion* and *Saint Joan*, he made numerous cuts and changes; and he authored or authorized drastic cuts and changes in other works.

If a movie producer films a good play, he told Kenneth Macgowan in 1934, he should 'assume that the author knows his job, and stand or fall by it. That is, of course, unless the author can stand by and [direct] his work himself, which is the ideal plan.' Macgowan's response: Shaw was 'ahead of his time as usual.'[46] But since he was too old for such work—born in 1856, he was seventy-seven when he wrote to Macgowan—if the producer chooses not to make that assumption, he should not undertake to film the play.

For a time, Shaw gave producers no opportunity to choose. Often, economic reasons dictated his rejection of movie offers. When films were in their infancy, he foresaw that they would become big business, organized by capitalists on the largest possible scale.[47] He regarded the economic aspect of movie making in exactly the term employed by movie makers to describe their enterprise, an industry. Like all industries, it is controlled by capitalists. 'If the capitalists let themselves be seduced from their pursuit of profits to the enchantments of art,' he realized, 'they would be bankrupt before they knew where they were. You cannot combine the pursuit of money with the pursuit of art.'[48] Though not seduced from their primary purpose, they employ people who pursue art, and like most employers they aim to pay their employees as little as necessary in return for as much as they can get. Shaw guided himself accordingly. It is his recognition of this characteristic of the film industry which underlies the famous quip—often repeated, often rephrased, and possibly apocryphal—that Shaw is said to have made to Samuel Goldwyn when he delineated their differences: 'You are interested in art, and I am interested in business.'[49] When dealing with businessmen, Shaw undertook to be as businesslike as they. He did all he could to prevent them from taking advantage of him. All movie producers denounce each other as crooks, and they are usually right, he joked in earnest. Therefore, if a producer would give him the name and address of a film producer who other producers agree is not a crook, Shaw would be greatly obliged.[50] Although he made such statements without rancour, he dealt with the crooks without illusions.

His terms involved answers to the questions Where? How much? and How long? Once talkies killed silent films, he believed, they simultaneously 'killed the old system of buying the world rights from the author.'[51] Refusing to sell world rights for the talkies, he insisted on dealing separately for production and distribution in separate countries or for separate languages that sometimes transcend boundaries (Germany, Austria, and German-speaking Switzerland, for instance). Instead of selling rights for a lump sum, he demanded standard percentage terms: 10 per cent of the gross sums paid by exhibitors to the manufacturer or to any intermediary between the exhibitor and manufacturer, unless the manufacturer were the distributor, in which case his royalty was 5 per cent of the gross sums paid by the public at the theatres where the film was shown.[52] To sweeten the terms, he declined advances. He demanded percentages of the gross rather than profits because: 'There may be no profit but there are always receipts and sometimes it may take ten lawsuits to determine what the profits are but you can always determine the receipts.'[53] Nor were his percentages outright sales. They were licenses for a specified, standard period of time, five years.[54]

Shaw held out for these apparently outrageous terms because he knew he could get them. As revealed earlier, silent film producers had already offered them to him. Such statements as those of movie financier Richard Norton, Lord Grantley, mislead: 'It is generally accepted in the trade that *seven* years is the minimum worthwhile period for a film agreement, to give the time for all the residual revenues (from re-issues, etc.) to come in. The previous Shaw films, especially *Pygmalion*, showed the importance of money from re-issues; to forgo it in advance can make the whole idea of a Shaw film uneconomic.'[55] Since *Pygmalion* turned a profit, since movie companies accepted Shaw's five year licence, and since Norton's view is that of the industry, his conclusion is questionable. Besides, if a film continued to earn a profit after five years, Shaw could and did renew the licence, for this action was mutually advantageous. If on the other hand, contractual assurances to the contrary, the film changed and misrepresented the author's work, the author could more quickly remove it from circulation.

With Shaw receiving a percentage of the gross, he was a shareholder rather than an employee. What was his attitude toward workers? If a Shavian film were to be made in a foreign language, he tried to ensure that his authorized translator would receive the same terms as he would for a stage production, half of his own royalties.[56] When he could not guarantee this, he inserted a contractual clause that the licensee must negotiate with his translator to use those portions of the screenplay the latter had already translated for the stage and to offer him employment to translate those passages of the screenplay not in the play.[57] As early as 1908, Shaw hoped that the Society of Authors would organize a screenwriters' union.[58] Asked whether the British film industry should recognize and make agreements with organizations which represented its technicians, he replied, 'Of course it should.'[59] When a union of movie extras created difficulties for producers J. Arthur Rank and Gabriel Pascal during the filming of *Cæsar and Cleopatra*, Shaw sided with the workers. If the producing company did not stick to its business of making pictures, he threatened, and began 'to engage in the class war with its extras ... then I shall rule it out of my future agreements. ... The war between employers and trade unions is a hundred years out of date.' Just as an employer who does not belong to a federation of employers is a fool, he added, so is an employee who does not belong to a union.[60]

G.B.S. AND B.I.P.

On 28 Oct. 1929, Lady Gregory's diary records, 'G.B.S. told me he had given one "talkie" to show how it should be done.'[1] She cites neither the play nor the people to whom G.B.S. gave it. By early 1930, however, Cecil Lewis had approached British Instructional Films about filming *How He Lied to Her Husband*; in March, Basil Dean of Associated Radio Pictures (R.K.O.'s London affiliate) wanted to discuss details of experimenting with a talkie of one of Shaw's plays; and by April, they had arranged such an experiment.[2] Possibly, this talkie was the same mentioned half a year earlier by Lady Gregory and the same about which Lewis approached British Instructional Films. But who was Cecil Lewis?

A teenage flying ace during World War I and a flight instructor in Peking in 1920, according to the book jacket of his autobiography *Never Look Back*, Lewis in 1922 became one of the four founders of the BBC. Shaw took an avuncular interest in the young man, to whom he wrote as early as 1923 with professional advice on radio production, friendly criticism of his plays, and invitations to visit.[3] Shaw decided to help young Lewis professionally by permitting him to make a talkie of *How He Lied to Her Husband*—if he could persuade a studio to employ him as its director and agree to film it uncut.

He did so. On 18 Aug. 1930, barely three years after the American premiere of *The Jazz Singer*, John Maxwell, head of British International Pictures, hired him to direct the first movie of a complete Shaw play.[4] What is more, Maxwell agreed to film it 'without transpositions interpolations omissions or any alterations misrepresenting the Author whether for better or worse except such as the Author may consent to or himself suggest'—a clause that would become standard in Shaw's film contracts. It is significant that *How He Lied to Her Husband* is a one-set, one-act play with three characters, for as Walter Mycroft, B.I.P. Scenario Editor, put it, 'If we were going *avant-garde* we would minimise the risk.' He assigned Frank Launder to prepare a scenario. 'Frank had the right attack,' says Mycroft. He devised a scene where the lover (Robert Harris), en route to the room of his lady (Vera Lennox), 'places his opera hat on the head of a piece of sculpture; young Mr Launder said the piece of sculpture was to be a bust of George Bernard Shaw himself. Which I thought would amuse Mr Shaw. Mr Shaw was not amused.'[5] This 'right attack,' which Donald P. Costello calls 'a little cinematic touch' and Robert C. Roman claims would have made the play 'conform to the needs of good cinema,'[6] Launder and the others failed to recognize, is not only not intrinsically or necessarily cinematic, it is also uncharacteristic of the Philistine husband, Bompas (Edmund Gwenn), who had fallen asleep during a performance of *Candida*[7] and would scarcely have a bust of its socialist author in his home. Shaw did not invariably object to references to himself in his plays, as *The Doctor's Dilemma* and *Fanny's First Play* testify. He objected only when they were inappropriate, as in B.I.P.'s proposed doctoring.

The decision to film *How He Lied to Her Husband* was of great importance. As Vera Lennox says, 'Practically every big star in London' wanted a role. 'It had been publicized that for the first time Shaw was going to permit one of his plays to be made into a talkie. And there were only three parts. I thought—everybody thought—that if you played in it, you were made. It was the tops.'[8] Since Shaw personally approved the cast, the excitement increased.[9]

Faced with Shaw's dictum against altering a word, Lennox confesses:

One day I really felt myself in difficulties. Mr Shaw's dialogue doesn't always flow comfortably. But this time I really was up a gum tree. So I worked on this speech, and I went to the director and said, 'Look, Cecil, I simply cannot get through this. I tried to alter it. Do I dare make this change?' He was as frightened as I was of changing one word, but he said, 'We'll risk it. The old boy was down here for rushes last night, so perhaps he won't be down tomorrow.' We took the shot with my slightly altered version of the speech. The next day, we shot as usual. Then came the time to see the rushes of the day before, when I made the alteration. The old boy came to the rushes. My heart fell through my boots. I thought the world was going to end. I sat between my director and George Bernard Shaw, and died. We had shot that particular scene seven times, and every time the alteration in the speech came, this great white head turned and looked down at me. You can perhaps imagine what I was feeling. After the seventh time the lights went up. We all stood up. It was rather like having royalty about one. All that happened was that he turned round and smiled at me and said,

'Perhaps it was a little easier to say that way,' and tapped me on the
shoulder. I could have kissed him.[10]

Except for the fight scene between the lover and husband, Lennox and
Harris both recall, Shaw did not interfere with the direction of the film.
During that scene, says Harris, 'He was so disgusted with the laborious
way in which I rose to my feet that he jumped onto the set, threw himself
down, and jumped up like a bouncing deer. Extraordinary performance,
at his age. Made me very ashamed of myself.' 'I remember him taking off
his coat,' says Lennox, 'more or less slinging it at somebody. "This is the
way you go at it! You've got to—!" The old boy himself! Shaw was
pounding out at Teddy Gwenn, and Teddy Gwenn was coming back with
a wallop! Cecil and I were having hysterics, laughing at them.'[11]
According to Blanche Patch, who also visited the set that day, Gwenn not
only came back, he knocked Shaw down. 'You see,' said Shaw, getting to
his feet, 'it's easy.'[12]
   The film's makers were inexperienced. Lewis had never directed a film
before.[13] While Edmund Gwenn had acted in movies, Harris recalls, 'I
don't think he had ever made a talking picture. I know I didn't. I don't
think Vera had done much filming. The camera man had never recorded a
sound picture. The whole thing was not very expert.'[14]
   The inexpert effort first opened in London on 12 Jan. 1931.[15] 'There
was no celebration,' says Lennox, 'and we weren't even invited.' Quietly
brought in, the film quietly disappeared. 'It was a bit of a let-down, after
the great build-up. It wasn't a catastrophe, it was more or less a dud.'[16] To
the London *Times*, the B.I.P. experiment conclusively proved 'the folly of
those who suppose that the right use, and the commercial use, of the talkie
invention is direct transference from stage to screen.'[17] In general, the
English critics found the film 'a dull, disappointing effort'.[18] *The New York
Times* took a more lenient view. Although it called the movie 'an
amateurish specimen of animated photography,' a piece of moviemaking
that 'could hardly be less imaginative than it is,' with direction that
seemed of the same period as the script's Victorian costumes and camera
work that sometimes cut off part of a head, it also pointed out—indicating
the experiment achieved partial success—that Shaw's 'characteristic wit
shines forth like a precious gem in a cast-iron setting' and that 'failing any
imaginative pictorial conception of his plays, it is better to have such
carbon copies than none at all.'[19]
   Of the film's unfriendly London reception, Shaw remarked: 'The poor
fellows had never read anything but a Hollywood sub-title.' Unlike the
usual talkie, which was merely a silent movie with spoken subtitles, *How
He Lied* contained continuous dialogue, 'except where Mr Gwenn

purposely makes a silence more dramatic than words could be.' Unlike the usual motion picture, 'the entire action takes place in the same room, the usual changes from New York to the Rocky Mountains, from Marseilles to the Sahara, from Mayfair to Monte Carlo, are replaced by changes from the piano to the sideboard, from the window to the door, from the hearth rug to the carpet.' In contrast to Hollywood films, *How He Lied* does not have the husband arrive in a taxi, open the door, climb the stairs, or any other 'baby padding'.[20] Two points are noteworthy. First, the only member of the three-character cast singled out for praise is Edmund Gwenn. Second, Shaw does *not* boast that a stationary camera rolls on while a play is performed, but that *drastic* changes of background are unnecessary for variety. Intercontinental changes of locale are *replaced by* camera changes within the same room.

Were Shaw's critics right? If so, to what extent does he share blame for the film's failure? To the extent that *How He Lied* was not adapted at all to the new medium, despite the fact that the film credits Lewis as adapter, Shaw is to blame. Except for insignificant cuts and variations of a few lines, stage play and screenplay are identical—hence, its absence from this volume.

Today, Edmund Gwenn's performance is the only one with any merit. Since the actors usually perform in too large a manner for the screen, they seem to overplay. Unaccustomed to acting in talkies, Harris speaks his lines with a virtually unvarying tempo and rhythm that soon become dull. Basically, however, blame attaches to the director, who did not make him pick up cues and did not attend to actionless silences. As Lennox candidly says, 'I knew I wasn't any good. In those days, theatre people hadn't realized that if you played a role on film as you played it on stage, the thickest slices of ham came out. I think the picture was stagey. It was badly directed. He directed it as if it were a play.'[21]

Indeed, the main reason for its failure is fledgling director Cecil Lewis. To film a play without adding new scenes, rearranging old ones, or putting them in different locations is difficult enough, but such difficulties are not insurmountable, particularly when the play is in one short act. Nor is it true, as Lewis says, blaming Shaw, that his assignment 'was clearly nothing more than a licence to film a stage play.'[22] A motion picture set in a single room is not intrinsically uncinematic. Once one decides to photograph a stage play intact—whether that play is *Rope* (Hitchcock), *The Homecoming* (Hall), *The Iceman Cometh* (Frankenheimer), or *How He Lied to Her Husband* (Lewis)—the transformation from stage to screen is the responsibility of the director, who can accomplish it through actors, camera, and editing. Lewis's failure to employ them satisfactorily is the major reason the movie seems like a photographed stage play. His blocking is stagey, with frequent use of cross-and-turn, and of characters who often just stand and talk to each other. Camera work is trite, and while photography and editing are not as static as the press claimed, they give that impression, for they fail to underscore or comment on the action. Lewis does not employ different camera angles or shots to reveal conflict, dominance, and submissiveness. Mainly, he uses a series of different kinds of long and medium shots, usually of two characters, who often face the camera and occasionally show profile or cheat with a three-quarter stance. He even fails to take advantage of cinematic implications in the play. At one point, after Aurora Bompas leaves her husband and lover (Henry) together, '*Bompas deliberately takes the poems from his breast pocket; looks at them reflectively; then looks at Henry, mutely inviting his attention. Henry refuses to understand, doing his best to look unconcerned.*' By using different camera set-ups and by appropriate editing, Lewis could have created a comically suspenseful sequence. To suggest one almost minimal possibility, he might have cut from a medium shot of the husband examining the poems and slyly glancing at his rival to a close-up of the poet refusing to understand, then to a long shot of both, in which the poet tries to look unconcerned. Instead, Lewis merely shows, in a single shot, Bompas reflectively examining the poems and looking at Henry. Because his technique is stagey, it is small wonder that reviewers regarded the movie as a photographed stage play.

According to Mycroft, 'The little film cost slightly more than £5,000 and, even at that tiny figure ... lost money. Shaw charged nothing for the story or his services. He was coming in on the profits.'[23] Since Shaw's contract called for a percentage of the gross, not profits, the last statement is incorrect. So, perhaps, is the first. According to Lewis, the movie 'didn't lose money.' It persuaded B.I.P. that he was a genius 'and resulted in my being offered a two-year contract as a film director.'[24]

Whoever is accurate, B.I.P. did sign Lewis to direct another G.B.S. film, this time full length, *Arms and the Man*. B.I.P did not do so because of a previous contractual commitment, for by the time the contract was signed (17 July 1932), the picture was more than half finished.[25]

Why *Arms and the Man?* According to Mycroft, John Maxwell had wanted to film *Pygmalion* but dropped the idea because the censor would 'never, never, never' permit 'Not bloody likely', and Mycroft suggested the other play.[26] Actually, the reason may be more complex. Although the court had ruled in Shaw's favour in March 1927, Jesse Levinson persisted in his effort to film *The Chocolate Soldier*. In August, he proposed to submit a movie adaptation for Shaw's approval, but Shaw refused to discuss the matter further.[27] When *The Jazz Singer* opened in New York in October, Shaw may have realized it was only a matter of time before the persistent Levinson persuaded an American studio to film the Straus musical, involve him in another expensive and time consuming law suit, and possibly make *Arms and the Man* worthless for movie purposes. One way to avoid these consequences would be to film *Arms and the Man* first. In June 1928, Shaw suggested a movie version to Adolph Menjou; in August, he discussed one with Rex Ingram; by October, he was negotiating with several English and American companies.[28] On 7 Dec. Levinson wrote Shaw he could persuade a motion picture studio (unnamed) to pay Shaw $25,000 if he agreed to make no claim against a *Chocolate Soldier* movie, for the studio had consented to use neither Shaw's name nor dialogue from *Arms and the Man* in the talkie or silent version (it was common practice then to make two versions, to accomodate theatres with and without sound projectors). Shaw would not reopen the discussion.[29]

But perhaps because Levinson's letter forced the issue, he opened it with Lawrence Langner of the Theatre Guild. On 2 July 1929, Langner sent him a detailed proposal for a movie of *Arms and the Man*.[30] Nothing came of it. By February 1930, Warner Brothers, with whom Shaw had been negotiating, was interested not in *Arms and the Man* but in *The Chocolate Soldier*, which they thought they could film without Shaw's consent.[31] Warners may have been the studio to which Levinson referred, for it had acquired First National Pictures, with whom Levinson had negotiated in 1926. On 15 Feb., Shaw again wrote to the Theatre Guild about a talkie of *Arms and the Man*. Samuel Goldwyn, he revealed, had been pressing him on the subject, but since Goldwyn wanted to cut the play to forty minutes he was not inclined to accept his offer. Although Langner kept the door open to future motion picture possibilities, he declined.[32]

In April 1930, before G.B.S. and B.I.P. signed to produce *How He Lied*, he twice reported that he had arranged a sound movie of *Arms and the Man*.[33] Possibly, his statements were aimed to prevent production of a *Chocolate Soldier* movie, for at this time a German affiliate of Movietone announced it would film *Der tapfere Soldat*. Shaw told Siegfried Trebitsch to advise Movietone that if it filmed *The Chocolate Soldier*, he would sue for infringement of his copyright, and he asked whether Trebitsch knew of a German firm he could trust to make a full length motion picture of *Helden* (Heroes, the German title of *Arms and the Man*) exactly as it stood and not a forty-minute scenario based on it. Apparently, Trebitsch succeeded in delaying the film, for the following year the German firm, probably fearful of a costly legal battle, asked Shaw's consent to film the comic opera. Absolutely and unequivocally, he refused.[34]

When G.B.S. and B.I.P. signed their agreement to film *Arms and the Man*, Shaw inserted two special clauses. B.I.P. would not mention *The Chocolate Soldier* in publicity of any kind, would use none of its music to accompany the film, and would neither directly nor indirectly suggest any connection between it and *Arms and the Man*. Also, since the title *Arms and the Man* is a quotation from an English classic and therefore unsuitable for use in any foreign language, the B.I.P. film must be shown abroad 'under the altered titles already in use for the play in foreign countries or failing such usage under new titles approved by the Author but under no circumstances shall the title be The Chocolate Soldier or any foreign equivalent or colorable imitation thereof.'[35]

Among the usual clauses was a prohibition against transpositions, interpolations, omissions, and alterations except those the author might accept or suggest. Did he approve or suggest any changes? 'Not a word was to be cut', says Lewis. Ditto, Mycroft: 'He would not agree to a single cut or change. All he would concede was the introduction of visual action, without dialogue, between the stage scenes, as it were.'[36] Understandably, writers on the subject have accepted their word.[37] On the evidence of Lewis's scenario, however, which contains marginal comments by Shaw,[38] they misrepresent the case. While Shaw refused to sanction some of Lewis's cuts and changes, he agreed to many and suggested a number of his own.

For the changes Shaw prohibited, he gave reasons. When Lewis, dramatizing the cavalry charge, has Sergius lead it against his will and pull frantically at his horse, Shaw exclaims, 'no!'—underscoring it three times—'Sergius's charge was quite genuine. Bluntschli compares him to Don Quixote charging the windmills. Read more carefully.' Where Lewis changes the business of Louka seeing Bluntschli's revolver on the ottoman to her seeing a bulging curtain, him behind it, Shaw explains, 'Louka should start as she sees the revolver on the ottoman. Then a close-up of the revolver only. Then Louka smiling cunningly as she guesses. This is necessary to prepare the effect of Raina sitting down on the revolver later on. Besides, if Louka saw the man himself or any part of him she would give him away. There is all the difference between finding the slot and actually seeing the quarry.'

Shaw discriminates among Lewis's cuts, such as the following (double brackets represent deletions from the play):

RAINA. ... Sergius: I think we two have found the higher love. When I think of you, I feel that I could never do a base deed, or think an ignoble thought.
[[SERGIUS. My lady and my saint! [*He clasps her reverently*].

RAINA [*returning his embrace*] My Lord and my—
SERGIUS. Sh-sh! Let me be the worshipper, dear. You little know
how unworthy even the best man is of a girl's pure passion.
RAINA. I trust you.]] I love you. You will never disappoint me,
Sergius.

Demands Shaw:

> *Why the cut here?*
> S. My lady & my saint
> R. My lord and my—(Louka sings)
> *The rest can be cut; but this is the climax.*

To many cuts and changes, Shaw often agreed. Approving the removal
of Raina's description of *Ernani*, which a worldwide film audience might
not understand, he confessed relief that Lewis had not introduced a
performance of the opera and chided him for having missed an
opportunity to waste money. Usually, though, he said nothing about cuts
he approved, such as Petkoff's remark that neither the Bulgarians nor the
Serbs would have been able to fight had not foreigners shown them how
(the point is made elsewhere). Excellent, said Shaw of some of Lewis's
changes, such as the garden as a relief to the library scene and Louka's
absence during the scene of Petkoff and the photograph.[39] The latter—
after which Louka returns in time for Raina to refer to her—'I think ... is
an improvement which I shall adopt,' Shaw noted in the margin.

Shaw makes more effective use of movie technique than Lewis does.
When Raina surreptitiously removes the photograph from her father's
pocket, it is Shaw not Lewis who indicates a close-up 'full size of the
screen with the portrait of Raina and the inscription.' When Sergius signs
a paper with great difficulty, it is Shaw not Lewis who inserts a close-up of
the process: 'arm on table, cheek on arm, tongue out convulsively
following the difficult strokes.' Where Lewis has Petkoff interrupt the four
younger people, the camera is on them when he begins to speak.
Unintelligible, advises Shaw, for unless the audience first sees who is
speaking, they will not know whose voice it is. In comedy especially,
Shaw's visual sense is keen. In one passage between Catherine and Louka,
Catherine calls, 'Louka!' Then: '(*stopping*) Yes, madam.' 'Is the library
door shut?' 'I think so madam.' 'If not, shut it as you pass through.' 'Yes,
madam (*going*).' 'Stop! (*Louka stops*).' Lewis removes all stage directions
and designates a close-up of Catherine with a voice-over by Louka.
Noticing that Lewis has missed the comic point, Shaw insists, 'The
overlay must be the other way about—Catherine visible but close up $\frac{1}{4}$

length of Louka repeatedly starting to go and turning as she is recalled.'
Not that Shaw is above a touch of the trite. In a bridge between the
bedroom and garden scenes, he proposes that when Raina gazes at a
portrait of Sergius, 'She presses it to her breast, but presently drops off to
sleep and has a vision of Bluntschli in her bed.'

At a certain point, words rather than pictures are necessary for
audience comprehension. During the battle of Slivnitza, Lewis has a silent
scene wherein the artillery unit discovers it has the wrong ammunition.
Says Shaw:

> The business here is amazement and laughter at the insane notion
> that the cavalry are going to charge the battery. It needs dialogue.
> 'Are those d--d fools going to charge us?' 'Impossible: not a man or
> a horse will get within thirty yards of it.' 'Cavalry on machine guns!
> we shall blow them to hell. They must be mad.' 'No: theyre only
> Bulgarians: they know no better. Be ready: theyre going to do it.
> Hurry up that ammunition there.'

Where Lewis merely has a close-up of a gunner's thumb pulling the
trigger of a machine gun, which fails to fire, Shaw revising the scenario
dramatizes the incident: 'This is not intelligible. You must have the
incident of the *sergeant* coming in a ghastly fright to Bluntschli. "Theyve
sent us the wrong cartridges, sir." "My God: we're done. Run for it,
everybody." Stampede of Servian gunners overtaken by the charge.'

Once—the only time, as far as I have discovered—Shaw was actually
present during the film's making. On this occasion, a rehearsal,[40] he tried
to show Anne Grey (Raina) how to perform a scene. Shaw played her role
so well, according to both Barry Jones (Bluntschli) and Maurice
Colbourne (Sergius), that Jones, turning to face her, was startled to find
himself looking at Shaw's white beard and not the actress's face.[41]

The sparse extant information about the making of *Arms and the Man*
suggests matters went badly. On 8 June 1932, after filming had begun, D.
Lewin Mannering, cast as Nicola, died of a heart attack, though contrary
to the vivid obituary in *The Times* the next day, he did not expire during a
take.[42] Shaw sent money for the actor's funeral and predicted a newspaper
article that would report more bad news on the film:

> Last Tuesday in Wales Maurice Colbourne, unable to control his
> horse, rode down Barry Jones and was himself thrown violently.
> His well filled head crashed against that of his colleague, which was
> entirely empty. Barry Jones perished immediately. Colbourne
> lingered in concussion until the following afternoon, when he

suddenly exclaimed 'Why the hell did I ever—' and fell back dead. In witnessing the accident Cecil Lewis, the [director], died of shock. When the news reached Elstree [Studios] Miss Grey said that life no longer meant anything to her. Her heart ceased beating; and she was removed to the B.I.P. mortuary, which is sadly overcrowded. Miss Angela Baddeley [Louka] turned pale, swallowed a pound and a half of veronal tablets, married Mr Mycroft, and expired in his arms. Miss Scudamore [Catherine] informs us that she is sorry for Mr Lewis's children, but in view of his having required two tests before giving her the part, congratulates his wife and considers his decease a bl--dy good job for the profession. The parts of Bluntschli and Sergius have been undertaken at a moment's notice by Mr Mycroft and Mr John Maxwell; and the ladies' parts have been filled by volunteers from the stenographic staff. The result will be a unique British film.[43]

Catastrophes of a different order followed. 'The biggest mistake was the studio's,' admits Mycroft, 'who thought it would be a good idea to shoot as much of the film as possible on location, North Wales masquerading as Bulgaria. Dialogue scenes in the open air are always difficult, and here, with so much dialogue, the result was quite artificial, made more so by the lack of technical refinements then available.'[44] In addition to the battle of Slivnitza, most of the second act was shot out of doors. Blanche Patch suggests another reason for the film's poor quality as 'lack of backing', which probably means inadequate budget. Shaw seems to concur: British experiments with his plays 'are hopeless: they have no money and want to put in minutes (mostly wasted) where months are needed.'[45] Possibly, Lewis did not sufficiently allow for cover shots of scenes that might turn out badly and B.I.P. did not have enough money for retakes of scenes that did turn out badly, for more than five weeks after Mannering's death, Shaw wrote to Roy Limbert, who ran the Malvern Festival, founded in 1929 chiefly to present Shaw's plays, that Arms and the Man might not be ready for its promised première in early August. B.I.P. 'talked about putting you off with a cut version, omitting all except the old stage version,' but Shaw refused to entertain such a notion. 'As it stood,' said he, 'the battle of Slivnitza was impossible and B.I.P. might be unable to fake anything presentable.'[46]

On 4 Aug. 1932, Arms and the Man opened at Malvern. Although The Times did not condemn it outright, the brevity and politeness of its respectful notice damned it with the faintest of praise.[47] Maurice Colbourne called the film 'a pronounced and dismal failure' and Allardyce Nicoll went further: 'No more dismal film has ever been shown to the public.'[48] It ended Lewis's film career and because it lost a great deal of money terminated B.I.P.'s association with G.B.S.[49]

What of Shaw's response? I do not think his article 'Arms and the Man on the Screen', which appeared in the Malvern Festival Book when the film premiered, demonstrates, as Costello claims, that he 'exulted' or showed 'enthusiasm' over the movie.[50] His letters to Roy Limbert, just alluded to, shed light on these published comments. On 17 July 1932, he tells Limbert he might have to scrap that article, for it discusses the superiorities of motion pictures to theatre. Perhaps he then revised it, for on 19 July he says he might have to revise it again. With these letters in mind, one recognizes two factors heretofore overlooked. First, Shaw dates the article 'July 1932', before the première. Second, he praises no one connected with the film and fails to mention a single performer or the director (his article on the How He Lied movie singled out Edmund Gwenn for praise and referred to Lewis in favourable terms). What he does say is that the movie version of Arms and the Man shows how physically and economically limited the theatre is in contrast to cinema. Whereas the stage play must be confined to three settings, two of them interiors, and only report through exposition such pivotal incidents as the battle of Slivnitza and the flight of the fugitive, the motion picture shows both. He does not say how well it does so. Nor does he evaluate the particular film at all. Instead, he discusses the cinema as medium. Unconfined to one location, characters can go in and out of doors, into gardens and across the countryside, 'with a freedom and variety impossible in the room with three walls which, however scene-painters may disguise it, is always the same old stage.' What he says about B.I.P. is accurate: they have indeed 'spent as many pounds on this picture as any manager could afford to spend pence on the plainest and cheapest performance of the play.' But note: the plainest and cheapest production, not the most expensive. Although he does not say that they should have spent more or that their methods were undeveloped and their facilities inadequate, he suggests as much in his concluding paragraph, which I quote in full (italics are mine):

> Later on, these advantages of the picture house may enable it to supersede the theatre for all except very specialized work. It is in fact already doing so, though the accompanying spread of the taste for and knowledge of dramatic art has reacted favorably on the business done in the old theatres in the old way. But the films, in spite of all their spendors and enchantments, are still in their infancy. When dramatic poets (as they call us authors in Germany) realize the possibilities of the screen, and the performers master its technique,

and the great producing corporations, still obsessed with the '[silent] movie' tradition, can be persuaded that a good play is not ready to be photographed until the actors have grown into it as completely as they do in the theatre after not only a month's rehearsal but a month's performance before the public, *then* every corner of the country in which a picture house can live will witness performances *compared to which this one of Arms and the Man will seem a mere sketch, in which the talent of the actors has produced a few happy moments under difficulties not yet, but presently to be, triumphantly overcome.*

In a consoling note to his protégé Cecil Lewis a week after the première, he called the uncut film 'magnificent beyond description', but his next statement clearly indicates that he was at least partly facetious or exaggerated, for he regarded it as magnificent only in comparison to other B.I.P. movies, one of which (*Lucky Girl*) he had just sampled. His response to it: 'My God!'[51]

When I saw *Arms and the Man*, it contained no battle scene and its few scenes not in the stage version were all brief and without dialogue; the rest was drastically cut. Total running time was eighty-five minutes. According to Mycroft, 'Having stuck out so long, the author capitulated when it was too late and the damage was irreparable—he agreed to cuts at last, and bits were chiselled out of the film. That, of course, only made it shorter; nothing could alter the fact that what was left was still just solid chunks of dialogue.'[52] Lewis's report is quite different:

> In order to salve what they could, British International Pictures, through their Distributors, shortened the film, to make it into a second feature. Cut to ribbons, without any continuity whatever, it was a travesty of the original. No author, however illustrious, can control what happens to a film when it reaches this stage. Shaw never knew of these cuts. He certainly did not authorize them. In the cutting room anything can happen and, by this time, nobody is much interested, except those who hope to cut their losses![53]

This shortened film—the only one in existence, as far as I know—more than travesties *Arms and the Man*, it emasculates it. Whatever Shaw's deficiencies as a neophyte adapter, whatever Lewis's as an inexperienced scenarist and virtually inexperienced director, both made a genuine effort to transform the play to a different medium. As the scenario reveals, they added scenes only discussed in the play, streamlined dialogue, and for visual variety changed settings when such changes flowed logically from the text. B.I.P.'s mutilations wreaked havoc with important thematic issues and made a mess of dramatic logic. Cutting the business of Bluntschli throwing his gun on the ottoman, they removed the preparation for Louka's discovery of it, which they retain and which naturally misses fire. Deleting the entire third act dialogue wherein Nicola reveals his psychological castration as a result of the social status quo, B.I.P. reduces the play's social and psychological issues to inaudible resonances. Also cut is a key thematic passage between the primarily romantic Sergius and the primarily realistic Bluntschli about the entirely realistic Nicola's announcement of his non-engagement: 'This is either the finest heroism or the most crawling baseness. Which is it, Bluntschli?' 'Never mind whether it's heroism or baseness. Nicola's the ablest man Ive met in Bulgaria. I'll make him manager of a hotel if he can speak French or German.' Considering Nicola's alternative and Louka's implacably disdainful attitude toward him, his decision to deny their engagement is realistic, and the point of it, emphasized by Bluntschli, is that such unrealistic moral conceptions as heroism and baseness are useless to judge conduct. Does the conduct do good or harm? It is the result that counts, not a heroic or base motive. To judge as Bluntschli does by the result of an action, B.I.P. appears to have understood none of these issues.

But Lewis must share blame with B.I.P. As Barry Jones puts it, since every actor but Anne Grey had played his role on stage, 'an experienced troupe was ready to be moulded in the different medium in which we were to portray the familiar characters.... We hoped for the baton of a Shaw maestro who had Shaw knowledge. And our Conductor admitted that he had never even seen the play. Thus we were a little like a pilotless ship.'[54]

Despite a witty choice of music at the end of the film, 'The Girl I Left Behind Me' as the camera frames Bluntschli and Raina, Lewis was too inexperienced, unimaginative, or untalented for the job at hand. Technically, the film is poor. When Sergius tells Catherine why he resigned his commission, his face is in shadow, his torso in light. As in *How He Lied to Her Husband*, Lewis fails to prevent his actors from performing in too large a manner for the screen; they thereby overact. As in the earlier film, much of his blocking is stagey. Instead of using camera and editor's shears to provide movement, Lewis uses cross-and-turn movement, or he has actors merely walk from one area of the set to another. When Bluntschli is about to explain why it is unprofessional to deploy cavalry against machine guns, for instance, Lewis does not use the camera and editor's scissors to create an exciting moment. Instead, he has Raina cross to Bluntschli in silence and only when she reaches him demand he tell her. On stage, the long moment could be intense; on screen, it is dead time, which numbs the scene, whereas a quick cut from one character to the other could have vitalized it.

Failing to exploit the film medium, Lewis even neglects to take advantage of suggestions in the play. He might have made comic capital by judicious reaction shots, such as Catherine's when Sergius describes the mother of Bluntschli's benefactress as an *old* lady. When Bluntschli tells Raina that death means sleep, which he prefers to climbing down the water pipe, Lewis uses neither pan nor reaction shot to reveal her response, which is imperceptible. Although the camera frames the pair at the end, the closing shot has little impact because they had been similarly framed throughout the previous scene. It is not Shaw's dialogue that makes the film seem stagey, it is the director's insufficient cinematic technique, combined with the studio's damaging, inept cuts.

G.B.S. AND R.K.O.

After G.B.S.'s ventures with B.I.P., his wife Charlotte persuaded him to take a trip around the world. On 16 Dec. 1932, they sailed on the Empress of Britain which on 23 March 1933 docked at San Francisco. The next morning he flew to San Simeon as guest of publisher William Randolph Hearst. On 28 March, he flew to Los Angeles.[1] In a bungalow especially built on the M.G.M. lot for actress Marion Davies, Hearst's mistress, Shaw was guest of honour at a luncheon. At the Shaw-Davies table were Charlie Chaplin, Louis B. Mayer, and Clark Gable,[2] who had completed *Polly of the Circus* with Davies the year before.

While in Hollywood, did Shaw discuss the possibility of filming his plays there? Although he consistently derided American producers, one producer, on the strength of published work with which Shaw was familiar,[3] held his respect: R.K.O.'s Kenneth Macgowan, formerly drama critic and associate editor of *Theatre Arts*, author of *The Theatre of Tomorrow* and (with designer Robert Edmond Jones) *Continental Stagecraft*, and with Jones and Eugene O'Neill founder of the Provincetown Players in New York. On 9 Feb. 1933, Macgowan had cabled Shaw, then on board the Empress of Britain, docked in Manila, about film rights to *Candida* and *Captain Brassbound's Conversion*.[4] Whether or not Shaw and Macgowan met in California, they corresponded, and Shaw indicated a disinclination to let R.K.O. film his plays. In an effort to persuade Shaw to change his mind, Macgowan—while Shaw was in California—asked two Englishwomen whose work Shaw knew, Clemence Dane and G. B. Stern, both novelists and playwrights, to write testimonials that in filming such dramas as Philip Barry's *The Animal Kingdom* and Dane's own *Bill of Divorcement*, R.K.O. made intelligent, faithful, and first rate adaptations. Both authors did so.[5] While sailing from California to New York, Shaw told Macgowan he doubted R.K.O.'s seriousness, for he saw no evidence that Hollywood understood how to film his plays. Yet he confessed his disappointment in English motion pictures of his plays—as if daring R.K.O. to do better. By the time Macgowan received Shaw's letter, he had the testimonials from Dane and Stern. On 12 May 1933, he sent them to Shaw and proposed that R.K.O. buy a ninety day option on *Captain Brassbound's Conversion* or other plays, submit a screenplay to Shaw by the end of that time, and complete the picture only if Shaw approved the script.[6] So intelligent was the proposal, Shaw continued discussions.

Beginning a flurry of transatlantic cables, Macgowan told Shaw on 18 Oct. that R.K.O. wanted *The Devil's Disciple* for John Barrymore, who had enthusiastically accepted the title role, and *Saint Joan* for Katharine Hepburn, then its most popular star. He offered alternative terms: a flat sum of $60,000 for both; or $10,000 for each, in advance of a 5 per cent royalty on the exhibitors' receipts up to $400,000 and 15 per cent thereafter. R.K.O.'s one stipulation was to cut each to eighty minutes, but (Shaw was assured) such abridgement would not materially affect the plays. If, as often alleged, Shaw was intransigent about cuts, discussions would have stopped immediately. He was not. They continued. Two days later, he agreed to the reduction of *The Devil's Disciple* to eighty minutes, but not *Saint Joan*, which he declared was suitable only as a long, single-feature film. His terms were a flat 10 per cent and a five-year licence. By 23 Oct. Macgowan had persuaded the studio to agree to one hundred minutes for *Joan*, but R.K.O. insisted on its usual seven-year licence. Although he could not obtain an agreement for a flat 10 per cent, he might—sweetening the refusal—obtain better than 15 per cent above $400,000. Four days later, Shaw cabled Macgowan to make R.K.O. stop haggling, forget about *Joan*, and get to work on *The Devil's Disciple* for the five-year licence and the flat 10 per cent, with—his own sweetener—no advance.[7]

Within the next few days, Macgowan urged R.K.O. to accept Shaw's terms. Not only was R.K.O. having difficulty in finding a script that both it and Barrymore would approve, he argued, but R.K.O. had Barrymore's services for two weeks, enough time for him to do his scenes in *The*

Devil's Disciple, which he had already approved. They would thus get him for $50,000, whereas if they delayed they would have to negotiate a new contract and perhaps meet his demand of $100,000 a film. R.K.O. could save another $8,000 on continuity and up to $15,000 on script changes, Macgowan pressed on, for the Shaw work could be quickly adapted. With the film requiring only four major sets, R.K.O. could complete it for about $250,000. In addition, it would have the publicity value of the first Shaw movie made in Hollywood and therefore the prospect of a larger gross, particularly in England. On 4 Nov. 1933, R.K.O. agreed to Shaw's terms.[8]

Because of the likelihood that the news would leak to the newspapers, R.K.O. wanted to launch its own publicity campaign immediately. Since it hoped to begin the movie within a month, work on the shooting script must start instantly, an impossibility if Shaw insisted on script approval. Upon Macgowan's guarantee that R.K.O. would make no material changes beyond cutting to eighty minutes and providing continuity, Shaw consented, provided the contract expressly stipulate that the movie will not show Dick Dudgeon to be in love with Judith Anderson and that he declare otherwise with the greatest possible emphasis.[9] On 14 Nov., writing to Barrymore directly, he explained that for Dick to adore Judith, 'a snivelling little goody-goody', would 'belittle him unbearably, and reduce the whole affair to third-rate Hollywood sobstuff. Unless I can knock this into R.K.O., the bargain may fall through.'[10] It did not. Shaw must have posted the letter to Barrymore before he received Macgowan's cable, sent the previous day. Because of Barrymore's commitment to M.G.M., R.K.O. could not make the picture until March, but it accepted Shaw's stipulation.[11] Although Barrymore's biographer implies the opposite,[12] Barrymore accepted it too. 'I have realized for a good many years,' he wrote to Shaw in a letter his biographer quotes but without this passage, that to act the role in any other way 'would not only make the man an ass but knock the play to pieces.'[13]

R.K.O. wasted no time in launching its publicity campaign. On 13 Nov., the same day Macgowan cabled acceptance, trade papers announced that R.K.O. had concluded an agreement to become the first American company to film a Shaw play, *The Devil's Disciple*, to star Barrymore. On 25 Nov. G.B.S. told the press how delighted he was with R.K.O. and the star.[14]

With production delayed, Shaw had ample time for script approval. R.K.O. assigned Lester Cohen to adapt the play. What corresponds to Act I and most of Act II was mimeographed on 9 Jan., the remainder on 18 Jan., 1934.[15] Immediately, each part went to the Production Code Administration, Hollywood's self-regulatory—that is, self-censorship—

organization. On 19 Jan., its head, Joseph I. Breen, told Merian C. Cooper, R.K.O.'s Head of Production, that the script was basically satisfactory under the terms of the Production Code, though he urged the removal of such blasphemies as 'Oh God' and 'Good God', and he suggested that a derogatory reference to King George III might be censored in England.[16]

To Shaw, however, the script was basically unsatisfactory. On 23 Jan., three days after Breen wrote approval, Shaw cabled disapproval. Do another movie for Barrymore, he told Macgowan, for until he revised Cohen's scenario, which he could not complete before May, it was useless.[17] The previous day, he had written more fully. After lecturing Macgowan on 'the differences between first rate work and shop routine,' he explained:

> I have only glanced through the opening pages of the scenario; but it has been enough to convince me that I must put in about a months work (or leisure) on it before any attempt is made to rehearse or shoot it. ...
>
> I see I shall have to educate Hollywood. It means well; but it doesnt know how to make an effect and leave it alone. It wallows in it fifteen seconds too long, and then starts to explain it. It can't find the spiritual *track* of a story and keep to it. And it cant tell a story. ... And it doesnt know the difference between a call boy and a playwright.[18]

With just the cable in hand, Macgowan replied in as positive a fashion as possible. Apologizing for the script's inadequacies, he expressed pleasure at the prospect of the master's invaluable revisions. By 12 Feb. he probably received the more detailed explanation. On that date, B. B. Kahane, President of R.K.O., suggested calling off the deal. Macgowan wasted no time in expressing his disagreement. R.K.O. was not to pay G.B.S. a salary to revise the script, he argued the same day.

> After all, perhaps Shaw will merely jazz up the stuff Lester Cohen wrote in the script. Perhaps Shaw may write a wholly new and pretty swell screen play—and a screen play by Bernard Shaw would be even better publicity than a play by him. I know, of course, that there is a chance that he may send us back a script that is of no use at all, but we shall lose nothing by waiting for it.

Even though the script will not be ready in time for R.K.O.'s April commitment to Barrymore, a new *Devil's Disciple* might persuade him to make a deal more financially advantageous to R.K.O. than the last, for 'I know that Barrymore is be-deviled to play in this Shaw piece, and I believe he will make some financial sacrifice to that end.' Macgowan's arguments persuaded Kahane.[19]

But Shaw called off the deal. After a thorough perusal of Cohen's screenplay, he decided that he and Hollywood were artistically incompatible. Whereas he was a skilled practitioner in the art of dramatic effectiveness, he told Macgowan, R.K.O.'s adapter was a blundering, illiterate novice whose techniques did not go beyond a lecture with demonstrations by magic-lantern. As for revising Cohen's work, he refused to assist in his own murder. R.K.O. might be right in preferring Cohen, but he could not account for such tastes. Forget and forgive was in order, Shaw concluded. Let R.K.O. forget; he would forgive.[20]

Beyond doubt, Macgowan's disappointment was genuine. Swallowing his pride, he attempted to change Shaw's mind. While Cohen's script was merely a preliminary scenario which was to serve as a groundwork for revisions and improvements, he argued, it was not unfaithful to the play. Statistics cannot prove artistic value, he admitted, but they demonstrate intent. Of the speeches in Shaw's play, Cohen retained 442 unaltered, deleted 143, changed the same number by cuts or additions, and added 201. Although this set of statistics might suggest that R.K.O. changed over half the play, Macgowan concluded that the script was three-quarters Shaw. The remaining quarter, said he, could easily be revised. To prevent the abandonment of the project, he proposed three courses of action: Shaw could revise or cut the Cohen speeches, suggest another writer, or approve a writer suggested by Macgowan.[21] Shaw refused all courses.

An examination of the R.K.O. script demonstrates the soundness of Shaw's judgement. A number of Cohen's cuts reveal failure to understand theme and character. After Burgoyne and Dick Dudgeon politely settle the hour of the latter's execution, for example, Shaw has Judith exclaim, 'Is it nothing to you what wicked thing you do if only you do it like a gentleman? Is it nothing to you whether you are a murderer or not, if only you murder a man in a red coat?' In undermining Burgoyne's superficial charm, and in prompting a response from an audience by having an audience in the play respond that way, Shaw stresses Burgoyne's moral inferiority, his kinship to Swindon, who is merely less charming than he, and the superiority of Dick, who saves rather than takes the life of another. Cohen cuts her speech.

Cohen's additions are dramatically trite or irrelevant. Showing Essie the stars and stripes, Dick proclaims it a symbol for which some will have to die. When Judith predicts Dick will die, Cohen shows her vision of his death, a remarkably mixed metaphor: his ascension to the gallows superimposed on dying flames. In a new scene, Cohen adds such stale jokes as the Sergeant telling Dick that unlike Judith some wives thank British soldiers for executing their husbands.

In Cohen's changes, the difference between G.B.S. and R.K.O. is particularly clear. After Dick makes a seditiously pro-American statement, everyone but Essie flees from the room. Noticing she alone remains, Shaw has him ironically exclaim, 'What! Have they forgotten to save your soul in their anxiety about their own bodies?' Cohen's version: 'What! In their haste to save their own necks, have they forgotten about your soul?' The apt antithesis soul/body becomes the inelegant necks/soul. One need not multiply examples to demonstrate that Shaw is a masterful stylist who employs language more gracefully than most dramatists, Hollywood or not. But such changes as Cohen's are often unnecessary, let alone less clever. As here, they cannot even claim to save time. Elsewhere, they are longer than the original, as when Dick meets Judith. Here is Cohen:

> RICHARD. You deserve your reputation. [*Looking into her eyes*] You are very beautiful.
> *Judith lowers her eyes, averts her head.*
> RICHARD. But I take it by the fact that you lower your eyes and avert your head—that you are a good woman. [*Smiling*] Such beauty should not be wasted—upon a melancholy and repressed manner.

Compare Shaw's pointed, dramatic economy. His Richard '*looks at her earnestly*' and says, 'You deserve your reputation; but I'm sorry to see by your expression that youre a good woman.' It is the Hollywood studio man, not the literary G.B.S. who is wordy.

Shaw's comparison of the typical Hollywood screenplay to a man who lectures with illustrated slides is exemplified by that same passage, where Cohen has the character describe what the spectators see. The entire script contains such numbing repetitiveness; for instance, its opening. After Cohen shows a column of British troops on the march, he has characters say that the roads are filled with British troops. In a new scene, Anderson carefully rehearses Christy to tell his mother that Anderson will visit her soon but not to tell her that her husband has been hanged. This new scene not only duplicates the play's opening scene, wherein Christy stupidly tells all, the screenplay includes and even expands the expository dialogue in that scene. Instead of employing the medium of cinema to cut quickly from one scene to another, thereby achieving economy and dramatic intensity, Cohen flattens the play's crisp, comic concision by, in Shaw's terms, wallowing in an effect long after it has been made.

Although R.K.O. kept its promise not to represent a romantic attachment between Dick and Judith, Cohen still ended the film on a romantic note. At the end of the play, as Dick and Judith shake hands, Essie calls, 'Theyre coming back. They want you.' Then: '*Jubilation in the market. The townsfolk surge back again in wild enthusiasm with their band, and hoist Richard on their shoulders, cheering him.*' Where does Cohen find the romance? Essie, of course. At the end of his screenplay:

> ESSIE [*clinging to Richard*] Oh Dick, they want you.
> *Just as Richard is being taken from her and hoisted onto the shoulders of the townsmen—*
> ESSIE [*calling up to him*] And so do I.
> *Now, as Richard is being jubilantly borne on the shoulders of the townsfolk—the music going full blast, great cries of 'The Devil's Disciple!'—amidst cheers and huzzahs, with Richard being carried straight into close up range of the camera—*
> *Final fade out.*

Even apart from the preposterous romantic note, is it at all likely that Puritan New Englanders would cheer Dick as the devil's disciple? Although they would applaud his defiance of King George, they would not hail his diabolism.

Artistically, as G.B.S. recognised, he and R.K.O. were hopelessly incompatible. Unable to understand the themes, characters, and style of Shavian drama, Hollywood was incapable of translating it to the motion picture medium, at which it was also deficient. Working, as they did, within the framework of American movies of the early 1930s, Macgowan and Cohen aimed to do well by Shaw. Even so, mutilation was the result. Hollywood's outlook and methods could not rise to the occasion.

GERMAN *PYGMALION*

In the production of two Shavian movies, England had failed him. In the preparation of one, Hollywood also failed. Shaw still hoped to find a scenarist capable of dealing faithfully with his plays. Unexpectedly, a possible solution came from the Continent.

Less than a week after Shaw cabled disapproval of the R.K.O. script, he received an inquiry from his French translators, Augustin and Henriette Hamon, about a French film of *Pygmalion*. Initially, he was dubious about permitting a non-English language version.[1] By July 1934, however, after the R.K.O. project dissolved, he was simultaneously discussing proposals for French and German *Pygmalion* films and seriously considered the former, which had been adapted by Riera and would star Gaby Morlay as Liza.[2]

On 19 May, Augustin Hamon had sent Shaw Riera's screenplay. On 4 June, in a long, well-reasoned letter, he stressed what Shaw would soon discover for himself, that script approval was no guarantee his wishes would be followed. After approval, the script could be revised by another hand, and during the filming or editing a director or producer could wreck the entire scenario and virtually create a new one. Since some sort of adaptation to another medium is essential, Shaw should find a reliable technician: an adapter who wants the author's wishes carried out and has the authority to do so. Such a person, claimed Hamon, was Riera, whose screenplay Shaw could judge for himself. Because the technical terms of a screenplay are in an international language, Riera's could become the basis of movie versions of *Pygmalion* in other languages. It was in his interest, Hamon argued, to ensure that his work would not suffer the cinematic desecration of Zola's *Nana*—an allusion to Samuel Goldwyn's talkie version released earlier in 1934. In rival Germany, fidelity would be impossible, partly because the film industry is no more honest there than anywhere else, but mainly because of the Hitler regime: Shaw's translator and chief interpreters were Jewish, and Shavian drama was anti-bourgeois and socialist. Although Shaw preferred to give Hamon authority to negotiate only for a French movie, Hamon wanted to arrange an Italian version, to be made simultaneously with the French (a common practice), also starring Gaby Morlay. Plus he wanted distribution rights elsewhere. In countries of the European Orient, he insisted, as well as in Baltic and North African nations, for instance, the intelligentsia spoke French better than English, and subtitles could bring the film to the common people. Moreover, it would not pay a producer in such countries to make a separate film of *Pygmalion*. Hamon suggested that Gaby Morlay's company pay a royalty of 20 per cent of the manufacturer's gross receipts, which would divide $7\frac{1}{2}$ per cent to Shaw, $7\frac{1}{2}$ per cent to the Hamons, and 5 per cent to Riera.[3]

No, replied Shaw half a year later, separate films in the Balkans and elsewhere could, if properly handled, pay for themselves. French language rights only: France, Belgium, French Switzerland, and Quebec.[4] Although Hamon persisted,[5] the project collapsed. Language rights proved an insurmountable barrier. So perhaps did Riera's adaptation.[6]

Many of Riera's cuts are sensible, aimed at preserving the essential quality of a scene and deleting slight repetitiveness and digressions, as in Doolittle's speech on the undeserving poor (double brackets indicate cuts):

> Dont say that, Governor. Dont look at it that way. What am I [[, Governors both? I ask you, what am I]]? I'm one of the undeserving poor: thats what I am. Think of what that means to a man. It means that he's up agen middle class morality all the time. If theres anything going, and I put in for a bit of it, it's always the same story: 'Youre undeserving; so you cant have it.' But my needs is as great as the most deserving widow's that ever got money out of six different charities in one week for the death of the same husband. I dont need less than a deserving man: I need more. I dont eat less hearty than him; and I drink more. I want a bit of amusement, cause I'm a thinking man. [[I want cheerfulness and a song and a band when I feel low. Well, they charge me just the same for everything as they charge the deserving.]] What is middle class morality? Just an excuse for never giving me anything. [[Therefore, I ask you, as two gentlemen, not to play that game on me.]] I'm playing straight with you. I aint pretending to be deserving. I'm undeserving; and I mean to go on being undeserving. I like it; and thats the truth. [[Will you take advantage of a man's nature to do him out of the price of his own daughter what he's brought up and fed and clothed by the sweat of his brow until she's growed big enough to be interesting to you two gentlemen?]] Is five pounds unreasonable? I put it to you; and I leave it to you.

While the deletions include flavourful language and rhythms, the words would be spoken, one must recall, in translation, not in Shavian English.

Some of Riera's cinematic technique is clever. To condense time, he skilfully edits shots and cuts and rearranges dialogue. When Higgins commands his housekeeper to remove Liza's clothes and burn them, send for new ones, and take her away, he has a medium shot of Higgins, Liza, Pickering, and Mrs Pearce; cuts to a close-up of Liza when Higgins orders Mrs Pearce to clean her; dissolves to a close-up of Liza covered with soap lather when Higgins tells Mrs Pearce to use Monkey Brand; and cuts to a medium shot of Liza in the bath tub, Mrs Pearce vigorously rubbing her back with soap, while Liza exclaims, 'If I'd known what I was letting myself in for, I wouldnt have come here. I always been a good girl;

[dialogue deleted] and I wont be put upon; and I have my feelings the same as anyone else.'

Several cuts are much less skilful. Riera underplays Liza's poverty by removing Mrs Eynsford Hill's bribe of sixpence, which Liza invites, to persuade her to explain why she called her son Freddy. Deleting Higgins's gift of the change in his pocket, he omits Liza's motive for taking the cab (because of the financial windfall, she splurges).

More often than not, Riera's cinematic devices sidetrack the momentum of dramatic action. While Higgins declaims about cleaning Liza and Mrs Pearce does so, he interrupts the latter activity with a digressive switch to a pub, where Doolittle sees a taxi arrive and its driver remove Liza's belongings. Later, as in the play, but now redundantly, Doolittle tells Higgins how he knew where his daughter was. To provide continuity between Acts IV and V, when Liza leaves Higgins's flat for his mother's house, Riera creates seemingly endless sequences with a great deal of walking—and one in which Liza 'bends avec the water'—which fail to further the action.

The worst rearrangement of scenes occurs at the ambassadorial garden party, where Doolittle appears, transformed by Ezra D. Wannafeller into a wealthy man. Transposing passages from the play's fifth act, Riera blurs the climax of Liza's triumph and diminishes the impact of Doolittle's entry later, when he is wanted so that a startled Liza can relapse into her gutter cry. To retain her surprise and shriek, Riera prevents them from meeting at the garden party. A seriously wrong addition occurs at the end, after Higgins tells Liza to buy him gloves and a tie. Although she tells him to buy them himself, a new sequence has her take a tie from a salesman and loosely knot it to judge the effect.

Chronologically overlapping proposals for a Franco-Italian version of *Pygmalion*, which did not develop, were proposals for a German version, which did. On 4 March 1934, after he cancelled *The Devil's Disciple*, Shaw recognized that if a *Pygmalion* movie were to be made, it could not be filmed as it stood; he himself must compose a scenario,[7] by which he meant a screenplay that was not yet a shooting script with purely technical directions for cameramen.[8] By 15 June, after he received Riera's adaptation, he stated that if he agreed to a German film, he would insist— as he had insisted with R.K.O.—that there be no romance between the two leads and that Liza must marry Freddy.[9]

Despite Hamon's warning about the impossibility of a faithful German movie, Shaw continued to negotiate. By September he evidently felt that negotiations would conclude satisfactorily: though he had not signed a contract, he began 'cutting Pygmalion to bits' for the German film.[10] On 1 Oct. he completed cuts of the play and the composition of new scenes.[11]

With three exceptions, this 1934 screenplay for the German *Pygmalion* is virtually the same as the screenplay for the 1938 British film. All three (see Appendixes D, E, and F) are new scenes added to the play text: a film sequence that follows Act II (written anew in 1938), the reception wherein Liza triumphs (drastically revised in 1938), and a scene that follows Act V (written anew in 1938). Because all constitute major revisions, I believe 1938 rather than 1934 represents the date of completion of the *Pygmalion* screenplay, which I will discuss later. At this point, I must anticipate that discussion by noting how Shaw in 1934 aimed to ensure that the German film would not romanticize the relationship between Higgins and Liza but suggest unmistakably that she will marry Freddy. First, as in 1938, Shaw explicitly says so in a parenthetical screen direction when Higgins first appears. Second, as in 1938, he adds film sequences when Liza leaves Higgins's residence after Act IV. She meets Freddy, who confesses having spent most of his nights on the street where she lives. He '*smothers her with kisses*' and declares they are engaged. After two policemen interrupt their embraces, she suggests they spend the evening driving in a taxi, where the police cannot interfere. Third, following Liza's departure at the end of Act V, Higgins strolls onto the balcony where he watches her kiss Freddy. He angrily shakes his fist at the couple. Liza thumbs her nose at him, Freddy takes off his hat to him '*in the Chaplin manner*' and as a wedding march plays they drive off. What could be clearer?

On 16 Feb. 1935, Shaw signed and sent a Memorandum of Agreement to producer Eberhard Klagemann, head of Klagemann Films, licensing until 31 Dec. 1939 a German movie version of *Pygmalion* for distribution in German-speaking countries. Shaw would receive 10 per cent of gross receipts paid by exhibitors. The film would follow Shaw's screenplay with no transposition, interpolation, omission, or alteration of any kind unless Shaw agreed or suggested it.[12]

A major film appeared forthcoming, and a Brechtian one at that. The German *Pygmalion* was directed by Erich Engel, who had staged the premières of Brecht's *In the Jungle* in 1923 and *The Threepenny Opera* in 1928, and who in 1949 would codirect with Brecht the East Berlin production of *Mother Courage and Her Children*. In 1923, moreover, Engel had directed a silent movie, *Mysteries of a Barbershop*, with a script (consisting of a more or less vague outline) by Brecht.[13] Music for *Pygmalion* was by Theo Mackeben, who conducted the orchestra for the 1928 *Threepenny Opera*. Gustaf Gründgens played Higgins. Famous for his Mephistopheles in Goethe's *Faust*, he was also the leader of the criminals in Fritz Lang's *M* (1931), a character reminiscent of Mack the Knife; in 1932, he sought Brecht's permission to direct *Saint Joan of the*

Stockyards.[14] Doolittle was Eugen Klöpfer, whom Brecht wanted to play the title role in *Baal.*[15]

Important actors performed other roles. The popular Jenny Jugo, who according to Martin Esslin 'was the German Loretta Young' (that is, a very pretty, clean-cut girl-next-door), played Liza. Pickering was Anton Edthofer, whom Esslin calls 'the most charming of the *bons vivants* of the Reinhardt theatres, a very refined, gentlemanly actor.' Mrs Higgins was Hedwig Bleibtreu, a dignified lady who had become a *doyenne* of German theatre.[16]

On 2 Sept. 1935[17] the film opened in Berlin where, Shaw was told, it was a blazing success. Although Klagemann wanted to produce *Cæsar and Cleopatra*, Shaw despite the blaze would not consider another film with him until he saw *Pygmalion.*[18] On 3 or 4 Jan 1936 he saw it.[19]

Despite Siegfried Trebitsch's repeated assurances that Klagemann faithfully followed Shaw's screenplay in every detail,[20] he did not do so. The picture's credits cite Shaw as author of the text but not of the screenplay, which is by Heinrich Oberländer and Walter Wasserman. The movie's opening scenes portray Liza as what Shaw accurately calls an impudent, cheeky, foulmouthed hoyden rather than the dirty, tired, and pitiable creature he depicted.[21] In contrast to Shaw's description, her person and clothing (despite a torn jumper) are clean. Throughout the film, she is self-possessed, aggressive, and unintimidated by, even indifferent to, the consequences of class differences between herself and Higgins. Upon his demand that she stay in his house for speech lessons, for example, she laughs, shrugs her shoulders, goes to the window, puts two fingers in her mouth, and whistles to her young friend Jonny (a character invented by the movie makers), who waits outside for her and whom she directs to bring her belongings.

In disregard of Shaw's screenplay, the motion picture introduces numerous new scenes which drastically change it. In one significant sequence of scenes, the change is in a Brechtian direction. Doolittle no longer receives a bequest from the American millionaire Ezra D. Wannafeller, on the basis of Higgins's claim that he was England's most original moralist. In the German picture, the transformation of Liza's boozing father links to the business difficulties of a firm that manufactures alcohol-free beverages. Under Higgins's tutelage, its Managing Director rehearses a speech to the company's stockholders. Because sales have been low, he states, the yearly dividend must drop by half of one per cent. Higgins corrects the speaker's delivery: his advice includes an admonition to be less dreamlike on the word *dividend* and he hints that the speech might be better written as well. Later, in an altogether uncharacteristic action,' he recommends that the Managing Director, who is about to launch a huge advertising campaign for the firm's alcohol-free beverages, hire Doolittle as chief speech-maker, since he can talk convincingly to the masses on the benefits of the company's product. For one or two speeches per month, the Managing Director offers him £1,000 per year. Unable to refuse so much money, he changes from a flagrant to a secret drinker.

Other new episodes are neither Brechtian nor Shavian. During a speech lesson, Higgins directs Liza to record sentences first with, then without four stones in her mouth. When she prepares for the second recording, she places the stones on a table, but one, unseen by her, falls to the floor. As she speaks into the microphone she notices only three stones on the table. 'Jesus!' she cries, and she shrieks that she has swallowed one. Angry at the interruption, Higgins tells her it does not matter, for he has more stones in the yard, and he directs her to continue her lessons.* In another new sequence, unrelated to anything in Shaw's play or screenplay, Higgins, Pickering, and Liza, all fashionably attired, visit a race track. While the men watch the race, a bored Liza takes a stroll. Seeing her friend Jonny sell ice cream on the other side of a railing, she yells to him. He admires her elegant apparel and leaves his cart to bring her some. While he is gone, a tall, burly man steals a cup of ice cream. Liza observes the theft and tells Jonny, who hurries to the man for payment. Instead, the man shoves him to the ground. Jonny rises and pushes the man's elbow so that he hits himself in the face with the ice cream. The man knocks Jonny down again. Furious, Liza yells at him, climbs over the railing in an unladylike manner, and flails him with her parasol. At this moment, Higgins comes by, stops the fight, and lectures her on such undignified behaviour. Taking advantage of the bully relaxing his guard because of the interruption, Liza hits him resoundingly on the head with her parasol.

Although the German film uses none of Shaw's new scenes between Liza and Freddy, it clearly establishes him as a romantic possibility for her. After she leaves Higgins's home, they sing and play a tuneful polka— she on a concertina, he on a ukelele. A fashionable, sporty young man, Freddy wears a black tee-shirt and white trousers, shoes, and socks; and he leaps smartly over a fence as he dashes to join Liza. In a new luncheon scene at Mrs Higgins's, near the end of the film, Liza confesses her father's occupation, her own, and Higgins's speech lessons. Mrs Hill, aghast, remembers where she saw Liza before and leaves with her children. Soon,

* Does the passage sound familiar? In the 1938 British film, Liza swallows a marble rather than a stone and Higgins dismisses the matter by saying he has plenty more. Despite the assertion of Leslie Ruth Howard, whose father played Higgins, that he improvised the rejoinder,[22] the dialogue in the German film suggests that improvisation played no role in this scene.

Freddy returns alone to tell Liza that regardless of her lowly origins he wants to marry her. But while the film builds up Freddy in this manner, it does so in order to knock him down and thereby establish decisively Higgins's victory over his romantic rival. From the start of the picture, Liza is matched with Higgins. Instead of a conflict between a middle-aged, mother-fixated bully and a class-intimidated eighteen-year-old girl who becomes an independent woman, the German movie portrays a self-reliant woman of the people and a handsome, virile-looking, wealthy professional man. Throughout, it suggests Cinderella and her prince, or to put the matter in terms of pop movies of the 1930's, the secretary and the boss she will marry. In the film's finale, the camera frames Liza and Higgins, and a romantic waltz begins to play in the background. Formally but flirtatiously, she asks the Herr Professor for advice on whether to marry Freddy, run a flower shop, or give speech lessons. Under the romantic music, Higgins says softly, 'Stay with me,' and adds—acknowledging her new status—'Miss Doolittle'. She smiles, the waltz swells, the film ends. In an illustrated souvenir programme of the picture, this unquestionably romantic conclusion becomes still clearer. A comic strip, with captions in rhymed doggerel, conveys the film's plot. The final panel shows Cupid holding hands with Liza and Higgins, who are dressed for a wedding. Above them are two arrows in a heart. The verse caption, anglicized, is: 'That Liza did depart,/Has struck him to the heart./But as you clearly see,/It all ends happily.'[23]

To help support this new end, the movie makers change the conclusion of the Doolittle plot. Unlike Shaw's play and screenplay, the parallel stories of Liza's and her father's social transformations do not merge. Instead of Doolittle arriving at the home of Mrs Higgins, Higgins visits that of Doolittle and the woman he is about to marry. In contrast to Shaw's play and screenplay, the film shows and names her, Betsy (a bizarre choice of name, since it like Liza derives from Elizabeth). At the end of the movie, father and daughter do not meet. Thus, the sight of him, clean and resplendently dressed, does not startle her into shrieking her old gutter cry—perhaps because such a relapse would undercut Liza's ladylike demeanour and her eligibility as an appropriate mate for the professor.

Among other devices, director Erich Engel employs music to symbolize Higgins's growing infatuation with Liza. When she first plays and sings a lively, rowdy drinking song on her concertina, Higgins threatens to throw the concertina out the window if she plays the vulgar song again. When she defiantly does so later, he chases her through several rooms in an effort to take the concertina from her. Following their argument after the ball, Higgins in a new scene meditates as he sits on a window sill, bathed by moonlight. Unconsciously, he whistles Liza's song. Still later, at his mother's house, as he waits for Liza to appear, his arm accidentally hits her concertina, which conveniently lies on a table beside him. The concertina makes a noise. He smiles fondly at it and pats it tenderly—an obvious forecast of what will come and an equally obvious revelation of the romantic feelings that have already arrived.

Although fidelity to Shaw's screenplay is not a virtue of the German *Pygmalion*, it has other virtues. Under Engel's guidance, the lighting creates beautiful chiaroscuro effects, and, with alternations of close-ups, medium shots, long shots, pans, and tracking shots, photography and editing combine to achieve a dynamic fluidity. Employing visual and auditory methods, Engel vivifies the text. When Mrs Hill hears Liza call her son by his first name, she produces a lorgnette to examine the flower girl. Just before Doolittle tells Higgins that they are men of the world and that Liza is to him what a small amount of money is to a gentleman like Higgins, the professor sits at a piano and plays what becomes background music for Doolittle's efforts to sell him his daughter, Schubert's *Serenade*. Particularly impressive is the Doolittle of Eugen Klöpfer, who plays the role not in a Shavian but in a Brechtian manner. When he points out that he has not asked Higgins or Pickering for money, for instance, he does so neither rhetorically nor in the panic-stricken manner of a man fearful of losing their attention. Rather, he simply refers to an obvious fact. Instead of an ingratiating Dickensian rogue acted broadly with flourish and relish, his Doolittle is realistically underplayed as a persuasive con man who is skilled at extracting money from the monied.

Unfortunately, and apart from the matter of fidelity to Shaw's screenplay, the German *Pygmalion* has failings as well. The ice-cream-in-the-face sequence is merely a variant of the trite pie-in-the-face standby of movie farces. The development that concerns Liza's concertina and polka is almost as stale. In terms of storytelling, the movie is flawed. When Engel shows Liza and Freddy singing and playing their concertina and ukulele, the audience must guess where they are. Although Pickering, at the end of the previous scene with Doolittle, had suggested that Liza might be at Mrs Higgins's, the only locale shown in the shot of Liza and Freddy is grass. The motion picture weakens the impact of Doolittle's changed fortunes by telegraphing them in advance. Before he tells Higgins what has happened to him, an interview with the Managing Director provides this information. Too frequently, the camera's shifts to and from different locales for the sake of visual variety dissipate a scene's dramatic momentum: Higgins's discussion with Liza about lessons is interrupted by an irrelevant shot of Jonny waiting outside for her, and cuts to and from Jonny's encounter with Doolittle in a tavern unnecessarily interrupt

G.B.S. in the U.S.A.   Luncheon party in Marion Davies's bungalow on the M.G.M. lot in Culver City. Charlie Chaplin, Bernard Shaw, Marion Davies, Louis B. Mayer, Clark Gable and George Hearst.

How He Lied to Her Husband   She tries to prevent a fight between He and Her Husband. Edmund Gwenn, Vera Lennox and Robert Harris.

British *Pygmalion*   Photograph taken at press showing at Leicester Square Theatre (London), 4 October 1938. Bernard Shaw, Anthony Asquith, Wendy Hiller, Leslie Howard, Gabriel Pascal.

British *Pygmalion*   The ball. Violet Vanbrugh, Iris Hoey, Esme Percy, Leslie Howard and Violet Tree.

the bathroom scene. More seriously, Liza's confession to the Hills is a mere red herring that interrupts the dramatic intensity of her argument with Higgins.

Needless to say, Shaw detested the German *Pygmalion*. Its makers, he accurately charged, altered his screenplay 'out of all recognition. They spoiled every effect, falsified all the characters, put in everything I left out and took out most of what I had put in.'[24] How could they get away with such actions? Shaw was far from the scene of what was literally the crime, breach of contract. Why did not Trebitsch interfere or at least tell Shaw what was happening, as he had in 1931 about a planned movie of *Der tapfere Soldat*? One can guess. As a Jew in Nazi Germany, Trebitsch was in no position to register an effective complaint. 15 Sept. 1935, less than two weeks after the movie opened—saw passage of the 'Nuremberg laws', which deprived Jewish Germans of their citizenship. On the screen and in printed records of the film, the credits significantly fail to include a translator's name. Jews were banned from Nazi Germany's film industry. Hamon's prognosis had been correct.

The German *Pygmalion* demonstrated the wisdom of three features of Shaw's movie contracts. Because he sold a five-year licence, he could refuse to renew it if the movie violated his contract. Because he strictly limited countries where the film could be distributed, he kept the market open for a new film version in a different language, and he threatened Klagemann with legal action if the German producer attempted to distribute the film in Poland.[25] Because he licensed only one film at a time, he could refuse to permit a motion picture maker to adapt another of his plays. Under no circumstances, said Shaw, would he trust Klagemann with *Cæsar and Cleopatra* or any other play of his.[26]

SAINT JOAN

On 1 Oct. 1934, Shaw completed the *Pygmalion* screenplay for Klagemann. In a burst of creative energy, he began a screenplay of *Saint Joan* on 15 Oct., only two weeks later, and he completed it on 13 Nov.[1] On 30 Nov., he gave a copy to Elisabeth Bergner,[2] who under the direction of her husband Paul Czinner planned to play the title role, which she had created in Germany, directed by Max Reinhardt. Early in December, he announced that she would film it in 1935.[3] Later, probably after conferences with Czinner, he revised the screenplay.[4] Very likely, he completed revisions by June 1935, when the press reported production would begin in the Fall.[5] In the Summer, however, Czinner sent the screenplay to the Vatican for approval. Censorship prevented the filming of *Saint Joan.*

Shaw was long familiar with the pernicious effects of stage censorship, which under the Lord Chamberlain's jurisdiction lasted from 1737 to 1969. In 1893, censorship had prevented a London production of *Mrs Warren's Profession*, whose subject was prostitution. When Arnold Daly brought the play into New York in 1905, the Secretary of the Society for the Suppression of Vice, Anthony Comstock (his name inspired Shaw to coin the word *comstockery*) denounced it as dirty, though he had not read it, and instigated legal action against the cast, who were subsequently acquitted.

In 1909, Shaw appeared before the Joint Select Committee of the Houses of Lords and Commons, convened to examine the issue of stage censorship. He urged its abolition. Dramatists, he argued, should have the same freedom journalists and novelists have, the same freedom the ordinary citizen has, and they should have no restraint which does not apply to all citizens. Should not a play be prohibited because it might offend the religious feelings of a large part of the community? No. Should ridicule of sacred personages or attacks upon religion be permitted on stage? Yes, for 'the danger of crippling thought, the danger of obstructing formation of the public mind by specially suppressing such representations is far greater than any real danger that there is from such representations.' The true difficulty is not to suppress them but to bring them about, for producers hesitate to invest money in a play with ideas contrary to the opinions of a large number of people.[6] What of morality and immorality? As 'a specialist in immoral and heretical plays,' he said in a statement rejected by the Committee, he defined immorality as 'Whatever is contrary to established manners and customs.' Therefore, immorality is not necessarily sinful.[7] Moreover, he told the Committee, 'from one end of the Bible to the other the words "moral" and "immoral" are not used.'[8] If one is likely to feel offended by sexual suggestiveness in the theatre, he advised a few years later, one should stay away.[9]

1909, the year Shaw testified on stage censorship, saw passage of the Cinematographic Act, which laid the groundwork for film censorship in England. Initially, the act aimed solely to protect movie audiences from fire hazards, but local authorities went further. By 1910, they commonly employed it to prohibit the showing of motion pictures on Sundays. In

1912, the Association of Cinematographic Exhibitors created the British Board of Film Censors and appointed as President Shaw's old nemesis, G. A. Redford, just retired as Examiner of Plays for the Lord Chamberlain's office. Although the Board operated under general principles rather than a fixed code, it had two specific tabus: nudity and the portrayal of Christ. If the Board found a film to be objectionable, it withheld its certificate of approval until the producer made necessary cuts. By 1916, the Board's licensing conditions expanded: 'No film shall be shown which is likely to be injurious to morality or to encourage or incite to crime, or to lead to disorder, or to be offensive to public feeling, or which contains any offensive representation of living persons.' By 1932, the courts recognized the almost unlimited censorship powers of the licensing Board.[10]

In the United States too, film censorship began in 1909, with the creation of the National Board of Censorship, later called the National Board of Review. Unlike that of its British counterpart, its initial impact soon dissipated. In 1922, the threat of censorship by the federal government prompted the Motion Picture Producers and Distributors of America to form a self-censorship agency. With former Postmaster General Will H. Hays as its first president, it soon became known as the Hays Office. When films on forbidden subjects were announced, the Hays Office pressured producers to sanitize them, but when box offices felt the impact of the Great Depression, producers deviated from Will Hays's moral dicta.[11] In early 1934, Catholic bishops organized the Legion of Decency, which aimed under a threat of boycott to protect Catholics from the influence of 'vile and unwholesome pictures'. Protestant and Jewish leaders supported its efforts. The bishops demanded and received assurances that producers would comply with the Hays Office's requirements. On 1 July 1934, the movie industry agreed to put all such matters into the hands of the new Production Code Administration, headed by Joseph I. Breen. The P.C.A. first reviewed a script submitted by the producer, then indicated whether it conformed to the requirements of the Production Code and if it did not, to cite particulars, so that the producer could make the necessary changes. Upon completion of the movie, the P.C.A. screened it and either gave a seal of approval or else indicated what cuts or changes were required for a seal. Although the P.C.A. neither had nor pretended to have legal status—Breen ended each letter with a statement that the producer was free to accept or disregard P.C.A. observations—it imposed a $25,000 fine upon violators.[12] More important, the producing companies which supported the P.C.A. owned or controlled theatres that exhibited movies.[13] Until Otto Preminger successfully defied the P.C.A. in 1953 with *The Moon is Blue*, theatres would not exhibit a film that did not carry a P.C.A. seal of approval.

For two decades, the P.C.A. successfully administered its code. Among the restrictions were prohibitions against profanity, including *damn* and *hell* (unless used in a religious context or quotation); *fanny* and *whore*; *hot* (if applied to a woman) and *fairy* (if applied to a man); blasphemy, including *God*, *Jesus*, and *Christ* (unless said reverently); the depiction of religion or the clergy as ridiculous or villainous; nudity, undressing, or indecent exposure; sex hygiene and venereal disease; mockery of the sanctity of marriage; and scenes of actual childbirth.[14] Such national restrictions did not prevent local censorship. When a company distributed a picture, it provided a copy of cutting continuity to assist exhibitors in repairing the film and in complying with local censorship regulations.[15]

Shaw's attitude toward movie censorship was no different from his attitude toward stage censorship. It perpetuated what he had described in the 1920's as stultifying mediocrity and a desolating romantic morality geared to mankind's lowest possible denominator. In 1935, he announced categorically that film censorship hands the guardianship of public morals 'to some frail and erring mortal man, and [makes] him omnipotent on the assumption that his official status will make him infallible and omniscient.'[16] Because a 'series of considered moral judgments ... are absurdly impractical,' he said five years earlier, the actual business of censorship 'reduces itself to the enforcement of a few rules of thumb through which any unscrupulous person can drive a coach and six, though they are intolerably obstructive and injurious to conscientious authors.'[17] Since 'the morals of the community are simply its habits,' he had said still earlier, 'Morality, in fact, is only popularity.'[18] Film censorship, like every form of censorship, is merely a pretext 'to suppress works which the authorities dislike'. As example, he cited the British ban on Eisenstein's *Potemkin*, opposed because it does not represent naval officers as 'popular and gallant angels in uniform'. The film's suppression 'has nothing to do with the morals of the film; it is simply a move in class warfare. The screen may wallow in every extremity of vulgarity and villainy provided it whitewashes authority. But let it show a single fleck on the whitewash, and no excellence, moral, pictorial, or histrionic, can save it from prompt suppression and defamation. That is what censorship means.'[19] What Shaw said of undesirable plays is true of undesirable movies: there is no such thing. Who would go to the expense of making a film unless it were desirable? As for the clamour about sex, 'sex appeal is a perfectly legitimate element in all the fine arts that deal directly with humanity. ... Its treatment under the censorship is often vulgar; yet I believe that on balance, the good that has been done by the films in associating sex appeal with beauty and cleanliness, with poetry and music, is incalculable.' If the clamourers create a public inquiry about sex in movies, then 'people who consider sex as sinful in itself must be excluded from it like other lunatics.'[20]

In mid-1935, a year after the formation of the P.C.A., events were set in motion which resulted in a ban on the motion picture version of *Saint Joan*. Unlike the ban on *Mrs Warren's Profession*, the prohibition of *Saint Joan* had nothing to do with immorality. Unlike the ban on numerous movies, sexual suggestiveness was not at issue. Unlike the ban on *Potemkin*, class warfare was not a factor. Nor did the proposed film expose religion or the clergy to ridicule. Quite the contrary, in fact, and therein lies the reason for its suppression. Its interpretation of history differed from the official view of one religious institution, the Catholic Church.

According to Elisabeth Bergner, the question of Catholic approval of *Saint Joan* came from Twentieth Century Fox, which would not finance or distribute it unless they were sure it would not incur Catholic disapproval. Paul Czinner discussed the matter with Jesuit Father Cyril Martindale, who agreed to act as intermediary between the movie makers and the appropriate Catholic examiners.[21] Since these examiners were not part of an official body of the Catholic Church but an organization called Catholic Action, with its headquarters in Rome, it is technically true, as Czinner asserted, that the Church itself did not censor the script.[22] It is also true that Catholic Action's spokesman, who made or summarized its objections, was a priest whose viewpoint was that of the Vatican.

On 27 Aug. 1935, Father M. Barbera, S. J., reported that it was impossible to approve the screenplay of *Saint Joan* by the 'mocking Irishman' Shaw. The two fundamental reasons, said he, are that Shaw omitted Joan's repeated appeals to the Pope and 'It is false that Joan retracted.' These Vatican interpretations of Joan's trial, he called 'historical facts' which Shaw altered. In the screenplay, said Father Barbera, accurately, Joan's words at the trial 'are utterly protestant'; then inaccurately, 'Never did Joan pronounce them.' Such statements 'represent in Shaw's intention, an attack to the R.C.C. The whole play is a satire against Church and State which are made to appear stupid and inept.' If the screenplay were changed to accord with these points, and others noted in its margins, it 'could pass'; 'if the final film appears to be according to the truth of the story [i.e., as interpreted by the Church], and does not contain anything against the prestige of the R.C.C., the Catholic Action (Azione Cattolica) will declare that the showing of such a picture has not met with any objections from the Catholic Authorities.'[23] Although the Church did not officially censor the script, in other words, the fulfilment of Catholic Action's demands would result in no objection from the Church.

In the British Library's copy of what I call Shaw's revised screenplay of *Saint Joan*—and this is one reason I believe it to be the later version—are crossings-out and marginal notations by Catholic Action,[24] which objects to such words as *backside, holy,* and *infernal,* perhaps because they are indecent or blasphemous, and to such phrases as *I am damned, by Saint Denis,* and *dear child of God,* perhaps for the same reasons. Cauchon's humane statement, 'The Church cannot take life' must become 'does not wish death'. Joan's insistence that God's ways are not the ways of men, who are unfit for her to live among, and that she will go through the fire to His bosom, must be revised to 'I appeal to god and the pope.' The scene wherein Cauchon insists that custom notwithstanding Joan will not be tortured, must be omitted for the reason not that it is false but that it is 'essentially damaging'.

Very likely, Czinner continued to negotiate with Catholic Action, for Shaw learned what had happened a year later, August 1936.[25] Furious, he refused to submit to any censorship. On 2 Sept. 1936, he sent a letter to *The New York Times,* published 14 Sept., which made public the Catholic ban on *Saint Joan.* Accurately summarizing and quoting the letter and marginal comments just mentioned, he defended his play and screenplay against charges of historical inaccuracy and called the censor's demands 'absurdities [which] represent not the wisdom of the Catholic Church, but the desperation of a minor official's attempts to reduce that wisdom to an office routine.' He concluded that Catholic Action was connected to the P.C.A.[26] When Czinner attempted to explain that neither the P.C.A. nor the Church had officially censored the script, Shaw stood by his original charges. Some organization named Catholic Action, he reaffirmed, was strong enough to intimidate an English producer into submitting *Saint Joan* for its approval, and its disapproval wrecked the entire enterprise. To call such disapprobation unofficial is nit-picking. While Joseph I. Breen may be correct in saying he did not read the screenplay, he nevertheless 'carried on confidential conversations about the play.' Shaw compared himself to a man run over by an automobile without a license number.[27]

In the meantime, according to Bergner, she invited the Scottish playwright James Bridie to adapt Shaw's play for the cinema, and she did so without telling either Shaw or Czinner. Prudently, Bridie wrote Shaw to ask his approval. He refused and told Bergner that everything was over and done with.[28]

As a result of her action and of Catholic Action, Czinner did not direct and she did not star in a film version of *Saint Joan,* based on Shaw's screenplay. Which action proved decisive, I do not know. Perhaps their combination did. Nor do I know, since Bergner does not date the Shaw-Bridie matter, whether it occurred before the *New York Times* controversy (thus, a brief outburst of temper) or after it (thus, the last straw). Not until 1957, seven years after Shaw's death, was a film version of *Saint Joan* made, produced and directed by Otto Preminger, who did not know that Shaw had written a screenplay based on his own play.[29] Preminger's screen writer was Catholic Graham Greene, who seriously altered Shaw's work to conform to the viewpoint of the Church.*

In adapting *Saint Joan* to the screen, Shaw—whether or not he recognized it—followed the Inquisitor's criterion, cut from the screenplay, for reducing Joan's indictment from sixty-four counts to twelve: 'If we persist in trying The Maid on trumpery issues ... she may escape us on the great main issue.' Shaw strictly adheres to the drama's main issue: the destruction by the combined powers of church and state of the advanced individual whose actions and statements threaten the religious and political *status quo*. Although he deletes Cauchon's and Warwick's declarations that Joan is a forerunner of Protestantism and nationalism, he does not delete those actions and statements which reveal her Protestantism and nationalism. In other words, he removes or reduces only explicit references. While one might regret the excision of witty and perceptive passages, their substance is implicit in what remains. On the other hand, the Epilogue is not expendable but essential to Shaw's theme, for it demonstrates that the value of the advanced individual takes centuries to achieve recognition and that even when recognized her actual presence would still disturb the religious and political *status quo*.

In harmony with the principle enunciated by the Inquisitor, Shaw retains and stresses the basic conflict between private judgment and constituted authority, an issue closely related to Protestantism. In screenplay and stage play, Joan successfully challenges Baudricourt's judgment, successfully challenges the authority of the French army's

---

* According to this view, the Church hierarchy was neither actually nor by extension party to the trial, which was unfair. According to Shaw, the trial was fair and the judges represented the Church. After the court accepts Joan's recantation, Greene adds dialogue in which Stogumber begs Warwick not to blame the Church but instead to blame the particular French priests who conducted the trial (absolution and blame remain attached when the court later finds Joan guilty). Greene also invents a speech for Warwick, who consoles Stogumber with the statement that Joan will burn before the Pope hears of the matter. In addition to absolving the Church from guilt, Greene removes the secular interpretation of one of Joan's miracles. In the play, we hear that Joan told a drunken soldier named Foul Mouthed Frank not to swear when he is at the point of death, whereupon he drunkenly fell down a well and drowned. In Greene's screenplay, Frank is lecherous rather than drunk or foulmouthed. As he passionately reaches for Joan, she remarks that he will soon die. Immediately, Frank stiffens, hands upraised, and expires, as if stricken by a divine hand.

commander, and in the film's new battle scenes successfully overrides the judgment of military authorities in the field. Then, in a sequence of reversals, she unsuccessfully challenges the authority of king, statesmen, soldiers, and clergy—the same group who had supported her when it suited their interests—and with more adverse consequences unsuccessfully challenges the authority of the Catholic court which tries and condemns her. Although Shaw deletes many passages from the Epilogue, he retains its key feature, an encapsulation of the dramatic thrust of the entire play, praise of Joan from former friends and enemies alike when she presents no practical threat to them, rejection when she suggests she return. Her final line, in screenplay and play, the question of how long it will take the world to welcome God's saints, strikingly enunciates the work's basic theme, the necessity to distinguish between saint and crank, genius and lunatic, advanced individual and social misfit.

Throughout, Shaw trims the play to emphasize the main issues and cut what is tangential. Since Stogumber's and Warwick's responses to Cauchon's comparison of Talbot to a mad bull are relatively unimportant, Shaw deletes the entire section. Vital to Shaw's thesis that Cauchon acts honorably according to his own viewpoint, however, is his next speech, which remains: 'The Church cannot take life. And my first duty is to seek this girl's salvation.' His assertion that his disinterment damages justice, faith, and the foundations of the Church is a minor theme, therefore removed, but his proximate avowal that he was just, merciful, and faithful to his light is major, therefore retained.

In its transition from stage play to screenplay, *Saint Joan* simplifies complexities and excises subtleties. The blue-pencilling of Joan's statements that she will never take a husband and does not wish to be regarded as a woman removes psychological complexities. Shaw deletes such religious subtleties as the Archbishop's definition of a miracle as an event which, no matter how rational its basis, creates or confirms faith. Perhaps deferring to the supposed prudery of movie audiences, Shaw removes a reference to Charles's mistress. Deferring to their lack of historical knowledge, he removes references to Pythagoras and Wycliffe.

Important to Shaw's *Saint Joan* is its historical milieu. Not only does Shaw utilize such historical or legendary aspects of Joan's story as her recognition of the Dauphin at court and the change of wind at Orleans, he also lifts from her interrogation and trial comments that resemble Shavian inventions. Is Joan in a state of grace? 'If I am not, may God bring me to it: if I am, may God keep me in it,' says Shaw's Joan; 'If I am not, may God place me there; if I am, may God keep me there,' says history's Joan. Does Saint Michael appear to Joan naked? 'Do you think God cannot afford clothes for him?' asks Shaw's Joan; 'Do you think God has not wherewithal to clothe him?' asks history's Joan.[30]

The historical milieu of *Saint Joan* is not just a matter of a few paraphrases. Shaw aims to recreate her time and to remind the spectator that if he were alive then, he would vote to burn her. To the latter end, the screenplay retains, albeit in abbreviated form, the gentle, persuasive reasonableness of the Inquisitor's address to the court. To the former, as Shaw says in the play's Preface, he permits 'the medieval atmosphere to blow through my play freely.' In such an atmosphere, as Joan innocently corrects Baudricourt when he utters a blasphemous oath, damnation in its literal sense matters; and soldiers, as he reminds her, are subject to their feudal lord, not their king. Of particular value in recreating the medieval atmosphere is Shaw's dramatic treatment of miracles. It is the credulous Baudricourt who calls the egg-laying a miracle; Joan knows nothing about it. Although the gullible Dauphin is impressed by Joan's miraculous-like identification of him and Bluebeard, the Archbishop and Joan herself know how she did it. The greedy archer and the fleeing soldiers ignorantly believe that miracles caused the disasters visited upon their armies, but Shaw shows Joan's generalship to be responsible. The only act she herself calls a miracle is when Charles asks whether she can turn lead into gold: 'I can turn thee into a king, in Rheims Cathedral,' she quips; 'and that is a miracle that will take some doing, it seems.' But she intimates that hard work will underlie such a miracle.

In adapting *Saint Joan* to the screen, Shaw judiciously cuts the text, streamlines the play. Replies become more direct, and each line of development moves without digression or repetition toward its climax. Thus:

CHARLES. Why doesnt he raise the siege, then?
LA HIRE. ⟦The wind is against him.
BLUEBEARD. How can the wind hurt him at Orleans? It is not on the Channel.
LA HIRE. It is on the river Loire; and⟧ the English hold the bridgehead. He must ship his men across the river and upstream, if he is to take them in the rear. Well, he cannot, because there is a devil of a wind blowing the other way.

And:

D'ESTIVET. Why did you jump from the tower?
⟦JOAN. How do you know that I jumped?
D'ESTIVET. You were found lying in the moat. Why did you leave the tower?⟧
JOAN. Why would anybody leave a prison if they could get out?

Shaw not only cuts the play, he takes advantage of the greater resources of motion pictures to extend the action, broaden the scope, and enrich the drama. On screen, he shows what the play only mentions: the destruction of the bridge at Orléans, the burning of Joan. Instead of relying on exposition to reveal Joan to be a brilliant general, he demonstrates her military activities, forming ideas the professional commanders do not think of, then implementing them successfully. He shows Joan's face when soldiers march by and when she hears her voices through the ringing of the angelus. On stage, separation scenes are sometimes necessary. At the beginning of Scene 2, for example, he employs such a scene to give Joan time to change from dress to armour. Unnecessary for a movie, Shaw trims this scene to keep only what is dramatically essential. Among the deletions is the time-filling account of the death of Foul Mouthed Frank, which Shaw's skill prevents from seeming a mere time-filler. Because of this cut, Shaw cleverly rearranges the dialogue so that La Hire's reference to Dunois needing a miracle at Orléans serves as cue for Bluebeard's idea to test Joan's ability to work miracles by masquerading as the Dauphin (in the play, it comes a page before La Hire's statement). In the screenplay's new battle scenes, Shaw roams freely over space and through time, as he begins a scene shortly before the previous one ends. Employing simultaneous action, he cuts between Warwick's tent and Charles's coronation at Rheims. As he shows what Warwick and Cauchon discuss, he conveys a greater sense of urgency to their need to destroy Joan.

But the screenplay of *Saint Joan* does not entirely improve upon the play. Apart from the loss of superb passages of dialogue, such as the Archbishop's explanation of miracles, several enriching aspects of the play are seriously minimized. First, the conception of Joan as a woman of the people, and the role of the common people whom she represents, diminish. No longer does she tell Charles, 'I come from the land, and have gotten my strength working on the land.' Neither does she contrast what common folk understand and what knights understand, nor remind Dunois that the townspeople and commoners followed her into battle and showed the nobles how to fight their enemies. Although this aspect of *Saint Joan* is secondary to other themes, its loss impoverishes the screenplay. A related loss is the deletion of the Saint from Hell. On stage, Shaw could not show the burning of Joan. He therefore brings the English soldier who comforted her into the Epilogue. With justice, Shaw might plead that because the film shows him at the burning it need not do so again *post mortem* and that his omission from the Epilogue intensifies its dramatic impetus. Nevertheless, without him, the Epilogue contains no representative of the common people (the Executioner, a member of a

58

professional class, is contemptuous of commoners) and no longer shows that after Joan's death, as in her life, it is only the common people who stand by her (only the Saint from Hell comforts her) and that the common people have no real power (though the infernal saint does not want to abandon her, he must when the clock calls). Another loss is the diminished role of La Hire, Joan's first ally at court (and he is only a captain, far lower in rank than the others).

Even so, the strengths of the *Saint Joan* screenplay more than compensate for these losses, which I may have overemphasized. Both the common English soldier and La Hire are present, and audiences see the former in action. Close-ups of hair-dos and apparel may suggest Joan's link to the commoners, and the screenplay does retain several references to suggest that link. In the play, none of these aspects is obvious. In the screenplay, all are present, but in a still more implicit form.

ENTER GABRIEL PASCAL

In 1935, Shaw embarked on three motion picture ventures. Klagemann's *Pygmalion*, produced that year, angered Shaw when he saw it in January 1936. The Czinner-Bergner *Saint Joan*, announced for production that year, collapsed in 1936. In late 1935, before he saw the German *Pygmalion* and before he learned of Catholic Action's actions, he embarked upon the third. A stage direction might have read: enter Gabriel Pascal.

Who was this Hungarian *émigré* known as Gabriel, or Gaby, Pascal? A major difficulty in answering this question is that all sources, including his widow Valerie, acquired their information directly or indirectly from Pascal, who drew freely upon his abundant imagination. Yet some of his stories, however fantastic, might be true—a possibility one should keep in mind, remote though it may sometimes seem. Complicating the problem, as S. N. Behrman puts it, Pascal 'never made the least effort to give his inventions the vulgar gloss of consistency,' or as Valerie Pascal suspects, he enjoyed telling contradictory tales about his past. Thus, he announced to Behrman on one occasion that he descended illegitimately from Talleyrand, on another from Metternich; to his wife that he was the kidnapped offspring of royalty or perhaps an orphan; to Robert Morley that he was the illegitimate son of a Bulgarian officer.[1] Like the signpost that gives three different directions to the Emerald City of Oz, some of the statements are surely false, but one might be true.

Just as George Bernard Shaw created G.B.S., this Hungarian *émigré* created Gaby Pascal, a fascinating, flamboyant, self-dramatizing impresario with an enormous amount of *élan*, charm, blarney, and sheer chutzpah. To S. I. Hsiung, who adapted such ancient Chinese plays as *Lady Precious Stream* into English and who played a bit role in the movie *Major Barbara*, he was a self-promoter whose surname would be more appropriate if it began with R instead of P; to S. N. Behrman, a charlatan and megalomaniac who was at the same time irresistible and engaging; to Rex Harrison, 'a marvellous gypsy rogue, with incredible panache and no guile, as open as a baby and as ruthless as a tiger.'[2] Shaw told his German translator that he reminded him of Frank Harris and warned his French translator that this likable, imaginative, and incomparable story teller was purely an adventurer.[3] In an exchange from *Pygmalion*, retained in Shaw's screenplay and in the film Pascal made from it, the Hungarian producer might have recognized a description of himself: 'Doolittle: either youre an honest man or a rogue.' 'A little of both, Henry, like the rest of us: a little of both.'

Gabriel Pascal's real name was not Gabriel Pascal, which is not Hungarian, but Gabor Lehöl, which is.[4] Various sources agree he was born in Transylvania, Hungary, and usually give 1894 as his year of birth.[5] According to two sources, he was Jewish; to one, he was reared as a Catholic; at least two others record his assertion that Jesuits raised him.[6] Since the three possibilities are not mutually exclusive, all may be true; or none may be. Piecing together various accounts of his childhood, Pascal was a shepherd boy in Transylvania who, believe it or not, ran off with or was abducted by gipsies, who taught him the skills of acrobatics and theft. Adopted by a Viennese or perhaps Hungarian family, he went to a military academy, then to an agricultural school, and received training in diplomacy.[7]

But he resolved upon a theatrical career. According to Pascal, a luminary no lower than Eleanora Duse was responsible. While holidaying in Florence with his wealthy family, each morning he saw a sad-eyed woman in a nearby garden. Climbing a wall to learn the reason for her unhappiness, he was stopped by a whip-wielding man in riding boots. Saved by the lovely lady, whom he learned to be Duse, he decided to become an actor.[8] His 'star of destiny', as he termed it, took him to the Hofburg Theatre in Vienna, which he determined to join. Confronting an astonished secretary with a demand for an audition before all the directors, so the story goes, he announced his name, fixed a one-week deadline, promised to appear each morning to remind the secretary, and on the seventh day would have him fired if he did not arrange the audition. Before the secretary could gather his wits to throw him out, Pascal left. Keeping his promise, he appeared every morning, indicated with his fingers how many days remained, then disappeared. On the sixth day, he reminded the secretary of his threat. By this time, the secretary wondered whether Pascal might know someone important. On the seventh morning, he arranged the audition, which Pascal passed.[9]

In 1914, he told an interviewer, he worked in films with Robert Wiene, who later made *The Cabinet of Dr. Caligari*.[10] What that work entailed, the interview does not say, but the two major Wiene filmographies list no Wiene film for that year. Although *Arme Eva* (Poor Eve), also titled *Frau Eva* (1915), might have been made in 1914, neither filmography lists Pascal among the credits for it or any other Wiene film.[11]

With the onset of World War I, Pascal became a cavalry officer in the Hungarian Hussars. Off to the Italian front he went, accompanied by two dachshunds and a mongrel, he told his wife; to Russia, he told S. N. Behrman, and when he fed his prisoners magnificently, their sulkiness changed to gratitude and they happily made up songs for him.[12]

After the war, he created G.P. Films, which distributed movies in Europe. As various sources have it, he produced and codirected *Populi Morituri* (People About to Die), dated variously 1921 and 1922, in which he played a leading role.[13] Yet investigation reveals Robert Reinert to have been the sole producer and director of this film, which was also released as *Sterbende Völke* (Dying Peoples), and fails to reveal Pascal's name among the actors.[14]

In the summer of 1925, on the French Riviera, he claims to have met Shaw. To avoid offending the sensitivities of vacationers, he rose at dawn one morning for a nude swim. In the water, goes the possibly apocryphal tale, he encountered another enthusiast of nude swimming, G.B.S., with whom he instantly became friends. After prophesying that Pascal would one day go broke, the sixty-nine year old swimmer invited Pascal to visit him when he did.[15]

From the Riviera, Pascal went to Berlin, in whose film world he made no mark; then to Holland where the millionaire munitions maker Sir Basil Zaharoff supposedly offered to finance his film ventures in China provided he did some spying on the side. Pascal refused, found himself stranded with no funds to pay his hotel bill, escaped without his luggage, and repaired his fortunes in England, where he produced *The Street of the Lost Souls*, starring Pola Negri.[16] The story about Pascal's association with Sir Basil is unverifiable, with the Negri film unverified. Apart from

Valerie Pascal, the only source that even mentions his name in connection with the one British film Pola Negri made—entitled *The Woman He Scorned*—says he helped publicize it.[17]

From England, he returned to Berlin, where he produced several successful films, particularly Lehar's operetta *Friederika*, which one source says he codirected, another that he did not.[18] With Hitler's accession to power in 1933, Pascal left Germany. His first major stop was Hollywood, where according to Valerie Pascal he refused to work on a movie unless the star on whose name backing depended were replaced by 'an unknown actress, Jean Arthur'.[19] But while Jean Arthur was not a star in 1933, she was hardly unknown. She had been in films since 1920 and played featured and leading roles since 1923.

Soon, Pascal travelled to India, to join a celebrated mystic, Shri Meher Baba, in the production of a movie about reincarnation. When nothing came of the film, Pascal was stranded there. Partly through the assistance of a sea captain whom he had befriended in Bombay, he reports, he returned to California, where he remembered his nude Riviera swim a decade earlier. Hiding in the toilet of a train, he went to New York; then, broke as Shaw had predicted he would be, to England to visit his fellow-swimmer.[20]

In London, he borrowed money from a friend. To put himself in the proper frame of mind for his meeting with Shaw, he went to a barber shop for a shave, breakfasted at the Savoy, and took a cab to Shaw's flat at No. 4, Whitehall Court. In his pocket when he rang the doorbell, as Shaw later confirmed, was a half crown coin. Pascal ordered Shaw's maid to tell her master that the brown-buttocked film producer from the French Riviera wanted to see him. Either Shaw remembered or (his secretary makes no mention of the Riviera encounter) he was curious about the foreign caller. In either case, he saw him.[21]

According to Pascal, who evidently charmed everyone in the Shaw household, he told Shaw he was the materialization of Dick Dudgeon, proclaimed himself disciple to G.B.S., and requested movie rights to *Pygmalion*. Although Shaw refused, the visitor clearly fascinated him. Pascal returned several times. Shaw continued to hedge. On 8 Dec. 1935, Pascal delivered an ultimatum: unless Shaw gave him the rights by 4.00 p.m. five days later (Friday, the 13th), he would leave England to make films in China. That Friday, Pascal waited nervously in his Duke Street flat. At 3.45 he packed his toothbrush. As Big Ben began to strike four, a messenger rang the doorbell. At the fourth stroke, he handed Pascal an envelope with the contract for *Pygmalion*.[22] Or so Pascal maintains. Allowing for his usual dramatic exaggeration, the story might possibly be true. A cover letter reveals that on that date Shaw sent but did not personally give him a Memorandum of Agreement.[23] Furthermore, Shaw's Engagement Diary records this entry for 13 Dec. 1935: 'Pascal, 11.30.'[24] If Shaw dispatched a messenger from Whitehall Court at that hour, he had more than enough time to reach Duke Street by four.

Why did Shaw bypass Universal Pictures, Alexander Korda, and Marion Davies, who all sought permission to film *Pygmalion*,[25] and take a chance on the unknown émigré? For one thing, he would have had to take a chance on anyone.[26] For another, as Blanche Patch puts it, Pascal's 'veneration for the plays was clearly sincere'.[27] In 1941, Shaw said as much: 'Until he descended on me out of the clouds I could find nobody who wanted to do anything with my plays on the screen but mutilate them, murder them, give their cadavers to the nearest scrivener,' and exhibit them 'with my name attached and the assurance that nobody need fear that it had any Shavian quality whatever, and was not real genuine Hollywood'. Pascal, on the other hand, believed that everything such people did was wrong, everything Shaw did was right. 'Naturally, I quite agreed with him'.[28]

Whatever misgivings Shaw may have had about Pascal must have vanished a few weeks later, for then he saw the German *Pygmalion*.

DUTCH *PYGMALION*

Pascal filmed the third *Pygmalion*, not the second. After Shaw gave him permission to film it in English, Filmex Cinetone of Amsterdam filmed it in Dutch. Its director was German-born Ludwig Berger, who had made films in Germany, France, and the United States (*The Vagabond King*) and would later make one in England (*The Thief of Bagdad*). Starring the popular Dutch actors Lily Bouwmeester as Liza and Johan de Meester as Higgins, *Pygmalion* opened in Amsterdam in March 1937. A huge critical and popular success, by the time it had run seven weeks in Amsterdam (population 800,000) 200,000 people had seen it, and it was still running. With typical entrepreneurial modesty, its producer, Rudolf Meyer, called it 'the best [film] ever made in Holland.' One reviewer dubbed it 'a revelation for the Dutch [film] industry'.[1]

Although Berger's *Pygmalion* may well have been the best Dutch film then made and a revelation for the country's small movie industry, Shaw—who saw it in early May 1937—loathed it.[2] Like the German motion picture makers, the Dutch flagrantly violated their contract by disregarding Shaw's screenplay and his explicit intentions.

A moderately amusing though entirely conventional film, Ludwig Berger's *Pygmalion* is simply not Shaw's *Pygmalion*. While the picture credits no adapter or screenwriter, someone—perhaps Berger—created and interpolated new film sequences.[3] In one, following a phonetics lesson with Higgins, Liza encounters some urchins from her former neighbourhood and gives them the same lessons. Since she does so in the middle of a busy thoroughfare, she blocks traffic. Attracted by honking automobile horns and the cries of irate drivers, a policeman removes her. In another new scene, undoubtedly influenced by the German film, Doolittle gives a temperance lecture; as his female audience coos with delight and applauds him, he squats below the lectern to sneak a drink. When Liza leaves Higgins's house, she does not meet Freddy, as Shaw's screenplay indicates. Instead, two sailors unsuccessfully try to pick her up.

Among the major changes is the diminution of social resonances. Liza's and her father's social transformations appear to consist of little more than her donning an expensive party dress and him a suit. Underlying their insufficient changes, they are relatively clean before their metamorphoses. Liza is picturesque-poor, not dirty. Her clean room does not show the results of poverty; it is merely monastic. Other changes resemble those of the German film. Plucky and self-assertive, Liza never appears frightened of what somebody of Higgins's social class can do to someone of hers. Even when she visits his mother for her preliminary test, her behaviour is not tentative but self-confident.

As one might expect, the basic alteration is romance between professor and pupil. Freddy is skinny and effeminate looking, with a cherubic face, pasty complexion, hair parted in the centre and plastered back. He offers no competition to the pipe-smoking Higgins, who conveys a very attractive and comfortable virility. Nor is their romance only a matter of casting. The movie makers use none of Shaw's new scenes between Liza and Freddy, who disappears after Mrs. Higgins's at-home. Does Higgins pop half a chocolate into Liza's mouth, almost choking her, before she can refuse it? Hardly. Liza looks longingly at the box of chocolates. As she leans forward encouragingly, so that he can deposit it in her mouth, romantic music plays in the background and they smile at each other. When Liza, following her bath, enters in a kimono, she acts coy and flirtatious toward Higgins, who seems pleased at her prettiness, she at his pleasure. After their argument following the reception, suggestions of romance accelerate as Berger makes better use of Liza and her concertina than the German film makers do. He shows Higgins in his bedroom, then cuts to Liza's bedroom, where accompanying herself on the concertina she sings *Sarais Marais*, about a pair of lovers who are separated from each other. In addition to the implications of the song's lyrics, the settings and their juxtaposition by montage link the characters in a bedroom milieu. As Liza sings and Higgins listens, each undresses. The director cuts back and forth between them. Her voice is heard as the camera cuts to him, listening as he dons pyjama tops, then cuts to a close-up of her, with bare shoulders. Despite the fact that they are in separate rooms, the montage creates an unmistakably romantic ambience. When she begins to cry near the end of her song, the camera cuts to him in bed, about to put out the light, listening to her tearful voice. The next day, waiting for Liza at his mother's, he sits grumpily in a chair, humming. The song? *Sarais Marais*, of course. And of course Liza enters to hear him. When they begin to argue, he grabs her wrists when she raises her fists in anger. The touch does something to both. He looks romantic. She begins to melt. They look into each other's eyes and draw closely together as if to kiss, only to be interrupted by Mrs. Higgins, who leaves with Liza for the wedding. Soon, Higgins joins them in church. Making his way past Pickering and his mother, he stations himself between her and Liza. While Doolittle slips the ring on his bride's finger, Higgins talks tenderly to Liza, his mother smiles knowingly at them, Liza looks flirtatiously at Higgins, whose gaze is romantic. The implication is obvious. With his mother's blessing, the couple will follow her father's example.

This Dutch trivialization of Shaw's play, only a year and a half after the German movie, gave Shaw further reason to be glad he restricted distribution rights and took care to license only a single film for five years. There remained Gabriel Pascal and a British *Pygmalion*.

BRITISH *PYGMALION*

Pascal had to wait about two years to get backing for *Pygmalion*. Contrary to Valerie Pascal's assertions,[1] studio heads did not regard Shavian drama as too highbrow for the general public and they did not consider Shaw box office poison after the failure of B.I.P.'s *Arms and the Man*. Actually, they continued to request movie rights to his plays. Why did Pascal encounter so many difficulties?

One reason was his inexperience.[2] Another was the nature of Shaw's agreement, which gave him the right to produce *Pygmalion* but did not give him the play's film rights, which Shaw retained. The distinction is vital. Any agreement Pascal might conclude to exercise his own right was subject to an agreement with the property's owner. Whereas Shaw was an astute businessman, Pascal, as his widow attests, was not.[3] Unlike Pascal, Shaw was not so anxious to have his plays filmed that he would agree to a financially disadvantageous or exploitative contract. As Pascal discovered, the stumbling blocks to a contract were Shaw's insistence on a five-year license, the right of the author and no one else to change the script, and a royalty of 10 per cent on gross receipts from exhibitors rather than distributors (often linked to them, sometimes though the companies' names and their legal incorporations differed). Thus, when Columbia Pictures demanded not a five-year licence for *Pygmalion* but an absolute assignment of film rights, an explicit waiver of authorial rights to permit the studio 'to make changes in the scenario and to omit portions thereof and make alterations therein, to transpose parts of the same and interpolate therein parts of other works; and ... to recut, re-edit, and re-assemble and reconstruct said photoplay in such manner as we in our sole discretion shall deem advisable,' and a 10 per cent royalty on amounts paid by distributors rather than exhibitors,[4] Shaw refused to sign.

Before Pascal found backing, he supported himself as best he could. His only employment that I could discover during this two year period was as producer of a potboiler called *Reasonable Doubt*,[5] which featured Marie Lohr, who was to play major roles in his *Pygmalion* and *Major Barbara*. However despondent he may have felt, his public stance was unfailingly optimistic. 'I have practically concluded' a distribution contract,[6] he would invariably announce, and 'Next week I start. I go now see the old man to talk cast.'[7] He went to English and American studios, also French and Italian, for one of his plans was to shoot *Pygmalion* simultaneously in all three languages (the French cast would have Gaby Morlay and Michel Simon as Liza and Doolittle).[8]

It was probably during the Summer of 1937 that Nicholas Davenport, a financier, economist, socialist, and playwright, agreed to form a syndicate, Pascal Films, to produce *Pygmalion*. He raised £10,000 and approached C. M. Woolf of General Film Distributors for £40,000 more plus a distribution contract. Though Woolf refused, a flour magnate named J. Arthur Rank, who had begun to expand his activities into film making, and Richard Norton, later Lord Grantley, became interested. Upon Pascal's agreement to be personally responsible for finding additional funds if they were needed, Woolf withdrew his opposition and scheduled *Pygmalion* for production at Pinewood Studios.[9] Shaw conferred with Pascal and Leslie Howard, who would play Higgins and codirect the film with Anthony Asquith; then with Pascal and Laurence Irving, grandson of Sir Henry, who would design the sets.[10]

Though Shaw was consulted on casting, his advice was not always taken. For the leading male role, he wanted Charles Laughton.[11] After Laughton, his preference was Cecil Trouncer,[12] who played the first policeman Liza and Freddy meet. Shaw considered Leslie Howard 'hopelessly wrong', for 'the public will like him and probably want him to marry Eliza, which is just what I don't want.'[13]

While Shaw dutifully forwarded Pascal a letter from Marion Davies, then thirty-eight, who wanted to play the eighteen-year old Liza[14] (this shows it is unlikely that, as her biographer states, Shaw initiated the idea[15]), Wendy Hiller was cast even before Pascal secured financial backing. Contrary to Pascal's assertion that he 'discovered' her,[16] she had already achieved success on London and New York stages in *Love on the Dole*, which Shaw had seen, and in the summer of 1936, at Shaw's suggestion, she played Liza at the Malvern Festival,[17] after which Shaw told her that only she could play Liza in the movie of *Pygmalion*,[18] a stipulation he made to Pascal.[19] Other actors cast early were Wilfrid Lawson as Doolittle, Marie Lohr as Mrs Higgins, and Leueen McGrath as Clara. Pascal suggested Philip Merivale for Pickering, Jean Cadell for Mrs Hill. Although Shaw approved Merivale, Scott Sunderland played the role. But he approved Jean Cadell only for Mrs Pearce: 'Her salary would be wasted on the other parts.' For Freddy, Pascal proposed John Mills, with whose work Shaw was unfamiliar.[20]

Mills might have played the role had not David Tree, grandson of Sir Herbert Beerbohm Tree, who under Shaw's direction had played Higgins in the play's first London production, decided his career needed a new direction. At the Oxford Repertory Company some years earlier, young Tree, playing Freddy as 'distilled essence of undergraduate', achieved a great success among the largely undergraduate audience. Next under contract to Alexander Korda, he played a series of bomb-throwing revolutionists. Though he considered himself terrible, Korda felt differently: 'Just the sort of thing you do so well.' Tree, who wanted a change, heard of Pascal and *Pygmalion*. Unable to contact the producer through usual channels, he went directly to his apartment one morning.

Pascal himself, scowling all over his face, opened the door dressed in his pyjamas. 'Vot you vant, young man?' 'I want to play Freddy in *Pygmalion.*' He was momentarily caught off his balance. 'Vy you tink you can play Freddy?' In answer, I quickly produced an Oxford newspaper review. He read it in silence, and then said suddenly: 'Come in, young man! I get dressed. Vee go see Bernashow.'

'Bernashow' turned out to be Bernard Shaw, who soon ascertained Tree's genealogy. Did Shaw think the young man could play Freddy? 'Why not?' he said. 'After all, you could scarcely make a greater mess of it than your grandfather made of Higgins.' Pascal then persuaded Korda to release Tree from his contract. With Tree cast as Freddy, Pascal or Shaw got the idea to cast his mother Viola as a journalist in the ballroom scene.[21]

Wishing to become part of this *Pygmalion* film, major names in the English theatre world accepted bit roles: O. B. Clarence played a vicar, Eileen Beldon a parlourmaid, Stephen Murray a policeman. For the ambassadorial reception, Shaw quipped, 'All the élite of the profession over forty rushed down to Pinewood to super in it. Apparently they are so hard up that they will do *anything* for ten guineas.'[22] In addition to Esme Percy in the substantial role of Higgins's former pupil and Violet Vanbrugh as the Ambassadress, Kathleen Nesbitt, Irene Brown, and Iris Hoey played bits. In roles of one line each were two young actors at the start of illustrious careers: Leo Genn as the prince charming who dances with Liza at the ball and Anthony Quayle as her hairdresser.

Behind the scenes were people who were or would soon become major figures. Arthur Honegger wrote the score. The editor was David Lean, later a director (*Great Expectations* and *Lawrence of Arabia*). Photography was by Harry Stradling, who had done *Carnival in Flanders* and would do *A Streetcar Named Desire.* Cameraman was Jack Hildyard, whose credits would include *The Bridge on the River Kwai* (directed by Lean). Assistant Director was Teddy Baird, who would produce *The Importance of Being Earnest* (directed by Asquith).

After what he regarded as a grotesque effort by Hollywood to adapt *The Devil's Disciple*, and the revolting German and Dutch movies of *Pygmalion*, Shaw was elated at the prospect of this new *Pygmalion* film: 'An all British film, made by British methods without interference by American script writers, no spurious dialogue but every word by the author, a revolution in the presentation of drama on the film. In short,' he concluded, ignoring the fact that its producer and prime mover was Hungarian, 'English *über Alles*'.[23]

On the eve of production, however, all of the all British financiers had not delivered the promised money. On 11 March 1938,[24] Norton gave a well publicized luncheon party with the announced purpose of celebrating the first day's shooting, the real aim to prod the reluctant investors, who attended with a mass of newspaper, society, and entertainment people. Only Norton, Pascal, and Shaw wondered whether the first day's shooting might also be the last. Leslie Howard and Wendy Hiller performed a short scene, the gala luncheon began, and speeches were made, during which, at the eleventh hour, the money materialized.[25]

Except for the first day's shooting, Shaw was absent during the making of *Pygmalion*. He advised from afar. 'The stills are magnificent', he wrote to Pascal on one occasion, and he predicted Wendy Hiller would be 'the film sensation of the next five years.'[26] On another: 'Wendy is perfect. But Higgins is fatally wrong', and then he suggested the sort of costume Leslie Howard should have had.[27] Through the producer, he suggested how Laurence Irving might enhance the film's ending: 'Not only must the drawingroom be pretty and the landscape, and the river if possible, visible through the windows with the suggestion of a perfect day outside, but the final scene on the embankment at Cheyne Walk must be a really beautiful picture. Its spaciousness must come out when the car is driven off. Irving must eclipse Whistler in this.'[28] Despite his frequent advice, he purposely stayed away from the set. 'I do not propose to interfere in the direction of the picture,' he told Pascal, 'since I cannot, at my age, undertake it myself.'[29] He was true to his word.

But he endeavoured to protect his own domain. Less than a year after he signed with Pascal, he discovered that the producer planned to introduce a jealousy scene between Higgins and Freddy, an addition which would immediately present Higgins in the role of lover.[30] He did more than veto the idea, he rewrote the end to make Liza's and Freddy's future together more explicit, and to show Higgins's acceptance of that future. Producer and directors wanted expansion of the ambassadorial reception scene, and Anthony Asquith persuaded Shaw to revise it.[31] To provide more suspense, Shaw added new characters, notably a former pupil of Higgins who might be skillful enough to discover Liza's origins. The recomposition of this scene stimulated him to suggest: 'Why not, by the way, [introduce] a black princess talking Hottentot (all clicks) with Higgins following her and taking down the clicks frantically in his notebook?'[32] Pascal did not act upon this idea. At first, Shaw resisted the addition of a scene between Acts II and III,[33] but he relented after his revised screenplay was typed and wrote a brief phonetics lesson.

Shaw did not agree to all the trio's suggestions. Perhaps because of economy, perhaps fear of redundancy, Pascal proposed to trim Shaw's new film sequences by the deletion of one of the two policemen Liza and Freddy encounter. Shaw was resolute: 'I must have two policemen ... and two scenes, because I must produce the impression of the two lovers having run at least as far as Cavendish Square from the first policeman and to Hanover Square from the second.'[34] He prevailed. Perhaps because Anthony Asquith wanted greater visual variety, with picturesque exteriors, he proposed new concluding sequences. Of what his proposal consisted, one can guess from Shaw's response:

> Anthony is a talented and inventive youth; but he doesnt know the difference between the end of a play' and the beginning. Just when the audience has had enough of everything except the ending between Higgins and Eliza, to go back to the dirty mob in Covent Garden and drag back Doolittle after he has been finished and done with would produce a boredom and distraction that would spoil the whole affair. As to taking Higgins and Eliza out of that pretty drawingroom to be shaken up in a car it shews an appalling want of theatre sense and a childish itch for playing with motor cars and forgetting all about the play and the public. So away all that silly stuff goes.[35]

In most of these particulars, Shaw had his way.

As I have just suggested, he did not win every battle. Indeed, he was not always aware there were battles. Before analyzing what the directors did with Shaw's screenplay, let us examine the screenplay, which in several important respects improves upon the play. And it masterfully employs the medium of cinema.

The play's major elements are its comedy, the transformation of Liza, and the social themes that derive in part from her metamorphosis. Since its comic dialogue and action are too obvious to require documentation (it has held the stage since 1913 and been reprinted often since 1914), I will not comment on them except insofar as Shaw's cinematic additions reinforce its generic basis.

Although the play *Pygmalion* raises the question of romance between Liza and Higgins only to reject such a notion and to stress its irrelevance, the screenplay goes further to deny it. While the play dramatizes neither scenes of wooing nor of flirtation between them, and while it ends with Higgins's acknowledgement that she will marry Freddy, generations of actors, audiences, and readers—not to mention adapters into German and Dutch movies and American musical comedy—steadfastly deny the play's denial of romance between professor and pupil. Why? Theatrical custom in regard to leading man and woman constitutes one reason (habitual expectations are difficult to shed), resonances of the Cinderella tale another. No doubt psychologists can find still other reasons, but one major cause may lie in the simple fact that after Act III, Freddy disappears from the play. Despite Liza's references to him thereafter, audiences do not see her alternative to Higgins. For this reason alone, her stated determination to marry what has become an offstage presence may fail to convince some people.

In the screenplay, Shaw remedies this possible deficiency. Apart from explicit statements that create different theatrical and cinematic expectations—that Higgins and Freddy contrast with each other in age (forty vs. twenty) and appearance (not youthful vs. very youthful and handsome)—and tell the director and screenplay reader that Freddy 'is the one who captivates and finally carries off Liza,' and any suggestion of romance between Liza and Higgins 'should be most carefully avoided', Shaw strengthens Freddy's role by enlarging it. In a new film scene, when Liza leaves Higgins's flat after what corresponds to Act IV, Freddy '*smothers her with kisses*', to which she '*responds. They stand there in one another's arms.*' He announces their engagement, and in the next scene they embrace again. In the following scene Liza wishes she could wander forever with him, and they embrace a third time. After the play's Act V come new film sequences. Mrs Higgins tells her son that after Liza's slavery to him, Freddy is the sort of man any woman would marry. Higgins predicts that he and Pickering will have to support them. He suggests that since he does not do such a thing and Pickering is too old for it, Freddy can make love to Liza. Outside Mrs Higgins's home, Freddy reappears and thanks Higgins for having promised to set Liza up in a flower shop—a premature expression of gratitude, she says, hushing him. The couple drive off with Mrs Higgins and leave the phonetics professor to visualize them selling flowers and vegetables in their shop.[36] To a policewoman who inquires whether anything is wrong, Higgins replies that what he has seen constitutes both a happy ending and a happy beginning. It is noteworthy that Higgins's final encounter is with a female member of the police force, a woman professionally employed, for she establishes a link to and thereby underscores Liza's independence from him. In this respect, one recalls Liza's statement about her marriage to Freddy, a reversal of the conventional phraseology (revised from the play's first production and first printed editions): she will marry him as soon as *she* is able to support *him*.

Not only does Shaw strengthen Freddy's role, he removes virtually every suggestion of Higgins's possible romantic interest in Liza, for such suggestions, because they keep the possibility in the air, may seem to refute subsequent denials. Shaw retains Higgins's statement that he is a confirmed bachelor. He deletes Pickering's insistence that Higgins must not take advantage of Liza, Doolittle's advice that Higgins marry her, and Higgins's confession to Liza: 'You never asked yourself, I suppose, whether *I* could do without you. ... I have grown accustomed to your voice and appearance. I like them, rather.' Whereas playwright Shaw has Higgins, acknowledging Liza's newly acquired independent spirit, refer to her as 'a tower of strength: a consort battleship', screenwriter Shaw, determined to prevent a suggestion of romance, deletes the word *consort.* Although he retains Mrs Higgins's curiosity—natural for a mother—as to the relationship between her son and Liza, he also keeps Higgins's explicit response, 'I dont mean a love affair.' When his mother laments the fact that he is uninterested in pretty young women, he insists—perhaps Freudianly, perhaps just flatteringly—that his idea of a lovable woman is one who resembles her and that he will never seriously like young women, who are all idiots.

More appropriate to the spirit of comedy is the end of the screenplay, for in it and not in the stage play, all the principals clearly get what they want. Freddy gets Liza, Liza gets a flower shop and a man who will not bully her, Higgins gets Liza's unromantic, egalitarian-based comradeship. Although Doolittle, as in the play, laments his fate, it is difficult to feel sorry for so jolly a character whose material situation has appreciably improved.

The play's social resonances carry into the screenplay, which in certain respects makes them more vivid. Higgins recognizes his wager to be about more than just speech. As a Covent Garden flower girl, he tells Pickering, Liza's 'kerbstone English ... will keep her in the gutter to the end of her days.' In changing her speech, he tells his mother, he is 'filling up the deepest gulf that separates class from class and soul from soul.' The screenplay shows more stages in Liza's social transformation: not only the dirty flower girl and the scrubbed pupil, as in the play, but also Liza at the reception, a graduation ceremony where, to employ Mrs Higgins's phrase, she, as well as Higgins's and her dressmaker's art, triumph. Thereafter, her newly acquired independence, when she is out of her society dress, is all the more striking.

As money is a key element in a play or screenplay about social classes, so is it in *Pygmalion.* Clara pinches pennies. Freddy's difficulty in getting a taxi suggests his family's economic straits, and to Liza a taxi ride is a treat, but in the screenplay, not the stage play, she inquires and is amazed at how much such a ride costs. Whereas Liza sells (and begs) in Covent Garden, she offers to buy (speech lessons) in Higgins's flat. Aiming to exploit her, Doolittle gets five pounds in what Higgins later refers to as a sale of Liza. At the ambassador's reception in the screenplay, Shaw emphasizes not Liza's beauty or Cinderella charm but Higgins's bet, which her exposure threatens to lose. Nepommuck, who is not in the stage play, derives his income from sniffing out lower-class imposters and blackmailing them to buy his silence.* In Higgins's screen vision of Liza's and Freddy's life together, they sell flowers and vegetables.

Far more effectively than the play, the screenplay reveals Liza's environment, which the play only suggests through expository dialogue. Unlike the play, the screenplay takes us into Liza's room, with its peeling wallpaper, its broken window mended with paper, and its wretched bed—in vivid contrast to her bedroom at Higgins's house, also unseen by stage audiences, which the screenplay shows to be 'light, clean, and cheerful'. In taking audiences into both rooms, Shaw does not merely 'open up' the play for the screen. Rather, he makes organic use of the film medium to reveal thematically relevant aspects of his characters' backgrounds.

Shaw makes numerous alterations in his play. Because he shows the heavy rain, Liza's triumph at the reception, and her departure from Higgins's flat, he cuts expository dialogue about them. He changes or cuts references unintelligible to a non-British audience: 'Lisson Grove prudery' becomes 'slum prudery' and such place and brand names as Hanwell, Hammersmith, and Monkey Brand disappear. Since Higgins's allusion to Milton's comment on Shakespeare might be unintelligible to mass movie audiences, out goes his reference to Doolittle's 'native woodnotes wild'. Although *Pygmalion* has fewer discursive passages than *Saint Joan*, Shaw deftly bluepencils many of them to streamline his comedy for world film audiences. In Doolittle's reappearance, Shaw cuts the second and less comic of his two long speeches—a wise decision, since it recapitulates points already made and prevents the film from progressing rapidly to the confrontation between Higgins and Liza. Of that confrontation, which constitutes the longest discursive passage in the play, Shaw deletes more than half. What is essential, he retains; for example, the difference between Higgins and Pickering, Liza's determination not to be passed over, her resolution to marry Freddy, and her independence. What is less dramatically essential or depicted elsewhere, he removes; for instance, the similarity between Higgins and Doolittle, Higgins's dependence on Liza, and his lecture on the difference between life at his

---

* His name probably derives from both John of Nepomuck, martyred in 1393 because he refused to tell what he heard in the confessional (Shaw's Nepommuck refuses to tell only for a price) and the Hungarian Johann Nepomuk Hummel, whose music stands in the same relationship to his teacher's (Mozart) as Shaw's character's ability to his teacher's, inferiority. Nepommuck calls himself 'the marvellous boy'—Wordsworth's designation of Thomas Chatterton, also an imposter (he pretended to have discovered a medieval poet, whose works he himself wrote).

flat and life in the gutter. An example of Shaw's effectiveness in streamlining dialogue in order to remove a point already made and reach a dramatic point more quickly, occurs when Mrs Pearce announces Liza:

> MRS PEARCE. ... She's quite a common girl, sir. Very common indeed. I should have sent her away, only I thought perhaps you wanted her to talk into your machines. [[I hope Ive not done wrong; but really you see such queer people sometimes—youll excuse me, I'm sure, sir—
> HIGGINS. Oh, thats all right, Mrs Pearce. Has she an interesting accent?
> MRS PEARCE. Oh something dreadful, sir, really. I don't know how you can take an interest in it]].
> HIGGINS [to Pickering] Let's have her up. Shew her up, Mrs Pearce.

In adapting the play to the screen, Shaw cuts what is necessary for stage but not for cinema. For instance, between Liza's departure to have a bath and her return, Shaw must give the actress time to change costume and make-up. During this separation scene, he fills the time first with a discussion of more than three and a half printed pages about Higgins's attitude toward women, his habit of swearing, and his unconcern with personal cleanliness. Then, Mrs Pearce announces Doolittle's arrival. Because an editor's shears or a laboratory technician's dissolve can cover the time lapse, screenwriter Shaw completely cuts the scene before the announcement. On stage, the parlourmaid comes further into the room and lowers her voice in order to make a confidential statement to Mrs Higgins. Since a cut from a longer to a closer view can do the job, the screenplay cuts the stage direction.

From the start of the screenplay, Shaw makes good use of the different medium. In the play, the action begins at 11.15 p.m., after the theatres have concluded their evening performances; in the screenplay, late afternoon, after the matinées have let out. Why? Partly, I infer, to show thunderclouds, which are clearer in the daylight, and partly to show Liza's neighbourhood and lodging more clearly, for they have poor illumination. Shaw not only shows people caught in the heavy shower and Freddy vainly attempting to get a cab—both more effective than exposition about them—he also has Liza, shawl over her head to protect herself from the rain, disappear in Freddy's footsteps, a clever coupling of the two characters that combines dramatic economy, cinematic freedom, and thematic suggestiveness. With great impact, Shaw employs editor's shears to cut freely through space and time: Liza in her room; Freddy on the street below, joined by her; the pair entering Cavendish Square; then

entering Hanover Square—the short, accelerating scenes conveying speed
and frustration as the lovers flee the phonetician's home and two
policemen. To secure emphasis and create suspense, he uses the different
angles of vision made possible in cinema. In the play, when a bystander
warns Liza that a man is transcribing her words, she springs up terrified
and cries that she has done nothing wrong. In the screenplay, the warning
comes in a view of the two central pillars of the portico, with several
people between, seen from the market. After the warning, Shaw cuts to
the reverse view, toward the market, as the crowd turns to look at
Higgins.

As stated earlier, the *Pygmalion* screenplay improves on the play in
several important respects. It does not do so in all respects. Unfortunately,
it diminishes the importance of Clara, who since Shaw cuts the relevant
passages is no longer a foil for Liza (unlike Liza, she attempts to flirt with
Higgins; like Liza, she affects a type of speech not her own). Thus, in the
screenplay she becomes the only Eynsford Hill not organically related to
the transformation of Liza—a dramatic weakness. Regrettably, the
screenplay loses some of the play's social resonances, such as Higgins's
observation that a woman of Liza's class 'looks like a worn out drudge of
fifty a year after she's married.'

In any case, Shaw's adaptation retains the essential qualities of the
original play, improves in several major areas, and employs the different
medium to great advantage. What of the English-language movie based
on it?

To begin with, the question wants modification, for the print of Pascal's
Pygmalion that was first released in the United States was considerably
different from the print released in England. Their credits reflect their
differences. Although both name Shaw as sole author of the screenplay
and dialogue, the American print adds a third name to the adapters cited
on the British print: W. P. Lipscomb, Cecil Lewis, and Ian Dalrymple. To
complicate matters further, the standard reference work on British films
adds a fourth name, Anatole de Grunwald.[37] Who did what to Shaw's
screenplay is unclear, but what is clear is that various hands tampered
with it. Before discussing the film in general, let me examine how and
why the American print differed from the English.

Apart from the fact that Shaw filmed a spoken preface which
charmingly introduced himself to American audiences, discussed movies,
and urged Americans to see *Pygmalion* about twenty times (see Appendix
C), the major differences derive from censorship by the P.C.A., whose
demands centred upon profanity and immorality. Such words as *baggage*,
slut, *damn*, and variants of *damn*, said the P.C.A., must be deleted and the
producers must eliminate statements and inferences that Liza's father

would sell her virtue, that she is illegitimate, and that he has been living in sin with her stepmother.[38] M.G.M., whose distribution company Loew's, Inc. released the film in America, capitulated. So did Pascal, despite such public protestations as, 'you can't translate Bernard Shaw or any genius to the screen if you make compromises. Otherwise you put water in your wine and—what the hell! The dialogue of a great writer is to him like champagne. You can't change it and keep it.'[39] But what else could he say when he aimed to promote his film?

The P.C.A. demands did not surprise Pascal, who had made protection shots to cover various passages to which they called attention after they had read the script.[40] Even so, he failed to provide against all contingencies. After the London première and before the American, he was in Hollywood, busily making changes—'cutting last two reels in half,'[41] among other deletions—in order to acquire the P.C.A. seal of approval. Happily, Liza's 'not bloody likely' did not offend, for by 1938 the phrase was a social gaffe, not an obscenity. But every *damning*, *damn*, and *damnation* was either replaced by an inoffensive word like *swearing* or else snipped out. The most substantive change focused on Doolittle, who was so laundered in the American print that not only did he not mention he was not married to the woman he lived with, he was not on his way to his own wedding in the final scene. Apparently, it did not matter to the censors that Doolittle's wedding motivates his appearance and that without this motivation he has no business on the screen. Sanitized without Shaw's knowledge, *Pygmalion* opened in New York in December 1938.*

A decade later, when Pascal rereleased *Pygmalion*, he asked the P.C.A. to permit restoration of the scene near the end where Doolittle invites

---

* Ironically, only a year later *Gone with the Wind* opened in Atlanta and made film history when Rhett Butler told Scarlett O'Hara that he did not give a damn what would happen to her. How did producer David O. Selznick get away with that *damn*? Although screenwriter Sidney Howard had changed the famous line to 'Frankly, my dear, I don't care,' Selznick decided that *damn* was essential. As his biographer tells it, 'Censor Joseph Breen refused to approve the word. David appealed to film czar Will Hays, arguing that the censorship system would be held up to ridicule if the famous line had to be bowdlerized. Hays permitted Rhett to say, 'Frankly, my dear, I don't give a damn.' But, because the use of profanity on the screen was still a punishable offence, David was required to pay a $5000 fine to the Producers Association. He figured it was worth it.'[42] In a year, the times had not changed, but *Gone with the Wind* had only a solitary *damn*, Selznick had more clout than Pascal, and the American film industry, whose P.C.A. was part of its *self*-regulation, regarded the best-selling novel and multi-million dollar American movie more reverently than a classic comedy and an English film.

Pickering to his wedding.[43] In terms that reveal both moral and other values, Breen refused. The scene contains ' "comedy treatment of illicit sex", which, as you know, the Code specifically prohibits. ... By and large, I think your picture when it was released by Metro suffered nothing from the deletion of this scene. ... If the picture is to be re-issued, the fact that this particular scene will not be in the picture, will not impair, one iota, its box-office value.'[44] So much for art. Or even drama. Only in the last dozen years or so was the British print of *Pygmalion* released in America. Let us examine this print.

One reason *Pygmalion* is a superior film is its acting, from the principals to the most minor roles. Although Wendy Hiller employs stage cockney rather than an authentic cockney accent (no doubt for the purpose of intelligibility), her performance captures more qualities and nuances than the most demanding Shavian would have any right to expect. Liza's insecurity and self-deprecation, her terror at how someone of Higgins's class could ruin her for life, her feeble attempt at ingratiation, her pathetic gratitude at Pickering's politeness, her terror at the bath, the eruption of her natural good humour at unexpected mishaps during her lessons, her frustrations and anger, her gumption when she brazens it out at Mrs Higgins's at-home, her loss of fear when she gets used to talking on a familiar subject, her rage at Higgins, her sense of independence and power—these are some of Liza's facets the actress realizes. Among the chief characters, Wilfrid Lawson hits the appropriate Dickensian notes of Doolittle, David Tree the likable naiveté of Freddy, Marie Lohr the dignity, sympathy, and sense of humour of Mrs Higgins, Jean Cadell the protective mother-surrogate quality of Mrs Pearce. Granting the inappropriateness of Leslie Howard, who is far softer, less brutal, and more charming, sophisticated, and sympathetic than the role as written, he adapts Higgins to his distinctive abilities and persona, and performs the role very well. Even the smaller parts are dazzlingly portrayed: Irene Brown's utterly self-assured Duchess, O. B. Clarence's confused Vicar, Violet Vanbrugh's regal Ambassadress, to name a few. Detail upon detail contributes to the film's superiority in acting. Although the movie cuts Mrs Pearce's denial when Doolittle refers to her as Higgins's wife, Jean Cadell wordlessly acts that denial so well that one does not miss the line. Wilfrid Lawson manages to convey disorientation when he notices a nodding Buddha (which conceals a hidden microphone) without missing a beat of his speech.

An important reason for the success of *Pygmalion*, says Wendy Hiller, was that 'the direction was in the expert hands of Anthony Asquith.'[45] According to David Tree, Pascal's 'great stroke of genius with *Pygmalion* was to surround himself with Anthony Asquith, who in my opinion was

the most underrated director that ever was, and David Lean as editor.'
What of Leslie Howard, who shares directing credit with Asquith? Says
Tree: 'Leslie Howard had his name up in the credits as a director of
Pygmalion, but as far as I saw, Leslie never took any part in the direction.
He was never there.' *Pygmalion* is really Asquith's picture.[46]

Anthony Asquith expertly translated *Pygmalion* into cinematic terms.
Cinematically and economically, the opening conveys milieu. As Donald
Costello describes it, 'The first shot is a close-up of a violet. The camera
pulls back to reveal Eliza holding her basket of flowers amid the hustle-
bustle of a typical Covent Garden scene; she is surrounded by a colourful
crowd engaged in inarticulate cockney chatter.'[47] Later, Higgins's
laboratory is introduced in different but also appropriately cinematic
terms: not a camera pulling back amid inarticulate speech, but rather a
montage of recording devices, amplifying apparatus, and a model of a
human ear, with suspenseful music to accompany the introduction of the
tools of this infrequently dramatized trade.

Asquith makes fine use of reaction shots: Mrs Eynsford Hill and Clara
when Liza calls Freddy by his name, bewilderment or shock when Liza
relates with precise diction that her father ladled gin down her aunt's
throat. More extensively, a great deal of the scene in which Higgins and
Pickering ignore Liza after the ball focuses on her reaction to their
conversation, which prepares the audience for her rebellion and
independence.

Asquith first presents Liza at the ball not when she emerges with
Higgins and Pickering from a car, as Shaw indicates, but after she has
deposited her wraps in the cloakroom, so that she confronts us suddenly,
almost shockingly, transformed into a radiant beauty, with dazzling face
and magnificent bare shoulders. Skilfully and without calling attention to
the device, Asquith shoots the camera from low or high angles to suggest
dominance or submissiveness. In the early part of the film it is Higgins but
not Liza whom he shoots from below. When she becomes an independent
human being, the camera, emphasizing her new stature, shoots her from
below for the first time. When Higgins's blackmailing pupil is about to tell
the Ambassadress Liza's identity, Asquith keeps the scene fluid and full of
suspense; he does not cut jerkily to Higgins for a reaction shot but rather
has him walk into the picture from behind a pillar, where, one may infer,
he has been listening, also in suspense.

The determining factor for the distance between actors and camera, the
movement of the camera, and the editing of different shots during any
particular moment, says Asquith, was the emphasis required by the
dialogue. Thus, 'when Higgins decides to take on the bet to turn the
flower-girl into a duchess, he strides about the room dynamically and the

camera follows his movements with the minimum of cuts.' Following the agreement is an argument between him and Mrs Pearce, with interruptions by Liza and Pickering. 'Here we used the other kind of movement—quick staccato inter-cutting of individual [close-ups], with the occasional added emphasis of people moving or turning into the shot.' According to Asquith, 'the dialogue must not be interfered with by any visual effect, however ingenious, and ... at the same time the eye should not be merely a sleeping partner to the ear.'[48] What is significant is not that his principles harmonize with Shaw's, but that his practice justifies them. As evidence of the exceptional variety employed by him and editor David Lean, one may turn to the second scene Asquith describes. In the film, this sequence—from Higgins's comment that Liza's English will doom her to the gutter through his command that Mrs Pearce take her away—contains two dozen speeches. But Asquith does not let the camera roll on while the characters talk. He shows a close-up of Liza listening to her fate, a medium close shot of Pickering and Higgins who boasts of what he can do, a medium shot of Higgins and Liza when they discuss terms, a panning shot as Higgins goes from Liza to Pickering accepting her offer and explaining its significance, and so forth. For these twenty-four speeches, Asquith and Lean edit eighteen different shots. Observing that the number of separate shots in this scene 'almost equals the number of speeches—an extraordinary fluidity—and three years before *Citizen Kane*,' Robert Gessner calls Asquith's *Pygmalion* 'the most fluid film between *Intolerance* and $8\frac{1}{2}$'[49]

The most fluid, not the best. Although *Pygmalion* is a superior motion picture, it is not the masterpiece that these comments, if untempered, might suggest. Some of it is poorly made, some trite.

While the set decorations and costumes of the Covent Garden scene are realistic, the background is obviously painted. In both Covent Garden and Higgins's flat, Liza's face is too clean, as is her costume in the latter scene, where according to Shaw her apron is *nearly* clean and her shabby coat tidied only *a little*. Perhaps to make Liza appear more attractive—and hint at romance?—she is laundered. Mrs Pearce touches her far too often, which she would not do if Liza were as dirty as Shaw indicates; and no one suggests there may be fleas in her hat, which Mrs Pearce and Higgins handle casually, for it is as clean as everything else about her. One wonders why she needs a bath. To reveal Higgins's obliviousness to Liza's displeasure at such comments as once she has had a good sleep she will feel less cheap, Shaw has him eat an apple as he casually orders her about. Instead of contrasting him chomping the apple and Liza staring at him speechless, the film merely frames them and though Leslie Howard picks up an apple and plays with it, he does nothing so vulgar as eat it. Both montages of Liza's lessons—before and after her visit to Mrs Higgins—last too long and contain such stale devices as Liza tossing in nightmarish sleep, an accumulation of records to indicate the passage of time, and her reading a book titled *Etiquette*. Another montage, in which Higgins discovers Liza has gone and looks for her, merely interrupts the dramatic action by irrelevant visual sequences, including a location shot at Piccadilly Circus in which Leslie Howard inquires among real flower girls.[50] Most of these montages, none of which Shaw devised, are dull, since one waits for the film to get on with the story. The famous 'not bloody likely' is less effective than it should be because, as David Tree explains, 'the camera concentrated on Leslie Howard in fits of laughter, which is just a terrible cliché. To have someone roaring with laughter, to show the audience that it's time they were laughing, was a very great mistake. Perhaps Leslie insisted that the camera should be on him.'[51]

Although the makers of the British *Pygmalion* did so to a far lesser extent than those of the German and Dutch, they too, for reasons not always clear, made numerous alterations in Shaw's screenplay. In some instances, they are appropriate. Before the action begins, a written message briefly explains, no doubt because mass movie audiences do not know, the identity of Pygmalion (without this explanation the title is meaningless). Whereas Shaw changed the time of the opening scene from night to late afternoon, the movie makers returned it to night, perhaps to contrast more sharply the elegant evening dress of the Eynsford Hills and Pickering with the clothes of the poorer people. The adapters restore some dialogue Shaw deleted. Re-enter the sarcastic bystander's reference to Park Lane, perhaps because they thought it would be intelligible to Americans. Instead of dropping the reference to Hanwell, as Shaw did, they make it intelligible by calling it Hanwell Insane Asylum.

Some changes appear to have been made for the purpose of building up the star actor. In the play, cut from the screenplay, Pickering asks Doolittle how he knew Liza was at Wimpole Street if he did not send her and why he brought her luggage if he intended to take her away. The movie makers restore these questions but give them to Higgins. The effect is to diminish emphasis on the supporting player and to increase emphasis, by increasing lines with initiative, on the star. Perhaps for a similar reason, they change the opening dialogue of the Wimpole Street scene. Shaw retains the dialogue that indicates Higgins has shown everything to Pickering, who has had enough for the morning, and cuts the passage about Higgins being more skilful in phonetics than Pickering is. The movie makers cut what Shaw kept, restore what he cut. Consequently, the star actor becomes more impressive. In Shaw's play and screenplay, Higgins gives Doolittle a £5 note. The film makes a tired

British *Pygmalion*   At the ball, Liza is about to dance with her prince charming. Wendy Hiller and Leo Genn (centre); Violet Vanbrugh, Iris Hoey, Esme Percy, Leslie Howard and Violet Tree (group left).

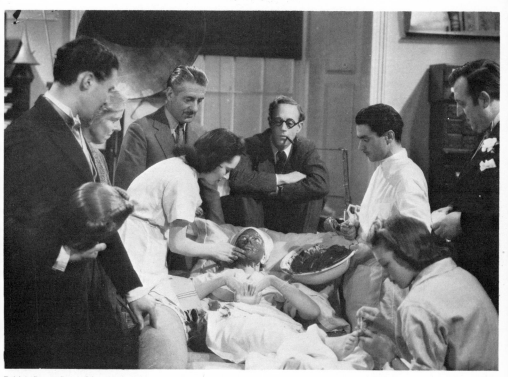

British *Pygmalion*   Liza receives beauty treatment. Anthony Quayle (holding wig), Jean Cadell, Scott Sunderland, Wendy Hiller and Leslie Howard.

British *Pygmalion*   Liza meets Mrs Eynsford Hill at Mrs Higgins's at-home. Leueen MacGrath, O. B. Clarence, Everley Gregg, Leslie Howard, Wendy Hiller, Marie Lohr and David Tree.

British *Pygmalion*   A terrified Liza brazens it out as she meets Mrs Higgins. Marie Lohr and Wendy Hiller.

joke of the transaction: at Higgins's prompting, Pickering gives him two £5 notes and when Doolittle refuses the second, Higgins unconsciously pockets it.

Other changes, also intended as improvements, also accomplish the opposite. After introducing Liza, the movie introduces Higgins, or rather his back, as he overhears various conversations. Since the audience has no idea who the listener is or why he would want to listen, the eavesdropping sequences are pointless. Instead of contrasting Liza with an old woman, who *'disciplined by experience'* can cope with such emergencies as a sudden downpour, and who suggests what Liza might become, as Shaw's screenplay does, the movie pairs her with a flower girl her own age so that after she leaves Higgins she can return to Covent Garden where her former friend, about to recognize her, realizes this well-dressed lady cannot be Liza. While touching in a conventional way, the scene is unnecessary since one needs no further dramatization that Liza has changed and since it interrupts the momentum of her flight with Freddy. In the film, Mrs Eynsford Hill prepares to give Liza a shilling, then changes her mind and gives her sixpence. In the screenplay, she wants to and does give sixpence but her daughter argues that a penny is sufficient. Allowing for inflation, the shilling is valid, but the elimination of the conflict between mother and daughter slackens the scene and further diminishes the dramatic importance of Clara.

More serious changes occur in Mrs Higgins's at-home scene with the appearance of four new characters, strangers to the audience. While the principals speak important dialogue, the parlourmaid's voice in the background announces the arrival of Reverend and Mrs Birchwood, and Major and Mrs Rawcroft. Once one sees the vicar's turned-around collar, one knows who he is, but when a few minutes later a strange man appears beside Liza, then an unfamiliar woman, the result is confusion. Equally important, the new characters are unnecessary. The major and his wife fulfil no function at all, and the vicar's shock could be conveyed as well by Mrs Eynsford Hill. In the same scene, the film transfers the passage wherein Higgins and Pickering explain their experiment to Mrs Higgins from after Liza's departure to before her entry, probably to climax the scene with Liza's social gaffe. However, the transposition creates several unfortunate consequences. First, in order to hear her son and Pickering, Mrs Higgins must ignore her guests, an uncharacteristic breach of etiquette. Second, key dramatic points vanish. Since Higgins wants to learn from his mother the extent to which Liza is presentable, he can do so only after she has gone. In the movie, he does not question his mother about Liza. Third, the rearrangement and elimination of these questions result in the deletion of a crucial thematic passage, which concerns what will happen to Liza after the outcome of the bet, for in Shaw's play and screenplay, but not in the film, Mrs Higgins pointedly emphasizes that the important issue is not merely to pass Liza off as a lady, but rather 'the problem of what is to be done with her afterwards,' and she explicitly points to Mrs Eynsford Hill as an example of the dubious advantages her son's experiment will give Liza, a fine lady's manners and habits but not her income. Moviegoers hear none of these, for both passages are cut.

Other important social issues disappear. Whereas Shaw cuts the second, less important of Doolittle's long speeches in his second scene, the movie cuts both. Doolittle states that Higgins has made him a slave to middle class morality, but the movie makers cut the speech that explains what middle class morality means. In deleting Higgins's 'This is an age of upstarts who have to be taught to speak like ladies and gentlemen,' the film weakens the theme's universality and strengthens the romantic Cinderella aspect. A result of these deletions is to simplify the play's focus, which narrows more exclusively to the relationship between Liza and Higgins.

Like the German and Dutch films, the English film defeated Shaw's determination to suggest no romance between Higgins and Liza. At the end, she returns to him. Despite assertions that 'Shaw himself ... added ... the final romantic ending'[52] and that Pascal got him 'to approve the final ending of the film,'[53] all evidence—including Valerie Pascal's explicit statement[54]—indicates he did neither, but discovered the changed ending only when he saw the completed picture at the special press showing on 4 Oct. 1938, two days before its London première, and by then it was a *fait accompli* about which he could do nothing. Pascal knew Shaw's wishes. Even apart from their expression in the screenplay, Shaw threatened to break with him unless he swore adherence to every comma of the screenplay.[55] But except for the first day's shooting, Shaw was absent while *Pygmalion* was made.

According to Anthony Asquith and his assistant Teddy Baird, the film makers shot three different endings. None was satisfied with the first, which conformed to Shaw's screenplay.[56] The second, a compromise between Shaw's screenplay and a conclusion which has Higgins confident that Liza will return to him, kept Shaw's dialogue in front of Mrs Higgins's home, where Liza hushes Freddy after he thanks Higgins for promising to set them up in a flower shop. Next, it transposed a passage from the end of Act V where Higgins orders her to buy food and clothing for him, and restored a passage from early editions of the play where after his mother promises to buy them he tells her not to bother since he is certain Liza will do so. Then the car drives off; Higgins laughs and walks away, cheerfully whistling.[57] But this ending may have seemed too inconclusive for the movie makers.

Once they determined on a romantic end, their problem was how to film it without writing new dialogue. Their ploy was to transfer dialogue from other portions of the play to the end. After Liza leaves for Doolittle's wedding, Higgins returns home. Accidentally, he turns on the record player, which conveniently holds a record of what Liza said when she first visited him, 'I aint dirty: I washed my face and hands afore I come, I did.' 'I shall make a duchess of this draggletailed guttersnipe,' predicts Higgins's voice, whereupon Liza's exclaims, 'Ah-ah-ah-ow-ow-oo!' His voice continues, 'In six months—in three.' After he switches off the machine, he hears Liza's voice again, this time in person and with perfect diction, stating she washed her face and hands before she came. As he did after the ball, Higgins requests his slippers. The scene fades out, the music swells, and the picture ends in a conventionally happy manner.

For basic reasons, the movie's end is ridiculous. It makes nonsense of the new sequences which return Freddy and have him and Liza kiss. Although the movie cuts portions of these scenes and rearranges others, it makes no sense to bring him back in the capacity of lover and then to drop the subject without a word of explanation. Moreover, as played by so powerful a persona as Wendy Hiller, Liza emerges as a fiercely independent human being, not as a neurotic who enjoys being bullied and abused by someone like Higgins. Her return to fetch slippers for Leslie Howard seems incredible.

To help make the sabotaged ending palatable, the movie foreshadows it. In addition to making Liza cleaner and more attractive in the early scenes, Higgins softer and more sympathetic, the film creates an ambience of sentimentality and romance. Laurence Irving's setting of Liza's room reveals little of the poverty Shaw describes, though its wall contains, as specified, a picture of a popular actor (Robert Montgomery). As Asquith photographs it, it looks untidy and a bit smudged, not wretched, and he introduces quaintness. Whereas Shaw specifies that the birdcage's tenant is dead, the movie makers give Liza an adorable parrot who three times says hello to her and whom she addresses while charming music plays. Far less often than in Shaw's screenplay does Liza say 'Aaaaaow'. As a result, she seems less vulgar, Higgins less pained at her utterances. Where Shaw has Higgins command, '(*explosively*) Woman: cease this detestable boohooing instantly,' Howard utters the line gently, with no explosiveness. When he and Liza discuss lessons, a tightly framed shot of them, his eyes half closed and her expression flirtatiously perky, clearly suggests romance. The film deletes Higgins's admission that his idea of a lovable woman is someone like his mother. When he grabs Liza's wrists as she is about to scratch him, the conflict does not give way to a near embrace, as in Holland, but the look in his eyes suggests that he wishes it would.

Symptomatic of such forshadowing are changes in the ambassadorial reception scene. Among some lively additions to this scene—including two gossip columnists who increase the suspense as to whether Karpathy (Pascal's new name for Nepommuck, presumably because it sounds more Hungarian) will discover Liza's identity—is a visit from a grand old lady and her son, a prince charming who in an exceptionally well directed scene climaxes the proceedings by dancing with Liza-Cinderella, to Honegger's lovely waltz music. With Liza more clearly established as Cinderella, the charm of Leslie Howard hints that off the dance floor he will be her prince. While it may be perverse to disapprove of what is so admirably done, the scene emphasizes what Shaw avoids, romance.

Nevertheless, this *Pygmalion* is a superior motion picture, for it withstands these changes. The cuts and alterations do not eliminate its social aspects, they make them less explicit. Despite the ending and the romantic ambience that surrounds Higgins and Liza, the movie is in other respects essentially faithful to Shaw. What makes it so impressive is what is Shavian about it, not what the movie makers have changed. Imperfect though it is, the Pascal-Asquith *Pygmalion* is a good, largely faithful adaptation.

What was Shaw's response to it? Privately, he said, 'The trouble with Leslie Howard is he thinks he's Romeo.'[58] Publicly, he endorsed the film. It lost none of its force in its transference to the screen, he maintained, and it was 'substantially' his own version.[59] After its London première, he filmed a preface for Americans, whom he told that Pascal put his play on the screen 'just as the author wrote it and as he wanted it produced.' Diderik Roll-Hanson, who incorrectly assumes Shaw was responsible for the movie's romantic end, is very likely correct when he asserts, 'For Shaw the important thing ·was not who married whom but the preservation of the satiric mood of his play.'[60] Compared to the German and Dutch versions, Pascal's *Pygmalion* was fidelity incarnate, but in commenting specifically on its ending, Shaw carefully avoided responsibility or endorsement. Why did he permit the substitution of a romantic reconciliation between Higgins and Liza?

> I did not.... Nothing of the kind was emphasized in my scenario, where I emphasized the escape of Eliza from the tyranny of Higgins by a quite natural love affair with Freddy.
>
> But I cannot at my age undertake studio work: and about 20 directors seem to have turned up there and spent their time trying to

sidetrack me and Mr Gabriel Pascal, who does really know chalk from cheese. They devised a scene to give a lovelorn complexion to Mr Leslie Howard: but it is too inconclusive to be worth making a fuss about.[61]

In other words, the film's ending differed from his own but in view of the movie as a whole it should not receive disproportionate emphasis.

Although the English press praised both stars, it was Wendy Hiller whose reviews were overwhelming[62] and whose performance *The Spectator* called 'one of the best ... of the year.'[63] 'The most important thing,' said the same review, 'is that it represents a triumph for Anthony Asquith,' to whom 'the laurel crown goes.' Others echoed such praise. 'Although *Pygmalion* has so much talk, and thus might seem to be a very difficult subject for the screen,' said *The London Mercury*, because of Asquith 'this film version makes more out of the text ... than a stage version would be likely to do.'[64] The general tenor of most English reviews is that directorial and histrionic skill made a success of apparently intractable material, Shavian dialogue and themes. But the reviewers did not compare the scripts of play and film or consider that a screenplay might seem inadequate not only because of what it contains but also because of preparatory or explanatory dialogue it omits. Siegfried Kracauer, who is among those theorists with tastes formed by silent movies, maintains that in *Pygmalion* it is the embassy's staircase, Liza's nightmares, and Higgins's recording gadgets that impress, not the witty dialogue and clash of characters.[65]

In the United States, the film's enthusiasts were more enthusiastic, its detractors more condemnatory. '*Pygmalion* could scarcely have avoided being important,' said *Time*. 'It could easily have avoided being good. As produced by Gabriel Pascal and acted by Wendy Hiller and Leslie Howard, it is not merely good but practically perfect.'[66] No *practically* about it, said New York's *Daily Mirror*, it is 'a perfect movie. It reveals [Shaw] as a scenarist fully equal to Hollywood. It's universal in its appeal.'[67] *The World-Telegram* urged readers to 'drop everything ... and lay your dough on the line without delay' at the box office because of a 'brilliant performance by Wendy Hiller' and 'a brilliant, witty, amusing, fast-moving, beautifully directed and acted film which easily takes its place among the cinema achievements of the year.'[68]

While praise of the film was not universal, no reviewer appears to have found fault with Wendy Hiller. 'If the shortcomings of the script are not felt as long as one looks at the screen,' said *The Nation*, 'we have to thank Wendy Hiller, who steals the show'. Chief shortcoming is that the script, like the play, 'stresses the transformation process at the expense of the more important values.' What values are more important? 'We do not see her falling in love with him.' Had the script shown this, believe it or not, it 'could have achieved depth.'[69] Another typically adverse criticism, reminiscent of Shaw's parody in *Fanny's First Play*, is that *Pygmalion* contains 'little or no action' and too much dialogue. 'Nothing happens, but every one continues to talk. No matter how shining the talk, no picture can stand up under that.' It is also 'about strange and often disagreeable people. And just to make things harder, its attitude toward every one and everything is somewhat mocking.'[70]

More justifiably, a typical adverse criticism was that the movie's Anglicisms presented stumbling blocks to American enjoyment. Nearly all its values, 'its subtleties of humor, of characterization and of social comment come through the unfamiliar medium of English as spoken in Great Britain. Superficially it becomes, for Americans, a stiff exercise in diction. For a good proportion of the general public that barrier may prove too difficult or at least very distracting.'[71] Another adverse criticism was that Leslie Howard, 'a sensitive actor on his own plane,' is 'too delicate' for this role.[72]

Several American critics commented on the film's end. Referring to Shaw's anti-Hollywood spoken preface to the film, the *Brooklyn Daily Eagle* satirically took Shaw to task for 'Kowtowing to the Americans' by attaching a 'sugar-sweet ending' to his play. Probably, Shaw was not 'as satisfied as the publicity men would have us believe.' But: 'Actually, G.B.S., we don't think you spoiled your play' by the romantic ending.[73] With a similar diagnosis, John Mason Brown reached a different conclusion: at the end the movie 'suddenly ceases to have any real connection with your play. It becomes unashamedly like all our worse movies.' Would Liza and Higgins marry? 'Not these two!'[74] *The Saturday Review of Literature* approximated Shaw's view: 'in spite of the altered denouement ... it is an excellent movie. It has the Shaw flavor, the Shaw bite; it preserves the point and the best part of the dialogue of the play.'[75]

Despite rave reviews, the American distributors—wary of comments on the film's intellectual humour and unintelligible British accents—took no chances. Dutifully featuring the raves, their advertisements stressed Cinderella, sex, comedy, and the quaint, popular author. A poster described Liza's transformation: 'From City Streets to Society Glamour Girl!'[76] One advertisement announced, 'LADIES KNOW MEN ALWAYS WANT THE WOMEN THEY CAN'T GET! Uproariously swell is this brilliant Bernard Shaw comedy—of a woman-proof bachelor who ignored girls who threw themselves at him—but was remarkably easy to be had—when he met a beauty who told him to go jump in the lake!' Several featured a caricature of G.B.S., with a comic-strip balloon that declared, 'Of course it's as good as they say. I wrote it!'[77]

Pascal's *Pygmalion* was an astonishing success. Before it opened in England it won the Volpi Cup at the Venice Film Festival.[78] Eight of New York's nine film critics voted it one of the ten best pictures of the year. It won two academy awards for 1938: best screenplay went to Shaw, best adaptation to Lipscomb, Lewis, and Dalrymple. Unquestionably, Valerie Pascal is correct in saying it broke box office records.[79] When Shaw in an unexpected turnabout permitted Pascal to dub the film into French and Italian,[80] it became a box office success in France and Italy too.[81]

The success of *Pygmalion* had several major results. It cemented the relationship between Shaw and Pascal,[82] who for all his deficiencies Shaw recognized to be as faithful a producer of Shavian films as he was likely to find. Moreover, said Shaw, its 'sensational success ... has suddenly brought me into vogue as a screen expert.'[83] Were it not for Pascal's *Pygmalion*, Shaw's screenwriting career might have ended at this point.

Ironically, the financial success of *Pygmalion* was not a financial success for either Shaw or Pascal, though they suffered for different reasons. For Shaw, the reason was taxation. As he explained, 'My royalty on the Pygmalion film brought me in over £20,000 in the first year, and thereby subjected me to income and surtax at the rate of 19/6d in the pound [i.e., nineteen shillings and sixpence, or 97½ per cent] not only on those royalties but on my entire income, plus my wife's....Another such stroke of luck would ruin me.'[84] For Pascal, the reason was poor business management. Costs were higher than he had anticipated. To raise more money, he had to give some of the royalties reserved for himself. When it disappeared, he had to raise more and to do so he had to part with more of his royalties. Each new sum became harder to raise than the last, the price he had to pay more usurious. The final cost of *Pygmalion* was £125,000. Despite its success, he earned nothing.[85] As Shaw predicted the day it opened in New York, the film's fortunes were made by the financiers and distributors.[86]

On 29 Oct. 1937, before shooting started on *Pygmalion*, Shaw sent Paul Czinner a Memorandum of Agreement which authorized him to direct Elisabeth Bergner in the *Saint Joan* film.[87] In May 1938, before *Pygmalion* opened, Shaw announced they would film it that summer. Did this mean that he had agreed to alter passages so as not to offend the Catholic Church? 'I have made no alterations and do not intend to make any.' Did he consider Elisabeth Bergner appropriate for Joan? Had he seen her in the role? 'We shall see. I have not seen Miss Bergner in the part, which she made famous in Germany. I am as curious to see her as St. Joan as you are.'[88]

That summer, he satisfied his curiosity. On 6 Aug. 1938, she played the first of seven performances of *Saint Joan* at the Malvern Festival. Shaw considered her performance a misrepresentation of the role[89] and, though she drew full houses, he regarded her as a total failure.[90] Elsewhere, he explains why: 'She wants to ... [leave] out everything except crying.'[91] Because he did not want such an interpretation filmed, he refused to let her play the role on the screen and told her to abandon all hope of doing so.[92] In a letter to Bergner, he asserted that her acting career was over, that she was now not an actress but a personality, and that she was on his blacklist.[93] Then *Pygmalion* opened. Its success gave Shaw an additional reason for giving *Saint Joan* to Pascal.

Who would play Joan? Pascal, exploring Hollywood for financial backing, suggested Greta Garbo. To Shaw, the notion reeked of Hollywood. 'If the heroine of the play were the Blessed Virgin they would probably have suggested Miss Mae West. ... We must have Wendy [Hiller]. ... She cannot refuse the part, which is unique; and even if she did, or if she dropped dead, I could produce two young English provincial Joans who would do better than any Hollywood siren.'[94]

Shaw tried to dissuade Pascal from seeking capital outside England, not because of Anglo-Irish chauvinism but because of America's thralldom to the P.C.A., whose prohibitions were linked to Catholic censors. Refusing to conciliate the Vatican, he imposed an absolute condition that Pascal film *Saint Joan* in total disregard of Catholic Action. Once the film was completed, he believed, America's twenty million Catholics would go to it as they go to saloons and girlie shows despite the Church's pleas not to do so. Although Hollywood distributors threaten not to release *Saint Joan* without a seal of approval, Shaw maintained, they would have to distribute it, not only because of the profit they would realize but also because he and Pascal had become insuppressible.[95] Shaw was wrong. They were very suppressible. Without the alterations demanded by the censors, Pascal could not find·backing. He tabled *Saint Joan*.

THE DEVIL'S DISCIPLE

In September 1938, in the same letter in which he refused to conciliate the Vatican on *Saint Joan*, Shaw suggested—thus revealing his simultaneous consideration of a *Devil's Disciple* movie—that Scott Sunderland (Pickering in *Pygmalion*) could play Burgoyne and the rest of the cast could be as American as Pascal wished.[1] In his address to American audiences of *Pygmalion*, filmed in October, he disclosed that he might film his 'American play', *The Devil's Disciple*. That month or the next, Pascal planned to meet John Barrymore, still interested in it, and he told Shaw they could, if they wished, get for the title role an actor who had been at the same table with Shaw and Marion Davies when they lunched at M.G.M. in 1933, Clark Gable.[2]

With a Hollywood *Devil's Disciple* again imminent, Shaw in early 1939[3] wrote new film sequences for the opening and perhaps recast or retained some of the scenes he had composed in 1915 for a silent movie version—but not those 'vivid scenes from the Boston tea party', which unfortunately are lost. The silent and talking introductory scenes, wrote Shaw in the margin of the 1939 typescript, were sufficient. 'The Boston tea business would cost a lot, be very troublesome, and not draw an extra penny.'[4]

Like *Saint Joan*, the Irishman's 'American play' has religion as a major theme and derives from historical events which concern successful rebellion against England. In both, charming and urbane aristocrat-soldiers are partly responsible for the legalized murder of an anti-British patriot, though in *The Devil's Disciple* a last-minute rescue saves the victim. Whereas *Saint Joan* establishes both the religious and political milieu of its action, however, *The Devil's Disciple* focuses almost exclusively on the religious. As Lawrence Langner observes, the play fails to deal with the underlying issues between England and her American colonies.[5] Uncharacteristically, Shaw does not bring in specifically historical references until the second scene of the third act. Partly because of its relatively few socio-historical resonances, *The Devil's Disciple* is less richly textured than *Saint Joan*. Though it carries its own delights and has been perennially popular, it is a lesser work than *Joan* or *Major Barbara*, each of which has religious and social themes.

The introductory film sequences of *The Devil's Disciple* suggest that Shaw may have decided to remedy this deficiency to the extent, to adopt his comment on *Saint Joan*, of permitting the historical atmosphere to blow freely through his screenplay. With cinematic flair, he economically and visually sketches the historical period: the signing of the Declaration of Independence and the replacement of the Union Jack by the Stars and Stripes, then a juxtaposition of the exterior of King George III's palace. In the first of two new dialogue sequences, not derived from exposition in the play, he creates a stupid, gabbling, and fussy monarch and a prime minister who patiently suffers his master in order to run the kingdom. But

Shaw provides more than a funny scene with conventional comic characters. Far more successfully than he does in the play, he evokes late eighteenth century England, which regarded the colonists not as civil libertarians in pursuit of their rights but as rebels against the lawful rule of their king. Deftly, he sketches eighteenth century details. George III refers to the exiled Stuart, Bonnie Prince Charlie, who though still called 'the young pretender' in contrast to his father, 'the old pretender', was at the time of the American Revolution no longer young. Shaw has King George refer to America as 'Robinson Crusoe's island'—an allusion to Defoe's eighteenth century novel which according to Shaw 'occupies in relation to the middle classes the same position that Karl Marx's Kapital does to the modern socialist proletariat' and whose every other page moralizes on 'the advantages and benefits and happinesses of the middle station of life.'[6] The ironic touch is apt, for the American Revolution was essentially middle class in origin. In the second dialogue sequence, Shaw dramatizes an expository passage in the play, the historical fact that Lord Germain did not wish to interrupt his departure for a weekend in the country to wait to sign the orders to General Howe to march north to Albany, where he would join forces with General Burgoyne, who was marching south, to put down the uprising—which their combined strength might have done. More hilarious in the showing than in the telling, the short scene ends on a thoroughly apt note which perhaps only an Irishman could imagine: Lord Germain, who is insufficiently interested in his official pursuits to learn to call New Amsterdam New York, leaves whistling 'Lillibulero', an English song about Irish Catholic subversives.

Are these sequences all that Shaw wrote for the film? I do not know. Nor do I know what cuts Shaw planned or made in the play's dialogue. When Pascal's English backers, General Film Distributors, discovered his efforts to make his next movie in Hollywood, they refused to finance him except to make British films.[7] Did he try but fail to secure American backing and then temporarily drop the project? The possibility exists.

In 1959, the Hecht-Hill-Lancaster company made *The Devil's Disciple* in Hollywood. When Walter Mycroft told them of Shaw's opening film sequences, they displayed no interest and 'someone prominently associated' with the production said, 'We've re-written Shakespeare, why shouldn't we re-write Shaw?'[8] As Costello observes, 'the result was the mutilation and murder' of Shaw's play.[9]

MAJOR BARBARA

Shaw plunged into cinematic activities with a zest that belied his eighty-odd years. The press reported one plan after another. *Candida*? Katharine Cornell refused—a sensible decision, thought Shaw, since the role was one of her most popular and a movie would kill stage revivals; besides, as the play lacks visual interest, it is unsuited to the screen.[1] Marlene Dietrich as *The Millionairess*? Shaw thought her foreign accent suitable and he met her to discuss the proposal.[2] Nothing came of it. *Cæsar and Cleopatra*? Shaw considered Robert Donat too young for Cæsar, Cecil Trouncer (the first policeman in *Pygmalion*) just right.[3] But Pascal's financial backers rejected it in favour of *The Doctor's Dilemma*, to star Wendy Hiller and Leslie Howard, or if Howard were unavailable, Ronald Colman, in his first major role in a British film.[4] In December 1938, Shaw gave Pascal permission to film it.[5] Though the press announced it would be their next movie, reports named none of these stars. Instead: Greer Garson, Jean Cadell, C. Aubrey Smith, Roland Young, Cedric Hardwicke, and Paul Lukas.[6] Pascal brought Greer Garson to meet Shaw.[7] Still, the project came to nothing.

What of the possibility that instead of an adaptation Shaw write an original screenplay? 'I'm 82,' he said in October 1938, 'certainly a bit too old to start on a new profession.'[8] Not quite certainly. A month later, he began what was initially designed as a historical film set in the seventeenth century. By the time he completed it, in May 1939, it became a play, *"In Good King Charles's Golden Days"*.[9] Did the original draft contain cinematic sequences? As far as Shaw's bibliographer knows, it does not survive.[10]

All previous reports notwithstanding, Shaw and Pascal agreed by July 1939 that their next movie would be *Major Barbara*.[11] The most important factor in this decision was Wendy Hiller's desire and availability to play the title role.[12]

But Shaw consented only for the one picture. The money Pascal raised for *Major Barbara*, he insisted, remembering Pascal's ruinous financial agreements during the filming of *Pygmalion*, must be for *Major Barbara* alone: 'I know the artistic value of your indifference to money; but if I gave you more than one agreement at a time you would raise the last penny on the whole lot and spend it on the first, leaving yourself penniless for the rest, whilst I should be tied up for years.'[13] Shaw implored Pascal not to make any personal sacrifice to secure financial backing, for, he confided, he himself could help if necessary.[14] Again, Pascal formed a syndicate with Nicholas Davenport, financed by J. Arthur Rank and C. M. Woolf of General Film Distributors.[15] Shaw agreed to permit the syndicate to use £12,774 of his royalties from *Pygmalion* until it raised all the necessary money.[16]

For *Major Barbara*, Shaw determined that unlike *Pygmalion*, adapters would not circumvent his intentions. Pascal too determined that his artistic wishes would not be thwarted. He would direct as well as produce *Major Barbara*.

From August 1939 through September 1940, Shaw cut passages and enthusiastically wrote numerous new sequences, including Barbara fainting by the Thames and expensive episodes at Undershaft's factory and town.[17] Other hands worked on the script. As its Scenario Editor, Marjorie Deans, explains, Pascal's production team included her, the film editor David Lean, and Anatole de Grunwald, who helped her prepare the shooting script but who did not receive screen credit. The trio read the play aloud and suggested cuts or minor alterations to Pascal. He decided which to show Shaw, who would then approve, disapprove, or suggest alternatives, but 'nothing was changed without his consent.' Although, as we shall see, this was not entirely the case, he authorized but did not author the scenes wherein a Chinaman brings laundry to Jenny Hill and Bill Walker meets a woman on a refuse dump. 'Shaw seldom objected to the introduction of silent "business" in the scenes themselves, or cutaways to establish time lapses.' He 'would seldom bother about anything except the dialogue.'[18]

The Shaw-Pascal collaboration on the *Major Barbara* screenplay provides unique examples of the contributions of each. It was Pascal who in mid-1939 suggested that the film begin with Barbara delivering a sermon and meeting Cusins.[19] Shaw embroidered the suggestion and began the film with a speech by Cusins, who then goes to hear Barbara's sermon and meets her. But he did not always accept Pascal's ideas: 'Stephen and Cusins playing baccarat and Undershaft living like a second lieutenant just come into a legacy, with nautch girls all complete, is beyond the wildest dreams of Sam Goldwyn. I cannot put on paper the imprecations with which I hurled it into the waste paper basket; so unless you kept a copy it is dead.'[20] Do not follow Undershaft's scent, he commanded, because except at a circus, one horse at a time is sufficient. Another scent Shaw refused to let Pascal follow was that of Bilton, whose role he wanted to expand.[21] When Pascal proposed to restore Peter Shirley, converted by Barbara, Shaw admonished him: 'Beware of the temptation to overdo every good effect. Enough is enough: another word and enough becomes too much: the fault of Hollywood'. Furthermore, he added, such a scene would spoil Barbara's conversion scene with Bill

Walker. 'Big effects must not be repeated.'[22]

Although Pascal submitted, even deleting the third-act reference to Shirley, he was adamant about a notion to have Undershaft take Bill Walker aside, give him his card, and tell him to visit him at his factory. On the same morning Barbara and her family visit Perivale St Andrews, Bill Walker does so too, receives a job, becomes converted to a new life, and demonstrates hope to working class audiences that a man like them can achieve a better life. While Shaw did not remind Pascal that Bilton was in the play partly for that purpose, he vetoed the suggestion and explained: 'To drag [Bill] back merely to give the actor another turn because he is so good is one of those weaknesses which an author must resist: to bring back an actor on the stage after he has made his effect in scenes where he was all important is to spoil his part and make a disappointment of him instead of a success.' Instead, Shaw added a passage before Barbara and Undershaft arrive at his factory, wherein he more completely reassures her that she did not lose Bill's soul. Delighted, Pascal accepted the new dialogue but begged Shaw to trust his dramatic instinct and proposed to surprise him with a small scene at the end where Bill, washed and clean shaven, would echo several earlier lines. 'I absolutely object to it,' said Shaw when he saw the film. 'Cut it out.'[23] Pascal did not. Bill's rehabilitation is in the film.

While Pascal shot the film, Shaw continued to cut and revise dialogue, as the need arose.[24] During shooting, Pascal conceived a prologue in which Shaw wrote that *Major Barbara* is a parable, a fictitious tale which is inspired and essentially true.[25] When the passage appeared on the screen (see Appendix H), the time consuming process of writing changed to a completed, handwritten document; then, the author's hand signed his name.

As before, Pascal demonstrated his flair for surrounding himself with prominent or soon-to-be-prominent people. Music was by William Walton, costumes by Cecil Beaton. As Assistants in Direction, he had David Lean (editor of *Pygmalion*), who was also responsible for Montage (of Undershaft's factory), and stage director Harold French, who was also Dialogue Supervisor (later he would direct movies of Somerset Maugham's *Quartet* and *Trio*). Cameramen were Jack Hildyard (who had worked on *Pygmalion*)[26] and Ronald Neame, later producer of such films as *Great Expectations* and *Oliver Twist* (both directed by Lean) and director (*The Horse's Mouth*, among others). Settings were by Vincent Korda, brother of Alexander and designer of many films, and John Bryan, later to design *Great Expectations* and produce *The Horse's Mouth*. Editor was Charles Frend, who co-edited *Arms and the Man* and later directed *Scott of the Antarctic*.

Before the camera were a trio from *Pygmalion*: Wendy Hiller, David Tree as Lomax, and Marie Lohr as Lady Britomart, though Constance Collier, who was in *Intolerance*, wanted that role and for a time Pascal considered Mrs Patrick Campbell, who was Liza in the London première of *Pygmalion*.[27] As what Shaw calls the *elderly* Undershaft, Pascal cast Robert Morley, then in his early thirties. Notable stage and screen figures undertook key roles: playwright-actor Emlyn Williams, who years later with his Charles Dickens readings began a trend in one-man impersonations, was Snobby Price; Robert Newton, already a seasoned actor, played Bill Walker; Donald Calthrop, known chiefly in films for his villains, was Peter Shirley; and Walter Hudd (Meek, based on Lawrence of Arabia, in Shaw's *Too True to Be Good*) played Stephen. Major players acted cameos: Sybil Thorndike was the General (Mrs Baines in the play), Stanley Holloway (Alec Guinness's chief accomplice in *The Lavender Hill Mob* and Doolittle in *My Fair Lady*) was the constable who escorts Cusins to the Salvation Army meeting, character actors Felix Aylmer and Miles Malleson were butlers. Like *Pygmalion*, *Major Barbara* was An Event. As theatre historian Joe Mitchenson says, 'Everybody wanted to be in that. They were well paid for it, but they loved the thought they were connected with a Shaw film, a prestige film.' Mitchenson was David Tree's double in the long shots, his collaborator Raymond Mander an extra in the scene where Barbara delivers her sermon.[28] At Shaw's suggestion,[29] Pascal cast the Chinese playwright S. I. Hsiung in his only film role, a non-speaking laundryman who brings a basket of wash to Jenny Hill, who was played by a young actress 'discovered' by Pascal, Deborah Kerr.

As Cusins, Pascal originally selected not Rex Harrison but Andrew Osborn, later a producer for the BBC. Accounts of casting and recasting the role differ. At first, Pascal wanted Leslie Howard, an understandable choice since the reunion of the producer and stars of the successful *Pygmalion* made good box office sense. According to Vincent Korda, Howard was interested only if he could codirect as well as star.[30] According to Marjorie Deans, previous commitments made Howard unavailable. Why Andrew Osborn? On 3 Sept. 1939, Great Britain declared war on Nazi Germany. As Deans says, 'It was very difficult to find actors at all early in 1940, especially young actors, and Andrew Osborn, a very promising young actor, was available.'[31] As David Tree recalls, once Pascal found he could not get Leslie Howard for the role, he decided 'to go through the *Spotlight* Casting Directory and choose the person who looked most like Leslie to play Cusins.'[32] At the time, Osborn resembled Leslie Howard.

According to Osborn, he was then playing the leading role at the

Whitehall Theatre in *Without the Prince*, which was a success. 'Pascal was running a whole whirl of screen tests. In fact, it was a bit of a joke in the profession. "Have you been tested by Gaby Pascal?" "Oh, goodness yes, of course." Apparently, he came to the Whitehall Theatre. I didn't know he was there. The next day he rang me up and said he would like to make a test. I thought, 'Well, it's come around to my turn now." ' Pascal wanted the screen test in two days and had the script delivered to Osborn after midnight. When Osborn looked through it in the daytime, he discovered that Pascal had not marked any scenes. Upon telephoning him to find out which scenes to prepare, Pascal said to learn the entire part. In one day? Unless he specified certain scenes and gave him enough time to learn them, said Osborn, it would be a waste of both their time. Pascal agreed, Osborn tested a few scenes, and Pascal 'never waited for them to be processed or screened. He just walked onto the little set we had, put his arm round my shoulder, gave me a cigar, and said, "Now we go to London and we have some lunch"; and that was it.' Pascal took him to meet Shaw, with whom he spent about twenty minutes. Shaw approved. Osborn got the role.[33]

They rehearsed several scenes and filmed a few location shots in Devon, without dialogue. Robert Morley describes rehearsals:

> During readings, Pascal bullied everyone. He certainly bullied Andy. Gaby was continually screaming, 'You are murdering my picture!' to various people in the small room where we were reading. Pascal said to Andrew, about his performance, 'It's all grey, like the sky outside.' And Andrew said, very calmly, 'I think grey is a rather nice colour.' We did manage to shoot a few scenes. Then, a few days after we returned from Devon, Gaby told me that he had got rid of Andrew.[34]

Why? According to Osborn, 'the war intervened'. Was not Pascal able to secure a temporary exemption, as he did for other actors? 'I don't really know. Whether in fact Pascal was quite glad to see the back of me, or whether he didn't want to try to get me released or not, I just wouldn't know. I was not sorry to see the back of it.' Despite the fact that the role had promised a great opportunity, 'things just turned a bit sour.' Osborn neither liked nor understood Pascal, with whom he never felt at ease and who did not provide the reassurance that a young actor in his first major film role required.[35] According to Morley, Pascal 'decided that he had undercast the part.'[36] Said David Tree: 'Gaby was persuaded that this young man was totally inadequate.'[37]

Who would replace Osborn as Cusins? Shaw suggested a young stage actor who had not yet made a film, Alec Guinness. David Tree reports that Pascal offered him the role but he turned it down, saying 'I think Cholly is about all I'm worth' and recommended Rex Harrison. Marjorie Deans maintains that Harrison 'was very much Pascal's own choice.'[38] In July 1940, Harrison accepted the role.[39]

'Shaw contributed not only the script for *Major Barbara*,' says Costello, 'but—a bit more than during the filming of *Pygmalion*—his personal presence. Shaw made visits to the Denham studios and to location filming.'[40] Though accurate to an extent, the statement is essentially misleading, for while two or three times is *a bit* more than one, they do not constitute much personal presence. To be precise, Shaw witnessed shooting on 26 July 1940 (his eighty-fourth birthday) and again on 12 Sept.[41] On what may have been a different occasion, he visited Denham Studios to film what was originally intended to be a separate short subject, an address to American audiences, but which became a preface to the American print of *Major Barbara*.[42] (see Appendix G). Could Shaw actually have contributed much personal directorial influence even if he wanted to? When Pascal began to shoot the film, Shaw was exactly two months shy of the birthday just mentioned, and when he completed the final print at the end of December, Shaw was in his eighty-fifth year.[43]

On his first visit—to the Albert Hall, where Pascal shot the Salvation Army meeting—Shaw became a participant. Unexpectedly carried away when the large band played, and feeling 'twenty years younger', he joined the extras who sang and waved their arms.[44] On 12 Sept. at Denham Studios, he became his directorial self again and sent Pascal a series of rehearsal notes. Because they refer to different scenes, it is unclear which he saw shot and which he saw in rushes. When Cusins speaks verse (quotations from Euripides' *The Bacchae*), wrote Shaw, he should not try to make it sound colloquial but should deliberately declaim it. Unlike her performance as Liza—whom Wendy Hiller understood, for her face changed with each new wave of emotion—her performance as Barbara betrayed little understanding, for 'her face never changes at all'.[45] Because Miles Malleson played Morrison as the stereotyped self-possessed butler, his role does not come off properly. He should be terrified of Lady Britomart and totally disconcerted by the startling reappearance of Undershaft, particularly since he must contrast with Felix Aylmer, as Undershaft's self-possessed valet. Although Emlyn Williams played Snobby as a conventional smart cockney from beginning to end, the role's acting value lies in its contrast between his honesty with Rummy and his hypocritical cant with the others. Playing his role on one note, that of an upper-class silly ass, David Tree missed those points where even the fool says something sensible, and he ought slowly and solemnly to pontificate about the amount of tosh in the Salvation Army. When Marie Lohr calls her family names, she should hurl them as a mighty goddess would throw thunderbolts, her eyes flashing at each target, and close-ups of her victims should intensify her imprecations. Only for Robert Newton did he find praise: 'He is very good. He is quite new to me: I never heard of him before.'[46]

On the only other occasion Shaw visited the set, if indeed it was separate from the last, he filmed his speech to Americans. Taking the utmost care that nothing should disturb the old man's day of filming, Pascal banished everyone from the set but the technicians and stars, who would be photographed with Shaw. Naturally, everyone wanted to be present. Mitchenson reports part of what happened:

> I thought, 'Well, I'm damned if I'm not going to see him at least.' So I hid behind the set. No Bernard Shaw, nobody arrived. I began to get a little nervous, and I thought, 'I'd better get off this.' So I came running around behind the cyclorama, and I bumped into Wendy, Rex, Bernard Shaw, and Pascal. I nearly knocked Bernard Shaw over. Pascal looked at me as much as to say, 'What the hell are you doing here!' I thought he would tell me off the next day. And Bernard Shaw looked at me and said, 'I do hope that I haven't hurt you.' I crept back and I did just listen a little, but I couldn't see.

Harrison reports that during Shaw's speech, the worried expression on Pascal's face betrayed something had gone amiss. Soon, Pascal flapped his arms about. Shaw was oblivious. 'Eventually Pascal crept up to the great man and touched him on the arm—G.B.S. looked round furiously, and Pascal confessed, "We've run out of film." '[47] After reloading the camera, Shaw completed his talk.

These are the only recorded times Shaw put in his personal appearance. Mainly, he made suggestions to Pascal, who visited and corresponded with him. Pascal reported changes in the setting; Shaw advised on acting.[48] He also commented on costumes: Undershaft should wear a dinner jacket when he first visits his estranged wife and the costumers should clothe Sarah 'as brilliantly as possible, as Barbara has to get her effect by dressing *against* her.'[49] Via Pascal, he advised conductor Muir Mathieson as to musical effects.[50] On one occasion, he called the stills 'first rate. It is an immense step from the stage, where however you may disguise it, the characters have to be in a row facing the audience the same way all the time, to the screen as you handle it.'[51] At the end of August or beginning of Sept. 1940, he saw a rough cut of the Salvation Army shelter scenes, without the music.[52] On 30 or 31 Dec. he saw the final print. As recorded earlier, he commanded Pascal to remove Bill Walker's return at the end. With the film completed, his admonition was ineffective. Only his personal presence, which was generally absent, might have helped.

By the time Pascal filmed *Major Barbara*, England was at war. In certain cases, officials provided for delayed induction, but performers and behind-camera personnel were no less patriotic than those not in the artistic professions. Many enlisted, many were called up, many wanted no exemptions. 26 May 1940 began the British evacuation of Dunkirk, and nine hundred ships rescued over a third of a million English and French troops. That day, Pascal began location shooting in Devon, which provided backgrounds for Undershaft's factory town (other location shots were Sheffield for the factory scenes and Tower Bridge for Bill Walker's meeting with Todger Fairmile). Pascal began studio shooting at Denham on 17 June.[53] On 10 July, the Nazi bombing of Britain began.

Literally, *Major Barbara* was filmed under fire. Furniture, properties, and technical equipment were inaccessible or destroyed by bombs. London exteriors for location shots were filmed one day, reduced to rubble the next, before shooting was completed. Transportation proved unreliable: bombs put railways out of commission for periods of time, land mines made roads unsafe. Actors therefore bedded down where they could, in or as close to the studio as possible: dressing rooms, pubs, the homes of friends.[54] Air raids continually interrupted shooting. Invariably, once the actors were ready to start and the cameras prepared to roll, a klaxon sounded, announcing the arrival of Nazi bombers, and cast and crew retreated to the shelter beneath the concrete floor of the sound stage.[55] One day, the company managed to complete only one take out of seventeen scheduled set-ups. Pascal claimed he counted 125 bombs that fell in the vicinity of Denham Studios during the picture's filming.[56] When Shaw shot his address to American audiences, he did not exaggerate when he remarked, 'at any moment a bomb may crash through this roof and blow me to atoms, because the German bombers are in the skies'. Then, impishly: 'I can't absolutely promise you such a delightful finish to this news item. Still, it may happen, so don't give up hope—yet.' As filming neared completion toward the end of the year, bombings intensified and the company spent most of its time in the air raid shelter.[57]

Often, Pascal did not join the others below but with Scenario Editor Deans remained on the lawn and employed the lost time to go over the script.[58] Aware of the absence of the flamboyant and colourful producer-director, the actors—while they sheltered from the enemy bombers—invented a fantastic life for him. Morley fabricated a luxurious, private shelter where Pascal retreated, with a built-in bar and music system, lined with tiger skins and attended by beautiful women. So believable was he,

Wendy Hiller became incensed that Pascal would selfishly enjoy a commodious retreat and not permit the others to join him. When she reprimanded him, he of course did not know what she was talking about.[59]

Another distortion which became accepted as fact concerned David Tree's leave from his anti-aircraft unit so that he could complete the film. Pascal was unable to complete Tree's scenes in time and, though he promised to arrange an extension of the leave, forgot to do so. When Tree reported late to his unit, he received a minor punishment for the infraction, a week's confinement to barracks.[60] In the studio, gossip transformed the story to the arrival of soldiers who arrested Tree on the set and took him away.[61] Canny enough to realize that the gossip made better copy, Pascal embroidered it. 'A military patrol arrived to arrest him,' he told the American press. 'I made all kinds of pretexts until I finished the last scene, then sent a letter to Tree's commander, offering myself as a prisoner in his place for the usual two weeks, since it was my fault.'[62]

On 15 July 1940, another disaster occurred: Donald Calthrop (Peter Shirley) died, *before* completing his final scene, though newspapers reported the opposite.[63] 'As the scene was incomplete,' says Hiller, 'another actor, whose name I do not know, was secured and made up to look like Donald Calthrop. Yet another actor was used to dub in the dialogue.'[64] Shaw helped save the situation with the practical suggestion that instead of composing new lines, Pascal transfer two of Shirley's speeches to Rummy Mitchens (that the sale of Bill's soul was 'dear at the money' and that Barbara in her innocence made too much of him).[65] Shirley's only remaining speech was transferred to a separate scene. In photographing it, Pascal and Lean did not show his face but shot him and Barbara from behind as they walked away from the shelter, and though she turned to him, he looked straight ahead. Unseen, a voice imitated Donald Calthrop as he told Barbara, 'Youve youth and hope. Thats two better than me.'

Apart from the war, the chief problem in the making of *Major Barbara* appears to have been Pascal's direction. 'He bullied everyone', says Morley. 'Gaby made me very nervous. He didn't make me feel I was very good.' Each morning his shouts greeted the actors and when they left 'Gaby was still screaming, "You are ruining my picture—you are crucifying me!" '[66] 'On more than one occasion,' says Hiller, 'I was called in to calm him down.'[67] As for Deborah Kerr, whose first movie this was, he reduced her to tears several times.[68] A temperamental person who frequently lost his temper, says Mitchenson, he frightened almost everyone. No one quite knew what he was going to do. At 'one awful moment' after the filming of Hiller's sermon, 'he suddenly looked at her and said, "It's no good. You're just a constipated virgin."' Pascal 'sacked practically everyone during the course of the film', including Harold French, David Tree and Marie Lohr. Despite the chaos that resulted from these frequent dismissals, Pascal's outbursts subsided and within a few hours he would kiss the people he had fired and act perfectly friendly again. He did not always direct his temperamental fits at the actors. During the filming of the breakfast scene, Mitchenson recalls, he became infuriated that a bowl of oranges came from Denham Village rather than Fortnum and Mason's. He ordered all actors to their dressing rooms until someone brought oranges from the London store. 'Eventually we were all back again, everything was relit, the oranges were there, and we went on filming. I asked one of the prop men, "What happened?" He said, "Well, all we did was to have our two hours off and took those oranges and brought them back and said they were from Fortnum's." '[69]

Pascal was devious—at times, it turned out, to his own detriment. To placate financier C. M. Woolf, since *Major Barbara* was behind schedule and over budget, he agreed to eliminate Barbara's Embankment scene, where she faints and is taken home in an ambulance.[70] To persuade Shaw to cut the scene, Pascal reported that Hiller disliked it and that he would not press her to film it. Shaw wrote to her, with reasons why she should play it, and told her to consider them, then decide for herself whether to cut it. The letter mystified Hiller, who 'had never expressed a dislike for any scene.'[71] After Pascal completed shooting, the deleted scene bothered him. During cutting, Deans remembers, 'we all realized that there was a change-of-mood gap between Barbara walking out disheartened from the shelter and coming into the breakfast scene. Gaby said, "We *must* have the Embankment scene! *I* will pay for it out of my own pocket, every penny!" And he did.' But little was left in his pocket. The scene he filmed was an abridgement of what Shaw wrote, and though Hiller fainted,no ambulance arrived.[72]

To compensate for those deficiencies of which he was aware, Pascal employed two directorial assistants. Harold French coached the actors in their dialogue and rehearsed them in their lines.[73] According to everyone with whom I have spoken, David Lean was entirely in charge of the actual shooting. Pascal 'was so much at sea' with the technical aspects of movie making, says David Tree, and S. I. Hsiung confirms this report, that when he insisted on certain camera angles which Lean knew would not work out satisfactorily, 'Lean and the crew sometimes turned over the camera to keep Gaby happy, without any film in it. They had a special name for these takes: "Gaby's takes", without film in the camera.' Lean would then quietly suggest he take cover shots in case 'Gaby's takes' did not come up to expectations.[74] This should not imply, however, that Pascal was not in command. To the contrary: all agree he was very much in control. The final word was always his.

Both David Tree and Wendy Hiller contrast the making of *Major Barbara* with that of *Pygmalion*. 'On *Pygmalion*, one knew that one was working with a really efficient director and the whole thing was very pleasant,' says Tree. 'With *Major Barbara*, it was exactly the opposite.' 'I was sadly missing the helpful direction of "Puffin" Asquith which I had on *Pygmalion*,' says Hiller. 'I desperately needed guidance. ... Pascal was no director.' Yet she also recognizes that without Pascal's 'almost demoniac energy the film would never have beaten all the difficulties of war-time production.'[75]

Scheduled for ten weeks, *Major Barbara* took six months to shoot. Because filming lasted longer than expected, costs mounted. Pascal even asked the actors to take a cut in salary, Morley remembers. 'At that time I had a terribly forceful agent. I told Pascal to negotiate with him. He told the agent that my performance was terrible and that I would be finished in films. My agent calmly replied, "Well, if that's true, he'd better get all he can out of this picture." So nobody actually took a cut.'[76] Nobody except Pascal. *Major Barbara* was originally budgeted at £125,000, which came from the Pascal-Davenport syndicate, Woolf's General Film Distributors, and the National Provincial Bank. By the summer of 1940, it became obvious that the budget was insufficient. In stages, Woolf advanced an additional £76,000 and the bank did the same—more than doubling the total budget, exclusive of distribution charges.[77] One can assume that Pascal acted as he had on *Pygmalion*: to secure additional funds, he gave up more and more portions of his own share or the priority on his return.

On 6 July 1940, when Shaw discovered how matters stood, he urged Pascal to finish shooting '*without a single retake*, until you have it complete. When it is finished ... go through the rushes and be satisfied with what is good enough, no matter how much better you could make it if you had another six months. ... You must finish, finish, finish at all sacrifice until *a* Barbara film is ready for release, no matter how far it may fall short of *the* film of which you dream.'[78] Insofar as he was capable of following such advice, Pascal followed it. Most of Shaw's new film sequences, he did not shoot.[79]

On the other hand, some scenes he shot were cut. Before examining the film Pascal made from Shaw's screenplay, let us analyze that screenplay.

From the outset, Shaw determined to update *Major Barbara* from its January 1906 setting to a period either modern or in the future.[80] Instead of riding in carriages, the Undershaft family rides in cars. The war in Manchuria becomes the front, the gun cotton shed the cordite shed.

Because of a new law, the technicality that permits Cusins to qualify as a bastard changes: though his parents' marriage has become legal in England, it was illegal when Cusins was born. Instead of the true armourer keeping faith by selling weapons indiscriminately 'to aristocrat and republican, to Nihilist and Tsar, to Capitalist and Socialist,' as he did before the Spanish Civil War and Russian Revolution, he sells them 'to Royalist and Republican, to Communist and Capitalist.' *Major Barbara* gains by such updating, which gives it more immediacy.

But the modernity of *Major Barbara* is generalized, not tied to 1940, when it was made. While the Battle of Britain raged, Shaw resisted Pascal's efforts to introduce specifically contemporary references. Whereas Shaw's text has Cusins respond to Undershaft's insistence that if he succeed to the inheritance he will have to change his name, 'Would any man named Adolphus—any man called Dolly!—object to be called something else?' Pascal, with Hitler in mind, tried different versions of Cusins's response so as to employ the name Adolf.[81] Whereas Shaw's text has Cusins recall giving a revolver and cartridges to a student who fought with Greece against Turkey, Pascal changed the reference to the Spanish Civil War, in which the student fought on the Loyalist side, and for a time Shaw seriously considered retaining the latter change: he amended a line to 'the blood of every Spanish *Falangist* he shot.'[82] But he dropped the idea and he rejected Pascal's suggestion to conclude the film with a topical reference, for 'there is nothing that I can put in at the end that will not be out of date a week hence.'[83] Time has proved him right. To today's audiences too young to remember the period, the reference to Grecian and Turkish enmity requires no footnote, but a reference to a Falangist would. Cusins's pleasure at the prospect of no longer having the comic names Adolphus or Dolly is still understandable and funny, but Adolf without Hitler is neither.

As I explain in more detail in my Note on the Text, for *Major Barbara*—unlike *Saint Joan* and *Pygmalion*—Shaw did not key new film sequences and bridges to a cut edition of the play. Instead, he wrote new film sequences and discussed with Pascal cuts, transpositions, and interpolations in the play text. Until what corresponds to the end of Act II, Pascal's different shooting scripts harmonize with Shaw's screen version published by Penguin Books in 1945, except that, unlike this screenplay, the latter does not incorporate Shaw's internal cuts. Because the various texts after Act II differ radically from each other, this screenplay then conforms to Shaw's published, uncut text. In preparing it, Shaw restored some cuts and cut some restorations.[84] It is difficult to believe that the practical Shaw did not recognize the desirability of making internal cuts in the second half of the screenplay, perhaps including a stale argument about fresh air that delays the dramatic action, unnecessary exposition about Jains, and a scene that takes too long to reveal that Shirley and Barbara leave each other after their tea. Faced with actual filming, Shaw authorized cuts, but one cannot tell which cuts he made or permitted solely for budgetary and related considerations. This *Major Barbara* screenplay, then, is bifurcated. Until Barbara and Shirley leave the Salvation Army shelter, it is a screenplay for filming; afterward, a screenplay with the fullest possible text, to be pruned for filming.

In the screenplay's new prologue, which dramatizes the meeting of Barbara and Cusins, Shaw, freed from the limitations of the stage, moves within minutes or seconds from an exterior where Cusins speaks on Greek religion, to another exterior where Barbara delivers a sermon, to the interior of the Salvation Army shelter, to a tram stop, to Wilton Crescent. He reverses time to show consecutively what occurs simultaneously: Barbara's scenes outside a restaurant and by the river precede concurrent episodes at the Salvation Army meeting and in Undershaft's flat.

Shaw does not have Bill Walker describe his encounter with Todger Fairmile: a new flashback dramatizes it. Because of the altercation between Undershaft and Cusins on how the Salvation Army by defanging workers aids capitalists is, as Shaw put it,[85] more stagey than cinematic, he deletes it entirely and cuts directly to Barbara's return from a meeting. Sensibly, he cuts inessential explanations and quickens the dramatic pace:

THE WOMAN. Whats your name?
THE MAN. Bronterre O'Brien Price. ⟦Usually called⟧ Snobby Price, for short.
⟦THE WOMAN. Snobby's a carpenter, aint it? You said you was a painter.
PRICE. Not that kind of snob, but the genteel sort. I'm too uppish, owing to my intelligence, and my father being a Chartist and a reading, thinking man: a stationer, too, I'm none of your common hewers of wood and drawers of water; and dont you forget it. [*He returns to his seat at the table, and takes up his mug*].⟧ Wots y o u r name?

Eliminating what is basically redundant or unnecessary, Shaw effectively streamlines such passages as Cusins's:

Father Undershaft: you are mistaken: I am a sincere Salvationist. You do not understand the Salvation Army. It is the army of joy, of love, of courage: [[it has banished the fear and remorse and despair of the old hell-ridden evangelical sects:]] it marches to fight the devil with trumpet and drum, with music and dancing[[, with banner and palm, as becomes a sally from heaven by its happy garrison]]. It picks the waster out of the public house and makes a man of him; it finds a worm wriggling in a back kitchen, and lo! a woman! [[Men and women of rank too, sons and daughters of the Highest.]] It takes the poor professor of Greek, the most artificial and self-suppressed of human creatures, [[from his meal of roots,]] and lets loose the rhapsodist in him; [[reveals the true worship of Dionysos to him;]] sends him down the public street drumming dithyrambs [*he plays a thundering flourish on the drum*].

Not all of Shaw's cuts are as fortunate as these, however. One misses—certainly, audiences who fail to perceive the point miss—Lady Britomart's comment, after Cusins explains that his mother is his father's dead wife's sister, that Cusins is his own cousin. But this infelicitous omission is the exception, not the rule.

Shaw's new scenes do more than dramatize exposition. In showing Barbara's and Cusin's meeting, Shaw deepens our perception of their characters and of his theme. He reveals the scholar's ineffectuality that is his alternative to Undershaft's offer of power, and in dramatizing Barbara's religious inspiration he more effectively than in the play lays the groundwork for her despair when her father 'buys' the Salvation Army. Though late in the play Barbara states, 'I escaped from the world into a paradise of enthusiasm and prayer and soul saving,' the play dramatizes only the soul saving; the screenplay's prologue and large Salvation Army meeting led by the General dramatize the paradise of enthusiasm and prayer as well. Some new film sequences are not even hinted at in the play, notably, Barbara fainting at the Embankment, a vivid dramatization of her emotional state after she leaves the shelter.

Most of the new film sequences occur in Shaw's revision of Act III. Instead of describing Perivale St Andrews, he takes advantage of the film's resources to present a countryside view of the firm's name, labyrinths of buildings and immense tubes, a sulphates shed that resembles a Snow King's cave, a grand square of churches and temples, and panoramic views from a rooftop restaurant of a forty-storey building. He takes spectators inside the Labour Church to show busts of socialist heroes and heroines, including Marx, the Webbs, and G.B.S. One of the more impressive new scenes is a performance of the quartet and chorus from *Moses in Egypt*, music by Rossini, new lyrics by Shaw, with orchestra and singers conducted by Arturo Toscannini. Written in November 1939,[86] the concert is not 'live' but a televised recording projected onto an immense screen.

Shaw's revised dialogue is not invariably effective. Hilarious is the new exchange between Lomax and Undershaft when the latter refers to where Japanese worship. 'The Shinto shop?' asks Lomax. 'We call it a temple,' says Undershaft. Less funny is his revision of an exchange between Cusins and Lady Britomart, which in the play pointedly creates comedy by antithesis, the unexpected, and inversion: 'I was possessed.' 'Youre not sober yet. Go home to bed at once.' 'I have never before ventured to reproach you, Lady Brit; but how could you marry the Prince of Darkness?' 'It was much more excusable to marry him than to get drunk with him.' Revised for the motion picture, antithesis and inversion blur; comedy diminishes, and the point dulls: 'You are his friend: you got drunk with him.' 'I did not marry him. I tolerate him because he was the instrument of Barbara's birth; but to me he is the Prince of Darkness.' 'You are getting drunker and drunker, Adolphus. Finish your breakfast and stop talking.'

Nor do his altered sequences always improve. The transposition of Cusins's recitation of passages from *The Bacchae* from the Salvation shelter scene to Undershaft's flat is to the good, since Cusins has had more time to know Undershaft and has become inebriated (both better motivations). Shaw's rearrangement of episodes in Act III, Scene 1 betters the play, where he employs much ingenuity to get characters off and into the single set. In the screenplay, because place can change quickly and frequently, the new, revised, and old sequences flow more realistically. A small but major revision, which stems from both new scenes and transpositions of old passages, weakens the screenplay. In the play, it is only when Cusins persuades Undershaft that he is technically a bastard that Undershaft considers him a possible successor. Since the play's denouement hinges on this question, the matter is crucial. Unfortunately, the screenplay undercuts the dramatic reversal and Undershaft's seriousness about this qualification by having him consider Cusins's succession at his flat after the Salvation Army meeting, *before* Cusins reveals his eligibility: 'Have you ever thought of going into business? My business: money and gunpowder?' If the speech merely represents a job offer, not the inheritance, the point is unclear. And unlikely too, for at the factory, before Cusins explains his illegitimacy, Undershaft promises him a temple of Dionysos or a small private oratory behind his office, then coyly drops the subject: 'I forgot that we have not come to that yet. The remark was prophetic.' For Shaw, who lectured Hollywood against weakening dramatic impact, this dialogue is, to say the least, unfortunate.

Additions strengthen the play's religious aspects. In a passage added to

Undershaft's speech before the departure to his factory, Shaw more convincingly than in the play dramatizes Barbara's reassurance as to Bill Walker and therefore more effectively prepares for her return to the colours at the end. With the creation of two new characters, Mog Habbijam and Todger Fairmile, Shaw provides what the play lacks: accounts of genuine religious conversions, each different from the other.

Shaw's screenplay strengthens social aspects as well. In a new passage, he clarifies the role of Lazarus:

> UNDERSHAFT.... It is part of the [Undershaft] tradition that they should take a partner with a Jewish name. It suggests financial ability; and he gets all the blame when our profits are considered exorbitant.
> CUSINS. A scapegoat, then?
> UNDERSHAFT. Exactly: a scapegoat.
> CUSINS. That is the role of the Jew in modern Capitalism.
> UNDERSHAFT. Yes; but it was an Undershaft invention. Most of these notions are.

Expanding the role of Morrison, the screenplay reveals him as the sort of worker who assumes the values of his employers and who understands their social code better than they do. Since factories exist in order to furnish his wages, he explains in the screenplay, one must put up with them. Whereas in the play Lady Britomart resolves the question of whether Morrison should announce Undershaft or whether he is at home in the house, in the screenplay the entire family turns to Morrison, who provides the socially correct answer.

To appreciate more fully Shaw's mixture of success and failure in adapting *Major Barbara* to the screen, one must examine its major themes and focus. Like the play, the screenplay is a dialectical network that fuses themes of the organization of society, the dilemma of the intellectual, and individual salvation. In dramatizing the conversion of Barbara and Cusins to Undershaft's principles, Shaw suggests not their defeat and the victory of capitalism, but rather the victory of all three figures, who get what they want. Undershaft finds a worthy successor and the young people aim to employ his social improvements as a stepping-stone to further social improvement and spiritual regeneration. On stage, Cusins and Barbara find it difficult to compete with Undershaft, who is witty, persuasive, and has more lines than either of them. In addition, the dramatic focus of the first act is primarily on him: 'Waiting for Andrew', as it were. Only later do they acquire stature. In the screenplay, Shaw retains what gives Undershaft strength, but adds a prologue which gives initial emphasis to

Cusins and Barbara, whose roles it strengthens. In his screenplay, Shaw achieves a better balance among the three principals.

The screenplay clarifies the social aspect. More than the play, it emphasizes that despite Undershaft's social advances, his factory is still a capitalistic enterprise that prevents rather than fosters radical social change for its workers. He calls seditious speeches at the Labour Church 'the Undershaft safety valve. Our people can talk here; and as long as men can talk politics they will never do anything else except work for their daily bread.' In addition to contrasting Cusins as the ineffectual intellectual at the beginning and the man of power at the end, the screenplay defines his role as social reformer more clearly than the play does. In the Salvation shelter, Shaw demonstrates the results of nineteenth century capitalism: miserable, character-destroying, soul-starving poverty. In Undershaft's factory town he shows material well-being to be the result of enlightened capitalism. Though desirable, this is not in Shaw's mind sufficient for society, which should be organized not primarily for the profit of an individual or an oligarchy, but, as Cusins declares, for the people, who should have power to force the governing oligarchy to work for the *general* good. Building upon Undershaft's accomplishment, he aims to transform capitalism to democratic socialism. In two ways, Shaw clarifies his aim and role, revision of dialogue and a new scene. In the play, Cusins tells Barbara that Undershaft's factory is run by 'the most rascally part of society, the money hunters, the pleasure hunters, the military promotion hunters' and Undershaft challenges him to fight 'the rascals.' Less rhythmically but more pointedly, Cusins in the screenplay tells Barbara it is run by 'Capitalist money hunters,' and Undershaft challenges him to fight 'the money hunters.' Shaw also makes one of Cusins's explanations more accurate. As a Greek teacher, he says in the play, he 'gave the intellectual man weapons against the common man.' In the screenplay, he 'gave the rich man an intellectual weapon against the poor man' and adds that he proposes to give the *poor* man – more thematically appropriate than the play's *common* man – not simply weapons but *material* weapons to force those in power to work for the general welfare. Expanding and clarifying this theme is a new scene, the televised extravaganza *Moses in Egypt*, which an announcer explicitly interprets: the Red Sea symbolizes 'the Socialist revolution on which our most glorious hopes and our deadliest fears are fixed.' Implying that capitalism, exemplified by Undershaft's factory, contains the seeds of its destruction, the chorus sings, 'We forge our own destruction/We shall be slain who slay,' and prophesies, 'Creation, not destruction,/Henceforth shall make us great.' Also important is the symbolic title. Moses is in Egypt, not the promised land, to which he hopes to lead the children of

Israel. Similarly, Perivale St Andrews is not the promised land of socialism, to which Cusins in a Fabian fashion hopes to give its workers the power to reach.

Dramatically, however, Shaw's screenplay fails to make Cusins's dilemma credible. In choosing an armaments factory as the arena in which a better world may be forged, Shaw deliberately links social improvement with a morally repulsive business, for the elimination of poverty must be the first step before any other may be taken, even if it takes a dealer in slaughter and mutilation to do it. In daring Cusins to make war on war, the armaments factory provides an apt background for the metaphor. Because Cusins loathes what a munitions factory stands for, he faces an 'abyss of moral horror' which he must overcome to accept Undershaft's offer. The screenplay fails to dramatize this abyss. While it vivifies the life Undershaft's factory provides, it does not vivify the death it creates. Shaw portrays The Good Life enjoyed by Undershaft's workers: a splendid restaurant, a mansion-like apartment building, magnificent churches, and superb recreational facilities. But the factory itself is '*a forest of cranes and huge tubular metal structures*,' a '*labyrinth of buildings and monster tubes*,' and a picturesque sulphur shed. As for death and devastation, Lady Britomart reflects the audience's perception of them when she declares, 'pipes and boilers. They mean nothing to me.' Shaw fails to dramatize the use to which Undershaft's goods are put. The only view of its horror is a few wounded, lifesize dummies. Although he describes them in more gory detail than he does their stage counterparts, straw wounds inadequately convey slaughter, particularly when juxtaposed beside scenes of The Good Life. Because the former does not register at all, Cusins's dilemma, though discussed, is undramatized. Because the latter registers forcefully – and Shaw neglects to dramatize the social stratification at the factory, to which Undershaft alludes – the need for social change is unrealized. In dramatic terms, Shaw fails to make a case against Undershaft.

The same holds for the conflict between Undershaft and Barbara. Play and screenplay make clear that religious institutions depend on capitalism to survive. The screenplay goes further, for in the Shinto temple scene, Shaw reminds us that religion 'is politically important.' The Shinto temple 'is the temple of the Totalitarian State,' ruled and owned by Undershaft, Shaw stresses. Despite this sequence, Barbara's challenge is as undramatized as Cusins's abyss. Although she aims at spiritual improvement in the factory town, Shaw dramatizes no spiritual poverty. Although she says that here 'salvation is really wanted,' for the bodies that are full have souls that are empty, neither she nor we see evidence of it. The only Undershaft worker brought on screen is the same one brought on stage, Bilton, whom social 'betters' fail to intimidate.

To suggest that the *Major Barbara* screenplay is a failure is as far from my mind as to suggest it is an entire success. As I said earlier, it is a mixture of both. What of Pascal's film derived from this screenplay?

Despite Blanche Patch's assertion, which is typical, that 'there has been more tinkering with *Pygmalion* than with any other work of his,'[87] there was far more 'tinkering' with *Major Barbara*. Whereas Pascal's *Pygmalion* changed the screenplay's end, it retained a great deal of its essence. On the other hand, *Major Barbara* disembowelled the final act and eliminated most of its essence. To assert, as Costello does, that 'Pascal transferred it to the screen with only moderate alterations,'[88] is to ignore the transformation of more than a third of the play and screenplay – a third, moreover, that is vital to its thematic and dramatic development.

A hint that changes occurred is the film's closing credits, on every print: Charles Victor played Bilton, O. B. Clarence (the vicar of *Pygmalion*) Pettigrew. Yet while Pascal filmed scenes with both,[89] in no print do audiences see Bilton, and Pettigrew (invented by Pascal, to escort the family through the factory town) survives, unintroduced, in three silent long shots. Running time of Pascal's personal print is 137 minutes.[90] At its official world première, 7 April 1941, running time was sixteen minutes less.[91] When it opened in the United States with Shaw's three-minute prologue, running time dropped to 115 minutes.[92] When it went to American neighbourhood and rural theatres, it was reduced to 100 minutes and it was similarly mutilated when it went to the provinces in England.[93] As recently as 1964, the 100-minute version played in New York.[94] More recently, at a 1973 showing by the Toronto Film Society, it ran only 95 minutes; and in 1979 the print circulating in Australia ran 97 minutes[95]—both far cries from the 137, 121, or even 115 minute versions.

Why these cuts? Although American censorship, to be discussed shortly, constitutes one reason, another was the film's length. Unlike today's motion pictures, which often last two or more hours, a movie in the late 1930s and early 1940s usually ran about an hour and a half. A film of two hours or more was considered a major event. As Shaw remarked at the time, English provincial (and American, one might add) film theatres believed that a movie program should consist of two pictures and a newsreel.[96] Their total running time? Roughly three hours. Insofar as *Major Barbara* is concerned, the result, to use Shaw's wartime word, was sabotage.[97] What was cut? Chiefly, the Salvation Army meeting at the Albert Hall, the expository dialogue between Lady Britomart and Stephen at the beginning of the film (which explains the Undershaft tradition, necessary to the plot), and most of the scenes in Undershaft's factory (whose dialogue conveys the bulk of the work's political and economic themes, the abyss of moral horror, and Cusins's social goals). Most of these deletions, moreover, were cut from the 121-minute version as well, and the others, though present in Pascal's 137-minute print, are greatly abridged.

Initially, Pascal's intentions were honourable. Of Undershaft's speech about six hundred and seventy fools huddled in Parliament, according to Deans, 'Gaby used to say: "Without this speech I don't not make the picture!" (two negatives were always better than one for him).'[98] This speech is in Pascal's print, not the others. Ditto, Undershaft's statements that he is not to blame if morality mongers prefer to preach rather than to buy his weapons to fight evil people; that the world would be better if people scrapped obsolete moralities and religions which fail to fit the facts of life, as munitions makers scrap weapons that turn out wrong; that a decent income and good living conditions are more effective methods of salvation than Barbara's; that voting merely changes the names of cabinet members but killing accomplishes genuine, lasting social change; the armourer's faith, and the Undershaft maxims. Although I shall have more to say about Pascal's rearrangement of these passages from the order in which Shaw put them, the point at present is that only in his print is there any moral dilemma. Not until 19 March 1977, when the Public Broadcasting System showed Pascal's print on television, were these subjects heard by American movie audiences; not until June 1977, when the National Film Theatre showed it, by English audiences.[99] Perhaps the distributors' pressures were too strong for Pascal to overcome. Perhaps they or the exhibitors cut the film without his knowledge. And perhaps a little of both.

Certainly, Pascal recut the negative for America.[100] With the P.C.A. censorship of *Pygmalion* fresh in his mind, he knew that American distribution required conformity to the Code. From Cusins's 'You are damnably discouraging,' he snipped the offensive third word. So as not to offend prudish moviegoers, he laundered Bill Walker's reference to Mog as a 'carroty slat' (slut) to 'carroty cat', but even this was initially too strong for the P.C.A., which reminded him that the new noun was 'specifically included in the list of words and phrases which must be deleted from pictures which are to bear the Association's certificate of approval.' On the basis of the word's context, however, Pascal persuaded them to back down.[101]

On other matters, they did not relent. The offensive areas were vulgarity and irreverence toward religion and religious institutions. In Snobby Price's reference to Peter Shirley as 'a jumped-up, jerked-off, orspittle-turned-out incurable of an old workin man,' Pascal had to replace the second phrase. 'Chucked out' was the inoffensive substitute.

Since Bill exclaims *Gawd!* in a way the censors considered irreverent, exit; in its place, enter the neutral *Cor!*[102] Particularly damaging to the film were the P.C.A.'s demands that it must not lead the audience to conclude 'that the distiller is saved and members of the Salvation Army can rejoice in his salvation simply because he contributed £50,000 toward the work of the organization' and that 'the head of a worthwhile religious organization' must not explicitly declare that because of his donation 'a cynical munitions maker ... will be in Heaven with the "seal of God on his brow" '. Pascal capitulated. Instead of the General asking her audience to rejoice in Bodger's salvation, she asked them to *hope* for his salvation. Instead of telling them that after death Undershaft will be with them and be known by God's seal on his brow, she had to ask them to 'hope and pray that he will be there with us still. Then we shall know them as we ourselves are known.'[103] Only after he cut and redubbed *Major Barbara* to conform to the P.C.A. demands did it receive a seal of approval. When he cabled Shaw that upon screening the film for the Hays Office at the end of April 1941 they approved it with no cuts,[104] he misled Shaw, for what he showed them was a print he had already cut. But the P.C.A. was not the end of North American censorship. British Columbia censors demanded and got the deletion of Cusins drunkenly rising, staggering toward a window, and falling asleep in a drunken stupor.[105]

Largely for reasons of cuts— because of wartime filming conditions and demands of censors, distributors, and exhibitors—*Major Barbara* is botched. With motivations and connections between scenes missing, parts of the film seem 'talky', because dialogue loses its relation to dramatic development. Since editing shears eliminated large and small episodes, the direction sometimes seems choppy and unfocused. What is remarkable is how good much of the film is.

Among the principals, Robert Newton (Bill) and Rex Harrison (Cusins) are outstanding. While Wendy Hiller (Barbara) is less convincing and less complex than in *Pygmalion*, she is still effective. Emlyn Williams (Snobby) is superficial, but other small roles are impeccably acted, particularly Donald Calthrop (Shirley) and Walter Hudd (Stephen). Unlike the Covent Garden backdrop of *Pygmalion*, all *Major Barbara* exteriors shot in the studio look realistic.

Except for sequences mutilated by cutting, David Lean's camera work and editing—and in this discussion of these technical aspects, I use *Lean* as shorthand for Lean, Pascal, Neame, Hildyard, and Frend—effectively and fluidly alternate close, medium, and long shots with each other and with pans and tracking shots for emphasis, commentary, and focus. In the prologue, for example, the first view of Barbara is from behind, as she faces her audience, including Cusins in the background. Shortly after she begins her sermon, Lean cuts to a medium shot of her, from the front, then to a close-up of Cusins—the first close-up in the film—as he observes her audience, listens to her words, sees her, and becomes enraptured. Immediately, Lean cuts to a close-up of Barbara—her first and the film's second—then to another close-up of Cusins. By means of camera distancing and editing, the photography links the two characters. After they enter the shelter and sit, the camera frames them in a tight medium shot, visually linking them again. Later, when Barbara breaks down Bill Walker's brutality as she tries to win his soul - a scene Shaw once described as 'a sort of very moving love scene'[106]—the camera frames them in the same way. But when Bill argues with her, separated from her by Cusins and his drum, the camera shows a medium shot of all three, emphasizing the separation, followed by alternate shots of Bill alone and Barbara alone, the drum in the foreground.

Lean makes fine use of reaction shots; for instance, Shirley's pleasure when Barbara makes Bill uncomfortable, Bill and Cusins catching each other's eye when Undershaft 'buys' the Salvation Army, and during Mog's account of what she was like before her conversion, a woman who resembles Mog's former self is so affected that, close to tears, she leaves.

An early use of reaction shots establishes a motif. When Barbara asks for converts during her sermon, two little girls, then a young boy and girl, are transfixed by her sincerity and oratory. They demonstrate that Cusins is not the only one she dazzles, and they also begin a motif between Barbara and children. Later, when she leads the band to the shelter, children wave and call to her. When Undershaft arrives to visit her and a girl stumbles, she picks her up and holds her in her arms as she greets her father. In his factory town, she stands among a group of children who play with toy boats, and she pats a little boy's head. While this motif further humanizes Barbara by revealing a maternal-like warmth in addition to her businesslike and commanding manner, it also helps reveal the differences between the dirty children in the slum and the clean children in Undershaft's village, and helps prepare her line in the last scene, a desire to go house-hunting.

Lean uses the medium of cinema to make fluid the transition from Wilton Crescent to the Salvation shelter. When Barbara and Undershaft conclude their wager, Cusins strikes a loud chord on an organ and the family sings 'Onward Christian Soldiers.' Brass instruments and drum take up and continue the same song as the picture of the family group dissolves into a shot of a Salvation Army flag; the camera pulls back to reveal a marching band, led by Barbara, who enter the shelter yard.

Through visual means, Pascal helps establish character, mood, and milieu. After Cusins has met Barbara, a new scene shows him in Army

British *Pygmalion*   Liza, at home, before a mirror. On the wall are pictures of Robert Montgomery and Johnny Downs. Wendy Hiller.

British *Pygmalion*   Higgins and a cowering Liza, surrounded by the crowd, including Pickering and Mrs Eynsford Hill (upper right). Leslie Howard, Wendy Hiller, Scott Sunderland and Everley Gregg.

British *Pygmalion* Liz[a]
and Higgins argue afte[r]
the ball. Wendy Hiller an[d]
Leslie Howard.

Dutch *Pygmalion* Higgins
and Liza after they argue.
Johan de Meester and Lily
Bouwmeester.

uniform, having difficulty opening a door and tripping in the gutter because he inexpertly carries a huge drum—in comic contrast to his later ease in opening a door for Undershaft and kissing Barbara, both while he carries the drum. As Shaw observes in a stage and screen direction, the latter cannot be accomplished without practice. While Bill wrestles with his soul, Lean at various points cuts to him in different locales inside and outside the shelter and thus gives the impression that he has paced restlessly. Deftly establishing a contrast between social classes, Pascal has Undershaft, wearing a well tailored topcoat, arrive at the shelter in a Rolls Royce, at which poorly clad slum children gawk.

Camera and music create suspense and build toward a climax. After the announcement of Undershaft's arrival, the camera follows Morrison, accompanied by an excited motif on the violin, from the drawing room to the top of the stairway. An extreme long shot shows Undershaft, his back toward the camera, removing his coat, which he gives to a maid. After a quick cut to the family, who wait in suspense, the camera cuts back to a long shot of Morrison as he leads Undershaft up the stairway, his back still toward us, and down the hall to the drawing room door. A medium shot shows Morrison opening the door for him, the music builds to a fanfare, and Morrison announces the visitor. The camera pans as Lady Britomart crosses to Undershaft, and when she reaches him he faces the camera for the first time and the music mellows.

Several small directorial details enhance the dramatic action. When Undershaft announces that Barbara will preach his gospel, he is standing – as if by chance, for Pascal wisely makes no special point of it – in a pulpit. When Barbara enters to meet Peter Shirley, Bill Walker's feet are propped on a stove, barring her way. Stopping and looking at him sternly, she silently intimidates him into removing his feet to let her pass.

But much of the film is ineffective. The condensed version of Barbara's Embankment scene carries no emotional conviction. Made at the last moment as a filler, the scene looks as though it were done on the cheap, which it was. Pascal sometimes botches effects. When Barbara urges Bill to come with her to brave manhood on earth and eternal glory in heaven, Shaw indicates a loud drum beat by Cusins as he enters, breaking the mood into which she has virtually hypnotized Bill. Instead, Pascal has Barbara plead, look up as the camera cuts to Cusins, who enters, and only then has him bang the drum, and not particularly loudly. Camera and actors linger where such lingering retards the dramatic action. Undershaft takes far too long to give the General his check. He removes and polishes his spectacles, takes out and unscrews the cap of his fountain pen, and signs. Obviously, suspense was the reason for such protraction. It was not the result, for he does no more than what the audience expects him to do, write on a piece of paper. Since the pace drops, the play stops. To have performed the business beneath the lines, rather than between them, would have been more exciting and more to the point: Undershaft's ease in buying the Salvation Army.

Some touches are trite. When Rummy tells Snobby that women's types of sins, unlike those of men, cannot be mentioned publicly but must be whispered in private, she whispers and mimes whispering with her hand – as if neither he nor the audience knew what whispering were.

To good effect, Pascal occasionally restores passages cut by Shaw; for instance, Lady Britomart's comments that it was more excusable to marry Undershaft than to get drunk with him and that Cusins is his own cousin. Probably to avoid confusing a mass, worldwide audience with incomprehensible dialogue, Pascal removes many Greek references. In the film, Cusins's cry 'Dionysos Undershaft has descended. I am possessed' becomes the more understandable 'Saint Undershaft and Saint Bodger have descended: the patron saints of peace and temperance.'

With good results, Pascal sometimes interpolates new sequences. To motivate Lomax's fit of laughter, a self-possessed Morrison brings Undershaft a glass of hot lemon and ginger which, says the butler, Undershaft takes at precisely 9.15 p.m., whereupon Undershaft observes that Morrison's memory seems to be better than his own. Despite Shaw's warning against breaking dramatic continuity by switching to something new in its midst, Pascal's new scene wherein Snobby's mother, her pride damaged by her son's lies, hurls him down the steps as he tries to sneak away from the shelter, demands who has been beating whom, and chases him is not only funny but also provides emotional satisfaction at the petty scoundrel's comeuppance.

Usually, however, Pascal's changes are for the worse. Bill's return at the end—happy, clean-shaven, and well employed—is contrived, trite, and unconvincing. Whereas Shaw has Bill reveal his encounter with Todger and Mog in a flashback, Pascal cuts from the shelter to that encounter, then cuts back to the shelter just before Bill's return. Although, one might argue, Shaw's method emphasizes a breakaway from and return to a single, stagey setting, that setting – since it is photographed and edited wth variety—does not seem stagey, and Shaw's way is economical. By contrast, Pascal's method is redundant, since after Bill returns he relates what the audience has seen. To open the scene at Undershaft's flat, Shaw has him upon entering offer Cusins a drink, since it is cold outside. Pascal starts the scene at the dinner table, where Undershaft repeats the General's quotation of his question, after she thanked God for his donation, 'You dont thank me?' The first time, the line is funny. Because we know Undershaft is on the platform, her repetition at the meeting is also funny. But it is not funny a third time, where it merely betrays the director's uncertainty as to how to begin the scene.

Moreover, Pascal compounds Shavian blunders. As in Shaw's screenplay, Undershaft, in his flat, invites Cusins to join his cannon business—before Cusins establishes his eligibility. In addition, Pascal later transposes two passages from after Cusins's revelation to before it. The first is Undershaft's Platonic paraphrase, which urges the Greek professor to become a maker of gunpowder. The second is his challenge, 'Dare you make war on war? Here are the means.' To make matters worse, Undershaft follows this challenge with a direct query as to whether Cusins will come into his business. As in Shaw's screenplay, the scenes in Undershaft's factory do not emphasize the destructive nature of its products. Pascal even cuts references to slaughter, such as telegrams which announce the 'good news' of the death of three hundred soldiers. The only weapons in the film are the antique Woolwich Infant and a clean, almost attractive bomb. What Pascal shows is modern industrial technology: huge machines, a hot ingot passing along rollers, the release of molten steel into a cauldron, a grinding wheel, nitrates, and admiring reaction shots of the family. Because he shows nothing to hate, Cusins's declaration that Undershaft is driving him against his natural hatred of war seems either an irrelevancy or an intellectual's disinclination to enter business.

Undoubtedly, one reason for this distortion is the time the film was made. As mentioned earlier, location shooting started the same day as the evacuation from Dunkirk. Studio shooting began on 17 June—a week after the Nazis invaded France, three days before they entered Paris, five days before the French government signed an armistice pact with them. On 10 July the Battle of Britain started. Before these events, everyone thought the idea of filming *Major Barbara* in modern dress was reasonable. Indeed, as Deans says, 'it would have been impossible to make scenes with genuine London crowd players at Tower Bridge and elsewhere if the idea had been otherwise.' But the events of June and July changed everything. 'Once France dropped out the feeling changed, and by the time we reached the factory sequences there was certainly no intention of representing it as a munitions factory actually in time of war.'[107] Although Miss Deans did not say this, it would have been virtually impossible to portray convincingly a munitions maker as a mephistophelian character at a time when Britain was literally fighting for her life, and it is inconceivable that Anglo-American audiences could have accepted such a characterization. Considering the time in which Pascal made *Major Barbara*, one cannot blame him for not trying to do so but instead to settle for shrewdness and cynicism. From today's viewpoint, however, the result is a loss of significant aspects of *Major Barbara*. Curiously, an anachronistic consequence of the film being made in 1940, of which I have found no contemporary reference, is that Peter Shirley would not be unemployed in wartime, when the younger men were mobilized.

Wartime notwithstanding, Pascal's rearrangement of the scenes in Undershaft's factory is dramatically illogical and prevents *Major Barbara* from being the superior film it could have been even within the limitations just discussed. Because of the rearranged scenes, Cusins observes that Undershaft's factory town needs only a cathedral to be a heavenly rather than a hellish city *after* the family's visit to the church-filled Piety Square. Apart from Pascal having Undershaft issue Cusins several invitations to join his firm before Cusins reveals his eligibility, Pascal rearranges the arguments about the moral dilemma to before those of the establishment of eligibility and the practical details of employment. Consequently, the issue of salary, not morality, becomes the critical problem. Since they are settled last, climactically, Cusins no longer announces that the real tug of war is to come. It has already gone.

A crucial factor that prevents *Major Barbara* from being a superior film is its weakening of Shaw's social criticism. Unlike play and screenplay, the film dilutes Undershaft's revelation that elected representatives serve capitalistic enterprises (double brackets indicate cuts, capital letters additions):

> The government of your country! *I* am the government of your country: I, and Lazarus. Do you suppose that you and half a dozen amateurs like you, can govern [[Undershaft and Lazarus]] A COUNTRY LIKE ENGLAND? [[No, my friend, you will do what pays u s . You will make war when it suits us and keep peace when it doesnt. You will find out that trade requires certain measures when we have decided on those measures. When I want anything to keep my dividends up, you will discover that my want is a national need. When other people want something to keep my dividends down, you will call out the police and military.]]

While England's conflict with Nazi Germany justifies the deletion of the sentence about making war, it does not justify the remaining cuts. Nor does it justify others, including Undershaft's explanation of *why* poverty is a crime, the social stratification and compartmentalization in his factory town, their result in a large profit for him, or the Jew's role as scapegoat. In fact, no one mentions that Lazarus is Jewish.

Although Pascal's visual contrast between the grime and dirt of

London's slums and the cleanliness and wholesomeness of Perivale St Andrews vividly portrays the superiority of benevolent capitalism and the point that poverty should be eliminated, he fails entirely to demonstrate that its elimination is only the first step toward social improvement. The film shows no Labour Church, no *Moses in Egypt* performance. When (in Pascal's print, for the entire episode is in no other) Undershaft recites his predecessors' maxims and asserts that they left nothing for him to say but 'Unashamed', Cusins does not state he will write something on the wall—an implicit recognition that Undershaft's is not the final word. Instead, distorting Shaw's view, Pascal transposes a passage from an entirely different context, that Undershaft might be a great man. More important, Cusins (in all prints) does not tell Barbara why he will join her father's firm or that he intends to give the people power to enable them to force the ruling oligarchy to work for the common good. He only tells her Undershaft's offer has beaten him and he will make war on war, though how he intends to do so is a mystery since Pascal cuts his repudiation of the armourer's faith and his announced new goal.

Because of these deletions and rearrangements, because most of the time consumed by the film's new scenes focuses on religion (Barbara's sermon, Bill's meeting with Todger, the great Salvation meeting), and because the religious and romantic passages suffer least from cuts, I find it impossible to agree with Costello's conclusion that in this film 'the social focus remains primary.'[108] Instead of a dialectical network of politics, economics, the role of the intellectual, social evolution, and religion, which exists in Shaw's play and screenplay, Pascal's movie is essentially about a religious girl whose fiancé gets a good job in her father's business. Despite its successful elements, *Major Barbara* simplifies Shaw's work in a way he had feared Hollywood might do.

In England, *Major Barbara* disappointed the reviewers, who generally felt that while it was reasonably satisfactory it was far below the level of *Pygmalion*. 'Despite some brilliant qualities we rarely forget that *Major Barbara* was written for a room with three walls,' said *The New Statesman and Nation*—a surprising assessment in view of the film's many exteriors. Perceptively, however, the review goes on to observe that in converting the play to the screen, Pascal made 'drastic cuts in Mr Shaw's argument.' Undershaft 'has gone oddly astray' and his profession, 'in the atmosphere of the present, [seems] to have entered on a new phase of respectability.' When Cusins and Barbara 'submit themselves, we have to guess what exactly it is they are taking on.' The montage of the factory and town 'hardly make up for arguments not taken over from the play,' whose cuts 'rather make hay of the play's last Act.' Such major flaws notwithstanding, the review concludes that the film 'is still first-rate entertainment. ... Whatever one may say against it, *Major Barbara* is unquestionably fun.' Despite reservations about the acting—Morley's Undershaft 'frequently seems to be confusing himself with Uplift' and 'Hiller is a shade too sweet ... she lacks edge and incisiveness'—*The Times* nevertheless praised the film's 'honesty of purpose and some highly amusing moments.'[109]

In the United States, where opinion divided sharply, *Major Barbara* like *Pygmalion* received on the whole a more favourable press, though like the English, American critics regarded it less highly than its predecessor.

Its admirers were unstinting in their praise. 'To call it a manifest triumph would be arrant stinginess with words,' said one, for it is 'a more triumphant picture than any the British have yet sent across.'[110] Major accolades went to the performers: 'extraordinarily good' and 'Robert Newton perhaps emerges with highest honours.'[111] The movie's American devotées responded to its witty and literate language and—surprisingly, in light of what was deleted—to its ideas, probably because both qualities were in short supply in American motion pictures. *Major Barbara* has 'a lot of talk,' said *Time*, but 'It is the kind of talk that cinema addicts seldom hear—brilliant, provocative, richly comic.' 'The most auspicious thing' about it, said *The New York Times*, 'is that it takes for granted that movie audiences have brains.' Its 1905 ideas were 'still ahead of the times—upon the screen.'[112]

Major Barbara had its detractors too. Despite the enormous amount of deletions—by Costello's count, the film retained only 210 of the 1,143 lines of the scenes in Undershaft's factory[113]—reviewers glibly resorted to clichés. 'After the Salvation Army episodes the action stops too often to let the characters discuss Shaw's sociological ideas.'[114] Instead of action and movement, 'there is only this eternal talk, talk, talk.'[115] Such notions take a long time to die. As recently as January 1976, when *Major Barbara* was revived in New York, Pauline Kael disregarded the facts to report blithely, 'Shaw had allowed *Pygmalion* to be cut and adapted for the screen, and it was a great success, but he got stubborn on this one and hung on to his dialogue.'[116]

Publicly, Shaw praised its producer-director: 'He shocks me by his utter indifference to the cost; but the result justifies him ... The man is a genius: that is all I have to say about him.'[117] The actors' responses vary. 'I was very proud to have done that film', Morley told me, but Hiller said she thought it so bad she left before it was over and has never seen it in its entirety.[118]

With customary accuracy, *Variety* predicted its box-office appeal. A 'class attraction,' it 'will hit substantial biz in metropolitan key runs and de luxers, but presents a problem for the nabes and hinterland spots. ... The picture will not hold up with American audiences generally.' The reasons: 'endless passages of dialogue that consume too much footage' for audience tastes, 'too full of Cockney dialect which is too strong for American audiences to consume in such a large dose,' and the religious satire—despite, one recalls, the censorship of its strongest aspect—'will not set well with the church-going element which ... makes up a very large majority of theatre audiences.'[119]

To compensate, distributors employed advertisements that stressed the success of *Pygmalion* (aiming at a bandwagon effect), the popular image of G.B.S., and of course sex. One advertisement displayed a cartoon of Shaw pushing a baby carriage with two dolls labelled *Pygmalion* and *Major Barbara* and a comic-strip ballon with Shavian words, 'Barbara's my biggest and best—and at my age, too!' Another showed a glamourized drawing of Rex Harrison and Wendy Hiller in a night gown with a plunging neckline, plus the caption, 'In *Pygmalion* Shaw showed you what a man could do with a woman. NOW in *Major Barbara* he shows you what a woman can do with a man!'[120]

Unlike *Pygmalion*, *Major Barbara* recieved no Academy Award. According to *Variety*, American business was 'only good to thin'.[121] In England it grossed less than it cost.[122] While I have found no evidence that it lost money, and while it was not the 'almighty flop' Shaw once called it,[123] it earned less than *Pygmalion*. As for Pascal, says S. N. Behrman, since it did not repeat the success of his previous Shaw film, 'his bankruptcy rather decreased in proportion.'[124]

ARMS AND THE MAN

In 1939, the year Shaw and Pascal agreed to film *Major Barbara*, the producer received a proposal to build motion picture studios in the Bahamas.[1] By November 1940, undoubtedly because of difficulties in making movies in wartime England, the idea became exceptionally desirable. Thrilled at the prospect of turning the Bahamas into a second Hollywood, Shaw approved and placed *Saint Joan*, *Candida*, and *The*

Devil's Disciple at Pascal's disposal.[2] On 6 Jan. 1941, Pascal left England to recut the negative of *Major Barbara* for American distribution and at the same time to pursue the Bahamas project.[3]

While in the United States, he abandoned it in favour of a scheme to establish a film industry in Vancouver, which unlike the Bahamas was on the same coast as Hollywood and could more easily avail itself of Hollywood's technical experts and stars.[4] On 2 May 1941, less than two weeks before the American premiere of *Major Barbara*, Shaw received a cable which announced that a group was ready to back Pascal to make films in Canada.[5] A month later, the press reported he would 'definitely' establish production headquarters there and in late August would start shooting an adaptation of Paul Gallico's novel *The Snow Goose*, which Shaw called a Donald Duck film. Next would come two Shaw movies, the first to be *The Millionairess*, *Captain Brassbound's Conversion*, or *Arms and the Man*; the second, *Saint Joan*.[6] In late 1941, the Canadian plan collapsed. One reason was the difficulty of financing the operation in wartime;[7] another, the heavy Canadian taxation that Shaw believed would prove ruinous.[8]

During negotiations for both the Bahamas and Canada, Pascal also negotiated with Hollywood studios.[9] To Shaw's admiration, he continually wheeled as he attempted to deal. 'The celerity with which you find a new plan of campaign when the old one breaks down,' said Shaw, 'is very reassuring.'[10] With equal celerity, Pascal planned different plays for his next film. At first, he determined to follow *Major Barbara* with *Saint Joan*, starring Katharine Hepburn.[11] Though she was interested, nothing developed. For several weeks, he importuned Katharine Cornell to play Jennifer in *The Doctor's Dilemma*,[12] but he wooed in vain. His chief difficulty in concluding a Hollywood contract was Shaw's refusal to commit himself to more than one movie at a time. In the 1930s and 1940s, Hollywood films were made by studios, which insisted on a long-term, multi-picture contract with a producer.[13] The impasse was complete. Pascal's decision to film *The Snow Goose* in addition to a Shaw play may have been an attempt to compromise in order to obtain backing, for the two works comprised a two-picture deal. In September 1941, the press reported that he was on the verge of signing a two-picture contract with R.K.O., *The Snow Goose* and *Arms and the Man*.[14]

For a time, *Arms and the Man* seemed almost certain to be produced. By August 1941, Pascal had raised £100,000 ($500,000).[15] On 3 Sept. Shaw completed new film sequences for it.[16]

Why *Arms and the Man*, which had already been filmed in English? One may infer several reasons. The B.I.P. movie did not play in America. Because of its critical and box office failure, B.I.P. very likely cut losses as much as possible by spending little on publicity and withdrawing it after a brief initial distribution. Shaw did not renew – and was probably not asked to renew – his five-year licence, and nine years was sufficiently long ago that a new version could be made. Also, M.G.M. was filming *The Chocolate Soldier*, starring Nelson Eddy and Rise Stevens (it opened in November 1941). Although M.G.M.'s *Chocolate Soldier* had Oscar Straus's music, it bypassed the copyright problem by fitting the songs into the text of Ferenc Molnar's play *The Guardsman*. If Shaw did not begin a competing movie soon, he may well have feared that, even though M.G.M.'s film was not based on his play, another *Arms and the Man* film might be impossible for a very long time.

In contrast to the 1932 movie of *Arms and the Man*, wherein Shaw merely advised Cecil Lewis on new film sequences, Shaw himself wrote such sequences for the 1941 picture, with those cinematic advantages he had extolled nine years earlier. Since I have already commented on the cuts Shaw recommended and authorized in 1932, I will not repeat myself here but will instead confine my examination of the 1941 *Arms and the Man* screenplay to Shaw's new scenes and to aspects of the play.

Instead of referring to important offstage events, Shaw brings them vividly onto the screen, notably the battle of Slivnitza, which includes the professional soldiers' surprise that cavalry would charge machine guns ('Those Bulgarian idiots are capable of anything'), the arrival of the sergeant with news about the wrong ammunition, Sergius leading a band of sabre-flourishing riders, Bluntschli crouching in a shell hole to escape the enemy's notice, then unhurriedly walking away after the charge has passed. More than dramatizing expository passages, Shaw enriches the comedy by the creation of scenes not suggested in the play. On the run, Bluntschli purchases bread from a peasant woman whose silence he tries to obtain first by overpaying her, then by warning her her countrymen will kill her if they hear she has sold food to the enemy. Cleverly, Shaw reveals the woman to be more astute than the Swiss realist. After she pockets his money, she tells her countrymen he robbed her bread. In another scene, a victory celebration, Bulgarian crowds cheer Petkoff and Sergius, whom the girls especially adore, and respond enthusiastically to patriotic speeches.

Although Shaw created new film sequences for *Arms and the Man*, he recognized as a dramatic storyteller that at a certain point condensation and acceleration, not expansion and diffusion, are effective. His new film sequences precede each of the play's three acts and interrupt the first. Once the movie reaches the final act, however, and the audience is interested in the characters and story, he insisted on no change of location. Alternations of close-ups, medium shots, and long shots, and changes from desk to stove to window, with landscape beyond, provide all the variety a director needs.[17]

Shaw himself uses cinema techniques advantageously. Creating suspense, he cuts back and forth between the pursued Bluntschli who observes Raina's lighted window and the action in her room. Skillfully employing camera and editor's shears for comic irony, he has Raina — in a new luncheon scene between Acts II and III— speak as though she were a dainty eater; cuts to her father, who dumps a whole chicken on his plate, then sets to work on it; cuts to a close-up of her father's daughter, who uses her fingers to pull a leg off her half chicken, then greedily gnaws at the leg; cuts to Bluntschli, who observes these actions with dismay; and cuts to the entire group, busily eating.

Many Shavian stage directions reproduced from the play can be more effective when enacted for the camera's eye than from the proscenium arch's unshifting view. When Raina surreptitiously removes her photograph from the pocket of her father's coat, with the assistance of Bluntschli, '*who covers it with a sheet of paper under the very nose of Sergius, who looks on amazed*', the stage director must convey these actions and emotions within a single long shot, as it were. With greater resources, the movie director might have the camera show in close-up the removal of the picture, pan as the photograph goes to Bluntschli's hand to beneath a sheet of paper, and continue panning to Sergius's amazed face. Without altering a line or stage direction, certain dramatic moments can become more effective on screen than on stage; for example, Raina's successful bluff when an officer enters her room to seek the fugitive: 'Nonsense, sir: you can see that there is no one on the balcony. (*She throws the shutters wide open and stands with her back to the curtain where the man is hidden, pointing to the moonlit balcony. A couple of shots are fired right under the window; and a bullet shatters the glass opposite Raina, who winks and gasps, but stands her ground ...*).'

In his new film sequences, Shaw augments the play's major theme, the contrast between the realistic and romantic views of life. In play and screenplay, the basically realistic Bluntschli insists that the chief distinction between soldiers is that the experienced carry food rather than ammunition, the inexperienced the opposite. Whereas the play asks the audience to accept his word, for it shows only him in a predicament that demonstrates this matter, the movie dramatizes his claim: neither of Bluntschli's sub-lieutenants carries cartridges for his revolver. Crucial to Shaw's theme are that even the basically romantic characters are secretly troubled by the failure of their ideals to conform to the facts of life, and that romance and reality coexist to different degrees in most people. Were these not so, Raina's conversion to Bluntschli's viewpoint would be unbelievable. Early in both screenplay and play, therefore, the audience learns that before Sergius's victory she wondered whether her heroic ideals were nothing but fantasies based on operas and that she often longs to say or do something to shock him. In the new film sequences, Shaw goes further. When Raina romantically tells her mother that since 'the guest is sacred' they must not betray Bluntschli, Catherine realistically responds, 'Dont be ridiculous, child. This isnt an opera: it's real life.' But when Catherine points out that Bluntschli cannot possibly escape in his enemy uniform, Raina realistically suggests giving him her father's old clothes. Next, with a touch that helps humanize Catherine and reveal her practicality, Shaw has her observe, 'now that I see the poor creature lying there helpless I dont feel I should like to see him murdered. But look at the mess he is making of your bed with his boots. His spurs will tear the sheets to pieces.'

In a new movie sequence, Shaw also reveals the practical use to which authorities employ romantic idealism. During patriotic speeches that follow the battle of Slivnitza, the Mayor attempts to stimulate enthusiasm by exaggerating the odds against which the Bulgarians beat 'the invading hosts of our deadly enemies the Serbs.' Carried away by the approving cries of the crowd, he exclaims that against these 'millions' of ruthless foes were a mere two hundred patriots. When a voice from the crowd corrects him by shouting, 'Two thousand', the interrupter is silenced, kicked, and forced to flee for his life. Then the Mayor, Sergius, and Petkoff rekindle the crowd's fervour so that they will hunt fugitive Serbian soldiers.

Unfortunately, one of Shaw's new film sequences is maladroit and trite. Fortunately, it is the only one. In one of several scenes that link Acts I and II, plenipotentiaries sign a peace treaty. Among the signatories are Petkoff and Sergius, who '*find writing their names a bit of a job.*' With this screen direction, Shaw unwisely dissipates the effectiveness of similar comic business in Act III, where the situation — which has built to it — renders it more appropriate: Sergius with great difficulty signs the documents prepared by Bluntschli. In the same between-acts scene, Shaw demonstrates triteness. In the Council Chamber is a ten-foot statue of Peace, with a wreath visible in its left hand. After all signatures are affixed to the peace treaty, the camera shows that the statue's right hand, held behind its back, carries a revolver.

With the exception of this single scene, Shaw's new film sequences are funny, further the dramatic action, harmonize with and augment the play's themes, and enhance the texture of *Arms and the Man*, which in its 1941 version promised to be a richly comic film.

Before he wrote them, Shaw encountered problems with Hollywood. After he completed them, problems intensified. In July, someone urged

Pascal to suggest that Shaw change the setting from Bulgaria to Canada. Shaw dismissed the notion out of hand: 'The population of Bulgaria is 6 million, the theatre going proportion of which is negligible. Their feelings may be disregarded.' Moreover, since no Canadian, American, or Briton considers a Canadian soldier nearly as romantic as a Swiss or Bulgarian one, and since the play is so well known in English-speaking countries that any such change would appear a bad joke, Pascal should leave the play as it is.[18]

Later, Shaw encountered a typical Hollywood problem, the star. With only partial accuracy, a newspaper report of 28 Sept. 1941 stated:

> Ginger Rogers can play the role of Raina in *Arms and the Man* if she so desires, says the producer. He reports she displayed considerable interest in the role when he discussed it with her a while back, and Mr Shaw is convinced that she can do it, too. In fact, Shaw has demonstrated his enthusiasm by completely rewriting the play and placing the proper emphasis upon the character in light of Miss Rogers's position in the Hollywood firmament.[19]

The accurate parts are that Ginger Rogers was interested in playing in the film, that Shaw wanted her to play Raina, and that he placed the proper emphasis on Raina, the leading female character. The rest is inaccurate, for Rogers really wanted to play Louka and to have Shaw rewrite the script in order to build Louka into the star role. Shaw rejected the notion. '*If Ginger is to be the star,*' he insisted, '*she must play Raina.*'[20] To revise *Arms and the Man* to make Louka the stellar part, 'with a dance and plenty of laughs for Miss Rogers,' would be to change the play into *The Chocolate Soldier*. 'That would suit Hollywood to perfection,' for they love that comic opera and lack the faintest comprehension of serious comedy. If she persists in wanting to play Louka and in demanding its expansion, Shaw instructed, 'do not argue with her: just throw her out of the window and tell her not to come back.'[21] While Pascal did not obey these commands to the letter, she did not return.

Nor did Pascal make the film, perhaps because Rogers could not have her way, perhaps because the studios refused to consider a one-Shaw-picture contract with him, perhaps because M.G.M.'s *Chocolate Soldier* would soon open, perhaps because of all three reasons.

As Shaw put it, Pascal 'achieved the surprising feat of going to America at the height of his reputation, fortified by a monopoly of my plays for filming, and coming back with nothing done and nothing doing.'[22] With Pascal, however, something was always doing. Once more, the something was *Saint Joan*.

Shaw's earlier disapproval notwithstanding, Pascal wanted Greta Garbo to play The Maid. Despite Shaw's determination that Joan should be 'a new Englishwoman on the threshold of a career,' not 'an old Hollywood star no longer in her first youth,' he thought that 'as the G.G. arrangement, like all Gabriel's arrangements, will probably come to nothing anyhow, we need not bother about it yet.'[23] Shaw was mistaken. On 17 March 1943, before he left the United States, Pascal signed Garbo to a contract.[24] Shaw wavered, for her engagement might have been the condition under which Pascal could secure financial backing. It was. Armed with her signature, he interested J. Arthur Rank in financing the film.[25] Shaw proposed Robert Newton for the English soldier who gives Joan the cross, Rex Harrison for Dunois, and if Harrison were unavailable, Robert Donat.[26] Pascal tried to persuade Granville Barker to return to acting and play the Inquisitor.[27]

Pascal's arrangement with Rank called for three films: *Saint Joan* with Garbo, then *Cæsar and Cleopatra* and *The Doctor's Dilemma*.[28] Shaw was anxious that Pascal should not rush into another disadvantageous agreement. The capital, he urged, must be more than sufficient to cover the movie's cost, else Pascal would find himself in the same position as before, forced to give up his share of the film's income to borrow money to complete the picture. Shaw wanted Rank to pay Pascal a salary plus 10 per cent of the gross receipts.[29] Although Pascal reported Rank's consent, the truth was different. Unless Pascal withdrew his demand for 10 per cent of the gross receipts, Rank told him privately, he would not finance the film. Pascal agreed.[30] At the end of July or beginning of August 1943, Shaw sent Rank a draft agreement for a motion picture of *Saint Joan*, to be directed by Pascal.[31] But again the *Joan* project collapsed. The British government felt that to make a movie about Englishmen burning a famous patriot of one of her allies would be injudicious until after the war.[32]

CÆSAR AND CLEOPATRA

Still, the agreement with Rank did not collapse. Once *Joan* was postponed, they turned to *Cæsar and Cleopatra*. Within the Rank Organisation, objections were raised to the large budget, estimated at £550,000, on a play that had never had a major financial success in London. Arguing that the movie would gain prestige on the American market and thereby help sell other films even if it did not recover its costs, Rank prevailed.[1] On 21 Nov. 1943, Shaw and Rank concluded an agreement to produce *Caesar and Cleopatra*. The screenplay would be entirely Shaw's, the direction entirely Pascal's, and neither film nor advertisements would in any way state or suggest that either was by anyone else.[2]

As Pascal discovered, Shaw intended obedience to the letter. When trade papers announced that *Caesar and Cleopatra* would be codirected by Brian Desmond Hurst, an experienced film director, Shaw twice called Pascal's attention to the contractual clause that forbade any sharing of authorship or direction.[3] Though Hurst's name was removed, he remained. Because Pascal produced and directed *Caesar*, as he did *Barbara*, says Deans, he needed assistance, but 'the fact of the matter was that he didn't want it. He wanted to do it all himself.' He was determined that no one could say, as they did of his earlier films, 'that somebody else had directed *Caesar and Cleopatra*, and that Pascal had nothing to do with it.' Whereas he employed Hurst in two capacities, he only used him in the first, to assist the Pascal team, Deans and for a short time W. P. Lipscomb (one of the *Pygmalion* adapters, who this time worked without screen credit), in pre-production preparation of the shooting script. When shooting began, Hurst was to have been Pascal's Assistant in Direction, the job David Lean and Harold French had on *Major Barbara*, but Pascal 'took absolutely no notice of him when they got into the studio. Gaby simply ignored Brian, and from the word Go did every bit of direction himself.'[4] When the film was completed, Hurst implored Shaw for screen credit. Though polite, Shaw adamantly refused to share credit with 'transcript writers or co-directors of any sort.' If Hurst could find a title that did not employ the word director, Shaw would not grudge him publicity. 'But please note that the scenario of Caesar is my work. Anything you have contributed to it, though it may suggest a title for you, must not be described as scenario.'[5] Hurst went uncredited.

Over three months before Shaw signed the agreement with Rank, he and Pascal began to cast the film, which at that time they expected to follow *Saint Joan*. 'We make *Caesar and Cleopatra*,' Pascal proclaimed in August 1943. 'John Gielgud is Caesar. Vivien Leigh is Cleopatra. ... Ralph Richardson is Britannus.'[6] One-third of the pronouncement proved accurate. On 5 Aug. 1943, a Hollywood gossip columnist announced that David O. Selznick had agreed to permit Vivien Leigh, bound to him by an exclusive contract, to play Cleopatra.[7] She did. For her services, Selznick would receive a substantial percentage of the film's receipts.[8] Neither

Richardson nor Gielgud played the other roles, however. Richardson did not know that Shaw had considered him for Britannus and does not recall that Pascal ever contacted him about it.[9] Cecil Parker played the part. On 29 Aug. 1943, Shaw told Gielgud that the movie of *Cæsar and Cleopatra* depended upon his availability to play Caesar. If he were unavailable, Shaw continued:

> I must turn down the whole project as I know no one who could follow Forbes Robertson in the part with any chance of getting away with it except yourself. As you are now playing the worst part in a very obsolete play I had hoped you would like to try the best part in a comparatively modern one. ... You will have to play Cæsar some day, just as you have had to play Hamlet and Macbeth. You owe him to your repertory.[10]

Refusing the role, and for good reason, while refusing as well to concede Shaw's assessment of his current role and play (Valentine in *Love for Love*), Gielgud replied on the same day:

> Cæsar ... is indeed a great part, and one that I should greatly like to try and play. But I do not like filming, and should be terrified of risking giving an indifferent performance. The technique is so different, and one would need a good six months concentration with nothing else to distract. To try and act in the theatre at the same time is I am sure impossible, especially now with transport and blackout complications, and *Love for Love* can hardly fail to run until the spring of next year. So I must reluctantly say no to the film, and hope that you will let me do the *play* some time not so far distant. Then if I were to please you in it (and not dislike myself in the part as well) perhaps the film could be undertaken with mutual confidence. If, however, you should think of somebody else—and of course I hope you won't—you will naturally please yourself in the arrangement of the plans for the film.[11]

When *Cæsar and Cleopatra* replaced *Saint Joan* as the next Shaw-Pascal film, Shaw reconsidered whether another actor might effectively follow Forbes Robertson. By March 1944, Claude Rains agreed to play the role.[12]

Pascal offered Apollodorus to David Tree, who was in his previous Shaw films, but Tree preferred to remain with his anti-aircraft regiment.[13] The role went to Stewart Granger. Pascal cast Basil Sydney as Rufio, Flora Robson as Ftatateeta, and Francis L. Sullivan as Pothinus. As usual in a Pascal-Shaw film, major actors played minor roles: Ernest Thesiger was Theodotus, Esme Percy (Karpathy in *Pygmalion*) the Major-Domo, Felix Aylmer (Undershaft's valet in *Barbara*) a nobleman, Stanley Holloway (the constable in *Barbara*) Belzanor, Leo Genn (the prince charming who danced with Liza) Bel Affris, Michael Rennie a Centurion, Renee Asherson (Katherine in Olivier's *Henry V*) Iras, and O. B. Clarence (who played bits in Pascal's other Shaw films) the Musician. Charles Victor, whose Bilton was cut from *Barbara*, survived in *Cæsar* as a porter. As a nonspeaking harpist, Pascal cast a fifteen-year old whom he found, he says, in a dance school in Golders Green. 'Say goodbye to her,' he claims to have told her classmates. 'And remember this day well—for you are seeing the birth of a star.'[14] Perhaps he did, but the girl, Jean Simmons, had already made her screen debut in 1943 at age fourteen in *Give Us the Moon*.

Pascal signed Oliver Messel to design costumes and settings. As art director, he had John Bryan, who had worked on *Barbara*. Four photographers shot the film: Frederick Young, who later photographed *Lawrence of Arabia*; Jack Hildyard, who was operating cameraman on both *Pygmalion* and *Barbara*; Robert Krasker, whose later work would include *The Third Man*; and Jack Cardiff, who would later photograph *The Red Shoes* and direct films, such as *Sons and Lovers*.

To compose the music, Pascal attempted without success to secure Prokoviev, Benjamin Britten, and William Walton.[15] Shaw urged Arthur Bliss.[16] He himself sent Bliss flattering letters. 'Remember that an orchestral suite by you will long survive Pascal's film', the former music critic told the composer, 'and become a standard concert piece quite independently of my play, like Grieg's *Peer Gynt* music.' Did Shaw want Egyptianized music? 'In Heaven's name, no,' and he punningly suggested the score be 'Blissful and British. If you feel tempted, think of what *Messiah* would have been if Handel had felt bound to compose Jewish and Syrian music for it.... Or even what my play would have been if I had Latinized Cæsar's dialogue.' Instead, 'Let yourself rip in your own way and it will all come right.'[17] Bliss began to compose a skeleton piano score. Then he met Pascal. 'One look at him,' said Bliss, 'made it self-evident that he would never be a sympathetic collaborator and I withdrew from the assignment.'[18] In the end, Pascal signed Georges Auric, one of the French composers known as 'Les Six' and whose film scores include René Clair's *A Nous la liberté* and Jean Cocteau's *Blood of a Poet*.

As with *Major Barbara*, Shaw wrote additional film sequences for *Cæsar and Cleopatra* and approved and suggested cuts, changes, and transpositions in the play.[19] Studio hands implored him to shorten the script. Recalling the destruction of *Major Barbara*, he refused to accommodate what he regarded as one-horse movie theatres which demanded two features plus a short comedy. He wanted this occasion to be made special, *Cæsar and Cleopatra* plus a newsreel, with perhaps a higher admission price. Any other policy would ruin the film and confirm Hollywood's notion that Shavian plays are unfit for pictures.[20] One demand was to delete the entire Syrian palace prologue, and Pascal did so in all but one of his shooting scripts.[21] Shaw was furious. To throw Claude Rains and the Sphinx at the audience before they knew who or where he was would be to ruin a £300,000 ship for a half pence worth of tar.[22] He repudiated Rank's suggestion that he add love interest.[23] As he later commented, his job as screenwriter was not to make love for people, who after the movie should go home and do it themselves; besides, since Shakespeare wrote the definitive drama of Cleopatra's love, his own work 'must ... remain a play for Puritans.'[24]

Initially, Shaw decided to compose only one new scene for the screen version, the preparation of Cleopatra's bath, completed 15 March 1944, to follow the play's first act[25]—not, as Deans asserts, to provide a change of time, locale, and mood in the middle of the second act.[26] 'Otherwise,' he reported, 'I had to make very few alterations for the screen version.'[27] One such alteration occurred in April 1944, shortly after he met Claude Rains, whose physique differed from Forbes Robertson's. Shaw therefore changed Cleopatra's line from 'You are old, and rather thin and stringy' to 'You are hundreds of years old; but you have a nice voice.' On the same occasion he changed Cæsar's line from 'am I a wolf?' to 'am I a wild beast?'[28]

Pascal also wanted a new scene to inform the audience of the time gap between Acts III and IV before Cleopatra refers to it. Although Shaw preferred a definite break at the end of the Pharos scene, he promised to consider the matter.[29] A year later (24 July 1945) he wrote the scene, in which a musician leads a harp girl on a camel and, as he lectures her, refers to the passage of time. Why did he take so long? Perhaps because he remained unconvinced that such a scene was necessary. On the same day he sent Pascal this scene, he sent another (whether the idea was his or Pascal's, I do not know), to precede Act II. Addressing Roman troops, a Centurion tells the audience where they are. Meanwhile, waiting a full year for the former scene to arrive, Pascal had a barber shop built so that as Rufio has his hair and beard spruced up for Cleopatra's banquet, someone might casually refer to the time that has elapsed. With the scenery already built, Shaw, against his judgment and only to justify the cost of the scenery, wrote a barber shop scene.[30] He did so on 8 Aug., only two weeks after he completed the other two scenes. By this time, Basil Sydney (Rufio) was no longer available. Pascal therefore fell back on

Shaw's earlier version, which he varied slightly. The old musician sat beside the harpist on a camel led by Pascal himself.[31] But this scene was cut from the film. Instead, the transition is provided by a few lines of the barber shop scene plus variations of several later lines, which reveal how long the Romans have held the palace, all spoken as voice-over while the Major-Domo leads a small entourage through a market-place.

The chief new film sequences connect Acts I and II. In the first, Shaw strengthens Cæsar and provides additional motivation for Ptolemy's speech to the council: Ftatateeta announces that Ptolemy and his advisors are to assemble because Caesar has summoned them. In the play, because no reason is given, one receives the impression that Cæsar merely interrupts a meeting. The same scene also motivates Cleopatra's presence in the Council Chamber: 'If that little beast is to be there I must be there too, or Caesar will think he is the Pharaoh.' Equally important, the scene reveals more clearly than the play a change in Cleopatra as a result of the previous night. When she converses with Ftatateeta, whose role the scene strengthens, she does so differently from the night before: no longer as one who stands in fear of a headmistress or who vengefully orders her about but as one on the threshold of adulthood. Yet Cleopatra is still not an adult, the scene reminds us. Her nurse calls her *child*, makes her take a bath, and instructs her on cosmetics. For these reasons, and because Ftatateeta's appearance in this scene and nowhere else shows '*her powerful and handsome body ... apparently naked except for a rich sash or sumptuous belt*,' Shaw tries to ensure, as his cover letter to Pascal states, that she, not Cleopatra, provides the film's sexual attraction. 'It is extremely important,' Shaw insists, 'that Cleopatra's charm shall be that of a beautiful child, *not of sex*. The whole play would be disgusting if Cæsar were an old man seducing a child.'[32]

Directly, this two-character dialogue changes to a mob scene, another new film sequence that contrasts disciplined Roman soldiers with a disordered Egyptian crowd. Carefully individualizing the crowd, Shaw has some in terror of Roman barbarism, others who recognize that Romans are as civilized as they. Next, in a new 'apparent anachronism' (the phrase is Shaw's, from a note that follows the play), which with others enforces the theme that mankind has made no real progress since Cæsar's time, a Centurion tells Roman occupation forces that they may fraternize with Egyptian women. By means of this address, Shaw informs the audience that the setting is Alexandria—the scene's main point—and foreshadows dangers to come.

With cinematic skill, Shaw interpolates his new sequences. When Cleopatra recognizes that the old gentleman is Cæsar, she throws herself into his lap and embraces him. Then:

All the wood and brass in the orchestra let fly with every note in the chromatic scale fortissimo. Meanwhile the strings put on their mutes; and the screen goes black. The din is infernal; but it moderates as the instruments drop out one by one, the extreme discords first, then the 13ths, 11ths, 9ths down to the diminished 7ths, on which the muted strings join in with Schubertian sweetness, and modulate back to the nocturne of the sphinx in the desert. Simultaneously the blackened-out screen lightens into the desert scene with the moon in the east (the left side of the screen). The moon, accompanied by the nocturne music, passes across the screen to the west to indicate the passing of the night. The music is broken twice by a syncopated throb and flash of summer lightning. Towards the end of the transit the moon fades; the sky brightens into dawning sunlight; and the oboe cuts in with a pastoral descant. Tall, straight lines of buildings appear with appropriate chords from the wind; and the scene dissolves into Cleopatra's bedchamber, and the music into a lullaby.

Not only does Shaw use the resources of music and camera to provide a transition in time, he also suggests a journey in space. He repeats a motif of a previous scene—a nocturne when Cæsar sees the Sphinx—and establishes a passage-of-time motif which he employs later after the escape from the Pharos: '*The lighthouse passes out of sight and leaves the sky, which darkens into light. The new moon appears in the east and crosses waxing and waning five times to appropriate music: a tune with five variations. When it rises for the fifth time it is on the desert with the old musician and the harp girl travelling through it.*' As before, the moon moves from left to right, accompanied by music.

Adapting the play to a different medium, Shaw cuts or rearranges sequences and passages from the order required for the theatre. When Cleopatra leaves the quay to have herself rolled into a blanket, playwright Shaw enlivens dead time with military alarms and preparations until she returns. Appropriate editing can eliminate dead time, recognizes screenwriter Shaw, who cuts from her departure to the beginning of the Pharos scene, then back to the quayside for her return. To bring Apollodorus into the group that includes the Persian and Belzanor and to provide expository information about Cæsar's battle, the play's last act begins with the establishment of the setting and much preliminary matter. In the screenplay, Shaw lets the camera establish the setting without dialogue, the editor's scissors bring Apollodorus into the group, and he cuts chit-chat that indicates its members know him. For cinematic economy, Shaw compresses Apollodorus's two fights with the Roman sentry into one, which avoids redundancy, and he eliminates unnecessary exposition about a password. When Britannus announces that the Egyptians have landed between them and the barricades, the play has Rufio exclaim, 'Curses! It is true. We are caught like rats in a trap.' The screen would magnify so melodramatic an outburst to laughable proportions (a danger incipient even on stage). Happily, Shaw deletes the speech.

By judicious cuts and changes, Shaw streamlines the play. He removes unnecessary expository details from the opening scene and retains the essential. He includes the account of the rivalry between Cleopatra and Ptolemy, needed to understand the plot, but he cuts inessential references to the rivalry between her younger sister and his younger brother. Probably to avoid confusing worldwide film audiences with a profusion of unfamiliar names, he cuts many (Cato, Juba, and Eupator, for instance) and changes Vercingetorix to the more comprehensible King of the Gauls. For dramatic impact, he deletes excessive explanation to make response directly follow statement:

> RUFIO. Swing it up by the crane then. ⟦We will send the eggs to the cook; drink our wine from the goblets, and the carpet will make a bed for Caesar.⟧
> APOLLODORUS. The crane!

With similar effectiveness, he removes digressions and repetitions:

> These knockers at your gate are also believers in vengeance and in stabbing. You have slain their leader: it is right that they shall slay you. ⟦If you doubt it, ask your four counsellors here.⟧ And then in the name of that right [*he emphasizes the word with great scorn*] shall I not slay them for murdering their Queen, and be slain in my turn by their countrymen as the invader of their fatherland? ⟦Can Rome do less than slay these slayers, too, to shew the world how Rome avenges her sons and her honor?⟧ And so, to the end of history, murder shall breed murder, always in the name of right and honor and peace, until the gods are tired of blood and create a race that can understand.

Thus, Shaw streamlines play into screenplay.

Yet *Cæsar and Cleopatra* retains more of Shaw's play than any other of his screenplays. The main reason is that this play is more essentially cinematic than the others. 'When I came to look at it,' said Shaw, 'I found I had written the play as a film.'[33] The play 'reads very much like a film-script', echoes Deans, who points out that Shaw's directions for changes of set are passages 'of highly imaginative, visual writing, describing the impression to be received rather than the way in which it is to be obtained. These passages are cinematic in the truest sense of the term.' An example she cites is his cinematic description of the transition between the Syrian palace prologue and Act I. The former ends with a mob in panic. Then, '*The torch is thrown down and extinguished in the rush. The noise of the fugitives dies away. Darkness and dead silence.*' The new scene begins with '*The same darkness*' and '*The same silence,*' which '*break softly into silver mist and strange airs as the windswept harp of Memnon plays at the dawning of the moon. It rises full over the desert; and a vast horizon comes into relief, broken by a huge shape which soon reveals itself in the spreading radiance as a Sphinx pedestalled on the sands.*' 'What is this,' Deans asks, 'but a singularly poetic description of a fade-out, both of sound and picture, from one scene, and of a fade-in to the next?' She also cites the transition from the Sphinx scene to the throne room scene, which she accurately says 'is described in terms much more obviously fitted to the technique of the screen than of the stage.'[34] As Shaw describes this transition, Cæsar follows Cleopatra across the desert. Then:

> *The moonlight wanes: the horizon again shews black against the sky, broken only by the fantastic silhouette of the Sphinx. The sky itself vanishes in darkness, from which there is no relief until the gleam of a distant torch falls on the great Egyptian pillars supporting the roof of a majestic corridor. At the further end of this corridor a Nubian slave appears carrying the torch. Cæsar, still led by Cleopatra, follows him. They come down the corridor, Cæsar peering keenly about at the strange architecture, and at the pillar shadows between which, as the passing torch makes them hurry noiselessly backwards, figures of men with wings and hawk's heads, and vast marble cats, seem to flit in and out of ambush.*

Regarded in the new context of cinema, it is difficult to believe Shaw wrote these passages in 1898.

The play contains numerous hints for the cameraman and editor. Where Shaw uses a split stage technique, as characters in one area observe and comment on characters in another, an editor might cut from one group to the other: from Cæsar and Rufio to Cleopatra and Ftatateeta (after the murder of Pothinus), from Cæsar and Britannus to Belzanor and the Persian (in Cæsar's departure scene). A camera could track the action as '*The guards, led by Belzanor, shoulder their way into the palace through the flying crowd of women, who escape through the courtyard gate.*' The

133

film might then cut to Ftatateeta, who screams against the sacrilege of men in the chambers of the Queen, and into the picture the Persian's knife would move until it reaches her throat. The camera could pull back as the Persian speaks to her. In brief, the original play is sometimes explicitly, sometimes implicitly, cinematic in nature.

While Pascal attempted to translate Shaw's screenplay into a movie, Shaw aimed, as much as possible for a man approaching ninety, to supervise. 'Now and again Shaw went over to watch them at work on the new picture,' says Blanche Patch,[35] but I have found only one specific reference to Shaw's presence on the set, 29 June 1944, when he grumbled about hundreds of people who were not working. 'Were they all on the payroll?' he asked. No: they came to see Shaw. He also complained of 'Vivien Leigh gabbling tonelessly such sounds as *cummineecho* and *oaljentlemin*!' ('the Romans will come and eat you' and 'Old gentleman').[36] Nevertheless, he added, 'You have surpassed yourself in this production already in one scene. When it is finished it will lick creation ... the film promises to be a wonder.'[37]

Once a week, Pascal visited Shaw to show him stills and discuss the production.[38] As before, they corresponded. When Shaw saw photographs of Raymond Lovell as Lucius Septimius, he wondered if it were possible to recast the role and retake his scenes, for Septimius should be under forty and look like 'an athlete and a swordsman without an ounce of fat on him,' not 'fat and overfed'.[39] It was not possible. When Claude Rains became jealous of the emphasis Pascal's camera and blocking gave other members of the cast, Shaw advised Pascal how to deal with him: 'Try to impress on C.R. that unless the other characters are made the very most of—they are all minor figures who are there to build him up—he will lose heavily.'[40] Rains wanted to wear a wreath in the Pharos scene. Pascal preferred he wear his helmet, then hand it to Britannus as a gentleman would give his opera hat to his valet, before he dives into the sea.[41] Shaw vetoed the wreath, since a key point in the scene 'is the change from the old baldheaded discouraged futile disillusioning superannuated dug-out before lunch to the ebullient impetuous steel nerved Cæsar after it.' He then suggested new business that would have Cæsar 'so excited by Apollodorus's dive that he snatches off his helmet and hurls it at Britannus like a ball at cricket; and Britannus fields it like a first class wicket keeper.'[42]

Shaw corresponded on diction, costume, and make-up. One note told Pascal to pronounce the heroine's name as Cleopahtra rather than Cleopaytra, unlike Americans, who call tomahto tomayter.[43] Another advised the correct pronunciation of Ftatateeta, which should become 'as easy as saying "left a message" or "laugh to scorn" or "lift a suitcase" or any other phrase with an ft in it.'[44] For Britannus's costume, he sketched a man in an academic robe, which should be blue. Britannus should have yellow or auburn long-flowing side whiskers, which he also sketched.[45]

On the Shawless set, Pascal prepared a superspectacle. 'He wanted to make one of those enormous *Ben Hur* epics, with vast crowds,' says Deans.[46] And he did: over a hundred name players and thousands of extras,[47] at a cost not only in salary but also in costume. He had exact copies made of Eygptian settings, which were immense: the palace to which Cleopatra brings Cæsar occupied over 28,000 square feet; its columns, each nineteen feet in diameter, weighed over a ton; the lighthouse, tall enough itself, was perched on a thirty-foot rostrum so that the camera could shoot a clear sky behind it; the immense quayside exterior of the palace accommodated vast crowds and a galley. Pascal even consulted an astronomer, who designed the formation of the stars in the Egyptian sky when the film takes place.[48]

Cæsar and Cleopatra was over two years in the making. In November 1943, Shaw and Rank concluded their agreement. Almost immediately thereafter, Pascal signed Vivien Leigh, then other actors. In March 1944, Shaw completed the first new film sequence. Shooting began in June 1944. But the picture's London première was not until December 1945.

Why so long? From the outset, the film encountered obstacles that dwarfed those of *Major Barbara*. Shooting began 12 June 1944, six days after D-Day; it ended in the summer of 1945. Four days after filming started, the Nazis began their V-2 rocket attacks on London, which interrupted the shooting schedule, damaged one of the sets, destroyed dressmaking workrooms, cracked the windows and ceiling of Pascal's home, and nearly killed several members of the production unit.[49] The war caused delays in transportation of personnel and materials. Where under ordinary circumstances a costume might take a few days to supply, under wartime conditions it took weeks. To build the sets, Pascal recruited plasterers from Ireland.[50] When teenaged costume makers were evacuated from London because of the bombings, further delays resulted. An up-to-date camera crane, suitable for a technicolour camera, which is heavier and bulkier than a black-and-white camera, proved impossible to manufacture and difficult to obtain when it was needed.[51] Because of coal rationing, insufficient fuel was available to heat water for baths at Flora Robson's home, and only dribbles of water ran from the studio showers. Since she could not properly wash off Ftatateeta's dark body make-up, she became browner each day.[52]

When six weeks after shooting began Pascal learned Vivien Leigh was pregnant, he rearranged the schedule to film her scenes first. When she miscarried, he rearranged it once more.[53] The English weather disrupted schedules further. For weeks during the summer of 1944, the sun refused to shine—a catastrophe for a movie with so much outdoor footage.[54] Because of both bombings and weather, Pascal decided to move the production—papier-mâché Sphinx included—to Egypt.[55] As Deans recalls, this decision generated a great deal of adverse criticism, often unfair. The studio Sphinx, said Pascal's detractors, 'took up shipping space the government needed for munitions being exported to Egypt, so it was almost treasonable. The fact was, Pascal would not have been *allowed* to use such shipping space. Transport was offered him in certain ships that were going over *empty* to collect arms and supplies and bring them either to England or Italy; and the studio Sphinx was left in the desert.'[56] Although the Egyptian government co-operated fully, it could not control the weather, which turned Britannically cool and rainy. To Pascal's dismay, Egyptian extras discovered that the papier-mâché shields, varnished with a type of fish glue, were edible. The property builders therefore had to construct three hundred more appetizing shields. Location shots in Egypt included long shots around the Sphinx, Roman troops marching through the desert, battle scenes in the desert, and shots of the Alexandrian harbour and the Pharos lighthouse.[57]

As shooting dragged on, costs mounted. Claude Rains's contract called for twelve weeks' work at $50,000 and an additional sum prorated on the $50,000 if shooting took longer. Because he would be liable to high English taxes if he worked more than six months, his agent inserted a clause that if he had to remain when the tax became applicable, the employer must pay it and give Rains his $50,000 plus pro rata after taxes. Rains stayed more than six months. For his services, J. Arthur Rank paid approximately $1,400,000, of which $100,000 went to the actor, the rest to the Royal Exchequer.[58] Because Vivien Leigh's services were extended, Selznick sued for more money. Settling out of court, Rank gave him 10 per cent of the gross.[59]

Accurate figures on film costs are difficult to obtain or verify. According to *Variety*, *Cæsar and Cleopatra* cost £1,200,000; to Rank's biographer, £1,278,000; the chairman of Pascal's company says the latter figure excludes the cost of technicolour prints; both *Film Daily* and *Motion Picture Daily* put the cost at £1,500,000.[60] The prevailing rate of exchange was four dollars to the pound. During wartime, the British press and public regarded such sums as reckless extravagance, and by a foreigner at that. A Member of Parliament denounced the waste and demanded that expenditures be restricted.[61]

Such factors as war, weather, and escalating expenses did not constitute the movie's only problem. Much ill will developed between Pascal and many of his colleagues, who regarded his outbursts not as the explosions of a genius but as temper tantrums and his majestic air as arrogance.[62] They were appalled at his mismanagement, which wasted time and money. Despite his knowledge that delays in completing Rains's scenes would cost many thousands of pounds, he failed to act accordingly. As Flora Robson recalls:

> Pascal wasted three days over an actor who had one line to say (it could have been done after Rains left). The line was an announcement such as 'The Queen!' After a day of takes, the actor was sacked, another fat man engaged. Clothes were altered to fit him, a new make-up arranged, there was another day of frustration, he was sacked, and the first man returned. The line could have been dubbed! Three days wasted, and Pascal had to pay Rains's tax!

Even apart from the tax, Pascal's inexpert scheduling created frustrations which lowered morale. When he decided one day that the next scene he would shoot was Cleopatra's discovery of Ftatateeta with her throat cut, he sent Robson to the make-up room. 'I warned Pascal that it *must be* the next scene,' says Robson, 'as the make-up man said I could not sit about waiting with a bloody throat. Pascal wanted it at once, so I spent an hour with my head hanging backwards. Pascal was not ready. In fact, he did several other scenes first, taking hours, then called me.' Since so much time passed, she had to return to make-up for repairs, with more hours wasted.[63] When the scene appeared on the screen, moreover, she was shot from the top of her head, her gashed throat not visible.

At times, because Vivien Leigh and Claude Rains were not on speaking terms with Pascal, both Frederick Young and Bluey Hill (Pascal's Australian assistant) acted as go-betweens.[64] Upset with Pascal's direction, which they felt made the film ponderous rather than light, Rains and Leigh asked high executives in the Rank Organisation to intervene. The executives, says Robson, 'came down to Denham *en masse* and asked to see the rushes (not a good test). They said they could find no fault. We carried on. 'What else can we do?' said Rains. Later, Robson complained to Shaw that he 'should not have a director of an English film who does not understand English. He makes actors overact to explain the meaning to *him*. What should be light is overemphasized and heavy!'[65]

Actors were not the only people with whom friction developed. Technicians went on strike and several of Pascal's assistants resigned.[66] Once production ended and before the movie opened, the film's technicians called a union meeting and passed a resolution never to work with Pascal again.[67]

Considering tensions created by the war and by the clash of

personalities, it would not be surprising if Pascal failed to complete the film. He did complete it, but not until September 1945—fifteen months after shooting began, nine months behind schedule.[68]

Unlike *Pygmalion* and *Major Barbara*, *Cæsar and Cleopatra* encountered no difficulty with American censors. The P.C.A. found nothing in the shooting script 'not basically in conformity with the requirements of our Production Code.' Yet it pointed out problem areas. When Ftatateeta takes Cleopatra to be bathed, Ftatateeta's sash should 'fully cover all the intimate parts of her body' and there should be no suggestion that Cleopatra, about to step into the bath, is really naked. Alluding to business at the beginning of the harp playing scene—her ladies giggle as Iras and Charmian pull down a blue tunic worn by a monkey whom they have dressed to resemble Britannus—it warned 'Care will ... be needed ... to avoid pointing up any reference to the animal's sex organs.'[69] Pascal took greater care than that: he did not use the scene. Anxious to please the P.C.A., who previously had ignored the context and meaning of Snobby Price's phrase 'jerked off' and heard only its obscene connotation, Pascal shrewdly altered the advice of Apollodorus, who is sophisticated about enology, from 'Try the Lesbian, Cæsar' to 'Sicilian'. Experience had taught Pascal to take as few chances as possible with the P.C.A.

Cæsar and Cleopatra is more faithful to Shaw's screenplay than either of Pascal's other Shavian films. Although it is a mediocre movie, the reason is not its fidelity but its director. Without Asquith and Lean, who had directed and edited *Pygmalion*, without Lean and French, who had guided the photography, editing, and acting of *Major Barbara*, Pascal assembled a production unit which, because they had not the ability or were not permitted, failed to serve him adequately or to supply the expertise he lacked. More than with either of his previous Shaw films, Pascal here was on his own. Although many of his directorial decisions and actions were sound, others were not.

As before, he tampered with the screenplay. While several of his cuts were judicious, as the final print reveals, more were injudicious. Deleting a third of Cæsar's long address to the Sphinx, he cut such inessentials as starry lamps in Gaul, Britain, Spain, and Thessaly, and retained the essential: affirmations that Cæsar's position compares to the Sphinx's and that both are strangers not to each other but to ordinary mortals. He removed an unnecessary portion of Cæsar's explanation of his disapproval of Pompey's murder: 'Was he not my son-in-law, my ancient friend [[, for 20 years the master of great Rome? Did not I, as a Roman, share his glory? Was the fate that forced us to fight for the mastery of the world, of our making]]? Am I Julius Cæsar, or am I a wild beast, that you fling me the grey head of the old soldier, the laurelled conqueror, and then claim my gratitude for it?'

Severely and injudiciously, Pascal abridges the opening Syrian palace scene, which therefore fails to reveal expository information that Cleopatra is missing and has run away, that she and her brother Ptolemy vie for the throne, and that Ftatateeta is her chief nurse and a powerful fighter. In fact, the scene completely eliminates Ftatateeta and reveals only the imminent arrival of the victorious Cæsar. A later cut removes the motivation for subsequent action: Apollodorus's suggestion that he take a message and present to Cæsar, who will give him the order for Cleopatra's release, for though she may not leave the palace, he can.

Other deletions result in thematic reductiveness. Movie audiences do not hear the Persian point out that Cæsar elevates men too humble to become serious rivals to him. Nor do they discover that his moral renunciation of vengeance has a practical side, for they do not hear why the murder of Pothinus was militarily impractical: 'Is it any magic of mine, think you, that has kept your army and this whole city at bay for so long? Yesterday, what quarrel had they with me that they should risk their lives against me? But today we have flung them down their hero, murdered; and now every man of them is set upon clearing out this nest of assassins—for such we are and no more.' Because Pascal eliminates explanatory dialogue, he makes the burning of the library a revelation of Cæsar's clever tactics and a mere plot ploy; he cuts Shaw's ironic contrast between Ptolemy's teacher Theodotus, who grieves at the burning of books but delights 'with viperish relish' at the decapitation of Pompey while his wife and child looked on, and Cleopatra's teacher Cæsar, who in explicit contrast to Theodotus values living people rather than books.

Ineffectively, Pascal transposes Shaw's new scene between Cleopatra and Ftatateeta. Partly for reasons already given and partly because it suggests a passage of time which helps justify the reference in Act II to Cleopatra having bewitched Cæsar into supporting her claim to the throne, Shaw puts it after Act I. Pascal places it in the middle of Act II, which thereby occurs in two days, not one. Although he achieves visual variety, he breaks the scene's dramatic momentum. Unwisely, he transposes a portion of the Syrian palace scene to a point before the Council Chamber scene. As placed by Shaw, the treachery planned in this prologue has dramatic point, for it leads to the discovery that Cleopatra has run away. As replaced by Pascal, it has no dramatic point but provides a facile transition to the next scene: after a reference to Ptolemy, the camera shows him.

More important is the changed end. As Shaw has it, play and screenplay conclude with the triumphant cry of Roman soldiers, who draw their swords and raise them: 'Hail, Cæsar!' Shaw's package is large but tidy: he begins with an announcement of Cæsar's victorious arrival, ends with his triumphant departure. The concluding note of Cæsar's triumph simultaneously suggests Cleopatra's defeat. Early in play and screenplay, the 'old gentleman' promises that if Cæsar thinks she is worthy he will make her the real ruler of Egypt. During her interview with Pothinus, she expresses her hope that Cæsar will appoint her viceroy when he leaves. Although Cæsar's legions kill her rival Ptolemy, Cæsar appoints his true disciple, Rufio, to govern Egypt. What Cleopatra gets is a throne without power plus a consolation prize, Mark Antony, and as Rufio tells her, to swop Cæsar for Antony is a bad bargain. In the movie, though, 'Hail, Cæsar!' is followed by a shot of Cleopatra, her eyes gleaming and her lips smiling as she anticipates the arrival of Mark Antony. Thus, Pascal suggests victory for the sexy charmer and minimizes the implication that she fails to get what she has killed for.

In his direction of the actors, Pascal is inadequate. Surely, Leigh is superb as a kittenish and altogether Shavian Cleopatra, Basil Sydney exceptional as the brusque watchdog Rufio, and Francis L. Sullivan fine as the shrewdly urbane politician Pothinus. For the most part, however, the acting has little verve, variety, or moment-to-moment reality. Too heavy-handedly, Rains plays Cæsar on virtually one note throughout. Instead of taking Apollodorus *'into his confidence in his most winning manner'*, as Shaw directs, he delivers the speech no differently from previous or subsequent passages. Instead of *'his imagination catching fire'* when he considers tracing the source of the Nile, he is so lethargic that nothing catches fire. Some acting is embarrassingly bad, as when a woman rushes toward the camera, waves her arms, grimaces, and yells that the Romans are coming. Pascal inserts trivializing business that fails to generate the comedy he obviously intends, as when Cæsar fails but Britannus succeeds in playing musical pipes. He employs stagey rather than cinematic movement. When Cleopatra, hidden in the Sphinx, calls 'Old gentleman', the camera does not cut to Cæsar's astonished face. Instead, he does a stage cross, listens, holds, and turns. When in the Council Chamber Cæsar has Rufio call for Ftatateeta, Pascal does not cut to her as she speaks. Instead, he waits for her to enter and stop before she talks. The staginess of this movie is directorial, not authorial.

In two significant instances, Pascal's casting is at fault. While Stewart Granger is a capable actor, his athletic persona suggests the kind of man Cleopatra says she adores, not the type of aesthete who proclaims, 'I do not keep a shop. Mine is a temple of the arts. My motto is Art for Art's sake.' With him in the role, one wonders why Cleopatra does not make a pass at him. As Deans observes, the casting of Robson as Ftatateeta 'tends to diminish rather than to heighten the comedy-angle of the part as Shaw originally conceived it … and the terror she strikes into the hearts of the Roman sentries [is] thus not so intrinsically funny as [it] might have been,' but she feels this casting makes her assassination of Pothinus more believable[70] (in my judgment, it is her fight with the Persian, which Pascal eliminates, and her battle with the sentry, if it were better staged, which would make it believable). Though a good actress, Robson in no way provides the sexual attraction Shaw explicity demanded for Ftatateeta.[71]

Technically, Pascal is maladroit. The Egyptians are generally no darker than the Romans. Cleopatra is as pale as, often paler than, Cæsar. Ftatateeta's complexion changes from scene to scene, perhaps because of lack of proper bathing facilities, mentioned earlier. While one cannot blame Pascal for this, one can blame him, when Cæsar talks of his pallor in the moonlight, for lighting Caesar's body while keeping his face in shadow. *Cæsar and Cleopatra* is the first Shavian film in Technicolour. Although Pascal has the sky change colour during the banquet scene according to Shaw's directives, he has it do so not gradually but suddenly, in a cut to a different camera set-up. For this reason, and also because he has not habituated us to regard the colour background in terms of emotional intensification, the changing colours in this scene look like mistakes.

For the most part, he uses his camera inexpertly. *Cæsar and Cleopatra* is not a visually spectacular film. It merely has large settings and crowds. Since the camera and editing scissors fail to take advantage of them, or of the possibilities inherent in the dialogue and action, the sets serve as expensive background for talk, which because of its elegance and wit sometimes overcomes its leaden milieu. Shaw's waxing and waning moons are unphotographed. Instead, the shot of Cleopatra in Cæsar's arms dissolves into an unimaginative daylight exterior as Roman troops march through the desert. Pascal realizes few of the cinematic possibilities in Shaw's directions. When Cæsar, led by Cleopatra, passes through a corridor, he does not peer keenly at the strange architecture or at what may lurk in the shadows, and the passing torch does not make winged, hawk-headed men hurry noiselessly backwards or huge marble cats seem to flit in and out of the shadows, as Shaw describes the sequence. Pascal's camera does not explore, focus, or highlight, and his lighting does not reveal. Because he fails to employ the medium of cinema, he fails to dramatize. When the women flee the Syrian palace, Pascal does no more than photograph a group of running ladies. His camera does not even individualize their terror. When Cæsar announces that Rufio will be governor of Egypt, the Roman soldiers simply call, 'Hail, Cæsar!' With no cinematographic means at his disposal, Shaw in 1906 had the female

Egyptian extras respond in outrage to the appointment, the Roman soldier extras react with great delight, with differentiating lines for members of each group (for instance, 'That vulgar common man!' 'Who did he say?' from the women; 'Did you hear that?' 'One of us! A freedman!' from the men).[72] With cinematic means, Pascal does not even show an Egyptian lady frowning, a Roman soldier smiling.

Usually, he fails to use the camera to enhance the emotional or comic dynamics of a scene. Anthony Harvey (Ptolemy) is skinny and small, Francis L. Sullivan (Pothinus) enormously fat and tall, but Pascal's camera does not adequately visualize Pothinus dwarfing Ptolemy. Nor does it demonstrate Cæsar as imposing when he commands Ftatateeta to be silent. Pascal employs surprisingly few reaction shots. When Bel Affris tells the group that the Romans will soon cut their throats, Pascal's camera shows no one's response. During a clash between the title characters—'But it is false—false. I swear it.' 'It is true, though you swore it a thousand times, and believed all you swore'—he does not emphasize their conflict by cross-cutting. Instead, framing them harmoniously, he drains the sequence of much of its dramatic impact. Apollodorus's journey with his royal passenger could be more interesting than what Pascal photographs, a single long shot of a boat moving from the harbour, the rower's back to the camera—which resembles nothing more than a filler. Not only does Pascal not show Granger's face as he sings, the voice does not sound a bit like his.

Pascal even botches his own good ideas. During the final part of Cæsar's address to the Sphinx, the shooting script has the camera pan from the Sphinx's head to between its paws, where a red mass of colour defines itself as a cluster of poppies on which Cleopatra lies. No such panning shot enlivens the film, which merely cuts from a long shot, Cæsar in the foreground, to a medium shot of Cleopatra, red poppies at her knees. In the sequence prior to the Council Chamber scene, the shooting script directs a camera to show a sign that reads 'Tax Receipts' and has a Roman Tax Officer give inarticulate instructions to minor tax officials. Inside the chamber, before Cæsar demands payment of his taxes, the Tax Officer shows him a papyrus scroll with tax returns and whispers *almost* inaudibly that the figures represent a surplus. If the film has a sign that says 'Tax Receipts', it is so carefully hidden or placed at such a distance that I missed it, and the Tax Officer's whisper to Cæsar is totally inaudible. Result? One does not know what this man is doing in the scene.

In battle scenes, where the director of a superspectacle should be at his best, Pascal is perhaps at his worst. While he hired extras, he did not employ them. For the battle at the Pharos, he does no more than show three successive long shots in which extras hack and thwack at each other, then a fourth just before and after Rufio dives into the water. Particularly inept is the battle between Romans and Egyptians, just before Cæsar's departure scene, which clocks in at a mere one minute and forty seconds.[73] The military strategy is unclear, and at times the action is too. Because Pascal fails adequately to establish that the movement of the Roman troops is from left to right, the Egyptians from right to left (this becomes evident only after repeated viewings), a very long shot of riders moving leftward, with no cuts to closer views of which army they represent, fails to register either victory or defeat. Although several long shots show that Ptolemy and Achillas observe the action, the camera is not close enough to their faces to demonstrate how they respond. In one shot, Cæsar looks stern, but one cannot tell why. Pascal leaves his audience unclear as to who are the Romans, who the Egyptians, and to which nation dead bodies belong. In short, he fails to dramatize the battle. After its end, as weird, haunting music plays, Cæsar prayerfully echoes his early speech to the Sphinx, 'I am he of whose genius you are the symbol: part brute, part woman, and part god,' to which a hollow voice, apparently the Sphinx's, drones in a stage whisper, 'Hail, Cæsar!'

Exactly what Shaw thought of these trite sequences is unrecorded. He did, however, comment on the film in general: 'As a specimen of technicolour it is good, and as an illustrated chapter of Roman history passable; but as C & C, NO.'[74] Perhaps for this reason, Shaw did not do for *Cæsar* what he did for *Pygmalion* and *Barbara*, appear personally in a filmed prologue. The main virtues of Pascal's *Cæsar* film are not immense settings and large crowds but dialogue and Vivien Leigh, which shows that for screen as well as stage Shaw wrote good lines and good parts.

How did Pascal regard the film? Seven years after its completion, he said, 'I dislike it very much and consider it a gorgeous bore.'[75] Perhaps, but only perhaps, one should regard this comment in its context: he had just completed *Androcles and the Lion* and said at the same time that until *Androcles*, which he was promoting, he thought *Pygmalion* his best movie.

In England, the adverse prerelease publicity concerning Pascal's lavish expenditures in a period of wartime belt-tightening created a climate so hostile in some quarters that Pascal would have had to be a combination of Griffith, Eisenstein, and Welles in order to mollify his detractors. Even so, he would not have placated all of them, particularly E. W. and M. M. Robson, whose book attacked the film. Complaining of its costs, they vilified Pascal, the actors, and especially Shaw. They derided Pascal for having cast 'an utterly negative and phantom Cæsar' (Rains had played *The Invisible Man* and *Phantom of the Opera*), a Cleopatra 'famous for the *negative* (that is, anti-social) character of Scarlett O'Hara,' an Apollodorus who had portrayed sadists and criminals. Shaw gratuitously slanders English officers and almost always treats English heads of state with disrespect. Is this film 'likely to be of encouragement or comfort to those who have suffered grievous loss in the war?' they ask, confident of a negative reply. Written before they saw the film, their purpose in writing the book was to prevent people from seeing the movie. If their readers do so anyhow, 'don't blame us. You have been warned.'[76] While the Robsons' hostility obviously differed in degree from that of most people, their indignation reflected that of a sector of the English population.

Some English reviews praised the film highly. A 'tremendous achievement that brings increased honour to the British screen and is worthy of the mighty attempt,' reported *The Daily Express*. A 'standard of artistry and realism hitherto unapproached by any British production ... worth every minute and every penny ... lavished upon it,' said *The Cinema*. Other reviews went to the opposite extreme. 'More than a disappointment', said *The News Chronicle*, it was 'a dismal ordeal.'[77] According to *The New Statesman and Nation*, Shaw's dialogue sounded stagey on the screen, Cæsar's address to the Sphinx 'seemed interminable', jokes fell flat, and Pascal's editing resembled 'desperate clockwork'.[78] The consensus fell between these extremes. Though 'entertaining enough to belie its long running time', as *The Spectator* said, it was by and large 'ordinary'.[79]

In the United States, critical opinion divided sharply. 'Exquisitely mounted,' said *Film Daily*, 'a classic delight for the discriminating theatregoer' and 'a treat to the eye' of the average one. 'As a spectacle, this Gabriel Pascal production does itself proud,' said *Time*. 'But all the munificent movie art does not conceal art of a rarer, riper kind: the dialogue for this superspectacle was written by a great master of prose and wit.'[80] Other reviews felt the spectacle did conceal the rarer and riper art. The comedy is 'drowned ... in a sea of trappings', said *Theatre Arts*. *The Journal-American* called the movie 'pretentious and overwhelming. ... After all it is the Shaw writing that should dominate a Shaw dramatization. Here, while his lines are present and accounted for, their deftness is frequently subordinated to visual dazzle.' To the contrary, said *The Sun*, 'All that beauty does not make up for all that talk.'[81]

Appraisals of Pascal varied. According to *The Hollywood Reporter*, which deplored the film's 'slow, draggy pace and the clumsy staging of action,' its inadequacies were 'largely attributable to Pascal's direction.' Not so, said *The New York Times*: Pascal 'has done a superior job in making a conversational drama both intellectual and spectacular. He has made the mere movement of peoples dynamic to the eye and he has

PYGMALION

1. Eliza war ein armes Ding,
   Das Blumen zu verkaufen ging.
   Sie sucht im Regen und im Schmutz
   Unter Passantenschirmen Schutz.

2. Professor Higgins, sprachgelehrt,
   Zu gern des Volkes Sprache hört.
   Von Kraftausdrücken ganz berückt,
   Hat das Notizbuch er gezückt.

3. Doch an Eliza ihn erschreckt
   Ihr toller Rinnsteindialekt.
   Durch sein System, das schwört er ihr,
   Wird eine Lady bald aus ihr.

4. Sie hat die Chance wahrgenommen
   Und ist in Higgins Haus gekommen.
   Man schrubbt sie ab und seift sie ein,
   Steckt sie in schöne Kleider rein.

5. Dann übt sie mit dem Mikrophon
   Den vornehmen Gesellschaftston.
   Ein Unterricht, den sie empfing,
   Von Higgins und von Pickering.

6. Herr Doolittle, der Müll abfährt,
   Die Tochter drohend rückbegehrt.
   Doch 5 Pfund Schmerzensgeld, sie haben
   Im Whiskyrausch den Zorn begraben.

7. Pick kann sich nicht dazu verstehen,
   Nur Experiment in ihr zu sehen.
   Er fürchtet, daß die ganze Sache
   Dem Higgins noch zu schaffen mache.

8. Mit Hofknicks und Konversation
   Betritt Eliza den Salon.
   Die Ladies unnahbar und kühl
   Betrachten sie durchs Glas mit Stil.

9. Von ihrer Grazie überrannt,
   Fand man sie plötzlich höchst charmant.
   Man flüstert heimlich hinterdrein,
   Der Vater soll ein Herzog sein.

10. Herr Higgins ist ein Egoist,
    Dem Hauptsach sein Triumph nur ist.
    Eliza schmerzlich hat entdeckt,
    Dass sie für ihn nur Wettobjekt

11. Da sie ihm nur Objekt der Wette,
    Wirft sie ihm hin Ring, Perlenkette.
    Erklärt ihm, daß sie auf ihn pfeift,
    Was Higgins wütend nicht begreift.

12. Daß ihm Eliza fortgeloffen,
    Das hat ihn in sein Herz getroffen.
    Doch wie ihr hier ganz deutlich seht,
    Die Sach' am Ende gut ausgeht.

man *Pygmalion*   Comic strip story of film, with captions in rhymed couplets.

German *Pygmalion*   Higgins reads phonetics transcript to Liza while bystanders observe. Jenny Jugo and Gustaf Gründgens.

British *Pygmalion*   Higgins about to pop a marble in Liza's mouth. Wendy Hiller and Leslie Howard.

carefully directed discourses for actual physical suspense.'[82] The same extremes characterize reviews of the actors. To one reviewer, Rains was 'delightful', Leigh 'perfect'; to another, they 'have not helped considerably'.[83] Whereas one reviewer found Robson 'indulging too often in eye-rolling melodrama,' another placed her among those who 'play their supporting roles well.'[84] For the most part, though, the actors received praise.

'The greatest British prestige film to date,' an American trade paper announced after its London press showing, '*Cæsar and Cleopatra* definitely puts Britain on the map as second to none in production value.'[85] Rank achieved the goal that prompted him to finance the picture. But what of box office? In its distinctive idiom, *Variety* pinpointed the film's commercial problems in America and suggested how to compensate for them:

> While a complete lack of love interest, either actual or intimated, is bound to react unfavorably on the b.o. potential, picture should do moderately well in this country. Exhibs will undoubtedly compensate in their advertising for the s.a. missing from the picture itself. Vivien Leigh's solid marquee power, plus Claude Rains' popularity with a large segment of American audiences, can be counted on to help, too.
>
> Wit of George Bernard Shaw, who is responsible for both the story and the screenplay, sparkles throughout. Unfortunately for the b.o. prospects, however, it is on the sophisticated side. ... With proper selling and advertising, however, exhibs need have no fear of the film's pulling power and can count on moderately good grosses.[86]

This prediction of what the exhibs would do proved understatement. 'The Motion Picture Event of the Century', trumpeted a typical advertisement.[87] Dominating another was a drawing of Vivien Leigh's face; beneath it, in another drawing, Claude Rains made love to the scantily clad, sensually posed heroine; to its right, another drawing portrayed a battle scene. With emphatic capitalization, the advertisement promised, 'NEVER BEFORE SUCH SEDUCTIVE BEAUTY SUCH RIOTOUS, LUXURIOUS LOVING AND LIVING!' Subordinate to sex was spectacle, which was therefore uncapitalized: 'Two worlds of magnificent pageantry and spectacular revelry meet in the mightiest picture ever filmed, a wonderful, glorious spectacle of the lashing legions of Rome and Egypt, and the clashing wills of their rulers!'[88]

Less than two months after its New York opening, *Variety* predicted that *Cæsar and Cleopatra* would lose approximately $3,000,000.

Negative cost of the film was £1,200,000 (about $4,800,000 at current rate of exchange). Additional charges ... include 10 per cent of the proceeds to George Bernard Shaw for the story and 10 per cent to David O. Selznick for appearance of Vivien Leigh, who is under Selznick contract.

British gross on 'Cleo', according to latest and most liberal estimates, will total $1,400,000. Out of this will come a 20 per cent distribution fee ($280,000) and 10 per cent for prints and advertising ($140,000). These figures subtracted from the British gross leave Rank with a $980,000 net.

The U.S. gross ... will be $2,500,000 or a shade less. Against this is charged UA's 30 per cent distribution fee ($750,000) and 30 per cent more for prints and advertising. Subtracting these two sums from the gross, gives a net in this country of $1,000,000.

Rest of the world will give a gross of $400,000, according to best estimates. From this must be subtracted 20 per cent for distribution ($80,000) and 10 per cent for prints and advertising ($40,000), leaving a net of $280,000.

Total income worldwide thus tallies $2,260,000. From this must be taken the 10 per cent for Shaw and 10 per cent for Selznick, a total of approximately $450,000, which leaves the world net at approximately $1,800,000. Subtracting that from the $4,800,000 negative cost, result is a red ink entry of approximately $3,000,000.[89]

Shaw's royalty statement for the period ending 24 June 1950[90] generally supports *Variety*'s assessment. Converted into dollars, it shows cumulative earnings of approximately $1,751,750 from the United States (less than *Variety*'s figure), $1,139,860 from England (less), and $857,840 from the rest of the world (more). Using the percentages given by *Variety*, one comes up with a loss of a bit more than $3,000,000. Fifteen years after its American release, according to United Artists, the film made only $1,885,847 in America, and an associate of J. Arthur Rank called it 'a disastrous loss'.[91]

But Shaw claimed that financially it 'was a real success'.[92] The reason: it cost $3,000,000, much less than the press announced.[93] Even if one accepts his figure, arithmetic reveals a loss of over a million dollars. Perhaps Shaw was unaware of the large percentages for distribution and advertising. Perhaps too, if the cost figure is false, the others are questionable, and possible interlocks between producer and distributors might disguise real profits. Although commonly regarded as the biggest financial failure in the history of British cinema, *Cæsar and Cleopatra*, Walter Mycroft observes, 'was run pretty close by another film at the same time, about which much less was said, this being a musical, *London Town*, which cost as much and had no merit whatever.'[94]

THE AFTERMATH

In England *Cæsar and Cleopatra* had two disastrous consequences for Pascal. First, J. Arthur Rank broke his contract for another film with him.[1] Second, the Association of Cine-Technicians in its April 1946 meeting submitted a resolution to its members that because of 'the inordinate length of time taken to produce *Cæsar and Cleopatra* ... Mr Gabriel Pascal should not be permitted to make any further films in this country.' Amended so that he 'should be severely censured and only allowed to make pictures in this country subject to special control,' the resolution passed by 218 votes to 33.[2] When the Press Officer of the A.C.T. invited Shaw to contribute to the debate on the subject, which would be reported in the Association's magazine, Shaw noted, 'I certainly could make a contribution to the subject, but am silenced by the law of libel, which forbids me to point out that the Denham studios are not up to date in every way.'[3]

Although the cancellation of Pascal's contract with Rank left him free to pursue other avenues, the A.C.T. resolution so curtailed such possibilities that it prevented him from making another motion picture in England. Eight months before A.C.T.'s resolution, Pascal announced that his next movie would be *The Doctor's Dilemma*.[4] Early in 1946, Marjorie Deans and Walter Mycroft prepared two draft shooting scripts of it.[5] By 13 August, Shaw and Pascal were on the verge of completing an agreement to film it for Alexander Korda. At the same time, the A.C.T. sent Korda a copy of its resolution.[6] He refused to discuss the matter with the A.C.T.—not because of friendliness to Pascal, since their relationship was cool, but because he did not want to set a precedent which, according to Korda's biographer, would 'inhibit large-scale production in Britain.'[7] Though his biographer does not say this, the precedent would also affect labour's voice in managerial decisions. Whether the A.C.T. pressures proved stronger than Korda admitted, or whether other factors were involved, the project did not materialize. Three years later, when it appeared that Pascal might film *The Devil's Disciple* in England with Montgomery Clift and either Jean Simmons or Deborah Kerr, the A.C.T. reminded his potential financiers of their resolution.[8] Pascal made no more movies in England.

Because of the situation in England and because Pascal was going to the United States in any case, to promote *Cæsar and Cleopatra*, he regarded a Hollywood production of his next Shaw film as more desirable than ever. Before the completion of *Cæsar and Cleopatra*, Shaw advised that since it would be a great pictorial success, to follow it with an indoor comedy would be a let-down, and *The Devil's Disciple* would prove unsympathetic to the Anglo-American alliance. The screen version of *Arms and the Man* was appropriately pictorial, said Shaw, and should prove just right for newly demobilized audiences.[9] Acting upon this advice, Pascal announced in America that it would be his next movie, perhaps to star Paulette Goddard and Cary Grant. Probably to bypass anticipated studio demands for a multi-picture contract, he also announced acquisition of English-language rights to Marcel Pagnol's *Birth of Love*.[10] Nothing came of these plans.

Americans did not share Shaw's view that *The Devil's Disciple* would disturb Anglo-American relationships. On 30 Aug. 1945, three days before the end of World War II, Manny Wolfe, head of R.K.O.'s Story Department, suggested the studio film it. 'There is more stimulation in one minute of *Devil's Disciple*,' he told producer William Dozier, 'than one may find in thirty minutes of so-called superficial chase action which takes place in the run-of-the-mill picture.'[11] When Pascal reached America, discussions probably took place, for in January 1946 he cabled Shaw to send him the opening film sequences he had written.[12]

Although Wolfe did not prevail at R.K.O., the prospect of filming this play remained alive. A year later, Pascal signed a contract to produce it under the auspices of Mary Pickford's Allied Artists. Almost immediately, announcements went out that Pickford would film Shaw's two plays set in America, *The Devil's Disciple* and *The Shewing-up of Blanco Posnet*, to be produced and directed by Pascal, and to star Jean Simmons in the first. How *The Shewing-up of Blanco Posnet* entered the agreement is a mystery (unless the press erred), since Shaw's cable of permission expressly stated that it must wait.[13]

Whereas Pascal succeeded in negotiating an agreement with Mary Pickford, he failed to raise money from the Bank of America. The problem was not, as Valerie Pascal says, that Shaw wanted the Bank of America 'to guarantee' his 10 per cent share of the gross receipts.[14] Rather, Shaw would not give the Bank of America first call on receipts and to receive his own royalties only after the film returned the bank's investment, an agreement which could earn him nothing.[15]

Although Shaw signed no contract for *The Devil's Disciple* with Allied Artists and gave Pascal permission to produce and direct it only if he could secure financial backing and a distribution agreement, Pascal on the strength of Shaw's cable signed a contract with Pickford, whose company advanced him money. When she tried to get him to explain how he intended to carry out his commitment, she could not do so. Consequently, she sued him and won payment of damages.[16]

Until he obtained financial backing as well as concluded a contract, Pascal never restricted himself to merely one project. Nor did he regard Hollywood and England as the only possible places to film Shavian plays. Among others were Ireland and Italy, which he explored simultaneously. In June 1946, while in America, he announced that he would make films in Europe, preferably in Italy.[17] In August, he was in Dublin, where he arranged a private showing of *Cæsar and Cleopatra* for Eamon de Valera, Prime Minister of the Irish Free State (which two years later became the Republic of Ireland), along with several cabinet members, including the Minister of Finance. At Pascal's urging, de Valera wrote Shaw his opinion of the film, which was enthusiastic. At the beginning of September, Pascal announced he was searching for an Irish girl to play the lead in *Saint Joan*, perhaps to be filmed in Ireland.[18]

A year later, on 10 Sept. 1947, the nonagenarian Irish screenwriter drafted an interview:

> I have had in mind for a long time the fitness of Ireland for film industry. The climate, the scenery, the dramatic aptitudes of the people, all point that way. The present domination of Hollywood over the mind of the world is to me deplorable: it is creating a barbarous sock-on-the-jaw morality from which Ireland must be rescued. Having already municipalized my Irish landed property I am ready to give Ireland the first call on my valuable film rights. I have in fact executed an agreement which will have that effect if the project meets with the necessary public approval and financial private support. Already I have been met more than half way in both respects. An experimental company, to be known presently as Irish Screen Arts Limited, is now in existence with sufficient Irish capital to exploit certain film rights of mine until it is in a position to build the necessary studios to operate exclusively in Ireland: a work which might well be undertaken by the Irish State.[19]

In the year between Pascal's visit to de Valera and the agreement to which Shaw alluded (signed 8 Sept. 1947) Pascal, despite official Irish film censorship, energetically planned to make in Ireland, with Irish actors, films by what one of his Irish associates called 'the greatest Irishman since Saint Patrick (who was not an Irishman at all).'[20] He formed a partnership with prominent Dubliners: solicitor Arthur Cox, architect John J. Robinson, accountant E. J. Shott, and famous patriot Dan Breen, who adorned the wall of his home, according to Walter Mycroft, with pictures of Wellington, Napoleon, and Hitler.[21] Kingpin of the enterprise was millionaire financier Joseph McGrath, who agreed to join the venture and with his friends finance it. Under Pascal's personal directorship, Irish Screen Arts Ltd. would build an eight-stage studio, begin with an investment of a quarter of a million pounds, and while the Irish studios were being built would start production in Italy of *Androcles and the Lion*, follow it in Ireland with *Saint Joan*. In approximately two years the government would assist in financial aid, to be obtained by the imposition of a tariff on films imported into Ireland.[22]

By June 1947, the enterprise began to founder. Upon advice that it could not possibly succeed financially, McGrath withdrew. In letters and cables to Pascal, de Valera, and Cox, Shaw delivered an ultimatum. Unless a quarter of a million pounds were available when Pascal left for Rome on 6 June, Shaw would withdraw. Pleading with Shaw, de Valera urged faith in Cox and Robinson. Although he could see no difficulty in raising the money, explained Cox, the problem was to locate a suitable entrepreneur willing to become the organization's active nucleus, 'but ... it will take time.'[23] Obviously sincere, Cox persuaded Shaw to withdraw his ultimatum. In September, Shaw placed all his unfilmed plays at the disposal of the Irish company, 'under the supreme direction of Gabriel Pascal ... whose peculiar talent is of the essence of this Agreement.'[24]

With *Androcles and the Lion*, Pascal and his colleagues planned to film, also in Italy, a life of Saint Francis, whose screenplay Pascal wanted Shaw to write. He refused: 'I think we [should] both let Saint Francis alone. You do not care a rap about him; and my view of him and of Savonarola and of Jesus is that their propaganda of Holy Poverty and amateur Communism was mischievous and ignorant.'[25] At the meeting of the Directors of Irish Screen Arts Ltd. on 23 Nov. 1947, Pascal told Breen, Cox, Robinson, and Shott that he had arranged with Universalia Films, which was producing a Franco-Italian Christians-to-the-lions epic called *Fabiola*, to co-ordinate the schedules of it and *Androcles* in order to use the same coliseum setting for both films. Pascal proposed Barry Fitzgerald for Androcles, Vittorio Gassman for the Captain, Francis L. Sullivan for Cæsar, and Jean Simmons for Lavinia (which she played when Pascal later produced it for R.K.O.). Roberto Rossellini, who had achieved worldwide fame for *Open City*, would direct the Saint Francis film.[26] A day or two later, Pascal dropped the Saint Francis project because he found the non-Shavian script to be unsuitable.[27] But the minutes of the meeting revealed that Irish Screen Arts Ltd. had raised only £41,000, far short of the necessary quarter of a million. Once Shaw read them, he recognized that the enterprise had failed and that he should proceed in Italy independently of the Irish group.[28] Pascal went there to try to arrange the *Androcles* movie. When he returned in January 1948,[29] it was clear that the project was dead.

But *Saint Joan* was not. More than a year and a half earlier, Shaw had seen photographs of Ingrid Bergman, whom he considered right for Joan. When Bergman decided to play Maxwell Anderson's *Joan of Lorraine*, which opened on Broadway 18 Nov. 1946, Shaw was undiscouraged. He regarded her action as 'a stupendous stroke of good luck' for him, since 'Anderson, without stepping on my grass, has given us a film advertisement that will make America rush to see Ingrid as the real and only possible St. Joan.'[30] When in early 1947 he cabled Pascal permission to negotiate for *The Devil's Disciple* in Hollywood, he told him that *Saint Joan* must wait until Bergman disentangled herself from Anderson's play.[31] It waited. With the collapse of Irish Screen Arts in late 1947, the Bergman possibility revived. On 16 July 1948, Pascal brought her to visit Shaw.[32] But a new obstacle arose: she had agreed to make a movie of Anderson's play (retitled *Joan of Arc*). 'Mere foolishness', said Shaw of the supposed problem, for he was no reason why she could not film both Joans. 'The two will advertise each other enormously, to A's benefit as well as ours.' Also to B's, who 'will get two big salaries instead of only one.' Still, Pascal might keep Deborah Kerr in reserve.[33] Reserve or no, the plan fell through. Neither actress played Shaw's Joan. Although Pascal returned to Dublin in November 1948[34] in an effort to revive the Irish venture, he was unsuccessful.

After Ireland, Italy, and Ingrid, Pascal tried to finance a production in Malta.[35] He failed. From Malta, he turned to Mexico, where he hoped to arrange a movie of *Androcles and the Lion* with Cantinflas as Androcles and Valerie Hidveghy, a Hungarian actress he had recently married, as Lavinia. 'Spanish and Hungarian accents do not matter,' said Shaw.[36] They wanted Diego Rivera to design the film.[37] Reconsidering, Shaw suggested that *The Shewing-up of Blanco Posnet*, his western, might be more appropriate for Mexico, but acted in Spanish. Even so, he doubted the Mexican venture would come off.[38] On 14 March 1950, Pascal left for Mexico.[39] Shaw's doubts were soon confirmed. In June and July, Pascal tried Italy once more, and once more without success.[40] During this time, he had someone draft film sequences for the opening of *Androcles*. Completed on 15 Aug. 1950,[41] portions of them were incorporated in an early draft of a screenplay by Ken Englund, who with director Chester Erskine wrote the screenplay Pascal produced for R.K.O. in 1953, after Shaw's death.[42]

Others approached Shaw with film proposals. In 1945, the Theatre Guild wanted to star Katharine Hepburn in *Saint Joan*. Committed to Pascal for *Joan*, Shaw told the Guild Hepburn was wrong for it, right for *The Millionairess*.[43] In 1952, Hepburn had a great success with the latter play; in 1945, nothing came of the movie proposal. In 1946, M.G.M. wanted *Candida* for Greer Garson.[44] Shaw refused. In 1947, Robert Montgomery wanted to star in *The Devil's Disciple*. Citing taxes as the reason, Shaw refused.[45] One offer, however, he did not refuse. Europa Films of Stockholm wanted to do *Pygmalion* in Swedish. Since Shaw saw no likelihood of Pascal going there, he agreed on 27 Dec. 1948. But Europa Films did not make the movie.[46]

Shaw urged Pascal to cast his lot elsewhere. Less than five months before he died, he warned the producer against 'laying out your life as if I were sure to live another fifty years, and putting all your eggs in that quite illusory basket accordingly. It is extremely unlikely that I shall live another three years, and not certain that I shall live another three days.' Unless Pascal wished to starve, he commanded, 'Never forget that dealings with very old people can be only transient.... Look for a young Shaw; for though Shaws do not grow on the gooseberry bushes there are as good fish in the sea as ever came out of it.... Devotion to an old crock like me is sentimental folly.'[47]

CODA

Before Gabriel Pascal arrived on the scene, and after *Cæsar and Cleopatra* opened to the public, Shaw engaged in numerous negotiations for motion pictures. Before Pascal completed his first Shavian movie, all film realizations of Shaw's plays were unsatisfactory. After Shaw's death, other Shavian movies were made. The three American efforts, already mentioned, were all disastrous—*Androcles and the Lion* (1953), *Saint Joan* (1957), and *The Devil's Disciple* (1959)—and the first, produced by Pascal, may well be the worst, since the second is to some extent redeemed by performances of actors like John Gielgud and Harry Andrews and the third to some extent by the acting of Laurence Olivier. Germany adapted *Arms and the Man* (Helden, 1958) and *Mrs. Warren's Profession* (Frau Warrens Gewarbe, 1959), but neither made a significant impact. Although two of the three Shavian films made in England after Shaw's death were unsatisfactory— *The Millionairess* (1961) and *Great Catherine* (1968)—one was not: *The Doctor's Dilemma* (1958). More than likely, the chief reason was its director, Anthony Asquith, who codirected *Pygmalion*. Yet despite his usual fluid and intelligent direction—as well as fine performances by such actors as Dirk Bogarde, Robert Morley, and Felix Aylmer—Asquith's second Shavian film failed to achieve the artistic, critical, or popular success of his first. Although Gabriel Pascal's Shavian films made during Shaw's lifetime were in many respects inadequately realized, the major motion picture versions of Shaw's plays were those (particularly the first two) produced by the Shaw-Pascal collaboration, which lasted ten years to the very day. On 13 Dec. 1935, Shaw signed the agreement that gave Pascal the right to film *Pygmalion*. On 13 Dec. 1945, exactly ten years later, Pascal's movie version of *Cæsar and Cleopatra* had its first public showing.

Footnotes

Abbreviations:

AH	Augustin Hamon
BC	Henry W. and Albert A. Berg Collection, New York Public Library
BFI	British Film Institute
BL	British Library, Additional Manuscripts
DC	Donald P. Costello, *The Serpent's Eye: Shaw and the Cinema* (Notre Dame, Indiana: University of Notre Dame Press, 1965)
DD	Valerie Pascal, *The Disciple and His Devil* (New York: McGraw-Hill Book Co., 1970)
DHL	Files of Dan H. Laurence
GP	Gabriel Pascal
HC	Hanley Collection, Humanities Research Centre, University of Texas at Austin
HL	Margaret Herrick Library of the Academy of Motion Picture Arts and Sciences
HRC	Humanities Research Centre, University of Texas at Austin
IAO	Interview with Andrew Osborn (24 Sept. 1976)
IDT	Interview with David Tree (2 Jan. 1976)
IJM	Interview with Joe Mitchenson (14 Sept. 1976)
IMD	Interview with Marjorie Deans (7 Jan. 1976)
IME	Interview with Martin Esslin (28 Sept. 1976)
IRH	Interview with Robert Harris (21 Sept. 1976)
IRM	Interview with Robert Morley (23 Sept. 1976)
ISIH	Interview with S. I. Hsiung (7 Feb. 1977)
IVL	Interview with Vera Lennox (20 Sept. 1976)
KM	Kenneth Macgowan
LC	Library and Museum of the Performing Arts, New York Public Library at Lincoln Centre
LSE	London School of Economics and Political Science, Shaw Material, Business Papers
MD	Files of Marjorie Deans
MGM	Files of Metro-Goldwyn-Mayer
MPAA	Files of the Motion Picture Association of America
MS	Marjorie Deans, *Meeting at the Sphinx: Gabriel Pascal's Production of Bernard Shaw's* Cæsar and Cleopatra (London: MacDonald and Co., n.d.)
NYT	*The New York Times*

RKO   Files of R.K.O. General Pictures
SA   Files of the Society of Authors
SNB   S. N. Behrman, *The Suspended Drawing Room* (New York: Stein and Day, 1965)
ST   Siegfried Trebitsch
VP   Files of Valerie Pascal
WHEB   Walter Hampden–Edwin Booth Theatre Collection and Library

PROLOGUE

1. G. Bernard Shaw, 'What I Think About the Film Industry', *Daily Film Renter*, 19 (1 Jan. 1946), 5.
2. Bernard Shaw, Untitled answers to written questions put by the editors, *The Cine-Technician*, 5 (Sept.–Oct. 1939), 72.
3. George Bernard Shaw, 'Authors and Their Rights', *The Screen Writer*, 3 (Aug. 1947), 1–2.
4. *The Bodley Head Bernard Shaw: Collected Plays with Their Prefaces*, Vol. 7 (London: The Bodley Head, 1974), p. 202.
5. DC, p. xxi.
6. Dan H. Laurence, ed., headnote, in Bernard Shaw, *Collected Letters 1898–1910* (London: Max Reinhardt, 1972), p. 281; Helmut Gernsheim, 'G.B.S. and Photography', *The Photographic Journal: Section A*, 91 (Jan. 1951), 31.
7. Shaw, letter to Sidney Webb, 18 Oct. 1898, in *Collected Letters*, p. 67.
8. Bernard Shaw, 'The Exhibitions', *The Amateur Photographer*, 34 (11 Oct. 1901), 282–284.
9. Letters to Emery Walker, 11 Aug. 1902; Frederick H. Evans, 28 Nov. 1902; Agnes F. Jennings, 4 Dec. 1902; Evans, 6 May 1903; Alvin Langdon Coburn, 26 July 1904, in *Collected Letters*, pp. 281–282, 289–291, 321, 435–436.
10. 'Literature and Art', in Shaw, *Platform and Pulpit*, ed. Dan H. Laurence (New York: Hrill & Wang, 1961), p. 41.
11. Letter (HC).
12. Letter, 19 Aug. 1912, in Bernard Shaw and Mrs Patrick Campbell, *Their Correspondence*, ed. Alan Dent (New York: Alfred A. Knopf, 1952), p. 36.
13. George Bernard Shaw, 'What the Films May Do to the Drama', *Metropolitan Magazine*, 42 (May 1915), 23, 54.
14. 'A Relief from the Romantic Film', in *Platform and Pulpit*, p. 178.
15. Archibald Henderson, *Table-Talk of G.B.S.* (New York: Harper and Brothers, 1925), p. 50; William Henry Hanemann, 'Oh, Shaw!' *Motion Picture Classic*, 28 (Nov. 1928), 49; 'Shaw Defends "The Big Parade" ', *The World* (New York), 23 May 1926, Sect. I, p. 2; Bernard Shaw, 'Best of the Year', *World Film News and Television Progress*, 1 (Jan. 1937), 3. Shaw refers to *Carnival in Flanders* by its French title, *La Kermesse héroïque*.
16. Note to Fenner Brockway, 3 April 1929, in Brockway, *Outside the Right* (London: George Allen & Unwin, 1963), p. 215.
17. Ivor Montagu, 'Old Man's Mumble: Reflections on a Semi-Century' *Sight and Sound*, 44 (Autumn 1975), 223.
18. LSE, Parcel 26.

SHAW AND SILENT MOVIES

1. Rachel Low, *The History of the British Film: 1918–1929* (London: George Allen & Unwin, 1971), p. 19.
2. Letter, 12 Dec. 1908 (HC).
3. Letter to G. H. Thring, 15 May 1912 (BL 56878).
4. See Bernard F. Dukore, *Bernard Shaw, Director* (Seattle: University of Washington Press, 1971).
5. Letter to Mrs Patrick Campbell, 25 June 1913, in Shaw and Campbell, p. 136.
6. Letter, Frederick Whelen to Shaw, 25 July 1913 (LSE, Parcel 13).
7. Letter to Miss Galbraith Welch, 23 Feb. 1915, quoted in *Americana, Maps, Prints, Literature & Fine Books* (Catalogue of Sotheby Parke Bernet, Inc., New York, for auction sale 30 April 1975), No. 321.
8. Postal card to Adrian Brunel, c. 28 August–17 Sept., 1916, in Brunel, *Nice Work: The Story of Thirty Years of British Film Production* (London: Forbes Robertson, 1949), p. 33.
9. 'What the Films May Do to the Drama', p. 54.
10. G. Bernard Shaw, 'The Cinema as a Moral Leveller', *The New Statesman: Special Supplement on the Modern Theatre*, 3 (27 June 1914), 1.
11. Letter to Gaylord Wilshire, Jr., 1922–1926 (privately owned).
12. George Bernard Shaw, 'What I Think of the Cinema', *Picture Plays*, n.v. (13 March 1920), 4.
13. 'What the Films May Do to the Drama', p. 154.
14. 'The Case for Equality', in Shaw, *Practical Politics: Twentieth Century Views on Politics and Economics*, ed. Lloyd J. Hubenka (Lincoln: University of Nebraksa Press, 1976), pp. 126–127.
15. George Bernard Shaw, 'Education and the Cinematograph', *The Bioscope Educational Supplement*, No. 2, 23 (18 June 1914), i.
16. Written text of lecture, 'Redistribution of Income', delivered 28 Oct. 1914 (BL 50687).
17. 'What I Think of the Cinema', p. 4.
18. 'What the Films May do to the Drama', pp. 23, 54.
19. Letter, Shaw to M. E. McNulty, 4 Dec. 1928 (HRC).
20. 'What the Films May Do to the Drama', p. 23.
21. Quoted in H. K. Reynolds, 'Shaw in Film Debut Derides Movies, Sees End of Own Career', *New York American*, 9 Oct. 1926, p. 1.
22. Henderson, *Table-Talk of G.B.S.*, pp. 48–50.
23. Ibid., p. 44.
24. 'The Cinema as a Moral Leveller', p. 1.
25. Robert C. Roman, 'G.B.S. on the Screen', *Films in Review*, 11 (Aug.–Sept. 1960), 407–408.
26. 'Shaw Poses for Movie Scene, Finicky as a Hollywood Star', *New York Evening Post*, 22 Feb. 1926 (clipping, DHL).
27. Thomas Quinn Curtis, 'A Wave of Made-in-France American Films', *New York Herald Tribune*, 26 Aug. 1962, Sect. IV, p. 4.
28. DeWitt Bodeen, 'Rex Ingram and Alice Terry, Part II: The Studio at Nice and the End of a Career', *Films in Review*, 26 (March 1975), 134, 141; Denis Gifford, *The British Film Catalogue: 1895–1970* (New York: McGraw-Hill, 1973), No. 08439; 'The Three Passions', *Bioscope*, 19 Dec 1928, p. 49; *Variety*, 8 May

1929 (clipping, HL). I have been unable to find reviews in either the New York or London *Times*. The photograph is in the James Anderson Collection, Vol. 6 (BFI).

29. Letter, Shaw to Blance Patch, 20 Aug. 1928 (HRC).

30. Letter, 12 Dec. 1908 (HC).

31. Post card to Percy Burton, 11 Aug. 1913, published in *Boston Transcript* (?), c. 1914, clipping in R. Lock scrapbook, New York Public Library (DHL).

32. For example: letters to Shaw from American Film Releases, 3 March 1913; United Kingdom Films, 6 Nov. 1913; Walter Peacock, 25 July 1916 (LSE, Parcel 13).

33. Letter, Calvert to Shaw, 20 Aug. 1915 (HC); cable, Shaw to Calvert, 4 Oct. 1915 (privately owned).

34. Letter to Shaw from Broadwest Films, Ltd., 29 Dec. 1916 (LSE, Parcel 13).

35. Letter to Shaw from Arthur Brentano, 3 Sept. 1919, ibid.

36. '$1,000,000 Refused by Shaw Because Tax is Too High', *New York American*, 28 March 1920, Sect. I, p. 4; Shaw's shorthand reply at foot of letter to Shaw from Herman Katz, 21 Oct. 1920 (transcription, DHL).

37. 'Shaw Cold Shoulders U.S. Film Rights Buyer', *The World* (New York), 23 Feb. 1926 (clipping, DHL).

38. Letter, Goldwyn to Shaw, 5 May 1919 (LSE, Parcel 13).

39. Quoted in Henry Neil, 'Keeping Young at Seventy', *Psychology*, 8 (Jan. 1927), 85; see also letter, Judge Neil to Shaw, 1 Nov. 1926 (BL 50519).

40. For instance: 'Shaw Picks to Pieces £10,000 Movie Offer', NYT, 27 May 1921, p. 19; H. K. Reynolds, 'U.S. Movies Capture Shaw at $100,000', *New York American*, 14 Nov. 1926 (clipping, DHL); 'Shaw Denies Tale of Rejected Play', *New York Evening Post*, 12 Oct. 1926, p. 8; 'Shaw Can't Recall Scenario Rejection', NYT, 12 Oct. 1926, p. 31.

41. '$1,000,000 Refused by Shaw', p. 4.

42. Quoted in Archibald Henderson, *Bernard Shaw: Playboy and Prophet* (New York: D. Appleton, 1932), p. 697.

43. Letter to Shaw, 10 Oct. 1927 (LSE, Parcel 13).

44. Henderson, *Table-Talk of G.B.S.*, p. 52.

45. Bernard Shaw, 'The Theatre and the Film', *The Referee*, 4 Sept. 1921, p. 5.

46. '$1,000,000 Refused by Shaw', p. 4. 'I Am a Classic But Am I a Shakespeare Thief?' (1920), in *Shaw on Theatre*, ed. E. J. West (New York: Hill & Wang, 1958), p. 132.

47. Letter, Shaw to J. E. Vedrenne, 27 June 1926 (HC).

48. Letter, Shaw to William Lestocq, 19 Feb. 1919 (HRC).

49. Henderson, *Table-Talk of G.B.S.*, pp. 46, 50.

50. Carbon copy of letter, Shaw to Anderson, Vay, Hubert & Blumberg, Ltd., 18 March 1914 (this is a dozen years earlier than the date given in DC, p. 27); letters, the British & Colonial Kinematographic Co. to Shaw, 25 May 1914, and Curtis Brown Agency to Shaw, 11 Aug. 1915; carbon copy of letter, Shaw to G. McL. Baynes, 16 Oct. 1915 (LSE, Parcel 13).

51. Robert A. Simon, 'Shaw and Super-Shaw', *New York Post*, 2 Jan. 1921 (clipping, DHL).

52. Quoted in H. K. Reynolds, 'Shaw in Film Debut', p. 3.

53. Letter, G. McL. Baynes to Shaw, 19 Nov. 1915 (LSE, Parcel 13).

54. Letter, Shaw to Horace B. Liveright, 7 May 1920 (LSE, Parcel 13).

55. DC, p. 153 lists the credits: Producer, Weteb Studios; Director, Vaclav

THE COLLECTED SCREENPLAYS OF BERNARD SHAW

Binovec; Screenplay, Suzanne Marwille; Settings, Frantisek Josef Leopold; Cameraman, Josef Kokeisl; Cast: Frank Rose-Ruzicka (Frank), Suzanne Marwille (Marta), V. Ch. Vladimirov (Theodor), and Ada Karlovsky, Alois Charvat, Joe Jahelka, J. Fiser, Vaclav Rapp.

56. H. K. Reynolds, 'U.S. Movies Capture Shaw'; 'Lasky Offer of $75,000 Tempts G. B. Shaw', NYT, 18 Nov. 1926, p. 26; Gene Tunney, *Arms for Living* (New York; Wilfred Funk, 1941), pp. 216-217. Archibald Henderson, *George Bernard Shaw: Man of the Century* (New York: Appleton-Century-Crofts, 1956), p. 102n., gives a somewhat but not essentially different account of the press reports.

57. Letter to me from K. M. Skallon, Secretary to Gene Tunney, 5 May 1976.

58. *The Devil's Disciple* in the first two cases, *You Never Can Tell* in the third, *Pygmalion* in the fourth. Letters: Anderson, Vay, Hubert & Blumberg, Ltd. to Shaw, 11 March 1914; Shaw to them, 18 March 1914; they to Shaw, 19 March 1914; G. McL. Baynes to Shaw, 15 Oct. 1915; Shaw to Baynes, 16 Oct. 1915 (carbon copy); Hugh A. Baynes to Associated Film Sales Corp., n.d. but attached to letter of 19 Oct. 1915; The Hungarian Film Factory to Shaw, 29 Nov. 1921 (LSE, Parcel 13).

59. Copy proof (1927) of Shaw's deposition in case of Levinson v. Shaw, 1926 (LSE, Parcel 11).

60. Plaintiff's statement, Writ issued 14 Oct. 1926, Levinson (Plaintiff) v. Shaw (Defendant), Statement of Claim, delivered 26 Oct. 1926; copy proof of Shaw's deposition (LSE, Parcel 11); Blanche Patch, *Thirty Years with G.B.S.* (London: Gollancz, 1951), p. 205; Henderson, *Shaw: Man of the Century*, p. 542.

61. Copy proof of Shaw's deposition, loc. cit.

62. Henderson, *Shaw: Man of the Century*, p. 542.

63. Plaintiff's statement, loc. cit.

64. Copy proof of Shaw's deposition, loc. cit.

65. Henderson, *Shaw: Man of the Century*, p. 543; Shaw, note on slip of paper (LSE, Parcel 11).

THE ARRIVAL OF SOUND

1. Wolf Von Eckardt and Sander L. Gilman, *Bertolt Brecht's Berlin* (Garden City, N.Y.: Anchor Books, 1975), p. 104; Low, p. 202. Vogt, Masolle, and Engel began to develop their system (Tri-Ergon) as early as 1919.

2. H. K. Reynolds, 'Shaw in Film Debut', p. 1. The title is of course in error.

3. Hayden Church, 'Shaw May Come Here—In Movies', *The World*, 5 Dec. 1926, Sect. I, p. 1; 'G. B. Shaw in Talking Film: May be Seen in America', NYT 29 Dec. 1926, p. 1; letter, Shaw to ST, 13 Jan 1927 (BC).

4. 'Problems of Speaking Films. The Experiment with *St. Joan*.' Interview with Mr Lewis Casson *The Observer*, 24 July 1927, p. 12; Raymond Mander and Joe Mitchenson, *Theatrical Companion to Shaw* (London: Rockliff, 1954), p. 321; the latter erroneously call this Shaw's first appearance in a talking film, as does DC, p. 7.

5. 'Problems of Speaking Films' loc. cit.; Walter Charles Mycroft, 'Shaw—and the Devil to Pay', *Films and Filming*, 5 (Feb. 1959), 14.

6. Letter (privately owned).

7. Harry M. Geduld, *The Birth of the Talkies* (Bloomington: Indiana University Press, 1975), p. 231.
8. Shown on *Lowell Thomas Remembers* (Honolulu, 20 May 1977, KHET-TV); Roman, pp. 409-410.
9. Hanemann, pp. 48-49.
10. 'Shaw Finds Talkies Opening New Field', NYT, 19 May 1929, Sect. I, p. 26.
11. Bernard Shaw, 'Films, Plays, and G. B. Shaw: An Interview', *Fame—The Box Office Check-Up*, n.v. (1937), 22.
12. Letter, Shaw to ST, 23 April 1930 (BC).
13. Shaw, Answers to questionnaire by Huntly Carter, 'Relation of the Cinema to the Theatre', 9 May 1932 (HRC).
14. Quoted in G. W. Bishop, 'The Living Talkies: An Interview with Bernard Shaw', *Theatre Guild Magazine*, 7 (Nov. 1929), 32; 'Shaw Finally Allows Play to Be a Talkie', NYT, 8 Aug. 1930, p. 1; Shaw, Answers to questionnaire by Huntly Carter, loc. cit.
15. Pola Negri, *Memoirs of a Star* (Garden City, N.Y.: Doubleday, 1970), pp. 321, 333.
16. 'Pola Negri to Screen Shaw's "Cleopatra" ', NYT, 1 Dec. 1928, p. 14.
17. Patch, p. 152.
18. Postal card, Shaw to ST, 11 Dec. 1928 (BC).
19. Cable, Pickford to Shaw, 6 Feb. 1930; draft reply by Shaw, n.d. (HRC); also DC, p. 26.
20. Engagement Diary, 2 Jan. 1930 (LSE, Parcel 26).
21. Post card, Shaw to Asquith, 10 April 1929 (HRC).
22. Letters: Shaw to ST, 7 Feb. 1931 (BC); Paul Kohner to Shaw, 11 Dec. 1928; Kohner to Blanche Patch, 8 Jan. 1929; John Dimitri Stephon to Shaw, 6 Feb. 1929 (LSE, Parcel 13).
23. Quoted in R. B. Marriott, ' "Films Are Not Children's Picture Books": Bernard Shaw Talks About *St. Joan* Film', *The Era*, 101 (5 May 1938), 1.
24. Letter to Theresa Helburn, 15 Feb. 1935, in Lawrence Langner, *G.B.S. and the Lunatic* (New York: Atheneum, 1963), p. 225.
25. Quoted in Bishop, p. 32.
26. Letter to Theresa Helburn, 15 Feb. 1935, in Langner, p. 225.
27. Bishop, p. 32.
28. George Bernard Shaw, 'The Art of Talking for the Talkies', *World Film News*, 1 (Nov. 1936), 7.
29. Asquith, 'The Play's the Thing', *Films and Filming*, 5 (Feb. 1959), 13.
30. Shaw, 'Films, Plays, and G. B. Shaw', p. 22.
31. Shaw, 'My First Talkie', (1931), in *Shaw on Theatre*, p. 205.
32. Asquith, 'The Play's the Thing', p. 13.
33. Roman, p. 406.
34. Shaw, 'Films, Plays, and G. B. Shaw', p. 22.
35. Letter to Huntly Carter, in Carter, *The New Spirit in the Cinema* (New York: Arno Press, 1970), p. 377.
36. Esslin, *An Anatomy of Drama* (London: Temple Smith, 1976), p. 12.
37. 'Memo: From G.B.S. to S.G.', NYT, 27 Sept. 1936, Sect. X, p. 4.
38. Patch, p. 119; Lewis, *Never Look Back: An Attempt at Autobiography* (London: Hutchinson, 1974), p. 108; Mycroft, p. 15; Roman, p. 412; DD, p. 82.
39. Untitled, in *Continental Daily Mail*, 9 Oct. 1938 (Ivo Currall's Scrapbook,

Vol. 21, p. 49, RADA).

40. Letter, Shaw to Peter Michael Watts, 3 Oct. 1946 (BBC Archive); Peter Noble, *Profiles and Personalities* (London: Brownlee, 1946), p. 106; p. 107 reproduces Shaw's handwritten note that certifies factual accuracy.

41. Shaw, 'Films, Plays, and G. B. Shaw', pp. 22, 26.

42. Glyn Roberts, 'Bernard Shaw Discusses the Cinema', *Film Weekly*, n.v. (12 Feb. 1938), 7.

43. Shaw, 'Films, Plays, and G. B. Shaw', p. 22; see also the section titled 'Cutting and Changing the Script', in Dukore, *Bernard Shaw, Director*.

44. Letter, Shaw to ST, 23 April 1930 (BC).

45. Ibid. Italics are Shaw's.

46. Kenneth Macgowan, *Behind the Screen: The History and Technique of the Motion Picture* (New York: Delta, 1965), pp. 386–387.

47. Letter, Shaw to Pinero, 12 Dec. 1908 (HRC).

48. Henderson, *Table-Talk of G.B.S.*, p. 45.

49. Howard Dietz, *Dancing in the Dark: Words by Howard Dietz* (New York: Quadrangle, 1974), p. 59. For variations on the phrasing, see: 'Memo: From G.B.S. to S.G.', p. 4; Henderson, *Shaw: Playboy and Prophet*, p. 705; DC, p. 9. Although Costello may be right in his claim that the statement was invented by Howard Dietz, then Samuel Goldwyn's press agent, Dietz in his autobiography does not claim credit.

50. Letters, Shaw to ST, 30 Dec. 1935 and 16 Jan. 1936 (BC).

51. Letter, Shaw to Theresa Helburn, 15 Feb. 1935, in Langner, p. 224.

52. Several contracts (SA).

53. Letter, addressee and date not given, in SNB, p. 77.

54. Several contracts (SA).

55. Mary and Alan Wood eds., *Silver Spoon* (London: Hutchinson, 1954), pp. 222-223.

56. Letter, Shaw to ST, 15 June 1934 (BC).

57. Memorandum of Agreement, 27 Dec. 1948, Shaw and A.B. Europa Film (Stockholm) to produce *Pygmalion* (courtesy A.B. Europa Film).

58. Letter, Shaw to Pinero, 12 Dec. 1908 (HRC).

59. Shaw, Untitled answers to written questions, p. 73.

60. Letter, Shaw to GP, 25 Sept. 1944, in DD, p. 109.

G.B.S. AND B.I.P.

1. Lady Augusta Gregory, *Lady Gregory's Journal*, ed. Lennox Robinson (New York: Macmillan, 1947), p. 216.

2. Letters: Dean to Shaw, 12 Mar. 1930; British Instructional Films to Shaw, 30 April 1930; note on this letter, Shaw to Blanche Patch (LSE, Parcel 13).

3. Letters and post cards, Shaw to Lewis, 31 May 1923 to 3 Jan. 1929 (HRC).

4. Copy, Memorandum of Agreement (SA).

5. Mycroft, p. 14.

6. DC, p. 32; Roman, p. 411.

7. References to *Candida* are in early editions of the play, which in part parodies *Candida*. It was written for Arnold Daly, who had a great success in America as Marchbanks. When Shaw prepared the Standard Edition of his works in 1931,

and when he prepared the movie, he deleted all references to *Candida* from *How He Lied*. Despite their omission, the characterization of the husband is the same and does not affect my conclusion. For a comparison of different versions of this play, see my 'Shaw Improves Shaw', *Modern Drama*, 6 (May 1963), 26-31.

8. IVL.

9. IRH.

10. IVL.

11. IRH; IVL.

12. Patch, p. 121.

13. 'Foreword' to DC, p. x; *Never Look Back*, p. 106.

14. IRH.

15. Mander and Mitchenson, p. 101, give the date as 10 Jan. but an advertisement in *The Times* that day says it will open on Monday 12th, when an advertisement appears.

16. IVL.

17. 'Mr Shaw's Talking Film', *The Times*, 13 Jan 1931, p. 10.

18. 'Shaw Talkie Disappoints', NYT, 13 Jan. 1931, p. 35.

19. Mordaunt Hall, 'Their Master's Voice', NYT, 25 Jan. 1931, Sect. VIII, p. 5; Hall, 'Mr. Shaw's First Film', NYT, 17 Jan 1931, p. 23.

20. .'My First Talkie', (1931), in *Shaw on Theatre*, pp. 205-206.

21. IVL.

22. 'Foreword' to DC, p. x.

23. Mycroft, p. 14.

24. *Never Look Back*, p. 106.

25. Copy, Memorandum of Agreement (SA); letter, Shaw to Lewis, 10 June 1932 (BC). Shooting began before 5 June.

26. Mycroft, p. 15.

27. Letter, Shaw to Levinson, 27 Aug. 1927 (in my possession).

28. 'Mr. Shaw and Mr. Menjou', NYT, 3 June 1928, Sect. VIII, p. 8; letters: Shaw to Blanche Patch, 28 Aug. 1928 (HRC); the Gaumont Co. to Patch, 20 Oct. 1928; instructions on this letter, Shaw to Patch, c. 22-25 Oct. 1928 (Colby College).

29. Letter, Levinson to Shaw, and note on letter, Shaw to Patch (LSE, Parcel 11).

30. Letter, Langner to Shaw, 2 July 1929, and attached 'Proposal of Arrangement for Talking Picture' (LSE, Parcel 13).

31. Letter, Holmes C. Walton to Shaw, 11 Feb. 1930, ibid.

32. Langner, pp. 222-223.

33. Letters: Shaw to Holmes C. Walton, 17 April 1930 (LSE, Parcel 13); Shaw to ST, 23 April 1930 (BC).

34. Letters: Shaw to ST, 24 and 28 April 1930 (BC).

35. Copy, Memorandum of Agreement (SA).

36. *Never Look Back*, p. 108; Mycroft, p. 15.

37. DC, p. 39; Roman, p. 412; Frank E. Thomas, Jr., 'An Examination of Four Plays by Bernard Shaw Adapted to the Film Medium' (M.A. Thesis, Cornell University, 1955). Apparently, Thomas did not see *Arms and the Man*, for he calls it a silent movie (p. 44).

38. Scenario (BC). Although it is undated, Shaw's letters that accompany it indicate that Lewis prepared it in early 1932. Unless otherwise stated, Shaw's comments are his holograph notations on this scenario.

39. Letter, Shaw to Lewis, 18 April 1932 (BC).

40. Barry Jones, who played Bluntschli, claims that one textual change derives from an ad lib he made during this rehearsal. After Raina exclaims, 'I am a Petkoff!' Shaw's text, retained in Lewis's scenario, has Bluntschli respond, 'What's that?' Instead, Jones facetiously inquired, 'A pet what?' So delighted was Shaw, says Jones, that he not only insisted Jones keep the ad lib in the film, he also employed the new line in subsequent editions of the play. See Barry Jones, 'Mr Shaw's First Film', in *The Elstree Story* (London: Clerke and Cockeran, 1948), p. 77. Although Jones's story is good, it is apparently inaccurate. The Standard Edition of *Plays Pleasant* (London: Constable, 1931), which includes the play, contains the altered line. So do Vol. 8 of *The Works of Bernard Shaw* (London: Constable, 1930) and Vol. 8 of *The Ayot St. Lawrence Edition: The Collected Works of Bernard Shaw* (New York: William H. Wise, 1931). As indicated above (n. 38), Lewis rprepared his scenario in early 1932. Rehearsals followed. Very likely, Lewis used an earlier edition of the play and Shaw instructed him to alter his scenario to conform to the changes Shaw made for more recent editions. Jones's inaccurate title derives chiefly from his refusal to recognize *How He Lied to Her Husband* as a film rather than as a photographed stage play (p. 76).

41. Jones, p. 79; Maurice Colbourne, *The Real Bernard Shaw* (New York: Philosophical Library, 1949), p. 95.

42. 'An Actor's Death at a Film Studio', *The Times*, 9 June 1932, p. 10; 'Wallace Evenett Fills Lewin Mannering's Role', *Kinematograph Weekly*, 184 (16 June 1932), 44. 'Of course *The Times* is nuts', Cecil Lewis wrote me on 10 Nov. 1976. 'Mannering did not die on the set.'

43. Letter, Shaw to Lewis, 10 June 1932 (BC).

44. Mycroft, p. 15.

45. Patch, p. 122; letter, Shaw to KM, 7 April 1933 (copy, SA).

46. Letters: Shaw to Limbert, 17 and 19 July 1932 (HRC).

47. '*Arms and the Man*: Film of Mr Shaw's Play', *The Times*, 8 Aug. 1932, p. 8.

48. Colbourne, p. 94; Nicoll, *Film and Theatre* (New York: T. Y. Crowell, 1936), p. 165.

49. Lewis, *Never Look Back*, p. 108; letter to me, 15 Nov. 1975; Mycroft, p. 15.

50. DC, p. 40. The article is reprinted in *Shaw on Theatre*, pp. 212–213.

51. Postal card, Shaw to Lewis, 11 Aug. 1932 (BC).

52. Mycroft, p. 15.

53. Letter, Lewis to me, 15 Nov. 1975.

54. Jones, pp. 76–77.

G.B.S. AND R.K.O.

1. St John Ervine, *Bernard Shaw: His Life, Work and Friends* (New York: Morrow, 1956), p. 529; Engagement Diary, 1933 (LSE, Parcel 26).

2. Photographs in my possession.

3. Copy of letter, Shaw to KM, 15 Feb. 1934 (SA).

4. RKO.

5. Letters: KM to Shaw, 12 May 1933; (copy) Dane to KM, 27 Mar 1933; (copy) Stern to KM, 27 April 1933; David T. O'Shea to Gordon E. Youngman, 23 Dec.

1933 (RKO).

6. Copies of letters, Shaw to KM. 7 April 1933 (SA); KM to Shaw, 12 May 1933 (RKO).

7. Copies of correspondence (SA).

8. Copies of telegrams, KM to Pandro S. Berman, 28 Oct. 1933, and to Ned E. Depinet, 31 Oct. 1933 (RKO); KM to Shaw, 4 Nov. 1933 (SA).

9. Copies of cables, KM to Shaw, 9 Nov. 1933; Shaw to KM, 10 Nov. 1933 (SA).

10. Quoted in Gene Fowler, *Good Night, Sweet Prince* (New York: Viking, 1943), p. 351.

11. Copy of cable, KM to Shaw, 13 Nov 1933 (SA).

12. Fowler, pp. 351–352.

13. Carbon copy of letter, Barrymore to Shaw, 4 Dec. 1933 (Gene Fowler Papers, Rare Books Room, Library of University of Colorado, Boulder.)

14. Clippings, *Variety* and *Hollywood Reporter* (RKO); 'Says RKO Beat British', NYT, 26 Nov. 1933, Sect. II, p. 2.

15. RKO. All references to this screenplay are to this copy.

16. Copy of letter, Breen to Cooper (RKO).

17. RKO.

18. 22 Jan. 1934 (copy, SA), quoted in Fowler, p. 352.

19. Copy of cable, KM to Shaw, 26 Jan. 1934; inter-office memos: Kahane to David T. O'Shea; KM to Kahane; Kahane to KM, 13 Feb. 1934 (RKO).

20. Copy of letter, Shaw to KM, 15 Feb 1934 (SA).

21. Copy of letter, KM to Shaw, 12 April 1934 (SA).

GERMAN *PYGMALION*

1. Letter, Shaw to AH, 29 Jan. 1934 (privately owned).

2. Shorthand draft of letter, Shaw to Paul Koretz, July 1934 (HRC), transcription DHL.

3. Letter, AH to Shaw, 4 June 1934 (LSE, Parcel 16).

4. Post card, Shaw to AH, 30 Jan. 1935 (privately owned).

5. Letter, AH to Shaw, 8 May 1936 (LSE, Parcel 16).

6. HRC. All references to Riera's adaptation are to this copy.

7. Letter, Shaw to ST (BC).

8. Letter, Shaw to AH, 8 Dec. 1937 (privately owned).

9. Letter, Shaw to ST (BC).

10. Letter, Shaw to ST, 22 Sept. 1934 (BC).

11. Holograph MS, dated on final page but crossed out, perhaps because Shaw later revised it (BL 50634). Further references to Shaw's new scenes in the 1934 scenario are to this MS, which dovetails the cuts Shaw made in the play text (Shaw's Corner, Ayot St Lawrence).

12. Memorandum of Agreement (HRC); postal card, Shaw to ST, 16 Feb. 1935 (BC).

13. W. Stuart McDowell, 'A Brecht-Valentin Production: *Mysteries of a Barbershop*', *Performing Arts Journal*, 1 (Winter 1977), 4; McDowell, 'Actors on Brecht: The Munich Years', *The Drama Review*, 20 (Sept. 1976), 106–108.

14. Klaus Völker, *Brecht Chronicle*, trans. Fred Wieck (New York: Seabury Press, 1975), p. 156.

15. IME.
16. IME.
17. Alfred Bauer, *Deutscher Spielfilm-Almanach 1929–1950* (Berlin: Filmblätter Verlag, 1950), p. 297.
18. Letters, Shaw to Rutland Boughton, 24 Oct. 1935 (BL 52365); Shaw to ST, 15 Dec. 1935 (BC).
19. Shaw's Engagement Diary for 1936 is unclear as to which date he actually saw the movie (LSE, Parcel 26).
20. Letters: Shaw to ST, 30 Dec. 1935 and 16 Jan. 1936 (BC).
21. Undated comments beside two sketches of Liza by Feliks Topolski (Iconography Collection, HRC).
22. Leslie Ruth Howard, *A Quite Remarkable Father* (Toronto: Longmans, Green, 1959), pp. 248–249.
23. 'Dass ihm Eliza fortgeloffen,/Das hat ihn in sein Herz getroffen./Doch wie ihr hier ganz deutlich seht,/Die Sach' am Ende gut ausgeht' (programme in my possession).
24. 'Films, Plays, and G. B. Shaw', p. 26.
25. Letter, Shaw to Floryan Sobieniowski, 7 Jan. 1936 (HRC).
26. Letter, Shaw to ST, 16 Jan. 1936 (BC).

SAINT JOAN

1. Dates on title and final pages (HRC). The scenario is keyed to a printed edition of the play (London: Constable, 1931) with a notation on the title page 'Cut for Scenario/Nov. 1934/GBS' (Shaw's Corner, Ayot St Lawrence).
2. Dated inscription (courtesy Mr and Mrs Charles Sharp).
3. Untitled clipping, NYT, c. 9 Dec. 1934 (DHL).
4. Both typescripts are in BL 50634. For discussion of evidence for first and revised drafts, see Note on the Texts.
5. Letters: Peter Ridgeway to Shaw, 17 June 1935; Eugene Leahy to Shaw, 17 July 1935 (BL 50521).
6. Extract from the Minutes of the Joint Committee, reprinted as *Shaw on Censorship*, Shavian Tract No. 3 (London: The Shaw Society, 1955), pp. 2–3, 7–8.
7. Reprinted in the Preface to *The Shewing-up of Blanco Posnet*, in *The Bodley Head Bernard Shaw*, Vol. 3, p. 698.
8. *Shaw on Censorship*, p. 6.
9. Letter to *The Times*, 8 Nov. 1913, reprinted in Allen Chappelow, *Shaw — 'The Chucker Out': A Biographical Exposition and Critique* (London: George Allen & Unwin, 1969), pp. 64–66.
10. Neville March Hunnings, *Film Censors and the Law* (London: George Allen & Unwin, 1967), pp. 48–55, 68, 73–75, 86.
11. Ibid., pp. 151–154; Charles John Gaupp, Jr., 'A Comparative Study of the Changes in Fifteen Film Plays Adapted from Stage Plays' (Ph.D. Dissertation, State University of Iowa, 1950), p. 3.
12. Hunnings, pp. 157–159; Gaupp, pp. 3–7.
13. Letter, Francis S. Harmon to GP, 28 Feb. 1938 (MPAA).
14. Gaupp, Appendixes 2 and 4.

15. Title page of Dialogue Cutting Continuity, *Pygmalion* (Library of Congress).
16. 'Film Censorship', in *Platform and Pulpit*, p. 262.
17. Letter to *The Times*, 17 Feb. 1930, p. 15.
18. Shaw, 'The Cinema as a Moral Leveller', p. 2.
19. 'Views of the Censorship', *British Film Journal*, 1 (Apr.-May 1928), 65.
20. 'Film Censorship', op. cit., pp. 261-262.
21. Interview with Elisabeth Bergner, 6 Jan. 1976; see also Bergner, *Bewundert viel und viel gescholten* (München: Bertelsmann Verlag, 1978), p. 165. In her autobiography, Bergner says that Father Martindale took Shaw's play to Rome; marginal comments by the Catholic examiners (see below) make it clear that he took Shaw's screenplay.
22. Advice on *St. Joan* Was Asked in Rome', NYT, 17 Sept. 1936, p. 1.
23. BL 50633.
24. BL 50634. Shaw's notes on these marginal comments are in BL 50633. See also Note on the Texts.
25. 'Advice on *St. Joan* Was Asked in Rome', loc. cit.; 'Miss Helburn Recalls Comments', NYT, 17 Sept. 1936, p. 18.
26. Reprinted as '*Saint Joan* Banned: Film Censorship in the United States', in *Shaw on Theatre*, pp. 244, 248, 250-251.
27. 'Advice on *St. Joan* Was Asked in Rome' loc. cit.; Shaw Stands Firm on Censor Charge', NYT, 27 Sept 1936, Part II, p. 14.
28. Bergner, *Bewundert viel*, pp. 165-167. Bergner does not give the date of Shaw's letter to her.
29. Interview, 14 Jan. 1967.
30. Shaw used T. Douglas Murray's translation of Jules Quicherat's transcription of Joan's trial: *Jeanne d'Arc, Maid of Orleans, Deliverer of France: Being the Story of Her Life, Her Achievements and Her Death, as Attested on Oath and Set Forth in the Original Documents* (London: Heinemann, 1907), pp. 24, 44.

ENTER GABRIEL PASCAL

1. SNB, p. 80; DD, p. 59; IRM.
2. ISIH; SNB, p. 80; Harrison, *Rex: An Autobiography* (London: Macmillan, 1974), p. 72.
3. Letters: Shaw to ST, 30 Dec. 1935 (BC); Shaw to AH, 21 Nov. 1936 (privately owned).
4. The sources of Gabor (which, anglicized, is Gabriel) are 'Shaw's Disciple', *The New Yorker* (31 May 1941), 12 (clipping, LC) and DD, p. 59. The source of Lehöl is 'Gabriel Pascal', *World Film News*, n.v. (Sept. 1936) 5 (clipping, BFI). IME confirms which names are Hungarian.
5. For example: Terry Ramsaye, ed., *1939-40 International Motion Picture Almanac* (New York: Quigley Publishing Co., n.d.), p. 489; 'Gabriel Pascal Dies at 60', *New York Herald Tribune*, 7 July 1954 (clipping, LC); *Hollywood Reporter*, 7 July 1954 and *Variety*, 7 July 1954 (clippings, HL). *Variety* gives his date of birth as 1898.
6. Respectively: George Vine, 'Missing Film Heir is Dead', *News Chronicle*, 21 June 1966 (clipping, BFI); ISIH; DD, p. 70; 'Shaw's Disciple', loc. cit.; William

Hawkins, 'Shaw Movie His "Finest" ', *New York World-Telegram*, 22 June 1946 (clipping, MPAA).

7. Leonard Lyons, 'The Lyons Den', *New York Post*, 20 Feb. 1955, (clipping, DHL); DD, pp. 60, 62; William Hawkins, 'Shaw Movie His "Finest" ', loc. cit.; 'Gabriel Pascal Dies at 60', loc. cit.; 'Shaw's Disciple', op. cit., pp. 12–13.

8. 'Shaw's Disciple', op. cit., p. 13.

9. DD, pp. 61–62.

10. Lesley Blanch, 'Warring Britain's New Movie, *Major Barbara*', *Vogue*, 97 (1 Apr. 1941), 106.

11. Francis Courtade, 'Biofilmographie de Robert Wiene', *l'Avant-scène du cinéma*, no. 160–161 (July–Sept. 1975), 28–30; 'Dokumentation: Robert Wiene', *Filmkundliche mitteilungen*, No. 1–2 (Feb. 1969), 21–48.

12. DD, p. 63; SNB, p. 70.

13. DD, p. 65; Ramsaye, p. 489.

14. Gerhard Lamprecht, *Deutsche Stummfilme 1921–1922* (Berlin: Deutsche Kinemathek eV, 1968).

15. DD, pp. 65–67; SNB, pp. 65–67.

16. DD, pp. 67–68.

17. 'Gabriel Pascal', *World Film News*, loc. cit.

18. Respectively: Ramsaye, p. 489; *Filmlexicon degli Autori e delle Opere* (Rome: Edizione di Bianco e Nero, 1962), Vol. 5, p. 370.

19. DD, pp. 68–69.

20. DD, pp. 69–72.

21. Untitled, in *Continental Daily Mail*, loc. cit.; DD, pp. 75–78; SNB, p. 69; Patch, p. 118.

22. GP, 'Shaw as a Scenario Writer', in *G.B.S. 90*, ed. Stephen Winsten (New York: Dodd, Mead, 1946), pp. 255, 259–260.

23. Cover letter, Shaw to GP, 13 Dec 1935 (VP); Memorandum of Agreement, 13 Dec. 1935 (Shaw Estate files of its New York attorney, Richard E. Coven).

24. LSE, Parcel 26.

25. Letters: Shaw to Blanche Patch, 29 March 1935 (HRC) and to ST, 15 Dec. 1935 (BC); Louella O. Parsons, 'Hollywood: Marion Davies and G.B. Go on Spoofing Jaunt', *New York American*, 11 March 1936, p. 8.

26. Letter, Shaw to ST, 30 Dec. 1935 (BC).

27. Patch, p. 123.

28. Letter to Stewart Robinson, 12 July 1941, quoted in 'The Personal Touch', *The Family Circle*, 19 (19 Sept. 1941), 3.

DUTCH *PYGMALION*

1. 'Pygmalion', *Motion Picture Herald*, 17 Apr. 1937, p. 46; 'Amsterdam Gets the Word', *The Star*, 1937 (clipping, HRC).

2. Photostatic copy of letter, Shaw to GP, 10 May 1937 (Bancroft Library, University of California, Berkeley).

3. Mycroft, p. 15, credits Berger with adaptation. So does DC, p. 43. Costello, whose basic source was Mycroft, did not see the film (letter to me, 4 Nov. 1976).

BRITISH *PYGMALION*

1. DD, p. 80.
2. Alan Wood, *Mr. Rank: A Study of J. Arthur Rank and British Films* (London: Hodder and Stoughton, 1952), p. 96.
3. DD, p. 79.
4. Letter, Columbia Pictures to GP, 17 Sept. 1937 (HRC).
5. 'Reasonable Doubt', *Monthly Film Bulletin*, 3 (31 Dec. 1936), 213; also *Filmlexicon*, Vol. 5, p. 370.
6. Letter, GP to Shaw, 18 June 1937 (HRC).
7. Quoted in SNB, p. 72.
8. Letter, AH to Shaw, 30 April 1937 (LSE, Parcel 16).
9. Wood, pp. 95–96.
10. Engagement Diaries, 10 Dec. 1937 and 25 Feb. 1938 (LSE, Parcel 26.)
11. R. J. Minney, *Recollections of George Bernard Shaw* (Englewood Cliffs, N.J.: Prentice Hall, 1969), p. 76.
12. Letter to GP, 1 Sept. 1938, quoted in DD, p. 83.
13. Letter to GP, 16 April 1938, quoted in DD, p. 83.
14. Letter, Shaw to Blanche Patch, 20 Mar. 1936 (HC).
15. Fred Lawrence Guiles, *Marion Davies: A Biography* (New York: McGraw-Hill, 1972), p. 287.
16. DD. p. 83; SNB, p. 72.
17. Wendy Hiller, 'Portrait of Pascal', *The Shaw Review*, 14 (Jan. 1971), 33–34; Patch, p. 124.
18. Letter, Ronald Gow (Wendy Hiller's husband) to me, 12 July 1964.
19. Patch, p. 124.
20. Copy of letter, GP to Shaw, Oct. 30, 1937; note by Shaw at foot of letter, 11 or 19 Nov. 1937 (MGM); quotation from DD, p. 81.
21. IDT; Tree, *Pig in the Middle* (London: Michael Joseph, 1966), pp. 11–13.
22. Letter, Shaw to Mrs Patrick Campbell, 20 Sept. 1938, in Shaw and Campbell, p. 372.
23. Letter to GP, 24 Feb. 1938, quoted in DD, p. 85.
24. 'Shaw's View', *Sunday Express*, 13 March 1938 (clipping, DHL).
25. DD, p. 81.
26. 18 Nov. 1937, quoted in SNB, p. 78.
27. Letter to GP, 24 March 1938, printed in Shaw, *Pygmalion* (New York: Dodd, Mead, 1939).
28. Letter to GP, 24 Feb. 1938, in DD, p. 84.
29. Copy of note to GP, 11 or 19 Nov. 1937, at foot of letter from GP to Shaw, 30 Oct. 1937 (MGM).
30. Letter, Shaw to AH, 21 Nov. 1936 (privately owned).
31. Wood, pp. 96–97.
32. Letter, 6 Mar. 1938, quoted in DD, p. 82.
33. Letter, Shaw to GP, 6 Mar. 1938 (VP).
34. Letter, Shaw to GP, 16 April 1938, quoted in DD, p. 81.
35. Letter, Shaw to GP, 24 Feb. 1938 (VP).
36. While a handwriting resembling Shaw's (it is unclear) writes 'Omit' this flashforward and a preceding flashback, it does not cross or line out the scenes, which is Shaw's usual practice when he intends to cut something. Whether or not

the handwriting is his, my conclusions concerning Liza and Freddy are unaffected by it.

37. Gifford, No. 10536.

38. Letter, Francis S. Harmon, P.C.A., to GP, 22 Mar. 1938; Memorandum by Geoffrey Shurlock, P.C.A., 7 Sept 1938; letter, Joseph I. Breen, P.C.A., to Louis B. Mayer, 9 Sept. 1938 (MPAA).

39. Quoted in Bosley Crowther, 'G. B. Shaw's Disciple', NYT, 23 Oct. 1938, Sect. IX, p. 5.

40. Letter, Francis S. Harmon to Joseph I. Breen, 13 Sept. 1938 (MPAA).

41. Cable, GP to Henry Andrew, n.d. but after 17 Oct. 1938 (MPAA).

42. Bob Thomas, *Selznick* (New York: Pocket Books, 1972), p. 165.

43. Letter, GP to Breen, 31 Mar 1948 (MPAA).

44. Letter, Breen to GP, 5 April. 1948 (MPAA).

45. Hiller, p. 34.

46. IDT.

47. DC. p. 55.

48. Asquith, 'Shakespeare, Shaw on the Screen', *The Cine Technician*, 4 (Nov.-Dec. 1938), 124.

49. Gessner, *The Moving Image: A Guide to Cinematic Literacy* (New York: Dutton, 1970), pp. 114-115.

50. 'They Made a Film in Piccadilly—And No One Noticed', *The Daily Mirror* (undated clipping, Mander and Mitchenson Theatre Collection).

51. IDT.

52. Roman, pp. 412-413.

53. DC, p. 68.

54. DD, p. 84.

55. Letter, Shaw to AH, 21 Nov. 1936 (privately owned).

56. Randoff Goodman, 'Interview with Anthony Asquith, and Edward Baird', *From Script to Stage* (San Francisco: Reinhart Press, 1971), p. 315.

57. Rehearsal script (courtesy David Tree).

58. Quoted by Flora Robson, letter to me, 22 Feb. 1977.

59. Shaw, Untitled answers, p. 73.

60. Roll-Hanson, 'Shaw's *Pygmalion*: the two Versions of 1916 and 1941', *Review of English Literature*, 8 (July 1967), 88.

61. Shaw, 'Bernard Shaw Flays Filmdom's "Illiterates"', *Reynolds News* (London), 22 Jan. 1939, in *The Bodley Head Bernard Shaw*, Vol. 4, pp. 822-823.

62. Cable, Shaw to GP, 29 Oct. 1938 (MGM).

63. Basil Wright, 'Pygmalion', *The Spectator*, 161 (14 Oct. 1938), 603.

64. Charles Davy, 'Films', *The London Mercury*, 39 (Nov. 1938), 63.

65. Kracauer, *Theory of Film: The Redemption of Physical Reality* (London: Oxford University Press, 1971), pp. 229, 285.

66. 'Cinema: Old Shaw, New Trick', *Time*, 32 (5 Dec 1938), 26.

67. '*Pygmalion* at the Astor', *Daily Mirror*, 8 Dec. 1938 (clipping, LC).

68. William Boehnel, '*Pygmalion* on Screen is Hailed as a Triumph', *New York World-Telegram*, 8 Dec. 1938 (clipping, LC).

69. Franz Hoellering, 'Films', *The Nation*, 147 (24 Dec. 1938), 701-702.

70. Eileen Creelman, 'The New Talkies', *New York Sun*, 8 Dec 1938 (clipping, LC).

71. Archer Winston, '*Pygmalion* Opens at the Astor Theatre', *New York Post*, 8

Dec. 1938 (clipping, LC).

72. Otis Ferguson, 'The Good with the Bad', *The New Republic*, 97 (28 Dec. 1938), 231.

73. Herbert Cohn, 'An Open Letter to G. B. Shaw in Re: *Pygmalion* at the Astor', *Brooklyn Daily Eagle*, 8 Dec. 1938 (clipping, LC).

74. Brown, 'Mr. Shaw's *Pygmalion* Acted on the Screen', *New York Post*, 16 Dec. 1938 (clipping, LC).

75. 'Shaw on the Screen', *The Saturday Review of Literature*, 19 (24 Dec. 1938), 8.

76. Poster (HRC).

77. Ads in press book (LC).

78. Letter, Shaw to Mrs Patrick Campbell, 20 Sept. 1938, in Shaw and Campbell, p. 372.

79. DD, p. 85.

80. Letter, Shaw to GP, 13 Oct. 1938 (BL 50522).

81. DC, pp. 77—78.

82. Postal card, Shaw to ST, 7 Dec. 1938 (BC).

83. Letter, Shaw to Lawrence Langner, 3 April 1940, in Langner, p. 411.

84. Letter, Shaw to D. Kilham Roberts, 17 Sept. 1942 (BL 50630).

85. SNB, pp. 72-73.

86. Postal card, Shaw to ST, 7 Dec. 1938 (BC).

87. HRC.

88. Marriott, p. 1.

89. Letter, Shaw to GP, 26 Aug. 1938 (VP).

90. Letter, Shaw to GP, 1 Sept. 1938 (VP).

91. Letter, Shaw to GP, n.d., quoted in DD, p. 105.

92. Letters, Shaw to GP, 26 Aug. 1938 and 1 Sept. 1938, loc. cit.

93. Bergner, *Bewundert viel*, pp. 185-186. Although Bergner does not date the letter, its context indicates that Shaw wrote it before October 1938.

94. Letter, Shaw to GP, Sept. 1, 1938 (VP), quoted in Leonard Lyons, 'The Lyons Den', *New York Post*, 16 Aug. 1953, p. 8M (DHL).

95. Letter, Shaw to GP, 1 Sept. 1938 (VP).

THE DEVIL'S DISCIPLE

1. Ibid.

2. Letter, GP to Shaw, 13 Oct. 1938 (BL 50522).

3. Letters, Marjorie Deans to me, 4 Nov. 1976 and 3 Jan. 1977. The latter quotes a cable from Pascal to her, Sept. 1941, which supports this date.

4. See above, pp. 13-14, and Note on the Text. These scenes differ from the treatment Pascal later prepared (MD).

5. Langner, p. 83.

6. 'Socialism and the Labor Party' (1920), in Shaw, *Practical Politics*, pp. 148-149.

7. Copy, cable from James and John Woolf and Richard Norton to GP, 29 Oct. 1938 (MGM).

8. Mycroft, p. 31.

9. DC, p. 30.

MAJOR BARBARA

1. Photostatic copy of letter, Shaw to GP, 26 Aug. 1938 (Bancroft Library, University of California, Berkeley).
2. Letter, Shaw to GP, 20 Feb. 1939 (VP); Engagement Diary, 6 July 1939 (LSE, Parcel 26).
3. Letter, Shaw to GP, 1 Sept. 1938 (VP).
4. Copies of cables, Nicholas Davenport to GP, GP to C. M. Woolf, both 16 Nov. 1938 (MGM).
5. HRC.
6. 'Pascal to Film Life of Amelia Earhart', NYT, 3 Feb. 1939 (clipping, LC).
7. Engagement Diary, 4 March 1939 (LSE, Parcel 26).
8. Quoted in Campbell Dixon, 'Shaw Praises His Own Film', *Daily Telegraph*, 5 Oct. 1938 (clipping, HRC).
9. Letter, Shaw to Roy Limbert, 24 Dec. 1938 (HRC); 'What Is It? G.B.S. Doesn't Know Yet', *The Christian Science Monitor*, 29 March 1939, p. 8; for dates of composition, see *The Bodley Head Shaw*, Vol. 7, p. 202.
10. Letter, Dan H. Laurence to me, 5 March 1976.
11. Letter, Shaw to ST, 13 July 1939 (HRC).
12. DC, p. 83.
13. Letter, Shaw to GP, 21 Aug. 1939 (VP).
14. Letter, Shaw to GP, 9 Nov. 1939 (VP).
15. Wood, p. 98.
16. Holograph note by Shaw at the foot of Reconciliation Statement between Shaw and Pascal Film Productions, Ltd., 16 Dec. 1939 (HRC).
17. Letters, Shaw to GP, 9 and 21 Aug., 21 Sept., and 21 Nov. 1939 (VP).
18. IMD; letter, Marjorie Deans to me, 21 April 1976.
19. DD, pp. 96–97.
20. Letter, Shaw to GP, 21 Aug. 1939, quoted in DD, p. 97.
21. Photocopy of letter, Shaw to GP, 31 Aug. 1939 (WHEB).
22. Letter, Shaw to GP, 21 Nov. 1939 (VP).
23. Photocopies of letters and postal card: GP to Shaw, 24 July 1940; Shaw to GP, 28 July 1940; GP to Shaw, 31 July 1940; Shaw to GP, 31 Dec. 1940 (WHEB).
24. Letters, Shaw to GP, 25 Sept. 1940 (VP); Pascal to Shaw, 5 Oct. 1940 (photocopy, WHEB).
25. Letter, GP to Shaw, 15 Aug. 1940 (BFI).
26. Letter, Jack Hildyard to me, 15 March 1977. I have seen no print of *Major Barbara* that carries his name.
27. Letter, Shaw to Mrs Patrick Campbell, 21 Aug. 1939, in Shaw and Campbell, pp. 384–385.
28. IJM.
29. ISIH.
30. Interview with Vincent Korda, 24 Dec. 1975.
31. IMD.
32. IDT.
33. IAO.
34. IRM.
35. IAO.

36. IRM.
37. IDT.
38. Photocopy of letter, Shaw to GP, 28 June 1940 (WHEB); IDT; IMD.
39. Copy of letter, GP to Shaw, 3 July 1940 (WHEB).
40. DC, p. 84.
41. Photocopy of letter, Shaw to GP, 28 July 1940 (WHEB); rehearsal notes, 12 Sept. 1940, Shaw to GP (VP).
42. Copy of letter, GP to United Artists, 14 July 1941 (Shaw Estate files of its New York attorney, Richard E. Coven).
43. IMD.
44. Letter, Shaw to GP, 28 July 1940, quoted in DD, p. 98 and SNB, p. 74.
45. DD, pp. 98-100.
46. Rehearsal notes, loc. cit.
47. IJM; Harrison, p. 70.
48. Letters: GP to Shaw, 5 Oct. 1940 (photocopy, WHEB); Shaw to GP, 23 June 1940 (VP).
49. Phototcopy of letter, GP to Shaw, 3 July 1940 (WHEB); letter, Shaw to Ronald Gow, n.d., quoted in Sidney P. Albert, 'More Shaw Advice to the Players of *Major Barbara*', *Theatre Survey*, 11 (May 1970), 79.
50. Photocopy of letter, GP to Shaw, 31 July 1940 (WHEB).
51. Postal card, Shaw to GP, 29 Aug. 1940 (photocopy, WHEB), reproduced in Shaw, *Major Barbara* (New York: Dodd, Mead, 1941), facing p. 24.
52. Letter, GP to Shaw, 15 Aug. 1940 (BFI); photostatic copy, postal card, Shaw to GP, 29 Aug. 1940 (WHEB).
53. Interview with Vincent Korda, 24 Dec. 1975; IDT; IMD.
54. Lesley Blanch, p. 73; Howard Barnes, 'The Screen: Old Mr Shaw Rings the Bell Once More', *New York Herald Tribune*, 18 May 1941 (clipping, LC); letter, Wendy Hiller to me, 30 June 1976; IJM.
55. Harrison, p. 69; 'War and Films: Script Writer's London Diary', *New York Herald Tribune*, 11 May 1941 (clipping, LC).
56. C. A. Lejeune, 'British Studios Weather Air Raids', NYT, 6 Oct. 1940, Sect. IX, p. 4; 'Movie Slowed by Air Raids', *Morning Telegraph*, 23 May 1941 (clipping, LC).
57. Robert Morley and Sewell Stokes, *Robert Morley: A Reluctant Autobiography* (New York: Simon and Schuster, 1966), p. 158.
58. 'War and Films', loc. cit.
59. IJM; IRM.
60. IDT.
61. IJM.
62. 'Movie Slowed by Air Raids', loc. cit.
63. 'Mr Donald Calthrop', *The Times*, 16 July 1940, p. 7; 'Donald Calthrop', *Variety*, 7 Aug. 1940 and Douglas Gilbert, 'Pascal and Shaw Stun Films', *New York World Telegram*, 10 May 1941 (clippings, LC).
64. Letter to me, 30 June 1976.
65. Letter, Marjorie Deans to me, 7 July 1976; photostatic copy of letter, GP to Shaw, 24 July 1940 (WHEB).
66. IRM; Morley and Stokes, p. 158.
67. Hiller, p. 35.
68. Letter, S. I. Hsiung to me, 1 Aug. 1976; ISIH.

69. IJM.
70. IMD.
71. Letter, 4 Dec. 1940, in Hiller, p. 35.
72. IMD.
73. Harrison, p. 68; IMD; IJM; ISIH.
74. IDT; ISIH.
75. IDT; Hiller, p. 35.
76. IRM.
77. 'Pascal Film Productions Ltd., *Major Barbara*', n.d. (LSE, Parcel 13).
78. Letter, quoted in DD, pp. 100-101.
79. GP, op. cit., p. 192; IMD.
80. Photostatic copy of letter, Shaw to GP, 15 Sept. 1939 (WHEB).
81. Second Rehearsal Script, 15 April 1940 (courtesy David Tree) and Shooting Script, n.d. (BL 50617).
82. Shooting Script, loc. cit.
83. Letter, Shaw to GP, 23 June 1940 (VP).
84. Letter, Shaw to Marjorie Deans, 11 Jan. 1944 (MD).
85. Letter, Shaw to GP, 25 Sept. 1940 (VP).
86. Letter, Shaw to GP, 21 Nov. 1939, quoted in DD, p. 98.
87. Patch, p. 125.
88. DC, p. 110.
89. Interview with Penelope Dudley Ward, 28 Dec. 1975; IDT; IMD; IJM.
90. To be exact, 136 minutes, 47 seconds: letter, Jeremy Boulton (BFI) to me, 13 April 1977.
91. BFI; brochure (Mander and Mitchenson Theatre Collection).
92. Ramsaye, p. 652.
93. Letter, Shaw to Gilbert Murray, 5 Sept. 1941 (British Drama League).
94. By my watch.
95. The former, *TFS* 25, Programme 7, p. 7 (BFI); the latter, by my watch.
96. Letter, Shaw to Murray, loc. cit.
97. Letter, Shaw to GP, 25 Sept. 1944 (VP).
98. Written addendum to transcript of IMD.
99. Letters to me from Benjamin J. Magliano (PBS), 19 April 1977, and Jeremy Boulton (BFI), 13 April 1977.
100. IMD; Francis S. Harmon, 'Memo for Files re: *Major Barbara*' 30 Oct. 1940 (MPAA).
101. Letters, Francis S. Harmon to GP, 13 and 19 Feb. 1941 (MPAA).
102. Ibid.
103. Letters, Harmon to GP, 13, 19, and 20 Feb. 1941 (MPAA).
104. Cable, GP to Shaw, received 2 May 1941 (BL 50522).
105. Report to Production Code Administration from Local Censor Board, British Columbia, received 6 Oct. 1941 (MPAA).
106. Letter, Shaw to Theresa Helburn, 10 Nov. 1928, quoted in Albert, p. 73.
107. IMD.
108. DC, p. 110.
109. William Whitebait, 'The Movies: *Major Barbara* at the Odeon', *The New Statesman and Nation*, 21 (12 April 1941), 387; '*Major Barbara*: Mr Shaw's Play as a Film', *The Times*, 2 April 1941, p. 6.
110. Bosley Crowther, 'The Screen in Review', NYT, 15 May 1941, p. 27.

111. Howard Barnes, '*Major Barbara*—Astor', *New York Herald Tribune*, 15 May 1941; John Beaufort, '*Major Barbara* as a Film', *Christian Science Monitor*, 15 May 1941 (clippings, LC).

112. 'Cinema: The New Pictures', *Time*, 37 (2 June 1941), 80; Bosley Crowther, 'G. B. Shaw Beats the Drum', NYT, 18 May 1941, Sect. IX, p. 3.

113. DC, p. 103.

114. Philip T. Hartung, 'For the Brain; For the Heart', *The Commonweal*, 34 (30 May 1941), 136.

115. Leo Mishkin, '*Major Barbara* Is Second G. B. Shaw Play to Be Transferred to Screen', *Morning Telegraph*, 15 May 1941 (clipping, LC).

116. 'In Brief', *The New Yorker*, 51 (12 Jan. 1976), 18. The commentary appeared anonymously, but in a letter to me dated 4 Feb. 1977, Fred Keefe of *The New Yorker* identifies its author as Kael.

117. Letter, Shaw to Stewart Robinson, 12 July 1941, loc. cit.

118. IRM; interview with Wendy Hiller, 27 Dec. 1975.

119. Walt, 'Major Barbara' *Variety*, 7 May 1941 (clipping, LC).

120. Press Book (Dept. of Rare Books, Cornell University Library).

121. Quoted in DC, p. 110.

122. Wood, p. 105.

123. Letter, Shaw to Marjorie Deans, 2 Jan. 1942 (MD).

124. SNB, p. 73.

ARMS AND THE MAN

1. DD, p. 102.

2. Letter, Shaw to GP, 7 Nov. 1940 (VP).

3. Photocopy of postal card, Shaw to GP, 31 Dec. 1940 (WHEB).

4. IMD.

5. Cable from GP (BL 50522).

6. NYT, 15 June 1941 (clipping, HL); letter, Shaw to GP, 22 July 1941 (VP).

7. IMD.

8. Letter, Shaw to GP, 1 Aug. 1941 (VP).

9. IMD.

10. Letter, Shaw to GP, 20 Oct. 1941 (VP).

11. Letter, GP to Shaw, 15 Aug. 1940 (BFI).

12. Cable, GP to Shaw, received 2 May 1941 (BL 50522); NYT, 25 May 1941 (clipping, LC).

13. IMD.

14. Thomas M. Pryor, 'By Way of Report', NYT, 28 Sept. 1941, Sect. IX, p. 3.

15. Letter, Shaw to ST, 25 Aug. 1941 (BC).

16. Dated in Shaw's hand at end of MS (BL 50643).

17. Injunction at foot of typescript of film sequences (BL 50643); letter, Shaw to GP, 20 Oct. 1941 (VP).

18. Letter, Shaw to GP, 22 July 1941, quoted in DD, p. 102.

19. Pryor, loc. cit.

20. Postal card, Shaw to Marjorie Deans, 13 Oct. 1941 (VP).

21. Letter, Shaw to GP, 20 Oct. 1941, quoted in DD, pp. 102–103.

22. Letter, Shaw to Marjorie Deans, 22 March 1943 (MD).

23. Ibid.
24. Cable, GP to Marjorie Deans, 18 March 1943, quoted in letter, Deans to me, 29 July 1978.
25. SNB, pp. 83-84; letter, Shaw to GP, 8 May 1943 (VP).
26. Letter, Shaw to GP, 8 May 1943 (VP).
27. Hesketh Pearson, *G.B.S. A Postscript* (New York: Harper, 1950), p. 115.
28. SNB, p. 84; DD, pp. 103-104.
29. Letter, Shaw to GP, 8 May 1943; postal card, Shaw to GP, 18 July 1943 (VP).
30. DD, p. 103.
31. Letter, Shaw to Marjorie Deans, 3 Aug. 1943 (MD).
32. DD, p. 106; SNB, p. 85.

CÆSAR AND CLEOPATRA

1. Wood, p. 162.
2. Memorandum of Agreement (SA).
3. Letters, Shaw to GP, 16 and 24 Jan. 1944 (VP).
4. IMD; letters, Deans to me, 19 Feb. 1977 and 24 June 1978.
5. Letter, Shaw to Brian Desmond Hurst, 9 Jan. 1945 (HRC).
6. Quoted in SNB, p. 85.
7. Louella O. Parsons, 'Vivien Leigh to Star in *Cæsar, Cleopatra*', *New York Journal American*, 5 Aug. 1943 (MPAA).
8. 'United Artists Will Release Pascal's Cæsar', *Motion Picture Herald*, 24 June 1944 (clipping, MPAA).
9. Letter, Sir Ralph Richardson to me, 3 July 1976.
10. Letter, Shaw to Gielgud, quoted in Ronald Hayman, *John Gielgud* (London: Heinemann, 1971), p. 143.
11. Letter, Gielgud to Shaw, 29 Aug. 1943 (HC). Printed with permission of author.
12. Dixon Campbell, 'Shaw Writes a New Scenario', *Daily Telegraph*, 22 March 1944 (clipping, HRC).
13. IDT.
14. Quoted in Leonard Lyons, 'The Lyons Den', *New York Post*, 20 Feb. 1955 (clipping, DHL).
15. MS, p. 102.
16. Postal card, Shaw to GP, 15 Feb. 1944 (VP).
17. Letters, Shaw to Bliss, 30 April and 7 May 1944, in Sir Arthur Bliss, *As I Remember* (London: Faber and Faber, 1970), pp. 166-167.
18. Ibid., p. 128.
19. IMD; Patch, p. 168.
20. Letter, Shaw to GP, 25 Sept. 1944 (VP).
21. See Note on the Text.
22. Postal card, Shaw to GP, 30 Dec. 1944, in DD, pp. 109-110.
23. Wood, pp. 162-163.
24. Quoted in Noble, p. 106.
25. Notation on typescript (BL 50610). Dates of composition of this and other scenes also derive from notations on typescripts.

26. MS, p. 50.

27. Quoted in Hayden Church, 'It's the Same Shaw—And He's Still Writing', NYT, 21 Oct. 1945, Sect. VI, p. 13.

28. Post card, Shaw to Rains, 27 April 1944 (Mugar Memorial Library, Boston University); letter, Shaw to Leigh, n.d., in Felix Barker, *The Oliviers* (Philadelphia: Lippincott, 1953), p. 264.

29. Letters, GP to Shaw, 23 July 1944; Shaw to GP, 28 July 1944, in MS, p. 52.

30. Holograph notation at head of typescript (BL 50610); letter, Shaw to GP, 9 Sept. 1945 (VP). See Appendix I for this scene.

31. IMD.

32. Letter, Shaw to GP, 15 March 1944. Quoted in Dan H. Laurence, *Shaw: An Exhibit* (Austin, Texas: HRC, 1977), No. 737.

33. Quoted in Church, 'It's the Same Shaw', op. cit., p. 13.

34. MS, p. 47.

35. Patch, p. 129.

36. Letter, Shaw to GP, 1 July 1944, quoted in DD, p. 108.

37. Quoted in MS, p. 42.

38. GP, p. 258; Patch, p. 129.

39. Letter, Shaw to GP, 25 Sept. 1944, quoted in DD, p. 107.

40. Letter, Shaw to GP, 28 July 1944 (VP).

41. Letter, GP to Shaw, 8 July 1944, quoted in MS, p. 40.

42. Postal card, Shaw to GP, 9 July 1944 (VP); first quotation in DD, p. 107, second in MS, p. 41.

43. Note, Shaw to GP, 7 May 1944, on bottom of postal card, GP to Shaw, 4 May 1944 (HRC).

44. Quoted in MS, p. 41.

45. Letters, Shaw to GP, 19 and 26 July 1944, quoted in MS, pp. 32, 37-38.

46. IMD.

47. 'Super Shaw Film Finds Critics Cold', *New York Daily News*, 13 Dec. 1945 (clipping, MPAA).

48. Wood, p. 163; MS, pp. 43, 112-113.

49. MS, pp. 41, 89-90, 93; letter, Jack Hildyard to me, 15 March 1977.

50. Sidney Skolsky, 'Hollywood Is My Beat', *New York Post*, 31 Jan. 1945; William Hawkins, 'Shaw Movie His "Finest" ', *New York World-Telegram*, 22 June 1946 (clippings, MPAA).

51. MS, pp. 89-90.

52. Janet Dunbar, *Flora Robson* (London: Harrap, 1960), p. 226.

53. Barker, p. 264; Wood, pp. 163-164.

54. Letter, Deans to me, 19 Feb. 1977.

55. DD, p. 109.

56. IMD.

57. MS, pp. 99-101.

58. 'Inside Stuff—Pictures', *Variety*, 20 Dec. 1944 (clipping, MPAA).

59. 'Vivien Leigh's Holdover by Rank Gives Selznick a Cut in "Cæsar and Cleo" ', *Variety*, 25 July 1945; ' "Cleo" $3,000,000 Into the Red', *Variety*, 30 Oct. 1946 (clippings, MPAA).

60. ' "Cleo" $3,000,000 Into the Red', loc. cit.; Wood, p. 167; Grantley, p. 209; Ernest Fredman, ' "Cæsar" Acclaimed as Smash Rank Hit', *Film Daily*, 12 Dec. 1945 and Peter Burnup, 'Cæsar and Cleopatra', *Motion Picture Daily*, 13 Dec.

1945 (clippings, MPAA).

61. DD, p. 112.

62. DD, p. 110.

63. Letter, Flora Robson to me, 22 Feb. 1977.

64. Letter, Frederick Young to me, 3 March 1977; Wood, p. 164.

65. Letter, Robson to me, 22 Feb. 1977.

66. Barker, p. 265; Wood, p. 164.

67. Letter, Deans to me, 19 Feb. 1977.

68. 'Thirteenth Annual Meeting', *The Cine-Technician*, 60 (May–June 1946), 60.

69. Letter, Joseph I. Breen to GP, 14 Sept. 1944 (MPAA).

70. MS, pp. 77–78.

71. Letter, Shaw to GP, 14 March 1944 (HRC).

72. *Bernard Shaw, Director*, p. 38. The MS of this and other dialogue for extras in *Cæsar and Cleopatra* is in HRC.

73. DC, p. 135.

74. Letter, Shaw to Georgina (Gillmore) Musters, 29 Nov. 1946 (privately owned).

75. Sol Jacobson, 'Androcles in Hollywood', *Theatre Arts*, 36 (Dec. 1952), 66.

76. E. W. and M. M. Robson, *Bernard Shaw Among the Innocents* (London: The Sydneyan Society, 1945), pp. 3, 10–11, 23–24. Since the book was published in December 1945 and the film's first public showing was 13 Dec. 1945, there is little doubt that the authors did not see the movie when they wrote their book. That little doubt is dispelled by the fact that the book makes no reference to anything that happens on screen but quotes exclusively from the play.

77. Quoted in Richards Vidmer, 'Shaw's "Cæsar" Filmed by Rank as Super-Super', *New York Herald-Tribune*, 13 Dec. 1945; C.A.W., 'Cæsar and Cleopatra' *The Cinema*, 12 Dec. 1945 (clippings, MPAA). Since the reviewers attended a special press showing on 11 Dec. a number of notices appeared on or before the date of its first public showing, 13 Dec.

78. William Whitebait, 'The Movies: *Cæsar and Cleopatra* at the Marble Arch Odeon', *The New Statesman and Nation*, 30 (15 Dec. 1945), 404–405.

79. Edgar Anstey, 'The Cinema: *Cæsar and Cleopatra*', *The Spectator*, 175 (21 Dec. 1945), 591.

80. 'Reviews', *Film Daily*, 6 Aug. 1946 (clipping, MPAA); 'Cinema: The New Pictures', *Time*, 48 (19 Aug. 1946), 98.

81. Hermine Rich Isaacs, 'The Films: Late Summer', *Theatre Arts*, 30 (Sept. 1946), 517; Rose Pelswick, 'Cæsar and Cleopatra', *New York Journal-American*, 6 Sept. 1946; Eileen Creelman, 'The New Movies', *The New York Sun*, 6 Sept. 1946 (clippings, MPAA).

82. Jack D. Grant, 'Shaw's "Cæsar, Cleopatra" Disaapointing Film Fare', *The Hollywood Reporter*, 6 Aug. 1946 (clipping, MPAA); Bosley Crowther, 'G. B. Shaw's "C. and C." ', NYT, 8 Sept. 1946, Sect. II, p. 1.

83. Bosley Crowther, 'The Screen in Review: Shaw's *Cæsar and Cleopatra* as Film Opens at the Astor', NYT, 6 Sept. 1946, p. 18; Isaacs, loc. cit.

84. Philip T. Hartung, 'The Screen: Happy Birthday, G.B.S.', *The Commonweal*, 44 (16 Aug. 1946), 434; Kate Cameron, 'The Astor Presents Shaw Comedy in Film', *New York Daily News*, 6 Sept. 1946 (clipping, MPAA).

85. Ernest Fredman, ' "Cæsar" Acclaimed as Smash Rank Hit', *Film Daily*, 12 Dec. 1945 (clipping, MPAA).

Caesar and Cleopatra   Cleopatra's music room. Jean Simmons (playing harp) and Vivien Leigh (fanned by slaves).

Caesar and Cleopatra
Apollodorus on the crane
with Cleopatra rolled inside
the carpet. Stewart Granger
(aloft), Cecil Parker, Basil
Sydney and Claude Rains.

Caesar and Cleopatra Caesar and an exultant Cleopatra in her palace. Vivien Leigh and Claude Rains.

Caesar and Cleopatra A centurion and Ftatateeta observe as Apollodorus puts a pilum out of harm's way. Michael Rennie, Stewart Granger and Flora Robson.

86. Herb, 'Cæsar and Cleopatra', *Variety*, 7 Aug. 1946 (clipping, LC).
87. DC, p. 143.
88. Torn advertisement from unidentified paper (HRC).
89. ' "Cleo" $3,000,000 Into the Red', loc. cit.
90. LSE, Parcel 13.
91. DC, p. 144.
92. Index card, dated by Shaw February 1949, pasted on royalty statement (LSE, Parcel 13).
93. 'Shaw Defends Producer of *Cæsar and Cleopatra*', *New York Herald-Tribune*, 30 April 1946 (clipping, MPAA).
94. Mycroft, p. 30.

THE AFTERMATH

1. Wood, p. 169.
2. '1945–1946 The Association of Cine-Technicians Thirteenth Annual Report Agenda for Thirteenth Annual General Meeting, Saturday, April 27th & Sunday, April 28th', p. 7 (Archives of the Association of Cinematograph, Television, and Allied Technicians); 'Thirteenth Annual Meeting', pp. 60–61.
3. Holograph note at foot of letter, Harold Byers to Shaw, 6 May 1946 (HRC).
4. 'Three More Shaw Films', *The Times*, 1 Aug. 1946, p. 7.
5. IMD; Mycroft, p. 31. Among the Shaw papers at the British Library is a draft shooting script of *The Doctor's Dilemma* (BL 50620). Although its title page bears Shaw's name and no one else's, it is virtually identical to the script prepared by Deans and Mycroft (MD), who apparently made minor revisions before they or Pascal sent it to Shaw. The presence of his name on the title page and the absence of theirs is attributable to Shaw's insistence that no name but his be connected with the authorship of his screen writing.
6. Letter, Shaw to GP, 13 Aug. 1946 (VP); 'A.C.T. Send Korda Resolution on Pascal "Control" ', *Cinema*, 14 Aug. 1946 (clipping, HRC).
7. 'Korda Flays the A.C.T. "Dictators" ', *The Daily Film Renter*, 20 (19 Aug. 1946), p. 3; Karol Kulik, *Alexander Korda: the Man Who Could Work Miracles* (New Rochelle, N.Y.: Arlington House, 1975), p. 274.
8. ' "Caesar" Man Takes Cash Discount', *Daily Express*, 24 Feb. 1949 (clipping, HRC).
9. Shaw, postal card to GP, 16 Nov. 1944 (VP).
10. Irene Thirer, 'Pascal Here with "Cæsar"—Will Film New Pagnol Work', *New York Post*, 17 June 1946 (clipping, MPAA).
11. Memo, Wolfe to Dozier (RKO).
12. Note, Shaw to Blanche Patch, 30 Jan. 1946 (Bucknell University Library).
13. Cable, Shaw to GP, received 2 Feb. 1947 (VP); DD, p. 115; 'M. Pascal to Make Shaw Films in U.S.', *The Times*, 5 Feb. 1947, p. 3; 'Pickford, Cowan Sign Pascal Pact for Two Shaw Pictures', *Variety*, 5 Feb. 1947 and untitled report, *The Hollywood Reporter*, 5 Feb. 1947 (clippings, HL); 'Pascal's Deal with Pickford-Cowan', *Kinematograph Weekly*, 360 (13 Feb. 1947), 8A.
14. DD, p. 115.
15. Copy of letter, Shaw to Swartz, Eiffron and Steinberg, 26 March 1947 (VP).
16. Letter, Shaw to Marjorie Deans, 30 May 1947 (MD); cable, Pickford to

Shaw, 2 Nov. 1947 (HRC); DD, p. 116; letter, Shaw to GP, n.d. (VP).

17. 'Pascal to Italy Where Workers Have Spirit', *Motion Picture Herald*, 163 (22 June 1946), 28.

18. Letter, de Valera to Shaw, 29 Aug. 1946 (BL 50526); Tom Sheehy, 'Pascal's Dublin Visit Stirs Talk of Irish Studios', *Motion Picture Herald*, 164 (28 Sept. 1946), 44.

19. 'Interview on Irish Films' (HRC).

20. Letter, Arthur Cox to Shaw, 5 Dec. 1947 (LSE, Parcel 13).

21. Mycroft, p. 31.

22. Letter, Cox to Shaw, 21 April 1947 (LSE, Parcel 13).

23. Draft of wire, Shaw to Cox, 3 June 1947 (HRC); postal card, Shaw to GP, 4 June 1947 (VP); letters, de Valera to Shaw, 9 June 1947 and Cox to Shaw, 10 June 1947 (LSE, Parcel 13).

24. Memorandum of Agreement (Rare Book Room, Cornell University Library).

25. Postal card, Shaw to GP, 24 Sept. 1947, in DD, p. 140.

26. Minutes of Meeting (LSE, Parcel 13).

27. Letter, Cox to Shaw, 25 Nov. 1947 (LSE, Parcel 13).

28. Copy of letter, Shaw to Cox, 30 Nov. 1947 (VP).

29. Engagement Diary, 1948 (LSE, Parcel 26).

30. Letter, Shaw to GP, quoted in DD, p. 106.

31. Cable, Shaw to GP, received 2 Feb. 1947 (VP).

32. Engagement Diary, 1948, loc. cit.

33. Letters, Shaw to GP, quoted in Leonard Lyons, 'The Lyons Den', *New York Post*, 14 Aug. 1953 (clipping, DHL).

34. Engagement Diary, 1948, loc. cit.

35. Letter, Shaw to GP, 15 Feb. 1949 (VP).

36. Letter, Shaw to GP, 27 Oct. 1949, quoted in DD, p. 195.

37. Jacobson, p. 68.

38. Letters, Shaw to GP, 5 and 6 March 1950 (VP).

39. Engagement Diary, 1950 (LSE, Parcel 26).

40. Letters, Shaw to GP, 18 June and 5 July 1950 (VP).

41. BL 50627. Beside the date is a pencilled entry, 'from W.P.J.' The last letter could be an L, which would suggest the author was W. P. Lipscomb. In ink is an entry which resembles Pascal's hand, 'for G.B.S.' Nothing suggests Shaw is the author.

42. Englund's typed draft is dated 27 Dec. 1950 (RKO). Reviewer Theodore Hoffman's title accurately describes what R.K.O. did to Shaw's play: 'Thrown to the Lions', *The New Republic*, 128 (15 June 1953), 22–23.

43. Langner, p. 80.

44. Letter, Paul Koretz to Shaw, 27 Aug. 1946 (BL 50526).

45. Lawrence Langner, *The Magic Curtain* (New York: Dutton, 1951), p. 421.

46. Postal card, Shaw to GP, received 1 Nov. 1947 (VP); Memorandum of Agreement (courtesy A.B. Europa Film); letter, Karin Gustafson-Svanbom to me, 9 March 1976.

47. Letter, Shaw to GP, 18 June 1950 (VP).

Saint Joan

The lights in the auditorium fade out.
Peals of bells as from many church towers, high and low notes increasing in
intensity. The main title of the film:

SAINT JOAN

The sound of the bells gradually diminishing provides a background to the
subsequent subtitles, fading out entirely at the end of the last subtitle:

THE HUNDRED YEARS WAR

1429

FAIR FRANCE

'the cities and the towns defaced
By wasting ruin of the cruel foe.'*

Background of waste and ruin.

Pastures near Domrémy. The edge of a bluff overlooking a vast plain. A church
tower rises from a clump of trees. A burnt out farmhouse, still smouldering, in the
middle distance. Sheep browsing.

Joan is sitting on the grass with her hands clasped round her ankles, gazing
intently at the burnt house. Her shepherd's crook is beside her. Also her sheep dog.
Her back is to the audience.

A marching song is heard, very distant, soldiers singing and drums marking
time.

---

* Shakespeare, *King Henry VI*, Part One, III, iii, 45–46. Joan of Arc is a
character in this play. In his typescript, Shaw misquotes the first line, substituting
'her' for 'the.'

> Rum tum trumpledum,
> Bacon fat and rumpledum,
> Old Saint mumpledum,
> Pull his tail and stumpledum
> O my Ma-ry-Ann!

She rises to her knees, and shades her eyes with her hand, listening and looking for the source of the sound.

She flings out her arm, waving to the soldiers, and marks time with her feet.

The dog, puzzled by these proceedings, and fearing something wrong with her, noses or paws at her anxiously.

She turns round and sits down, caressing the dog reassuringly, and shewing her face to the audience for the first time.

Joan is an ablebodied country girl of 17 or 18, with an uncommon face; eyes very wide apart and bulging as they often do in very imaginative people, a long well-shaped nose with wide nostrils, a short upper lip, resolute but full-lipped mouth, and handsome fighting chin.

The angelus is rung in the church tower.

Joan rises and stands at attention, like a soldier, but with clasped hands and radiant face.

Her expression changes to one of intense determination. She snatches up her crook and strides down the hill, leaving the dog to look after her sheep.

Fade to:

A sunny stone chamber on the first floor of the castle of Vaucouleurs. The morning sun.

Captain Robert de Baudricourt, a military squire, handsome and physically energetic, but with no will of his own, is disguising that defect in his usual fashion by storming terribly at his steward, a trodden worm, scanty of flesh, scanty of hair, who might be any age from 18 to 55, being the sort of man whom age cannot wither because he has never bloomed.

The captain is seated at a plain strong oak table. The steward stands facing him, if so deprecatory a stance as his can be called standing. The mullioned thirteenth century window is open behind him. A turret with a narrow arched doorway leads to a winding stair which descends to the courtyard.

ROBERT. No eggs! Thousand thunders, man, what do you mean by no eggs?

STEWARD. Sir: It is not my fault. It is the act of God.

ROBERT. You blame your Maker for it.

STEWARD. Sir: what can I do? I cannot lay eggs.

ROBERT [*sarcastic*] Ha! You jest about it.

STEWARD. No, sir, God knows. We all have to go without eggs just as you have, sir. The hens will not lay.

ROBERT. Indeed! [*Rising*] My three Barbary hens and the black are the best layers in Champagne. And you tell me that there are no eggs! [*Driving the steward to the wall*] Who stole them? The milk was short yesterday, too.

STEWARD. [*desperate*] No, sir: nobody will steal anything. But there is a spell on us: we are bewitched.

ROBERT. That story is not good enough for me. Robert de Baudricourt burns witches and hangs thieves. Go. Bring me four dozen eggs and two gallons of milk before noon, or Heaven have mercy on your bones! [*He resumes his seat with an air of finality*].

STEWARD. Sir: I tell you there will be no eggs—not if you were to kill me for it—as long as The Maid is at the door.

ROBERT. The Maid! What maid?

STEWARD. The girl from Lorraine, sir. From Domrémy.

ROBERT [*rising in fearful wrath*] Thirty thousand thunders! Fifty thousand devils! Do you mean to say that that girl, who had the impudence to ask to see me two days ago is here still?

STEWARD. I have told her to go, sir. She wont.

ROBERT. I did not tell you to tell her to go: I told you to throw her out. You have fifty men-at-arms and a dozen lumps of able-bodied servants to carry out my orders. Are they afraid of her?

STEWARD. She is so positive, sir.

ROBERT [*seizing him by the scruff of the neck*] You parcel of curs: you are afraid of her.

STEWARD [*hanging limp in his hands*] No sir: we are afraid of you; but she puts courage into us. She really doesnt seem to be afraid of anything. Perhaps you could frighten her, sir.

ROBERT [*grimly*] Perhaps. Where is she now?

STEWARD. Down in the courtyard, talking to the soldiers as usual. She is always talking to the soldiers except when she is praying.

ROBERT. Praying, you idiot? I know the sort of girl that is always talking to soldiers. She shall talk to me a bit.

With these words he turns towards the spiral staircase and walks out of the picture. The steward follows.

Cut to:

A view of the courtyard. It is a sunny day in early spring. The snow is melting, dripping from the roofs. Cocks crow, cows low. At intervals the clanging of hammer blows from a smithy can be heard. A few cannons, no longer in service, stand in a corner. Birds sing. Far in the background a group of soldiers can be seen through a wooden grille; they are seated and in their midst appears a figure in light garb, apparently a girl.

ROBERT [*stopping at the doorstep, shouts fiercely*] Hallo, you there!

A GIRL'S VOICE [*bright, strong and rough*] Is it me, sir?

ROBERT. Yes, you.

THE VOICE. Be you captain?

ROBERT. Yes, damn your impudence, I be captain. Come up here. [*To the soldiers, who have sprung to their feet in consternation and stand at attention*] Shove her along quick.

The girl dashes through the wooden gate into the courtyard, splashing through pools of water, straight towards Robert.

STEWARD [*edging into the picture, whispering*] She wants to go and be a soldier herself. She wants you to give her soldier's clothes. Armor, sir! And a sword! Actually! [*He steals behind Robert*].

Joan appears in the doorway. Her voice is normally a hearty coaxing voice, very confident, very appealing, very hard to resist.

JOAN [*bobbing a curtsey*] Good morning, captain squire. Captain: you are to give me a horse and armor and some soldiers, and send me to the Dauphin. Those are your orders from my Lord.

ROBERT [*outraged*] Orders from y o u r lord! And who the devil is your lord?

JOAN. My Lord is the King of Heaven.

ROBERT. Why, the girl's mad. [*To the steward*] Why didn't you tell me so, you blockhead?

STEWARD. Sir: do not anger her: give her what she wants.

JOAN. Squire, it is the will of God that you are to do what He has put into my mind.

ROBERT. It is the will of God that I shall send you back to your father with orders to put you under lock and key and thrash the madness out of you.

JOAN. You think you will, squire; but you will find it all coming quite different. You said you would not see me; but here I am.

STEWARD [*appealing*] Yes, sir. You see, sir.

ROBERT. Hold your tongue!

STEWARD [*abjectly*] Yes, sir.

ROBERT [*to Joan, with a sour loss of confidence*] So you are presuming on my seeing you, are you?

JOAN [*sweetly*] Yes, squire.

ROBERT [*feeling that he has lost ground, inflates his chest imposingly to cure the unwelcome and only too familiar sensation*] I am going to assert myself.

JOAN [*busily*] Please do, squire. The horse will cost sixteen francs. It is a good deal of money: but I can save it on the armor. I am very hardy; and I do not need beautiful armor made to my measure like you wear. I shall not want many soldiers: the Dauphin will give me all I need to raise the siege of Orleans.

ROBERT [*flabbergasted*] To raise the siege of Orleans!

JOAN [*simply*] Yes, squire: that is what God is sending me to do. Three men will be enough. They have already promised to come with me. Polly and Jack and—

ROBERT. Polly!! You impudent baggage, do you dare call squire Bertrand de Poulengey Polly to my face?

JOAN. His friends call him so, squire: Jack—

ROBERT. That is Monsieur John of Metz, I suppose?

JOAN. Yes, squire. Jack will come willingly. So will Dick the Archer and their servants John of Honecourt and Julian. There will be no trouble for you, squire: I have arranged it all: you have only to give the order.

ROBERT [*contemplating her in a stupor of amazement*] Well, I a m damned!

JOAN [*with unruffled sweetness*] No, squire: God is very merciful; and the blessed saints Catherine and Margaret, who speak to me every day [*he gapes*], will intercede for you. You will go to paradise; and your name will be remembered for ever as my first helper.

ROBERT [*to the steward, still much bothered, but changing his tone as he pursues a new clue*] Is this true about Monsieur de Poulengey?

STEWARD [*eagerly*] Yes, sir. They both want to go with her.

ROBERT [*thoughtful*] Mf!

Camera pans to the other side of the hall where one sees a well kept courtyard.

ROBERT [*shouts to a passing soldier*] Hallo! Send Monsieur de Poulengey to me, will you? [*He turns to Joan*]. Wait in the yard.

JOAN [*smiling brightly at him*] Right, squire. [*She goes out*].

STEWARD [*anxious that the matter should go on*] Sir, think of those hens, the best layers in Champagne; and—

ROBERT. Think of my boot; and take your backside out of reach of it.

The steward retreats hastily.

From the other side —from the courtyard —appears Bertrand de Poulengey, a lymphatic French gentleman-at-arms, aged 36 or thereabout, employed in the department of the provost-marshal, dreamily absent-minded, seldom speaking unless spoken to, and then slow and obstinate in reply; altogether in contrast to the self-assertive, loud-mouthed, superficially energetic, fundamentally will-less Robert.

Poulengey salutes, and stands awaiting orders.

ROBERT [*genially*] It isnt service, Polly. [*Poulengey relaxes*]. It's about this girl you are interested in. First, she's mad. That doesnt matter. Second, I know her class. Her father is a farmer. He might have a cousin a lawyer, or in the Church. People of this sort can give a lot of bother to the authorities. That is to say, to m e . Now no doubt it seems to you a very simple thing to take this girl away, humbugging her into the belief that you are taking her to the Dauphin. But if you get her into trouble, you may get m e into no end of a mess. So, Polly, hands off her.

POULENGEY [*with deliberate impressiveness*] I should as soon think of the Blessed Virgin herself in that way, as of this girl.

ROBERT. You are not going to tell me that you take her crazy notion of going to the Dauphin seriously, are you?

POULENGEY [*slowly*] There is something about her. They are pretty foulmouthed in the guardroom, some of them. But there hasnt been a word that has anything to do with her being a woman. They have stopped swearing before her. There is something. Something. It may be worth trying.

ROBERT. Oh, come, Polly! pull yourself together.

He accompanies him up the spiral stairs. The camera follows. (During the following dialogue they stop occasionally, talking, then proceed again, etc.).

ROBERT. Commonsense was never your strong point; but this is a little too much.

POULENGEY [*unmoved*] What is the good of commonsense? If we had any commonsense we should join the Duke of Burgundy and the English king. They hold half the country, right down to the Loire. They have Paris. The Dauphin is in Chinon, like a rat in a corner, except that he wont fight. We dont even know that he i s the Dauphin: his mother says he isnt. The queen denies the legitimacy of her own son!

ROBERT [*shrugging his shoulders*] Well, she married her daughter to the English king.

POULENGEY. The English will take Orleans: nothing can save our side now but a miracle.

They are now one or two steps below the entrance to the stone room.

ROBERT. Oh! You think the girl can work miracles, do you?

POULENGEY. Her words and her ardent faith in God have put fire into me.

ROBERT [*giving him up*] Whew! You are as mad as she is.

POULENGEY [*obstinately*] We want a few mad people now. See where the sane ones have landed us!

They have now arrived at the top, facing the stone room.

ROBERT [*undecided*] Do you think I ought to have another talk to her?
Cut to:
Corner in the yard, near the smithy.
The clanging of the hammer can now be plainly heard. Joan —illuminated by the fire in the smithy —watches how a cannon is being repaired. A few soldiers and the steward stand about her.
POULENGEY'S VOICE. Joan!
Camera pans to Poulengey leaning out of window on the first floor just above Joan.
JOAN [*raising her voice above the hammering in the smithy*] Will he let us go, Polly?
POULENGEY. Come up.
Joan brightly winks to the steward, confident of victory. She hurries across the court, the steward following to show her the way.
The room on the first floor.
Poulengey sits down. Robert remains standing to inflate himself more imposingly. Joan comes in.
POULENGEY [*gravely*] Sit down, Joan.
JOAN [*checked a little, and looking to Robert*] May I?
ROBERT. Do what you are told.
Joan curtsies and sits down on a stool between them. Robert outfaces his perplexity with his most peremptory air.
ROBERT. What is your name?
JOAN [*chattily*] They always call me Jenny in Lorraine. Here in France I am Joan. The soldiers call me The Maid.
ROBERT. What is your surname?
JOAN. Surname? What is that? My father sometimes calls himself d'Arc; but I know nothing about it.
ROBERT. What did you mean when you said that St Catherine and St Margaret talked to you every day?
JOAN. They do.
ROBERT. What are they like?
JOAN [*suddenly obstinate*] I will tell you nothing about that: they have not given me leave.
ROBERT. But you actually see them; and they talk to you just as I am talking to you?
JOAN. No: it is quite different. I cannot tell you: you must not talk to me about my voices.
ROBERT. How do you mean? voices?
JOAN. I hear voices telling me what to do. They come from God.
ROBERT. They come from your imagination.
JOAN. Of course. That is how the messages of God come to us.
POULENGEY. Checkmate.
ROBERT. No fear! [*To Joan*] So God says you are to raise the siege of Orleans?
JOAN. And to crown the Dauphin in Rheims Cathedral.
ROBERT [*gasping*] Crown the D—! Gosh!
JOAN. And to make the English leave France.
ROBERT [*sarcastic*] Anything else?
JOAN [*charming*] Not just at present, thank you, squire.

ROBERT. I suppose you think raising a siege is as easy as chasing a cow out of a meadow. [*Grimly*] Did you ever see English soldiers fighting?

JOAN. They are only men. God made them just like us; but He gave them their own country and their own language; and it is not His will that they should come into our country and try to speak our language.

ROBERT. Who has been putting such nonsense into your head? Dont you know that soldiers are subject to their feudal lord, and that it is nothing to them or to you whether he is the duke of Burgundy or the king of England or the king of France? What has their language to do with it?

JOAN. We are all subject to the King of Heaven; and He gave us our countries and our languages, and meant us to keep to them. If it were not so it would be murder to kill an Englishman in battle; and you, squire, would be in great danger of hell fire. You must not think about your duty to your feudal lord, but about your duty to God.

POULENGEY. It's no use, Robert: she can choke you like that every time.

ROBERT. Can she, by Saint Denis! We shall see. [*To Joan*] We are not talking about God: we are talking about practical affairs. I ask you again, girl, have you ever seen English soldiers fighting, plundering, burning? Have you heard no tales of their Black Prince who was blacker than the devil himself?

JOAN. You must not be afraid, Robert—

ROBERT. Damn you, I am not afraid. And who gave you leave to call me Robert?

JOAN. You were called so in church in the name of our Lord. All the other names are your father's or your brother's or anybody's.

ROBERT. Tcha!

JOAN. At Domrémy we had to fly to the next village to escape from the English soldiers. Three of them were left behind, wounded. I came to know these three poor goddams quite well.

ROBERT. Do you know why they are called goddams?

JOAN. No. Everyone calls them goddams.

ROBERT. It is because they are always calling on their God to condemn their souls to perdition. That is what goddam means in their language. How do you like it?

JOAN [*rises impetuously, and goes at him, unable to sit quiet any longer*] Squire, you will live to see the day when there will not be an English soldier on the soil of France; and there will be but one king there: not the feudal English king, but God's French one.

ROBERT. Rot! [*To Poulengey*] But the Dauphin might swallow it. And if she can put fight into him, she can put it into anybody.

POULENGEY. There is something about the girl—

ROBERT [*turning to Joan*] Now listen you to me; and [*desperately*] dont cut in before I have time to think.

JOAN [*plumping down on the stool again, like an obedient schoolgirl*] Yes, squire.

ROBERT. Your orders are, that you are to go to Chinon under the escort of this gentleman and his friends.

JOAN [*radiant, clasping her hands*] Oh, squire! Your head is all circled with light, like a saint's.

POULENGEY. How is she to get into the royal presence?

ROBERT [*who has looked up for his halo rather apprehensively*] I dont know:

how did she get into m y presence? If the Dauphin can keep her out he is a better man than I take him for.

JOAN. And the dress? I may have a soldier's dress, maynt I, squire?

ROBERT. Have what you please.

JOAN [*wildly excited by her success*] Come, Polly. [*She dashes out*].

ROBERT [*shaking Poulengey's hand*] Goodbye, old man, I am taking a big chance. But as you say, there is something about her.

POULENGEY. Yes: there is something about her. Goodbye. [*He goes out*].

Robert, still very doubtful whether he has not been made a fool of by a crazy female, and a social inferior to boot, scratches his head and slowly comes back from the door.

STEWARD'S VOICE [*shouting*] Sir, sir!

ROBERT. What now?

STEWARD [*dashes up the spiral stairs; he points to basket full of eggs*] The hens are laying like mad, sir. Five dozen eggs!

In his excitement he trips over the last step, falling full length into the room. A few eggs smash on the floor.

ROBERT [*crosses himself and stammers*] Christ in Heaven! [*Aloud but breathless*] She did come from God.

A close-up of Robert as he says these last portentous words.

Slow dissolve.

Beautiful, far-flung evening scenery.

In the distance a number of horsemen; they appear practically as silhouettes, but their armor glistens in the rays of the setting sun.

The horseman in the centre is noticeably smaller of stature and slimmer than the others.

Evening bells are heard from afar; the wind moves the brushwood in the foreground.

Slow dissolve.

A coat-of-arms hewn in stone above a portal of the Castle of Chinon.

Dissolve.

A reception room in the castle. The camera moves down as from the ceiling of the room, bringing into focus a page, who opens the door.

PAGE [*announcing*] The Dauphin.

At the announcement, four people who wait for him stand perfunctorily at court attention.

The Archbishop of Rheims, close to 50, is a full-fed prelate with nothing of the ecclesiastic about him except his imposing bearing.

The Lord Chamberlain, Monseigneur de la Trémouille, is a monstrous arrogant wineskin of a man.

Gilles de Rais, a young man of 25, very smart and self-possessed, sports the extravagance of a little curled beard dyed blue at a clean-shaven court. He is determined to make himself agreeable, but lacks natural joyousness, and is not really pleasant. In fact when he defies the Church some eleven years later he is accused of trying to extract pleasure from horrible cruelties, and hanged. So far, however, there is no shadow of the gallows on him.

Captain La Hire is a war dog with no court manners and pronounced camp ones.

The Dauphin, aged 26, really King Charles the Seventh since the death of his father, but as yet uncrowned, comes in through the curtains with a paper in his hands. He is a poor creature physically; and the current fashion of shaving closely, and hiding every scrap of hair under the headcovering or headdress, both by women and men, makes the worst of his appearance. He has little narrow eyes, near together, a long pendulous nose that droops over his thick short upper lip, and the expression of a young dog accustomed to be kicked, yet incorrigible and irrepressible. But he is neither vulgar nor stupid; and he has a cheeky humor which enables him to hold his own in conversation. Just at present he is excited, like a child with a new toy.

CHARLES. Oh, Archbishop, do you know what Robert de Baudricourt is sending me from Vaucouleurs?

THE ARCHBISHOP [*contemptuously*] I am not interested in the newest toys.

CHARLES [*indignantly*] It isnt a toy.

LA TRÉMOUILLE. It is my business to know what is passing between you and the garrison at Vaucouleurs. [*He snatches the paper from the Dauphin's hand, and begins reading it with some difficulty, following the words with his finger and spelling them out syllable by syllable.*]

CHARLES [*mortified*] You all think you can treat me as you please because I owe you money, and because I am no good at fighting. But I have the blood royal in my veins.

THE ARCHBISHOP. Even that has been questioned, your Highness. One hardly recognizes in you the grandson of Charles the Wise.

CHARLES. I want to hear no more of my grandfather. He was so wise that he used up the whole family stock of wisdom for five generations, and left me the poor fool I am, bullied and insulted by all of you.

THE ARCHBISHOP. Control yourself, sir. These outbursts of petulance are not seemly.

CHARLES. A lecture! Thank you. What a pity it is that though you are an archbishop saints and angels dont come to see y o u !

THE ARCHBISHOP. What do you mean?

CHARLES. Aha! Ask that bully there [*pointing to La Trémouille*].

LA TRÉMOUILLE [*furious*] Hold your tongue. Do you hear?

CHARLES. Oh, I hear. You neednt shout. Why dont you go and shout at the English? and bully them instead of bullying me?

LA TRÉMOUILLE [*raising his fist*] You young—

CHARLES [*running behind the Archbishop*] Dont you raise your hand to me. It's high treason.

THE ARCHBISHOP [*resolutely*] Come, come! this will not do. My Lord Chamberlain: please! please! we must keep some sort of order. [*To the Dauphin*] And you, sir: if you cannot rule your kingdom, at least try to rule yourself.

CHARLES. Another lecture! Thank you.

LA TRÉMOUILLE [*handing over the paper to the Archbishop*] Here: read the accursed thing for me. He has sent the blood boiling into my head: I cant distinguish the letters.

CHARLES [*coming back and peering round la Trémouille's left shoulder*] I will read it for you if you like. I c a n read, you know.

LA TRÉMOUILLE [*with intense contempt, not at all stung by the taunt*] Yes: reading is about all you are fit for. Can you make it out, Archbishop?

THE ARCHBISHOP. I should have expected more commonsense from De

Baudricourt. He is sending some cracked country lass here—

CHARLES [*interrupting*] No: he is sending a saint: an angel. And she is coming to me: to m e , the king, and not to you, Archbishop. She knows the blood royal if you dont. [*He struts past Bluebeard and La Hire*].

THE ARCHBISHOP. This creature is not a saint. She is not even a respectable woman. She does not wear women's clothes. She is dressed like a soldier, and rides round the country with soldiers.

CHARLES. You havnt read the end of the letter.

THE ARCHBISHOP [*reading the letter*] De Baudricourt says she will raise the siege of Orleans, and beat the English for us.

LA TRÉMOUILLE. Rot!

BLUEBEARD [*coming between the Archbishop and Charles*] At the head of your troops in Orleans you have Jack Dunois: the invincible Dunois, the darling of all the ladies, the wonderful bastard. Is it likely that the country lass can do what he cannot do?

CHARLES. Why doesnt he raise the siege, then?

LA HIRE. The English hold the bridgehead. He must ship his men across the river and upstream, if he is to take them in the rear. Well, he cannot, because there is a devil of a wind blowing the other way. What he needs is a miracle.

BLUEBEARD. We can easily find out whether she is an angel or not. Let us arrange when she comes that I shall be the Dauphin, and see whether she will find me out.

CHARLES. Yes: I agree to that. If she cannot find the blood royal I will have nothing to do with her.

THE ARCHBISHOP [*who has read the end of the letter and become more thoughtful*] Since his Highness desires it, let her attend the Court.

Charles goes out, followed by Bluebeard and La Hire.

LA TRÉMOUILLE. I wonder will she pick him out!

THE ARCHBISHOP. Of course she will.

LA TRÉMOUILLE. How?

THE ARCHBISHOP. She will know what everybody in Chinon knows: that the Dauphin is the meanest-looking and worst-dressed figure in the Court, and that the man with the blue beard is Gilles de Rais.

LA TRÉMOUILLE. I never thought of that.

THE ARCHBISHOP. You are not so accustomed to miracles as I am. It is part of my profession.

Cut to:

Close-up of Bluebeard, standing theatrically on the dais before the throne.

Chatter and laughter on all sides.

The camera moves back, gradually revealing the entire throne room. Bluebeard, like the courtiers, enjoys the joke rather obviously.

There is a curtained arch in the wall behind the dais: but the main door, guarded by men-at-arms, is at the other side of the room. Charles is in the middle of a group of courtiers in the centre of the room. La Hire is on his right, the Archbishop on his left. La Trémouille stands on the dais by the side of the throne. The Duchess de la Trémouille, surrounded by a group of ladies in waiting, is behind the Archbishop.

The chatter of the courtiers makes such a noise that nobody notices the appearance of the page at the door.

THE PAGE. The Duke of—[*Nobody listens*]. The Duke of—[*The chatter continues. Indignant at his failure to command a hearing, he snatches the halberd of the nearest man-at-arms, and thumps the floor with it. The chatter ceases; and everybody looks at him in silence*]. Attention! [*He restores the halberd to the man-at-arms*]. The Duke of Vendôme presents Joan the Maid to his Majesty.

CHARLES [*putting his finger on his lip*] Ssh! [*He hides behind the nearest courtier, peering out to see what happens*].

BLUEBEARD [*majestically*] Let her approach the throne.

Joan, dressed as a soldier, with her hair bobbed and hanging thickly round her face, is led in by a bashful and speechless nobleman, from whom she detaches herself to stop and look round eagerly for the Dauphin.

THE DUCHESS [*to the nearest lady in waiting*] My dear! Her hair!

All the ladies explode in uncontrollable laughter.

BLUEBEARD [*trying not to laugh, and waving his hand in deprecation of their merriment*] Ssh—ssh! Ladies! Ladies!!

JOAN [*not at all embarrassed*] I wear it like this because I am a soldier. Where be Dauphin?

A titter runs through the Court as she walks to the dais.

BLUEBEARD [*condescendingly*] You are in the presence of the Dauphin.

Joan looks at him sceptically for a moment, scanning him hard up and down to make sure. Dead silence, all watching her. Fun dawns in her face.

JOAN. Coom, Bluebeard! Thou canst not fool me. Where be Dauphin?

A roar of laughter breaks out as Gilles, with a gesture of surrender, joins in the laugh, and jumps down from the dais beside La Trémouille. Joan, also on the broad grin, turns back, searching along the row of courtiers, and presently makes a dive, and drags out Charles by the arm.

JOAN [*releasing him and bobbing him a little curtsey*] Gentle little Dauphin, I am sent to you to drive the English away from Orleans and to crown you king in the cathedral at Rheims.

CHARLES [*triumphant, to the Court*] You see, all of you: she knew the blood royal. Who dare say now that I am not my father's son? [*To Joan*] But if you want me to be crowned at Rheims you must talk to the Archbishop, not to me. There he is [*he is standing behind her*]!

JOAN [*turning quickly, overwhelmed with emotion*] Oh, my lord! [*She falls on both knees before him, with bowed head, not daring to look up*] My lord: you are filled with the glory of God Himself; but you will touch me with your hands, and give me your blessing, wont you?

THE ARCHBISHOP [*touched, putting his hand on her head*] Child: you are in love with religion.

JOAN [*startled: looking up at him*] Am I? I never thought of that. Is there any harm in it?

THE ARCHBISHOP. There is no harm in it, my child. But there is danger.

JOAN [*rising, with a sunflush of reckless happiness irradiating her face*] There is always danger, except in heaven. Oh, it must be a most wonderful thing to be Archbishop.

The Court smiles broadly: even titters a little.

THE ARCHBISHOP [*drawing himself up sensitively*] Gentlemen: your levity is rebuked by this maid's faith. I am, God help me, all unworthy; but your mirth is a deadly sin.

Their faces fall. Dead silence.

BLUEBEARD. My lord: we were laughing at her, not at you.

The courtiers take heart at this. There is more tittering.

JOAN [*scandalized*] You are an idle fellow, and you have great impudence to answer the Archbishop.

LA HIRE [*with a huge chuckle*] Well said, lass! Well said!

JOAN [*impatiently to the Archbishop*] Oh, my lord, will you send all these silly folks away so that I may speak to the Dauphin alone?

LA HIRE [*goodhumoredly*] I can take a hint. [*He salutes; turns on his heel; and goes out*].

THE ARCHBISHOP. Come, gentlemen. The Maid comes with God's blessing, and must be obeyed.

The courtiers withdraw, some through the arch, others at the opposite side. The Archbishop marches across to the door, followed by the Duchess and La Trémouille. As the Archbishop passes Joan, she falls on her knees, and kisses the hem of his robe fervently. He shakes his head in instinctive remonstrance; gathers the robe from her; and goes out. She is left kneeling directly in the Duchess's way.

THE DUCHESS [*coldly*] Will you allow me to pass, please?

JOAN [*hastily rising, and standing back*] Beg pardon, maam, I am sure.

The Duchess passes on. Joan stares after her; then whispers to the Dauphin.

JOAN. Be that Queen?

CHARLES. No. She thinks she is.

JOAN [*again staring after the Duchess*] Oo-oo-ooh! [*Her awestruck amazement at the figure cut by the magnificently dressed lady is not wholly complimentary*].

LA TRÉMOUILLE [*very surly*] I'll trouble your Highness not to gibe at my wife. [*He goes out. The others have already gone*].

JOAN [*to the Dauphin*] Who be old Gruff-and-Grum?

CHARLES. He is the Duke de la Trémouille.

JOAN. What be his job?

CHARLES. He pretends to command the army. And whenever I find a friend I can care for, he kills him.

JOAN. Why dost let him?

CHARLES [*petulantly moving to the throne side of the room to escape from her magnetic field*] How can I prevent him? He bullies me. They all bully me.

JOAN. Art afraid?

CHARLES. Yes: I am afraid. It's no use preaching to me about it. It's all very well for these big men with their armor that is too heavy for me, and their swords that I can hardly lift. They like fighting; but I am quiet and sensible and only want to be left alone. So if you are going to say "Son of St Louis: gird on the sword of your ancestors, and lead us to victory" you may spare your breath to cool your porridge; for I am not built that way; and there is an end of it.

JOAN [*trenchant and masterful*] Blethers! We are all like that to begin with. I shall put courage into thee.

CHARLES. But I dont want to have courage put into me. Put courage into the others, and let them have their bellyful of fighting; but let me alone.

JOAN. It's no use, Charlie: if thou fail to make thyself king, thoult be a begger: what else art fit for? Come! Let me see thee sitting on the throne. I have looked forward to that.

CHARLES. What is the good of sitting on the throne when the other fellows give all the orders? However! [*he sits enthroned, a piteous figure*] here is the king for you! Look your fill at the poor devil.

JOAN. Thourt not king yet, lad: thourt but Dauphin. The people count no man king of France until he be crowned in Rheims Cathedral. And thou needs new clothes, Charlie. Why does not Queen look after thee properly?

CHARLES. We're too poor. She wants all the money we can spare to put on her own back. Besides, I like to see her beautifully dressed; and I dont care what I wear myself: I should look ugly anyhow.

JOAN. There is some good in thee, Charlie; but it is not yet a king's good.

CHARLES. We shall see. I am not such a fool as I look. I have my eyes open; and I can tell you that one good treaty is worth ten good fights. These fighting fellows lose all on the treaties that they gain on the fights. If we can only have a treaty, the English are sure to have the worst of it, because they are better at fighting than at thinking.

JOAN. If the English win, it is they that will make the treaty. Thou must fight, Charlie! We must take our courage in both hands: aye, and pray for it with both hands too.

CHARLES [*descending from his throne and again crossing the room to escape from her dominating urgency*] Oh do stop talking about praying. I want to be just what I am. Why cant you mind your own business, and let me mind mine?

JOAN. What is my business? Helping mother at home. What is thine? Petting lapdogs and sucking sugarsticks. I call that muck. I tell thee it is God's business we are here to do: not our own. I have a message to thee from God; and thou must listen to it, though thy heart break with the terror of it.

CHARLES. I dont want a message; but can you tell me any secrets? Can you do any cures? Can you turn lead into gold, or anything of that sort?

JOAN. I can turn thee into a king, in Rheims Cathedral; and that is a miracle that will take some doing, it seems.

CHARLES. Will the consecration pay off my mortgages? I have pledged my last acre to that fat bully Trémouille.

JOAN. The land is thine to rule righteously, and not to pledge at the pawnshop as a drunken woman pledges her children's clothes. I come from God to tell thee to kneel in the cathedral and become king. The very clay of France will become holy: her soldiers will be the soldiers of God: the rebel dukes will be rebels against God: the English will return to their lawful homes. Wilt be a poor little Judas, and betray me and Him that sent me?

CHARLES [*tempted at last*] Oh, if I only dare!

JOAN. I shall dare in God's name! Art for or against me?

CHARLES [*excited*] I'll risk it, I warn you I shant be able to keep it up; but I'll risk it. You shall see. [*Running to the main door and shouting*] Hallo! Come back, everybody. [*To Joan, as he runs back to the arch opposite*] Mind you stand by and dont let me be bullied. [*Shouting through the arch*] Come along, will you: the whole Court. [*He sits down in the royal chair as they all hurry in to their former places, chattering and wondering*]. Now I'm in for it; but no matter: here goes! [*To the page*] Call for silence, you little beast, will you?

THE PAGE [*snatching a halberd as before and thumping with it repeatedly*] Silence for His Majesty the King. The King speaks. [*Peremptorily*] Will you be silent there? [*Silence*].

CHARLES [*rising*] I have given the command of the army to The Maid. The Maid is to do as she likes with it.

General amazement. La Hire, delighted, slaps his steel thighpiece with his gauntlet.

LA TRÉMOUILLE [*turning threateningly towards Charles*] What is this? *I* command the army.

Joan quickly puts her hand on Charles's shoulder as he instinctively recoils. Charles, with a grotesque effort culminating in an extravagant gesture, snaps his fingers in the Chamberlain's face.

JOAN. Thou't answered, old Gruff-and-Grum. [*Suddenly flashing out her sword as she divines that her moment has come*] Who is for God and His Maid? Who is for Orleans with me?

LA HIRE [*carried away, drawing also*] For God and His Maid! To Orleans!

ALL THE KNIGHTS [*following his lead with enthusiasm*] To Orleans!

Joan, radiant, falls on her knees in thanksgiving to God. They all kneel, except the Archbishop, who gives his benediction with a sigh, and La Trémouille, who collapses, cursing.

The points of the swords dissolve to:

A pennon fluttering in the east wind on the banks of the Loire (during the dissolve one hears the whistling wind).

A sudden pan of the camera brings the face of Dunois, ages 26, into focus. He looks at the pennon.

Over the head of Dunois one sees the silver Loire, commanding a long view in both directions. In the background stand the walls of Orleans, the towers and spires of the city against the evening sky. The pennon flutters from a lance rammed into the ground.

Dunois' shield with its bend sinister (the sign of illegitimacy) lies beside the lance. He has his commander's baton in his hand. He is well built, carrying his armor easily. His broad brow and pointed chin give him an equilaterally triangular face, already marked by active service and responsibility, with the expression of a good-natured and capable man who has no affectations and no foolish illusions. His page is sitting on the ground, elbows on knees, cheeks on fists, idly watching the water.

DUNOIS [*looks at the pennon, and shakes his fist at it*] Change, curse you, change, English harlot of a wind, change to the west, I tell you. [*With a growl he paces in silence, but soon begins again*] False wind from over the water, will you never blow again?

THE PAGE [*bounding to his feet*] See! There! There she goes!

DUNOIS [*startled from his reverie: eagerly*] Where? Who? The Maid?

THE PAGE. No: the kingfisher.

DUNOIS [*furiously disappointed*] Is that all? You infernal young idiot: I have a mind to pitch you into the river.

A SENTRY'S VOICE WESTWARD. Halt! Who goes there?

JOAN'S VOICE. The Maid.

DUNOIS. Let her pass.

Joan, in splendid armor, rushes in in a blazing rage.

JOAN [*bluntly*] Be you Bastard of Orleans?

DUNOIS [*cool and stern, pointing to his shield*] You see the bend sinister. Are you Joan the Maid?

JOAN. Sure.

DUNOIS. Where are your troops?

JOAN. Miles behind. They have cheated me. They have brought me to the wrong side of the river.

DUNOIS. I told them to.

JOAN. Why did you? The English are on the other side!

DUNOIS. The English are on both sides.

JOAN. But Orleans is on the other side. We must fight the English there. Which is the way to the bridge?

DUNOIS. You are impatient, Maid.

JOAN. Is this a time for patience? Our enemy is at our gates. Oh, why are you not fighting? I will deliver you from fear. I—

DUNOIS [*laughing heartily, and waving her off*] No, no, my girl: if you delivered me from fear I should be a good knight for a story book, but a very bad commander of the army. Come! let me begin to make a soldier of you. [*He takes her to the water's edge*]. Do you see those two forts at the end of the bridge?

With these words the camera pans, bringing into view the two forts in the distance; little of the bridge comes into focus.

JOAN. Are they ours or the goddams'?

DUNOIS. Be quiet, and listen to me. If I were in either of those forts with only ten men I could hold it against an army. The English have more than ten times ten goddams in those forts to hold them against us.

JOAN. They cannot hold them against God. God did not give them the land under those forts: they stole it from Him. He gave it to us. I will take those forts.

DUNOIS. Single-handed?

JOAN. Our men will take them. I will lead them.

DUNOIS. Not a man will follow you.

JOAN. I will not look back to see whether anyone is following me.

DUNOIS [*recognizing her mettle, and clapping her heartily on the shoulder*] Good. You have the makings of a soldier in you. You are in love with war.

JOAN [*startled*] Oh! And the Archbishop said I was in love with religion.

DUNOIS. I, God forgive me, am a little in love with war myself, the ugly devil! I am like a man with two wives. Do you want to be like a woman with two husbands?

JOAN [*matter-of-fact*] I will never take a husband. A man in Toul took an action against me for breach of promise; but I never promised him. I am a soldier! Bastard: I dare you to follow me.

DUNOIS. You must not dare a staff officer, Joan: only company officers are allowed to indulge in displays of personal courage. However, all in good time. Our men cannot take those forts by a sally across the bridge. They must come by water, and take the English in the rear on this side.

JOAN [*her military sense asserting itself*] Then make rafts and put big guns on them; and let your men cross to us.

DUNOIS. The rafts are ready; and the men are embarked. But they cannot come up against both wind and current. We must wait until God changes the wind. Come: let me take you to the church. You must pray for a west wind. My prayers are not answered. Yours may be.

JOAN. Oh yes: I will pray: I will tell St Catherine: she will make God give me a west wind. Quick: shew me the way to the church.

THE PAGE [*sneezes violently*] At-cha!!!

JOAN. God bless you, child! Coom, Bastard.

They go off. The page rises to follow. He picks up the shield, and is taking the spear as well when he notices the pennon, which is now streaming eastward.

THE PAGE [*dropping the shield and calling excitedly after them*] Seigneur! Seigneur! Mademoiselle!

DUNOIS [*running back*] What is it? The kingfisher? [*He looks eagerly for it up the river*].

JOAN. Oh, a kingfisher! Where?

THE PAGE. No: the wind, the wind, the wind [*pointing to the pennon*]: that is what made me sneeze.

DUNOIS [*looking at the pennon*] The wind has changed. God has spoken. [*Kneeling and handing his baton to Joan*] You command the king's army. [*Rising*] You dared me to follow. Dare you lead?

JOAN [*bursting into tears and flinging her arms round Dunois, kissing him on both cheeks*] Dunois, dear comrade in arms, help me. My eyes are blinded with tears.

DUNOIS [*dragging her away*] Make for the flash of the guns.

JOAN [*in a blaze of courage*] Ah!

DUNOIS [*dragging her along with him*] For God and Saint Denis!

THE PAGE [*shrilly*] The Maid! The Maid! God and The Maid! Hurray-ay-ay!

Cut to:

Cannonade. Distant shouts.

The river Loire at Orleans, with the bridge in the distance and the tower, rather like a castle chessman, at the end farthest from the city.

On a huge raft with a cannon mounted on it Joan, the Duc d'Alençon, and Dunois stand watching the tower as the raft half drifts, half sails with a big lugsail towards it. The raft is crowded with men-at-arms.

The master gunner is laying the cannon. His assistant stands by with his linstock burning. There is a continual din of distant shouting and talking on the raft, not loud enough to drown Joan's voice when, after looking eagerly from the cannon to the tower and back again a few times, she pounces at the cannon, pushing the gunner away.

JOAN. No. Too high. You cant reach it. The shot must bounce up off the water. Let me. Let me. [*She lays the cannon herself. Silence on the raft, all watching*]. Now, now! [*She snatches the linstock and fires the cannon, which is loaded with black powder and makes a thick smoke*].

D'ALENÇON. Good shot, Maid. Youve breached the tower.

JOAN [*exultant*]. I knew I should. I can do that every time. Ah!!

An arrow strikes her in the throat. She screams and falls. A shout of triumph from the enemy.

Dunois and D'Alençon rush to her.

She cries piteously, like a baby.

The gunner plucks the arrow away (it has wounded her neck and stuck in her coat of mail), eliciting a piercing scream from her.

She cries still more piteously.

D'ALENÇON. Those cursed English archers.

DUNOIS. A surgeon there. She will bleed to death.

JOAN. No. No surgeon. Lift me: I want to pray. [*Dunois and D'Alençon lift her to her knees whilst the cannoneer makes a bandage of tow to put round her neck. Joan clasps her hands in supplication*]. O blessed Madame St Margaret, O dear Madame St Catherine, do not let me bleed to death. My work is not done. Oh, you must not—you will not—

THE GUNNER. By God, the flow of blood has stopped. The wound has healed. Look! [*He throws away the bandage*].

D'ALENÇON. A miracle! On your knees! God is on this raft.

The men-at-arms kneel, crossing themselves.

JOAN [*smiling in ecstasy and springing to her feet*] The pain is gone: I have my strength again. Gloria in excelsis Deo. Up, up, up: to work, to work.

The men-at-arms rise and shout defiance at the enemy.

Cut to:

The top of the circular tower against the sky. The battlements are of timber. In the middle is a rough rail round the stairhead into the interior, and a flagstaff with the English standard.

The battlements are manned by English archers, each with his long bow, and his supply of arrows stuck in the battlement beside him. They stand at an equal distance between each, and shoot rhythmically together in volleys. At each flight, they give the English Hurrah! *to terrify the French.*

FIRST VOLLEY. Hurrah!

They take fresh arrows and draw their bows to the ear.

SECOND VOLLEY. Hurrah!

They notch and draw again.

THIRD VOLLEY. Hurrah!

Lord Salisbury comes up by the stairs.

SALISBURY. Attention! [*They turn and stand at attention*]. Where is the man whose arrow struck the Maid?

An archer steps forward and salutes, grinning.

SALISBURY [*taking a purse from his belt*] You know, all of you, that the Maid is a witch, accurst of God and his saints. [*They salute*]. You know that the only way to destroy a witch's damnable magic is to draw her blood. [*They salute again*]. This purse contains ten gold pieces. This man has drawn the blood of the witch: we have nothing to fear now. The gold is his. Take it in God's holy name. [*He holds out the purse to the archer*].

The highly gratified archer stretches out his hand to take the purse.

A cannon ball splinters a battlement; strikes Salisbury and the archer down, groaning and mortally wounded, scattering the gold pieces in all directions; and shivers the flagstaff, bringing down the standard.

All stare horrorstricken until the report of the cannon follows.

The archers, panicstricken, lower their heads and rush to the stairs, down which they disappear.

The last archer: that is, the least frightened, is tempted by the gold whilst waiting for the stairs to clear.

He picks up two pieces and looks at them doubtfully.

Joan's cannon fires another shot.

The archer shudders; flings away the gold; crosses himself; and runs to the stairs.

Salisbury groans and expires.

The archer is already dead.

Cut to:

The raft with the cannon, as before, but at the bank near the bridge. The men-at-arms are leaping ashore.

D'ALENÇON. That last shot has cleared the top of the tower. They are on the run.

DUNOIS. They will scatter into the country and escape us. We must stop the rout.

JOAN. Thoult do nowt of the sort, Jack. If they scatter into the country so much the better for us. The danger is that theyll cross the bridge to take cover in the town. Thou must blow up the bridge.

DUNOIS. Blow up the Loire bridge! Youre mad.

JOAN. A broken bridge is soon mended. Master Gunner: land thy cannon but leave thy powder aboard and bring what more thou canst lay hands on. The rest of you fetch straw and anything that will burn up quickly and heap it over the powder. I want a fireship.

DUNOIS. But what for? What will you do with it?

JOAN. Anchor it under the bridge; set fire to the straw; and get ashore quick as best we can, sink or swim.

THE SOLDIERS [jubilant] Ay, ay. The Maid is right. Powder there. Straw there. God and the Maid.

Bags of powder and trusses of straw are thrown on board.
Joan sets to stack them.
Soldiers jump from the shore back to the raft to help her.

DUNOIS. I should never have thought of that.

D'ALENÇON. Neither should I.

DUNOIS. We are no use here. We must lead the attack on the tower. Come. [*He springs ashore and hurries off*].

D'ALENÇON. Carry on, Maid. We'll clear out the tower.

The bridgehead, at the foot of the tower. English and Burgundian archers (the Burgundian archers have crossbows) in confusion and terror. Some are still pouring out through the tower gate. Sir William Glasdale and a couple of other knights on horseback arrive and rally them. The movement of the men ceases. They look to him for a lead.

GLASDALE. Steady there, steady. Stand there, will you. All across the bridge, into the town. Follow me.

KNIGHTS. À Glasdale! À Glasdale! Follow up. Across the bridge. This way.

SOLDIERS. À Glasdale! À Glasdale!

They stream off across the bridge.
A big explosion, followed by several minor ones.
Appalling shrieks from the wounded. Cries of terror.
A torrent of fugitives surges back upon the tail of the advance.

FUGITIVES. Fly, fly. Back for your lives. The witch.

AN ENGLISH SERGEANT [collaring a fugitive] What are we to fly for? Stand up to it, you curs. À Glasdale! À Glasdale! What has frightened you, man?

All stop to listen.

THE FUGITIVE. Hell has opened under Glasdale's feet. He has fallen into the bottomless pit, man and horse and hundreds with him. The witch and all her devils are clawing them. Fly.

THE SERGEANT [releasing him] Holy Savior! [He turns and runs].

They all run madly from the bridge.
Dissolve to:
The top of the tower by moonlight. The two corpses lie where they fell. Joan's

standard flies from the broken flagstaff. Joan kneeling in prayer with an expression of intense pity. D'Alençon rushes up the stairway.

D'ALENÇON. What are you doing here? I have been searching for you everywhere.

JOAN. I am praying for the souls of these two poor men.

D'ALENÇON. Pray them into hell, blast them! Dont you see that they are English goddams?

JOAN. Dont be angry with me.

D'ALENÇON. But youve seen hundreds of dead men today. Why need you bother about these two?

JOAN. They looked so lonely. I had to pray for them.

D'ALENÇON. Psha! You must learn when to be a saint and when to be a soldier; for you cant be both at the same time.

JOAN. But the battle is over; and we have won. God has saved France.*

Dissolve to:

A sunny day. A beflagged street in Orleans, the town gate in the background. Church bells ring in victory. A large crowd in the streets, on the roofs, people waving out of the windows. Women, men, children, the aged —all shout themselves hoarse in jubilant cries of The Maid!

Riding in the middle of a procession of victorious troops entering the city, mounted on a white charger, is The Maid. She holds the white banner, blackened by the smoke of battle, torn and slashed.

Close-up: in contrast to the elaborate harness of her horse is the happy and at the same time shyly smiling face of The Maid, acknowledging the acclamations of the crowd.

This close-up of Joan dissolves to:

A close-up of a book with beautiful pictures, a strong, manly hand turning the leaves.

The cries and shouts fade out during the dissolve. Silence. The camera moves back.

A tent in the English camp. An imposing nobleman, aged 46, is seated in a handsome chair turning over the leaves of an illuminated Book of Hours. A bullnecked English chaplain of 50 is sitting on a stool at a table, hard at work writing. The nobleman is enjoying himself: the chaplain is struggling with suppressed wrath.

During the whole of the following scene, the hubbub from the camp at intervals invades the tent. The neighing of horses, the stamping of galloping hooves, shouts, words of command, etc. Rays of the sun illuminate the interior of the tent.

THE NOBLEMAN. Now this is what I call workmanship. There is nothing on earth more exquisite than a bonny book, with well-placed columns in beautiful borders, and illuminated pictures.

THE CHAPLAIN. I must say, my lord, you take our situation very coolly. Very coolly indeed.

THE NOBLEMAN [*supercilious*] What is the matter?

THE CHAPLAIN. The matter, my lord, is that we English have been defeated.

* In the first version of Shaw's *Saint Joan* screenplay, the scene changes at this point to the palace of the Cardinal of Winchester, a new film sequence. See Appendix B for the discarded scene.

THE NOBLEMAN. That happens, you know. It is only in history books and ballads that the enemy is always defeated.

THE CHAPLAIN. But we are being defeated over and over again. Jargeau, Meung, Beaugency, just like Orleans. [*He throws down his pen*]. By God, if this goes on any longer I will fling my cassock to the devil, and take arms myself, and strangle the accursed witch with my own hands.

THE NOBLEMAN. Easy, man, easy: we shall burn the witch and beat the bastard all in good time. Indeed I am waiting at present for the Bishop of Beauvais, to arrange the burning with him. '

A page appears. Behind him, outside, a view of the camp: tents, soldiers, etc.

THE PAGE. The Right Reverend the Bishop of Beauvais: Monseigneur Cauchon.

Cauchon, aged about 60, comes in. The page withdraws. The two Englishmen rise.

THE NOBLEMAN [*with effusive courtesy*] My dear Bishop, how good of you to come! Allow me to introduce myself: Richard de Beauchamp, Earl of Warwick, at your service.

CAUCHON. Your lordship's fame is well known to me.

WARWICK. This reverend cleric is Master John de Stogumber.

THE CHAPLAIN [*glibly*] John Bowyer Spenser Neville de Stogumber. Keeper of the Private Seal to His Eminence the Cardinal of Winchester.

CAUCHON. Messire John de Stogumber: I am always the very good friend of His Eminence. [*He extends his hand to the chaplain, who kisses his ring*].

WARWICK. Do me the honor to be seated. [*He gives Cauchon his chair, placing it at the head of the table*].

Cauchon accepts the place of honor with a grave inclination. Warwick fetches another chair carelessly, and sits in his former place. The chaplain goes back to his chair.

Though Warwick has taken second place in calculated deference to the Bishop, he assumes the lead in opening the proceedings as a matter of course. He is still cordial and expansive; but there is a new note in his voice which means that he is coming to business.

WARWICK. Well, my Lord Bishop, you find us in one of our unlucky moments. Charles is to be crowned at Rheims, practically by the young woman from Lorraine.

During these words, dissolve to:

Coronation day in Rheims.

The procession to the cathedral through the medieval street. Men-at-arms line the pavements and keep the surging crowd pressed back against the houses. Windows and roofs crowded with sightseers. Priests chanting. Folk shouting and throwing flowers.

The procession is headed by Charles on horseback with his peers and churchmen. Behind them a gap in the procession is filled by Joan carrying her banner on her white horse. After her a car representing the city of Orleans. Then archers on foot, etc.

Cut to:

The square in front of the cathedral, of course without the equestrian statue of Joan which now stands there.

Another view of the procession as it enters the cathedral.

Cut to:

The cathedral choir. Coronation anthem being sung.
Charles enthroned in royal robes.
The Archbishop pours the holy oil on his head from a little vial.
Joan sets the crown on his head; then falls on her knees and kisses his hand.
The music rises to a climax.
Dissolve to:
The tent.

WARWICK. I suppose it will make a great difference to Charles's position.

CAUCHON. Undoubtedly. It is a masterstroke of The Maid's.

THE CHAPLAIN [*agitated*] We were not fairly beaten, my lord. No Englishman is every fairly beaten.

CAUCHON raises his eyebrow slightly, then quickly composes his face.

WARWICK. Our friend here takes the view that the young woman is a witch. It would, I presume, be the duty of your reverend lordship to denounce her to the Inquisition, and have her burnt for that offence.

CAUCHON. I am afraid the bare fact that an English army has been defeated by a French one will not convince the court of the Inquisition that there is any witchcraft in the matter. [*Disappointment on the faces of Warwick and the chaplain*] The names on The Maid's white banner were not the names of Satan and Beelzebub, but the blessed names of our Lord and His holy mother.

WARWICK [*looking very dubious*] Well, what are we to infer from all this, my lord? Has The Maid converted you?

CAUCHON. If she had, my lord, I should have known better than to have trusted myself here within your grasp.

WARWICK [*blandly deprecating*] Oh! My lord!

CAUCHON. She is not a witch. She is a heretic.

WARWICK [*speaking after a moment's thought*] My lord: I wipe the slate as far as the witchcraft goes. None the less, we must burn the woman.

CAUCHON. The Church cannot take life. And my first duty is to seek this girl's salvation.

WARWICK. No doubt. But you do burn people occasionally.

CAUCHON. No. When The Church cuts off an obstinate heretic as a dead branch from the tree of life, the heretic is handed over to the secular arm. The Church has no part in what the secular arm may see fit to do.

WARWICK. Precisely. And I shall be the secular arm in this case. Well, my lord, hand over your dead branch; and I will see that the fire is ready for it.

CAUCHON. No, my lord: the soul of this village girl is of equal value with yours or your king's before the throne of God; and if there be a loophole through which this baptized child of God can creep to her salvation, I shall guide her to it.

THE CHAPLAIN [*rising in a fury*] You are a traitor.

CAUCHON [*springing up*] You lie, priest. [*Trembling with rage*] If you dare do what this woman has done—set your country above the holy Catholic Church—you shall go to the fire with her.

THE CHAPLAIN. My lord: I—I went too far. I—[*he sits down with a submissive gesture*].

WARWICK [*who has risen apprehensively*] My lord: I apologize to you for the word used by Messire John de Stogumber. It does not mean in England what it does in France. In your language traitor means betrayer: one who is perfidious, treacherous, unfaithful, disloyal. In our country it means simply one who is not

201

wholly devoted to our English interests.

CAUCHON. I am sorry: I did not understand. [*He subsides into his chair with dignity*].

WARWICK [*resuming his seat, much relieved*] I must apologize on my own account if I have seemed to take the burning of this poor girl too lightly. When one has seen whole countrysides burnt over and over again as mere items in military routine, one has to grow a very thick skin. Otherwise one might go mad: at all events, I should.

THE CHAPLAIN. I speak under correction; only this: but The Maid is full of deceit: she pretends to be devout. Her prayers and confessions are endless. How can she be accused of heresy when she neglects no observance of a faithful daughter of The Church?

CAUCHON [*flaming up*] A faithful daughter of The Church! The Pope himself at his proudest dare not presume as this woman presumes. She acts as if she herself were The Church. She brings the message of God to Charles; and The Church must stand aside. S h e crowns him in the cathedral of Rheims. She sends letters to the king of England giving him God's command through h e r to return to his island on paid of God's vengeance, which s h e will execute. Has she ever in all her utterances said one word of The Church? Never. It is always God and herself. It is not the Mother of God now to whom we must look for intercession, but to Joan the Maid. What will the world be like when The Church's accumulated wisdom and knowledge and experience, its councils of learned, venerable pious men, are thrust into the kennel by every ignorant dairymaid? What will it be when every girl thinks herself a Joan? I shudder to the very marrow of my bones when I think of it. If she does not recant in the dust before the world, and submit herself to the last inch of her soul to her Church, to the fire she shall go.

Warwick obviously considers the result of the conversation to be sufficient for the day. He rises.

WARWICK. My lord: we seem to be agreed.

CAUCHON [*rising also, but in protest*] I will uphold the justice of the Church. I will strive to the utmost for this woman's salvation.

THE CHAPLAIN [*implacably*] I would burn her with my own hands.

Dissolve to:

The ambulatory in the cathedral of Rheims. A pillar bears one of the stations of the cross. Joan is kneeling in prayer before the station. Dunois comes into the ambulatory.

Footsteps and voices echo.

DUNOIS. Come, Joan! you have had enough praying. The streets are full. They are calling for The Maid.

JOAN. No: let the king have all the glory.

DUNOIS. He only spoils the show, poor devil. Come!

Joan shakes her head reluctantly. Dunois raises her.

A short interval.

JOAN. Dear Jack: I think you like me as a soldier likes his comrade.

DUNOIS. You need it, poor innocent child of God. You have not many friends at court.

JOAN. Why do all these courtiers hate me? I have set them right. I have made Charles a real king. Then why do they not love me?

DUNOIS [*rallying her*] Sim-ple-ton! Do ambitious politicians love the climbers who take the front seats from them? Why, I should be jealous of you myself if I were ambitious enough.

JOAN [*looks at him anxiously*] Jack, only for my voices I should lose all heart. That is why I had to steal away to pray here alone after the coronation. I'll tell you something, Jack. It is in the bells I hear my voices. Not today, when they all rang: that was nothing but jangling. But here in this corner, where the echoes linger, or in the fields, where they come from a distance through the quiet of the countryside. [*The cathedral clock chimes the quarter*] Hark! [*She becomes rapt*]. Do you hear? "Dear-child-of-God." But it is at the hour, when the great bell goes, it is then that St Margaret and St Catherine and sometimes even the blessed Michael will say things that I cannot tell beforehand. Then, oh then—

DUNOIS [*interrupting her kindly but not sympathetically*] Then, Joan, we shall hear whatever we fancy in the booming of the bell. I should think you were a bit cracked if I hadnt noticed that you give me very sensible reasons for what you do, though I hear you telling others you are only obeying Madame St Catherine.

JOAN [*crossly*] Well, I have to find reasons for you, because you do not believe in my voices. But the voices come first; and I find the reasons after.

DUNOIS. Are you angry, Joan?

JOAN. Yes. [*Smiling*] No: not with you. I wish you were one of the village babies.

DUNOIS. Why?

JOAN. I could nurse you for a while.

DUNOIS. You are a bit of a woman after all.

JOAN. No: not a bit: I am a soldier and nothing else. Soldiers always nurse children when they get a chance.

DUNOIS. That is true. [*He laughs*].

They go to the nave. The sound of their retreating footsteps is lost in the distance.

Dissolve to:

The portal.

Dunois opens the door; sunlight floods in. He goes out onto the steps with Joan. A crowd outside cheers: The Maid! The Maid!

Dissolve to:

The Archbishop's palace. The view is taken from a hall onto the terrace. In the garden, shrines; in the background, the cathedral. It is a sunny afternoon, but a strong wind moves the trees outside. Clouds hurry across the sky.

When the scene opens Charles is seen hastening towards the Archbishop, who is just returning from a walk in the garden.

CHARLES. Archbishop: The Maid wants to start fighting again.

The camera moves back, bringing Joan, Dunois, Bluebeard and La Hire, in the hall, into the picture.

THE ARCHBISHOP. Have we ceased fighting, then? Are we at peace?

CHARLES. No: but let us be content with what we have done. Let us make a treaty. Our luck is too good to last.

JOAN. Luck! God has fought for us; and you call it luck!

THE ARCHBISHOP [*sternly*] Maid: the king addressed himself to me, not to you. You forget yourself. You very often forget yourself.

JOAN [*unabashed, and rather roughly*] Then speak, you; and tell him that it is not God's will that he should take his hand from the plough.

THE ARCHBISHOP. If I am not so glib with the name of God as you are, it is because I interpret His will with the authority of the Church and of my sacred

203

office. When you first came you respected it, and would not have dared to speak as you are now speaking.

CHARLES. Yes: she thinks she knows better than everyone else.

JOAN. I never speak unless I know I am right.

BLUEBEARD | [exclaiming | Ha ha!
CHARLES | together] | Just so.

THE ARCHBISHOP. How do you know you are right?

JOAN. My voices—

CHARLES. Oh, your voices, your voices. Why dont the voices come to me? I am king, not you.

JOAN. What voices do you need to tell you what the blacksmith can tell you: that you must strike while the iron is hot? I tell you we must make a dash at Compiègne and relieve it as we relieved Orleans. Then Paris will open its gates; or if not, we will break through them. What is your crown worth without your capital?

LA HIRE. That is what I say too. We shall go through them like a red hot shot through a pound of butter. What do you say, Bastard?

They all turn their heads to Dunois enquiringly after his opinion.

JOAN. Jack: tell them what you think.

DUNOIS. I think that God was on your side; for I have not forgotten how the wind changed, and how our hearts changed when you came. But I tell you as a soldier that God is no man's daily drudge, and no maid's either.

JOAN. But—

DUNOIS. Sh! I have not finished. [*Addressing everybody*] I know how much God did for us through The Maid, and how much He left me to do by my own wits; and I tell you that your little hour of miracles is over, and that from this time on he who plays the war game best will win. But Joan goes ahead and trusts to God: she thinks she has God in her pocket. Up to now she has had the numbers on her side; and she has won. But I see that some day she will go ahead when she has only ten men to do the work of a hundred. And then she will find that God is on the side of the big battalions. She will be taken by the enemy. And the lucky man that makes the capture will receive sixteen thousand pounds from the Earl of Ouareek.

JOAN [*flattered*] Sixteen thousand pounds! Eh, laddie, have they offered that for me? There cannot be so much money in the world.

DUNOIS. There is, in England. And now tell me, all of you, which of you will lift a finger to save Joan after she is locked in a dungeon, and the bars and bolts do not fly open at the touch of St Peter's angel? She will not be worth the life of a single soldier to us.

JOAN. Jack: you are right. I am not worth one soldier's life if God lets me be beaten; but France may think me worth my ransom after what God has done for her through me.

CHARLES. I have no money; and this coronation has cost me the last farthing I can borrow.

JOAN. I put my trust in the Church.

THE ARCHBISHOP. Woman: they will drag you through the streets, and burn you as a witch.

JOAN [*running to him*] Oh, my lord, I a witch! Your blessing would protect me.

THE ARCHBISHOP. I have no blessing for you while you are proud and disobedient.

JOAN. Oh, I am a poor girl. I am so ignorant that I do not know A from B. How could I be proud? And how can you say that I am disobedient when I always obey my voices, because they come from God.

THE ARCHBISHOP. The voice of God on earth is the voice of the Church Militant; and all the voices that come to you are the echoes of your own wilfulness.

JOAN. It is not true.

THE ARCHBISHOP [*flushing angrily*] You tell the Archbishop that he lies!

JOAN. I never said you lied. It was you that as good as said my voices lied. When have they ever lied? If you will not believe in them: even if they are only the echoes of my own commonsense, are they not always right? and are not your earthly counsels always wrong?

THE ARCHBISHOP [*indignantly*] It is waste of time admonishing you. The Bastard has told you that if you persist in setting up your military conceit above the counsels of your commanders—

DUNOIS [*interposing*] To put it quite exactly, if you attempt to relieve the garrison in Compiègne without the same superiority in numbers you had at Orleans—

THE ARCHBISHOP [*continuing*] The army will disown you, and will not rescue you. And His Majesty the King has told you that the throne has not the means of ransoming you.

CHARLES. Not a penny.

THE ARCHBISHOP. You stand alone: absolutely alone.

DUNOIS. That is the truth, Joan. Heed it.

JOAN. Where would you all have been now if I had heeded that sort of truth? I thought France would have friends at the court of the king of France; and I find only wolves fighting for pieces of her poor torn body. But I am wiser now; and nobody is any the worse for being wiser. Do not think you can frighten me by telling me that I am alone. France is alone; and God is alone. I see now that the loneliness of God is His strength. Well, my loneliness shall be my strength too; it is better to be alone with God: His friendship will not fail me, nor His counsel, nor His love. In His strength I will dare, and dare, and dare, until I die. I will go out now to the common people, and let the love in their eyes comfort me for the hate in yours.

She goes from them. They stare after her in glum silence.

Joan, silent, determined and rapt, continues her exit through the trees and flowers straight towards the audience to the limit of the focus.

Fade out.

The screen is dark.

The noise of battle.

Fade in:

Dust clouds, horsemen in flight.

VOICES. Back to the town!

JOAN [*galloping into the picture*] No, charge the enemy, for God and France!

A few of her faithfuls attempt to tear back her horse by the bridle: too late!

Burgundian soldiers charge up, surrounding Joan.

Fights with sword and spears on all sides.

A Burgundian soldier grasps Joan close, and tears her out of the saddle.

A close-up of Joan falling.

The expression on her face, an anxious question to her voices —shouts of victory from the Burgundians.
Dissolve to:
The courtyard of the castle at Rouen.
Warwick, Cauchon and two other clerics. A sunny morning.
CAUCHON. I wish your lordship good-morrow.
WARWICK. Good-morrow to your lordship.
CAUCHON [*introducing the monk, who is on his right*] This, my lord, is Brother John Lemaître, of the order of St Dominic. He is acting as deputy for the Chief Inquisitor into the evil of heresy in France. Brother John: the Earl of Warwick.
WARWICK. Your Reverence is most welcome.
The Inquisitor smiles patiently, and bows. He is a mild elderly gentleman, but has evident reserves of authority and firmness.
CAUCHON [*introducing the Canon, who is on his left*] This gentleman is Canon John D'Estivet, of the Chapter of Bayeux. He is acting as Promoter.
WARWICK. Promoter?
CAUCHON. Prosecutor, you would call him in civil law.
WARWICK. Ah! prosecutor. Quite, quite. I am very glad to make your acquaintance, Canon D'Estivet.
D'Estivet bows. He is on the young side of middle age, well mannered, but vulpine beneath his veneer.
WARWICK. May I ask what stage the proceedings have reached? It is fully four months since I bought The Maid from the Burgundians for a very handsome sum. It is very nearly three months since I delivered her up to you, my Lord Bishop, as a person suspected of heresy.
CAUCHON. We have not been idle, my lord. We have held fifteen examinations of The Maid: six public and nine private.
THE INQUISITOR [*always patiently smiling*] Everything is now in order, and we proceed to trial this morning.
WARWICK [*graciously*] Well, that is good news, gentlemen. I will not attempt to conceal from you that our patience was becoming strained. In fact I must tell you now plainly that her death is a political necessity which I regret but cannot help. If the Church lets her go—
CAUCHON [*with fierce and menacing pride*] If the Church lets her go, woe to the man, were he the Emperor himself, who dares lay a finger on her! The Church is not subject to political necessity, my lord.
WARWICK [*looking hard at Cauchon*] I should be sorry to have to act without the blessing of the Church.
CAUCHON. And yet they say Englishmen are hypocrites! You play for your side, my lord, even at the peril of your soul. I dare not go so far myself. I fear damnation.
WARWICK. If we feared anything we could never govern England, my lord.
They look hard at one another.
CAUCHON. It will be very good of your lordship to withdraw and allow the court to assemble.
Warwick goes.
Cauchon, the Inquisitor and D'Estivet begin to walk towards the camera, which moves away from them.
A passage with a number of archers comes into view. They hurry along this

passage into a great stone hall in the castle, arranged for a trial-at-law. There are two raised chairs side by side for the Bishop and the Inquisitor as judges. Rows of chairs radiating from them are for the canons, the doctors of law and theology, and the Dominican monks, who act as assessors. The table is for the scribes, with stools. There is also a heavy rough wooden stool for the prisoner. The court is shielded from the weather by screens and curtains. There are arched doors.

Cauchon takes one of the judicial seats; and D'Estivet sits at the scribes' table, studying his brief.

The Inquisitor takes the other judicial chair on Cauchon's left.

Thirty to forty assessors hurry into the hall, headed by Chaplain de Stogumber and Canon de Courcelles, a young priest of 30. The scribes sit at the table, leaving a chair vacant opposite D'Estivet. Some of the assessors take their seats: others stand chatting, waiting for the proceedings to begin formally. De Stogumber, aggrieved and obstinate, will not take his seat: neither will the Canon, who stands on his right.

CAUCHON [*to the chaplain*] Good morning, Master de Stogumber.

THE CHAPLAIN. I have to make a protest, my lord.

CAUCHON. You make a great many.

THE CHAPLAIN. Here is Master de Courcelles, Canon of Paris, who associates himself with me in my protest.

CAUCHON. Well, what is the matter?

COURCELLES. My lord: we have been at great pains to draw up an indictment of The Maid on sixty-four counts. We are now told that they have been reduced, without consulting us.

THE INQUISITOR. Master de Courcelles: I am the culprit. I am overwhelmed with admiration for the zeal displayed in your sixty-four counts; but in accusing a heretic, as in other things, enough is enough. Therefore I have thought it well to have your sixty-four articles cut down to twelve—

COURCELLES [*thunderstruck*] Twelve!!!

THE INQUISITOR. Pray take your places, gentlemen; and let us proceed to business.

All who have not taken their seats, do so.

THE CHAPLAIN. Well, I protest. [*He sits down*].

THE INQUISITOR. Heresy, gentlemen, heresy is the charge we have to try.

The Inquisitor drops his blandness and speaks very gravely.

In the foreground of the picture a row of heads of the assessors, etc. Further back, the Inquisitor.

THE INQUISITOR [*continuing*] You are going to see before you a young girl, pious and chaste; for I must tell you, gentlemen, that the things said of her by our English friends are supported by no evidence, whilst there is abundant testimony that her excesses have been excesses of religion and charity and not of worldliness and wantonness. This girl is not one of those whose hard features are the sign of hard hearts, and whose brazen looks and lewd demeanor condemn them before they are accused. The devilish pride that has led her into her present peril has left no mark on her countenance. It has even left no mark on her character; so that you will see a diabolical pride and a natural humility seated side by side in the selfsame soul. Therefore be on your guard. God forbid that I should tell you to harden your hearts; for her punishment if we condemn her will be so cruel that we should forfeit our own hope of divine mercy were there one grain of malice against her in our hearts. But if you hate cruelty—[*The picture now shews the heads of assessors on the other side, and again further backwards, the Inquisitor*] and if any man here does not hate it I command him on his soul's salvation to quit this holy court—I say, if you hate cruelty, remember that nothing is so cruel in its consequences as the toleration of heresy. Remember also that no court of law can be so cruel as the common people are to those whom they suspect of heresy. The heretic in the hands of the Holy Office is safe from violence, is assured of a fair trial, and cannot suffer death, even when guilty, if repentance follows sin. Innumerable lives of heretics have been saved because the Holy Office has taken them out of the hands of the people, and because the people have yielded them up, knowing that the Holy Office would deal with them. [*Close-up of the Inquisitor*] Gentlemen: I am compassionate by nature as well as by my profession; and though the work I have to do may seem cruel to those who do not know how much more cruel it would be to leave it undone, I would go to the stake myself sooner than do it if I did not know its righteousness, its necessity, its essential mercy. I ask you [*view of the entire court*] to address yourself to this trial in that conviction. Anger is a bad counsellor: cast out anger. Pity is sometimes worse: cast out pity. But do not cast out mercy. Remember only that justice comes first. [*Close-up of the Inquisitor. The camera pans to Cauchon*]. Have you anything to say, my lord, before we proceed to trial?

CAUCHON. You have spoken for me, and spoken better than I could.

THE INQUISITOR. Let the accused be brought in.

LADVENU [*calling*] The accused. Let her be brought in.

Joan, chained by the ankles, is brought in by a guard of English soldiers. With them is the Executioner and his assistants. They lead her to the prisoner's stool, and place themselves behind it after taking off her chain. She wears a page's black suit. Her long imprisonment and the strain of the examinations which have preceded the trial have left their mark on her; but her vitality still holds: she confronts the court unabashed, without a trace of the awe which their formal solemnity seems to require.

The following trail scene may be enlivened by a succession of close-ups strung together by quick dissolves and cuts.

THE INQUISITOR [*kindly*] Sit down, Joan. [*She sits on the prisoner's stool*]. You look very pale today. Are you not well?

JOAN. Thank you kindly: I am well enough. But the Bishop sent me some carp; and it made me ill.

CAUCHON. I am sorry. I told them to see that it was fresh.

JOAN. You meant to be good to me, I know; but it is a fish that does not agree with me. The English thought you were trying to poison me—

| CAUCHON | [*together*] | What! |
| THE CHAPLAIN | | No, my lord. |

JOAN [*continuing*] The English are determined that I shall be burnt as a witch; and they sent their doctor to cure me; but he was forbidden to bleed me because the silly people believe that a witch's witchery leaves her if she is bled. Why do you leave me in the hands of the English? I should be in the hands of the Church. And why must I be chained by the feet to a log of wood? Are you afraid I will fly away?

D'ESTIVET. Woman: it is not for you to question the court!

COURCELLES. When you were left unchained, did you not try to escape by

Caesar and Cleopatra   Advertisement in unidentified American magazine.

Caesar and Cleopatra   On the set at Denham Studios. Gabriel Pascal, Cecil Parker and Bernard Shaw.

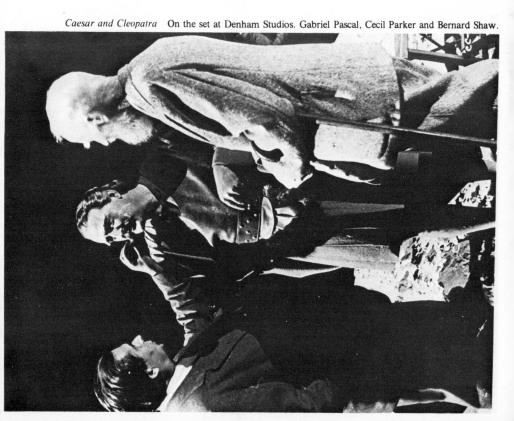

Caesar and Cleopatra The men rise when they hear Pothinus's death cry. Stewart Granger, Vivien Leigh, Basil Sydney and Claude Rains.

Arms and the Man Petkoff and Catherine respond to Sergius embracing Louka. Frederick Lloyd, Margaret Scudamore, Angela Baddeley and Maurice Colbourne.

jumping from a tower sixty feet high? If you cannot fly like a witch, how is it that you are still alive?

JOAN. I suppose because the tower was not so high then. It has grown higher every day since you began asking me questions about it.

D'ESTIVET. Why did you jump from the tower?

JOAN. Why would anybody leave a prison if they could get out?

D'ESTIVET. You tried to escape?

JOAN. Of course I did.

D'ESTIVET [rising] That is a confession of heresy. I call the attention of the court to it.

JOAN. Heresy, he calls it! Am I a heretic because I try to escape from prison?

D'ESTIVET. If you are in the hands of the Church, and you wilfully take yourself out of its hands, you are deserting the Church; and that is heresy.

JOAN. It is great nonsense. Nobody could be such a fool as to think that.

D'ESTIVET. You hear, my lord, how I am reviled in the execution of my duty by this woman. [He sits down indignantly].

CAUCHON. I have warned you before, Joan, that you are doing yourself no good by these pert answers.

JOAN. But you will not talk sense to me. I am reasonable if you will be reasonable.

THE INQUISITOR [interposing] This is not yet in order. You forget, Master Promoter, that the proceedings have not been formally opened. The time for questions is after she has sworn on the Gospels to tell us the whole truth.

JOAN. I have said again and again that I will tell you all that concerns this trial. But I cannot tell you the whole truth: God does not allow the whole truth to be told. You do not understand it when I tell it. I am weary of this argument: we have been over it nine times already. I have sworn as much as I will swear; and I will swear no more.

COURCELLES. My lord: she should be put to the torture.

THE INQUISITOR. You hear, Joan? That is what happens to the obdurate. Has she been shewn the instruments?

THE EXECUTIONER. They are ready, my lord. She has seen them.

JOAN. If you tear me limb from limb until you separate my soul from my body you will get nothing out of me beyond what I have told you. Besides, I cannot bear to be hurt; and if you hurt me I will say anything you like. But I will take it all back afterwards; so what is the use of it?

LADVENU. There is much in that. We should proceed mercifully.

COURCELLES. But the torture is customary.

THE INQUISITOR. If the accused will confess voluntarily, then its use cannot be justified.

COURCELLES. But she refuses to take the oath.

LADVENU [disgusted] Do you want to torture the girl for the mere pleasure of it?

COURCELLES [bewildered] But it is not a pleasure. It is the law. It is always done.

CAUCHON [decisively] It will not be done today if it is not necessary.

COURCELLES. Your lordship is merciful, of course. But it is a great responsibility to depart from the usual practice.

JOAN. Thou art a rare noodle, Master. Do what was done last time is thy rule, eh?

COURCELLES [*rising*] Thou wanton: dost thou dare call me noodle?
THE INQUISITOR. Patience, Master, patience: I fear you will soon be only too terribly avenged.
COURCELLES [*mutters*] Noodle indeed! [*He sits down, much discontented*].
THE INQUISITOR. Meanwhile, let us not be moved by the rough side of a shepherd lass's tongue.
JOAN. Nay: I am no shepherd lass.
THE INQUISITOR. This is not a time for vanity, Joan. You stand in great peril.
JOAN. I know it: have I not been punished for my vanity? If I had not worn my cloth of gold surcoat in battle like a fool, that Burgundian soldier would never have pulled me off my horse; and I should not have been here.
THE CHAPLAIN. If you are so clever at woman's work why do you not stay at home and do it?
JOAN. There are plenty of other women to do it; but there is nobody to do my work.
CAUCHON. Come! we are wasting time on trifles. Joan: I am going to put a most solemn question to you. Take care how you answer; for your life and salvation are at stake on it. Will you for all you have said and done, be it good or bad, accept the judgment of God's Church on earth? Will you submit your case to the Church?
JOAN. I am a faithful child of the Church. I will obey the Church—
CAUCHON [*hopefully leaning forward*] You will?
Joan.—provided it does not command anything impossible.
Cauchon sinks back in his chair with a heavy sigh.
D'ESTIVET. She imputes to the Church the error and folly of commanding the impossible.
JOAN. If you command me to declare that all that I have done and said, and all the visions and revelations I have had, were not from God, then that is impossible: I will not declare it for anything in the world. And in case the Church should bid me do anything contrary to the command I have from God, I will not consent to it, no matter what it may be.
THE ASSESSORS [*shocked and indignant*] Oh! The Church contrary to God! Flat heresy. This is beyond everything!
D'ESTIVET [*throwing down his brief*] My lord: do you need anything more than this?
CAUCHON. Woman: you have said enough to burn ten heretics. Will you not be warned? Will you not understand?
THE INQUISITOR. If the Church Militant tells you that your revelations and visions are sent by the devil to tempt you to your damnation, will you not believe that the Church is wiser than you?
JOAN. I believe that God is wiser than I; all the things that you call my crimes have come to me by the command of God. I say that I have done them by the order of God. If any Churchman says the contrary I shall not mind him.
LADVENU [*pleading with her urgently*] You do not know what you are saying, child. Do you want to kill yourself? Listen. Do you not believe that you are subject to the Church of God on earth?
JOAN. Yes. When have I ever denied it?
LADVENU. Good. That means, does it not, that you are subject to our Lord the Pope, to the cardinals, the archbishops, and the bishops for whom his lordship

stands here today?

JOAN. God must be served first.

D'ESTIVET. Then your voices command you not to submit yourself to the Church Militant?

JOAN. My voices do not tell me to disobey the Church; but God must be served first.

CAUCHON. And you, and not the Church, are to be the judge?

JOAN. What other judgment can I judge by but my own?

THE ASSESSORS [scandalized] Oh! [They cannot find words].

CAUCHON. Dare you pretend, after what you have said, that you are in a state of grace?

JOAN. If I am not, may God bring me to it: if I am, may God keep me in it!

LADVENU. That is a very good reply, my lord.

D'ESTIVET. With great respect, I must emphasize the gravity of two blasphemous crimes. First, she wears men's clothes, which is indecent, unnatural, and abominable. Second, she has intercourse with evil spirits.

JOAN. Is the blessed St Catherine an evil spirit? Is St Margaret? Is Michael the Archangel?

COURCELLES. How do you know that the spirit which appears to you is an archangel? Does he not appear to you as a naked man?

JOAN. Do you think God cannot afford clothes for him?

The assessors cannot help smiling, especially as the joke is against Courcelles.

THE INQUISITOR. For the last time, will you put off that impudent attire, and dress as becomes your sex?

JOAN. I will not.

D'ESTIVET [pouncing] The sin of disobedience, my lord.

JOAN [distressed] But my voices tell me I must dress as a soldier.

LADVENU. Joan, Joan: does not that prove to you that the voices are the voices of evil spirits? Can you suggest to us one good reason why an angel of God should give you such shameless advice?

JOAN. Why, yes: what can be plainer commonsense? I was a soldier living among soldiers. I am a prisoner guarded by soldiers. If I were to dress as a woman they would think of me as a woman; if I dress as a soldier they think of me as a soldier, and I can live with them as I do at home with my brothers. That is why St Catherine tells me I must not dress as a woman until she gives me leave.

COURCELLES. When will she give you leave?

JOAN. When you take me out of the hands of the English soldiers. Do you want me to live with them in petticoats?

LADVENU. My lord: what she says is, God knows, very wrong and shocking; but there is a grain of worldly sense in it such as might impose on a simple village maiden.

JOAN. If we were as simple in the village as you are in your courts and palaces, there would soon be no wheat to make bread for you.

CAUCHON. That is the thanks you get for trying to save her, Brother Martin.

LADVENU. Joan: we are all trying to save you. His lordship is trying to save you. The Inquisitor could not be more just to you if you were his own daughter. But you are blinded by a terrible pride and self-sufficiency.

JOAN. Why do you say that? I have said nothing wrong. I cannot understand.

THE INQUISITOR. The blessed St Athanasius has laid it down in his creed that those who cannot understand are damned. The simplicity of a darkened mind is no better than the simplicity of a beast.

JOAN. There is great wisdom in the simplicity of a beast, let me tell you; and sometimes great foolishness in the wisdom of scholars.

LADVENU. Joan: do you see that man who stands behind you [*he indicates the Executioner*]?

JOAN [*turning and looking at the man*] Your torturer? But the Bishop said I was not to be tortured.

LADVENU. That man is not only the torturer: he is also the Executioner. [*Calling on the Executioner*] Are you prepared for the burning of a heretic this day?

THE EXECUTIONER. Yes, Master.

LADVENU. Is the stake ready?

THE EXECUTIONER. It is. In the market-place. The English have built it too high for me to get near her and make the death easier.

JOAN [*horrified*] But you are not going to burn me now?

THE INQUISITOR. You realize it at last.

LADVENU. There are eight hundred English soldiers waiting to take you to themarket-place the moment the sentence of excommunication has passed the lips of your judges.

JOAN [*looking round desperately for rescue*] Oh God!

LADVENU. Do not despair, Joan. The Church is merciful. You can save yourself.

JOAN [*hopefully*] Yes: my voices promised me I should not be burnt. St Catherine bade me be bold.

CAUCHON. Woman: are you quite mad? Do you not yet see that your voices have deceived you?

JOAN. Oh no: that is impossible.

LADVENU [*pressing the point hard*] Have your voices kept a single promise to you since you were taken at Compiègne? The devil has betrayed you. The Church holds out its arms to you.

JOAN [*despairing*] Oh, it is true: it is true: my voices have deceived me. I have been mocked by devils. I have dared and dared; but only a fool will walk into a fire: God, who gave me my commonsense, cannot will me to do that.

LADVENU. Now God be praised that He has saved you at the eleventh hour! [*He hurries to the vacant seat at the scribes' table, and snatches a sheet of paper, on which he sets to work writing eagerly*].

CAUCHON. Amen!

JOAN. What must I do?

CAUCHON. You must sign a solemn recantation of your heresy.

JOAN. Sign? I cannot write.

CAUCHON. You have signed many letters before.

JOAN. Yes; but someone held my hand and guided the pen. I can make my mark.

THE CHAPLAIN [*who has been listening with growing alarm and indignation*] My lord: do you mean that you are going to allow this woman to escape us?

THE INQUISITOR. Master de Stogumber, you know the law.

THE CHAPLAIN [*rising, purple with fury*] I know what the Earl of Warwick will do when he hears of it. There are eight hundred men at the gate who will see that this abominable witch is burnt in spite of your teeth.

THE ASSESSORS [*meanwhile*] What is this? This is an intolerable fellow. He must be mad or drunk.

THE INQUISITOR [*rising*] Silence, pray! Gentlemen: pray silence! Master Chaplain: bethink you of your holy office: I direct you to sit down.

THE CHAPLAIN [*folding his arms doggedly, his face working convulsively*] I will NOT sit down.

THE INQUISITOR [*placidly resuming his seat*] If you will not sit, you must stand: that is all.

THE CHAPLAIN. I will NOT stand [*he flings himself back into his chair*].

LADVENU [*rising with the paper in his hand*] My lord: here is the form of recantation for The Maid to sign.

CAUCHON. Read it to her.

JOAN. Do not trouble. I will sign it.

THE INQUISITOR. You must know what you are putting your hand to.

LADVENU [*reading quietly*] "I, Joan, commonly called The Maid, a miserable sinner, do confess that I have most grievously sinned in the following articles. I have pretended to have revelations from God and the angels and the blessed saints, and perversely rejected the Church's warnings that these were temptations by demons. I have blasphemed abominably by wearing an immodest dress, contrary to the Holy Scripture and the canons of the Church. Also I have clipped my hair in the style of a man. I have incited men to slay each other, invoking evil spirits to delude them, and stubbornly and most blasphemously imputing these sins to Almight God. All of which sins I now renounce and abjure and I will never return to my errors, but will remain in communion with our Holy Church and in obedience to our Holy Father the Pope of Rome. All this I swear by God Almighty and the Holy Gospels, in witness whereto I sign my name to this recantation."

THE INQUISITOR. You understand this, Joan?

JOAN [*listless*] It is plain enough, sir.

THE INQUISITOR. And it is true?

JOAN. It may be true. If it were not true, the fire would not be ready for me in the market-place.

LADVENU [*taking up his pen and a book, and going to her quickly lest she should compromise herself again*] Come, child: let me guide your hand. Take the pen. [*She does so; and they begin to write, using the book as a desk*] J.E.H.A.N.E. So. Now make your mark by yourself.

JOAN [*makes her mark, and gives him back the pen, tormented by the rebellion of her soul against her mind and body*] There!

LADVENU [*replacing the pen on the table, and handing the recantation to Cauchon with a reverence*] Praise be to God, my brothers, the lamb has returned to the flock; and the shepherd rejoices in her more than in ninety and nine just persons. [*He returns to his seat*].

THE INQUISITOR [*taking the paper from Cauchon*] We declare thee by this act set free from the danger of excommunication in which thou stoodest. [*He throws the paper down to the table*]. But that thou mayst repent thy errors in solitary contemplation, and be shielded from all temptation to return to them, we, for the good of thy soul and for a penance, do condemn thee to eat the bread of sorrow and drink the water of affliction to the end of thy earthly days in perpetual imprisonment.

JOAN [*rising in terrible anger*] Perpetual imprisonment! Am I not then to be set free?

LADVENU [*mildly shocked*] Set free, child, after such wickedness as yours! What are you dreaming of?

JOAN. Give me that writing. [*She rushes to the table; snatches up the paper; and tears it into fragments*] Light your fire: do you think I dread it as much as the life of a rat in a hole? My voices were right.

LADVENU. Joan! Joan!

JOAN. Yes: they told me you were fools [*the word gives great offence*]. You promised me my life; but you lied [*indignant exclamations*]. You think that life is nothing but not being stone dead. I could do without my warhorse; I could drag about in a skirt; I could let the banners and the trumpets and the knights and soldiers pass me and leave me behind as they leave the other women, if only I could still hear the wind in the trees, the larks in the sunshine, and the blessed blessed church bells that send my angel voices floating to me on the wind. But without these things I cannot live; and by your wanting to take them away from me, or from any human creature, I know that your counsel is of the devil, and that mine is of God.

THE ASSESSORS [*in great commotion*] Blasphemy! blasphemy! She is possessed. The devil is in our midst.

D'ESTIVET [*shouting above the din*] She is a relapsed heretic. I call for her excommunication.

THE CHAPLAIN [*to the Executioner*] Light your fire, man. To the stake with her.

   The Executioner and his assistants hurry out through the courtyard.

LADVENU. You wicked girl: if your counsel were of God would He not deliver you?

JOAN. His ways are not your ways. He wills that I go through the fire to His bosom; for I am His child, and you are not fit that I should live among you. That is my last word to you.

   The soldiers seize her.

CAUCHON [*rising*] Not yet.

   They wait. Cauchon turns to the Inquisitor with an inquiring look. The Inquisitor nods affirmatively, also rising. They intone the sentence antiphonally.

CAUCHON. We decree that thou art a relapsed heretic.

THE INQUISITOR. Cast out from the unity of the Church.

CAUCHON. Sundered from her body.

THE INQUISITOR. We declare that thou must be excommunicate.

CAUCHON. And now we abandon thee to the secular power.

   The Inquisitor resumes his seat.

CAUCHON. If any true sign of penitence appear in thee, we permit our Brother Martin to administer to thee the sacramet of penance.

THE CHAPLAIN. Into the fire with the witch! [*He rushes at her, and helps the soldiers to push her out*].

   The assessors rise in disorder. Excited exclamation and shouts.

CAUCHON. This is irregular. The representative of the secular arm should be here to receive her from us.

THE INQUISITOR. That man is an incorrigible fool.

CAUCHON. Brother Martin: see that everything is done in order.

LADVENU. My place is at her side, my lord. You must exercise your own authority. [*He hurries out*].

Fade out.

The screen is dark. The sound of church bells from near and afar, high pitched, booming, and clashing peals clang together for several seconds. Then:

Gradual fade in (the bells continue):

A chattering mob of sightseers crowding the steps of a church in a street between the Palace and the market place.

A British man-at-arms, off duty, is out to see the fun. He is not on the steps but in the foreground.

The noise of the approaching show is heard. All become silent and turn in that direction. Some are eager and curious, some are gaping stupidly, a few picked faces register pity or horror.

A squad of mounted soldiers forces a way through the crowd. Following them a body of men-at-arms marching in ordered files. Then Joan, in a white shift, hurried along by three or four soldiers. De Stogumber is close on her heels, pushing her savagely as she hangs back, piteously begging for a cross. Ladvenu is with him, full of pity, but useless. She is trying to stop; but the men-at-arms drag, and De Stogumber pushes, not continuously but with violent gestures.

JOAN. A cross. I want a cross. There is one in the church. You have no right to keep my Savior from me.

THE CHAPLAIN. Witch. Sorceress. Strike her on her blaspheming mouth. To the fire with her.

LADVENU [*remonstrating*] Brother, brother—

JOAN [*as she is dragged away*] Oh, is there no child of Christ here who will give me a blessed cross—[*she is pushed so violently that she falls. A soldier drags her up again*].

THE SOLDIER. Come on, will you.

THE CHAPLAIN [*kicking at her*] On, strumpet. On, sorceress. To the fire. To the fire.

She is whirled away. Further ordered files bring up the rear. The crowd closes in behind them and follows. Ladvenu remains, heartbroken, waiting for the crowd to clear off the church steps.

The man-at-arms, who is troubled with a lively desire to kick De Stogumber, also remains.

Among the stragglers are several porters with bundles of faggots on their shoulders. Some of them are women.

Ladvenu, the steps being now clear, rushes into the church.

The man-at-arms suddenly pounces on the last straggling porter, an old woman; tears the bundle from her shoulders and takes a stick out of it; lifts the bundle and thumps it on her shoulders again; gives her a coin.

OLD WOMAN. God save your honor. Long live the goddams!

She hobbles off.

The man-at-arms sets the stick leaning against the lowest church step, and strikes it in the middle with his foot, breaking it in two.

He picks up the pieces; sits down on the steps; takes an old bowstring out of his pouch; and ties the two pieces of stick into the form of a cross.

Ladvenu hurries out of the church carrying a processional cross —a gold cross on a long black staff.

MAN-AT-ARMS. Thats no use, father. She cant take that into the fire with her. I bet she prefers this. Here! [*holding out the sticks*] consecrate it for her.

LADVENU [*touching it*] In the name of the Father, the Son and the Holy Ghost, Amen. And for this be all your sins forgiven to you. [*He rushes off after the procession*

The man-at-arms runs after him.

Cut to:

Long shot.

The market place, Rouen; many men-at-arms.

Crowd, the stake.

Close-up of the stake and platform.

Wisps of smoke are curling round the platform.

The executioner comes up the ladder.*

THE EXECUTIONER [*seizing Ladvenu and drawing him to the ladder*] Now, father. Down quickly. The fires I make are not to be trifled with.

JOAN. Oh yes, father, go. Go quickly; and God bless you for ever and ever.

THE EXECUTIONER. Quick, before the oil catches.

He drags Ladvenu down the ladder.

Joan is left without the cross.

An expression of anguish comes on her face.

THE VOICE OF THE MAN-AT-ARMS. Hi, Judy, look! Catch!

Joan's face lights up as she looks. She stretches out her arms hungrily for the cross of two sticks. It flies up from below. She catches it and hugs it to her breast.

There is a moment of terrible expectation.

Then the oil catches and a great wall of flame shoots up and hides her.

JOAN [*in the fire*] Jesus! Jesus! Jesus!

Dissolve to:

The great stone hall in the castle where the trial was held.

Nobody is present; the evening sun casts long and narrow shadows.

WARWICK'S VOICE. Hallo. [*Silence*] Hallo, there! [*Silence*].

Warwick appears in the background under the arch.

WARWICK. Hallo! [*Silence*].

The silence is broken by someone frantically howling and sobbing.

WARWICK. What in the devil's name—?

The chaplain staggers in from the back, passing Warwick, his face streaming with tears. He stumbles to the prisoner's stool, and throws himself upon it with heartrending sobs.

WARWICK [*going to him*] What is it, Master John?

THE CHAPLAIN [*clutching at his hand*] My lord, my lord: for Christ's sake pray for my wretched guilty soul.

WARWICK [*soothing him*] Yes, yes.

THE CHAPLAIN [*blubbering miserably*] I did not know what it would be like; when you see the thing you have done; when it is blinding your eyes, stifling your nostrils, tearing your heart, then—then—[*Falling on his knees*] O God, take away this sight from me! O Christ, deliver me from this fire that is consuming me! She cried to T h e e in the midst of it. She is in T h y bosom; and I am in hell for evermore.

WARWICK [*summarily hauling him to his feet*] Come come, man! you must pull yourself together. We shall have the whole town talking of this. [*He throws him not too gently into a chair at the table*] If you have not the nerve to see these things, why do you not do as I do, and stay away?

THE CHAPLAIN [*bewildered and submissive*] She asked for a cross. A soldier gave her two sticks tied together. Thank God he was an Englishman!

WARWICK. Hush! Someone is coming.

Ladvenu appears in the archway. He carries a bishop's cross. He is very grave and composed.

WARWICK. I am informed that it is all over, Brother Martin.

LADVENU [*enigmatically*] We do not know, my lord. It may have only just begun.

WARWICK. What does that mean, exactly?

LADVENU. I took this cross from the church for her that she might see it to the last. When the fire crept round us, and she saw that if I held the cross before her I should be burnt myself, she warned me to get down and save myself. My lord: a girl who could think of another's danger in such a moment was not inspired by the devil. When I had to snatch the cross from her sight, she looked up to heaven. And I do not believe that the heavens were empty. I firmly believe that her Savior appeared to her then in His tenderest glory. She called to Him and died. This is not the end for her, but the beginning.

Silence.

The distant bell continues to ring.

THE CHAPLAIN [*rising frantically, shrieking*] I will go pray among her ashes. [*He rushes wildly out*]. I am no better than Judas: I will hang myself.

WARWICK. Quick, Brother Martin: follow him: he will do himself some mischief. After him, quick.

Ladvenu hurries out.

Warwick alone. He walks towards the camera, with the expression of an undefined sentiment. From the side, a door is heard opening, and somebody enters. Warwick looks up: it is the Executioner.

THE EXECUTIONER. I am come to tell your lordship that your orders have been obeyed.

Warwick nods, wrapt in thought.

WARWICK. Master Executioner: I have your word, have I, that nothing remains, not a bone, not a nail, not a hair?

THE EXECUTIONER. Her heart would not burn, my lord; but everything that was left is at the bottom of the river. You have heard the last of her.

WARWICK [*with a wry smile, thinking of what Ladvenu said*] The last of her? Hm! I wonder!

Warwick says these words in a significant close-up, which slowly dissolves to the title:

EPILOGUE

Superimposed over this title appears the subtitle:

A NIGHT IN JUNE 1456

The title gradually dissolves to a wide terrace window. The outlines of a park can be distinguished in the darkness outside.

Distant thunder; flashes of lightning on the horizon. The camera moves back into the room, revealing Charles lying in bed. The bed is raised on a dais of two steps; its canopy bears the royal arms in embroidery. Except for the canopy and the huge down pillows there is nothing to distinguish it from a broad settee with bed clothes and a valance.

Charles is asleep. On his left is a little table with a picture of the Virgin, lighted by candles. A distant clock strikes the half-hour softly. An open book lies on the bed; it contains pictures of Fouquet's Boccaccio.

The camera pans and again brings the wide terrace window in the background into the picture. It is a very high window. Flashes of lightning, distant thunder.

Suddenly a gust of wind throws open the casements. The candles flicker. For several moments, bright flashes of lightning, illuminating a figure standing on the threshold.

CHARLES [*crying out in his sleep*] Who is there? Help! Murder!

JOAN. Easy, Charlie, easy. No one can hear thee. Thourt asleep.

She is dimly seen in a pallid light by the bedside. The window is still open; the wind sweeping through the trees outside makes a rushing sound in the leaves.

CHARLES [*peeping from underneath the bedclothes*] Joan! Are you a ghost, Joan?

The light grows brighter; she is plainly visible. He sits up.

JOAN. I am but a dream that thourt dreaming. Thou looks older, lad.

CHARLES. Am I really asleep?

JOAN. Fallen asleep over thy silly book.

CHARLES. Are you really dead?

JOAN. As dead as anybody ever is, laddie. I am out of the body.

CHARLES. Did it hurt much?

JOAN. Did what hurt much?

CHARLES. Being burnt.

JOAN. Oh, t h a t ! I cannot remember very well. I think it did at first; but then it all got mixed up; and I was not in my right mind. How hast been ever since?

CHARLES. Oh, not so bad. Do you know, I actually lead my army out and win battles?

JOAN. No! Did I make a man of thee after all, Charlie? Now tell me what has happened since you wise men knew no better than to make a heap of cinders of me?

CHARLES. Your case was tried over again. And the courts have declared that the sentence on you is broken, annihilated, annulled: null, non-existent, without value or effect.

JOAN. I was burned, all the same. Can they unburn me?

CHARLES. If they could, they would think twice before they did it. But I think you might say a word of thanks to me for having had justice done at last.

CAUCHON [*appearing at the window between them*] Liar!

CHARLES. Thank you.

JOAN. Why, if it isnt Peter Cauchon!

CAUCHON. I arraign the justice of Man. It is not the justice of God.

JOAN. Still dreaming of justice, Peter? See what justice came to with me! But what has happened to thee? Art dead or alive?

CAUCHON. Dead. Dishonored. They pursued me beyond the grave. They excommunicated my dead body: they dig it up and flung it into the common sewer. Yet God is my witness I was just: I was merciful: I was faithful to my light: I could do no other than I did.

CHARLES [*scrambling out of the sheets and enthroning himself on the side of the bed*] You people with your heads in the sky spend all your time trying to turn the world upside down; but I take the world as it is, and say that top-side-up is right-side-up; and I keep my nose pretty close to the ground.

JOAN. Be the English gone?

DUNOIS [*coming through the darkness on Joan's left, the candles relighting themselves at the same moment, and illuminating his armor and surcoat cheerfully*] The English are gone.

JOAN. Praised be God! Jack: wert thou God's captain to thy death?

DUNOIS. I am not dead. My body is very comfortably asleep in my bed at Chateaudun; but my spirit is called here by yours. I give you best, lassie. I wrote a fine letter to set you right at the new trial. Perhaps I should never have let the priests burn you; but I was busy fighting; and it was the Church's business, not mine. There was no use in both of us being burned, was there?

A long gentle knocking is heard.

CHARLES. Come in.

The door opens; and an old priest, white-haired, bent, with a silly but benevolent smile, comes in and trots over to Joan.

THE NEWCOMER. Excuse me, gentle lords and ladies. Do not let me disturb you. Only a poor old harmless English rector. Formerly chaplain to the cardinal: to my lord of Winchester. [*He looks at them inquiringly*] Did you say anything? I am a little deaf, unfortunately. Also a little—well, not always in my right mind, perhaps.

JOAN. Poor old John! What brought thee to this state?

THE CHAPLAIN. I tell my folks they must be very careful. I say to them, "If you only saw what you think about you would think quite differently about it. It would give you a great shock." And they all say "Yes, parson: we all know you are a kind man, and would not harm a fly." That is a great comfort to me, for once I did a very cruel thing, because I did not know what cruelty was like. I had not seen it, you know. That is the great thing: you must see it. And then you are redeemed and saved.

JOAN. Well, if I saved all those he would have been cruel to if he had not been cruel to me, I was not burnt for nothing, was I?

THE CHAPLAIN. Oh no; it was not you. My sight is bad: I cannot distinguish your features: but you are not she: oh no: she was burned to a cinder: dead and gone.

THE EXECUTIONER [*stepping from behind the bed curtains on Charles's right, the bed being between them*] She is more alive than you, old man. I was a master at my craft: better than the master of Paris; but I could not kill The Maid. She is up and alive everywhere.

WARWICK [*sallying from the bed curtains on the other side, and coming to Joan's left hand*] Madam: my congratulations on your rehabilitation. I feel that I owe you an apology.

JOAN. Oh, please dont mention it.

WARWICK [*pleasantly*] The burning was purely political.

JOAN. I bear no malice, my lord.

WARWICK. Just so. Very kind of you to meet me in that way. The truth is, these political necessities sometimes turn out to be political mistakes; and this one was a veritable howler; for your spirit conquered us, madam, in spite of our faggots.

A clerical-looking gentleman in black frockcoat and trousers, and tall hat, in the fashion of the year 1920, suddenly appears before them in the corner on their right. They all stare at him. Then they burst into uncontrollable laughter.

THE GENTLEMAN. Why this mirth, gentlemen?

WARWICK. I congratulate you on having invented a most extraordinarily comic dress.

THE GENTLEMAN. I do not understand. You are all in fancy dress: I am properly dressed.

DUNOIS. All dress is fancy dress, is it not, except our natural skins?

THE GENTLEMAN. Pardon me: I am here on serious business, and cannot engage in frivolous discussions. [*He takes out a paper, and assumes a dry official manner*]. I am sent to announce to you that Joan of Arc, formerly known as The Maid, having been the subject of an inquiry instituted by the Bishop of Orleans—

JOAN [*interrupting*] Ah! They remember me still in Orleans.

THE GENTLEMAN [*emphatically, to mark his indignation at the interruption*]— by the Bishop of Orleans into the claim of the said Joan of Arc to be canonized as a saint—

JOAN [*again interrupting*] But I never made any such claim.

THE GENTLEMAN [*as before*]—the Church has examined the claim exhaustively in the usual course, and, having admitted the said Joan successively to the ranks of Venerable and Blessed—

JOAN [*chuckling*] Me venerable!

THE GENTLEMAN.—has finally declared her to have been endowed with heroic virtues and favored with private revelations, and calls the said Venerable and Blessed Joan to the communion of the Church Triumphant as Saint Joan.

JOAN [*rapt*] Saint Joan!

THE GENTLEMAN. On every thirtieth day of May, being the anniversary of the death of the said most blessed daughter of God, there shall in every Catholic church to the end of time be celebrated a special office in commemoration of her; and it shall be lawful to dedicate a special chapel to her, and to place her image on its altar in every such church. And it shall be lawful and laudable for the faithful to kneel and address their prayers through her to the Mercy Seat.

JOAN. Oh no. It is for the saint to kneel. [*She falls on her kness, still rapt*].

THE GENTLEMAN [*putting up his paper, and retiring beside the Executioner*] In Basilica Vaticana, the sixteenth day of May, nineteen hundred and twenty.

DUNOIS [*raising Joan*] Half an hour to burn you, dear Saint: and four centuries to find out the truth about you!

The Archbishop and the Inquisitor are now seen on the right and left of Cauchon.

CAUGHON [*kneeling to her*] The girls in the field praise thee; for thou hast raised their eyes; and they see that there is nothing between them and heaven.

DUNOIS [*kneeling to her*] The dying soldiers praise thee, because thou art a shield of glory between them and the judgment.

THE ARCHBISHOP [*kneeling to her*] The princes of the Church praise thee, because thou hast redeemed the faith.

WARWICK [*kneeling to her*] The cunning counsellors praise thee, because thou hast cut the knots in which they have tied their own souls.

THE CHAPLAIN [*kneeling to her*] The foolish old men on their deathbeds praise thee, because their sins against thee are turned into blessings.

THE INQUISITOR [*kneeling to her*] The judges in the blindness and bondage of the law praise thee, because thou hast vindicated the vision and the freedom of the living soul.

THE EXECUTIONER [*kneeling to her*] The tormentors and executioners praise thee, because thou hast shewn that their hands are guiltless of the death of the soul.

CHARLES [*kneeling to her*] The unpretending praise thee, because thou hast taken upon thyself the heroic burdens that are too heavy for them.

JOAN. Woe unto me when all men praise me! I bid you remember that I am a saint, and that saints can work miracles. And now tell me: shall I rise from the dead, and come back to you a living woman?

A gust of wind: the candles are extinguished. Darkness blots out the room.

JOAN. What! Must I burn again? Are none of you ready to receive me?

The voices exclaim in dark irregular chorus.

CAUCHON. The heretic is always better dead. And mortal eyes cannot distinguish the saint from the heretic.

DUNOIS. Forgive us, Joan: we are not yet good enough for you. I shall go back to my bed.

WARWICK. We sincerely regret our little mistake; but political necessities, though occasionally erroneous, are still imperative.

THE CHAPLAIN. Oh, do not come back: you must not come back.

THE GENTLEMAN. The possibility of your resurrection was not contemplated in the recent proceedings for your canonization. I must return to Rome for fresh instructions.

In the darkness they are heard discreetly stealing away.

Gradually the screen lights up again: outlines revealed by the rays of the moon. Charles and Joan alone have stayed behind.

CHARLES [*seated on the bed, yawning*] Poor old Joan! They have all run away from you. And what can I do but go back to bed too? [*He does so*].

JOAN [*sadly*] Goodnight, Charlie.

CHARLES [*mumbling in his pillows*] Goo ni. [*He sleeps. The darkness envelops the bed*].

The first stroke of midnight is heard softly from a distant bell. The last remaining rays of light gather into a white radiance descending on Joan. The hour continues to strike.

JOAN. O God that madest this beautiful earth, when will it be ready to receive Thy saints? How long, O Lord, how long?

From afar, the voices of a choir, accompanied by organ and orchestral music. Dissolve to final title:

THE END

Pygmalion

Note

This scenario is not technically complete; but it indicates exactly what the producer has to work on in the studio, with all the omissions from and additions to the text of the original play. These are so extensive that the printed play should be carefully kept out of the studio, as it can only confuse and mislead the producer and the performers.

The film begins with a summer thunderstorm in London.*

First, a sky over chimney pots and church towers, with masses of thundercloud and a black cloud moving toward the sun.

Cut to:

Piccadilly Circus, London. Flower sellers (women in shawls with baskets) seated round the base of the Eros monument. Among them Liza Doolittle, the only young one. The rest are elderly or middle aged. All, including Liza, are too poorly clad and dirty to be attractive. Liza is a pathetic draggle tailed creature. She offers bunches of violets to the passers-by, like the rest; but there is no business, as the sky is darkening, and people are looking up anxiously at the clouds, loosening the bands of their umbrellas, and hurrying on. The flower sellers are still offering their wares; but no words can be distinguished through the traffic noises.

Cut to:

Liza and her next neighbor, an elderly woman. The audience now has a better look at Liza; but her good looks are not yet discoverable: she is dirty and her ill combed hair is dirty. Her shawl and skirt are old and ugly. Her boots are deplorable, her hat, an old black straw with a band of violets, indescribable. The older woman, though also dirty with London grime, and no better dressed, is slightly more disciplined by experience. She is busy packing her basket and covering it. Liza is listless, discouraged, and miserable.

OLD WOMAN. Now then, Liza: wake up. It's going to rain something chronic. You going to sit there and get soaked?

LIZA. O Gawd, I avnt sold a bloody thing since five o'clock, I avnt. Whats the good of doing anything in this weather?

OLD WOMAN. Come now: talking like that wont elp. Better get home dry than wet.

The old woman takes up her basket and hurries off.

---

* When the film was first released in the United States in 1938, Shaw prefaced it with a spoken address to American audiences. For the text of Shaw's speech, see Appendix C.

Thunder, much nearer, after a flash.

Liza looks up, and hastily stirs herself to pack her basket. She finishes by putting her hat into the basket and drawing her shawl over her head. Then she rushes off.

View of Piccadilly Circus again; but it is now raining with the first heavy drops of a thunder shower.

People putting up umbrellas, turning up the collars of their coats, and beginning to run. Also hailing taxis and scrambling into them.

Liza, with her basket under her arm, makes a rush for it and vanishes.

Another street scene continuing the business of people caught in a heavy shower.

Freddy, a goodlooking young gentleman aged 20, is on the kerb, hailing taxi after taxi; but they are all engaged.

FREDDY. Tax! [*The cab does not stop*]. Tax! [*Another failure*]. Tax! [*Another*]. Oh, damn! [*He rushes off*].

Liza comes running with her shawl over her head and her basket under her arm. She disappears in Freddy's footsteps.

Note

In the book the play begins at 11.15 p.m. after the theatres close.

In the film the play begins in the late afternoon, as the theatres are closing after their matinées. Consequently nobody is in evening dress.

Under the portico of the church of St Paul in Covent Garden, London. (Note that this is not St Paul's Cathedral by Christopher Wren, but the smaller church by Inigo Jones). *The portico is on the sidewalk, level with it and sheltering it from the rain. Its great columns divide the view of it into sections.*

General view of it from the market, with the crowd of people sheltering from heavy rain. Mrs Hill, her daughter, Higgins and the rest are in position; but they are not distinguishable in this shot.

The church clock chimes the first quarter. The clangor must be fairly loud, but not unmusical.

Under the portico looking out as from the church wall through the columns to Covent Garden market. Thus all the shelterers have their backs to the audience except Higgins, who stands in the middle with his back to them listening and making notes, cocking his ears right and left alternately as he listens. There is a babel of conversation but nothing distinguishable.

The figure of Higgins should be on the scale of a close-up. The row of backs behind him should be on that of a longer shot, so as to give him comparative magnitude.

Higgins is not youthful. He is a mature, well built, impressive, authoritative man of 40 or thereabouts, with a frock coat, a broadbrimmed hat, and an Inverness cape.

It is important that in age and everything else he should be in strong contrast to Freddy, who is 20, slim, goodlooking, and very youthful.

(The producer should bear in mind from the beginning that it is Freddy who captivates and finally carries off Eliza, and that all suggestion of a love interest between Eliza and Higgins should be most carefully avoided).

A section of the crowded portico viewed from the market. Close-up to the two central pillars. The space between them must be enough to manoeuvre four principals in front of the sheltering crowd.

An elderly lady (Mrs Eynsford Hill) and her daughter (Clara) are in front glumly watching the rain. The mother is slight, refined, and well bred. The daughter, young and blooming, is more thickly built and comparatively bumptious. Their dress is in good taste but not new and not expensive.

THE DAUGHTER [*in the space between the central pillars, close to the one on her left*] I'm getting chilled to the bone. What can Freddy be doing all this time?

THE MOTHER [*on her daughter's right*] Not so long. But he ought to have got us a cab by this.

Freddy rushes in out of the rain from the Southampton Street side, and comes between them closing a dripping umbrella. He is wet round the ankles.

THE DAUGHTER. Well, havnt you got a cab?

FREDDY. Theres not one to be had for love or money.

THE MOTHER. Oh, Freddy, there must be one. You cant have tried.

THE DAUGHTER. It's too tiresome. Do you expect us to go and get one ourselves?

THE MOTHER. You really are very helpless, Freddy. Go again; and dont come back until you have found a cab.

FREDDY. Oh, very well: I'll go, I'll go. [*He opens his umbrella and dashes off, but comes into collision with Liza, who is hurrying in for shelter, knocking her basket out of her hands. A blinding flash of lightning, followed instantly by a rattling peal of thunder, orchestrates the incident*].

LIZA. Nah then, Freddy: look wh' y' gowin, deah.

FREDDY. Sorry [*he rushes off*].

LIZA [*picking up her scattered flowers and replacing them in the basket*] Theres menners f' yer! Tǝ-oo banches o voylets trod into the mad. [*She sits down on the plinth of the column, sorting her flowers, on the lady's right*].

THE MOTHER. How do you know that my son's name is Freddy, pray?

LIZA. Ow, eez yǝ-ooa san, is e? Wal, fewd dan y' dǝ-ooty bawmz a mather should, eed now bettern to spawl a pore gel's flahrzn than ran awy athaht pyin. Will ye-oo py me f'them? [*Here, with apologies, this desperate attempt to represent her dialect without a phonetic alphabet must be abandoned as unintelligible outside London*].

THE DAUGHTER. Do nothing of the sort, mother. The idea!

THE MOTHER. Please allow me, Clara. Have you any pennies?

THE DAUGHTER. No. Ive nothing smaller than sixpence.

LIZA [*hopefully*] I can give you change for a tanner, kind lady.

THE MOTHER [*to Clara*] Give it to me. [*Clara parts reluctantly*]. Now [*to the girl*] This is for your flowers.

LIZA. Thank you kindly, lady.

THE DAUGHTER. Make her give you the change. These things are only a penny a bunch.

THE MOTHER. Do hold your tongue, Clara. [*To the girl*] You can keep the change.

LIZA. Oh, thank you, lady.

THE MOTHER. Now tell me how you know that young gentleman's name.

LIZA. I didnt.

THE MOTHER. I heard you call him by it. Dont try to deceive me.

LIZA [*protesting*] Who's trying to deceive you? I called him Freddy or Charlie same as you might yourself if you was talking to a stranger and wished to be pleasant. [*She sits down beside her basket*].

THE DAUGHTER. Sixpence thrown away! Really, mamma, you might have spared Freddy t h a t . [*She retreats in disgust behind the pillar*].

An elderly gentleman of the amiable military type rushes into the shelter, and closes a dripping umbrella. He is in the same plight as Freddy, very wet about the ankles. He is in evening dress, with a light overcoat. He takes the place left vacant by the daughter.

THE GENTLEMAN. Phew! [*he goes to the plinth beside Liza, puts up his foot on it; and stoops to turn down his trouser ends*].

THE MOTHER. Oh dear! [*She retires sadly and joins her daughter*].

LIZA [*taking advantage of the military gentleman's proximity to establish friendly relations with him*] Cheer up, Captain; and buy a flower off a poor girl.

THE GENTLEMAN. I'm sorry. I havnt any change.

LIZA. I can give you change, Captain.

THE GENTLEMAN. For a sovereign? Ive nothing less.

LIZA. Garn! Oh do buy a flower off me, Captain. I can change half-a-crown. Take this for tuppence.

THE GENTLEMAN. Now dont be troublesome: theres a good girl. [*Trying his pockets*] I really havnt any change—Stop: heres three hapence, if thats any use to you [*he retreats to the other pillar*].

LIZA [*disappointed, but thinking three halfpence better than nothing*] Thank you, sir.

THE BYSTANDER [*to the girl*] You be careful: give him a flower for it. Theres a bloke here behind taking down every blessed word youre saying. [*All turn to the man who is taking notes*].

Cut to:

Under the portico looking out through the columns to Covent Garden market, the crowd turning round to look at Higgins.

Cut to:

The whole width of the portico viewed from the market. The crowd with Liza making a frantic scene in front of them. Pickering in the foreground watching the row. Single figures or pairs detach themselves momentarily to speak to Liza or to one another. Finally Higgins pushes through to her.

LIZA [*springing up terrified*] I aint done nothing wrong by speaking to the gentleman. Ive a right to sell flowers if I keep off the kerb. [*Hysterically*] I'm a respectable girl: so help me.

General hubbub, mostly sympathetic to Liza, but deprecating her excessive sensibility. Cries of Dont start hollerin. Who's hurting you? Nobody's going to touch you. Whats the good of fussing? Steady on. Easy easy, etc., *come from the elderly staid spectators, who pat her comfortingly. Less patient ones bid her shut her head, or ask her roughly what is wrong with her. A remoter group, not knowing what the matter is, crowd in and increase the noise with question and answer:* Whats the row? What-she do? Where is he? A tec taking her down. What! him? Yes: him over there: Took money off the gentleman, etc.

LIZA [*breaking through them to the gentleman, crying wildly*] Oh, sir, dont let him charge me. You dunno what it means to me. Theyll take away my character and drive me on the streets for speaking to gentlemen. They—

THE NOTE TAKER [*coming forward on her right, the rest crowding after him*] There! there! there! there! who's hurting you, you silly girl? What do you take me for?

THE BYSTANDER. It's aw rawt: e's a gentleman: look at his bə-oots.

Close-up between the two central pillars, viewed from the market.

LIZA [*still hysterical*] I take my Bible oath I never said a word—

THE NOTE TAKER [*overbearing but good-humored*] Oh, shut up, shut up. Do I look like a policeman?

LIZA [*far from reassured*] Then what did you take down my words for? How do I know whether you took me down right? You just shew me what youve wrote about me. [*The note taker opens his book and holds it steadily under her nose, though the pressure of the mob trying to read it over his shoulders would upset a weaker man*]. Whats that? That aint proper writing. I cant read that.

THE NOTE TAKER. I can. [*Reads, reproducing her pronunciation exactly*] "Cheer ap, Keptin; n' baw ya flahr orf a pore gel.'

LIZA [*much distressed*] It's because I called him Captain. I meant no harm. [*To the gentleman*] Oh, sir, dont let him lay a charge agen me for a word like that. You—

THE GENTLEMAN. Charge! I make no charge. [*To the note taker*] Really, sir, if you are a detective, you need not begin protecting me against molestation by young women until I ask you. Anybody could see that the girl meant no harm.

THE BYSTANDERS GENERALLY [*demonstrating against police espionage*] Course they could. What business is it of yours? You mind your own affairs. He wants promotion, he does. Taking down people's words! Girl never said a word to him. What harm if she did? Nice thing a girl cant shelter from the rain without being insulted, etc., etc., etc. [*She is conducted by the more sympathetic demonstrators back to her plinth, where she resumes her seat and struggles with her emotion*].

THE BYSTANDER. He aint a tec. He's a blooming busybody: thats what he is. I tell you, look at his bə-oots.

THE NOTE TAKER [*turning on him genially*] And how are all your people down at Selsey?

THE BYSTANDER [*suspiciously*] Who told you my people come from Selsey?

THE NOTE TAKER. Never you mind. They did. [*To the girl*] How do you come to be up so far east? You were born in Lisson Grove.

LIZA [*appalled*] Oh, what harm is there in my leaving Lisson Grove? It wasn't fit for a pig to live in; and I had to pay four-and-six a week. [*In tears*] Oh, boo—hoo—oo—

THE NOTE TAKER. Live where you like; but stop that noise.

THE GENTLEMAN [*to the girl*] Come, come! he cant touch you: you have a right to live where you please.

LIZA [*subsiding into a brooding melancholy over her basket, and talking very low-spiritedly to herself*] I'm a good girl, I am.

THE SARCASTIC BYSTANDER [*not attending to her*] Do you know where *I* come from?

THE NOTE TAKER [*promptly*] Hoxton.

Titterings. Popular interest in the note taker's performance increases.

THE SARCASTIC ONE [*amazed*] Well, who said I didnt? Bly me! you know everything, you do.

THE FLOWER GIRL [*still nursing her sense of injury*] Aint no call to meddle with me, he aint.

THE BYSTANDER [*to her*] Of course he aint. Dont you stand it from him. [*To the note taker*] See here: what call have you to know about people what never offered to meddle with you?

LIZA. Let him say what he likes. I dont want to have no truck with him.

THE BYSTANDER. You take us for dirt under your feet, dont you? Catch you taking liberties with a gentleman!

THE SARCASTIC BYSTANDER. Yes: tell him where he come from if you want to go fortune-telling.

THE NOTE TAKER. Cheltenham, Harrow, Cambridge, and India.

THE GENTLEMAN. Quite right.

Great laughter. Reaction in the note taker's favor. Exclamations of He knows all about it. Told him proper. Hear him tell the toff where come from? *etc.*

LIZA [*resenting the reaction*] He's no gentleman, he aint, to interfere with a poor girl.

Long shot shewing the whole portico crowded with shelterers. They all move off except Liza, Higgins, and Pickering, who are left alone between two of the pillars as before. The sky brightens during the exodus and London is again bathed in sunshine.

Back to close-up between the two central pillars, viewed from the market.

THE DAUGHTER [*out of patience, pushing her way rudely to the front and displacing the gentleman, who politely retires to the other side of the pillar*] What on earth is Freddy doing? I shall get pneumownia if I stay in this draught any longer.

THE NOTE TAKER [*to himself, hastily making a note of her pronunciation of 'monia' as mownia*] Earls Court.

THE DAUGHTER [*violently*] Will you please keep your impertinent remarks to yourself.

THE NOTE TAKER. Did I say that out loud? I didnt mean to. I beg your pardon. Your mother's Epsom, unmistakably.

THE MOTHER [*advancing between her daughter and the note taker*] How very curious! I was brought up in Largelady Park, near Epsom.

THE NOTE TAKER [*to the daughter*] You want a cab, do you?

THE DAUGHTER. Dont dare speak to me.

THE MOTHER. Oh please, please, Clara. [*Her daughter repudiates her with an angry shrug and retires haughtily*]. We should be so grateful to you, sir, if you found us a cab. [*The note taker produces a whistle*]. Oh, thank you. [*She joins her daughter*].

The note taker blows a piercing blast.

THE SARCASTIC BYSTANDER. There! I knowed he was a plainclothes copper.

THE BYSTANDER. That aint a police whistle: that a sporting whistle.

LIZA [*still preoccupied with her wounded feelings*] He's no right to take away my character. My character is the same to me as any lady's.

THE NOTE TAKER. I dont know whether youve noticed it; but the rain stopped about two minutes ago.

THE BYSTANDER. So it has. Why didnt you say so before? and us losing our time listening to your silliness! [*He walks off towards the Strand*].

THE MOTHER. It's quite fine now, Clara. We can walk to a motor bus. Come. [*She gathers her skirts above her ankles and hurries off towards the Strand*].

THE DAUGHTER. But the cab—[*her mother is out of hearing*]. Oh, how tiresome! [*She follows angrily*].

All the rest have gone except the note taker, the gentleman, and the flower girl, who sits arranging her basket, and still pitying herself in murmurs.

LIZA. Poor girl! Hard enough for her to live without being worrited and chivied.

THE GENTLEMAN [*returning to his former place on the note taker's left*] How do you do it, if I may ask?

THE NOTE TAKER. Simply phonetics. The science of speech. Thats my profession: also my hobby. Y o u can spot an Irishman or a Yorkshireman by his brogue. *I* can place any man within six miles. I can place him within two miles in London. Sometimes within two streets.

LIZA. Ought to be ashamed of himself, unmanly coward!

THE GENTLEMAN. But is there a living in that?

THE NOTE TAKER. Oh yes. Quite a fat one. This is an age of upstarts who have to be taught to speak like ladies and gentlemen. Now I can teach them—

LIZA. Let him mind his own business and leave a poor girl—

THE NOTE TAKER [*explosively*] Woman: cease this detestable boohooing instantly; or else seek the shelter of some other place of worship.

LIZA [*with feeble defiance*] Ive a right to be here if I like, same as you.

THE NOTE TAKER. A woman who utters such depressing and disgusting sounds has no right to be anywhere—no right to live. Remember that you are a human being with a soul and the divine gift of articulate speech: that your native language is the language of Shakespear and Milton and The Bible; and dont sit there crooning like a bilious pigeon.

Close-up of Liza.

LIZA [*quite overwhelmed, looking up at him in mingled wonder and deprecation without daring to raise her head*] Ah-ah-ah-ow-ow-ow-oo!

Back to close-up between the two central pillars, viewed from the market.

THE NOTE TAKER [*whipping out his book*] Heavens! what a sound! [*He writes; then holds out the book and reads, reproducing her vowels exactly*]. Ah-ah-ah-ow-ow-ow-oo!

LIZA [*tickled by the performance, and laughing in spite of herself*] Garn!

THE NOTE TAKER. You hear this creature with her kerbstone English: the English that will keep her in the gutter to the end of her days. Well, sir, in three months I could pass that girl off as a duchess at an ambassador's garden party. I could even get her a place as lady's maid or shop assistant, which requires better English.

LIZA. What's that you say?

THE NOTE TAKER [*turning crushingly on her*] Yes, you squashed cabbage leaf, you disgrace to the noble architecture of these columns, you incarnate insult to the English language: I could pass you off as the Queen of Sheba. [*To the Gentleman*] Can you believe that?

THE GENTLEMAN. Of course I can. I am myself a student of Indian dialects; and—

THE NOTE TAKER [*eagerly*] Are you? Do you know Colonel Pickering, the author of Spoken Sanscrit?

THE GENTLEMAN. I a m Colonel Pickering. Who are you?

THE NOTE TAKER. Henry Higgins, author of Higgins's Universal Alphabet.

PICKERING [*with enthusiasm*] I came from India to meet you.

HIGGINS. I was going to India to meet you.

PICKERING. Where do you live?

HIGGINS. 27A Wimpole Street.

PICKERING. I'm at the Carlton. Come and dine with me.

HIGGINS. Right you are.

LIZA [*to Pickering, as he passes her*] Buy a flower, kind gentleman. I'm short for my lodging.

PICKERING. I really havnt any change. I'm sorry [*he goes away*].

HIGGINS [*shocked at the girl's mendacity*] Liar. You said you could change half-a-crown.

LIZA [*rising in desperation*] You ought to be stuffed with nails, you ought. [*Flinging the basket at his feet*] Take the whole blooming basket for sixpence.

The church clock strikes the second quarter.

BOYS' VOICES [*singing within the church: they are practising the 102nd Psalm*] Hear my prayer O Lord; and let my cry come unto Thee. Hide not Thy face from me in the day when I am in trouble, etc., etc., etc.

HIGGINS [*hearing the voice of God, rebuking him for his Pharisaic want of charity to the poor girl*] A reminder. [*He raises his hat solemnly; then throws a handful of money into the basket and follows Pickering*].

Under the portico looking out through the two pillars to the roadway with the market beyond (the previous scene from the opposite end).

LIZA [*picking up a half-crown*] Ah-ow-ooh! [*Picking up a couple of florins*] Aaah-ow-ooh! [*Picking up several coins*] Aaaaaah-ow-ooh! [*Picking up a half-sovereign*] Aaaaaaaaaaaah-ow-ooh!!!

A taxi rolls up and stops.

FREDDY [*springing out of the cab*] Hallo! [*To the girl*] Where are the two ladies that were here?

LIZA [*taking her hat out of the basket and putting it on*] They walked to the bus when the rain stopped.

FREDDY. And left me with a cab on my hands! Damnation!

LIZA [*with grandeur*] Never mind, young man. *I'*m going home in a taxi. [*She sails off to the cab. The driver puts his hand behind him and holds the door firmly shut against her. Quite understanding his mistrust, she shews him her handful of money*]. A taxi fare aint no object to me, Charlie. [*He grins and opens the door*]. Here. What about the basket?

THE TAXIMAN. Give it here. Tuppence extra.

LIZA. No: I dont want nobody to see it. [*She crushes it into the cab and gets in, continuing the conversation through the window*] Goodbye, Freddy.

FREDDY [*dazedly raising his hat*] Goodbye.

TAXIMAN. Where to?

LIZA. Bucknam Pellis [Buckingham Palace].

TAXIMAN. What d'ye mean—Bucknam Pellis?

LIZA. Dont you know where it is? In the Green Park, where the King lives. [*To Freddy*] Goodbye, Freddy. Dont let me keep you standing there. Goodbye.

FREDDY. Goodbye. [*He goes*].

TAXIMAN. Here? Whats this about Bucknam Pellis? What business have you at Bucknam Pellis?

LIZA. Of course I havnt none. But I wasnt going to let him know that. You drive me home.

TAXIMAN. And wheres home?

LIZA. Angel Court, Drury Lane, next Meiklejohn's oil shop.

TAXIMAN. That sounds more like it, Judy. [*He drives off*].
Dissolve to:
The entrance to Angel Court, a narrow little archway between two shops, one of them Meiklejohn's oil shop. When it stops there, Eliza gets out, dragging her basket with her.
LIZA. How much?
TAXIMAN [*indicating the taximeter*] Cant you read? A shilling.
LIZA. A shilling for two minutes!!
TAXIMAN. Two minutes or ten: it's all the same.
LIZA. Well, I dont call it right.
TAXIMAN. Ever been in a taxi before?
LIZA [*with dignity*] Hundreds and thousands of times, young man.
TAXIMAN [*laughing at her*] Good for you, Judy. Keep the shilling, darling, with best love from all at home. Good luck! [*He drives off*].
LIZA [*humiliated*] Impidence!
She picks up the basket and trudges up the alley through the archway.
Angel Court in perspective from under the archway. A typical little London alley.
Back view of Liza wearily dragging along with her basket.
She disappears into a doorway.
No dialogue.
Liza's lodging. A small room with very old wall paper hanging loose in the damp places. A broken pane in the window is mended with paper. A portrait of a popular actor and a fashion plate of ladies' dresses, all wildly beyond poor Liza's means, both torn from newspapers, are pinned up on the wall. A birdcage hangs in the window; but its tenant died long ago: it remains as a memorial only.
These are the only visible luxuries: the rest is the irreducible minimum of poverty's needs: a wretched bed heaped with all sorts of coverings that have any warmth in them, a draped packing case with a basin and jug on it and a little looking glass over it, a chair and table, the refuse of some suburban kitchen, and an American alarum clock on the shelf above the unused fireplace.
Liza comes in and dumps her basket on the floor with a sigh of relief. She takes off her shawl and spreads it on the bed. She sits at the table and takes handfuls of money from the pocket of her apron. She balances the silver in one hand, covers it with the other, and jingles it at her ear like a child's rattle.
Close-up of Liza jingling the money at her ear. Her habitual anxious poor woman's expression changes very gradually into a happy smile. This fades out into:
Close-up of Liza, still in her dirty make-up, wearing her best hat, with three enormous ostrich feathers. She looks dreadfully ugly in it, but very self-satisfied. This fades out into:
Close-up of Liza in a coronet and diamonds, like Queen Alexandra, but with an expression of extreme hauteur. She is still ridiculous in her dirty make-up (no picture must anticipate her change to a blooming young beauty after her first bath). *This again fades out into:*
Her bedroom again after nightfall. The candle is lighted; and on the table is a big thick cup and a knife, the remains of her supper. (She has treated herself to a cup of cocoa and a "doorstep"). The hat with the three feathers is on the table. She is sitting at the table.
She sweeps the crumbs of the doorstep into her palm with the knife, and throws

them into her mouth. She drinks up the last of the cocoa.

The rises and puts the hat away carefully in the packing case. She takes off her skirt and spreads it on the bed. She takes the candle from the chimney board and puts it on the chair, within reach of the bed. She sits on the bed and pulls off her boots and stockings. She goes to bed without any further change. She blows out the candle.

The darkness fades into:

Next day at 11 a.m. Higgins's laboratory in Wimpole Street. It is a room on the first floor, looking on the street, and was meant for the drawing room. The double doors are in the middle of the back wall; and persons entering find in the corner to their right two tall file cabinets at right angles to one another against the walls. In this corner stands a flat writing-table, on which are a phonograph, a laryngoscope, a row of tiny organ pipes with a bellows, a set of lamp chimneys for singing flames with burners attached to a gas plug in the wall by an indiarubber tube, several turning-forks of different sizes, a life-size image of half a human head, shewing in section the vocal organs, and a box containing a supply of wax cylinders for the phonograph.

Further down the room, on the same side, is a fireplace, with a comfortable leather-covered easy-chair at the side of the hearth nearest the door, and a coal-scuttle. There is a clock on the mantel-piece. Between the fireplace and the phonograph table is a stand for newspapers.

On the other side of the central door, to the left of the visitor, is a cabinet of shallow drawers. On it is a telephone and the telephone directory. The corner beyond, and most of the side wall, is occupied by a grand piano, with the keyboard at the end furthest from the door, and a bench from the player extending the full length of the keyboard. On the piano is a dessert dish heaped with fruit and sweets, mostly chocolates.

The middle of the room is clear. Besides the easy-chair, the piano bench, and two chairs at the phonograph table, there is one stray chair. It stands near the fireplace. On the walls, engravings: mostly Piranesis and mezzotint portraits. No paintings.

Pickering is seated at the table, putting down some cards and a tuning-fork which he has been using. Higgins is standing up near him, closing two or three file drawers which are hanging out. He appears in the morning light as a robust, vital, appetizing sort of man of forty or thereabouts, dressed in a professional-looking black frock-coat with a white linen collar and black silk tie. He is of the energetic, scientific type, heartily, even violently interested in everything that can be studied as a scientific subject, and careless about himself and other people, including their feelings. He is, in fact, but for his years and size, rather like a very impetuous baby 'taking notice' eagerly and loudly, and requiring almost as much watching to keep him out of unintended mischief. His manner varies from genial bullying when he is in a good humor to stormy petulance when anything goes wrong; but he is so enitrely frank and void of malice that he remains likeable even in his least reasonable moments.

HIGGINS [*as he shuts the last drawer*] Well, I think thats the whole show.

PICKERING. It's really amazing. I havnt taken half of it in, you know.

HIGGINS. Would you like to go over any of it again?

PICKERING [*rising and coming to the fireplace, where he plants himself with his back to the fire*] No, thank you: not now. I'm quite done up for this morning.

Higgins goes to the piano and eats candies.

Mrs Pearce, his housekeeper, comes in. She is middleaged, and very respectable and dignified.

HIGGINS. Whats the matter?

MRS PEARCE [*hesitating, evidently perplexed*] A young woman asks to see you, sir.

HIGGINS. A young woman! What does she want?

MRS PEARCE. Well, sir, she says youll be glad to see her when you know what she's come about. She's quite a common girl, sir. Very common indeed. I should have sent her away, only I thought perhaps you wanted her to talk into your machines.

HIGGINS [*to Pickering*] Lets have her up. Shew her up, Mrs Pearce [*he rushes across to his working table and picks out a cylinder to use on the phonograph*].

MRS PEARCE [*only half resigned to it*] Very well, sir. It's for you to say. [*She goes downstairs*].

HIGGINS. This is rather a bit of luck. I'll shew you how I make records. We'll set her talking; and I'll take it down first in Bell's Vissible Speech; then in broad Romic; and then we'll get her on the phonograph so that you can turn her on as often as you like with the written transcript before you.

MRS PEARCE [*returning*] This is the young woman, sir.

Liza enters in state. She has a hat with three ostrich feathers, orange, sky-blue, and red. She has a nearly clean apron, and the shoddy coat has been tidied a little. The pathos of this deplorable figure, with its innocent vanity and consequential air, touches Pickering, who has already straightened himself in the presence of Mrs Pearce. But as to Higgins, the only distinction he makes between men and women is that when he is neither bullying nor exclaiming to the heavens against some feather-weight cross, he coaxes women as a child coaxes its nurse when it wants to get anything out of her.

HIGGINS [*brusquely, recognizing her with unconcealed disappointment, and at once, babylike, making an intolerable grievance of it*] Why, this is the girl I jotted down yesterday when I was sheltering from the rain. [*To Liza*] Be off with you: I dont want you.

LIZA. Dont you be so saucy. You aint heard what I come for yet. [*To Mrs Pearce, who is waiting at the door for further instructions*] Did you tell him I come in a taxi?

MRS PEARCE. Nonsense, girl! what do you think a gentleman like Mr Higgins cares what you came in?

LIZA. Oh, we a r e proud! He aint above giving lessons, not him: I heard him say so. Well, I aint come here to ask for any compliment; and if my money's not good enough I can go elsewhere.

HIGGINS. Pickering: shall we ask this baggage to sit down, or shall we throw her out of the window?

LIZA [*running away in terror to the piano, where she turns at bay*] Ah-ah-oh-ow-ow-ow-oo! [*Wounded and whimpering*] I wont be called a baggage when Ive offered to pay like any lady.

Motionless, the two men stare at her from the other side of the room, amazed.

PICKERING [*gently*] But what is it you want?

LIZA. I want to be a lady in a flower shop. But they wont take me unless I can talk more genteel. He said he could teach me. Well, here I am ready to pay him— not asking any favor—and he treats me zif I was dirt.

HIGGINS [*thundering at her*] Sit down.

MRS PEARCE [*severely*] Sit down, girl. Do as youre told.

LIZA. Ah-ah-ah-ow-ow-oo! [*She stands, half rebellious, half bewildered*].

PICKERING [*very courteous*] Wont you sit down? [*He places the stray chair near the hearthrug between himself and Higgins*].

LIZA [coyly] Dont mind if I do. [*She sits down. Pickering returns to the hearthrug*].

HIGGINS. Whats your name?

LIZA. Liza Doolittle.

HIGGINS [*declaiming gravely*]

   Eliza, Elizabeth, Betsy and Bess,

   They went to the woods to get a bird's nes':

PICKERING. They found a nest with four eggs in it:

HIGGINS.   They took one apiece, and left three in it.

They laugh heartily at their own fun.

PICKERING. Higgins: I'm interested. What about the ambassador's garden party? I'll say youre the greatest teacher alive if you make that good. I'll bet you all the expenses of the experiment you cant do it. And I'll pay for the lessons.

LIZA. Oh, you are real good. Thank you, Captain.

HIGGINS [*tempted, looking at her*] It's almost irresistible. She's so deliciously low—so horribly dirty—

LIZA [*protesting extremely*] Ah-ah-ah-ah-ow-ow-oo-oo!!! I aint dirty: I washed my face and hands afore I come, I did.

HIGGINS. You dont know what washing means. Never mind. [*Becoming excited as the idea grows on him*] I shall make a duchess of this draggletailed guttersnipe.

LIZA [*strongly deprecating this view of her*] Ah-ah-ah-ow-ow-oo!

HIGGINS [*carried away*] Yes: in six months—in three if she has a good ear and a quick tongue—I'll take her anywhere and pass her off as anything. We'll start today: now! this moment! Take her away and clean her, Mrs Pearce. Is there a good fire in the kitchen?

MRS PEARCE [*protesting*] Yes; but—

HIGGINS [*storming on*] Take all her clothes off and burn them. Ring up Whitely or somebody for new ones. Wrap her up in brown paper til they come.

LIZA. Youre no gentleman, youre not, to talk of such things. I'm a good girl, I am; and I know what the likes of you are, I do.

HIGGINS. We want none of your slum prudery here, young woman. Youve got to learn to behave like a duchess. Take her away, Mrs Pearce. If she gives you any trouble, wallop her.

LIZA [*rising and squaring herself determinedly*] I'm going away. He's off his chump, he is. I dont want no balmies teaching me.

HIGGINS. Oh, indeed! I'm mad, am I? Very well, Mrs Pearce: you neednt order the new clothes for her. Throw her out.

LIZA [*whimpering*] Nah-ow. You got no right to touch me.

MRS PEARCE. You see now what comes of being saucy. [*Indicating the door*] This way, please.

LIZA [*almost in tears*] I didnt want no clothes. I wouldnt have taken them.

HIGGINS [*intercepting her on her reluctant way to the door*] Youre an ungrateful wicked girl. This is my return for offering to take you out of the gutter and dress you beautifully and make a lady of you.

MRS PEARCE. Stop, Mr Higgins. I wont allow it. Go home to your parents, girl;

and tell them to take better care of you.

LIZA. I aint got no parents. They told me I was big enough to earn my own living and turned me out.

MRS PEARCE. Wheres your mother?

LIZA. I aint got no mother. Her that turned me out was my sixth stepmother. But I done without them. And I'm a good girl, I am.

HIGGINS. Very well, then, what on earth is all this fuss about? The girl doesnt belong to anybody—is no use of anybody but me. [*He goes to Mrs Pearce and begins coaxing*]. You can adopt her, Mrs Pearce: I'm sure a daughter would be a great amusement to you. Now dont make any more fuss. Take her downstairs; and—

MRS PEARCE. But whats to become of her? Is she to be paid anything? Do be sensible, sir.

HIGGINS. Oh, pay her whatever is necessary: put it down in the housekeeping book. [*Impatiently*] What on earth will she want with money? She'll have her food and her clothes. She'll only drink if you give her money.

LIZA [*turning on him*] Oh you a r e a brute. It's a lie: nobody ever saw the sign of liquor on me.

PICKERING [*in good-humored remonstrance*] Does it occur to you, Higgins, that the girl has some feelings?

HIGGINS [*looking critically at her*] Oh no, I dont think so. Not any feelings that we need bother about. [*Cheerily*] Have you, Eliza?

LIZA. I got my feelings same as anyone else.

HIGGINS [*to Pickering, reflectively*] You see the difficulty?

PICKERING. Eh? What difficulty?

HIGGINS. To get her to talk grammar. The mere pronunciation is easy enough.

LIZA. I dont want to talk grammar. I want to talk like a lady in a flower-shop.

MRS PEARCE. Will you please keep to the point, Mr Higgins. I want to know on what terms the girl is to be here. Is she to have any wages? And what is to become of her when youve finished your teaching? You must look ahead a little.

HIGGINS [*impatiently*] Whats to become of her if I leave her in the gutter? Tell me that, Mrs Pearce.

MRS PEARCE. Thats her own business, not yours, Mr Higgins.

HIGGINS. Well, when Ive done with her, we can throw her back into the gutter; and then it will be her own business again; so thats all right.

LIZA. Oh, youve no feeling heart in you: you dont care for nothing but yourself. [*She rises and takes the floor resolutely*]. Here! Ive had enough of this. I'm going [*making for the door*]. You ought to be ashamed of yourself, you ought.

HIGGINS [*snatching a chocolate cream from the piano, his eyes suddenly beginning to twinkle with mischief*] Have some chocolates, Eliza.

LIZA [*halting, tempted*] How do I know what might be in them? Ive heard of girls being drugged by the like of you.

Higgins whips out his penknife; cuts a chocolate in two; puts one half into his mouth and bolts it; and offers her the other half.

HIGGINS. Pledge of good faith, Eliza. I eat one half: you eat the other. [*Liza opens her mouth to retort: he pops the half chocolate into it*]. You shall have boxes of them, barrels of them, every day. You shall live on them. Eh?

LIZA [*who has disposed of the chocolate after being nearly choked by it*] I wouldnt have ate it, only I'm too ladylike to take it out of my mouth.

HIGGINS. Listen, Eliza. I think you said you came in a taxi.

LIZA. Well, what if I did? Ive as good a right to take a taxi as anyone else.

HIGGINS. You have, Eliza; and in future you shall have as many taxis as you want. You shall go up and down and round the town in a taxi every day. Think of that, Eliza.

MRS PEARCE. Mr Higgins: youre tempting the girl. It's not right. She should think of the future.

HIGGINS. At her age! Nonsense! Time enough to think of the future when you havnt any future to think of. No, Eliza: think of chocolates, and taxis, and gold, and diamonds.

LIZA. No: I dont want no gold and no diamonds. I'm a good girl, I am.

HIGGINS. You shall remain so, Eliza, under the care of Mrs Pearce. And you shall marry an officer in the Guards, with a beautiful moustache: the son of a marquis, who will disinherit him for marrying you, but will relent when he sees your beauty and goodness—

PICKERING. Excuse me, Higgins; but I really must interfere. Mrs Pearce is quite right. [*To Eliza*] Miss Doolittle—

LIZA [*overwhelmed*] Ah-ah-ow-oo!

HIGGINS. There! Thats all youll get out of Eliza. Ah-ah-ow-oo! No use explaining. As a military man you ought to know that. Giver her her orders: thats enough for her. Eliza: you are to live here for the next six months, learning how to speak beautifully, like a lady in a florist's shop. If youre good and do whatever youre told, you shall sleep in a proper bedroom, and have lots to eat, and money to buy chocolates and take rides in taxis. If youre naughty and idle you will sleep in the back kitchen among the black beetles, and be walloped by Mrs Pearce with a broomstick. At the end of six months you shall go to Buckingham Palace in a carriage, beautifully dressed. If the King finds out youre not a lady, you will be taken by the police to the Tower of London, where your head will be cut off as a warning to other presumptuous flower girls. If you are not found out, you shall have a present of seven and sixpence to start life with as a lady in a shop. If you refuse this offer you will be a most ungrateful wicked girl; and the angels will weep for you. [*To Pickering*] Now are you satisfied, Pickering? [*To Mrs Pearce*] Can I put it more plainly and fairly, Mrs Pearce?

MRS PEARCE [*patiently*] I think youd better let me speak to the girl properly in private. I dont know that I can take charge of her or consent to the arrangement at all. Of course I know you dont mean her any harm; but when you get what you call interested in people's accents, you never think or care what may happen to them or you. Come with me, Eliza.

HIGGINS. Thats all right. Thank you, Mrs Pearce. Bundle her off to the bathroom.

LIZA [*reluctantly and suspiciously*] Youre a great bully, you are. I wont stay here if I dont like. I wont let nobody wallop me. I never asked to go to Bucknam Pellis, I didnt. I was never in trouble with the police, not me. I'm a good girl—

MRS PEARCE. Dont answer back, girl. You dont understand the gentleman. Come with me. [*She leads the way to the door, and holds it open for Liza.*].

LIZA [*as she goes out*] Well, what I say is right. I wont go near the King, not if I'm going to have my head cut off. If I'd known what I was letting myself in for, I wouldnt have come here. I always been a good girl; and I never offered to say a word to him; and I dont owe him nothing; and I dont care; and I wont be put upon; and I have my feelings the same as anyone else—

Mrs Pearce shuts the door; and Liza's plaints are no longer audible.

Cut to:

Liza and Mrs Pearce on the stairs, Mrs Pearce leading the way upstairs. Liza is still grumbling the last three or four lines of her speech: I always been a good girl, etc., etc.

The landing above. Two doors.

MRS PEARCE [*opening one of the doors.*] I will have to put you here. This will be your bedroom. [*They go in*].

Inside the room. A good servant's bedroom, light, clean, and cheerful. The two women enter.

LIZA. O-oh, I couldnt sleep here, missus. It's too good for the likes of me. I should be afraid to touch anything. I aint a duchess yet, you know.

MRS PEARCE. You have got to make yourself as clean as the room: then you wont be afraid of it. [*She goes to another door*]. And you must call me Mrs Pearce, not missus. [*She goes through it, Liza following*].

A bathroom, with a couple of bath gowns hanging up. Mrs Pearce comes in, followed by Liza.

LIZA. Gawd! whats this? Is this where you wash clothes? Funny sort of copper I call it.

MRS PEARCE. It is not a copper. This is where we wash ourselves, Eliza, and where I am going to wash you.

LIZA. You expect me to get into that and wet myself all over! Not me. I should catch my death. I knew a woman did it every Saturday night; and she died of it.

MRS PEARCE. Mr Higgins has the gentlemen's bathroom downstairs; and he has a bath every morning, in cold water.

LIZA. Ugh! He's made of iron, that man.

MRS PEARCE. If you are to sit with him and the Colonel and be taught you will have to do the same. They wont like the smell of you if you dont. But you can have the water as hot as you like. There are two taps: hot and cold.

LIZA [*weeping*] I couldnt. I dursnt. Its not natural: it would kill me. Ive never had a bath in my life: not what youd call a proper one.

MRS PEARCE. Well, dont you want to be clean and sweet and decent, like a lady? You know you cant be a nice girl inside if youre a dirty slut outside.

LIZA. Boohoo!!!!

MRS PEARCE. Now stop crying and go back into your room and take off all your clothes. Then wrap yourself in this [*Taking down a gown from its peg and handing it to her*] and come back to me. I will get the bath ready.

LIZA [*all tears*] I cant. I wont. I'm not used to it. Ive never took off all my clothes before. It's not right: it's not decent.

MRS PEARCE. Nonsense, child. Dont you take off all your clothes every night when you go to bed?

LIZA [*amazed*] No. Why should I? I should catch my death. Of course I take off my skirt.

MRS PEARCE. Do you mean that you sleep in the underclothes you wear in the daytime?

LIZA. What else have I to sleep in?

MRS PEARCE. You will never do that again as long as you live here. I will get you a proper nightdress.

LIZA. Do you mean change into cold things and lie awake shivering half the night? You want to kill me, you do.

MRS PEARCE. I want to change you from a frowzy slut to a clean respectable girl fit to sit with the gentlemen in the study. Are you going to trust me and do what I tell you or be thrown out and sent back to your flower basket?

LIZA. But you dont know what the cold is to me. You dont know how I dread it.

MRS PEARCE. Your bed wont be cold here: I will put a hot water bottle in it. [*Pushing her into the bedroom*] Off with you and undress.

LIZA. Oh, if only I'd a known what a dreadful thing it is to be clean I'd never have come. I didnt know when I was well off. I—[*Mrs Pearce pushes her through the door, but leaves it partly open lest her prisoner should take to flight*].

Mrs Pearce puts on a pair of white rubber sleeves, and fills the bath, mixing hot and cold and testing the result with the bath thermometer. She perfumes it with a handful of bath salts and adds a palmful of mustard. She then takes a formidable looking long handled scrubbing brush and soaps is profusely with a ball of scented soap.

Liza comes back with nothing on but the bath gown huddled tightly round her, a piteous spectacle of abject terror.

MRS PEARCE. Now come along. Take that thing off.

LIZA. Oh I couldnt, Mrs Pearce: I reely couldnt. I never done such a thing.

MRS PEARCE. Nonsense. Here: step in and tell me whether it's hot enough for you.

LIZA. Ah-oo! Ah-oo! It's too hot.

MRS PEARCE [*deftly snatching the gown away and throwing Liza down on her back*] It wont hurt you. [*She sets to work with the scrubbing brush*].

Liza's screams are heartrending.

The shot fades out in a tempest of yells from Liza and vigorous lathering by Mrs Pearce.

Note

Liza is of course dressed from the waist to the knees; but she is masked by Mrs Pearce during the moment between the snatching off of the bathing gown and the concealment of her bathing drawers by the side of the bath.

Fade in:

The laboratory as before.

Higgins and Pickering seated reading.

Mrs Pearce, with her rubber sleeves still on, enters with Japanese clothes hanging on her arm.

HIGGINS. Oh! That you, Mrs Pearce? What the devil has been going on upstairs? Somebody was screaming the house down.

MRS PEARCE. Thats all right, sir: it wont occur again. Might she use these Japanese things you brought back from abroad? She's perfectly clean now. I really cant put her back into her old things. It's only until the new clothes come.

HIGGINS. Certainly, Mrs Pearce. Anything you like. Is that all?

MRS PEARCE. No sir. I am sorry to have to tell you that the trouble's beginning already. There a dustman downstairs, Alfred Doolittle, wants to see you. He says you have his daughter here.

PICKERING. Phew! I say.

HIGGINS. Send the blackguard up.

Major Barbara Cusins pours vodka into the fire. Robert Morley and Rex Harrison.

Major Barbara Shaw meets the actor cast as Cusins before Rex Harrison was engaged (on the wall are a poster, by Aubrey Beardsley, of the 1894 production of *Arms and the Man*, directed by Shaw, and a photograph of William Morris). Bernard Shaw, Gabriel Pascal and Andrew Osborn.

Major Barbara   Todger Fairmile makes Bill Walker pray while Mog prays. Robert Newton, Cathleen Cordell and Torin Thatcher.

Major Barbara   Bill Walker pulls Jenny Hill's hair while she prays. Deborah Kerr and Robert Newton.

MRS PEARCE. Dont give her up to him, sir. I dont like his looks. I'll take care of the girl, sir.

Mrs Pearce goes out.

PICKERING. He may not be a blackguard, Higgins.

HIGGINS. Nonsense. Of course he's a blackguard.

PICKERING. Whether he is or not, I'm afraid we shall have some trouble with him.

HIGGINS [*confidently*] Oh no: I think not. If theres any trouble he shall have it with me, not I with him.

Alfred Doolittle is an elderly but vigorous dustman, clad in the costume of his profession, including a hat a back brim covering his neck and shoulders. He has well marked and rather interesting features, and seems equally free from fear and conscience. He has a remarkably expressive voice, the result of a habit of giving vent to his feelings without reserve. His present pose is that of wounded honor and stern resolution.

Note

The first appearance of Doolittle should be impressive and threatening. The audience should have a good look at him as he appears in the doorway.

A strong point must be made of the change in his expression from the outraged avenging father to the irresistibly charming old rascal on the line "Well, what w o u l d a man come for? Be human, Governor."

After this change, Doolittle should be thoroughly l i k e d by the audience.

This must be managed by close-ups. At his exit also a feature must be made of the look at Mrs Pearce and the wink at Higgins.

DOOLITTLE [*at the door, uncertain which of the two gentlemen is his man*] Professor Iggins?

HIGGINS. Here. Good morning. Sit down.

DOOLITTLE. Morning, Governor. [*He sits down magisterially*] I come about a very serious matter, Governor.

HIGGINS [*to Pickering*] Brought up in Hounslow. Mother Welsh, I should think. [*Doolittle opens his mouth, amazed. Higgins continues*] What do you want, Doolittle?

DOOLITTLE [*menacingly*] I want my daughter: thats what I want. See?

HIGGINS. Of course you do. Youre her father, arnt you? You dont suppose anyone else wants her, do you? I'm glad to see you have some spark of family feeling left. She's upstairs. Take her away at once.

DOOLITTLE [*rising, fearfully taken aback*] What!

HIGGINS. Take her away. Do you suppose I'm going to keep your daughter for you?

DOOLITTLE [*remonstrating*] Now, now, look here, Governor. Is this reasonable? Is it fairity to take advantage of a man like this? The girl belongs to me. You got her. Where do I come in? [*He sits down again*].

HIGGINS. Your daughter had the audacity to come to my house and ask me to teach her how to speak properly so that she could get a place in a flower shop. This gentleman and my housekeeper have been here all the time. [*Bullying him*] How dare you come here and attempt to blackmail me? You sent her here on purpose.

DOOLITTLE [*protesting*] No, Governor.

HIGGINS. You must have. How else could you possibly know that she is here?

DOOLITTLE. Dont take a man up like that, Governor.

HIGGINS. The police shall take you up. This is a plant—a plot to extort money by threats. I shall telephone for the police. [*He goes resolutely to the telephone and opens the directory*].

DOOLITTLE. Have I asked you for a brass farthing? I leave it to the gentleman here: have I said a word about money?

HIGGINS [*throwing the book aside and marching down on Doolittle with a poser*] What else did you come for?

DOOLITTLE [*sweetly*] Well, what w o u l d a man come for? Be human, Governor.

HIGGINS. So you came to rescue her from worse than death, eh?

DOOLITTLE [*appreciatively: relieved at being so well understood*] Just so, Governor. Thats right.

HIGGINS. Well: take her away.

DOOLITTLE. Have I said a word about taking her away? Have I now?

HIGGINS [*determinedly*] Youre going to take her away, double quick. [*He crosses to the hearth and rings the bell*].

DOOLITTLE [*rising*] No, Governor. Dont say that. I'm not the man to stand in my girl's light. Heres a career opening for her, as you might say; and—

Mrs Pearce opens the door and awaits orders.

HIGGINS. Mrs Pearce: this is Eliza's father. He has come to take her away. Give her to him. [*He goes back to the piano, with an air of washing his hands of the whole affair*].

DOOLITTLE. No. This is a misunderstanding. Listen here—

MRS PEARCE. He cant take her away, Mr Higgins: how can he? You told me to burn her clothes.

DOOLITTLE. Thats right. I cant carry the girl through the streets like a blooming monkey, can I? I put it to you.

HIGGINS. You have put it to me that you want your daughter. Take your daughter. If she has no clothes go out and buy her some.

DOOLITTLE [*desperate*] Wheres the clothes she come in? Did I burn them or did your missus here?

MRS PEARCE. I am the housekeeper, if you please. I have sent for some clothes for your girl. When they come you can take her away. You can wait in the kitchen. This way, please.

Doolittle, much troubled, accompanies her to the door; then hesitates; finally turns confidentially to Higgins.

DOOLITTLE. Listen here, Governor. You and me is men of the world aint we?

HIGGINS. Oh! Men of the world, are we? Youd better go, Mrs Pearce.

MRS PEARCE. I think so, indeed, sir. [*She goes, with dignity*].

PICKERING. The floor is yours, Mr Doolittle.

DOOLITTLE [*to Pickering*] I thank you, Governor. [*To Higgins, who takes refuge on the piano bench, a little overwhelmed by the proximity of his visitor; for Doolittle has a professional flavor of dust about him*] Well, the truth is, Ive taken a sort of fancy to you, Governor; and if you want the girl, I'm not so set on having her back home again but what I might be open to an arrangement. Regarded in the light of a young woman, she's a fine handsome girl. As a daughter she's not worth her keep; and so I tell you straight. All I ask is my rights as a father; and youre the last man alive to expect me to let her go for nothing; for I can see youre one of the straight sort, Governor. Well, whats a five-pound notle to you? and what Eliza to me? [*He turns to his chair and sits down judicially*].

PICKERING. I think you ought to know, Doolittle, that Mr Higgins's intentions are entirely honorable.

DOOLITTLE. Course they are, Governor. If I thought they wasn't, I'd ask fifty.

HIGGINS [*revolted*] Do you mean to say that you would sell your daughter for £50?

DOOLITTLE. Not in a general way I wouldnt; but to oblige a gentleman like you I'd do a good deal, I do assure you.

PICKERING. Have you no morals, man?

DOOLITTLE [*unabashed*] Cant afford them, Governor. Neither could you if you was as poor as me. Not that I mean any harm, you know. But if Liza is going to have a bit out of this, why not me too?

HIGGINS [*troubled*] I dont know what to do, Pickering. There can be no question that as a matter of morals it's a positive crime to give this chap a farthing. And yet I feel a sort of rough justice in his claim.

DOOLITTLE. Thats it, Governor. Thats all I say. A father's heart, as it were.

PICKERING. Well, I know the feeling; but really it seems hardly right—

DOOLITTLE. Dont say that, Governor. Dont look at it that way. What am I, Governors both? I ask you, what a m I? I'm one of the undeserving poor: thats what I am. Think of what that means to a man. It means that he's up agen middle class morality all the time. If theres anything going, and I put in for a bit of it, it's always the same story: "Youre undeserving; so you cant have it." But my needs is as great as the most deserving widow's that ever got money out of six different charities in one week for the death of the same husband. I dont need less than a deserving man: I need more. I dont eat less hearty than him; and I drink a lot more. I want a bit of amusement, cause I'm a thinking man. I want cheerfulness and a song and a band when I feel low. Well, they charge me just the same for everything as they charge the deserving. What is middle class morality? Just an excuse for never giving me anything. Therefore, I ask you, as two gentlemen, not to play that game on me. I'm playing straight with you. I aint pretending to be deserving. I'm undeserving; and I mean to go on being undeserving. I like it; and thats the truth. Will you take advantage of a man's nature to do him out of the price of his own daughter what he's brought up and fed and clothed by the sweat of his brow until she's growed big enough to be interesting to you two gentlemen? Is five pounds unreasonable? I put it to you; and I leave it to you.

HIGGINS. Pickering: shall I give him a fiver?

PICKERING. He'll make a bad use of it, I'm afraid.

DOOLITTLE. Not me, Governor, so help me I wont. Dont you be afraid that I'll save it and spare it and live idle on it. There wont be a penny of it left by Monday: I'll have to go to work same as if I'd never had it. It wont pauperize me, you bet. Just one good spree for myself and the missus, giving pleasure to ourselves and employment to others, and satisfaction to you to think it's not been throwed away. You couldnt spend it better.

HIGGINS [*taking out his pocket book and coming between Doolittle and the piano*] This is irresistible. Lets give him ten. [*He offers two notes to the dustman*].

DOOLITTLE. No, Governor. She wouldnt have the heart to spend ten; and perhaps I shouldnt neither. Ten pounds is a lot of money: it makes a man feel prudent like; and then goodbye to happiness. You give me what I ask you, Governor: not a penny more, and not a penny less.

HIGGINS [*to Doolittle*] Five pounds I think you said.

DOOLITTLE. Thank you kindly, Governor.

HIGGINS. Youre sure you wont take ten?

DOOLITTLE. Not now. Another time, Governor.

HIGGINS [*handing him a five-pound note*] Here you are.

DOOLITTLE. Thank you, Governor. Good morning. [*He hurries to the door, anxious to get away with his booty. When he opens it he is confronted with a dainty and exquisitely clean young Japanese lady in a simple blue cotton kimono printed cunningly with small white jasmine blossoms. Mrs Pearce is with her. He gets out of her way deferentially and apologizes*]. Beg pardon, miss.

THE JAPANESE LADY. Garn! Dont you know your own daughter?

DOOLITTLE	exclaiming	Bly me! it's Eliza!
HIGGINS	simul-	Whats that? This!
PICKERING	taneously	By Jove!

DOOLITTLE [*with fatherly pride*] Well, I never thought she'd clean up as good looking as that, Governor. She's a credit to me, aint she? And she'll soon pick up your free-and-easy ways.

LIZA. I'm a good girl, I am; and I wont pick up no free-and-easy ways.

HIGGINS. Eliza: if you say again that youre a good girl, your father shall take you home.

LIZA. Not him. You dont know my father. All he come here for was to touch you for some money to get drunk on.

DOOLITTLE. Well, what else would I want money for? To put into the plate in church, I suppose. [*She puts out her tongue at him. He is so incensed by this that Pickering presently finds it necessary to step between them*]. Dont you give me none of your lip; and dont let me hear you giving this gentleman any of it neither, or youll hear from me about it. See?

HIGGINS. Have you any further advice to give her before you go, Doolittle? Your blessing, for instance.

DOOLITTLE. No, Governor: I aint such a mug as to put up my children to all I know myself. Hard enough to hold them in without that. If you want Eliza's mind improved, Governor, you do it yourself with a strap. So long, gentlemen. [*He turns to go*].

HIGGINS [*impressively*] Stop. Youll come regularly to see your daughter. It's your duty, you know. My brother is a clergyman; and he could help you in your talks with her.

DOOLITTLE [*evasively*] Certainly, I'll come, Governor. Not just this week, because I have a job at a distance. But later on you may depend on me. Afternoon, gentlemen. Afternoon, maam. [*He touches his hat to Mrs Pearce, who disdains the salutation and goes out. He winks at Higgins, thinking him probably a fellow sufferer from Mrs Pearce's difficult disposition, and follows her*].

LIZA. Dont you believe the old liar. He'd as soon you set a bulldog on him as a clergyman. You wont see him again in a hurry.

PICKERING. We dont want to, Eliza. Do you?

LIZA. Not me. I dont want never to see him again, I dont. Aint you going to call me Miss Doolittle any more?

PICKERING. I beg your pardon, Miss Doolittle. It was a slip of the tongue.

LIZA. Oh, I dont mind; only it sounded so genteel. I should just like to take a taxi to the corner of Tottenham Court Road and get out there and tell it to wait for me, just to put the girls in their place a bit. I wouldnt speak to them, you know.

PICKERING. Better wait til we get you something really fashionable.

HIGGINS. Besides, you shouldnt cut your old friends now that you have risen in the world. Thats what we call snobbery.

LIZA. You dont call the like of them my friends now, I should hope. Theyve took it out of me often enough with their ridicule when they had the chance; and now I mean to get a bit of my own back. But if I'm to have fashionable clothes, I'll wait.

MRS PEARCE [*coming back*] Now, Eliza. The new things have come for you to try on.

LIZA. Ah-ow-oo-ooh! [*She rushes out*].

MRS PEARCE [*following her*] Oh, dont rush about like that, girl. [*She shuts the door behind her*].

HIGGINS. Pickering: we have taken on a stiff job.

PICKERING [*with conviction*] Higgins: we have.*

Dissolve to:

The study the following day.

Liza, in her new clothes, and feeling her inside put out of step by a lunch, dinner, and breakfast of a kind to which it is unaccustomed, is seated with Higgins and the Colonel, feeling like a hospital out-patient at a first encounter with the doctors.

Higgins, constitutionally unable to sit still, discomposes her still more by striding restlessly about. But for the reassuring presence and quietude of her friend the Colonel she would run for her life, even back to Drury Lane.

HIGGINS. Say your alphabet.

LIZA. I know my alphabet. Do you think I know nothing? I dont need to be taught like a child.

HIGGINS [*thundering*] Say your alphabet.

PICKERING. Say it, Miss Doolittle. You will understand presently. Do what he tells you; and let him teach you in his own way.

LIZA. Oh well, if you put it like that—Ahyee,bəy-ee, cəy-ee, dəy-ee—

HIGGINS [*with the roar of a wounded lion*] Stop. Listen to this, Pickering. This is what we pay for as elementary education. This unfortunate animal has been locked up for nine years in school at our expense to teach her to speak and read the language of Shakespear and Milton. And the result is Ahyee, Bə-yee, Cə-yee, Də-yee. [*To Eliza*] Say A, B, C, D.

LIZA [*almost in tears*] But I'm saying it. Ahyee, Bəyee, Cə-yee—

HIGGINS. Stop. Say a cup of tea.

LIZA. A cappətə-ee.

HIGGINS. Put your tongue forward until it squeezes against the top of your lower teeth. Now say cup.

LIZA. C-c-c—I cant. C-Cup.

---

*In the 1934 manuscript and the 1938 mimeographed script, Shaw suggested an entr'acte sequence in a woodland setting. See Appendix D for the discarded scene.

PICKERING. Good. Splendid, Miss Doolittle.

HIGGINS. By Jupiter, she's done it at the first shot. Pickering: we shall make a duchess of her. [*To Liza*] Now do you think you could possibly say tea? Not tǝ-yee, mind: if you ever say bǝ-yee cǝ-yee dǝ-yee again you shall be dragged round the room three times by the hair of your head. [*Fortissimo*] T, T, T, T.

LIZA [*weeping*] I cant hear no difference cep that it sounds more genteel-like when you say it.

HIGGINS. Well, if you can hear that difference, what the devil are you crying for? Pickering: give her a chocolate.

PICKERING. No, no. Never mind crying a little, Miss Doolittle: you are doing very well; and the lessons wont hurt. I promise you I wont let him drag you round the room by your hair.

HIGGINS. Be off with you to Mrs Pearce and tell her about it. Think about it. Try to do it by yourself: and keep your tongue well forward in your mouth instead of trying to roll it up and swallow it. Another lesson at half-past four this afternoon. Away with you.

Liza, still sobbing, rushes from the room.

Dissolve to:

Mrs Higgins's drawing room, in a flat on Chelsea Embankment. The room has three windows looking on the river; and the ceiling is not so lofty as it would be in an older house of the same pretension. The windows are open, giving access to a balcony with flowers in pots. If you stand with your face to the windows, you have the fireplace on your left, and the door in the right-hand wall close to the corner nearest the windows.

Mrs Higgins was brought up on Morris and Burne Jones; and her room, which is very unlike her son's room in Wimpole Street, is not crowded with furniture and little tables and nicknacks. In the middle of the room there is a big ottoman; and this, with the carpet, the Morris wall-papers, and the Morris chintz window curtains and brocade covers of the ottoman and its cushions, supply all the ornament, and are much too handsome to be hidden by odds and ends of useless things. A few good oil-paintings from the exhibitions in the Grosvenor Gallery thirty years ago (the Burne Jones, not the Whistler side of them) are on the walls. The only landscape is a Cecil Lawson on the scale of a Rubens. There is a portrait of Mrs Higgins as she was when she defied fashion in her youth in one of the beautiful Rossettian costumes which, when caricatured by people who did not understand, led to the absurdities of popular estheticism in the eighteen-seventies.

In the corner diagonally opposite the door Mrs Higgins, now over sixty and long past taking the trouble to dress out of the fashion, sits writing at an elegantly simple writing-table with a bell button within reach of her hand. There is a Chippendale chair further back in the room between her and the window nearest her side. At the other side of the room, further forward, is an Elizabethan chair roughly carved in the taste of Inigo Jones. On the same side a piano in a decorated case. The corner between the fireplace and the window is occupied by a divan cushioned in Morris chintz.

It is between four and five in the afternoon.

The door is opened violently; and Higgins enters.

MRS HIGGINS [*dismayed*] Henry! [*Scolding him*] What are you doing here today? It is my at-home day: you promised not to come.

HIGGINS. Ive picked up a girl.

MRS HIGGINS. Does that mean that some girl has picked you up?
HIGGINS. Not at all. I dont mean a love affair. [*He sits on the settee*].
MRS HIGGINS. What a pity!
HIGGINS. Why?
MRS HIGGINS. Well, you never fall in love with anyone under forty-five. When will you discover that there are some rather nice-looking young women about?
HIGGINS. Oh, I cant be bothered with young women. My idea of a lovable woman is somebody as like you as possible. I shall never get into the way of seriously liking young women: some habits lie too deep to be changed. [*Rising abruptly and walking about, jingling his money and his keys in his trouser pockets*] Besides, theyre all idiots.
MRS HIGGINS. Do you know what you would do if you really loved me, Henry?
HIGGINS. Oh bother! What? Marry, I suppose.
MRS HIGGINS. No. Stop fidgeting and take your hands out of your pockets. [*With a gesture of despair, he obeys and sits down again*]. Thats a good boy. Now tell me about the girl.
HIGGINS. She's coming to see you.
MRS HIGGINS. I dont remember asking her.
HIGGINS. You didnt. *I* asked her. If youd known her you wouldnt have asked her.
MRS HIGGINS. Indeed! Why?
HIGGINS. Well, it's like this. She's a common flower girl. I picked her off the kerbstone.
MRS HIGGINS. And invited her to my at-home!
HIGGINS [*rising and coming to her to coax her*] Oh, thatll be all right. Ive taught her to speak properly; and she has strict orders as to her behavior. She's to keep to two subjects: the weather and everybody's health—Fine day and How do you do, you know—and not to let herself go on things in general. That will be safe.
MRS HIGGINS. Safe! To talk about our health! about our insides! perhaps about our outsides! How could you be so silly, Henry?
HIGGINS [*impatiently*] Well, she must talk about something. [*He controls himself and sits down again*]. Oh, she'll be all right: dont you fuss. Pickering is in it with me. Ive a sort of bet on that I'll pass her off as a duchess in six months. I started on her some months ago; and she's getting on like a house on fire. I shall win my bet. She has a quick ear; and she's been easier to teach than my middle-class pupils because she's had to learn a complete new language. She talks English almost as you talk French.
MRS HIGGINS. Thats satisfactory, at all events.
HIGGINS. Well, it is and it isnt.
MRS HIGGINS. What does that mean?
HIGGINS. You see, Ive got her pronunciation all right; but you have to consider not only h o w a girl pronounces, but w h a t she pronounces; and that's where—
They are interrupted by the parlormaid, announcing guests.
THE PARLORMAID. Mrs and Miss Eynsford Hill. [*She withdraws*].
HIGGINS. Oh Lord! [*He rises and makes for the door; but before he reaches it his mother introduces him*].

Mrs and Miss Eynsford Hill are the mother and daughter who sheltered from the rain in Covent Garden. The mother is well bred, quiet, and has the habitual anxiety of straitened means. The daughter has acquired a gay air of being very much at home in society: the bravado of genteel poverty.

MRS EYNSFORD HILL [*to Mrs Higgins*] How do you do? [*They shake hands*].

MISS EYNSFORD HILL. How d'you do? [*She shakes*].

MRS HIGGINS [*introducing*] My son Henry.

MRS EYNSFORD HILL. Your celebrated son! I have so longed to meet you, Professor Higgins.

HIGGINS [*glumly, making no movement in her direction*] Delighted. [*He backs against the piano and bows brusquely*].

MISS EYNSFORD HILL [*going to him with confident familiarity*] How do you do?

HIGGINS [*staring at her*] Ive seen you before somewhere. I havnt the ghost of a notion where; but Ive heard your voice. [*Drearily*] It doesnt matter. Youd better sit down.

MRS HIGGINS. I'm sorry to say that my celebrated son has no manners. You mustnt mind him.

MISS EYNSFORD HILL [*gaily*] I dont. [*She sits in the Elizabethan chair*].

MRS EYNSFORD HILL [*a little bewildered*] Not at all. [*She sits on the ottoman between her daughter and Mrs Higgins, who has turned her chair away from the writing-table*].

HIGGINS. Oh, have I been rude? I didnt mean to be.

He goes to the central window, through which, with his back to the company, he contemplates the river and flowers in Battersea Park on the opposite bank as if they were a frozen desert.

The parlormaid returns, ushering in Pickering.

THE PARLORMAID. Colonel Pickering. [*She withdraws*].

PICKERING. How do you do, Mrs Higgins?

MRS HIGGINS. So glad youve come. Do you know Mrs Eynsford Hill—Miss Eynsford Hill? [*Exchange of bows. The Colonel brings the Chippendale chair a little forward between Mrs Hill and Mrs Higgins and sits down*].

PICKERING. Has Henry told you what weve come for?

HIGGINS [*over his shoulder*] We were interrupted: damn it!

MRS HIGGINS. Oh Henry, Henry, really!

MRS EYNSFORD HILL [*half rising*] Are we in the way?

MRS HIGGINS [*rising and making her sit down again*] No, no. You couldnt have come more fortunately: we want you to meet a friend of ours.

HIGGINS [*turning hopefully*] Yes, by George! We want two or three people. Youll do as well as anybody else.

The parlormaid returns, ushering Freddy.

THE PARLORMAID. Mr Eynsford Hill.

HIGGINS [*almost audibly, past endurance*] God of Heaven! another of them.

FREDDY [*shaking hands with Mrs Higgins*] Ahdedo?

MRS HIGGINS. I dont think you know my son, Professor Higgins.

FREDDY [*going to Higgins*] Ahdedo?

HIGGINS [*looking at him much as if he were a pickpocket*] I'll take my oath Ive met y o u before somewhere. Where was it?

FREDDY. I dont think so.

HIGGINS [*resignedly*] It dont matter, anyhow. Sit down.

He shakes Freddy's hand, and almost slings him on to the ottoman with his face to the windows; then comes round to the other side of it.

HIGGINS. Well, here we are, anyhow! [*He sits down on the ottoman next Mrs Eynsford Hill on her left*]. And now what the devil are we going to talk about until Eliza comes?

MRS HIGGINS. Henry: you are the life and soul of the Royal Society's soirées; but really youre rather trying on more commonplace occasions.

HIGGINS. Am I? Very sorry. [*Beaming suddenly*] I suppose I am, you know. [*Uproariously*] Ha, ha!

THE PARLORMAID [*opening the door*] Miss Doolittle. [*She withdraws*].

HIGGINS [*rising hastily and running to Mrs Higgins*] Here she is, mother. [*He stands on tiptoe and makes signs over his mother's head to Liza to indicate to her which lady is her hostess*].

Liza, who is exquisitely dressed, produces an impression of such remarkable distinction and beauty as she enters that they all rise, quite fluttered. Guided by Higgins's signals, she comes to Mrs Higgins with studied grace.

LIZA [*speaking with pedantic correctness of pronunciation and great beauty of tone*] How do you do, Mrs Higgins? [*She gasps slightly in making sure of the H in Higgins, but is quite successful*]. Mr Higgins told me I might come.

MRS HIGGINS [*cordially*] Quite right: I'm very glad indeed to see you.

PICKERING. How do you do, Miss Doolittle?

LIZA [*shaking hands with him*] Colonel Pickering, is it not?

MRS EYNSFORD HILL. I feel sure we have met before, Miss Doolittle. I remember your eyes.

LIZA. How do you do? [*She sits down on the ottoman gracefully in the place just left vacant by Higgins*].

MRS EYNSFORD HILL [*introducing*] My daughter Clara.

LIZA. How do you do?

CLARA [*impulsively*] How do you do? [*She sits down on the ottoman beside Liza, devouring her with her eyes*].

FREDDY [*coming to their side of the ottoman*] Ive certainly had the pleasure.

MRS EYNSFORD HILL [*introducing*] My son Freddy.

LIZA. How do you do?

Freddy bows and sits down in the Elizabethan chair, infatuated.

HIGGINS [*suddenly*] By George, yes: it all comes back to me! [*They stare at him*]. Covent Garden! [*Lamentably*] What a damned thing!

MRS HIGGINS. Henry, please! [*He is about to sit on the edge of the table*] Dont sit on my writing-table: youll break it.

HIGGINS [*sulkily*] Sorry.

He goes to the divan, stumbling into the fender and over the fire-irons on his way; extricating himself with muttered imprecations; and finishing his disastrous journey by throwing himself so impatiently on the divan that he almost breaks it. Mrs Higgins looks at him, but controls herself and says nothing.

A long and painful pause ensues.

MRS HIGGINS [*at last, conversationally*] Will it rain, do you think?

LIZA. The shallow depression in the west of these islands is likely to move slowly in an easterly direction. There are no indications of any great change in the barometrical situation.

FREDDY. Ha! ha! how awfully funny!

LIZA. What is wrong with that, young man? I bet I got it right.

FREDDY. Killing!

MRS EYNSFORD HILL. I'm sure I hope it wont turn cold. Theres so much influenza about. It runs right through our whole family regularly every spring.

LIZA [darkly] My aunt died of influenza; so they said.

MRS EYNSFORD HILL [clicks her tongue sympathetically]!!!

LIZA [in the same tragic tone] But it's my belief they done the old woman in.

MRS HIGGINS [puzzled] Done her in?

LIZA. Y-e-e-e-es, Lord love you! Why should s h e die of influenza? She come through diphtheria right enough the year before. I saw her with my own eyes. Fairly blue with it, she was. They all thought she was dead; but my father he kept ladling gin down her throat til she came to so sudden that she bit the bowl off the spoon.

MRS EYNSFORD HILL [startled] Dear me!

LIZA [piling up the indictment] What call would a woman with that strength in her have to die of influenza? What become of her new straw hat that should have come to me? Somebody pinched it; and what I says is, them as pinched it done her in.

MRS EYNSFORD HILL. What does doing her in mean?

HIGGINS [hastily] Oh, thats the new small talk. To do a person in means to kill them.

MRS EYNSFORD HILL [to Liza, horrified] You surely dont believe that your aunt was killed?

LIZA. Do I not! Them she lived with would have killed her for a hat-pin, let alone a hat.

MRS EYNSFORD HILL. But it cant have been right for your father to pour spirits down her throat like that. It might have killed her.

LIZA. Not her. Gin was mother's milk to her. Besides, he's poured so much down his own throat that he knew the good of it.

MRS EYNSFORD HILL. Do you mean that he drank?

LIZA. Drank! My word! Something chronic.

MRS EYNSFORD HILL. How dreadful for you!

LIZA. Not a bit. It never did him no harm what I could see. But then he did not keep it up regular. [Cheerfully] On the burst, as you might say, from time to time. And always more agreeable when he had a drop in. When he was out of work, my mother used to give him fourpence and tell him to go out and not come back until he'd drunk himself cheerful and loving-like. Theres lots of women has to make their husbands drunk to make them fit to live with. [Now quite at her ease] You see, it's like this. If a man has a bit of a conscience, it always takes him when he's sober; and then it makes him low-spirited. A drop of booze just takes that off and makes him happy. [To Freddy, who is in convulsions of suppressed laughter] Here! what are you sniggering at?

FREDDY. The new small talk. You do it so awfully well.

LIZA. If I was doing it proper, what was you laughing at? [To Higgins] Have I said anything I oughtnt?

MRS HIGGINS [interposing] Not at all, Miss Doolittle.

LIZA. Well, thats a mercy, anyhow. [Expansively] What I always say is—

HIGGINS [rising and looking at his watch] Ahem!

LIZA [looking round at him; taking the hint; and rising] Well: I must go. [They all *rise. Freddy goes to the door*]. So pleased to have met you. Goodbye. [*She shakes hands with Mrs Higgins*].

MRS HIGGINS. Goodbye.

LIZA. Goodbye, Colonel Pickering.

PICKERING. Goodbye, Miss Doolittle. [*They shake hands*].

LIZA [*nodding to the others*] Goodbye, all.

FREDDY [*opening the door for her*] Are you walking across the Park, Miss Doolittle? If so—

LIZA [*with perfectly elegant diction*] Walk! Not bloody likely. [*Sensation*]. I am going in a taxi. [*She goes out*].

    Pickering gasps and sits down.

FREDDY [*to the heavens at large*] Well, I ask you—[*He gives it up, and comes to Mrs Higgins*]. Goodbye.

MRS HIGGINS [*shaking hands*] Goodbye. Would you like to meet Miss Doolittle again?

FREDDY [*eagerly*] Yes, I should, most awfully.

MRS HIGGINS. Well, you know my days.

FREDDY. Yes. Thanks awfully. Goodbye. [*He goes out*].

CLARA. May I come too?

MRS HIGGINS. Of course, dear. Goodbye.

CLARA. Thanks awfully. Goodbye. [*She goes, after a shake-hands*].

MRS EYNSFORD HILL. Goodbye, Mr Higgins.

HIGGINS. Goodbye. Goodbye.

MRS EYNSFORD HILL [*to Pickering*] It's no use. I shall never be able to bring myself to use that word.

PICKERING. Dont. It's not compulsory, you know. Youll get on quite well without it.

MRS EYNSFORD HILL. Only, Clara is down on me if I am not positively reeking with the latest slang. Goodbye.

PICKERING. Goodbye. [*They shake hands*].

MRS EYNSFORD HILL [*to Mrs Higgins*] Thank you, dear, for a most exciting afternoon. Goodbye. [*She goes out*].

HIGGINS [*eagerly*] Well? Is Eliza presentable? [*He swoops on his mother and drags her to the ottoman, where she sits down in Liza's place with her son on her left*].

    Pickering returns to his chair on her right.

MRS HIGGINS. You silly boy, of course she's not presentable. She's a triumph of your art and of her dressmaker's; but if you suppose for a moment that she doesnt give herself away in every sentence she utters, you must be perfectly cracked about her. And now tell me, Colonel Pickering: what is the exact state of things in Wimpole Street?

PICKERING [*cheerfully: as if this completely changed the subject*] Well, I have come to live there with Henry. We work together at my Indian Dialects; and we think it more convenient—

MRS HIGGINS. Quite so. I know all about that; it's an excellent arrangement. But where does this girl live?

HIGGINS. With us, of course. Where s h o u l d she live?

MRS HIGGINS. But on what terms? Is she a servant? If not, what is she?

PICKERING [*slowly*] I think I know what you mean, Mrs Higgins.

HIGGINS. Well dash me if *I* do! Ive had to work at the girl every day for months to get her to present pitch. Besides, she's useful. She knows where my things are, and remembers my appointments and so forth.

MRS HIGGINS. How does your housekeeper get on with her?

HIGGINS. Mrs Pearce? Oh, she's jolly glad to get so much taken off her hands; for before Eliza came, s h e used to have to find things and remind me of my appointments. But she's got some silly bee in her bonnet about Eliza. She keeps saying "You dont think, sir": doesnt she, Pick?

PICKERING. Yes: thats the formula. "You dont think, sir." Thats the end of every conversation about Eliza.

MRS HIGGINS. You certainly are a pretty pair of babies, playing with your live doll.

HIGGINS. Playing! The hardest job I ever tackled: make no mistake about that, mother. But you have no idea how frightfully interesting it is to take a human being and change her into a quite different human being by creating a new speech for her. It's filling up the deepest gulf that separates class from class and soul from soul.

PICKERING [*drawing his chair closer to Mrs Higgins and bending over to her eagerly*] Yes: it's enormously interesting. I assure you, Mrs Higgins, we take Eliza very seriously. Every week—every day almost—there is some new change. [*Closer again*] We keep records of every stage—dozens of gramophone disks and photographs—

HIGGINS [*assailing her at the other ear*] Yes, by George: it's the most absorbing experiment I ever tackled. She regularly fills our lives up: doesnt she, Pick?

PICKERING. We're always talking Eliza.

HIGGINS. Teaching Eliza.

PICKERING. Dressing Eliza.

MRS HIGGINS. What!

HIGGINS. Inventing new Elizas.

	[*speaking together*]	
HIGGINS.		You know, she has the most extraordinary quickness of ear:
PICKERING.		I assure you, my dear Mrs Higgins, that girl
HIGGINS.		just like a parrot. Ive tried her with every
PICKERING.		is a genius. She can play the piano quite beautifully.
HIGGINS.		possible sort of sound that a human being can make:
PICKERING.		We have taken her to classical concerts and to music
HIGGINS.		Continental dialects, African dialects, Hottentot
PICKERING.		halls; and it's all the same to her; she plays everything
HIGGINS.		clicks, things it took me years to get hold of; and
PICKERING.		she hears right off when she comes home, whether it's
HIGGINS.		she picks them up like a shot, right away, as if she had
PICKERING.		Beethoven and Brahms or Lehar and Lionel Monckton;

HIGGINS. ⎱ [*speaking* ⎰ been at it all her life.
PICKERING. ⎰ *together*] ⎱ though six months ago, she'd never as much as touched a piano—

MRS HIGGINS [*putting her fingers in her ears, as they are by this time shouting one another down with an intolerable noise*] Sh-sh-sh—sh! [*They stop*].

PICKERING. I beg your pardon. [*He draws his chair back apologetically*].

HIGGINS. Sorry. When Pickering starts shouting nobody can get a word in edgeways.

MRS HIGGINS. Be quiet, Henry. Colonel Pickering: dont you realize that when Eliza walked into Wimpole Street, something walked in with her?

PICKERING. Her father did. But Henry soon got rid of him.

MRS HIGGINS. It would have been more to the point if her mother had. But as her mother didnt something else did.

PICKERING. But what?

MRS HIGGINS [*unconsciously dating herself by the word*] A problem.

PICKERING. Oh, I see. The problem of how to pass her off as a lady.

HIGGINS. I'll solve that problem. Ive half solved it already.

MRS HIGGINS. No, you two infinitely stupid male creatures: the problem of what is to be done with her afterwards.

HIGGINS. I dont see anything in that. She can go her own way, with all the advantages I have given her.

MRS HIGGINS. The advantages of that poor woman who was here just now! The manners and habits that disqualify a fine lady from earning her own living without giving her a fine lady's income! Is that what you mean?

PICKERING [*indulgently, being rather bored*] Oh, that will be all right, Mrs Higgins. [*He rises to go*].

HIGGINS [*rising also*] We'll find her some light employment.

PICKERING. She's happy enough. Dont you worry about her. Goodbye. [*He shakes hands as if he were consoling a frightened child, and makes for the door*].

HIGGINS. Anyhow, theres no good bothering now. The thing's done. Goodbye, mother. [*He kisses her, and follows Pickering*].

PICKERING [*turning for a final consolation*] There are plenty of openings. We'll do whats right. Goodbye.

HIGGINS [*to Pickering as they go out together*] Lets take her to the Shakespear exhibition at Earls Court.

PICKERING. Yes: lets. Her remarks will be delicious.

HIGGINS. She'll mimic all the people for us when we get home.

PICKERING. Ripping. [*Both are heard laughing as they go downstairs*].

MRS HIGGINS [*rises with an impatient bounce, and returns to her work at the writing-table. She sweeps a litter of disarranged papers out of her way; snatches a sheet of paper from her stationery case; and tries resolutely to write. At the third line she gives it up; flings down her pen; grips the table angrily and exclaims*] Oh, men! men!! men!!!*

Dissolve to:

The street before an Embassy in London one summer evening after dark. The hall door has an awning and a carpet across the sidewalk to the kerb, because a grand reception is in progress. A small crowd is lined up to see the guests arrive.

* In the 1934 screenplay, a shorter ballroom scene follows. See Appendix E.

A Rolls-Royce car drives up. Pickering in evening dress, with medals and orders, alights, and hands out Liza, in opera cloak, evening dress, diamonds, fan, flowers and all accessories. Higgins follows. The car drives off; and the three go up the steps and into the house, the door opening for them as they approach.

Inside the house. A spacious hall from which the grand staircase rises. On the left are the arrangements for the gentlemen's cloaks. The male guests are depositing their hats and wraps there.

On the right is a door leading to the ladies' cloakroom. Ladies are going in cloaked and coming out in splendor. Pickering whispers to Liza and points out the ladies' room. She goes into it. Higgins and Pickering take off their overcoats and take tickets for them from the attendant.

One of the guests, occupied in the same way, has his back turned. Having taken his ticket, he turns round and reveals himself as an important looking young man with an astonishingly hairy face. He has an enormous moustache, flowing out into luxuriant whiskers. Waves of hair cluster on his brow. His hair is cropped closely at the back, and glows with oil. Otherwise he is very smart. He wears several worthless orders. He is evidently a foreigner, guessable as a whiskered Pandour from Hungary; but in spite of the ferocity of his moustache he is amiable and genially voluble.

Recognizing Higgins, he flings his arms wide apart and approaches him enthusiastically.

WHISKERS. Maestro, maestro. [*He embraces Higgins and kisses him on both cheeks*]. You remember me?

HIGGINS. No I dont. Who the devil are you?

WHISKERS. I am you pupil: your first pupil, your best and greatest pupil. I am little Nepommuck, the marvellous boy. I have made your name famous throughout Europe. You teach me phonetic. You cannot forget ME.

HIGGINS. Why dont you shave?

NEPOMMUCK. I have not your imposing appearance, your chin, your brow. Nobody notice me when I shave. Now I am famous: they call me Hairy Faced Dick.

HIGGINS. And what are you doing here among all these swells?

NEPOMMUCK. I am interpreter. I speak 32 languages. I am indispensable at these international parties. You are great cockney specialist: you place a man anywhere in London the moment he open his mouth. I place any man in Europe.

A footman hurries down the grand staircase and comes to Nepommuck.

FOOTMAN. You are wanted upstairs. Her Excellency cannot understand the Greek gentleman.

NEPOMMUCK. Thank you, yes, immediately.

The footman goes and is lost in the crowd.

NEPOMMUCK [*to Higgins*] This Greek diplomatist pretends he cannot speak nor understand English. He cannot deceive me. He is the son of a Clerkenwell watchmaker. He speaks English so villainously that he dare not utter a word of it without betraying his origin. I help him to pretend; but I make him pay through the nose. I make them all pay. Ha Ha! [*He hurries upstairs*].

PICKERING. Is this fellow really an expert? Can he find out Eliza and blackmail her?

HIGGINS. We shall see. If he finds her out I lose my bet.

Liza comes from the cloakroom and joins them.

PICKERING. Well, Eliza, now for it. Are you ready?

LIZA. Are you nervous, Colonel?

PICKERING. Frightfully. I feel exactly as I felt before my first battle. It's the first time that frightens.

LIZA. It is not the first time for me, Colonel. I have done this fifty times—hundreds of times—in my little piggery in Angel Court in my day-dreams. I am in a dream now. Promise me not to let Professor Higgins wake me; for if he does I shall forget everything and talk as I used to in Drury Lane.

PICKERING. Not a word, Higgins. [*To Liza*] Now, ready?

LIZA. Ready.

PICKERING. Go.

They mount the stairs, Higgins last. Pickering whispers to the footman on the first landing.

FIRST LANDING FOOTMAN. Miss Doolittle, Colonel Pickering, Professor Higgins.

SECOND LANDING FOOTMAN. Miss Doolittle, Colonel Pickering, Professor Higgins.

At the top of the staircase the Ambassador and his wife, with Nepommuck at her elbow, are receiving.

HOSTESS [*taking Liza's hand*] How d'ye do?

HOST [*same play*] How d'ye do? How d'ye do, Pickering?

LIZA [*with a beautiful gravity that awes her hostess*] How do you do? [*She passes on to the drawingroom*].

HOSTESS. Is that your adopted daughter, Colonel Pickering. She will make a sensation.

PICKERING. Most kind of you to invite her for me. [*He passes on*].

HOSTESS [*to Nepommuck*] Find out all about her.

NEPOMMUCK [*bowing*] Excellency—[*he goes into the crowd*].

HOST. How d'ye do, Higgins? You have a rival here tonight. He introduced himself as your pupil. Is he any good?

HIGGINS. He can learn a language in a fortnight—knows dozens of them. A sure mark of a fool. As a phonetician, no good whatever.

HOSTESS. How d'ye do, Professor?

HIGGINS. How do you do? Fearful bore for you this sort of thing. Forgive my part in it. [*He passes on*].

The drawingroom and its suite of salons. The reception is in full swing. Liza passes through. She is so intent on her ordeal that she walks like a somnambulist in a desert instead of a débutante in a fashionable crowd. They stop talking to look at her, admiring her dress, her jewels, and her strangely attractive self. Some of the younger ones at the back stand on their chairs to see.

The Host and Hostess come in from the staircase and mingle with their guests. Higgins, gloomy and contemptuous of the whole business, comes into the group where they are chatting.

HOSTESS. Ah, here is Professor Higgins: he will tell us. Tell us about the wonderful young lady, Professor.

HIGGINS [*almost morosely*] What wonderful young lady?

HOSTESS. You know very well. They tell me there has been nothing like her in London since people stood on their chairs to look at Mrs Langtry.

Nepommuck joins the group, full of news.

HOSTESS. Ah, here you are at last, Nepommuck. Have you found out all about the Doolittle lady?

NEPOMMUCK. I have found out all about her. She is a fraud.

HOSTESS. A fraud! Oh no.

NEPOMMUCK. YES, yes. She cannot deceive me. Her name cannot be Doolittle.

HIGGINS. Why?

NEPOMMUCK. Because Doolittle is an English name. And she is not English.

HOSTESS. Oh, nonsense! She speaks English perfectly.

NEPOMMUCK. Too perfectly. Can you shew me any English woman who speaks English as it should be spoken? Only foreigners who have been taught to speak it speak it well.

HOSTESS. Certainly she terrified me by the way she said How d'ye do. I had a schoolmistress who talked like that; and I was mortally afraid of her. But if she is not English what is she?

NEPOMMUCK. Hungarian.

ALL THE REST. Hungarian!

NEPOMMUCK. Hungarian. And of royal blood. I am Hungarian. My blood is royal.

HIGGINS. Did you speak to her in Hungarian?

NEPOMMUCK. I did. She was very clever. She said "Please speak to me in English; I do not understand French." French! She pretends not to know the difference between Hungarian and French. Impossible: she knows both.

HIGGINS. And the blood royal? How did you find that out?

NEPOMMUCK. Instinct, maestro, instinct. Only the Magyar races can produce that air of the divine right, those resolute eyes. She is a princess.

HOST. What do you say, Professor?

HIGGINS. I say an ordinary London girl out of the gutter and taught to speak by an expert. I place her in Drury Lane.

NEPOMMUCK. Ha ha ha! Oh, maestro, maestro, you are mad on the subject of cockney dialects. The London gutter is the whole world for you.

HIGGINS [to the Hostess] What does your Excellency say?

HOSTESS. Oh, of course, I agree with Nepommuck. She must be a princess at least.

HOST. Not necessarily legitimate, of course. Morganatic perhaps. But that is undoubtedly her class.

HIGGINS. I stick to my opinion.

HOSTESS. Oh, you are incorrigible.

The group breaks up, leaving Higgins isolated. Pickering joins him.

PICKERING. Where is Eliza? We must keep an eye on her.

Liza joins them.

LIZA. I dont think I can bear much more. The people all stare so at me. An old lady has just told me that I speak exactly like Queen Victoria. I am sorry if I have lost your bet. I have done my best; but nothing can make me the same as these people.

PICKERING. You have not lost it, my dear. You have won it ten times over.

HIGGINS. Let us get out of this. I have had enough of chattering to these fools.

PICKERING. Eliza is tired; and I am hungry. Let us clear out and have supper somewhere.

The scene fades as the three make for the stairs.

Fade into:

The Wimpole Street laboratory. Midnight. Nobody in the room. The clock on the mantelpiece strikes twelve. The fire is not alight: it is a summer night.

Presently Higgins and Pickering are heard on the stairs.

HIGGINS [*calling down to Pickering*] I say, Pick: lock up, will you? I shant be going out again.

PICKERING. Right. Can Mrs Pearce go to bed? We dont want anything more, do we?

HIGGINS. Lord, no!

Liza opens the door and is seen on the lighted landing dressed as in the previous shot. She comes to the hearth, and switches on the electric lights there. She is tired; her pallor contrasts strongly with her dark eyes and hair; and her expression is almost tragic. She takes off her cloak; puts her fan and gloves on the piano; and sits down on the bench, brooding and silent. Higgins, in evening dress, with overcoat and hat, comes in, carrying a smoking jacket which he has picked up downstairs. He takes off the hat and overcoat; throws them carelessly on the newspaper stand; disposes of his coat in the same way; puts on the smoking jacket; and throws himself wearily into the easy-chair at the hearth. Pickering, similarly attired, comes in. He also takes off his hat and overcoat, and is about to throw them on Higgins's when he hesitates.

PICKERING. I say: Mrs Pearce will row if we leave these things lying about in the drawing room.

HIGGINS. Oh, chuck them over the bannisters into the hall. She'll find them there in the morning and put them away all right. She'll think we were drunk.

PICKERING. We are, slightly. Are there any letters?

HIGGINS. I didnt look. [*Pickering takes the overcoats and hats and goes downstairs. Higgins begins half singing half yawning an air from La Fanciulla del Golden West. Suddenly he stops and exclaims*] I wonder where the devil my slippers are!

Liza looks at him darkly; then rises suddenly and leaves the room.

Higgins yawns again, and resumes his song.

Pickering returns, with the contents of the letter-box in his hand.

PICKERING. Only circulars, and this coroneted billet-doux for you. [*He throws the circulars into the fender, and posts himself on the hearthrug, with his back to the grate*].

HIGGINS [*glancing at the billet-doux*] Money-lender. [*He throws the letter after the circulars*].

Liza returns with a pair of large down-at-heel slippers. She places them on the carpet before Higgins, and sits as before without a word.

HIGGINS [*yawning again*] Oh Lord! What an evening! What a crew! What a silly tomfoolery! [*He raises his shoe to unlace it, and catches sight of the slippers. He stops unlacing and looks at them as if they had appeared there of their own accord*]. Oh! theyre there, are they?

PICKERING [*stretching himself*] Well, I feel a bit tired. It's been a long day. Rather too much of a good thing. But youve won your bet, Higgins. Eliza did the trick, and something to spare, eh?

HIGGINS [*fervently*] Thank God it's over!

Liza flinches violently; but they take no notice of her; and she recovers herself and sits stonily as before.

PICKERING. Were you nervous? *I* was. Eliza didnt seem a bit nervous.

HIGGINS. Oh, s h e wasnt nervous. I knew she'd be all right. No: it's the strain of putting the job through all these months that has told on me. It was interesting enough at first, while we were at the phonetics; but after that I got deadly sick of it. If I hadnt backed myself to do it I should have chucked the whole thing up two months ago. It was a silly notion: the whole thing has been a bore.

PICKERING. Oh come! the reception was frightfully exciting. My heart began beating like anything.

HIGGINS. Yes, for the first three minutes. But when I saw we were going to win hands down, I felt like a bear in a cage, hanging about doing nothing. I tell you, Pickering, never again for me. No more artificial duchesses. The whole thing has been simple purgatory.

PICKERING. Youve never been broken in properly to the social routine. [*Strolling over to the piano*] I rather enjoy dipping into it occasionally myself: it makes me feel young again. Anyhow, it was a great success: an immense success. I was quite frightened once or twice because Eliza was doing it so well. You see, lots of the real people cant do it at all: theyre such fools that they think style comes by nature to people in their position; and so they never learn.

HIGGINS. Yes: thats what drives me mad: the silly people dont know their own silly business. [*Rising*] However, it's over and done with; and now I can go to bed at last without dreading tomorrow.

Liza's beauty becomes murderous.

PICKERING. I think I shall turn in too. Still, it's been a great occasion: a triumph for you. Goodnight. [*He goes*].

HIGGINS [*following him*] Goodnight. [*Over his shoulder, at the door*] Put out the lights, Eliza; and tell Mrs Pearce not to make coffee for me in the morning: I'll take tea. [*He goes out*].

Liza tries to control herself and feel indifferent as she rises and walks across to the hearth to switch off the lights. By the time she gets there she is on the point of screaming. She sits down in Higgins's chair and holds on hard to the arms. Finally she gives way and flings herself furiously on the floor, raging.

HIGGINS [*in despairing wrath outside*] What the devil have I done with my slippers? [*He appears at the door*].

LIZA [*snatching up the slippers, and hurling them at him one after the other with all her force*] There are your slippers. And there. Take your slippers; and may you never have a day's luck with them!

HIGGINS [*astounded*] What on earth—! [*He comes to her*]. Whats the matter? Get up. [*He pulls her up*]. Anything wrong?

LIZA [*breathless*] Nothing wrong—with y o u . Ive won your bet for you, havnt I? Thats enough for you. *I* dont matter, I suppose.

HIGGINS. Y o u won my bet! You! Presumptuous insect! *I* won it. What did you throw those slippers at me for?

LIZA. Because I wanted to smash your face. I'd like to kill you, you selfish brute. Why didnt you leave me where you picked me out of—in the gutter? You thank God it's all over, and that now you can throw me back again there, do you? (*She crisps her fingers frantically*].

HIGGINS [*looking at her in cool wonder*] The creature is nervous, after all.

LIZA [*gives a suffocated scream of fury, and instictively darts her nails at his face*]!!

HIGGINS [*catching her wrists*] Ah! would you? Claws in, you cat. How dare you shew your temper to me? Sit down and be quiet. [*He throws her roughly into the easy-chair*].

LIZA [*crushed by superior strength and weight*] Whats to become of me? Whats to become of me?

HIGGINS. How the devil do I know whats to become of you? What does it matter what becomes of you?

LIZA. You dont care. I know you dont care. You wouldnt care if I was dead. I'm nothing to you—not so much as them slippers.

HIGGINS [*thundering*] T h o s e slippers.

LIZA [*with bitter submission*] Those slippers. I didnt think it made any difference now.

A pause. Liza hopeless and crushed. Higgins a little uneasy.

HIGGINS [*in his loftiest manner*] Why have you begun going on like this? May I ask whether you complain of your treatment here?

LIZA. No.

HIGGINS. Has anybody behaved badly to you? Colonel Pickering? Mrs Pearce? Any of the servants?

LIZA. No.

HIGGINS. I presume you dont pretend that *I* have treated you badly?

LIZA. No.

HIGGINS. I am glad to hear it. [*He moderates his tone*]. Perhaps youre tired after the strain of the day. Will you have a glass of champagne? [*He moves towards the door*].

LIZA. No. [*Recollecting her manners*] Thank you.

HIGGINS [*good-humored again*] This has been coming on you for some days. I suppose it was natural for you to be anxious about the reception. But thats all over now. [*He pats her kindly on the shoulder. She writhes*]. Theres nothing more to worry about.

LIZA. No. Nothing more for y o u to worry about. [*She suddenly rises and gets away from him by going to the piano bench, where she sits and hides her face*]. Oh God! I wish I was dead.

HIGGINS [*staring after her in sincere surprise*] Why? In heaven's name, why? [*Reasonably, going to her*] Listen to me, Eliza. All this irritation is purely subjective.

LIZA. I dont understand. I'm too ignorant.

HIGGINS. It's only imagination. Low spirits and nothing else. Nobody's hurting you. Nothing's wrong. You go to bed like a good girl and sleep it off. Have a little cry and say your prayers: that will make you comfortable.

LIZA. I heard y o u r prayers. "Thank God it's all over!"

HIGGINS [*impatiently*] Well, d o n t you thank God it's all over? Now you are free and can do what you like.

LIZA [*pulling herself together in desperation*] What am I fit for? What have you left me fit for? Where am I to go? What am I to do? Whats to become of me?

HIGGINS [*enlightened, but not at all impressed*] Oh, t h a t s whats worrying you, is it? [*He thrusts his hands into his pockets, and walks about in his usual manner, rattling the contents of his pockets, as if condescending to a trivial subject out of pure kindness*]. I shouldnt bother about it if I were you. I should imagine you wont have much difficulty in settling yourself somewhere or other, though I hadnt quite realized that you were going away. [*She looks quickly at him : he does not look at her, but examines the dessert stand on the piano and decides that he will eat an apple*]. You might marry, you know. [*He bites a large piece out of the apple and munches it noisily*]. You see, Eliza, all men are not confirmed old bachelors like me and the Colonel. Most men are the marrying sort (poor devils!); and youre not bad-looking : it's quite a pleasure to look at you sometimes—not now, of course, because youre crying and looking as ugly as the very devil; but when youre all right and quite yourself, youre what I should call attractive. That is, to the people in the marrying line, you understand. You go to bed and have a good nice rest; and then get up and look at yourself in the glass; and you wont feel so cheap.

 Liza again looks at him, speechless, and does not stir.

 The look is quite lost on him : he eats his apple with a dreamy expression of happiness, as it is quite a good one.

HIGGINS [*a genial afterthought occurring to him*] I daresay my mother could find some chap or other who would do very well.

LIZA. I was above that before you came interfering with me.

HIGGINS [*waking up*] What do you mean?

LIZA. I sold flowers. I didnt sell myself. Now youve made a lady of me I'm not fit to sell anything else. I wish youd left me where you found me.

HIGGINS [*slinging the core of the apple decisively into the grate*] Tosh, Eliza. Dont you insult human relations by dragging all this cant about buying and selling into it. You neednt marry the fellow if your dont like him.

LIZA. What else am I to do?

HIGGINS. Oh, lots of things. What about your old idea of a florist's shop? Pickering could set you up in one: he has lots of money. [*Chuckling*] He'll have to pay for all those togs you have been wearing today; and that, with the hire of the jewellery, will make a big hole in two hundred pounds. Why, six months ago you would have thought it the millennium to have a flower shop of your own. Come! youll be all right. I must clear off to bed: I'm devilish sleepy. By the way, I came down for something: I forget what it was.

LIZA. Your slippers.

HIGGINS. Oh yes, of course. You shied them at me. [*He picks them up, and is going out when she rises and speaks to him*].

LIZA. Before you go, sir—

HIGGINS [*dropping the slippers in his surprise at her calling him Sir*] Eh?

LIZA. Do my clothes belong to me or to Colonel Pickering?

HIGGINS [*coming back into the room as if her question were the very climax of unreason*] What the devil use would they be to Pickering?

LIZA. He might want them for the next girl you pick up to experiment on.

HIGGINS [*shocked and hurt*] Is t h a t the way you feel towards us?

LIZA. I dont want to hear anything more about that. All I want to know is whether anything belongs to me. My own clothes were burnt.

HIGGINS. But what does it matter? Why need you start bothering about that in the middle of the night?

LIZA. I want to know what I may take away with me. I dont want to be accused of stealing.

HIGGINS [*now deeply wounded*] Stealing! You shouldnt have said that, Eliza. That shews a want of feeling.

LIZA. I'm sorry. I'm only a common ignorant girl; and in my station I have to be careful. There cant be any feelings between the like of you and the like of me. Please will you tell me what belongs to me and what doesnt?

HIGGINS [*very sulky*] You may take the whole damned houseful if you like. Except the jewels. Theyre hired. Will that satisfy you? [*He turns on his heel and is about to go in extreme dudgeon*].

LIZA [*drinking in his emotion like nectar, and nagging him to provoke a further supply*] Stop, please. [*She takes off her jewels*]. Will you take these to your room and keep them safe? I dont want to run the risk of their being missing.

HIGGINS [*furious*] Hand them over. [*She puts them into his hands*]. If these belonged to me instead of to the jeweller, I'd ram them down your ungrateful throat. [*He perfunctorily thrusts them into his pockets, unconsciously decorating himself with the protruding ends of the chains*].

LIZA [*taking a ring off*] This ring isnt the jeweller's: it's the one you bought me in Brighton. I dont want it now. [*Higgins dashes the ring violently into the fireplace, and turns on her so threateningly that she crouches over the piano with her hands over her face, and exclaims*] Dont you hit me.

HIGGINS. Hit you! You infamous creature, how dare you accuse me of such a thing? It is you who have hit me. You have wounded me to the heart.

LIZA [*thrilling with hidden joy*] Im glad Ive got a little of my own back, anyhow.

HIGGINS [*with dignity, in his finest professional style*] You have caused me to lose my temper: a thing that has hardly ever happened to me before. I prefer to say nothing more tonight. I am going to bed.

LIZA. [*pertly*] Youd better leave a note for Mrs Pearce about the coffee; for she wont be told by me.

HIGGINS [*formally*] Damn Mrs Pearce; and damn the coffee; and damn you; and [*suddenly dropping his beautiful elocution and raving furiously*] damn my own folly in having lavished my hard-earned knowledge and the treasure of my regard and intimacy on a heartless guttersnipe. [*He goes out with impressive decorum, and spoils it by slamming the door savagely*].

Liza goes down on her knees on the hearthrug to look for the ring. When she finds it she considers for a moment what to do with it. Finally she flings it down on the dessert stand and goes upstairs in a tearing rage.

The stairs. Liza going up to her room.

The landing. Liza goes into her room.

The bedroom as before, except that its furniture has been increased by a big wardrobe and a sumptuous dressing-table.

Liza comes in and switches on the electric light. She goes to the wardrobe; opens it; and pulls out a walking dress, a hat, and a pair of shoes, which she throws on the bed. She takes off her evening dress and shoes; then takes a padded hanger from the wardrobe; adjusts it carefully in the evening dress; and hangs it in the wardrobe, which she shuts with a slam. She puts on her walking shoes, her walking dress, and hat. She takes her wrist watch from the dressing-table and fastens it on. She pulls on her gloves; takes her vanity bag; and looks into it to see that her purse is there before hanging it on her wrist. She makes for the door.

She takes a last look at herself in the glass.

Close-up of her reflection in the glass, registering fierce resentment and determination.

She suddenly puts out her tongue at herself.

The bedroom. She leaves the room, ready equipped for going out. At the door she puts out the electric light. Blackout.

Note

All through this scene Liza expresses in all her movements her raging resolution to begone as an act of vengeance on the heartless Higgins. But her self-command is perfect.

Exterior of the house. Freddy, in evening dress and overcoat, is at the railings, gazing up at the second floor, in which one of the windows is still lighted.

The light goes out.

FREDDY. Goodnight, darling, darling, darling.

The hall door steps. The fanlight lights up. The door opens; and Liza appears. She puts out the fanlight; comes out on the steps; and closes the door, giving it a considerable bang behind her.

At the railings, closer up. Liza finds Freddy there.

LIZA. Whatever are you doing here?

FREDDY. Nothing. I spend most of my nights here. It's the only place where I'm happy. Dont laugh at me, Miss Doolittle.

LIZA. Dont you call me Miss Doolittle, do you hear? Liza's good enough for me. [*She breaks down and grabs him by the shoulders*]. Freddy: you dont think I'm a heartless guttersnipe, do you?

FREDDY. Oh no, no, darling: how can you imagine such a thing? You are the loveliest, dearest—

He loses all self-control and smothers her with kisses. She, hungry for comfort, responds. They stand there in one another's arms.

An elderly police constable arrives.

CONSTABLE [*scandalized*] Now then! Now then!! Now then!!!

They release one another hastily.

FREDDY. Sorry, constable. Weve only just become engaged.

They run away.

The constable shakes his head, reflecting on his own courtship and on the vanity of human hopes. He moves off in the opposite direction with slow professional steps.

Cavendish Square.

Freddy and Liza halt to consider their next move.

LIZA [*out of breath*] He didnt half give me a fright, that copper. But you answered him proper.

FREDDY. I hope I havnt taken you out of your way. Where were you going?

LIZA. To the river.

FREDDY. What for?

LIZA. To make a hole in it.

FREDDY. Eliza, darling. What do you mean? Whats the matter?

LIZA. Never mind. It doesnt matter now. Theres nobody in the world now but you and me, is there?

FREDDY. Not a soul.

They indulge in another embrace, and are again surprised by a much younger constable.

SECOND CONSTABLE. Now then, you two! Whats this? Where do you think you are? Move along here, double quick.

FREDDY. As you say, sir, double quick. [*They run away*].

Hanover Square.

Liza and Freddy rush in, and stop for breath.

FREDDY. I had no idea the police were so devishly prudish.

LIZA. It's their business to hunt girls off the streets.

FREDDY. We must go somewhere. We cant wander about the streets all night.

LIZA. Cant we? I think it'd be lovely to wander about for ever.

FREDDY. Oh, darling.

They embrace again, oblivious of the arrival of a crawling taxi. It stops.

TAXIMAN. Can I drive you and the lady anywhere, sir?

They start asunder.

LIZA. Oh, Freddy, a taxi. The very thing.

FREDDY. But, damn it, Ive no money.

LIZA. I have plenty. The Colonel thinks you should never go out without ten pounds in your pocket. Listen. We'll drive about all night; and in the morning I'll call on old Mrs Higgins and ask her what I ought to do. I'll tell you all about it in the cab. And the police wont touch us there.

FREDDY. Righto! Ripping. [*To the Taximan*] Wimbledon Common.

He follows Liza into the cab. They drive off.

Dissolve to:

Mrs Higgins's drawing room. She is at her writing-table as before. The parlor-maid comes in.

THE PARLORMAID [*at the door*] Mr Henry, maam, is downstairs with Colonel Pickering.

MRS HIGGINS. Well, shew them up.

THE PARLORMAID. Mr Henry is in a state, maam. I thought I'd better tell you.

MRS HIGGINS. If you had told me that Mr Henry was not in a state it would have been more surprising. Go upstairs and tell Miss Doolittle that Mr Henry and the Colonel are here. Ask her not to come down til I send for her.

THE PARLORMAID. Yes, maam.

Higgins bursts in. He is, as the parlormaid has said, in a state.

HIGGINS. Look here, mother: heres a confounded thing!

MRS HIGGINS. Yes, dear. Good morning. [*He checks his impatience and kisses her, whilst the parlormaid goes out*]. What is it?

HIGGINS. Eliza's bolted. What am I to do?

MRS HIGGINS. Do without, I'm afraid, Henry. The girl has a perfect right to leave if she chooses.

HIGGINS. But I cant find anything. I dont know what appointments Ive got. I'm—[*Pickering comes in. Mrs Higgins puts down her pen and turns away from the writing-table*].

PICKERING [*shaking hands*] Good morning, Mrs Higgins. Has Henry told you?

The parlormaid comes in and breaks off the conversation.

THE PARLORMAID. Mr Henry: a gentleman wants to see you very particular. He's been sent on from Wimpole Street.

HIGGINS. Oh, bother! I cant see anyone now. Who is it?

THE PARLORMAID. A Mr Doolittle, sir.

PICKERING. Doolittle! Do you mean the dustman?

THE PARLORMAID. Dustman! Oh no, sir: a gentleman.

HIGGINS [*springing up excitedly*] By George, Pick, it's some relative of hers that she's gone to. Somebody we know nothing about. [*To the parlormaid*] Send him up, quick.

THE PARLORMAID. Yes, sir. [*She goes*].

HIGGINS [*eagerly, going to his mother*] Genteel relatives! now we shall hear something. [*He sits down in the Chippendale chair*].

MRS HIGGINS. Do you know any of her people?

PICKERING. Only her father: the fellow we told you about.

THE PARLORMAID [*announcing*] Mr Doolittle. [*She withdraws*].

Doolittle enters. He is resplendently dressed as for a fashionable wedding, and might, in fact, be the bridegroom. A flower in his buttonhole, a dazzling silk hat, and patent leather shoes complete the effect. He is too concerned with the business he has come on to notice Mrs Higgins. He walks straight to Higgins, and accosts him with vehement reproach.

DOOLITTLE [*indicating his own person*] See here! Do you see this? Y o u done this.

HIGGINS. Done what, man?

DOOLITTLE. This, I tell you. Look at it. Look at this hat. Look at this coat.

PICKERING. Has Eliza been buying you clothes?

DOOLITTLE. Eliza! not she. Why would she buy me clothes?

MRS HIGGINS. Good morning, Mr Doolittle. Wont you sit down?

DOOLITTLE [*taken aback as he becomes conscious that he has forgotten his hostess*] Asking your pardon, maam. [*He approaches her and shakes her proffered hand*]. Thank you. [*He sits down on the ottoman, on Pickering's right*]. I am that full of what has happened to me that I cant think of anything else.

HIGGINS. What the dickens h a s happened to you?

DOOLITTLE. I shouldnt mind if it had only h a p p e n e d to me: anything might happen to anybody and nobody to blame but Providence, as you might say. But this is something that y o u done to me: yes, y o u , Enry Iggins.

HIGGINS. Have you found Eliza?

DOOLITTLE. Have you lost her?

HIGGINS. Yes.

DOOLITTLE. You have all the luck, you have. I aint found her; but she'll find me quick enough now after what you done to me.

MRS HIGGINS. But what has my son done to you, Mr Doolittle?

DOOLITTLE. Done to me! Ruined me. Destroyed my happiness. Tied me up and delivered me into the hands of middle class morality.

HIGGINS [*rising intolerantly and standing over Doolittle*] Youre raving. Youre drunk. Youre mad. I gave you five pounds. After that I had two conversations with you, at half-a-crown an hour. Ive never seen you since.

DOOLITTLE. Oh! Drunk am I? Mad am I? Tell me this. Did you or did you not write a letter to an old blighter in America that was giving five millions to found Moral Reform Societies all over the world, and that wanted you to invent a universal language for him?

HIGGINS. What! Ezra D. Wannafeller! He's dead. [*He sits down again carelessly*].

DOOLITTLE. Yes: he's dead; and I'm done for. Now did you or did you not write a letter to him to say that the most original moralist at present in England, to the best of your knowledge, was Alfred Doolittle, a common dustman?

HIGGINS. Oh, after your first visit I remember making some silly joke of the kind.

DOOLITTLE. Ah! you may well call it a silly joke. It put the lid on me right enough. Just give him the chance he wanted to shew that Americans is not like us: that they reckonize and respect merit in every class of life, however humble. Them words is in his blooming will, in which, Henry Higgins, thanks to your silly joking, he leaves me a share in his Predigested Cheese Trust worth three thousand a year on condition that I lecture for his Wannafeller Moral Reform World League as often as they ask me up to six times a year.

HIGGINS. The devil he does! Whew! [*Brightening suddenly*] What a lark!

PICKERING. A safe thing for you, Doolittle. They wont ask you twice.

DOOLITTLE. It aint the lecturing I mind. I'll lecture them blue in the face, I will, and not turn a hair. It's making a gentleman of me that I object to. Who asked him to make a gentleman of me? I was happy. I was free. I touched pretty nigh everybody for money when I wanted it, same as I touched you, Enry Iggins. Now I am worrited; tied neck and heels; and everybody touches m e for money. It's a fine thing for you, says my solicitor. Is it? says I. You mean it's a good thing for you, I says. When I was a poor man and had a solicitor once when they found a pram in the dust cart, he got me off, and got shut of me and got me shut of him as quick as he could. Same with the doctors: used to shove me out of the hospital before I could hardly stand on my legs, and nothing to pay. Now they finds out that I'm not a healthy man and cant live unless they looks after me twice a day. In the house I'm not let do a hand's turn for myself: somebody else must do it and touch me for it. A year ago I hadnt a relative in the world except two or three that wouldnt speak to me. Now Ive fifty, and not a decent week's wages among the lot of them. I have to live for others and not for myself: thats middle class morality. Y o u talk of losing Eliza. Dont you be anxious: I bet she's on my doorstep by this: she that could support herself easy by selling flowers if I wasnt respectable. And the next one to touch me will be you, Enry Iggins. I'll have to learn to speak middle class language from you, instead of speaking proper English. Thats where y o u l l come in; and I daresay thats what you done it for.

MRS HIGGINS. I think this solves the problem of Eliza's future. You can provide for her now.

HIGGINS [*jumping up*] Nonsense! he cant provide for her. He shant provide for her. She doesnt belong to him. I paid him five pounds for her. Doolittle: either youre an honest man or a rogue.

DOOLITTLE [*tolerantly*] A little of both, Henry, like the rest of us: a little of both.

HIGGINS. Well, you took that money for the girl; and you have no right to take her as well.

MRS HIGGINS. Henry: dont be absurd. If you want to know where Eliza is, she is upstairs.

HIGGINS [*amazed*] Upstairs!!! Then I shall jolly soon fetch her downstairs. [*He makes resolutely for the door*].

MRS HIGGINS [*rising and following him*] Be quiet, Henry. Sit down.

HIGGINS. I—

MRS HIGGINS. Sit down, dear; and listen to me.

HIGGINS. Oh very well, very well, very well. [*He throws himself ungraciously on the ottoman, with his face towards the windows*]. But I think you might have told us this half an hour ago.

MRS HIGGINS. Eliza came to me this morning. She told me of the brutal way you two treated her.

HIGGINS [*bounding up again*] What!

PICKERING [*rising also*] My dear Mrs Higgins, she's been telling you stories. We didnt treat her brutally. We hardly said a word to her; and we parted on particularly good terms.

HIGGINS. We said nothing except that we were tired and wanted to go to bed. Did we, Pick?

PICKERING [*shrugging his shoulders*] That was all.

MRS HIGGINS [*ironically*] Quite sure?

PICKERING. Absolutely. Really, that was all.

MRS HIGGINS. You didnt thank her, or pet her, or admire her, or tell her how splendid she'd been.

HIGGINS [*impatiently*] But she knew all about that. We didnt make speeches to her, if thats what you mean.

PICKERING [*conscience stricken*] Perhaps we were a little inconsiderate. Is she very angry?

MRS HIGGINS [*returning to her place at the writing-table*] Well, I'm afraid she wont go back to Wimpole Street, but she says she is quite willing to meet you on friendly terms and to let bygones be bygones.

HIGGINS [*furious*] Is she, by George? Ho!

MRS HIGGINS. If you promise to behave yourself, Henry, I'll ask her to come down. If not, go home; for you have taken up quite enough of my time.

HIGGINS. Oh, all right. Very well. Pick: you behave yourself. Let us put on our best Sunday manners for this creature that we picked out of the mud. [*He flings himself sulkily into the Elizabethan chair*].

MRS HIGGINS. Remember your promise, Henry. [*She presses the bell-button on the writing-table*]. Mr Doolittle: will you be so good as to step out on the balcony for a moment. I dont want Eliza to have the shock of your news until she has made it up with these two gentlemen. Would you mind?

DOOLITTLE. As you wish, lady. Anything to help Henry to keep her off my hands. [*He disappears through the window*].

The parlormaid answers the bell. Pickering sits down in Doolittle's place.

MRS HIGGINS. Ask Miss Doolittle to come down, please.

THE PARLORMAID. Yes, maam. [*She goes out*].

MRS HIGGINS. Now, Henry: be good.

HIGGINS. I am behaving myself perfectly.

PICKERING. He is doing his best, Mrs Higgins.

Liza enters, sunny, self-possessed, and giving a staggeringly convincing exhibition of ease of manner. She carries a little work-basket, and is very much at home. Pickering is too much taken aback to rise.

LIZA. How do you do, Professor Higgins? Are you quite well?

HIGGINS [*choking*] Am I—[*He can say no more*].

LIZA. But of course you are: you are never ill. So glad to see you again, Colonel Pickering. [*He rises hastily; and they shake hands*]. Quite chilly this morning, isnt it? [*She sits down on his left. He sits beside her*].

HIGGINS. Dont you dare try this game on me. I taught it to you; and it doesnt take me in. Get up and come home; and dont be a fool.

Liza takes a piece of needlework from her basket, and begins to stitch at it, without taking the least notice of this outburst.

MRS HIGGINS. Very nicely put, indeed, Henry. No woman could resist such an invitation.

HIGGINS. You let her alone, mother. Let her speak for herself. You will jolly soon see whether she has an idea that I havnt put into her head or a word that I havnt put into her mouth. I tell you I have created this thing out of the squashed cabbage leaves of Covent Garden; and now she pretends to play the fine lady with me.

MRS HIGGINS [*placidly*] Yes, dear; but youll sit down, wont you?

Higgins sits down again, savagely.

LIZA [*to Pickering, taking no apparent notice of Higgins, and working away deftly*] Will y o u drop me altogether now that the experiment is over, Colonel Pickering?

PICKERING. Oh dont. You mustnt think of it as an experiment. It shocks me, somehow.

LIZA. Oh, I'm only a squashed cabbage leaf—

PICKERING [*impulsively*] No.

LIZA [*continuing quietly*]—but I owe so much to you that I should be very unhappy if you forgot me.

PICKERING. It's very kind of you to say so, Miss Doolittle.

LIZA. It's not because you paid for my dresses. I know you are generous to everybody with money. But it was from you that I learnt really nice manners; and that is what makes one a lady, isnt it? You see it was so very difficult for me with the example of Professor Higgins always before me. I was brought up to be just like him, unable to control myself, and using bad language on the slightest provocation. And I should never have known that ladies and gentlemen didnt behave like that if you hadnt been there.

HIGGINS. Well!!

PICKERING. Oh, thats only his way, you know. He doesnt mean it.

LIZA. Oh, *I* didnt mean it either, when I was a flower girl. It was only my way. But you see I did it; and thats what makes the difference after all.

PICKERING. No doubt. Still, he taught you to speak; and I couldnt have done that, you know.

LIZA [*trivially*] Of course: that is his profession.

HIGGINS. Damnation!

LIZA [*continuing*] It was just like learning to dance in the fashionable way: there was nothing more than that in it. But you know what begun my real education?

PICKERING. What?

LIZA [*stopping her work for a moment*] Your calling me Miss Doolittle that day when I first came to Wimpole Street. That was the beginning of self-respect for me. [*She resumes her stitching*]. And there were a hundred little things you never noticed, because they came naturally to you. Things about standing up and taking off your hat and opening doors—

PICKERING. Oh, that was nothing.

LIZA. Yes: things that shewed you thought and felt about me as if I were something better than a scullery-maid; though of course I know you would have been just the same to a scullery-maid if she had been let into the drawing room. You never took off your boots in the dining room when I was there.

PICKERING. You mustnt mind that. Higgins takes off his boots all over the place.

LIZA. I know. I am not blaming him. It is his way, isnt it? But it made s u c h a difference to me that you didnt do it. You see, really and truly, apart from the things anyone can pick up (the dressing and the proper way of speaking, and so on), the difference between a lady and a flower girl is not how she behaves, but how she's treated. I shall always be a flower girl to Professor Higgins, because he always treats me as a flower girl, and always will; but I know I can be a lady to you, because you always treat me as a lady, and always will.

MRS HIGGINS. Please dont grind your teeth, Henry.

PICKERING. Well, this is really very nice of you, Miss Doolittle.

LIZA. I should like you to call me Eliza, now, if you would.

PICKERING. Thank you. Eliza, of course.

LIZA. And I should like Professor Higgins to call me Miss Doolittle.

HIGGINS. I'll see you damned first.

MRS HIGGINS. Henry! Henry!

PICKERING. Youre coming back to Wimpole Street, arnt you? Youll forgive Higgins?

HIGGINS [rising] Forgive! Will she, by George! Let her go. Let her find out how she can get on without us. She will relapse into the gutter in three weeks without me at her elbow.

Doolittle appears at the centre window. With a look of dignified reproach at Higgins, he comes slowly and silently to his daughter, who, with her back to the window, is unconscious of his approach.

PICKERING. He's incorrigible, Eliza. You wont relapse, will you?

LIZA. No: not now. Never again. I have learnt my lesson. I dont believe I could utter one of the old sounds if I tried. [*Doolittle touches her on her left shoulder. She drops her work, losing her self-possession utterly at the spectacle of her father's splendor*] A-a-a-a-a-ah-ow-ooh!

HIGGINS [*with a crow of triumph*] Aha! Just so. A-a-a-a-ahowooh! A-a-a-a-ahowooh! A-a-a-ahowooh! Victory! Victory! [*He throws himself on the divan, folding his arms, and spraddling arrogantly*].

DOOLITTLE. Can you blame the girl? Dont look at me like that, Eliza. It aint my fault. Ive come into some money. I'm dressed something special today. I'm going to St George's, Hanover Square. Your stepmother is going to marry me.

LIZA [*angrily*] Youre going to let yourself down to marry that low common woman!

PICKERING [*quietly*] He ought to, Eliza. [*To Doolittle*] Why has she changed her mind?

DOOLITTLE [*sadly*] Intimidated, Governor. Intimidated. Middle class morality claims its victim. Wont you put on your hat, Liza, and come and see me turned off?

LIZA. If the Colonel says I must, I—I'll [*almost sobbing*] I'll demean myself. And get insulted for my pains, like enough.

DOOLITTLE. Dont be afraid: she never comes to words with anyone now, poor woman! respectability has broke all the spirit out of her.

PICKERING [*squeezing Liza's elbow gently*] Be kind to them, Eliza. Make the best of it.

LIZA [*forcing a little smile for him through her vexation*] Oh well, just to shew theres no ill feeling. I'll be back in a moment. [*She goes out*].

DOOLITTLE [*sitting down beside Pickering*] I feel uncommon nervous about the ceremony, Colonel. I wish youd come and see me through it.

PICKERING. But youve been through it before, man. You were married to

Eliza's mother.

DOOLITTLE. Who told you that, Colonel?

PICKERING. Well, nobody told me. But I concluded—naturally—

DOOLITTLE. No: that aint the natural way, Colonel: it's only the middle class way. My way was always the undeserving way. But dont say nothing to Eliza. She dont know: I always had a delicacy about telling her.

PICKERING. Quite right. We'll leave it so, if you dont mind.

DOOLITTLE. And youll come to the church, Colonel, and put me through straight?

PICKERING. With pleasure. As far as a bachelor can.

MRS HIGGINS. May I come, Mr Doolittle? I should be very sorry to miss your wedding.

DOOLITTLE. I should indeed be honored by your condescension, maam; and my poor old woman would take it as a tremenjous compliment. She's been very low, thinking of the happy days that are no more.

MRS HIGGINS [*rising*] I'll order the car and get ready. [*The men rise, except Higgins*]. I shant be more than fifteen minutes. [*As she goes to the door Liza comes in, hatted and buttoning her gloves*]. I'm going to the church to see your father married, Eliza. You had better come with me. Colonel Pickering can go on with the bridegroom.

Mrs Higgins goes out. Liza comes to the middle of the room between the centre window and the ottoman. Pickering joins her.

DOOLITTLE. Bridegroom! What a word! It makes a man realize his position, somehow. [*He takes up his hat and goes towards the door*].

PICKERING. Before I go, Eliza, do forgive Higgins and come back to us.

LIZA. I dont think dad would allow me. Would you, dad?

DOOLITTLE [*sad but magnanimous*] They played you off very cunning, Eliza, them two sportsmen. It if had been only one of them, you could have nailed him. But you see, there was two; and one of them chaperoned the other, as you might say. [*To Pickering*] It was artful of you, Colonel; but I bear no malice: I should have done the same myself. I been the victim of one woman after another all my life; and I dont grudge you two getting the better of Eliza. I shant interfere. It's time for us to go, Colonel. So long, Henry. See you in St George's, Eliza. [*He goes out*].

PICKERING [*coaxing*] Do stay with us, Eliza. [*He follows Doolittle*].

Liza goes out on the balcony to avoid being alone with Higgins. He rises and joins her there. She immediately comes back into the room and makes for the door; but he goes along the balcony quickly and gets his back to the door before she reaches it.

HIGGINS. Well, Eliza, youve had a bit of your own back, as you call it. Have you had enough? and are you going to be reasonable? Or do you want any more?

LIZA. You want me back only to pick up your slippers and put up with your tempers and fetch and carry for you.

HIGGINS. I havnt said I wanted you back at all.

LIZA. Oh, indeed. Then what are we talking about?

HIGGINS. About you, not about me. If you come back I shall treat you just as I have always treated you. I cant change my nature; and I dont intend to change my manners. My manners are exactly the same as Colonel Pickering's.

LIZA. Thats not true. He treats a flower girl as if she was a duchess.

HIGGINS. And I treat a duchess as if she was a flower girl. The question is not whether I treat you rudely, but whether you ever heard me treat anyone else better.

LIZA [*with sudden sincerity*] I dont care how you treat me. I dont mind your swearing at me. I shouldnt mind a black eye: Ive had one before this. But [*standing up and facing him*] I wont be passed over.

HIGGINS. Then get out of my way; for I wont stop for you. You talk about me as if I were a motor bus.

LIZA. So you are a motor bus: all bounce and go, and no consideration for anyone. I cant talk to you: you turn everything against me: I'm always in the wrong. But you know very well all the time that youre nothing but a bully. You know I cant go back to the gutter, as you call it, and that I have no real friends in the world but you and the Colonel. You know well I couldnt bear to live with a low common man after you two; and it's wicked and cruel of you to insult me by pretending I could. You think I must go back to Wimpole Street because I have nowhere else to go but father's. But dont you be too sure that you have me under your feet to be trampled on and talked down. I'll marry Freddy, I will, as soon as I'm able to support him.

HIGGINS [*thunderstruck*] Freddy!!! that young fool! That poor devil who couldnt get a job as an errand boy even if he had the guts to try for it! Woman: do you not understand that I have made you a consort for a king?

LIZA. Freddy loves me: that makes him king enough for me. I dont want him to work: he wasnt brought up to it as I was. I'll go and be a teacher.

HIGGINS. Whatll you teach, in heaven's name?

LIZA. What you taught me. I'll teach phonetics.

HIGGINS. Ha! ha! ha!

LIZA. I'll offer myself as an assistant to that hairy-faced Hungarian.

HIGGINS [*rising in a fury*] What! That blackmailer! that humbug! that toadying ignoramus! You take one step in his direction and I'll wring your neck. [*He lays hands on her*]. Do you hear?

LIZA [*defiantly non-resistant*] Wring away. What do I care? I knew youd strike me some day. [*He lets her go, stamping with rage at having forgotten himself and recoils so hastily that he stumbles back into his seat on the ottoman*]. Aha! Now I know how to deal with you. What a fool I was not to think of it before! You cant take away the knowledge you gave me. You said I had a finer ear than you. And I can be civil and kind to people, which is more than you can. Aha! [*Purposely dropping her aitches to annoy him*] Thats done you, Enry Iggins, it az. Now I dont care t h a t [*snapping her fingers*] for your bullying and your big talk. I'll advertize it in the papers that your duchess is only a flower girl that you taught, and that she'll teach anybody to be a duchess just the same in six months for a thousand guineas. Oh, when I think of myself crawling under your feet and being trampled on and called names, when all the time I had only to lift up my finger to be as good as you, I could just kick myself.

HIGGINS [*wondering at her*] You damned impudent slut, you! But by George, Eliza, I said I'd make a woman of you; and I have. I like you like this.

LIZA. Yes: you turn round and make up to me now that I'm not afraid of you, and can do without you.

HIGGINS. Of course I do, you little fool. Five minutes ago you were like a millstone round my neck. Now youre a tower of strength: a battleship.

Mrs Higgins returns, dressed for the wedding. Liza instantly becomes cool and elegant.

MRS HIGGINS. The car is waiting, Eliza. Are you ready?

LIZA. Quite. Is the Professor coming?

MRS HIGGINS. Certainly not. He cant behave himself in church. He makes remarks out loud all the time on the clergyman's pronunciation.

LIZA. Then I shall not see you again, Professor. Goodbye. [*She goes to the door*].

MRS HIGGINS [*coming to Higgins*] Goodbye, dear.*

HIGGINS. Goodbye, mother. [*He is about to kiss her, when he recollects something*]. Oh, by the way, Eliza, order a ham and a Stilton cheese, will you? And buy me a pair of reindeer gloves, number eights, and a tie to match that new suit of mine. You can choose the color. [*His cheerful, careless, vigorous voice shews that he is incorrigible*].

LIZA [*disdainfully*] Number eights are too small for you if you want them lined with lamb's wool. You have three new ties that you have forgotten in the drawer of your washstand. Colonel Pickering prefers double Gloucester to Stilton; and you dont notice the difference. I telephoned Mrs Pearce this morning not to forget the ham. What you are to do without me I cannot imagine. [*She sweeps out*].

MRS HIGGINS. Really, neither can I.

HIGGINS. Oh, she'll come home to Wimpole Street all right enough. But fancy her wanting to marry that young idiot Freddy. Can you understand it?

MRS HIGGINS. Perfectly. After Eliza's six months slavery with you Freddy is just the sort of boy any girl would want to marry. But how is the poor lad to keep her? He has no profession.

HIGGINS. Pickering and I will have to keep them both. He can clean our boots, I suppose.

MRS HIGGINS. I dont believe he knows how to clean his own boots, poor lad!

HIGGINS. Well, he can make love to her. I dont do that sort of thing; and Pickering's too old.

MRS HIGGINS. Did she say anything to you about setting up as a teacher?

HIGGINS [*grimly*] She did.

MRS HIGGINS. What did you say?

HIGGINS. I wrung her neck.

MRS HIGGINS. Henry!!

HIGGINS. I did. Freddy cant wring her neck: he's not big enough.

MRS HIGGINS. Henry: you dont know it and cant help it; but you are a terrible elocutionary bully. Thats why Eliza wants the kindly little baby man whom she can bully.

HIGGINS. Anyhow, he takes that part of the job off our hands. [*The motor horn squawks impatiently*]. Thats for you. Theyre waiting.

MRS HIGGINS. Oh, bother! Goodbye, dear [*expecting a kiss*].

HIGGINS. I am going down with you.

He opens the door for her; and they go out together.

Cut to:

Mrs Higgins's limousine standing opposite her garden gate in Cheyne Walk. Inside the car are Liza and Freddy looking out for Mrs Higgins.

Higgins and his mother come out. He is overcoated and hatted exactly as in the

---

* In the 1934 screenplay, a shorter, different end follows. See Appendix F.

first scene in Covent Garden.

Liza disappears into the back of the limousine to allow Freddy to alight and open the door for Mrs Higgins.

HIGGINS [*staring at Freddy*] Hallo! What the devil are y o u doing here?

FREDDY. Miss Doolittle invited me.

MRS HIGGINS. How do you do, Mr Hill? I think you may call her Eliza now. [*She gets into the car*].

FREDDY [*still holding the car door open*] Coming, Professor?

LIZA. No, he is not coming. Get in quick. We are late.

FREDDY. By the way, Professor, thanks awfully for promising to set us up in a flower shop. Her old dream, you know. A lady in a flower shop. We are most grateful.

LIZA. Sh-sh-sh, Freddy: I havnt asked him yet.

She pulls him into the car. Liza slams the door of the limousine, which drives off, leaving Higgins on the pavement, stranded and amazed.

HIGGINS. A squashed cabbage leaf! A lady in a flower shop!

Dissolve to:

A vision of the past.

Covent Garden: a section of the portico viewed from the market.

Liza crouching over her basket, and looking her dirtiest and most wretched. Higgins along, looking at her.

LIZA. Poor girl! Hard enough for her to live without being worried and chivied. Ought to be ashamed of himself, unmanly coward. Let him mind his own business and leave a poor girl alone.

The old music from the church. Higgins takes his hat off. The scene fades out and is replaced by:

A vision of the future.

A florist's shop in South Kensington, full of fashionable customers. Liza behind the counter, serving in great splendor. The name of the shopkeeper, F. HILL, is visible. Half the shop is stocked with vegetables. Freddy, in apron and mild muttonchop whiskers, is serving. Dreamlike silence. Fade out into:

Mrs Higgins's garden gate in Cheyne Walk.

Higgins standing rapt. A policewoman comes along. She stops and looks curiously at Higgins, who is quite unconscious of her, and visibly rapt.

POLICEWOMAN. Anything wrong, sir?

HIGGINS [*waking up*] What?

POLICEWOMAN. Anything wrong, sir?

HIGGINS [*impressively*] No: nothing wrong. A happy ending. A happy beginning. Good morning, madam.

POLICEWOMAN [*impressed*] Good morning, sir.

Higgins raises his hat and stalks away majestically. The policewoman stands at attention and salutes.

THE END

Major Barbara   Barbara gives a sermon. Wendy Hiller and Deborah Kerr.

Major Barbara   On the set, at Denham Studios, when Shaw filmed what was originally intended to be a separate short subject, an address to American audiences, but which became a preface to the American print of *Major Barbara*. Wendy Hiller, Rex Harrison, Bernard Shaw and Gabriel Pascal.

Major Barbara   Bill Walker flaunts his victory before a despairing Barbara. Wendy Hiller and Robert Newton.

Major Barbara   On location at the Albert Hall, London. Rex Harrison, Robert Morley, Bernard Shaw and Gabriel Pascal.

The Devil's Disciple

Title on art backing of original Congress House:

July 4th 1776
THE DECLARATION OF
AMERICAN INDEPENDENCE

Dissolve to:
Close-up of Thomas Jefferson. Silent scene.
Indoors, signing the declaration. Silent and businesslike.
Cut to:
Close-up of his signature and then of the heading Declaration of Independence *engrossed.*
Dissolve to:
Medium shot, flag pole.
British Royal Standard flying. It comes down and is replaced by the American flag, revealing the thirteen stars and thirteen stripes of the first Federation.
Dissolve to:
The exterior of St James's Palace. Day.
Superimpose title:

The King's Palace. London. 1777.

Dissolve to:
The interior of one of the Royal Apartments.
King George III is fussing about and gabbling. The Prime Minister, Lord North, is in attendance.
GEORGE III. Eh? What, what? A fuss about the Colonies? Is it kind of you, North, to bother me about such things? Havnt I enough to attend to?
LORD NORTH. Unfortunately, your Majesty, the New England States have a considerable estimate of their own importance.
GEORGE III. What, what? Stuff and nonsense! States! What do you mean by States? Colonies are not States: they are parts of my State. Crumbs of it. Crumbs. What do you mean by New England? Where is it? Is it an island? Is it Robinson Crusoe's island? I never heard of it.
North patiently unfolds a map on the table, a table already crowded with documents. As he does this:
LORD NORTH. Your Majesty, New England is a substantial part of North

America. Lord Germain believes that the New England States are the pith of the matter.

GEORGE III. What, what? North America. Columbus's discovery. Let me see. Let me see. America is important, you know, North, quite important. Let me see. [*Looking at map*] Thats a devilish big place, you know, North: devilish big. I had no idea it was so big.

LORD NORTH. Very big, sir: and all this side of it is in rebellion.

GEORGE III. What, what! Rebellion. Gone Jacobite! Has that drunken blackguard the Pretender broken out again?

LORD NORTH. They never heard of the Pretender, sir. They are dissatisfied.

GEORGE III. Damn their impudence! What about?

LORD NORTH. Taxes. And restrictions on their trade. They are actually fighting us: it is most serious. Sir John Burgoyne has been instructed to march south from Quebec along the line of the Hudson River, while Sir William Howe will be ordered to proceed north from New York City, to effect a junction.

GEORGE III. What, what? Burgoyne. Thats a clever chap; but I dont like him. I feel that he is always laughing in his sleeve at me. Quite right to send him to America: quite right.

LORD NORTH. The two generals are to act together. When they join, the rebels will be cut off and outnumbered. Their victory will be a certainty. Burgoyne is already on the march. Lord Germain has in hand a special dispatch for Howe.

GEORGE III. Take care he sends that dispatch. Germain is a lazy, idle, good-for-nothing dog. Never does today what he can put off till tomorrow. But it doesnt matter. Burgoyne can deal with any colonial mob singlehanded. Let me hear no more of it.

Lord North shrugs his shoulders and rolls up the map hopelessly.

Dissolve to:

Lord Germain's room in Whitehall. Day. Lord Germain and his Secretary. Lord Germain is dressed for the road, and is in a state of agitation, striding about the room.

LORD GERMAIN. Not ready yet! But you know I go into the country on a Friday.

SECRETARY. The fair copy will be in order for signature in about an hour, my lord.

LORD GERMAIN. Wont do at all, I want to get down to the country. Have it for me when I return on Tuesday—er—Wednesday. [*He pauses for a moment by a map of America on the wall*]. Whereabouts is Johnny?

SECRETARY [*pointing*] General Burgoyne is there.

LORD GERMAIN. Oh, t h e r e ! Well, he can stay there until I come back to town. That place is thousands of miles away from New Amsterdam.

SECRETARY. New York now, my lord.

LORD GERMAIN. My grandfather always called it New Amsterdam. Cant get it out of my head, somehow. Doesnt matter, does it? Anyhow, I'm off. [*Exit Lord Germain, whistling* Lillibulero].

Dissolve to:

Medium long shot. Advance guard on the march.

Medium shot. General Sir John Burgoyne and Major Swindon on horseback, marching with the column.

Close-up of Burgoyne.

Medium shot. Soldiers marching.

Medium shot. Fife band marching. Tune: The Girl I Left Behind Me.

Dissolve to:

The kitchen of Dudgeon's farm house on the outskirts of the town of Westerbridge. Dawn.

Close-up of Mrs Dudgeon, asleep in a chair.

Major Barbara

PROLOGUE*

Sunday morning in an open space at the East End of London. Bitter winter weather. A placard seven feet high stands beside an empty packing case upside down, with a reading desk in front of it: the two forming a tribune for a speaker. With this equipment a desperately small meeting is being addressed, or rather read to, by a young university don in spectacles, very smart in a new overcoat and spotless muffler, supported by a few undergraduates, male and female, very cold, and all trying not to look dispirited by their failure to attract the public, which consists of one policeman on duty and three or four East End workers waiting for the public houses to open, and deciding very doubtfully that the lecture to which they are listening is better than no entertainment at all. The scene is extremely depressing.

The placard is inscribed in the largest letters, UNIVERSITY EXTENSION OPEN AIR MEETINGS. UNDER THE AUSPICES OF THE WORKERS' EDUCATION ASSOCIATION. FIVE STAGES OF GREEK RELIGION. LECTURER ADOLPHUS CUSINS D.C.L., LITT.D., REGIUS PROFESSOR OF GREEK IN THE UNIVERSITY OF OXFORD. ALL SUNDAY MORNINGS IN FEBRUARY.

CUSINS [*reading with very distinct articulation but not looking at his audience*] The ancient Greeks considered it unseemly to give public praise to women for their good looks, but apparently thought it did no harm to young men. Note that, unlike our own popular playwrights in England and the United States, the great Athenians scorned what we call love interest and regarded sex appeal as indecent.

A BYSTANDER. S'truth! [*He shrugs his shoulders and moves off*].

CUSINS. Listen to the words put into the mouth of Aeschylus by Aristophanes. He boasts of how he made the Greeks crave

Like lions to dash at the face of the foe, and leap to the call of the trumpet.
But no Sthenoboia I have given you, no: no Phaedra, no heroine strumpet.
If I have once put a woman in love in one act of one play may my
    teaching be scouted—

He is interrupted by the strains of a Salvation Army band playing a brisk march. Instantly the three remaining East Enders brighten up and hurry away in the direction of the sound.

CUSINS [*giving up in despair and thrusting his MS into his pocket*] No use. [*He descends from his platform and addresses himself to the police officer while his*

* For Shaw's spoken preface to American audiences and handwritten preface to British audiences of the film, see Appendixes G and H.

281

friends pack up the tribune and dismount the placard] I am afraid this open air experiment is no good. Or else I havnt the knack of attracting an audience. If it hadnt been for you I expect they would have stoned me. I am afraid I must have bored you terribly.

POLICEMAN [*civil and respectful*] Oh no, sir: no no. Only it sounded a bit heathenish at first, almost as if you believed in them queer old gods: I talked to my missus about it. You see, sir, she's keen on the Salvation Army, and likes good serious talk. But when you said that morning that God was there all along, whatever they called him, I knew it was all right.

CUSINS. I never thought much of myself as a speaker; but I have never lost my whole audience before.

POLICEMAN. Not at all, sir: I have heard worse. But there are two things that no speaker can stand up against.

CUSINS. And what are they, may I ask?

POLICEMAN. One is a band: the other is a fight. The Salvation Army knows that: it always has a band. And this Sunday theres a special attraction. Theres Major Barbara.

CUSINS. Major Barbara! How can a woman be a major?

POLICEMAN. She can, sir, in the army, or a sergeant, or a colonel, or even a general. If you want a tip or two as to how to gather a meeting and hold it you might do worse than follow that band to the Salvation Barracks and hear her take the Sunday service.

CUSINS. Egad, I will. I have a fancy for collecting religious experiences. Which way?

POLICEMAN. Come with me, sir. I'm off duty now that your meeting is over.

They go off together to the exterior of the Salvation Barracks. The meeting inside is overflowing into the doorway, which is crowded.

CUSINS. It's full up. We cant get in.

POLICEMAN. I can, sir. Keep close behind me. [*He pushes into the crowd*]. Now then: by your leave. This gentleman is on business. By your leave.

They push through to the interior of the hall. Room is made for them silently at the end of one of the forms. Barbara is on the platform speaking. Whilst she speaks Cusins's face shews that he is fascinated and keenly interested by Barbara herself, though not, like the rest, by what she is saying.

BARBARA. Amid all the poverty and ugliness of our lives here, the sin and the suffering, the grime and the smoke, the toil and the struggle, you know, and I know, that God is with us always and everywhere. We do not need a cathedral to worship Him in. Here in this old shed no less than beneath God's open sky we can draw nearer to Him. Some of you feel Him near you even now, and feel, too, how much you need Him. Wont you let Him come into your life now, today, as so many have done before? You want His strength, His guidance, His comfort: you need His forgiveness and friendship. Some of you turn away from Him in bitterness at the hardship of your lives, saying that you do not want God: you want happiness and beauty. God will give you both. There is no beauty like the beauty of the newly saved who has found the unspeakable happiness that only the consciousness of God's presence and love can give. We in the Army have our daily trials. Most of us are as poor as you are. But we are all happy; and the mark of that happiness is on us for you to see. The rich are not happy. The poor have only to reach out their hands for God's happiness and take it. Is there anyone here who has courage enough to raise his hand as a sign that he would like us to pray for him? Make the decision now: in your need and loneliness God is waiting for you. Someone here must feel that he should raise his hand, but that it isnt easy. It is the easiest thing in the world: he has often done it to beckon to his child or to stop a tram. He feels too shy perhaps. Never mind: I will pray for him; and God will give him the courage of a lion. Come: do not keep God waiting: thousands have done it; and if you can find me one who has done it and been sorry afterwards I will put off this dear uniform and never pray again. Come come! I know there is someone. [*Scanning their faces along the row her look meets that of Cusins. His hand shoots up instantly*]. Ah! I have found him. Let the brave gentleman come to the front: make room for him, please. [*Cusins passes up, all staring at him*]. Give me your hand, my brother. I will take you to our little room for confession where we will pray together. Friends; you will sing "How sweet the name of Jesus sounds!"

They rise and sing while she leads Cusins out through a side door into a small cloakroom, with overcoats hanging up and a table heaped with women's outdoor belongings. Along the table is a form, the only sitting accommodation in the place. Barbara sits and places sins beside her.

BARBARA. Now before we pray a little together, may I tell you to forget that we have never met before. You must not be shy and distant with me. I can see that all's well with you. I can see in your face the new happiness that has just come into your life. You are a new man: you are saved. You feel that, dont you?

CUSINS [*grimly determined*] Listen to me, Major Barbara. I am here on false pretences. It is true that a new happiness has come into my life: a happiness that I have never quite believed in—that at any rate I thought would never come into my life. It has come.

BARBARA. Thank God!

CUSINS. Take care. It has not made me a better man: it has made me an utterly unscrupulous one.

BARBARA. What do you mean?

CUSINS. Look at me. Look deep into my eyes. Is the new happiness that you see there the kind of happiness you are thinking of?

BARBARA [*looking hard*] It must be. There is no other happiness like it. It gladdens my heart because, under God, I have brought it there.

CUSINS. Good. Now let me warn you that though I am a scholar and a gentleman I am as poor as a church mouse, like all scholars. I am no good for anything in the way of worldly success.

BARBARA. Oh, what does that matter? We are all poor here. We never think of money or success. When all our money is spent on the Army we pray for more; and it comes: it always comes. Take your mind off such things. And now, shall we pray together?

CUSINS. I never pray—at least not in your way. The new thing that has come to me is not that I am saved. I was saved when I was five years old, when I first swallowed your religion. Since then I have swallowed twenty religions: that is my life's work. I know all their catchwords. They are nothing to me: I am interested in the essence of all religions, not in their catchwords or in yours.

BARBARA. Let us find it for you here. We can.

CUSINS. Nonsense! I have more to teach you about religion than you can yet imagine.

BARBARA. You think so. Then why have you come here with me? Why did you hold up your hand?

CUSINS. Because I have impulses that I cannot explain. They come very seldom. But when they come, nothing can stop me. There is an end of my conscience, of my prudence, of my reason. Such an impulse seized me the moment I saw you. Your are poor; you are ignorant; our table manners are different; our relatives will not mix; everything is against our associating with oneanother. No matter: to be with you I will join the Army: I will put on the uniform and beat the drum: in short, I am hopelessly and for ever in love with you and will follow you to the end of the world until you marry me. Is that plain?

BARBARA [*rising, calm and greatly amused*] Perfectly. And now will you begin by seeing me home? I should like to put you through your first trial by shewing you where I live and introducing you to my family.

CUSINS. I do not care where you live; and I will face ten families for you.

BARBARA [*putting on her cloak and gathering her bag*] So you shall. God has some little surprises for you, my friend. Come.

They go out by a door which leads to an alley beside the building, where they can sidetrack the crowd.

CUSINS. Have we far to go? What about a taxi?

BARBARA. We dont run to taxis in this part of the world. Most of us here have never been in one. We must walk to a tram.

They go off accordingly to a tram-stop in a main east end thoroughfare.

BARBARA. Here we are. Look out for a number 23.

CUSINS. But we are on the wrong side, are we not? This is the side for the trams going west.

BARBARA. We are going west.

CUSINS. Oh, I beg pardon. Where do you live?

BARBARA. In a place called Wilton Crescent.

CUSINS. Quite a fashionable address. I did not know that there is a Wilton Crescent at the east end. The only one I know is at Hyde Park Corner close to Belgrave Square. Where all the dukes and earls live. Have you ever been as far west as Hyde Park Corner?

BARBARA. Occasionally. I know the Wilton Crescent you mean. I live there.

CUSINS. But—but—but—

BARBARA. Why not? Plenty of poor people live there. How do you know that I am not a scullery maid? Here is number 23. [*She runs to the tram-car to secure a seat*]. Jump in.

They get into the car. It drives off; and in due course they arrive on the doorstep of the house in Wilton Crescent.

CUSINS. I ring the servants' bell, I suppose. Had I not better leave you before they open?

BARBARA. Dont ring. I have a latchkey. [*She produces it*].

CUSINS. By the way, I had better know your name before I go in.

BARBARA. You have not mentioned yours. And it is I who have to introduce you.

CUSINS. My name is Adolphus Cusins.

BARBARA. Adolphus! What a name! I shall call you Dolly.

CUSINS. My relatives do. I wish they didnt. Introduce me as Professor Cusins.

BARBARA. Allude to me as Miss Undershaft.

CUSINS [*thunderstruck*] Undershaft!!! The Canon King! The rival of Krupp and of Skoda! The multi-millionaire!!

BARBARA. Do not faint, Dolly. I have not seen him since I was that high [*indicating a height of about three feet*]. You will find my mother, Lady Britomart Undershaft, much more terrifying. [*She unlocks the door and goes in*].

CUSINS. So this is one of the little surprises you promised! Heaven help me! [*He goes in; and the door closes behind them*].

So ends the prologue.

Dissolve to:

Some weeks later in the library upstairs, where Lady Britomart Undershaft sits at her writing table after dinner. A large and comfortable settee is in the middle of the room with a copy of The Speaker, a Liberal weekly journal, on it. A person sitting on it (it is vacant at present) would have, on his right, the writing table, with the lady herself busy at it; the heavily curtained windows on his left with a smaller writing-table and an armchair near them; the door behind him towards his right; and additional sitting accommodation for half a dozen persons.

Lady Britomart is a mature governing class aristocrat, well dressed and yet careless of her dress, well bred and quite reckless of her breeding, well mannered and yet appallingly outspoken and indifferent to the opinion of her interlocutors, amiable and yet peremptory, arbitrary, and high-tempered to the last bearable degree, and withal a very typical managing matron of the upper class, treated as a naughty child until she grew into a scolding mother, and finally settling down with plenty of practical ability and worldly experience, limited in the oddest way with domestic and class limitations, conceiving the universe exactly as if it were a large house in Wilton Crescent, though handling her corner of it very effectively on that assumption, and being quite enlightened and liberal as to the books in the library, the pictures on the walls, the music in the portfolios, and the articles in the papers.

Her son Stephen comes in. He is a gravely correct young man, taking himself very seriously, and, though still in some awe of his mother from childish habit and bachelor shyness, quite untroubled by doubts or diffidence.

STEPHEN. Whats the matter?

LADY BRITOMART. Presently, Stephen.

Stephen submissively walks to the settee and sits down. He takes The Speaker.

LADY BRITOMART. Dont begin to read, Stephen. I shall require all your attention.

STEPHEN. It was only while I was waiting—

LADY BRITOMART. Dont make excuses, Stephen. [*He puts down The Speaker*]. Now! [*She finishes her writing; rises; and comes to the settee*]. I have not kept you waiting v e r y long, I think.

STEPHEN. Not at all, mother.

LADY BRITOMART. Bring me my cushion. [*He takes the cushion from the chair at the desk and arranges it for her as she sits down on the settee*]. Sit down. [*He sits down and fingers his tie nervously*]. Dont fiddle with your tie, Stephen: there is nothing the matter with it.

STEPHEN. I beg your pardon. [*He fiddles with his watch chain instead*].

LADY BRITOMART. Now are you attending to me, Stephen?

STEPHEN. Of course, mother.

LADY BRITOMART. I am going to speak to you very seriously. I wish you would let that chain alone.

STEPHEN [*hastily relinquishing the chain*] Have I done anything to annoy you, mother? If so, it was quite unintentional.

LADY BRITOMART [*astonished*] Nonsense! [*With some remorse*] My poor boy, did you think I was angry with you?

STEPHEN. What is it, then, mother? You are making me very uneasy.

LADY BRITOMART [*squaring herself at him rather aggressively*] Stephen: I really cannot bear the whole burden of our family affairs any longer. You must advise me: you must assume the responsibility.

STEPHEN. I!

LADY BRITOMART. Yes, you, of course. You were twenty-four last June. Youve been at Harrow and Cambridge. Youve been to India and Japan. You must know a lot of things, now; unless you have wasted your time most scandalously. Well, a d v i s e me.

STEPHEN [*troubled*] Really, mother, I know so little about our family affairs. It is so impossible to mention some things to you—[*he stops, ashamed*].

LADY BRITOMART. I suppose you mean your father.

STEPHEN [*almost inaudibly*] Yes.

LADY BRITOMART. My dear: we cant go on all our lives not mentioning him. You are old enough now to be taken into my confidence, and to help me to deal with him about the girls.

STEPHEN. But the girls are all right. They are engaged.

LADY BRITOMART [*complacently*] Yes: I have made a very good match for Sarah. Charles Lomax will be a millionaire when he is thirty-five. But in the meantime his trustees cannot under the terms of his father's will allow him more than £800 a year. And what about Barbara? I thought Barbara was going to make the most brilliant career of all of you. And what does she do? Joins the Salvation Army; discharges her maid; lives on a pound a week; and walks in one evening with a professor of Greek whom she has picked up in the street, and who pretends to be a Salvationist because he has fallen head over ears in love with her.

STEPHEN. I was rather taken aback when I heard they were engaged. Cusins is a very nice fellow: nobody would ever guess that he was born in Australia; but—

LADY BRITOMART. Oh, Adolphus Cusins will make a very good husband. After all, nobody can say a word against Greek. Let snobbish people say what they please: Barbara shall marry, not the man they like, but the man *I* like.

STEPHEN. Of course I was thinking only of his income. However, he is not likely to be extravagant.

LADY BRITOMART. Dont be too sure of that, Stephen. I know your quiet, simple, refined people like Adolphus: quite content with the best of everything! No: Barbara will need at least £2000 a year. Besides, my dear, y o u must marry soon. I am trying to arrange something for you. [*Stephen closes his lips and is silent*]. Now dont sulk, Stephen.

STEPHEN. I am not sulking, mother. What has all this got to do with my father?

LADY BRITOMART. My dear Stephen: where is the money to come from? You know how poor my father is. Really, if he were not the Earl of Stevenage, he would have to give up society. He says, naturally enough, that it is absurd that he should be asked to provide for the children of a man who is rolling in money. You see, Stephen, your father must be fabulously wealthy.

STEPHEN. You need not remind me of that, mother. I have hardly ever opened a newspaper in my life without seeing our name in it. The Undershaft torpedo! The

Undershaft quick firers! the Undershaft submarine! and now the Undershaft aerial battleship! At Harrow they called me the Woolwich Infant. At Cambridge it was the same. A little brute spoilt my Bible—your first birthday present to me—by writing under my name, "Son and heir to Undershaft and Lazarus, Death and Destruction Dealers: address, Christendom and Judea." But that was not so bad as the way I was kowtowed to everywhere because my father was making millions by selling cannons.

LADY BRITOMART. That is why your father is able to behave as he does, openly defying every social and moral obligation. He is above the law.

STEPHEN. He does not actually break the law.

LADY BRITOMART. Not break the law! He is always breaking the law. He broke the law when he was born: his parents were not married.

STEPHEN. Mother! Is that true?

LADY BRITOMART. Of course it's true: that was why we separated.

STEPHEN. But this is so frightful to me, mother. To have to speak to you about such things.

LADY BRITOMART. Now be a good boy, Stephen, and listen to me. The Undershafts are descended from a foundling who was adopted by an armorer and gun-maker. That was long ago, in the reign of James the First. Ever since then, the cannon business has always been left to an adopted foundling named Andrew Undershaft. Your father was adopted in that way; and he pretends to consider himself bound to keep up the tradition and adopt somebody to leave the business to. Of course I was not going to stand that. There may have been some reason for it when the Undershafts could only marry women in their own class, whose sons were not fit to govern great estates. But there could be no excuse for passing over my son.

STEPHEN. Then it was on my account that your home life was broken up, mother. I am sorry.

LADY BRITOMART. Well, my dear, there were other differences. I really cannot bear an immoral man. Your father didnt exactly d o wrong things: he said them and thought them: that was what was so dreadful. He really had a sort of religion of wrongness. Your father was a very attractive man in some ways. I did not dislike him myself: far from it. But I couldnt forgive Andrew for preaching immorality while he practised morality.

STEPHEN. All this simply bewilders me, mother. Right is right; and wrong is wrong; and if a man cannot distinguish them properly, he is either a fool or a rascal: thats all.

LADY BRITOMART [touched] Thats my own boy! Now: what do you advise me to do?

STEPHEN. We cannot take money from him.

LADY BRITOMART. After all, Stephen, our present income comes from Andrew.

STEPHEN [shocked] I never knew that.

LADY BRITOMART. The Stevenages could not do everything for you. We gave you social position. Andrew had to contribute s o m e t h i n g . He had a very good bargain, I think.

STEPHEN [bitterly] We are utterly dependent on him and his cannons, then?

LADY BRITOMART. Certainly not: the money is settled. But he provided it. So you see it is not a question of taking money from him or not: it is simply a question of how much.

STEPHEN. Of course if you are determined—

LADY BRITOMART. I am not determined: I ask your advice; and I am waiting for it.

STEPHEN [*obstinately*] I would die sooner than ask him for another penny.

LADY BRITOMART [*resignedly*] You mean that *I* must ask him. Very well, Stephen: it shall be as you wish. I have asked your father to come here this evening. [*Stephen bounds from his seat*]. Dont jump, Stephen: it fidgets me.

STEPHEN [*in utter consternation*] Do you mean to say that my father is coming here tonight?

LADY BRITOMART [*looking at her watch*] I said nine. [*He gasps. She rises*]. Ring the bell, please. [*Stephen goes to the smaller writing table: presses a button on it; and sits at it with his elbows on the table and his head in his hands, outwitted and overwhelmed*].

STEPHEN. He may be here at any moment!

LADY BRITOMART. I have to prepare the girls. I asked Charles Lomax and Adolphus to dinner on purpose. Andrew had better see them in case he should cherish any delusions as to their being capable of supporting their wives. [*The butler enters: Lady Britomart goes behind the settee to speak to him*]. Morrison: go up to the drawing room and tell everybody to come down here at once. [*Morrison withdraws. Lady Britomart turns to Stephen*]. Now remember, Stephen: I shall need all your countenance and authority. [*He rises and tries to recover some vestige of these attributes*]. I dont know how Barbara will take it. Ever since they made her a major in the Salvation Army she has developed a propensity to have her own way and order people about which quite cows me sometimes. Its not ladylike: I'm sure I dont know where she picked it up. Dont look nervous, Stephen. *I* am nervous enough, goodness knows; but I dont shew it.

Sarah and Barbara come in with their respective young men, Charles Lomax and Adolphus Cusins. Sarah is slender, bored, and mundane. Barbara is robuster, jollier, much more energetic. Sarah is fashionably dressed: Barbara is in Salvation Army uniform. Lomax, a young man about town, is like many other young men about town. He is afflicted with a frivolous sense of humor which plunges him at the most inopportune moments into paroxysms of imperfectly suppressed laughter. Lomax likes Sarah and thinks it will be rather a lark to marry her. Consequently he has not attempted to resist Lady Britomart's arrangements to that end.

All four look as if they had been having a good deal of fun in the drawing room. The girls enter first, leaving the swains outside. Sarah comes to the settee. Barbara comes in after her and stops at the door.

BARBARA. Are Cholly and Dolly to come in?

LADY BRITOMART [*forcibly*] Barbara: I will not have Charles called Cholly: the vulgarity of it positively makes me ill.

BARBARA. It's all right, mother. Are they to come in?

LADY BRITOMART. Yes, if they will behave themselves.

BARBARA [*through the door*] Come in, Dolly; and behave yourself.

Barbara comes to her mother's writing table. Cusins enters smiling, and wanders towards Lady Britomart.

SARAH [*calling*] Come in, Cholly. [*Lomax enters, controlling his features very imperfectly, and places himself vaguely between Sarah and Barbara*].

LADY BRITOMART [*peremptorily*] Sit down, all of you. [*They sit. Cusins crosses to the window and seats himself there. Lomax takes a chair. Barbara sits at the writing table and Sarah on the settee*]. I dont in the least know what you are laughing at, Adolphus. I am surprised at you, though I expected nothing better from Charles Lomax.

CUSINS [*in a remarkably gentle voice*] Barbara has been trying to teach me the West Ham Salvation March.

LADY BRITOMART. I see nothing to laugh at in that; nor should you if you are really converted.

CUSINS [*sweetly*] You were not present. It was really funny.

LOMAX. Ripping.

LADY BRITOMART. Be quiet, Charles. Now listen to me, children. Your father is coming here this evening.

General stupefaction. Lomax, Sarah, and Barbara rise: Sarah scared, and Barbara amused and expectant.

LOMAX [*remonstrating*] Oh I say!

LADY BRITOMART. You are not called on to say anything, Charles.

SARAH. Are you serious, mother?

LADY BRITOMART. Of course I am serious. It is on your account, Sarah, and also on Charles's. [*Silence. Sarah sits, with a shrug. Charles looks painfully unworthy*]. I hope you are not going to object, Barbara.

BARBARA. I! why should I? My father has a soul to be saved like anybody else. He's quite welcome as far as I am concerned. [*She sits on the table, and softly whistles "Onward, Christian Soldiers"*].

LOMAX [*still remonstrant*] But really, dont you know! Oh I say!

LADY BRITOMART [*frigidly*] What do you wish to convey, Charles?

LOMAX. Well, you must admit that this is a bit thick.

LADY BRITOMART [*turning with ominous suavity to Cusins*] Adolphus: you are a professor of Greek. Can you translate Charles Lomax's remarks into reputable English for us?

CUSINS [*cautiously*] If I may say so, Lady Brit, I think Charles has rather happily expressed what we all feel. Homer, speaking of Autolycus, uses the same phrase; $\pi \upsilon \kappa \iota \nu \grave{o} \nu$ $\delta \acute{o} \mu o \nu$ $\epsilon \lambda \theta \epsilon \widehat{\iota} \nu$ means a bit thick.*

LOMAX [*handsomely*] Not that I mind, you know, if Sarah dont. [*He sits*].

LADY BRITOMART [*crushingly*] Thank you. Have I y o u r permission, Adolphus, to invite my own husband to my own house?

CUSINS [*gallantly*] You have my unhesitating support in everything you do.

SARAH. Do you mean that he is coming regularly to live here?

LADY BRITOMART. Certainly not. There are limits.

SARAH. Well, he cant eat us, I suppose. *I* dont mind.

LOMAX [*chuckling*] I wonder how the old man will take it.

LADY BRITOMART. Much as the old woman will, no doubt, Charles.

LOMAX [*abashed*] I didnt mean—at least—

LADY BRITOMART. You didnt t h i n k , Charles. You never do; and the result is, you never mean anything. And now please attend to me, children. Your father will be quite a stranger to us.

LOMAX. I suppose he hasnt seen Sarah since she was a little kid.

LADY BRITOMART. Not since she was a little kid, Charles, as you express it

---

* The Greek phrase is pronounced *pukinon domon elthein.*

with that elegance of diction and refinement of thought that seem never to desert you. Accordingly—er—[*impatiently*] Now I have forgotten what I was going to say. Adolphus: will you kindly tell me where I was.

CUSINS [*sweetly*] You were saying that as Mr Undershaft has not seen his children since they were babies, he will form his opinion of the way you have brought them up from their behavior tonight, and that therefore you wish us all to be particularly careful to conduct ourselves well, especially Charles.

LADY BRITOMART [*with emphatic approval*] Precisely.

LOMAX. Look here, Dolly: Lady Brit didnt say that.

LADY BRITOMART [*vehemently*] I did, Charles. Adolphus's recollection is perfectly correct. It is most important that you should be good; and I do beg you for once not to pair off into opposite corners and giggle and whisper while I am speaking to your father.

BARBARA. All right, mother. We'll do you credit. [*She comes off the table, and sits in her chair with ladylike elegance*].

LADY BRITOMART. Remember, Charles, that Sarah will want to feel proud of you instead of ashamed of you.

LOMAX. Oh I say! theres nothing to be exactly proud of, dont you know.

LADY BRITOMART. Well, try and look as if there was.

Morrison, pale and dismayed, breaks into the room in unconcealed disorder.

MORRISON. Might I speak a word to you, my lady?

LADY BRITOMART. Nonsense! Shew him up.

MORRISON. Yes, my lady. [*He goes*].

LOMAX. Does Morrison know who it is?

LADY BRITOMART. Of course. Morrison has always been with us.

LOMAX. It must be a regular corker for him, dont you know.

LADY BRITOMART. Is this a moment to get on my nerves, Charles?

LOMAX. But this is something out of the ordinary, really—

MORRISON [*at the door*] The—er—Mr Undershaft. [*He retreats in confusion*].

Andrew Undershaft comes in. All rise. Lady Britomart meets him in the middle of the room behind the settee.

Andrew is, on the surface, a stoutish, easygoing elderly man, with kindly patient manners, and an engaging simplicity of character. But he has a watchful, deliberate, waiting, listening face, and formidable reserves of power, both bodily and mental, in his capacious chest and long head. His gentleness is partly that of a strong man who has learnt by experience that his natural grip hurts ordinary people unless he handles them very carefully, and partly the mellowness of age and success. He is also a little shy in his present very delicate situation.

LADY BRITOMART. Good evening, Andrew.

UNDERSHAFT. How d'ye do, my dear.

LADY BRITOMART. You look a good deal older.

UNDERSHAFT [*apologetically*] I a m somewhat older. [*Taking her hand with a touch of courtship*] Time has stood still with you.

LADY BRITOMART [*throwing away his hand*] Rubbish! This is your family.

UNDERSHAFT [*surprised*] Is it so large? I am sorry to say my memory is failing very badly in some things. [*He offers his hand with paternal kindness to Lomax*].

LOMAX [*jerkily shaking his hand*] Ahdedoo.

behave yourself. If not, leave the room.

LOMAX. I'm awfully sorry, Lady Brit; but really you know, upon my soul! [*He*

UNDERSHAFT. I can see you are my eldest. I am very glad to meet you again, my boy.

LOMAX [*remonstrating*] No, but look here dont you know—[*Overcome*] Oh I say!

LADY BRITOMART [*recovering from momentary speechlessness*] Andrew: do you mean to say that you dont remember how many children you have?

UNDERSHAFT. Well, I may as well confess: I recollect only one son. But so many things have happened since, of course—er—

LADY BRITOMART [*decisively*] Andrew: you are talking nonsense. Of course you have only one son. That is Charles Lomax, who is engaged to Sarah.

UNDERSHAFT. My dear sir, I beg your pardon.

LOMAX. Notatall. Delighted, I assure you.

LADY BRITOMART. This is Stephen.

UNDERSHAFT [*bowing*] Happy to make your acquaintance, Mr Stephen. Then [*going to Cusins*] y o u must be my son. [*Taking Cusins' hands in his*] How are you, my young friend? [*To Lady Britomart*] He is very like you, my love.

CUSINS. You flatter me, Mr Undershaft. My name is Cusins: engaged to Barbara. [*Very explicitly*] That is Major Barbara Undershaft, of the Salvation Army. That is Sarah, your second daughter. This is Stephen Undershaft, your son.

UNDERSHAFT. My dear Stephen, I b e g your pardon.

STEPHEN. Not at all.

UNDERSHAFT. Mr Cusins: I am much indebted to you for explaining so precisely. [*Turning to Sarah*] Barbara, my dear—

SARAH [*prompting him*] Sarah.

UNDERSHAFT. Sarah, of course. [*They shake hands. He goes over to Barbara*] Barbara—I a m right this time, I hope?

BARBARA. Quite right. [*They shake hands*].

LADY BRITOMART [*resuming command*] Sit down, all of you. Sit down, Andrew. [*She comes forward and sits on the settee. Cusins also brings his chair forward on her left. Barbara and Stephen resume their seats. Lomax gives his chair to Sarah and goes for another*].

UNDERSHAFT. Thank you, my love.

LOMAX [*conversationally, as he brings a chair forward between the writing table and the settee, and offers it to Undershaft*] Takes you some time to find out exactly where you are, dont it?

UNDERSHAFT [*accepting the chair, but remaining standing*] That is not what embarrasses me, Mr Lomax. My difficulty is that if I play the part of a father, I shall produce the effect of an intrusive stranger; and if I play the part of a discreet stranger, I may appear a callous father.

LADY BRITOMART. There is no need for you to play any part at all, Andrew. You had much better be sincere and natural.

UNDERSHAFT [*submissively*] Yes, my dear: I daresay that will be best. [*He sits down comfortably*]. Well, here I am. Now what can I do for you all?

LADY BRITOMART. You need not do anything, Andrew. You are one of the family. You can sit with us and enjoy yourself.

A painfully conscious pause. Barbara makes a face at Lomax, whose too long suppressed mirth immediately explodes in agonized neighings.

LADY BRITOMART [*outraged*] Charles Lomax: if you can behave yourself, *sits on the settee between Lady Britomart and Undershaft, quite overcome*].

BARBARA. Why dont you laugh if you want to, Cholly? It's good for your inside.

LADY BRITOMART. Barbara: you have had the education of a lady. Please let your father see that; and dont talk like a street girl.

UNDERSHAFT. Never mind me, my dear. As you know, I am not a gentleman; and I was never educated.

LOMAX [*encouragingly*] Nobody'd know it, I assure you. You look all right, you know.

CUSINS. Let me advise you to study Greek, Mr Undershaft. Greek scholars are privileged men. Few of them know Greek; and none of them know anything else; but their position is unchallengeable.

BARBARA. Dolly: dont be insincere. Cholly: fetch your concertina and play something for us.

LOMAX [*jumps up eagerly, but checks himself to remark doubtfully to Undershaft*] Perhaps that sort of thing isnt in your line, eh?

UNDERSHAFT. I am particularly fond of music.

LOMAX [*delighted*] Are you? Then I'll get it. [*He goes upstairs for the instrument*].

UNDERSHAFT. Do you play, Barbara?

BARBARA. Only the tambourine. But it's useful for taking collections at the end of our meetings.

UNDERSHAFT [*looks whimsically at his wife*]!!

LADY BRITOMART. It is not my doing, Andrew. Barbara is old enough to take her own way. She has no father to advise her.

BARBARA. Oh yes she has. There are no orphans in the Salvation Army.

UNDERSHAFT. Your father there has a great many children and plenty of experience, eh?

BARBARA [*looking at him with quick interest and nodding*] How did y o u come to understand that? [*Lomax is heard at the door trying the concertina*].

LADY BRITOMART. Come in, Charles. Play us something at once.

Lomax sits down in his former place, and preludes.

UNDERSHAFT. One moment, Mr Lomax, I am rather interested in the Salvation Army. Its motto might be my own: Blood and Fire.

LOMAX [*shocked*] But not your sort of blood and fire, you know.

UNDERSHAFT. My sort of blood cleanses: my sort of fire purifies.

BARBARA. So do ours. Come down tomorrow to my shelter—the West Ham shelter—and see what we're doing. We're going to march to a great meeting in the Assembly Hall at Mile End. Come and see the shelter and then march with us: it will do you a lot of good. Can you play anything?

UNDERSHAFT. In my youth I earned pennies, and even shillings occasionally, in the streets and in public house parlors by my natural talent for stepdancing. Later on, I became a member of the Undershaft orchestral society, and performed passably on the tenor trombone.

LOMAX [*scandalized —putting down the concertina*] Oh I say!

BARBARA. Many a sinner has played himself into heaven on the trombone, thanks to the Army.

LOMAX [*to Undershaft*] Yes: but getting into heaven is not exactly in your line, is it?

LADY BRITOMART. Charles!!!

LOMAX. Well; but it stands to reason, dont it? The cannon business may be necessary and all that: we cant get on without cannons; but it isnt right, you know. On the other hand, there may be a certain amount of tosh about the Salvation Army. But still you cant deny that it's religion; and you cant go against religion, can you? At least unless youre downright immoral, dont you know.

UNDERSHAFT. You hardly appreciate my position, Mr Lomax. M y morality— m y religion—must have a place for cannons and torpedoes in it.

STEPHEN [coldly —almost sullenly] You speak as if there were half a dozen moralities and religions to choose from, instead of one true morality and one true religion.

UNDERSHAFT. For me there is only one true morality; but it might not fit you, as you do not manufacture aerial battleships. There is only one true morality for every man; but every man has not the same true morality.

LOMAX [overtaxed] Would you mind saying that again? I didnt quite follow it.

CUSINS. It's quite simple. As Euripides says, one man's meat is another man's poison morally as well as physically.

UNDERSHAFT. Precisely.

LOMAX. Oh, t h a t ! Yes, yes, yes. True. True.

STEPHEN. In other words, some men are honest and some are scoundrels.

BARBARA. There are no scoundrels.

UNDERSHAFT. Indeed? Are there any good men?

BARBARA. No. Not one. There are neither good men nor scoundrels: there are just children of one Father; and the sooner they stop calling one another names the better. I know them. Ive had scores of them through my hands: criminals, philanthropists, missionaries, county councillors, all sorts. Theyre all just the same sort of sinner; and theres the same salvation ready for them all.

UNDERSHAFT. May I ask have you ever saved a maker of cannons?

BARBARA. No. Will you let me try?

UNDERSHAFT. Well, I will make a bargain with you. If I go to see you tomorrow in your Salvation Shelter, will you come the day after to see me in my cannon works?

BARBARA. Take care. It may end in your giving up the cannons for the sake of the Salvation Army.

UNDERSHAFT. Are you sure it will not end in your giving up the Salvation Army for the sake of the cannons?

BARBARA. I will take my chance of that.

UNDERSHAFT. And I will take my chance of the other. [They shake hands on it]. Where is your shelter?

BARBARA. In West Ham. At the sign of the cross. Ask anybody in Canning Town. Where are your works?

UNDERSHAFT. In Perivale St Andrews. At the sign of the sword. Ask anybody in Europe.

LADY BRITOMART. Really, Barbara, you go on as if religion were a pleasant subject. Do have some sense of propriety.

UNDERSHAFT. I do not find it an unpleasant subject, my dear. It is the only one that capable people really care for.

LADY BRITOMART [looking at her watch] Well, if you are determined to have it, I insist on having it in a proper and respectable way. Charles: ring for prayers.

General amazement. Stephen rises in dismay.

LOMAX [*rising*] Oh I say!

UNDERSHAFT [*rising*] I am afraid I must be going.

LADY BRITOMART. You cannot go now, Andrew: it would be most improper. Sit down.

UNDERSHAFT. My dear: I have conscientious scruples. May I suggest a compromise? If Barbara will conduct a little service in the drawing room, I will attend it willingly. I will even take part, if a trombone can be procured.

LADY BRITOMART. Dont mock, Andrew.

UNDERSHAFT [*shocked —to Barbara*] You dont think I am mocking, my love, I hope.

BARBARA. No, of course not; and it wouldnt matter if you were: half the Army came to their first meeting for a lark. [*Rising*] Come along. [*She throws her arm round her father and sweeps him out, calling to the others from the threshold*]. Come, Dolly. Come, Cholly.

    Cusins rises.

LADY BRITOMART. I will not be disobeyed by everybody. Adolphus: sit down [*He does not*]. Charles: you may go. You are not fit for prayers: you cannot keep your countenance.

LOMAX. Oh I say! [*He goes out*].

LADY BRITOMART [*continuing*] But you, Adolphus, can behave yourself if you choose to. I insist on your staying.

CUSINS. My dear Lady Brit: there are things in the family prayer book that I couldnt bear to hear you say.

LADY BRITOMART. What things, pray?

CUSINS. Well, you would have to say before all the servants that we have done things we ought not to have done, and left undone things we ought to have done, and that there is no health in us. I cannot bear to hear you doing yourself such an injustice, and Barbara such an injustice. As for myself, I flatly deny it: I have done my best. I shouldnt dare to marry Barbara—I couldnt look you in the face—if it were true. So I must go to the drawing room.

LADY BRITOMART [*offended*] Well, go. [*He starts for the door*]. And remember this, Adolphus [*he turns to listen*]: I have a very strong suspicion that you went to the Salvation Army to worship Barbara and nothing else. And I quite appreciate the very clever way in which you systematically humbug me. I have found you out. Take care Barbara doesnt. Thats all.

CUSINS [*with unruffled sweetness*] Dont tell on me. [*He steals out*].

LADY BRITOMART. Sarah: if you want to go, go. Anything's better than to sit there as if you wished you were a thousand miles away.

SARAH [*languidly*] Very well, mamma. [*She goes*].

    Lady Britomart, with a sudden flounce, gives way to a little gust of tears.

STEPHEN [*going to her*] Mother: whats the matter?

LADY BRITOMART [*swishing away her tears with her handkerchief*] Nothing. Foolishness. You can go with him, too, if you like, and leave me with the servants.

STEPHEN. Oh, you mustnt think that, mother. I—I dont like him.

LADY BRITOMART. The others do. That is the injustice of a woman's lot. A woman has to bring up her children; and that means to restrain them, to deny them things they want, to set them tasks, to punish them when they do wrong, to do all the unpleasant things. And then the father, who has nothing to do but pet them and spoil them, comes in when all her work is done and steals their affection from her.

STEPHEN. He has not stolen our affection from you.

LADY BRITOMART [*violently*] I wont be consoled, Stephen. There is nothing the matter with me. [*She rises and goes towards the door*].

STEPHEN. Where are you going, mother?

LADY BRITOMART. To the drawing room, of course. [*She goes out. "Onward, Christian Soldiers," on the concertina, with tambourine accompaniment, is heard when the door opens*]. Are you coming, Stephen?

STEPHEN. No. Certainly not. [*She goes. He sits down on the settee, with compressed lips and an expression of strong dislike*].

Dissolve to:

The yard of the West Ham shelter of the Salvation Army is a cold place on a January morning. The building itself, an old warehouse, is newly whitewashed. Its gabled end projects into the yard in the middle, with a door on the ground floor, and another in the loft above it without any balcony or ladder, but with a pulley rigged over it for hoisting sacks. Those who come from this central gable end into the yard have the gateway leading to the street on their left, with a stone horse-trough just beyond it, and, on the right, a penthouse shielding a table from the weather. There are forms at the table; and on them are seated a man and a woman, both much down on their luck, finishing a meal of bread (one thick slice each, with margarine and golden syrup) and diluted milk.

The man, a workman out of employment, is young, agile, a talker, a poser, sharp enough to be capable of anything in reason except honesty or altruistic considerations of any kind. The woman is a commonplace old bundle of poverty and hard-worn humanity. She looks sixty and probably is forty-five. If they were rich people, gloved and muffed and well wrapped up in furs and overcoats, they would be numbed and miserable; for it is a grindingly cold raw January day; and a glance at the background of grimy warehouses and leaden sky visible over the whitewashed walls of the yard would drive any idle rich person straight to the Mediterranean. But these two, being no more troubled with visions of the Mediterranean than of the moon, and being compelled to keep more of their clothes in the pawnshop, and less on their persons, in winter than in summer, are not depressed by the cold: rather are they stung into vivacity, to which their meal has just now given an almost jolly turn. The man takes a pull at his mug, and then gets up and moves about the yard with his hands deep in his pockets, occasionally breaking into a stepdance.

THE WOMAN. Feel better arter your meal, sir?

THE MAN. No. Call that a meal! Good enough for you, praps; but wot is it to me, an intelligent workin man.

THE WOMAN. Workin man! Wot are you?

THE MAN. Painter.

THE WOMAN [*sceptically*] Yus, I dessay.

THE MAN. Yus, you dessay! I know. Every loafer that cant do nothink calls isself a painter. Well, I'm a real painter: grainer, finisher, three pounds, ten a week when I can get it.

THE WOMAN. Then why dont you go and get it?

THE MAN. I'll tell you why. Fust: I'm intelligent—fffff! it's rotten cold here [*he dances a step or two*]—yes: intelligent beyond the station o life into which it has pleased the capitalists to call me; and they dont like a man that sees through em. Second, an intelligent bein needs a doo share of appiness; so I drink somethink cruel when I get the chawnce. Third, I stand by my class and do as little as I can so's to leave arf the job for me fellow workers. Fourth, I'm fly enough to know wots inside the law and wots outside it; and inside it I do as the capitalists do: pinch wot I can lay me ands on.

THE WOMAN. Whats your name?

THE MAN. Price. Bronterre O'Brien Price. Snobby Price, for short. Wots y o u r name?

THE WOMAN. Rummy Mitchens, sir.

PRICE [quaffing the remains of his milk to her] Your elth, Miss Mitchens.

RUMMY [correcting him] Missis Mitchens. Mrs Romola Mitchens.

PRICE. Wot! Oh Rummy, Rummy! Respectable married woman, Rummy, gittin rescued by the Salvation Army by pretendin to be a bad un. Same old game!

RUMMY. What am I to do? I cant starve. Them Salvation lasses is dear good girls; but the better you are, the worse they likes to think you were before they rescued you. Why shouldnt they av a bit o credit, poor loves? theyre worn to rags by their work. And where would they get the money to rescue us if we was to let on we're no worse than other people? You know what ladies and gentlemen are.

PRICE. Thievin swine! Wish I ad their job, Rummy, all the same.

RUMMY. Who saved you, Mr Price? Was it Major Barbara?

PRICE. No: I come here on my own. I'm going to be Bronterre O'Brien Price, the converted painter. I know wot they like. I'll tell em how I blasphemed an gambled and wopped my poor old mother—

RUMMY [shocked] Used you to beat your mother?

PRICE. Not likely. She used to beat me. You come and listen to the converted painter, and youll hear how she was a pious woman that taught me me prayers at er knee, an how I used to come home drunk and drag her out o bed be er snow white airs, an lam into er with the poker.

RUMMY. Thats whats so unfair to us women. Your confessions is just as big lies as ours: but you men can tell your lies right out at the meetins and be made much of for it; while the sort o confessions we az to make az to be wispered to one lady at a time. It aint right, spite of all their piety.

PRICE. Right! Do you spose the Army'd be allowed if it went and did right? Not much. It combs out air and makes us good little blokes to be robbed and put upon. But I'll play the game as good as any of em. I'll see somebody struck by lightnin, or hear a voice sayin "Snobby Price: where will you spend eternity?" I'll av a time of it, I tell you.

Jenny Hill, a pale, overwrought, pretty Salvation lass of eighteen, comes in through the yard gate, leading Peter Shirley, a half hardened, half worn-out elderly man, weak with hunger.

JENNY [supporting him] Come! pluck up. Youll be all right.

PRICE [rising and hurrying officiously to take the old man off Jenny's hands] Poor old man! Cheer up, brother: youll find rest and peace and appiness ere. Hurry up with the food, miss: e's fair done. [Jenny hurries into the shelter]. Ere, buck up, daddy! she's fetchin y'a thick slice o breadn treacle, an a mug o skyblue. [He seats him at the corner of the table].

RUMMY [gaily] Keep up your old art! Never say die!

SHIRLEY. I'm not an old man. I'm only forty-six. The grey patch come in my hair before I was thirty. Am I to be turned on the streets to starve for it? and my job given to a young man that can do it no better than me?

PRICE [*cheerfully*] No good jawrin about it. Youre ony a jumped-up, jerked-off, orspittle-turned-out incurable of an ole workin man: who cares about you? Eh? Make the thievin swine give you a meal: theyve stole many a one from you. Get a bit o your own back. [*Jenny returns with the usual meal*]. There you are, brother. Awsk a blessin an tuck that into you.

SHIRLEY [*looking at it ravenously but not touching it, and crying like a child*] I never took anything before.

JENNY [*petting him*] Come, come! the Lord sends it to you: he wasnt above taking bread from his friends; and why should you be? Besides, when we find you a job you can pay us for it if you like.

SHIRLEY [*eagerly*] Yes, yes: thats true. I can pay you back: it's only a loan. [*Shivering*] Oh Lord! oh Lord! [*He turns to the table and attacks the meal ravenously*].

JENNY. Well, Rummy, are you more comfortable now?

RUMMY. Bless you, lovey! youve fed my body and saved my soul, havnt you? [*Jenny, touched, kisses her*]. Sit down and rest a bit: you must be ready to drop.

JENNY. Ive been going hard since morning. But theres more work than we can do. I mustnt stop.

RUMMY. Try a prayer for just two minutes. Youll work all the better after.

JENNY [*her eyes lighting up*] Oh isnt it wonderful how a few minutes prayer revives you! I was quite lightheaded at twelve o'clock, I was so tired; but Major Barbara just sent me to pray for five minutes; and I was able to go on as if I had only just begun. [*To Price*] Did you have a piece of bread?

PRICE [*with unction*] Yes, miss; but Ive got the piece that I value more; and thats the peace that passeth hall hannerstennin.

RUMMY [*fervently*] Glory Hallelujah!

Bill Walker, a rough customer of about twenty-five, appears at the yard gate and looks malevolently at Jenny.

JENNY. That makes me so happy. When you say that, I feel wicked for loitering here. I must get to work again.

She is hurrying to the shelter, when the new-comer moves quickly up to the door and intercepts her. His manner is so threatening that she retreats as he comes at her truculently, driving her down the yard.

BILL. Aw knaow you. Youre the one that took awy maw girl. Youre the one that set er agen me. Well, I'm gowin to ev er aht. Tell er Bill Walker wants er. She'll knaow wot thet means. You stop to jawr beck at me; and Aw'll stawt on you: d'ye eah? Theres your wy. In you gow. [*He takes her by the arm and slings her towards the door of the shelter. She falls on her hand and knee. Rummy helps her up again*].

PRICE [*rising, and venturing irresolutely towards Bill*] Easy there, mate. She aint doin you no arm.

BILL. Oo are you callin mite? [*Standing over him threateningly*] Youre gowin to stend ap for er, aw yer? Put ap your ands.

RUMMY [*running indignantly to him to scold him*] Oh, you great brute— [*He instantly swings his left hand back against her face. She screams and reels back to the trough, where she sits down, covering her bruised face with her hands and rocking herself and moaning with pain*].

297

JENNY [*going to her*] God forgive you! How could you strike an old woman like that?

BILL [*seizing her by the hair so violently that she also screams, and tearing her away from the old woman*] You Gawd forgimme again an Aw'll Gawd forgive you one on the jawr thetll stop you pryin for a week. [*Holding her and turning fiercely on Price*] Ev you ennything to sy agen it?

PRICE [*intimidated*] No, matey: she aint anything to do with me.

BILL. Good job for you, you stawved cur. [*To Jenny*] Nah are you gowin to fetch aht Mog Ebbijem; or em Aw to knock your fice off you and fetch her meself?

JENNY [*writhing in his grasp*] Oh please someone go in and tell Major Barbara— [*she screams again as he wrenches her head down: and Price and Rummy flee into the shelter*].

BILL. You want to gow in and tell your Mijor of me, do you?

JENNY. Oh please dont drag my hair. Let me go.

BILL. Do you or downt you? [*She stifles a scream*]. Yus or nao?

JENNY. God give me strength—

BILL [*striking her with his fist in the face*] Gow an shaow her thet, and tell her if she wants one lawk it to cam and interfere with me. [*Jenny, crying with pain, goes into the shed. He goes to the form and addresses the old man*]. Eah: finish your mess; an git aht o maw wy.

SHIRLEY [*springing up and facing him fiercely, with the mug in his hand*] You take a liberty with me, and I'll smash you over the face with the mug and cut your eye out. Come shovin and cheekin and bullyin in here, where the bread o charity is sickenin in our stummicks!

BILL [*contemptuously, but backing a little*] Wot good are you, you aold palsy mag? Wot good are you?

SHIRLEY. As good as you and better. I'll do a day's work agen you or any fat young soaker of your age. What do y o u know? Not as much as how to beeyave yourself—layin your dirty fist across the mouth of a respectable woman!

BILL. Downt provowk me to ly it acrost yours: d'ye eah?

SHIRLEY [*with blighting contempt*] Yes: you like an old man to hit, dont you, when youve finished with the women. I aint seen you hit a young one yet.

BILL [*stung*] You loy, you aold soupkitchener, you. There was a yang menn eah. Did Aw offer to itt him or did Aw not?

SHIRLEY. Was he starvin or was he not? Was he a man or only a crosseyed thief an a loafer? Would you hit my son-in-law's brother?

BILL. Oo's ee?

SHIRLEY. Todger Fairmile o Balls Pond. Him that won £20 off the Japanese wrastler at the music hall by standin out 17 minutes 4 seconds agen him.

BILL [*sullenly*] Aw'm nao music awl wrastler. Ken he box?

SHIRLEY. Yes: an you cant.

BILL. Wot! Aw cawnt, cawnt Aw? Wots thet you sy [*threatening him*]?

SHIRLEY [*not budging an inch*] Will you box Todger Fairmile if I put him on to you?

BILL [*subsiding with a slouch*] Aw'll stend ap to enny menn alawv, if he was ten Todger Fairmawls. But Aw dont set ap to be a perfeshnal. An eah Aw emm, talkin to a rotten aold blawter like you sted o givin her wot for. [*Working himself into a rage*] Aw'm gowin in there to fetch her aht. [*He makes vengefully for the shelter door*].

SHIRLEY. Youre goin to the station on a stretcher, more likely. You mind what youre about: the major here is the Earl o Stevenage's granddaughter.

BILL [*checked*] Garn!

SHIRLEY. Youll see.

BILL [*his resolution oozing*] Well, Aw aint dan nathin to er.

SHIRLEY. Spose she said you did! who'd believe you?

BILL [*very uneasy, skulking back to the corner of the penthouse*] Gawd! theres no jastice in this cantry. Aw'm as good as er.

SHIRLEY. Tell her so. It's just what a fool like you would do.

Barbara, brisk and businesslike, comes from the shelter with a note book, and addresses herself to Shirley. Bill, cowed, sits down in the corner on a form, and turns his back on them.

BARBARA. Good morning.

SHIRLEY [*standing up and taking off his hat*] Good morning, miss.

BARBARA. Sit down: make yourself at home. [*He hesitates; but she puts a friendly hand on his shoulder and makes him obey*]. Now then! since youve made friends with us, we want to know all about you. Name and trade.

SHIRLEY. Peter Shirley. Fitter. Chucked out two months ago because I was too old.

BARBARA [*not at all surprised*] Youd pass still. Why didnt you dye your hair?

SHIRLEY. I did. Me age come out at a coroner's inquest on me daughter.

BARBARA. Steady?

SHIRLEY. Teetotaller. Never out of a job before. Good worker. And sent to the knackers like an old horse!

BARBARA. No matter: if you did your part God will do his.

SHIRLEY [*suddenly stubborn*] My religion's no concern of anybody but myself.

BARBARA [*guessing*] *I* know. Secularist?

SHIRLEY [*hotly*] Did I offer to deny it?

BARBARA. Why should you? My own father's a Secularist, I think. Our Father—yours and mine—fulfils himself in many ways; and I daresay he knew what he was about when he made a Secularist of you. So buck up, Peter! we can always find a job for a steady man like you. [*Shirley, disarmed and a little bewildered, touches his hat. She turns from him to Bill*]. Whats y o u r name?

BILL [*insolently*] Wots thet to you?

BARBARA [*calmly making a note*] Afraid to give his name. Any trade?

BILL. Oo's afride to give is nime? [*Doggedly, with a sense of heroically defying the House of Lords in the person of Lord Stevenage*] If you want to bring a chawge agen me, bring it. [*She waits, unruffled*]. Moy nime's Bill Walker.

BARBARA [*as if the name were familiar: trying to remember how*] Bill Walker? [*Recollecting*] Oh, I know: youre the man that Jenny Hill was praying for inside just now. [*She enters his name in her note book*].

BILL. Oo's Jenny Ill? And wot call as she to pry for me?

BARBARA. I dont know. Perhaps it was you that cut her lip.

BILL [*defiantly*] Yus, it w a s me that cat her lip. Aw aint afride o y o u .

BARBARA. How could you be, since youre not afraid of God? Youre a brave man, Mr Walker. It takes some pluck to do our work here; but none of us dare lift our hand against a girl like that, for fear of her father in heaven.

BILL [*sullenly*] I want nan o your kentin jawr. I spowse you think Aw cam eah to beg from you, like this demmiged lot eah. Not me. Aw downt want your bread

299

and scripe and ketlep. Aw dont blieve in your Gawd, no more than you do yourself.

BARBARA [*sunnily apologetic and ladylike, as on a new footing with him*] Oh, I beg your pardon for putting your name down, Mr Walker. I didnt understand. I'll strike it out.

BILL [*taking this as a slight, and deeply wounded by it*] Eah! you let maw nime alown. Aint it good enaff to be in your book?

BARBARA [*considering*] Well, you see, theres no use putting down your name unless I can do something for you, is there? Whats your trade?

BILL [*still smarting*] Thets nao concern o yours.

BARBARA. Just so. [*Very businesslike*] I'll put you down as [*writing*] the man who—struck—poor little Jenny Hill—in the mouth.

BILL [*rising threateningly*] See eah. Awve ed enaff o this.

BARBARA [*quite sunny and fearless*] What did you come for?

BILL. Aw cam for maw gel, see? Aw cam to tike her aht o this and to brike er jawr for er.

BARBARA [*complacently*] You see I was right about your trade. [*Bill, on the point of retorting furiously, finds himself, to his great shame and terror, in danger of crying instead. He sits down again suddenly*]. Whats her name?

BILL [*dogged*] Er nime's Mog Ebbijem: thets wot her nime is.

BARBARA. Mog Habbijam! Oh, she's gone to Canning Town, to our barracks there.

BILL [*fortified by his resentment of Mog's perfidy*] Is she? [*Vindictively*] Then Aw'm gowin to Kennintahn arter her. [*He crosses to the gate; hesitates; finally comes back at Barbara*]. Are you loyin to me to git shat o me?

BARBARA. I dont want to get shut of you. I want to keep you here and save your soul. Youd better stay: youre going to have a bad time today, Bill.

BILL. Oo's gowin to give it to me? Y o u, preps?

BARBARA. Someone you dont believe in. But youll be glad afterwards.

BILL [*slinking off*] Aw'll gow to Kennintahn to be aht o reach o your tangue. [*Suddenly turning on her with intense malice*] And if Aw downt fawnd Mog there, Aw'll cam beck and do two years for you, selp me Gawd if Aw downt!

BARBARA [*a shade kindlier, if possible*] It's no use, Bill. She's got another bloke.

BILL. Wot!

BARBARA. He fell in love with her when he saw her with her soul saved, and her face clean, and her hair washed.

BILL [*surprised*] Wottud she wash it for, the carroty slat? It's red.

BARBARA. It's quite lovely now, because she wears a new look in her eyes with it. It's a pity youre too late. The new bloke has put your nose out of joint, Bill.

BILL. Aw'll put his nowse aht o joint for him. Not that Aw care a carse for er, mawnd thet. But Aw'll teach her to drop me as if Aw was dirt. And Aw'll teach him to meddle with maw judy. Wots iz bleedin nime?

BARBARA. Sergeant Todger Fairmile.

SHIRLEY [*rising with grim joy*] I'll go with him, miss. I want to see them two meet. I'll take him to the infirmary when it's over.

BILL [*to Shirley, with undissembled misgiving*] Is thet im you was speakin on?

SHIRLEY. Thats him.

BILL. Im that wrastled in the music awl?

SHIRLEY. He's gev em up now for religion; so he's a bit fresh for want of exercise. He'll be glad to see you. Come along.
BILL. Wots is wight?
SHIRLEY. Thirteen four. [*Bill's last hope expires*].
BARBARA. Go and talk to him, Bill. He'll convert you.
SHIRLEY. He'll convert your head into a mashed potato.
BILL [*sullenly*] Aw aint afride of im. Aw aint afride of ennybody. Bat e can lick me. She's dan me. [*He sits down moodily on the edge of the horse trough*].
SHIRLEY. You aint goin. I thought not. [*He resumes his seat*].
BARBARA [*calling*] Jenny!
JENNY [*appearing at the shelter door with a plaster on the corner of her mouth*] Yes, Major.
BARBARA. Send Rummy Mitchens out to clear away here.
JENNY. I think she's afraid.
BARBARA [*her resemblance to her mother flashing out for a moment*] Nonsense! she must do as she's told.
JENNY [*calling into the shelter*] Rummy: the Major says you must come.
   Jenny comes to Barbara, purposely keeping on the side next Bill, lest he should suppose that she shrank from him or bore malice.
BARBARA. Poor little Jenny! Are you tired? [*Looking at the wounded cheek*] Does it hurt?
JENNY. No: it's all right now. It was nothing.
BARBARA [*critically*] It was as hard as he could hit, I expect. Poor Bill! You dont feel angry with him, do you?
JENNY. Oh no, no, no: indeed I dont, Major, bless his poor heart! [*Barbara kisses her; and she runs away merrily into the shelter. Bill writhes with an agonizing return of his new and alarming symptoms, but says nothing. Rummy Mitchens comes from the shelter*].
BARBARA [*going to meet Rummy*] Now Rummy, bustle. Take in those mugs and plates to be washed; and throw the crumbs about for the birds.
   Rummy takes the three plates and mugs; but Shirley takes back his mug from her, as there is still some milk left in it.
RUMMY. There aint any crumbs. This aint a time to waste good bread on birds.
PRICE [*appearing at the shelter door*] Gentleman come to see the shelter, Major. Says he's your father.
BARBARA. All right. Coming. [*Snobby goes back into the shelter, followed by Barbara*].
RUMMY [*stealing across to Bill and addressing him in a subdued voice, but with intense conviction*] I'd av the lor of you, you flat eared pignosed potwalloper, if she'd let me. Youre no gentleman, to hit a lady in the face. [*Bill, with greater things moving in him, takes no notice*].
SHIRLEY [*following her*] Here! in with you and dont get yourself into more trouble.
RUMMY [*with hauteur*] I aint ad the pleasure o being hintroduced to you, as I can remember. [*She goes into the shelter with the plates*].
SHIRLEY. Thats the—
BILL [*savagely*] Downt you talk to me, d'ye eah? You lea me alown, or Aw'll do you a mischief. Aw'm not dirt under y o u r feet, ennywy.
SHIRLEY [*calmly*] Dont you be afeerd. You aint such prime company that you

need expect to be sought after. [*He is about to go into the shelter when Barbara comes out, with Undershaft on her right*].

BARBARA. Oh, there you are, Mr Shirley! [*Between them*] This is my father: I told you he was a Secularist, didnt I? Perhaps youll be able to comfort one another.

UNDERSHAFT [*startled*] A Secularist! Not the least in the world: on the contrary, a confirmed mystic.

BARBARA. Sorry. By the way, papa, what is your religion? in case I have to introduce you again.

UNDERSHAFT. My religion? Well, my dear, I am a Millionaire. That is my religion.

BARBARA. Then I'm afraid you and Mr Shirley wont be able to comfort one another after all. Youre not a Millionaire, are you, Peter?

SHIRLEY. No; and proud of it.

UNDERSHAFT [*gravely*] Poverty, my friend, is not a thing to be proud of.

SHIRLEY [*angrily*] Who made your millions for you? Me and my like. Whats kep us poor? Keepin you rich. I wouldnt have your conscience, not for all your income.

UNDERSHAFT. I wouldnt have your income, not for all your conscience, Mr Shirley. [*He goes to the penthouse and sits down on a form*].

BARBARA [*stopping Shirley adroitly as he is about to retort*] You wouldnt think he was my father, would you, Peter? Will you go into the shelter and lend the lasses a hand?

SHIRLEY [*bitterly*] Yes: I'm in their debt for a meal, aint I?

BARBARA. Oh, not because youre in their debt, but for love of them, Peter, for love of them. [*He cannot understand, and is rather scandalized*] There! dont stare at me. In with you; and give that conscience of yours a holiday [*bustling him into the shelter*].

Barbara turns to her father.

UNDERSHAFT. Never mind me, my dear. Go about your work; and let me watch it for a while.

BARBARA. All right.

UNDERSHAFT. For instance, whats the matter with that outpatient over there?

BARBARA [*looking at Bill, whose attitude has never changed, and whose expression of brooding wrath has deepened*] Oh, we shall cure him in no time. Just watch. [*She goes over to Bill and waits. He glances up at her and casts his eyes down again, uneasy, but grimmer than ever*]. It w o u l d be nice to just stamp on Mog Habbijam's face, wouldnt it, Bill?

BILL [*starting up from the trough in consternation*] It's a loy: Aw never said so. [*She shakes her head*]. Oo taold you wot was in moy mawnd?

BARBARA. Only your new friend.

BILL. Wot new friend?

BARBARA. The devil, Bill. When he gets round people they get miserable, just like you.

BILL [*with a heartbreaking attempt at devil-may-care cheerfulness*] Aw aint miserable. [*He sits down again, and stretches his legs in an attempt to seem indifferent*].

BARBARA. Well, if youre happy, why dont you look happy, as we do?

BILL [*his legs curling back in spite of him*] Aw'm eppy enaff, Aw tell you. Woy cawnt you lea me alown? Wot ev I dan to y o u ? Aw aint smashed your fice, ev Aw?

BARBARA [*softly: wooing his soul*] It's not me thats getting at you, Bill.

BILL. Oo else is it?

BARBARA. Somebody that doesnt intend you to smash women's faces, I suppose. Somebody or something that wants to make a man of you.

BILL [*blustering*] Mike a menn o me! Aint Aw a menn? eh? Oo sez Aw'm not a menn?

BARBARA. Theres a man in you somewhere, I suppose. But why did he let you hit poor little Jenny Hill? That wasnt very manly of him, was it?

BILL [*tormented*] Ev dan wiv it, Aw tell you. Chack it. Aw'm sick o your Jenny Ill and er silly little fice.

BARBARA. Then why do you keep thinking about it? Why does it keep coming up against you in your mind? Youre not getting converted, are you?

BILL [*with conviction*] Not ME. Not lawkly.

BARBARA. Thats right, Bill. Hold out against it. Put out your strength. Dont lets get you cheap. Todger Fairmile said he wrestled for three nights against his salvation harder than he ever wrestled with the Jap at the music hall. He gave in to the Jap when his arm was going to break. But he didnt give in to his salvation until his heart was going to break. Perhaps youll escape that. You havnt any heart, have you?

BILL. Woy aint Aw got a awt the sime as ennybody else?

BARBARA. A man with a heart wouldnt have bashed poor little Jenny's face, would he?

BILL [*almost crying*] Ow, lea me alown! Ev Aw ever offered to meddle with y o u ? Neggin and provowkin me lawk this! [*He writhes convulsively from his eyes to his toes*].

BARBARA [*with a steady soothing hand on his arm and a gentle voice that never lets him go*] It's your soul thats hurting you, Bill, and not me. Weve been through it all ourselves. Come with us, Bill. [*He looks wildly round*]. To brave manhood on earth and eternal glory in heaven. [*He is on the point of breaking down*]. Come. [*A drum is heard in the shelter; and Bill, with a gasp, escapes from the spell as Barbara turns quickly. Adolphus enters from the shelter with a big drum*]. Oh! there you are, Dolly. Let me introduce a new friend of mine, Mr Bill Walker. This is my bloke, Bill: Mr Cusins. [*Cusins salutes with his drumstick*].

BILL. Gowin to merry im?

BARBARA. Yes.

BILL [*fervently*] Gawd elp im! Gaw-aw-aw-awd elp im!

BARBARA. Why? Do you think he wont be happy with me?

BILL. Awve aony ed to stend it for a mawnin: e'll ev to stend it for a lawftawm.

CUSINS. That is a frightful reflection, Mr Walker. But I cant tear myself away from her.

BILL. Well, Aw ken. [*To Barbara*] Eah! do you knaow where Aw'm gowin to, and wot Aw'm gowin to do?

BARBARA. Yes: youre going to heaven; and youre coming back here before the week's out to tell me so.

BILL. You loy. Aw'm gowin to Keninntahn, to spit in Todger Fairmawl's eye. Aw beshed Jenny Ill's fice; an nar Aw'll git me aown fice beshed and cam beck and shaow it to er. Ee'll itt me ardern Aw itt er. Thatll mike us square. [*To

Adolphus] Is thet fair or is it not? Youre a genlmn: you oughter knaow.

BARBARA. Two black eyes wont make one white one, Bill.

BILL. Cawnt you never keep you mahth shat? Oy awst the genlmn.

CUSINS [*reflectively*] Yes: I think youre right, Mr Walker. Yes: I should do it. It's curious: it's exactly what an ancient Greek would have done.

BARBARA. But what good will it do?

CUSINS. Well, it will give Mr Fairmile some exercise; and it will satisfy Mr Walker's soul.

BILL. Rot! there aint nao sach a thing as a saoul. Ah kin you tell wevver Awve a saoul or not? You never seen it.

BARBARA. Ive seen it hurting you when you went against it.

Bill [*with compressed aggravation*] If you was maw gel and took the word aht o me mahth lawk thet, Aw'd give you sathink youd feel urtin, Aw would. [*To Adolphus*] You tike maw tip, mite. Stop er jawr; or youll doy afoah your tawm. [*With intense expression*] Wore aht: thets wot youll be: wore aht. [*He goes away through the gate*].

CUSINS [*looking after him*] I wonder!

BARBARA. Dolly! [*indignant, in her mother's manner*].

CUSINS. Yes, my dear, it's very wearing to be in love with you. If it lasts, I quite think I shall die young.

BARBARA. Should you mind?

CUSINS. Not at all. [*He is suddenly softened, and kisses her over the drum, evidently not for the first time, as people cannot kiss over a big drum without practice. Undershaft coughs*].

BARBARA. It's all right, papa, weve not forgotten you. Dolly: explain the place to papa: I havnt time. [*She goes busily into the shelter*].

Undershaft and Adolphus now have the yard to themselves. Undershaft, seated on a form, and still keenly attentive, looks hard at Adolphus. Adolphus looks hard at him.

UNDERSHAFT. I fancy you guess something of what is in my mind, Mr Cusins. [*Cusins flourishes his drumsticks as if in the act of beating a lively rataplan, but makes no sound*]. Exactly so. But suppose Barbara finds you out!

CUSINS. You know, I do not admit that I am imposing on Barbara. I am quite genuinely interested in the views of the Salvation Army. The fact is, I am a sort of collector of religions; and the curious thing is that I find I can believe them all. By the way, have you any religion?

UNDERSHAFT. Yes.

CUSINS. Anything out of the common?

UNDERSHAFT. Only that there are two things necessary to Salvation. Money and gunpowder.

CUSINS. Barbara wont stand that. You will have to choose between your religion and Barbara.

UNDERSHAFT. So will you, my friend. She will find out that that drum of yours is hollow.

CUSINS. Father Undershaft: you are mistaken: I am a sincere Salvationist. You do not understand the Salvation Army. It is the army of joy, of love, of courage: it marches to fight the devil with trumpet and drums, with music and dancing. It picks the waster out of the public house and makes a man of him: it finds a worm wriggling in a back kitchen, and lo! a woman! It takes the poor professor of

Greek, the most artificial and self-suppressed of human creatures, and lets loose
the rhapsodist in him; sends him down the public street drumming dithyrambs
[*he plays a thundering flourish on the drum*].
UNDERSHAFT. You will alarm the shelter.
CUSINS. Oh, they are accustomed to these sudden ecstasies. However, if the
drum worries you— [*he pockets the drum-sticks; unhooks the drum; and stands it
on the ground opposite the gateway*]. Barbara is quite original in her religion.
UNDERSHAFT [*triumphantly*] Aha! Barbara Undershaft would be. Her
inspiration comes from within herself. [*In towering excitement*] It is the
Undershaft inheritance. I shall hand on my torch to my daughter. She shall make
my converts and preach my gospel—
CUSINS. What! Money and gunpowder!
UNDERSHAFT. Yes, money and gunpowder. Freedom and power. Command
of life and command of death.
CUSINS [*urbanely: trying to bring him down to earth*] This is extremely
interesting, Mr Undershaft. Of course you know that you are mad.
UNDERSHAFT [*with redoubled force*] And you?
CUSINS. Oh, mad as a hatter. You are welcome to my secret since I have
discovered yours. But I am astonished. Can a madman make cannons?
UNDERSHAFT. Would anyone else than a madman make them? And now [*with
surging energy*] question for question. Can a sane man make a man of a waster or
a woman of a worm? Are there two mad people or three in this shelter today?
CUSINS. You mean Barbara is as mad as we are?
UNDERSHAFT [*pushing him lightly off and resuming his equanimity suddenly
and completely*] Pooh, Professor! let us call things by their proper names. I am a
millionaire; you are a Greek scholar; Barbara is a savior of souls. What have we
three to do with the common mob of slaves and idolators?
CUSINS. Take care! Barbara is in love with the common people. So am I. Have
you never felt the romance of that love?
UNDERSHAFT [*cold and sardonic*] Have you ever been in love with Poverty, like
St Francis? Have you ever been in love with Dirt, like St Simeon? Have you ever
been in love with disease and suffering, like our nurses and philanthropists? Such
passions are unnatural. This love of the common people may please an earl's
granddaughter and a university professor; but I have been a common man and a
poor man; and it has no romance for me. Leave it to the poor to pretend that
poverty is a blessing: we know better than that. We three must stand together
above the common people: how else can we help their children to climb up beside
us? Barbara must belong to us, not to the Salvation Army.
CUSINS. Well, I can only say that if you think you will get her away from the
Salvation Army by talking to her as you have been talking to me, you dont know
Barbara.
UNDERSHAFT. My friend: I never ask for what I can buy.
CUSINS [*in a white fury*] Do I understand you to imply that you can buy
Barbara?
UNDERSHAFT. No; but I can buy the Salvation Army.
CUSINS. Tell that to Barbara if you dare. Here she is.
  *Barbara, Snobby Price, beaming sanctimoniously, and Jenny Hill, with a
tambourine full of coppers, come from the shelter and go to the drum, on which
Jenny begins to count the money. Peter Shirley comes into the yard and observes.*

Barbara is excited and a little overwrought.

BARBARA [*to Undershaft*] Weve just had a splendid experience. [*To Price*] Ive hardly ever seen them so much moved as they were by your confession, Mr Price.

PRICE. I could almost be glad of my past wickedness if I could believe that it would elp to keep hathers stright.

BARBARA. It will, Snobby. How much, Jenny?

JENNY. Four and tenpence, Major.

BARBARA. Snobby, if you had given your poor mother just one more kick, we should have got the whole five shillings!

PRICE. If she heard you say that, miss, she'd be sorry I didnt. Oh what a joy it will be to her when she hears I'm saved.

UNDERSHAFT. Shall I contribute the odd twopence, Barbara? The millionaire's mite, eh? [*He takes a couple of pennies from his pocket*].

BARBARA. How did you make that twopence?

UNDERSHAFT. As usual. By selling cannons, torpedoes, and submarines.

BARBARA. Put it back in your pocket. You cant buy your salvation here for twopence: you must work it out.

UNDERSHAFT. Is twopence not enough? I can afford a little more, if you press me.

BARBARA. Two million millions would not be enough. Your kind of money is no use. Take it away. [*She turns to Cusins*]. Dolly: you must write another letter for me to the papers. [*He makes a wry face*]. Yes: I know you dont like it; but it must be done. The General says we must close this shelter if we cant get more money. I force the collections at the meetings until I am ashamed: dont I, Snobby?

PRICE. It's a fair treat to see you work it, miss. The way you got them up from three-and-six to four-and-ten with that hymn, penny by penny and verse by verse, was a caution. Not a Cheap Jack on Mile End Waste could touch you at it.

BARBARA. Yes; but I wish we could do without it. What are those hatfuls of pence and halfpence? We want thousands! tens of thousands! hundreds of thousands! I want to convert people, not to be always begging for the Army in a way I'd die sooner than beg for myself. How are we to feed them? I cant talk religion to a man with bodily hunger in his eyes. [*Almost breaking down*] It's frightful.

JENNY [*running to her*] Major, dear—

BARBARA [*rebounding*] No: dont comfort me. It will be all right. We shall get the money.

UNDERSHAFT. How?

JENNY. By praying for it, of course. [*She goes to the gate and looks out into the street*].

BARBARA. The General has come to march with us to our big meeting this afternoon; and she is very anxious to meet you, for some reason or other. Perhaps she'll convert you.

UNDERSHAFT. I shall be delighted, my dear.

JENNY [*at the gate: excitedly*] Major! Major! heres that man back again.

BARBARA. What man?

JENNY. The man that hit me. Oh, I hope hes coming back to join us.

Bill comes through the gate, his hands deep in his pockets and his chin sunk between his shoulders, like a cleaned out gambler. He halts between Barbara and the drum.

BARBARA. Hullo, Bill! Back already!

BILL [*nagging at her*] Bin talkin ever sence, ev you?

BARBARA. Pretty nearly. Well, has Todger paid you out for poor Jenny's jaw?

BILL. No he aint. You want to know where the dirt come from, dont you?

BARBARA. Yes.

BILL. Well, Awll teoll you. [*Bill, being a cockney proletarian, pronounces I as ee-aw, and is himself called Beeyaw by his intimates*].

Dissolve to:

A street in Canning Town, an eastern suburb of London where the main thoroughfare is broad and spacious but the people poor and the shops cheap. Todger Fairmile and Mog Habbijam are holding a Salvation Army meeting at a corner near a flourishing public house. As it is Sunday morning the public house is closed; and Todger and Mog, being recent converts, have not yet found out that when its doors open it will profit by a crowd, no matter how that crowd has been induced to assemble. It is an attractive meeting. The brass band, ten strong, plays very handsomely; and its leader, who plays the soprano cornet (the old cornetto revived by the Army, and the most difficult instrument in the band) is quite a virtuoso. Mog, a shapely lass with a natural border of red gold hair under her bonnet, is well worth looking at; and Todger, the ex-wrestler, in the prime of his athletic youth, is not a figure to be passed by without stopping on an idle Sunday morning. The crowd is therefore not at all an exclusively pious one: all sorts of people are looking and listening, except ladies and gentlemen, who are not indigenous in Canning Town —or Kennintahn, as the natives call it. Mog, radiant in the first flush of her conversion, is addressing it.

MOG. Dear friends: we shall have another hymn presently. You dont know how it warms our hearts to hear so many of you joining in and knowing the dear words. I want to share my happiness with you. It is within your reach: you have only to stretch out your hands and take it. Listen to me, dear friends. A month ago I was the unhappiest girl in London. I wanted pleasure, pleasure, pleasure. I drank: I swore: I was unclean in my mind and in my body. And I was so miserable that I would walk out with any man, if he had money enough to treat me in every public house we passed. Not one of you would have let your daughters speak to me or your sons be seen with me. I thought I was a grand girl enjoying myself all the time. And I was lost and miserable, miserable, miserable. One day when I went to a public house for another drink, I found an Army meeting going on outside. Just as you have here. I stopped to laugh and mock at it. Just as some of you are stopping here today. Do you know who was conducting that meeting? Here he is: Sergeant Todger Fairmile: the greatest fighter in the Isle of Dogs. I laughed and mocked and put out my tongue at him; but he saw how unhappy I was. "You poor dirty unhappy little slut" he said "God has chosen you this day to have your sins cleansed and your soul lifted out of the mire of hell and saved." And he put his hand on me; and it was as strong as the hand of God, not because his hand is so strong, but because it was really the hand of God. And from that hour heaven opened to me and I became as happy as an angel. Oh, dear friends, dont you envy me? If that could happen to such a wretch as I was, how much more easily will it happen to you! Dear Sergeant: tell them. My heart's overflowing: I cant speak.

TODGER. You all know who I am, Todger Fairmile, champion wrestler, boxer, and swimmer. Some of you have put money on me and won it.

BYSTANDER. Yes; and some of us put our money the other way and lost it.

TODGER. Youll lose no more that way: I shall ask you for a penny or two in the lass's tambourine presently. Ive been promoted sergeant in the Salvation Army.

ANOTHER BYSTANDER. Yes: its easier than fighting, isnt it?

TODGER. No, my friend, it's not easier; but it's ever so much happier. And who told you that I have given up fighting? I was born a fighter; and, please God, I'll die a fighter. But the ring was too small for a champion like me. It was no satisfaction to me to knock out some poor fellow, or to get his shoulders down on the mat for a purse of money. It was too easy; and there was no future in it for either of us, though we were both facing eternity. One day I gave an exhibition spar for the benefit of a charity. Our General was there; and I was introduced to her. She said I was a wonderful young man; and she asked me was I saved. "No" says I "but I can go fifteen rounds with Tommy Farr if youll put up the money." "Of course you can," she says. "God built you big enough for a trifle like that. But will you go, not fifteen rounds, but eternity, with the devil for no money at all? He is the champion the Army has to fight. Have you pluck enough for that?" I tried hard to make light of it; but it stuck; and a week after I took the count for the first time and joined up. And now I fight the devil all the time; and I'll say for him that he fights fairer and harder than some champions I have tackled. But God is against him. And in that sign we shall conquer. And now shall we have another hymn?

He turns to the band who take up their instruments. The Salvationists open their hymnbooks.

While Todger's back is turned Bill Walker pushes his way through the crowd and takes Todger by the arm.

BILL. Youre Todger Firemawl, are you?

TODGER. Sergeant Fairmile, at your service, sir.

BILL. You took awy maw judy, did you? Nime of Mog Ebbijam.

MOG. Bill!! Dont you know me?

BILL. Blaow me! Its er voice. Wot ev you dan t'yseeawf? Wotz e dan to you?

MOG. Sergeant: it's Bill Walker, that was my bloke. And I'm so changed he doesnt know me.

TODGER. We'll make the same change in you, Bill. Is that what youve come for?

BILL [*turning to Todger*] Awv cam to ev me fice chynged rawt enaff; an' youre the menn that's gaoin to chynge it. Tike thet. [*He spits in Todger's face*]. Nah, eah's maw jawr. Itt it. Itt it your best. Brike it.

TODGER. Oh, that I should be found worthy to be spit upon for the Gospel's sake!

MOG. You shouldnt have done that, Bill. Youve spit in the face of your salvation.

BILL [*to Todger*] Listen eah you. D'yew knaow a slip of a girl nimed Jinny Ill?

TODGER. We do. Has she converted you?

BILL. Keep your mawnd orf this conversion business and listen to wot Awm teollin you. Aw browk Jinny Ill's jawr this mawnin.

TODGER. No you didnt, Bill. It's not so easy to break a jaw as you think. You havnt the punch for it. You hit her in the face like the fine bold fellow you are; and now you want to forgive yourself; and you find you cant unless I give you your blow back harder than you can hit. [*To the crowd*] Dear friends: this man is on the way to his salvation. Let us kneel down and pray for him. [*The Salvationists kneel. Bill and Todger remain standing*]. Kneel down, Bill.

BILL [*furiously*] The hell I will!

Todger throws him down on his face; and kneels on his shoulders. Mog kneels beside him. Both pray devoutly with bent heads while the band plays a hymn.

BILL. Eah! wot you think Awm mide of?

MOG [*praying*] Oh Lord: break his stubborn spirit; but dont urt iz dear eart.

BILL [*scrambling up and feeling his ribs*] Never you mawnd maw deah awt. Wot abaht maw ribs? you and your fourteen staown blowk! [*Roar of laughter from the profane section of the crowd*] Larf awy: Aw see Aw kin git naow jastice eah. Well, Aw'll settle wiv Jinny Ill in me aown wy, spawt o the lot o you. [*He elbows his way through the crowd, and trudges off on his way back to the West Ham shelter*].

Dissolve to:

The yard of the West Ham shelter.

BILL [*finishing his tale*] Sao naow you knaow all the good that move dan me.

BARBARA [*her eyes dancing*] Wish I'd been there, Bill.

BILL. Yus: youd a got in a hextra bit o talk on me, wouldnt you?

JENNY. I'm so sorry, Mr Walker.

BILL [*fiercely*] Downt you gaow bein sorry for me: youve no call. Listen eah. Wot Aw did Aw'll py for. Aw trawd to gat me aown jawr browk to settisfaw you—

JENNY [*distressed*] Oh no—

BILL [*impatiently*] Teoll y' Aw did. Weoll, if Aw cawnt settisfaw you one wy, Aw ken anather. Listen! Eahs me last quid. Tike it; and lets ev no more o your forgivin an pryin and your Mijor jawrin me.

JENNY. Oh, I couldnt take it, Mr Walker. But if you would give a shilling or two to poor Rummy Mitchens! you really did hurt her; and she's old.

BILL [*contemptuously*] Not lawkly. Aw'd give her anather as soon as look at er. Let her ev the lawr o me as she threatened! S h e aint forgiven me: not mach. It's this Christian gime o yours that Aw wownt ev plyed agen me. Aw waownt ev it, Aw teoll you; sao tike your manney and stop thraowin your silly barshed fice hap agen me.

JENNY. Major: may I take a little of it for the Army?

BARBARA. No: the Army is not to be bought. We want your soul, Bill; and we'll take nothing less.

BILL [*bitterly*] Aw knaow. Me an maw few shillins is not good enaff for you. Youre a earl's grendorter, you are. Nathink less than a anderd pahnd for you.

UNDERSHAFT. Come, Barbara! you could do a great deal of good with a hundred pounds. If you will set this gentleman's mind at ease by taking his pound, I will give the other ninety-nine.

Bill, dazed by such opulence, instinctively touches his cap.

BARBARA. Oh, youre too extravagant, papa. Bill offers twenty pieces of silver. All you need offer is the other ten. That will make the standard price to buy anybody who's for sale. I'm not; and the Army's not. [*To Bill*] Youll never have another quiet moment, Bill, until you come round to us. You cant stand out against your salvation.

BILL [*sullenly*] Aw cawnt stend aht agen music awl wrastlers and awtful tangued women. Awve offered to py. Aw can do no more. Tike it or leave it. There it is. [*He throws the pound on the drum, and sits down on the horse-trough. The money*

fascinates Snobby Price, who takes an early opportunity of dropping his cap on it].
*The General comes from the shelter. She is an earnest looking woman of forty,
with a caressing, urgent voice, and an appealing manner.*
BARBARA. This is my father, General. [*Undershaft comes from the table, taking
his hat off with marked civility*]. Try what you can do with him. He wont listen to
me, because he remembers what a fool I was when I was a baby. [*She leaves them
together and chats with Jenny*].
THE GENERAL. Have you been shewn over the shelter, Mr Undershaft? You
know the work we're doing, of course.
UNDERSHAFT [*very civilly*] The whole nation knows it, Madam.
THE GENERAL. No, sir: the whole nation does not know it, or we should not
be crippled as we are for want of money to carry our work through the length
and breadth of the land. Let me tell you that there would have been rioting this
winter in London but for us.
UNDERSHAFT. You really think so?
THE GENERAL. I know it. I remember last year, when you rich gentlemen
hardened your hearts against the cry of the poor. They broke the windows of
your clubs in Pall Mall.
UNDERSHAFT [*gleaming with approval of their method*] I remember quite well.
THE GENERAL. Well, wont you help me to get at the people? They wont break
windows then. Come here, Price. Let me shew you to this gentleman [*Price comes
to be inspected*]. Do you remember the window breaking?
PRICE. My ole father thought it was the revolution, maam.
THE GENERAL. Would you break windows now?
PRICE. Oh no, maam. The windows of eaven av bin opened to me. I know now
that the rich man is a sinner like myself.
RUMMY [*appearing above at the loft door*] Snobby Price!
SNOBBY. Wot is it?
RUMMY. Your mother's askin for you. She's heard about your confession [*Price
turns pale*].
THE GENERAL. Go, Mr Price, and pray with her.
JENNY. You can go through the shelter, Snobby.
PRICE [*to the General*] I couldnt face her now, maam, with all the weight of my
sins fresh on me. Tell her she'll find her son at ome, waitin for her in prayer. [*He
skulks off through the gate, incidentally stealing the pound on his way out by
picking up his cap from the drum*].
THE GENERAL [*with swimming eyes*] You see how we take the anger and the
bitterness against you out of their hearts, Mr Undershaft.
UNDERSHAFT. It is certainly most convenient and gratifying to all large
employers of labor, Madam.
THE GENERAL. Barbara: Jenny: I have good news: most wonderful news.
[*Jenny runs to her*]. My prayers have been answered.
JENNY. Yes, yes.
BARBARA [*moving nearer to the drum*] Have we got money enough to keep the
shelter open?
THE GENERAL. I hope we shall have enough to keep all the shelters open. Lord
Saxmundham has promised us five thousand pounds—
BARBARA. Hooray!
JENNY. Glory!

THE GENERAL. —if—

BARBARA. 'If!' If what?

THE GENERAL. —if five other gentlemen will give a thousand each to make it up to ten thousand.

BARBARA. Who is Lord Saxmundham? I never heard of him.

UNDERSHAFT [*who has pricked up his ears at the peer's name, and is now watching Barbara curiously*] A new creation, my dear. You have heard of Sir Horace Bodger?

BARBARA. Bodger! Do you mean the distiller? Bodger's whisky!

UNDERSHAFT. That is the man. He is one of the greatest of our public benefactors. He restored the cathedral at Hakington. They made him a baronet for that. He gave half a million to the funds of his party: they made him a baron for that.

SHIRLEY. What will they give him for the five thousand?

UNDERSHAFT. There is nothing left to give him. So the five thousand, I should think, is to save his soul.

THE GENERAL. Heaven grant it may! Oh Mr Undershaft, you have some very rich friends. Cant you help us towards the other five thousand? We are going to hold a great meeting this afternoon at the Assembly Hall in the Mile End Road. If I could only announce that one gentleman had come forward to support Lord Saxmundham, others would follow. Dont you know somebody? couldnt you? wouldnt you? [*her eyes fill with tears*] oh, think of those poor people, Mr Undershaft: think of how much it means to them, and how little to a great man like you.

UNDERSHAFT [*sardonically gallant*] Madam: you are irresistible. I cant disappoint you; and I cant deny myself the satisfaction of making Bodger pay up. You shall have your five thousand pounds.

THE GENERAL. Thank God!

UNDERSHAFT. You dont thank me?

THE GENERAL. Oh sir, dont try to be cynical: dont be ashamed of being a good man. The Lord will bless you abundantly; and our prayers will be like a strong fortification round you all the days of your life. [*With a touch of caution*] You will let me have the cheque to shew at the meeting, wont you? Jenny: go in and fetch a pen and ink. [*Jenny runs to the shelter door*].

UNDERSHAFT. Do not disturb Miss Hill: I have a fountain pen. [*Jenny halts. He sits on the table and writes the cheque. Cusins rises to make room for him. They all watch him silently*].

BILL [*cynically, aside to Barbara, his voice and accent horribly debased*] Wot prawce selvytion nah?

BARBARA. Stop. [*Undershaft stops writing: they all turn to her in surprise*]. General: are you really going to take this money?

THE GENERAL [*astonished*] Why not, dear?

BARBARA. Why not! Do you know what my father is? Have you forgotten that Lord Saxmundham is Bodger the whisky man? Do you know that the worst thing I have had to fight here is not the devil, but Bodger, Bodger, Bodger, with his whisky, his distilleries, and his tied houses? Are you going to make our shelter another tied house for him, and ask me to keep it?

BILL. Rotten dranken whisky it is too.

THE GENERAL. Dear Barbara: Lord Saxmundham has a soul to be saved like any of us.

BARBARA. I know he has a soul to be saved. Let him come down here; and I'll do my best to help him to his salvation. But he wants to send his cheque down to buy us, and go on being as wicked as ever.

UNDERSHAFT [*with a reasonableness which Cusins alone perceives to be ironical*] My dear Barbara: alcohol is a very necessary article. It heals the sick—

BARBARA. It does nothing of the sort.

UNDERSHAFT. Well, it makes life bearable to millions of people who could not endure their existence if they were quite sober. It enables Parliament to do things at eleven at night that no sane person would do at eleven in the morning. Is it Bodger's fault that this inestimable gift is deplorably abused by less than one per cent of the poor? [*He turns again to the table; signs the cheque; and crosses it*].

THE GENERAL. Barbara: will there be less drinking or more if all those poor souls we are saving come tomorrow and find the doors of our shelters shut in their faces? Lord Saxmundham gives us the money to stop drinking—to take his own business from him.

CUSINS [*impishly*] Pure self-sacrifice on Bodger's part, clearly! Bless dear Bodger! [*Barbara almost breaks down as Adolphus, too, fails her*].

UNDERSHAFT [*tearing out the cheque and pocketing the book as he rises and goes past Cusins to the General*] I also, General, may claim a little disinterestedness. Think of my business! think of the widows and orphans! [*The General shrinks; but he goes on remorselessly*] the oceans of blood, not one drop of which is shed in a really just cause! All this makes money for me: I am never richer, never busier than when the papers are full of it. Well, it is your work to preach peace on earth and goodwill to men. [*The General's face lights up again*]. Every convert you make is a vote against war. [*Her lips move in prayer*]. Yet I give you this money to help you to hasten my own commercial ruin. [*He gives her the cheque*].

CUSINS [*mounting the form in an ecstasy of mischief*] The millennium will be inaugurated by the unselfishness of Undershaft and Bodger. Oh be joyful! [*He takes the drum-sticks from his pocket and flourishes them*].

THE GENERAL [*taking the cheque*] The longer I live the more proof I see that there is an Infinite Goodness that turns everything to the work of salvation sooner or later. Who would have thought that any good could have come out of war and drink? [*She is affected to tears*].

JENNY [*running to the General and throwing her arms round her*] Oh dear! how blessed, how glorious it all is!

CUSINS [*in a convulsion of irony*] Let us seize this unspeakable moment. Let us march to the great meeting at once. Excuse me just an instant. [*He rushes into the shelter. Jenny takes her tambourine from the drum head*].

THE GENERAL. Mr Undershaft: have you ever seen a thousand people fall on their knees with one impulse and pray? Come with us to the meeting. Barbara shall tell them that the Army is saved, and saved through you.

CUSINS [*returning impetuously from the shelter with a flag and a trombone, and coming between the General and Undershaft*] You shall carry the flag down the first street, General [*he gives her the flag*]. Mr Undershaft is a gifted trombonist: he shall intone an Olympian diapason to the West Ham Salvation March. [*Aside to Undershaft, as he forces the trombone on him*] Blow, Machiavelli, blow. [*Cusins rushes to the drum, which he takes up and puts on*].

UNDERSHAFT. I will do my best. I could vamp a bass if I knew the tune.

CUSINS. It is a wedding chorus from one of Donizetti's operas; but we have converted it. We convert everything to good here, including Bodger. You remember the chorus. "For thee immense rejoicing—immenso giubilo—immenso giubilo." [*With drum obbligato*] Rum tum ti tum tum, tum tum ti ta—

BARBARA. Dolly: you are breaking my heart.

CUSINS. What is a broken heart more or less here? Dionysos Undershaft has descended. I am possessed.

THE GENERAL. Come, Barbara: I must have my dear Major to carry the flag with me.

JENNY. Yes, Yes, Major darling.

CUSINS [*snatches the tambourine out of Jenny's hand and mutely offers it to Barbara*].

BARBARA [*coming forward a little as she puts the offer behind her with a shudder, whilst Cusins recklessly tosses the tambourine back to Jenny, and goes to the gate*] I cant come.

JENNY. Not come!

THE GENERAL [*with tears in her eyes*] Barbara: do you think I am wrong to take the money?

BARBARA [*impulsively going to her and kissing her*] No, no: God help you, you must: you are saving the Army. Go; and may you have a great meeting!

JENNY. But arnt you coming?

BARBARA. No. [*She begins taking off the silver S brooch from her collar*].

THE GENERAL. Barbara: what are you doing?

JENNY. You cant be going to leave us.

BARBARA [*quietly*] Father: come here.

UNDERSHAFT [*coming to her*] My dear! [*Seeing that she is going to pin the badge on his collar, he retreats to the penthouse in some alarm*].

BARBARA [*following him*] Dont be frightened. [*She pins the badge on and steps back towards the table, shewing him to the others*] There! It's not much for £5000, is it?

THE GENERAL. Barbara: if you wont come and pray w i t h us, promise me you will pray f o r us.

BARBARA. I cant pray now. Perhaps I shall never pray again.

THE GENERAL. Barbara!

JENNY. Major!

BARBARA [*almost delirious*] I cant bear any more. Quick march!

CUSINS [*calling to the procession in the street outside*] Off we go. Play up, there! I m m e n s o g i u b i l o . [*He gives the time with his drum; and the band strikes up the march, which rapidly becomes more distant as the procession moves briskly away*].

THE GENERAL. I must go, dear. Youre overworked; you will be all right tomorrow. We'll never lose you. Now Jenny; step out with the old flag. Blood and Fire! [*She marches out through the gate with her flag*].

JENNY. Glory Hallelujah! [*flourishing her tamrine and marching*].

UNDERSHAFT [*To Cusins, as he marches out past him easing the slide of his trombone*] "My ducats and my daughter"!

CUSINS [*following him out*] Money and gunpowder!

BARBARA. Drunkenness and Murder! My God: why hast thou forsaken me?

She sinks on the form with her face buried in her hands. The march passes away into silence. Bill Walker steals across to her.

BILL [*taunting*] Wot prawce selvytion nah?

SHIRLEY. Dont you hit her when she's down.

BILL. She itt me wen aw wiz dahn. Waw shouldnt Aw git a bit o me aown beck? [*Turning to the drum, he misses the money*] Ellow! Weres me money gorn? Bly me if Jenny Ill didnt tike it arter all!

RUMMY [*screaming at him from the loft*] You lie, you dirty blackguard! Snobby Price pinched it when he took up his cap. I was up here all the time an see im do it.

BILL. Wot! Stowl maw manney! Waw didnt you call thief on him, you silly aold macker you?

RUMMY. To serve you aht for ittin me acrost the fice. It's cost y'pahnd, that az. [*Raising a pæan of squalid triumph*] I done you. I'm even with you. Ive ad it aht o y— [*Bill snatches up Shirley's mug and hurls it at her. She slams the loft door and vanishes. The mug smashes against the door and falls in fragments*].

BARBARA [*turning to him more composedly, and with unspoiled sweetness*] You cant afford to lose it, Bill. I'll sent it to you.

BILL [*his voice and accent suddenly improving*] Not if Aw wiz to stawve for it. Aw aint to be bought.

SHIRLEY. Aint you? Youd sell yourself to the devil for a pint o beer; only there aint no devil to make the offer.

BILL [*unshamed*] Sao Aw would, mite, and often ev, cheerful. But she cawnt baw me. [*Approaching Barbara*] You wanted maw saoul, did you? Well, you aint got it.

BARBARA. I nearly got it, Bill. But weve sold it back to you for ten thousand pounds.

SHIRLEY. And dear at the money!

BARBARA. No, Peter: it was worth more than money.

BILL [*salvationproof*] It's nao good: you cawnt get rahnd me nah. Aw downt blieve in it; and Awve seen tody that Aw was rawt. [*Going*] Sao long, aol soupkitchener! Ta, ta, Mijor Earl's Grendorter! [*Turning at the gate*] Wot prawce selvytion nah? Snobby Prawce! Ha! ha!

BARBARA [*offering her hand*] Goodbye, Bill.

BILL [*taken aback, half plucks his cap off; then shoves it on again defiantly*] Git aht. [*Barbara drops her hand, discouraged. He has a twinge of remorse*]. But thets aw rawt, you knaow. Nathink pasnl. Naow mellice. Sao long, Judy. [*He goes*].

BARBARA. No malice. So long, Bill.

SHIRLEY [*shaking his head*] You make too much of him, miss, in your innocence.

BARBARA [*going to him*] Peter: I'm like you now. Cleaned out, and lost my job.

SHIRLEY. Youve youth an hope. Thats two better than me.

BARBARA. I'll get you a job, Peter. Thats hope for you: the youth will have to be enough for me. [*She counts her money*]. I have just enough left for two teas and my bus home. [*He frowns and rises with offended pride. She takes his arm*]. Dont be proud, Peter: it's sharing between friends. And promise me youll talk to me and not let me cry. [*She draws him towards the gate*].

Dissolve to:

Outside an unpretentious eating-house somewhere between West Ham and

314

London bridge. Customers entering and leaving. The winter evening has fallen and the street lamps are alight. The shops are lighted up. Barbara and Shirley come out.

BARBARA. I must say goodnight now, Peter. Heres your tramfare. I'll walk home.

SHIRLEY. But you cant walk home: youre miles from your home. And youve had nothing in there except a cup of tea. Ive had to eat your food for you. Youve been on your feet all day. You cant walk home on an empty stomach.

BARBARA. If I feel tired I can take a taxi: there is plenty of money at home to pay for it. But I must be alone: I've things to think about. Dont mind my sending you away, Peter: I shall not forget my promise to get you a job.

SHIRLEY. I dont like leaving you. I dont feel that youre fit to be left.

BARBARA. Thank you, dear Peter. But it will be all right: I can take care of myself.

SHIRLEY. I'll bet you can. Better than me. Well, goodnight; and thank you kindly for looking for the job for me. I'll dye my hair this time.

BARBARA. Yes, do, Peter. Goodnight.

They shake hands; and Shirley goes his way. Barbara stands a moment, thinking; then moves off.

Dissolve to:

A wharf by the riverside. Moonlight. Tide flowing and rivercraft passing. Barbara comes slowly to the brink, and gazes intently at the stream. She takes off her bonnet; looks at it affectionately; kisses it and throws it into the river.

A uniformed watchman hurries in and grips her arm.

WATCHMAN. Now then: whats the game? Ive been watching you. I saw you throw your bonnet into the river. Dont give your mind to throwing yourself after it and giving me the job of fishing you out, because you wont be let do it. [*Shaking her arm*] See?

BARBARA [*smiling wanly*] That is what you thought, is it? Even if I wanted to throw away my own life, Ive no right to risk yours.

The Watchman, startled by her ladylike speech and manner, releases her arm, and steps back respectfully.

WATCHMAN. Youll excuse me, miss; but are you quite yourself this evening?

BARBARA. I'm not at all sure. This morning I was Major Barbara of the Salvation Army in West Ham. Now I'm only Miss Undershaft, of Stevenage House, Wilton Crescent. But you see Ive just drowned Major Barbara; so I suppose I must be Miss Undershaft. Do you think I can find a taxi to take me home? Ive walked a long way, and become quite tired suddenly.

WATCHMAN. There are no taxis about here: the best I can do for you is an ambulance. The ambulance can carry you to the station. They can telephone there to your home for somebody to take charge of you.

BARBARA. Thank you: if youll be so good. I'm quite sane and quite sober; but Ive had a great shock today; and—and— [*she faints into the arms of the watchman*].

WATCHMAN [*saving her from falling*] Steady, miss, steady. [*He eases her down on the flags, and kneels beside her. He blows his whistle three times. He feels her pulse. The ambulance arrives with two bearers, running*].

FIRST BEARER. She's dry.

SECOND BEARER. She's dressed like a Salvation lass. Where's her bonnet?

315

WATCHMAN. She hasnt been in the water: I stopped her just in time. It's only a faint. She's coming round. Get her to the station as quick as you can. Be civil to her: her people are big West End swells. I'll telephone them. [*They lift Barbara on to the ambulance and carry her off*].

Dissolve to:

The meeting to which Undershaft and Cusins have marched. Charrington's great hall in the Mile End Road is crowded; and the pavement outside is blocked by people waiting in vain for admission. Two Salvationists come from the hall and set up a huge placard inscribed THE HALL IS FULL. YOU CANNOT COME IN; BUT YOU CAN PRAY FOR US. *The people slowly turn away, disappointed.*

Inside the hall a combination of Salvation Army bands is accompanying the hymn "Climbing up the Golden Stairs," which the whole congregation is singing with impetuous enthusiasm. The General is standing in front of the platform, in the middle, not singing, but waiting for her turn. Jenny Hill is singing frantically, Cusins, in the middle of the back row, is leading the percussion, Undershaft is vamping a trombone accompaniment.

At the end of the hymn the General raises her hand. Immediately there is dead silence.

THE GENERAL. Friends: we have a duty tonight which we must not forget. God has answered our prayers wonderfully by sending us a great gift; one that will enable us to get through many winters as bitter as this one has been without stinting one of His children of their little ration of bread and milk, or their warm blanket in the shelter. You all know the name of the nobleman who, under God, was the instrument of the first half of that gift. You will pray for him and rejoice in his salvation. You do not know the name of that other generous servant of God who has made up the whole sum for us; and I may not tell it to you. For he is one of those who does not let his right hand know what his left doeth. Friends: he is here among us tonight. [*Tremendous applause*] This afternoon, when he announced his magnificent offering to me, I exclaimed "Thank God!" He smiled and said "You do not thank me." I told him to come to this meeting and he would hear how we thanked him. He has come; and you have kept my word for me. You may not know him on this side of the grave; but when we cross the river [*with a gesture*]—over there—he will be with us still. And we shall know him by the seal of God on his brow. We will now sing our old favorite "Abide with me."

All rise to begin the hymn. Undershaft steals away from the platform and disappears. Cusins, his drum not being as appropriate to "Abide with me" as it was to the golden stairs, slips out after him.

Both of them make for a greenroom where the tables and chairs and the hooks round the walls are heaped with the coats and wraps and hats of the choir.

Undershaft throws his trombone on the pile of coats on the table, and is mopping his forehead with his handkerchief when Cusins arrives.

UNDERSHAFT. Phui! This is more than I bargained for. I can stand no more of it. [*He snatches up his coat and hat from a chair, and puts them on*]. Come with me to my flat. I have something to say to you.

CUSINS. But I want to call at Wilton Crescent to ask if Barbara has got home safely.

UNDERSHAFT. Never mind Barbara: she can look after herself. Her uniform will protect her better than ten policemen. Come on. It is about Barbara I want to speak to you. [*He hurries out. Cusins has to do likewise*].

Cut to:

In the best room in Undershaft's very comfortable flat in Whitehall Court his valet is placing a tray of drinks on the sideboard. There is a decanter of red wine, and another full of a fluid which deceptively resembles the purest sparkling water. A glowing fire warms the room pleasantly.

Undershaft and Cusins come in, Undershaft pocketing his latchkey.

CUSINS. Nice and warm in here.

UNDERSHAFT [*to the valet, who helps them to get rid of their greatcoats and headgear*] Any messages?

THE VALET. No, sir. Anything to eat, sir?

UNDERSHAFT. No. Something to drink only.

THE VALET. All ready, sir.

UNDERSHAFT [*to Cusins*] It was devilishly cold outside. Try a nip of brandy. Help yourself.

CUSINS. Brandy! Good gracious, no. Lady Britomart is a temperance fanatic. I am allowed nothing stronger than water. [*He pours out a glass of the colorless fluid*]. My throat is horribly dry. I dont know how to sing; and the effect of my attempts at the meetings is to give me incipient laryngitis. [*He swallows a liberal gulp of the fluid*]. Aow! [*Choking*] Kkk! What's this? Oh Lord! Red hot firewater. Kkk! Aow! [*He throws what he has left in the glass into the fire, which flames up alarmingly*].

UNDERSHAFT. Take care. You will set the chimney on fire.

CUSINS. It has set my throat on fire. What on earth is it?

UNDERSHAFT. It is only vodka: it wont hurt you.

CUSINS. Give me something cold, for heaven's sake.

UNDERSHAFT [*pouring out a glass of the red wine*] Try my special temperance burgundy.

CUSINS [*swallows the whole glassful greedily*]!!!

UNDERSHAFT. Steady! Steady!

THE VALET. Go easy with that, sir. Mr Undershaft calls it a temperance burgundy: but I should be sorry to venture on more than one glass of it myself.

CUSINS [*pouring himself out another glass*] Nonsense! After that fiery stuff it is like milk. [*He empties the glass*]. Ah! that's better.

UNDERSHAFT. Are you all right now?

CUSINS. Perfectly.

UNDERSHAFT. Good. By the way, you wont mind my getting rid of this. [*He takes the S brooch from his collar and throws it on the table*].

CUSINS. That means you are getting rid of Barbara.

UNDERSHAFT. Not at all.

CUSINS. Yes. She has refused to swallow Bodger's whisky. Do you think she is any more likely to swallow your money and gunpowder?

UNDERSHAFT. She has swallowed a good deal of it already, my friend. What do you suppose she has been living on all these years?

CUSINS. You think you will end by making us swallow them.

UNDERSHAFT. We all have to swallow them. There are mystical powers above and behind the three of us that will make short work of your scruples.

CUSINS [*somewhat aggressively. He is no longer sober*] Do you think I dont know all about the mystical powers, Machiavelli? You remember what Euripides says about your money and gunpowder?

UNDERSHAFT. No. Does he mention me?

CUSINS [*declaiming*]

One and another
In money and guns may outpass his brother;
And men in their millions float and flow
And seethe with a million hopes as leaven;
And they win their will or they miss their will;
And their hopes are dead or are pined for still;
But whoe'er can know
As the long days go
That to live is happy, has found his heaven.

[*Colloquially*] My translation. What do you think of it?

UNDERSHAFT. I think, my friend, that if you wish to know, as the long days go, that to live is happy, you must first acquire money enough for a decent life, and power enough to be your own master.

CUSINS. You are damnably discouraging. [*Again declaiming*]

Is it so hard a thing to see
That the spirit of God – – whate'er it be – –
The Law that abides and changes not, ages long,
the Eternal and Nature-born: t h e s e things be strong?
What else is Wisdom? What of Man's endeavor,
Or God's high grace, so lovely and so great?
To stand from fear set free? To breathe and wait?
To hold a hand uplifted over Fate?
And shall not Barbara be loved for ever?

UNDERSHAFT. Euripides mentions Barbara, does he?

CUSINS. It is a fair translation. The word means loveliness.

UNDERSHAFT. May I ask – – as Barbara's father – – how much a year she is to be loved for ever on?

CUSINS. As Barbara's father, that is more your affair than mine. I can feed her by teaching Greek: that is about all.

UNDERSHAFT. Do you consider it a good match for her?

CUSINS [*with polite obstinacy*] Mr Undershaft: when I am sober I am in many ways a weak, timid, ineffectual person: and my health is far from satisfactory. At present I am very far from sober, thanks to your Intemperance Burgundy. But, drunk or sober, whenever I feel that I must have anything, I get it, sooner or later. I feel that way about Barbara. I dont like marriage; I feel intensely afraid of it; and I dont know what I shall do with Barbara or what she will do with me; but I feel that I and nobody else must marry her. Please regard that as settled. Not that I wish to be arbitrary; but why should I waste your time in discussing what is inevitable?

UNDERSHAFT. You mean that you will stick at nothing, not even the conversion of the Salvation Army to the worship of Dionysos.

CUSINS. The business of the Salvation Army is to save, not to wrangle about the name of the Pathfinder. Dionysos or another: what does it matter?

UNDERSHAFT [*taking Cusins affectionately by the shoulders*] Professor Cusins: you are a young man after my own heart.

CUSINS [*returning his embrace*] Mr Undershaft: you are, as far as I am able to gather, a most infernal old rascal; but you appeal very strongly to my sense of ironic humor.

UNDERSHAFT. Good. We shall get on very well together. Have you ever thought of going into business? My business: money and gunpowder? Barbara's money will come from it. Why not help to earn it? Have you thought of that at all?

CUSINS. Look here, Machiavelli: I am interested in thought reading, and have, in fact, made some experiments in it. But I object to your trying it on me. When my head is clear I will tell you exactly what I think. Just at present I am delightfully drunk and happy. And the room is very hot. Might we have the window open for a moment?

UNDERSHAFT. Certainly. [*Calling*] James! I should like a breath of fresh air myself. [*To the Valet, who has come forward*] Draw back those curtains; and open the window, will you?

THE VALET [*doubtfully*] It's a very windy night, sir.

UNDERSHAFT. So much the better. It's only for a minute to freshen the room.

The Valet draws the curtains apart and opens the window, which has no sash, and opens like double doors. The wind rushes in.

CUSINS [*inhaling a full breath*] Oh, what a relief! [*He reels*]. Hullo! Wha's ma'er? Room's going round.

UNDERSHAFT [*holding him up*] Steady, man, steady.

CUSINS. Wha's 'appening? The waves, the waves. How d'we get on ship? [*Undershaft saves him from falling*]. Stea'y, Macklevelly, stea'y. Ha! ha! ha! Fernal ole laskl; buppeal velly slongly my sense of ile—ile—ile— [*with a supreme effort to say it*] ilonnic humor. Ha! ha! ha! ha! O ha! ha! ha! ha!

UNDERSHAFT [*to the Valet*] Lend a hand, will you?

THE VALET. Right, sir.

UNDERSHAFT. Get his feet on the rug: the floor's like wax.

CUSINS [*quoting The Frogs, by Aristophanes*] Brekekekex co-ax co-ax. Brekekekex co-ax.

THE VALET. What's he trying to say, sir?

UNDERSHAFT. Greek, I expect. Come come, Euripides! Pull yourself together.

CUSINS. No, no, no. 'Sglaceful. Not Ulipplees, Allisloffnes. Brekklekkex co-ax co-ax co— [*Calling*] Steward! [*Looking at the Valet*] Oh, there you are, steward. Ole man dlunk, bline dlunk. Purrimabed. [*Sentimentally*] Be kind to him, steward. Gooni' o' man. Gooni', S'eward. Gooni'. Ni, ni [*he falls fast asleep; and they have to let him down flat on the floor*].

UNDERSHAFT. What the deuce are we to do with him?

THE VALET [*dubiously*] I am afraid he's here for the night, sir.

They carry him to bed.

Dissolve to:

The dining room at Wilton Crescent next morning. Breakfast is ready. Morrison in attendance. Lady Britomart comes in.

LADY BRITOMART. Nobody down yet!

MORRISON. No, my lady.

LADY BRITOMART. Miss Barbara has gone, I suppose.

MORRISON. No, my lady. Miss Barbara is not up yet.

LADY BRITOMART. What! Are you sure?

MORRISON. Quite sure, my lady. Miss Barbara came in late last night and said she was not to be called.

LADY BRITOMART. Not to be called!!!

MORRISON. Yes, my lady. She said she was very tired and must have twelve hours sleep.

LADY BRITOMART. Was she quite well?

MORRISON. A little pale, my lady, and without her bonnet. I hadnt much time to notice; for she went straight upstairs, and left me to settle with the taxi and the policeman.

LADY BRITOMART. Policeman! What are you talking about, Morrison?

MORRISON. He came with her in the taxi. He asked questions, my lady. Was she Miss Undershaft? Was it all right? And an account to settle for the taxi, and for an ambulance, and some tea at the police station. I thought it best to pay and say nothing.

LADY BRITOMART. An ambulance! There must have been some accident. You are quite sure she was not hurt?

MORRISON. She seemed all right, my lady.

LADY BRITOMART. But you say she was brought home by a policeman.

MORRISON. I think he wanted to make sure who she was: whether he had her name and address all right, as it were.

LADY BRITOMART. Hm! What have you laid all those covers for? Have the young ladies invited anyone to breakfast?

MORRISON. You are expecting Mr Cusins and Mr Lomax, my lady. The car is ordered for half-past ten to take the party to—to—to—

LADY BRITOMART. Well? To where?

MORRISON. To Mr Undershaft's premises, I think, my lady.

LADY BRITOMART. To the factory, you mean?

MORRISON [apologetically] Well, yes, my lady.

LADY BRITOMART. The factory pays your wages, Morrison.

MORRISON. Yes, my lady. That is what factories are for. We must put up with them. Bacon and eggs, my lady, as usual?

LADY BRITOMART. No: I'll have a sausage this morning.

Morrison serves the sausage. Lomax comes in.

LADY BRITOMART. You are late, Charles. Where is Adolphus?

LOMAX [*taking a seat at the table*] He will be here soon. He was out all night. He wasnt quite himself when he came home. [*To Morrison*] Eggs and bacon, please. [*He is served*].

LADY BRITOMART. When you say he wasnt quite himself, Charles, what exactly do you mean?

Cusins enters, in an ordinary lounge suit.

LADY BRITOMART. Good morning, Adolphus. Charles was just telling me that when you came home this morning you were not quite yourself. May I ask what was the matter with you?

CUSINS [*taking his seat at the table*] Only a hangover. [*To Morrison*] Coffee, please. Nothing to eat. [*To Lady Britomart*] I got blind drunk last night.

LADY BRITOMART. Blind drunk!!!

CUSINS. I went home with your husband. Have you ever tasted vodka, Lady Brit?

LADY BRITOMART. Certainly not.

CUSINS. It looks exactly like spring water. The strongest spirits taste like milk after it.

Sarah bounces in, fresh from her morning toilet.

SARAH. Good morning. [*She kisses her mother, then kisses Lomax*]. Morning, Dolly. [*To Morrison*] Buttermilk and kippers, please. [*She sits*].

CUSINS. A new Spanish burgundy, warranted free from added alcohol: a Temperance burgundy in fact, finished me. Its richness in natural alcohol made any addition superfluous.

LOMAX. You know, there is a certain amount of tosh about alcohol. Burgundy is either burgundy or it isnt. If it is, it's hot stuff unless you are used to it.

CUSINS. Quite true. Ive never been really drunk before. I rather liked it last night. I regret it now.

Barbara comes in, in ordinary dress, black and simple, contrasting with Sarah.

BARBARA. Good morning everybody. [*To Morrison*] Porridge: lots of porridge. And grape fruit. I'm as hungry as a hunter.

LOMAX. Oh, I say! Youve chucked the uniform.

LADY BRITOMART. You mean that Barbara has changed her dress, Charles. Why not say so?

LOMAX. No: I'm afraid I mean something more than that. I mean she has chucked her salvation things.

BARBARA. Cholly means exactly what he says, mother. We are all going to the factory of money and gunpowder, death and destruction, on which we are living. The uniform would be out of place there. Tell us about the meeting, Dolly.

CUSINS. It was an amazing meeting. We prayed for Bodger: it was most touching. Then we prayed for the anonymous donor of the £5000. Your father would not let his name be given.

LOMAX. That was rather fine of the old man, you know. Most chaps would have wanted the advertisement.

CUSINS. He said all the charitable institutions would be down on him like vultures on a battlefield if he gave his name.

LADY BRITOMART. That is Andrew all over. He never does a proper thing without giving an improper reason for it.

CUSINS. I cant blame him. All my life Ive been doing improper things for proper reasons.

BARBARA. Tell me the truth, Dolly. Were you really ever in earnest about the Army? Would you have joined if you had never seen me?

CUSINS. Well—er—Well, possibly as a collector of religions—

LOMAX. Not as a drummer though. You know, Dolly, you are a very clearheaded brainy chap; and you must have felt what even I feel, that there is a certain amount of tosh about the Salvation Army. Now the claims of the Church of England—

LADY BRITOMART. Thats enough, Charles. Speak of something suited to your mental capacity.

LOMAX. But surely the Church of England is suited to all our capacities.

LADY BRITOMART. That is its worst fault: a thoroughtly English one.

LOMAX. You are so awfully strongminded, Lady Brit.

LADY BRITOMART. Dont dare to say so. If there is one thing in the world that I am not, it is a strongminded woman.

Morrison returns.

LADY BRITOMART. What is it?

MORRISON. Mr Undershaft had just drove up to the door, my lady.

LADY BRITOMART. Well, let him in.

MORRISON. Shall I announce him, my lady? or is he at home here in a manner of speaking?

LADY BRITOMART. That is a very difficult question, Morrison. What do you advise, Adolphus? You are his friend: you got drunk with him.

CUSINS. I did not marry him. I tolerate him because he was the instrument of Barbara's birth; but to me he is the Prince of Darkness.

LADY BRITOMART. You are getting drunker and drunker, Adolphus. Finish your breakfast and stop talking.

LOMAX. Has the old man a latchkey?

LADY BRITOMART. Another word, Charles; and I'll box your ears. What do you say, Sarah?

SARAH. As Morrison has raised the question I should leave him to solve it.

BARBARA. Of course: Morrison knows better than anybody. Dont you, Morrison?

MORRISON. Well, miss, the occasion is new to me. But as he has not come to breakfast, I could shew him into the library with your ladyship's leave.

LADY BRITOMART. Yes, do, Morrison.

Morrison goes.

LADY BRITOMART. Children: go and get ready.

BARBARA. Ive not finished my porridge.

LADY BRITOMART. Take it with you.

Barbara does so and goes out with Sarah.

LADY BRITOMART. Charles: tell Stephen to come to the library in five minutes or so.

LOMAX. Righto. [*He goes*].

LADY BRITOMART. I wish Charles would not say righto: we shall have Morrison saying it next. Adolphus: are you sober enough to tell them to send round the carriage in fifteen minutes?

CUSINS [*rising*] I will try. I will take an emetic, I think.

LADY BRITOMART. Do, Adolphus: do

He goes.

Meanwhile Morrison has gone down the grand stairs to the entrance hall and opened the hall door. Undershaft comes in.

UNDERSHAFT. Morning, Morrison. You quite well, eh?

MORRISON [*taking Undershaft's overcoat and hat*] Quite well, thank you, sir. Glad to see you home again, sir.

UNDERSHAFT. Home again? Hm! You are more at home here than I am by this time, eh?

MORRISON. Oh, I am only part of the house, sir.

UNDERSHAFT. Where is her ladyship?

MORRISON. In the library, sir.

UNDERSHAFT. I forget where the library is. Which door?

MORRISON. Where you were the night before last, sir. Shall I shew you?

UNDERSHAFT [*following him*] Yes, yes. I am only a visitor here.

Morrison leads the way upstairs to the library.

MORRISON. I will tell her ladyship, sir. [*He closes the library door, leaving Undershaft alone*].

Undershaft examines the room like a stranger, making faces expressive of strong distaste. He hates the place.

Lady Britomart bounces in. Undershaft clears his countenance, and puts on his best husbandly manner.

UNDERSHAFT. Good morning, dear. How fortunate to find you alone!

LADY BRITOMART. Dont be sentimental, Andrew. Sit down.

They sit side by side on the settee.

LADY BRITOMART [*attacking instantly*] Sarah must have £800 a year until Charles Lomax comes into his property. Barbara will need more, especially if she has a lot of children; and she will need it permanently, because Adolphus is only a professor and hasnt any property.

UNDERSHAFT [*resignedly*] Yes, my dear: I will see to it. Anything else? for yourself, for instance?

LADY BRITOMART. I want to talk to you about Stephen.

UNDERSHAFT [*rather wearily*] Dont, my dear. Stephen doesnt interest me.

LADY BRITOMART. He does interest me. He is our son.

UNDERSHAFT. Do you really think so? He has induced us to bring him into the world; but he chose his parents very incongruously, I think. I see nothing of myself in him, and less of you.

LADY BRITOMART. Andrew: Stephen is an excellent son, and a most steady, capable, highminded young man. You are simply trying to find an excuse for disinheriting him.

UNDERSHAFT. My dear Biddy: the Undershaft tradition disinherits him. It would be dishonest of me to leave the cannon foundry to my son.

LADY BRITOMART. It would be most unnatural and improper of you to leave it to anyone else, Andrew. Do you suppose this wicked and immoral tradition can be kept up for ever? Do you pretend that Stephen could not carry on the foundry just as well as all the other sons of the big business houses?

UNDERSHAFT. Yes: he could learn the office routine without understanding the business, like all the other sons; and the firm would go on by its own momentum until the real Undershaft—probably an Italian or a German—would invent something new, and cut him out.

LADY BRITOMART. There is nothing that any Italian or German could do that Stephen could not do. And Stephen at least has breeding.

UNDERSHAFT. The son of a foundling! Nonsense!

LADY BRITOMART. My son, Andrew! And even you may have good blood in your veins for all you know.

UNDERSHAFT. True. Probably I have. That is another argument in favor of a foundling.

LADY BRITOMART. Andrew: dont be aggravating. And dont be wicked. At present you are both.

UNDERSHAFT. This conversation is part of the Undershaft tradition, Biddy. Every Undershaft's wife has treated him to it ever since the house was founded. It is mere waste of breath. If the tradition be ever broken it will be for an abler man than Stephen.

LADY BRITOMART [*pouting*] Then go away.

UNDERSHAFT [*deprecatory*] Go away!

LADY BRITOMART. Yes: go away. If you will do nothing for Stephen, you are not wanted here. Go to your foundling, whoever he is; and look after him.

UNDERSHAFT. The fact is, Biddy—

LADY BRITOMART. Dont call me Biddy. I dont call you Andy.

UNDERSHAFT. I will not call my wife Britomart: it is not good sense. Seriously, my love, the Undershaft tradition has landed me in a difficulty. I am getting on in years; and my partner Lazarus has at last made a stand and insisted that the succession must be settled one way or the other. Of course he is quite right. But I havnt found a fit successor yet.

LADY BRITOMART [*obstinately*] There is Stephen.

UNDERSHAFT. Thats just it: all the foundlings I can find are exactly like Stephen.

LADY BRITOMART. Andrew!!

UNDERSHAFT. I want a man with no relations and no schooling: that is, a man who would be out of the running altogether if he were not a strong man. And I cant find him. Every blessed foundling nowadays is snapped up in his infancy by Barnardo homes, or School Board officers, or Boards of Guardians; and if he shews the least ability he is fastened on by schoolmasters; trained to win scholarships like a racehorse; crammed with secondhand ideas; drilled and disciplined in docility and what they call good taste; and lamed for life. If you want to keep the foundry in the family, you had better find an eligible foundling and marry him to Barbara.

LADY BRITOMART. Ah! Barbara! Your pet! You would sacrifice Stephen to Barbara.

UNDERSHAFT. Cheerfully. And you, my dear, would boil Barbara to make soup for Stephen.

LADY BRITOMART. Andrew: this is not a question of our likings and dislikings: it is a question of duty. It is your duty to make Stephen your successor.

UNDERSHAFT. Just as much as it is your duty to submit to your husband. Come, Biddy! these tricks of the governing class dont go down with me. I am one of the governing class myself; and it is waste of time giving tracts to a missionary. I have the power in this matter; and I am not to be humbugged into using it for your purposes.

LADY BRITOMART. Andrew: you can talk my head off; but you cant change wrong into right. And your tie is all on one side. Put it straight.

UNDERSHAFT [*disconcerted*] It wont stay unless it's pinned [*he fumbles at it with childish grimaces*]—

   Stephen comes in.

STEPHEN [*at the door*] I beg your pardon [*about to retire*].

LADY BRITOMART. No: come in, Stephen. [*Stephen comes forward to his mother's writing table*].

UNDERSHAFT [*not very cordially*] Good morning.

STEPHEN [*coldly*] Good morning.

UNDERSHAFT [*to Lady Britomart*] He knows all about the tradition, I suppose?

LADY BRITOMART. Yes. [*To Stephen*]. It is what I told you the night before last, Stephen.

UNDERSHAFT [*sulkily*] I understand you want to come into the cannon business.

STEPHEN. *I* go into trade! Certainly not.

UNDERSHAFT [*opening his eyes, greatly eased in mind and manner*] Oh! in that case—

LADY BRITOMART. Cannons are not trade, Stephen. They are enterprise.

STEPHEN. I have no intention of becoming a man of business in any sense. I have no capacity for business and no taste for it. I intend to devote myself to politics.

UNDERSHAFT [*rising*] My dear boy: this is an immense relief to me. And I trust it may prove an equally good thing for the country. I was afraid you would consider yourself disparaged and slighted. [*He moves towards Stephen as if to shake hands with him*].

LADY BRITOMART [*rising and interposing*] Stephen: I cannot allow you to throw away an enormous property like this.

STEPHEN [*stiffly*] Mother: there must be an end to treating me as a child, if you please. [*Lady Britomart recoils, deeply wounded by his tone*]. Until the night before last I did not take your attitude seriously, because I did not think you meant it seriously. But I find now that you left me in the dark as to matters which you should have explained to me years ago. I am extremely hurt and offended. Any further discussion of my intentions had better take place with my father, as between one man and another.

LADY BRITOMART. Stephen! [*She sits down again, her eyes filling with tears*].

UNDERSHAFT [*with grave compassion*] You see, my dear, it is only the big men who can be treated as children.

STEPHEN. I am sorry, mother, that you have forced me—

UNDERSHAFT [*stopping him*] Yes, yes, yes, yes: thats all right, Stephen. She wont interfere with you any more: your independence is achieved: you have won your latchkey. Dont rub it in; and above all, dont apologize. [*He resumes his seat*]. Now what about your future, as between one man and another—I beg your pardon, Biddy: as between two men and a woman.

LADY BRITOMART [*who has pulled herself together strongly*] I quite understand, Stephen. By all means go your own way if you feel strong enough. [*Stephen sits down magisterially in the chair at the writing table with an air of affirming his majority*].

UNDERSHAFT. It is settled that you do not ask for the succession to the cannon business.

STEPHEN. I hope it is settled that I repudiate the cannon business.

UNDERSHAFT. Come, come! dont be so devilishly sulky: it's boyish. Freedom should be generous. Besides, I owe you a fair start in life in exchange for disinheriting you. You cant become prime minister all at once. Havnt you a turn for something? What about literature, art, and so forth?

STEPHEN. I have nothing of the artist about me, either in faculty or character, thank Heaven!

UNDERSHAFT. A philosopher, perhaps? Eh?

STEPHEN. I make no such ridiculous pretension.

UNDERSHAFT. Just so. Well, there is the army, the navy, the Church, the Bar. The Bar requires some ability. What about the Bar?

STEPHEN. I have not studied law. And I am afraid I have not the necessary push—I believe that is the name barristers give to their vulgarity—for success in pleading.

UNDERSHAFT. Rather a difficult case, Stephen. Hardly anything left but the stage, is there? [*Stephen makes an impatient movement*]. Well, come! is there anything you know or care for?

STEPHEN [*rising and looking at him steadily*] I know the difference between right and wrong.

UNDERSHAFT [*hugely tickled*] You dont say so! What! no capacity for business, no knowledge of law, no sympathy with art, no pretension to philosophy; only a simple knowledge of the secret that has puzzled all the philosophers, baffled all the lawyers, muddled all the men of business, and ruined most of the artists: the secret of right and wrong. Why, man, youre a genius, a master of masters, a god! At twentyfour, too!

STEPHEN [*keeping his temper with difficulty*] You are pleased to be facetious. I pretend to nothing more than any honorable English gentleman claims as his birthright [*he sits down angrily*].

UNDERSHAFT. Oh, thats everybody's birthright. Look at poor little Jenny Hill, the Salvation lassie! she would think you were laughing at her if you asked her to stand up in the street and teach grammar or geography or mathematics or even drawing room dancing; but it never occurs to her to doubt that she can teach morals and religion. You are all alike, you respectable people. You cant tell me the bursting strain of a ten-inch gun, which is a very simple matter; but you all think you can tell me the bursting strain of a man under temptation. You darent handle high explosives; but youre all ready to handle honesty and truth and justice and the whole duty of man, and kill one another at that game. What a country! What a world!

LADY BRITOMART [*uneasily*] What do you think he had better do, Andrew?

UNDERSHAFT. Oh, just what he wants to do. He knows nothing and he thinks he knows everything. That points clearly to a political career. Get him a private secretaryship to someone who can get him an Under Secretaryship; and then leave him alone. He will find his natural and proper place in the end of the Treasury Bench.

STEPHEN [*springing up again*] I am sorry, sir, that you force me to forget the respect due to you as my father. I am an Englishman and I will not hear the Government of my country insulted. [*He thrusts his hands in his pockets, and walks angrily across to the window*].

UNDERSHAFT [*with a touch of brutality*] The government of your country! *I* am the government of your country: I, and Lazarus. Do you suppose that you and half a dozen amateurs like you, sitting in a row in that foolish gabble shop, can govern Undershaft and Lazarus? No, my friend: you will do what pays u s . You will make war when it suits us, and keep peace when it doesnt. You will find out that trade requires certain measures when we have decided on those measures. When I want anything to keep my dividends up, you will discover that my want is a national need. When other people want something to keep my dividends down, you will call out the police and military. And in return you shall have the support and applause of my newspapers, and the delight of imagining that you are a great statesman. Government of your country! Be off with you, my boy, and play with your caucuses and leading articles and historic parties and great leaders and burning questions and the rest of your toys. *I* am going back to my counting-house to pay the piper and call the tune.

STEPHEN [*actually smiling, and putting his hand on his father's shoulder with indulgent patronage*] Really, my dear father, it is impossible to be angry with you. You dont know how absurd all this sounds to me. You are very properly proud of having been industrious enough to make money; and it is greatly to your credit that you have made so much of it. But it has kept you in circles where you are valued for your money and deferred to for it, instead of in the doubtless very old-fashioned and behind-the-times public school and university where I formed my habits of mind. It is natural for you to think that money governs England; but you must allow me to think I know better.

UNDERSHAFT. And what does govern England, pray?

STEPHEN. Character, father, character.

UNDERSHAFT. Whose character? Yours or mine?

STEPHEN. Neither yours nor mine, father, but the best elements in the English national character.

UNDERSHAFT. Stephen: Ive found your profession for you. Youre a born journalist. I'll start you with a high-toned weekly review. There!

Before Stephen can reply Sarah, Barbara, Lomax, and Cusins come in ready for walking. Barbara crosses the room to the window and looks out. Cusins drifts amiably to the armchair. Lomax remains near the door, whilst Sarah comes to her mother.

Stephen goes to the smaller writing table and busies himself with his letters.

SARAH. Go and get ready, mamma: the car is waiting.

Lady Britomart leaves the room.

UNDERSHAFT [*to Sarah*] Good day, my dear. Good morning, Mr Lomax.

LOMAX [*vaguely*] Ahdedoo.

UNDERSHAFT [*to Cusins*] Quite well after last night, Euripides, eh?

CUSINS. As well as can be expected.

UNDERSHAFT. Thats right. [*To Barbara*] So you are coming to see my death and devastation factory, Barbara?

BARBARA [*at the window*] You came yesterday to see my salvation factory. I promised you a return visit.

LOMAX [*coming forward between Sarah and Undershaft*] Youll find it awfully interesting. Ive been through the Woolwich Arsenal; and it gives you a ripping feeling of security, you know, to think of the lot of beggars we could kill if it came to fighting. [*To Undershaft, with sudden solemnity*] Still, it must be rather an awful reflection for you, from the religious point of view as it were. Youre getting on, you know, and all that.

SARAH. You dont mind Cholly, papa, do you?

LOMAX [*much taken aback*] Oh I say!

UNDERSHAFT. Mr Lomax looks at the matter in a very proper spirit, my dear.

LOMAX, Just so. Thats all I meant, I assure you.

SARAH. Are you coming, Stephen?

STEPHEN. Well, I am rather busy—er—[*Magnanimously*] Oh well, yes: I'll come. That is, if there is room for me.

UNDERSHAFT. I can take two with me in a little motor I am experimenting with for field use. You wont mind its being rather unfashionable. It's not painted yet; but it's bullet proof.

LOMAX [*appalled at the prospect of confronting Wilton Crescent in an unpainted motor*] Oh I say!

SARAH. Our own car for me, thank you. Barbara doesnt mind what she's seen in.

LOMAX. I say, Dolly, old chap: do you really mind the car being a guy? Because of course if you do I'll go in it. Still—

CUSINS. I prefer it.

LOMAX. Thanks awfully, old man. Come, my ownest. [*He hurries out. Sarah follows him*].

CUSINS [*moodily walking across to Lady Britomart's writing table*] Why are we two coming to this Works Department of Hell? that is what I ask myself.

BARBARA. I have always thought of it as a sort of pit where lost creatures with blackened faces stirred up smoky fires and were driven and tormented by my father. It is like that, dad?

UNDERSHAFT [*scandalized*] My dear! It is a spotlessly clean and beautiful hillside town.

CUSINS. With a Methodist chapel? Oh do say theres a Methodist chapel.

UNDERSHAFT. There are several, all of different persuasions. My men are all strongly religious. In the High Explosives Sheds they object to the presence of Agnostics as unsafe.

BARBARA. And yet they obey all your orders?

UNDERSHAFT. I never give them any orders. When I speak to one of them it is "Well, Jones, is the baby doing well? and has Mrs Jones made a good recovery?" "Nicely, thank you, sir." And thats all.

CUSINS. But Jones has to be kept in order. How do you maintain discipline among your men?

UNDERSHAFT. I dont. They do. You see, the one thing Jones wont stand is any rebellion from the man under him, or any assertion of social equality between the wife of the man with 4 shillings a week less than himself, and Mrs Jones! Of course they all rebel against me, theoretically. Practically, every man of them keeps the man just below him in his place. I never meddle with them. I never bully them. I dont even bully Lazarus. I say that certain things are to be done; but I dont order anybody to do them. I dont say, mind you, that there is no ordering about and snubbing and even bullying. The men snub the boys and order them about; the carmen snub the sweepers; the artisans snub the unskilled laborers; the foremen drive and bully both the laborers and artisans; the assistant engineers find fault with the foremen; the chief engineers drop on the assistants; the departmental managers worry the chiefs; and the clerks have tall hats and hymnbooks and keep up the social tone by refusing to associate on equal terms with anybody. The result is a considerable profit, some of which is spent in this house.

CUSINS [*revolted*] You really are a—well, what I was saying yesterday.

BARBARA. What was he saying yesterday?

UNDERSHAFT. Never mind, my dear. He thinks I have made you unhappy. Have I?

BARBARA. Do you think I can be happy in this vulgar silly dress? I! who have worn the uniform. Do you understand what you have done to me? Yesterday I had a man's soul in my hand. I set him in the way of life with his face to salvation. But when we took your money he turned back to drunkenness and derision. [*With intense conviction*] I will never forgive you that. If I had a child, and you destroyed its body with your explosives—if you murdered Dolly with your horrible guns—I could forgive you if my forgiveness would open the gates of heaven to you. But to take a human soul from me, and turn it into the soul of a wolf! that is worse than any murder.

UNDERSHAFT. Does my daughter despair so easily? Can you strike a man to the heart and leave no mark on him? Did he not spit in Todger's eye to save his honor? Did he not give up his hard earned pound to save his soul? Do you not know what a pound means to such a man: more than ten thousand pounds to me! Will he ever strike a woman again as he struck Jenny Hill? It is your faith that is failing, not his. You have sent him on the road to his salvation: it may not be your road; but he will not turn back. You have finished with Bill: your work is done in the Army. So put on your hat and come and have a look at m y work.

BARBARA [*her face lighting up*] Oh, you are right: he can never be lost now: where was my faith?

CUSINS. Oh, clever clever devil!

BARBARA. You may be a devil; but God speaks through you sometimes. [*She takes her father's hands and kisses them*]. You have given me back my happiness: I feel it deep down now, though my spirit is troubled.

UNDERSHAFT. You have learnt something. That always feels at first as if you had lost something.

BARBARA. Well, take me to the factory of death; and let me learn something more. There must be some truth or other behind all this frightful irony. Come, Dolly. [*She goes out*].

CUSINS. My guardian angel! [*To Undershaft*] Avaunt! [*He follows Barbara*].

STEPHEN [*quietly, at the writing table*] You must not mind Cusins, father. He is a very amiable good fellow; but he is a Greek scholar and naturally a little eccentric.

UNDERSHAFT. Ah, quite so. Thank you, Stephen. Thank you. [*He goes out*].

Stephen smiles patronizingly; buttons his coat responsibly; and crosses the room to the door. Lady Britomart, dressed for out-of-doors, opens it before he reaches it. She looks round for the others; looks at Stephen; and turns to go without a word.

STEPHEN [*embarrassed*] Mother—

LADY BRITOMART. Dont be apologetic, Stephen. And dont forget that you have outgrown your mother. [*She goes out*].

The entrance hall. They all come downstairs in the order in which they left the library. Morrison is waiting for them; and nothing is said while the men get into their overcoats and hats, with Morrison helping Undershaft. When they are all ready Morrison opens the door and finds an armored car waiting.

MORRISON [*authoritatively*] Higher up, please, higher up. You cant park yourself here.

UNDERSHAFT. All right, all right. That is my car, Morrison.

MORRISON. I beg your pardon, sir.

UNDERSHAFT. Room for two besides myself. My dear—

LADY BRITOMART. Most certainly not. I go in my own car. Take Barbara and Alolphus: they are accustomed to disreputable conveyances.

UNDERSHAFT. Can you drive a car, Mr Lomax?

LOMAX. Ra-therrr.

LADY BRITOMART. Andrew: have you no regard for your children's lives? His licence was endorsed last week for driving to the public danger with his arm round Sarah.

LOMAX. But I assure you I can drive quite safely with one hand.

LADY BRITOMART. Possibly. But you cannot see your way safely through the traffic in Knightsbridge while you are kissing Sarah. The magistrate said so; and I agree with the magistrate. You and Sarah will come in my car; and I shall sit between you. Stephen will sit in front. Now dont dawdle.

Sarah, Lomax and Stephen obediently hurry out.

LADY BRITOMART. The military lorry will have to shew us the way—unless you two are frozen to death in it. [*She goes out*].

UNDERSHAFT [*to Barbara*] It is not a military lorry, my dear. You will be quite comfortable.

Barbara and Adolphus go out.

UNDERSHAFT [*following*] Good morning, Morrison.

MORRISON. Shall we see you again this evening, sir? I have your room ready for you, sir.

UNDERSHAFT [*dashing out*] No, by George! Goodbye.

MORRISON [*regretfully*] Goodbye, sir.

Left alone, Morrison shuts the door and throws off his professional manner. He shakes his head over the unfortunate domestic incompatibility of the heads of the household; then takes a newspaper from the hall table, and goes off to have an easy time in his own quarters.

Dissolve to:

A road skirting a green hill, up the opposite slopes of which, parallel to the road, runs what appears to be a white wall, ending at the top in a tower with steps winding up it spirally. In enormous black letters on the white wall are the names UNDERSHAFT up one side and LAZARUS down the other.

Along the road come Undershaft's armored car followed by Lady Britomart's limousine. The limousine stops, honking violently. The armored car stops. The occupants alight, except Lady Britomart.

UNDERSHAFT. What is the matter? Have you broken down?

LOMAX [*who has a camera in his hand*] Sorry to stop you; but Sarah wants a photograph of your shop front.

BARBARA. So do I. I shall send it to the Society for saving our countryside from disfiguring advertisements. This is the whited wall in the Bible. How could you spoil that hill with it merely to flaunt your name on it?

LADY BRITOMART [*putting her head out of the window of the limousine*] You must have all that knocked down and taken away instantly, Andrew. I will not have our name daubed all over the home counties.

UNDERSHAFT. They are not walls, my love. They are the chimneys of my smelting works. When they are swept twice a year we get some tons of silver out of the soot, which is quite clean and white. The name of the firm can be read for ten miles with a good glass: it is one of the sights of the county. People feel as Sarah does that they must photograph it. For twenty square miles you cannot escape from it. The advertisement is worth several thousands a year to us, and, incidentally, my dear, to you.

LADY BRITOMART. In short, you did it for our sakes.

UNDERSHAFT. No: for the sake of the firm. Everything is for the sake of the firm here.

LOMAX. Sort of Totalitarian State, what?

UNDERSHAFT. Precisely, Mr Lomax.

LADY BRITOMART. Monstrous. [*She disappears into the limousine*].

SARAH. Was Lazarus a foundling, papa? Why did they give him a Jewish name?

UNDERSHAFT. Oh no. The Undershafts are the foundlings. It is part of the tradition that they should take a partner with a Jewish name. It suggests financial ability; and he gets all the blame when our profits are considered exorbitant.

CUSINS. A scapegoat, then?

UNDERSHAFT. Exactly: a scapegoat.

CUSINS. That is the role of the Jew in modern Capitalism.

UNDERSHAFT. Yes; but it was an Undershaft invention. Most of these notions are.

LADY BRITOMART [*reappearing*] If you dont drive on I will get out the walk. I will not sit here listening to Andrew glorying in his wickedness.

Her children scramble back to their cars.

LOMAX. Righto! [*He gets in*].

CUSINS [*with one foot on the step of the armored car*] I must allow myself to point out, Machiavelli, that the adoption plan is not only an Undershaft tradition: it is a Japanese custom. [*He get in*].

UNDERSHAFT. It is a very sensible one. We have a Japanese temple in the village. The Shinto religion suits us exactly. I, of course, am its Mikado. [*He gets in*].

The cars move off, and arrive presently at the works of Undershaft and Lazarus in a forest of cranes and huge tubular metal structures of one sort or another. Factory and office buildings all about.

Undershaft and his family alight with their betrotheds, and stare about them at the labyrinth of buildings and monster tubes.

LADY BRITOMART. I refuse to walk another step through all these sheds and pipes and boilers. They mean nothing to me. I have never asked you to come and look at the kitchen range and the scullery sink. Why is that roof making noises like a whale with asthma?

UNDERSHAFT. It is breathing, my love.

LADY BRITOMART. What is it breathing?

UNDERSHAFT. Just what you are breathing. Common air.

LOMAX. Arent you overdoing this ventilation business a bit? Sarah inherits that from you: she is crazy on open windows. I am always telling her that there is a certain amount of tosh about fresh air. I say shut your windows and stop blowing your nose.

SARAH. Shut up, Cholly. A handkerchief lasts me a week: it lasts you half a day.

LADY BRITOMART. You have been brought up stuffily, Charles. My daughters are fresh air girls. I hope Andrew appreciates that fact.

UNDERSHAFT. Come in and see what this shed does with the air it breathes. It is worth seeing.

They go into the shed, Cusins bringing up the rear with Undershaft.

CUSINS. Nitrogen from the air, I suppose?

UNDERSHAFT. Yes. Salts of ammonia.

They follow the others in.

The interior of the shed is like a scene in a pantomime representing a Snow King's cave. It rains sulphate of ammonia.

LADY BRITOMART. This is ridiculous. Is it snow, or salt, or what?

CUSINS. Nitrates to make explosives.

UNDERSHAFT. Or sulphates to fertilize the fields your farmers are exhausting and destroying. You can use them both ways. If you prefer explosives that is your affair, not mine.

CUSINS. And it took a European war to stir mankind up to discover how to get harvests from the air!

LADY BRITOMART. Dont be wicked, Adolphus. You are encouraging Andrew. This is rather pretty, and no doubt very wonderful; but it is immoral; and I refuse to admire it. I have had enough of this. I am going home.

UNDERSHAFT. Not yet, my love. You must see where our men live. [*Leading the way out*] Come, Euripides: you think that nitrates are good for nothing but death. You shall see the sort of life they produce.

They go out, Lady Britomart coming last with Stephen.

LADY BRITOMART. Stephen: you have not uttered a single word since we arrived. Do you want your father to think you have nothing to say about those dreadful names across the hill?

STEPHEN. I thought at first that they were in horribly bad taste. But somehow the place is very wonderful. Undershaft and Lazarus are very big people. I had rather say nothing until I have seen everything.

He goes out, his mother following, shaking her head; for he is impressed and shaken, and shews it.

Dissolve to:

A grand square. The buildings are churches and temples in various styles of architecture. There is a Russian Greek Church brilliantly tinselled, a mosque, a Shinto temple, an Indian Jain temple, various Free Church meeting houses, two Church of England edifices, Protestant with spire and Anglican with tower, and a Roman Catholic church in Italian XII century taste with Virgin and crosses. And there is a round Labor Church, with the inscription "NO MAN IS GOOD ENOUGH TO BE ANOTHER MAN'S MASTER."

Undershaft and his party arrive.

CUSINS. What on earth is all this?

UNDERSHAFT. Its official name is The Meeting Place of All the Religions. But as that is too long a title for everyday use the men call it Piety Square.

LADY BRITOMART. You should not allow it, Andrew. You should learn how to keep your employees in order.

BARBARA. Is the real meeting place of all the religions a cannon foundry?

UNDERSHAFT. Yes: they are all agreed on that. You are yourself a major in a fighting army.

BARBARA. I am nothing now. When I fought it was to fight the devil, not to kill.

UNDERSHAFT. Fighting that is not to kill is not fighting at all. And they all call their adversaries the devil. There is a Salvation barracks here for you, if you wish, dear. And you, Euripides, shall have a temple of Dionysos. Or perhaps a little private oratory at the back of your office.

CUSINS. My office! What do you mean?

UNDERSHAFT. Pardon: I forgot that we have not come to that yet. The remark was prophetic. Shall we have a closer look at the buildings?

SARAH. Whats the Indian one? May we go in?

UNDERSHAFT. It is a Jain temple: a reproduction of the most famous one in the world. You may not worship there without washing yourself all over; but you can see everything quite well without overstepping the thresholds of the shrines.

SARAH. Let us go in. I think I should like to be a Jain.

LOMAX [*sings*] My Jane, my Jane, my pretty Jane, why dost thou look so shy?

LADY BRITOMART. Will nothing make you behave yourself, Charles? Remember that this is a sacred place, though the misguided worshippers are heathen idolators.

They go into the temple, and stop before one of the shrines, in which is a seated image. It fascinates them.

BARBARA. How utterly wonderful! Perfect peace! Perfect beauty! I think I shall become a Jain too. What god is it?

UNDERSHAFT. It is not a god. It is supposed to be only a wiseacre of some sort; but it is really a symbol. I am afraid it is worshipped and prayed to as a god, though the Jains hold that God is something beyond us with which they dare not meddle.

LOMAX [*even he is impressed*] It's quite awfully peaceful. Bad for the cannon trade, though, isnt it?

UNDERSHAFT. Not at all. We made these figures here.

CUSINS. Y o u made those marvellous figures! I refuse to believe it.

UNDERSHAFT. One of our troubles here used to be the waste of good gummetal involved in making cannons. This went on until I had to visit India on business. I was greatly struck by these figures, especially as they were quite new; for I had enough waste metal here to supply all India with them. I found they were made in a certain place by a certain set of native workmen, and nowhere else. I went to that place and bought up the whole concern, workmen and all. The wages I offered were of course far beyond anything they had ever dreamt of. I promised them a temple as well: you are now in it. Sometimes, when my nerves are overwrought I come in here and sit for an hour before this shrine while a priest recites prayers in a language of which I do not understand one word. It soothes me as nothing else does. This Jain religion is far ahead of anything we have in the west.

STEPHEN. You mean, I presume, except the Church of England.

UNDERSHAFT. We have two: a Protestant Low Church and an Anglican Ritualist. But somehow I never go into them.

LADY BRITOMART. Andrew: you grow wickeder and wickeder. Children: come away at once. There is some uncanny magic about this place: that figure will convert us all to Indian idolatry if we stay here any longer. Come.

She leads the way out. They follow reluctantly.

Exterior of the Shinto temple. The party as before.

UNDERSHAFT. This is where our Japanese experts worship.

LOMAX. The Shinto shop?

UNDERSHAFT. We call it a temple. There is nothing special inside except a priest who will expect you to give him a penny for a stick of incense to burn at the altar.

LADY BRITOMART. I shall most certainly do nothing of the sort. I will not go in.

UNDERSHAFT. You need not. But the temple is politically important to us here.

STEPHEN. How, pray?

UNDERSHAFT. Well, as Mr Lomax said, it is the temple of the Totalitarian State.

CUSINS. Do not forget that I am a collector of religions. Machiavelli. I happen to know all about Shinto. I know, for instance, that the Shinto Totalitarian State is personified by the divine emperor, descended from the sun, who owns everything.

UNDERSHAFT. Precisely.

CUSINS. Then does the Japanese Mikado own everything here?

UNDERSHAFT. No. I own everything here. As a foundling I may be descended from the sun. At all events I am the divine emperor.

LADY BRITOMART. Oh, this is beyond bearing. Andrew: I cannot breathe here. I must get back to some part of England where you dont own everything, and where everyone knows that you are a vulgar tradesman and not a divine emperor. Children: come away at once.

STEPHEN. I think not, mother. I will see this thing through.

CUSINS. I confess to being enormously amused. The discovery of Machiavelli as a divine emperor was worth living for.

LOMAX. Well, I can't help feeling that there is a certain amount of tosh about this last Shinto touch. I am not saying anything against it, you know.

LADY BRITOMART. You may think it a joke; but it is no joke to me. I am a Liberal; and without an atmosphere of freedom I suffocate.

BARBARA. It is easy to be a Liberal in Wilton Crescent on a divine emperor's millions. Not so easy at the East End, where women earn tuppence hapenny an hour, and families pay four shillings a week for an attic or a damp cellar to live in. I have seen enough of the toy temples where Indians worship you. Shew me where our own people live, and where they worship God.

UNDERSHAFT. I have reserved that for the last, my dear. We shall finish up with the places where the workers own everything, and I own nothing. You shall see how they live in their own houses, buy at their own shops, eat at their own restaurants, amuse themselves in their own theatres, and send their children to their own schools. It makes it very difficult for them to leave my employment. But then they do not want to leave it.

LADY BRITOMART. Slavery, I call it.

UNDERSHAFT. You would, my dear. But there is plenty of your pet political freedom here. Let me shew you.

They pass on to the Labor Church.

LADY BRITOMART. What is written up there round the top?

CUSINS. "No man is good enough to be another man's master." A famous maxim of William Morris, a great poet, a great communist, a great craftsman, and a great manufacturer. I still buy his curtains and wallpapers. I cannot afford his printed books. They cost hundreds.

LADY BRITOMART. Then he was also a very great hypocrite. Not good enough to be another man's master! He was everyman's master. I remember him quite well. He wore a blue shirt and no tie.

They go in.

The Labor Church, pillared and roofed like a church, has a platform instead of an altar, and a vast organ over it. Busts in all directions of the heroes and heroines of Labor.

UNDERSHAFT. Here are all the great revolutionists and socialists for you. That is Morris himself in the middle before the platform: Saint William of Kelmscott they call him. And all the rest: Robert Owen, Marx and Engels and Ferdinand Lassalle, Wells and Shaw and the Webbs; Hyndman and Cunninghame Graham and Kropotkin; Tolstoy and some new Russians called Bolsheviks: all of them the reddest of Reds. Revolutionary agitators draw the largest audiences here: they are usually the best speakers. I seldom speak in public; but when I do I speak here.

STEPHEN. But do you allow seditious speeches to be made here?

UNDERSHAFT. Of course: that is what the place is for. It is the Undershaft safety valve. Our people can talk here; and as long as men can talk politics they will never do anything else except work for their daily bread.

BARBARA. May I hold a prayer meeting here?

UNDERSHAFT. If you like. But there are Salvation barracks available. You will get a better attendance in them.

LOMAX. This place must cost a lot of money. Have you to pay for it?

UNDERSHAFT. It pays for itself. There is a charge for admission at our concerts.

SARAH. Have you an orchestra?

UNDERSHAFT. We have the best orchestra in the world, and the best conductors, and the best singers. We pay them handsomely for one performance, which we televise and record so that we can reproduce it as often as we like.

LOMAX. I say: could you give us a spot of it now?

UNDERSHAFT. Yes: I have had my favorite record put in ready for you. The announcer will explain. Let us sit in this row: it is the best for hearing.

They do so.

UNDERSHAFT. You will find a switch at the back of the seat in front of you. Push it over to the right.

LADY BRITOMART [*fingering it*] This one?

UNDERSHAFT. Yes. Dont be afraid: it wont hurt you.

Lady Britomart pushes the switch over. Instantly the empty platform becomes an orchestra of a hundred performers in evening dress tuning their instruments. Behind them is the chorus, a small body of good singers, not a mob of amateurs. In front are seated four principal singers. The conductor's desk is vacant. The announcer comes on, and with a gesture signals to the band for silence. The tuning stops.

ANNOUNCER. What you are about to hear is a fragment from a dead opera by the Italian composer Giacomo Rossini, who in Europe a hundred years ago ranked as high as Handel in our own country. The subject is the miraculous passage through the Red Sea by the Israelites in their flight from Egypt.

But nowadays this has no appeal to our own destiny and our own troubles, consequently no importance for us. To make it live again we have interpreted the Red Sea as a symbol of the Socialist revolution on which our most glorious hopes and our deadliest fears are fixed. In the same agonizing throes of faith, hope, and terror must Moses have confronted the waves of the mighty sea that raged between his people and the promised land. We have not altered a note of the music: we have only given it such a wealth of orchestration as Rossini would himself have given it had the great resources of Undershaft and Lazarus been within his reach. The words alone are brought up to date. For Rossini at his greatest today there is only one conductor: Arturo Toscanini.

Toscanini enters, baton in hand, and takes his place at the conductor's desk.

ANNOUNCER. Ladies and gentlemen: Arturo Toscanini. [*He leaves the platform*].

Toscanini raises his baton; and the quartet and chorus from Rossini's Moses in Egypt follows, accompanied by the Wagnerian orchestra. At the famous modulation into G major the organ is added. The words are as follows.

RECITATIVE AND CHORUS

BASS SOLO.	*In this our hour of darkness* *We warsmiths of the cannons* *Where do we stand today?*
CHORUS.	*We forge our own destruction* *We shall be slain who slay.*
BASS SOLO.	*Then from the gods who fail us* *Ourselves must win the sway.*

I
QUARTET AND CHORUS

BASS SOLO.	*O thou great soul of all:* *Say where but here within us* *The answer to our call* *Shall we, thy servants, find?*
CHORUS.	*Say where but here within us* *Shall we the answer find?*
SOLO QUARTET.	*Say where?*
CHORUS.	*In ourselves.*

II

TENOR SOLO.	*Shall we not then arise* *And in our hearts the power* *We sought for in the skies* *Find ready to our hands?*
CHORUS.	*In heart and brain discover* *The godhead in our hands.*
SOLO QUARTET.	*Where else?*
CHORUS.	*In our hands.*

III

SOPRANO SOLO.	*From Women's tortured hearts* *Their slaughtered sons lamenting* *I cry against these arts* *That slay what we create.*
CHORUS.	*Creation, not destruction,* *Shall henceforth make us great.*
SOLO QUARTET.	*Dare we hope?*
CHORUS.	*Yes: we dare.*

IV
Soloists and Chorus with Organ ad lib.

ALL.	To thee the god within us We trust the world to win us. Creation, not destruction, Henceforth shall make us great.

SOPRANO SOLO.   Us great.
CHORUS.   Henceforth.

The players and singers vanish, leaving the platform empty as before.
UNDERSHAFT. Well? what did you think of it?
LADY BRITOMART. I loathed it. My mother used to play Thalberg's variations on that air; and she tried to force me to learn them too. I have hated music ever since.
LOMAX. I could hear that it was classical music. It made a devil of a noise.
UNDERSHAFT [*rising*] Come! it is time for lunch: you must all be hungry.
They all rise eagerly and make for the door.
LADY BRITOMART. I hope we can depend on your cookery, Andrew.
UNDERSHAFT. You shall have what my workers eat.
LADY BRITOMART [*stopping*] Is there nothing better here, Andrew?
UNDERSHAFT. There is nothing better anywhere. Do not be afraid. Come!
Cut to:
A park surrounding a colossal modern forty storey mansion. The party arrives at the entrance in its cars, and alights there.
LOMAX. Is this part of the show?
UNDERSHAFT. It is part of the show. It is where our younger workers prefer to live. The young wives insist on service flats, though we have plenty of bungalows for them.
BARBARA. Service flats! Do you mean that the young women dont know how to cook and wash and do their own housework?
UNDERSHAFT. Not at all. They have been most thoroughly and carefully taught how to do every kind of domestic work. The result is that nothing will induce them to do it. They know too much about it. They prefer to earn wages in the workshops and be waited on by professional servants when they go home.
LADY BRITOMART. I'll stop my subscription to the Domestic Training Institution at once. I never heard of such a thing.
They go in. In the entrance hall there are several automatic lifts: one marked EXPRESS. Undershaft presses the button of the Express lift, which comes down.
UNDERSHAFT. Youll lunch on the thirty-second floor [*he opens the grill of the lift, and ushers them in*].
The lift ascends. When they leave it, Undershaft conducts them to a handsome salon with big windows. A table is ready for lunch with a luxurious display of linen and silver and flowers.
LADY BRITOMART [*surveying the table critically*] The table is laid for five only. We are six.
UNDERSHAFT. You forget, my love, that I dont lunch. It is a modern habit I have never been able to acquire. A penny roll and a glass of milk in my office is enough for me. I must leave you now for an hour or so to see after my office business. It will be a relief for you to get rid of me for a while.
ALL EXCEPT BARBARA AND LADY BRITOMART [*politely murmuring*] Oh no. Not at all.
BARBARA [*explosively*] Yes it will. We cant talk about all these upsetting things in front of you. I want an hour's respite and some food.
UNDERSHAFT. You shall have both, my love. But first let me shew you where my older workpeople live. You can see it all from this window.

They crowd to the window he indicates.

The view from the window is of a green valley dotted with bungalows of various design: each with its verandah and garden.

LOMAX. Garden city notion, what?

UNDERSHAFT. They call it a garden suburb. I'm sorry to say they are all incorrigible snobs. You must be careful what you say when they are listening. Now if youll come to this window youll see where to find me in my own office.

They move expectantly to the opposite window. It commands a view of an ancient slag heap, now an apparently natural hill dotted with separate wooden sheds, and surmounted by a parapet and firestep on which is mounted an obsolete black cannon, short in the barrel and thick in the breech, without ornament of any kind.

UNDERSHAFT. That is where we handle high explosives. Any of those sheds may blow up at any moment. An explosion costs nothing but a shed and perhaps a casualty or two. The hill is called Thundercrest: it is the oldest part of the concern; and the Undershafts still like to do a good deal of their buisness there in the old shed that was meant for the clerk of the works. I leave the official bureau with its filing cabinets and board room and luxurious furniture and carpets and so on to Lazarus, who thoroughly enjoys them. I am more at home in the shed.

SARAH. Whats the big black thing peeping over the wall at the top?

UNDERSHAFT. That old thing is the gun that made me famous. It was called the Woolwich Infant; but it was designed by me and made by me. It is a sort of keepsake: one of the few things I am really sentimental about. That is where youll find me when you have finished here. The chauffeur will drive you over. Remember the name: Thundercrest. [*He goes out*].

CUSINS. I am rather impressed by the possibility of any of those sheds blowing up at any moment. It has a horrible fascination for me; but I think I shall take Barbara home first.

LADY BRITOMART. You had better all go home. But I shall stay. I had rather be blown to bits than let Andrew think he has frightened me.

SARAH. Your sentiments are mine, respected parent.

BARBARA [*very emphatically*] AND mine.

Lunch is brought in.

BARBARA. At last. Grub.

All except Lady Britomart rush hungrily to seat themselves at table, anyhow.

LADY BRITOMART. Dont rush, children. Really, you are picking up your father's manners already. [*She takes the head of the table with dignity*].

They all eat greedily, exhausted by the wonders of Undershaft and Lazarus.

Dissolve to:

Thundercrest. A gun emplacement along the ridge of the hill, with the old fat black cannon (the Woolwich Infant) in the middle, aiming southward over a firestep which fortifies the whole length of the emplacement and is evidently much older than the cannon. On the grey masonry of its breastwork are slate panels with incised inscriptions, illegible except at close quarters. In utmost contrast to the ultra-modernity and fresh paint of the model factory town hidden on the far side of the hill, Thundercrest is centuries old. It is used only as a dumping place for junk. Old ammunition boxes, handy for visitors to sit on, abound. The quaintest objects are lifesize dummy soldiers in early Victorian uniforms, lying about anyhow and anywhere in their red coats, cockaded peaked headgear, epaulets, and belts on which the pipeclay has long lost its lustre. Many of them have suffered gaping grapeshot wounds from which their straw entrails protrude grotesquely. One of them, fearfully gashed across the abdomen, has fallen in front of a very unimposing old brick edifice at the west end of the emplacement, with the word MANAGER over the door in the ugliest pre-Morrisian lettering. At the opposite end is one of the shabby old huts with which the hill is dotted. It is raised on posts and entered by a flight of wooden steps. The door is labelled DANGER in red!! Near the cannon is a new-looking modern shell with a red band painted on it.

The visiting party arrives, looking with some wonder at the prevailing disorder and decay.

Undershaft comes from the office, with a sheaf of telegrams in his hand.

UNDERSHAFT. Well, have you seen everything? I'm sorry I was called away. [*indicating the telegrams*] Good news from the front.

STEPHEN. Another victory?

UNDERSHAFT. Oh, I dont know. Which side wins does not concern us here. No: the good news is that the aerial battleship is a tremendous success. At the first trial it has wiped out a fort with three hundred soldiers in it [*he pockets the telegrams*].

CUSINS [*from the platform*] Dummy soldiers?

UNDERSHAFT [*striding across to Stephen and kicking the disemboweled dummy out of his way*] No: the real thing.

Cusins and Barbara exchange glances. Then Cusins sits on the step and buries his face in his hands. Barbara gravely lays her hand on his shoulder. He looks up at her in whimsical desperation.

UNDERSHAFT. Well, Stephen, what do you think of the place?

STEPHEN. Oh, magnificent. A perfect triumph of modern industry. Frankly, my dear father, I have been a fool: I had no idea of what it all meant: of the wonderful forethought, the power of organization, the administrative capacity, the financial genius, the colossal capital it represents. I have been repeating to myself as I came through your streets "Peace hath her victories no less renowned than War." I have only one misgiving about it all.

UNDERSHAFT. Out with it.

STEPHEN. Well, I cannot help thinking that all this provision for every want of your workmen may sap their independence and weaken their sense of responsibility. Are you sure so much pampering is really good for the men's characters?

UNDERSHAFT. Well you see, my dear boy, when you are organizing civilization you have to make up your mind whether trouble and anxiety are good things or not. If you decide that they are, then, I take it, you simply dont organize civilization; and there you are, with trouble and anxiety enough to make us all angels! But if you decide the other way, you may as well go through with it. However, Stephen, our characters are safe here. A sufficient dose of anxiety is always provided by the fact that we may be blown to smithereens at any moment.

At the same moment the door of the shed is thrown abruptly open; and a foreman in overalls and list slippers comes out on the little landing and holds the door for Lomax, who appears in the doorway.

LOMAX [*with studied coolness*] My good fellow: you neednt get into a state of nerves. Nothing's going to happen to you; and I suppose it wouldnt be the end of the world if anything did. A little bit of British pluck is what y o u want, old chap. [*He descends and strolls across to Sarah*].

UNDERSHAFT [*to the foreman*] Anything wrong, Bilton?

BILTON [*with ironic calm*] Gentleman walked into the high explosives shed and lit a cigaret, sir: thats all.

UNDERSHAFT. Ah, quite so, [*Going over to Lomax*] Do you happen to remember what you did with the match?

LOMAX. Oh come! I'm not a fool. I took jolly good care to blow it out before I chucked it away.

BILTON. The top of it was red hot inside, sir.

LOMAX. Well, suppose it was! I didnt chuck it into any of y o u r messes.

UNDERSHAFT. Think no more of it, Mr Lomax. By the way, would you mind lending me your matches.

LOMAX [*offering his box*] Certainly.

UNDERSHAFT. Thanks. [*He pockets the matches*].

LOMAX [*lecturing to the company generally*] You know, these high explosives dont go off like gunpowder, except when theyre in a gun. When theyre spread loose, you can put a match to them without the least risk: they just burn quietly like a bit of paper. [*Warming to the scientific interest of the subject*] Did you know that, Mr Undershaft? Have you ever tried?

UNDERSHAFT. Not on a large scale, Mr Lomax. Bilton will give you a sample of gun cotton when you are leaving if you ask him. You can experiment with it at home. [*Bilton looks puzzled*].

SARAH. Bilton will do nothing of the sort, papa. I suppose it's your business to blow up our enemies; but you might at least stop short of blowing up poor Cholly. [*Bilton gives it up and retires into the shed*].

LOMAX. My ownest, there is no danger. [*He sits beside her on the shell*].

LADY BRITOMART. Andrew: you shouldnt have let me see this place. To think of it being yours! and that you have kept it to yourself all these years!

UNDERSHAFT. It does not belong to me. I belong to it. It is the Undershaft inheritance.

LADY BRITOMART. It is not. Your cannons and chemicals may be the Undershaft inheritance; but the estate belongs to us. I wont give it up. I dont ask it any longer for Stephen—

STEPHEN [*interrupting her sharply*] I have not asked for it myself. The place is wonderful; but there is a Stevenage tradition as well as an Undershaft one. My future is in the Cabinet or Foreign Office, not in the counting house.

LADY BRITOMART. And leave Barbara to starve! Why should not Adolphus succeed to the inheritance? I could manage the town for him; and he can look after the cannons, if they are really necessary.

UNDERSHAFT. I should ask nothing better if Adolphus were a foundling. He is exactly the sort of new blood that is wanted in English business. Unfortunately he's not a foundling. [*He makes for the office door*].

CUSINS. How do you know? [*They all turn and stare at him*]. I think—Mind! I am not committing myself in any way as to my future course—but I t h i n k the foundling difficulty can be got over.

UNDERSHAFT. What do you mean?

CUSINS. Well, I have something to say which is in the nature of a confession.

SARAH.
LADY BRITOMART.
BARBARA. } Confession!
STEPHEN.

LOMAX. Oh I say!

CUSINS. Yes, a confession. Listen, all. Until I met Barbara I thought myself in the main an honorable, truthful man, because I wanted the approval of my conscience more than I wanted anything else. But the moment I saw Barbara, I wanted her far more than the approval of my conscience.

LADY BRITOMART. Adolphus!

CUSINS. It is true. You accused me yourself, Lady Brit, of joining the Army to worship Barbara; and so I did. She bought my soul like a flower at a street corner; but she bought it for herself.

UNDERSHAFT. What! Not for Dionysos or another?

CUSINS. Dionysos and all the others are in herself. I adored what was divine in her, and was therefore a true worshipper. But I was romantic about her too. I thought she was a woman of the people, and that a marriage with a professor of Greek would be far beyond the wildest social ambitions of her rank.

LADY BRITOMART. Adolphus!!

LOMAX. Oh I say!!!

CUSINS. When I learnt the horrible truth—

LADY BRITOMART. What do you mean by the horrible truth, pray?

CUSINS. That she was enormously rich; that her grandfather was an earl; that her father was the Prince of Darkness—

UNDERSHAFT. Chut!

CUSINS. —and that I was only an adventurer trying to catch a rich wife, then I stooped to deceive her about my birth.

BARBARA [rising] Dolly!

LADY BRITOMART. Your birth! Now Adolphus, dont dare to make up a wicked story for the sake of these wretched cannons. Remember: I have seen photographs of your parents; and the Agent General for South Western Australia knows them personally and has assured me that they are most respectable married people.

CUSINS. Their marriage was legal in Australia, but not in England. My mother is my father's deceased wife's sister; and in this island I was consequently a foundling. [Sensation].

STEPHEN. But such marriages have been made legal in England.

CUSINS. Not until I was grown up. I was born and bred a bastard. That is all the tradition requires. What do you say, Machiavelli?

UNDERSHAFT. You are an educated man. That is against the tradition.

CUSINS. Once in ten thousand times it happens that the schoolboy is a born master of what they try to teach him. Greek has not destroyed my mind: it has nourished it. Besides, I did not learn it at an English public school.

UNDERSHAFT. Hm! Well, I cannot afford to be too particular: you have cornered the foundling market. Let it pass. You are eligible, Euripides: you are eligible.

BARBARA. Dolly: yesterday morning, when Stephen told us all about the tradition, you became very silent; and you have been strange and excited ever since. Were you thinking of your birth then?

CUSINS. When the finger of Destiny suddenly points at a man in the middle of his breakfast, it makes him thoughtful.

UNDERSHAFT. Aha! You have had your eye on the business, my young friend, have you?

CUSINS. Take care! There is an abyss of moral horror between me and your accursed aerial battleships.

UNDERSHAFT. Never mind the abyss for the present. Let us settle the practical details and leave your final decision open. You know that you will have to change your name. Do you object to that?

CUSINS. Would any man named Adolphus—any man called Dolly!—object to be called something else?

UNDERSHAFT. Good. Now, as to money! I propose to treat you handsomely from the beginning. You shall start at a thousand a year.

CUSINS [*with sudden heat, his spectacles twinkling with mischief*] A thousand! You dare offer a miserable thousand to the son-in-law of a millionaire! No, by Heavens, Machiavelli! you shall not sweat me. You cannot do without me; and I can do without you. I must have two thousand five hundred a year for two years. At the end of that time, if I am a failure, I go. But if I am a success, and stay on, you must give me the other five thousand.

UNDERSHAFT. What other five thousand?

CUSINS. To make the two years up to five thousand a year. The two thousand five hundred is only half pay in case I should turn out a failure. The third year I must have ten per cent on the profits.

UNDERSHAFT [*taken aback*] Ten per cent! Why, man, do you know what my profits are?

CUSINS. Enormous, I hope: otherwise I shall require twentyfive per cent.

UNDERSHAFT. But, Mr Cusins, this is a serious matter of business. You are not bringing any capital into the concern.

CUSINS. What! no capital! Is my mastery of Greek no capital? Is my access to the subtlest thought, the loftiest poetry yet attained by humanity, no capital? My character! my intellect! my life! my career! what Barbara calls my soul! are these no capital? Say another word; and I double my salary.

UNDERSHAFT. Be reasonable—

CUSINS [*peremptorily*] Mr Undershaft: you have my terms. Take them or leave them.

UNDERSHAFT [*recovering himself*] Very well. I note your terms; and I offer you half.

CUSINS [*disgusted*] Half!

UNDERSHAFT [*firmly*] Half.

CUSINS. You call yourself a gentleman; and you offer me half!!

UNDERSHAFT. I do not call myself a gentleman; but I offer you half.

CUSINS. This to your future partner! your successor! your son-in-law!

BARBARA. You are selling your own soul, Dolly, not mine. Leave me out of the bargain, please.

UNDERSHAFT. Come! I will go a step further for Barbara's sake. I will give you three fifths; but that is my last word.

CUSINS. Done!

LOMAX. Done in the eye! Why, *I* get only eight hundred, you know.

CUSINS. By the way, Mac, I am a classical scholar, not a mathematical one. Is three fifths more than half of less?

UNDERSHAFT. More, of course.

CUSINS. I would have taken two hundred and fifty. How you can succeed in business when you are willing to pay all that money to a University don who is obviously not worth a junior clerk's wages!—well! What will Lazarus say?

UNDERSHAFT. Lazarus is a gentle romantic Jew who cares for nothing but string quartets and stalls at fashionable theatres. He will be blamed for your rapacity in money matters, poor fellow! as he has hitherto been blamed for mine. You are a shark of the first order, Euripides. So much the better for the firm!

BARBARA. Is the bargain closed, Dolly? Does your soul belong to him now?

CUSINS. No: the price is settled: that is all. The real tug of war is still to come. What about the moral question?

LADY BRITOMART. There is no moral question in the matter at all, Adolphus. You must simply sell cannons and weapons to people whose cause is right and just, and refuse them to foreigners and criminals.

UNDERSHAFT [determinedly] No: none of that. You must keep the true faith of an Armorer, or you dont come in here.

CUSINS. What on earth is the true faith of an Armorer?

UNDERSHAFT. To give arms to all men who offer an honest price for them, without respect of persons or principles: to Royalist and Republican, to Communist and Capitalist, to Protestant and Catholic, to burglar and policeman, to black man white man and yellow man, to all sorts and conditions, all nationalities, all faiths, all follies, all causes and all crimes. Have you read these letters cut into the wall behind you? They are the last words of the wisdom of the Undershafts since their beginnings on this spot. Here is the first: IF GOD GAVE THE HAND, LET NOT MAN WITHHOLD THE SWORD. The second: ALL HAVE THE RIGHT TO FIGHT: NONE HAVE THE RIGHT TO JUDGE. The third: TO MAN THE WEAPON: TO HEAVEN THE VICTORY. The fourth had no literary turn; so he wrote nothing; but he sold cannons to Napoleon under the nose of George the Third. The fifth: PEACE SHALL NOT PREVAIL SAVE WITH A SWORD IN HER HAND. The sixth, my master, was the best of all. NOTHING IS EVER DONE IN THIS WORLD UNTIL MEN ARE PREPARED TO KILL ONE ANOTHER IF IT IS NOT DONE. After that, there was nothing left for me to say. So I shall write up, simply, UNASHAMED.

CUSINS. My good Machiavelli, I shall certainly write something up on the wall; only, as I shall write it in Greek, you wont be able to read it. But as to your Armorer's faith, if I take my neck out of the noose of my own morality I am not going to put it into the noose of yours. I shall sell cannons to whom I please and refuse them to whom I please. So there!

UNDERSHAFT. From the moment when you become Andrew Undershaft, you will never do as you please again. Dont come here lusting for power, young man.

CUSINS. If power were my aim I should not come here for it. You have no power.

UNDERSHAFT. None of my own, certainly.

CUSINS. I have more power than you, more will. You do not drive this place: it drives you. And what drives the place?

UNDERSHAFT [enigmatically] A will of which I am a part.

BARBARA [startled] Father! Do you know what you are saying? or are you laying a snare for my soul?

CUSINS. Dont listen to his metaphysics, Barbara. The place is driven by Capitalist money hunters; and he is their slave.

UNDERSHAFT. Not necessarily. Remember the Armorers' Faith. I will take an order from a good man as cheerfully as from a bad one. If you good people prefer preaching and shirking to buying my weapons and fighting the money hunters, dont blame me. I can make cannons: I cannot make courage and conviction. Bah! you tire me, Euripides, with your morality mongering. Ask Barbara: s h e understands. [*He takes Barbara's hands, looking powerfully into her eyes*] Tell him, my love, what power really means.

BARBARA. [*hypnotized*] Before I joined the Salvation Army, I was in my own power; and the consequence was that I never knew what to do with myself. When I joined it, I had not time enough for all the things I had to do.

UNDERSHAFT [*approvingly*] Just so. And why was that, do you suppose?

BARBARA. Yesterday I should have said, because I was in the power of God [*She withdraws her hands from his with a power equal to his own*]. But you came and shewed me that I was in the power of Bodger and Undershaft. Today I feel— oh! how can I put it into words? Sarah: do you remember the earthquake at Cannes, when we were little children?—how little the surprise of the first shock mattered compared to the dread and horror of waiting for the second? That is how I feel in this place today. I stood on the rock I thought eternal; and without a word of warning it reeled and crumbled under me. I was safe with an infinite wisdom watching me, an army marching to Salvation with me; and in a moment, at a stroke of your pen in your cheque book, I stood alone; and the heavens were empty. That was the first shock of the earthquake: I am waiting for the second.

UNDERSHAFT. Come, come, my daughter! dont make too much of your little tinpot tragedy. What do we do here when we spend years of work and thought and thousands of pounds of solid cash on a new gun or an aerial battleship that turns out just a hairsbreadth wrong after all? Scrap it. Scrap it without wasting another hour or another pound on it. Well, you have made for yourself something that you call a morality or a religion or what not. It doesnt fit the facts. Well, scrap it. Scrap it and get one that does fit. That is what is wrong with the world at present. It scraps its obsolete steam engines and dynamos; but it wont scrap its old prejudices and its old religions and its old political constitutions. Whats the result? In machinery it does very well; but in morals and religion and politics it is working at a loss that brings it nearer bankruptcy every year. Dont persist in that folly. If your old religion broke down yesterday, get a newer and a better one for tomorrow.

BARBARA. Oh how gladly I would take a better one to my soul! But you offer me a worse one. [*Turning on him with sudden vehemence*] Justify yourself: shew me some light through the darkness of this dreadful place, with its beautifully clean workshops, and respectable workmen, and model homes.

UNDERSHAFT. Cleanliness and respectability do not need justification, Barbara: they justify themselves. I see no darkness here, no dreadfulness. In your Salvation shelter I saw poverty, misery, cold and hunger. You gave them bread and treacle and dreams of heaven. I give from three pound ten a week to twelve thousand a year. They find their own dreams; but I look after the drainage.

BARBARA. And their souls?

UNDERSHAFT. I save their souls just as I saved yours.

BARBARA. Y o u saved my soul! What do you mean?

UNDERSHAFT. I fed you and clothed you and housed you. I took care that you should have money enough to live handsomely—more than enough; so that you could be wasteful, careless, generous. That saved your soul from the seven deadly sins.

BARBARA [*bewildered*] The seven deadly sins!

UNDERSHAFT. Yes, the deadly seven. [*Counting on his fingers*] Food, clothing, firing, rent, taxes, respectability and children. Nothing can lift those seven millstones from Man's neck but money; and the spirit cannot soar until the millstones are lifted. I lifted them from your spirit. I enabled Barbara to become Major Barbara; and I saved her from the crime of poverty.

CUSINS. Do you call poverty a crime?

UNDERSHAFT. The worst of crimes. Poverty blights whole cities; spreads horrible pestilences; strikes dead the very souls of all who come within sight, sound, or smell of it. What y o u call crime is nothing: a murder here and a theft there, a blow now and a curse then: what do they matter? they are only the accidents and illnesses of life: there are not fifty genuine professional criminals in London. But there are millions of poor people, abject people, dirty people, sick people, ignorant people, ill fed, ill clothed people, poisoning us, forcing us to organize unnatural cruelties for fear they should rise against us and drag us down into their abyss. Only fools fear crime: we all fear poverty. Pah! [*turning to Barbara*] you talk of your half-saved ruffian in West Ham: you accuse me of dragging his soul back to perdition. Well, bring him to me here; and I will drag his soul back again to salvation for you. Not by words and dreams; but by three pound ten the five day week, a sound house in a healthy street, and a permanent job. In three weeks he will have a bowler hat and a chapel sitting: before the end of the year he will shake hands with a duchess at a Primrose League meeting, and join the Conservative Party.

BARBARA. And will he be the better for that?

UNDERSHAFT. You know he will. Dont be a hypocrite, Barbara. He will be better fed, better housed, better clothed, better behaved; and his children will be pounds heavier and bigger. That will be better than an American cloth mattress in a shelter, chopping firewood, eating bread and treacle, and being forced to kneel down from time to time to thank heaven for it: knee drill, I think you call it. It is cheap work converting starving men with a Bible in one hand and a slice of bread in the other. I will undertake to convert West Ham to Mahometanism on the same terms. Try your hand on m y men: their souls are hungry because their bodies are full.

BARBARA. And leave the east end to starve?

UNDERSHAFT [*his energetic tone dropping into one of bitter and brooding remembrance*] *I* was an east ender. I moralized and starved until one day I swore that I would be a full-fed free man at all costs; that nothing should stop me except a bullet, neither reason nor morals nor the lives of other men. I said "Thou shalt starve ere I starve"; and with that word I became free and great. I was a dangerous man until I had my will: now I am a useful, beneficient, kindly person. That is the history of most self-made millionaires, I fancy. When it is the history of every Englishman we shall have an England worth living in.

LADY BRITOMART. Stop making speeches, Andrew. This is not the place for them.

UNDERSHAFT [*punctured*] My dear: I have no other means of conveying my ideas.

LADY BRITOMART. Your ideas are nonsense. You got on because you were selfish and unscrupulous.

UNDERSHAFT. Not at all. I had the strongest scruples about poverty and starvation. Your moralists are quite unscrupulous about both: they make virtues of them. I had rather be a thief than a pauper. I had rather be a murderer than a slave. I dont want to be either; but if you force the alternative on me, then, by Heaven, I'll choose the braver and more moral one. I hate poverty and slavery worse than any other crimes whatsoever. And let me tell you this. Poverty and slavery have stood up for centuries to your sermons and speeches and leading articles: they will not stand up to my machine guns. Dont preach at them: dont reason with them. Kill them.

BARBARA. Killing. Is that your remedy for everything?

UNDERSHAFT. It is the final test of conviction, the only lever strong enough to overturn a social system, the only way of saying Must. Let six hundred and seventy fools loose in the streets; and three policemen can scatter them. But huddle them together in a chamber in Westminster; and let them go through certain ceremonies and call themselves certain names until at last they get the courage to kill; and your six hundred and seventy fools become a government. Your pious mob fills up ballot papers and imagines it is governing its masters; but the ballot paper that really governs is the paper that has a bullet wrapped up in it.

CUSINS. That is perhaps why, like most intelligent people, I never vote.

UNDERSHAFT. Vote! Bah! When you vote, you only change the names of the Cabinet. When you shoot, you pull down governments, inaugurate new epochs, abolish old orders and set up new. Is that historically true, Mr Learned Man, or is it not?

CUSINS. It is historically true. I loathe having to admit it. I repudiate your sentiments. I abhor your nature. I defy you in every possible way. Still, it is true. But it ought not to be true.

UNDERSHAFT. Ought! ought! ought! ought! ought! Are you going to spend your life saying ought, like the rest of our moralists? Turn your oughts into shalls, man. Come and make explosives with me. Whatever can blow men up can blow society up. The history of the world is the history of those who had courage enough to embrace this truth. Have you the courage to embrace it, Barbara?

LADY BRITOMART. Barbara: I positively forbid you to listen to your father's abominable wickedness. And you, Adolphus, ought to know better than to go about saying that wrong things are true. What does it matter whether they are true if they are wrong?

UNDERSHAFT. What does it matter whether they are wrong if they are true?

LADY BRITOMART. Children: come home instantly. Andrew: I am exceedingly sorry I allowed you to call on us. You are wickeder than ever. Come at once.

BARBARA [shaking her head] It's no use running away from wicked people, mamma.

LADY BRITOMART. It is every use. It shews your disapprobation of them.

BARBARA. It does not save them.

LADY BRITOMART. I see that you are going to disobey me. Sarah: are you coming home or are you not?

SARAH. I daresay it's very wicked of papa to make cannons; but I dont think I shall cut him on that account.

LOMAX [*pouring oil on the troubled waters*] The fact is, you know, there is a certain amount of tosh about this notion of wickedness. It doesnt work. You must look at facts. Not that I would say a word in favor of anything wrong; but then, you see, all sorts of chaps are always doing all sorts of things; and we have to fit them in somehow, dont you know. What I mean is that you cant go cutting everybody; and thats about what it comes to. [*Their rapt attention to his eloquence makes him nervous*]. Perhaps I dont make myself clear.

LADY BRITOMART. You are lucidity itself, Charles. Because Andrew is successful and has plenty of money to give to Sarah, you will flatter him and encourage him in his wickedness.

LOMAX [*unruffled*] Well, where the carcase is, there will the eagles be gathered, dont you know. [*To Undershaft*] Eh? What?

UNDERSHAFT. Precisely. By the way, may I call you Charles?

LOMAX. Delighted. Cholly is the usual ticket.

UNDERSHAFT [*to Lady Britomart*] Biddy—

LADY BRITOMART [*violently*] Dont dare call me Biddy. Charles Lomax: you are a fool. Adolphus Cusins: you are a Jesuit. Stephen: you are a prig. Sarah: you are a nonentity. Barbara: you are a lunatic. Andrew: you are a vulgar tradesman. Now you all know my opinion; and my conscience is clear, at all events [*she sits down on an ammunition box with a vehemence that almost splits it*].

UNDERSHAFT. My dear: you are the incarnation of morality. [*She snorts*]. Your conscience is clear and your duty done when you have called everybody names. Come, Euripides! it is getting late; and we all want to go home. Make up your mind.

CUSINS. Understand this, you old demon. You have me in a horrible dilemma. I want Barbara.

UNDERSHAFT. Like all young men, you greatly exaggerate the difference between one young woman and another.

BARBARA. Quite true, Dolly.

CUSINS. I also want to avoid being a rascal.

UNDERSHAFT [*with biting contempt*] You lust for personal righteousness, for self-approval, for what you call a good conscience, for what Barbara calls salvation, for what I call patronizing people who are not so lucky as yourself.

CUSINS. I do not: all the poet in me recoils from being a good man. But there are things in me that I must reckon with. Pity—

UNDERSHAFT. Pity! The scavenger of misery.

CUSINS. Well, love.

UNDERSHAFT. I know. You love the needy and the outcast: you love the oppressed races, the negro, the Indian ryot, the underdog everywhere. Do you love the Japanese? Do you love the French: Do you love the English?

CUSINS. No. Every true Englishman detests the English. We are the wickedest nation on earth; and our success is a moral horror.

UNDERSHAFT. That is what comes of your gospel of love, is it?

CUSINS. May I not love even my father-in-law?

UNDERSHAFT. Who wants your love, man? By what right do you take the liberty of offering it to me? I will have your due heed and respect, or I will kill you. But your love! Damn your impertinence!

CUSINS [*grinning*] I may not be able to control my affections, Mac.

UNDERSHAFT. You are fencing, Euripides. You are weakening: your grip is slipping. Come! try your last weapon. Pity and love have broken in your hand: forgiveness is still left.

CUSINS. No: forgiveness is a beggar's refuge. I am with you there: we must pay our debts.

UNDERSHAFT. Well said. Come! you will suit me. Remember the words of Plato.

CUSINS. Plato! Y o u dare quote Plato to m e !

UNDERSHAFT. Plato says, my friend, that society cannot be saved until either the Professors of Greek take to making gunpowder, or else the makers of gunpowder become Professors of Greek.

CUSINS. Oh, tempter! cunning tempter!

UNDERSHAFT. Come! choose, man, choose.

CUSINS. But perhaps Barbara will not marry me if I make the wrong choice.

BARBARA. Perhaps not.

CUSINS [desperately perplexed] You hear!

BARBARA. Father: do you love nobody?

UNDERSHAFT. I love my best friend.

LADY BRITOMART. And who is that, pray?

UNDERSHAFT. My bravest enemy. That is the man who keeps me up to the mark.

CUSINS. You know, the creature is really a sort of poet in his way. Suppose you stop talking and make up your mind, my young friend.

CUSINS. But you are driving me against my nature. I hate war.

UNDERSHAFT. Hatred is the coward's revenge for being intimidated. Dare you make war on war? Here are the means: Mr Lomax is sitting on them.

LOMAX [springing up] Oh I say! You dont mean that this thing is loaded, do you? My ownest: come off it.

SARAH [sitting placidly on the shell] If I am to be blown up, the more thoroughly it is done the better. Dont fuss, Cholly.

LOMAX [to Undershaft, strongly remonstrant] Your own daughter, you know!

UNDERSHAFT. So I see. [To Cusins] Well, my friend, may we expect you here at six tomorrow morning?

CUSINS [firmly] Not on any account. I will see the whole establishment blown up with its own dynamite before I will get up at five. My hours are healthy, rational hours: eleven to five.

UNDERSHAFT. Come when you please: before a week you will come at six and stay until I turn you out for the sake of your health. [Calling] Bilton! [He turns to Lady Britomart, who rises]. My dear: let us leave these two young people to themselves for a moment. [Bilton appears at the door of the shed]. I am going to take you through the cordite shed.

BILTON [barring the way] You cant take anything explosive in here, sir.

LADY BRITOMART. What do you mean? Are you alluding to me?

BILTON [unmoved] No, maam. Mr Undershaft has the other gentleman's matches in his pocket.

LADY BRITOMART [abruptly] Oh! I beg your pardon. [She goes into the shed].

UNDERSHAFT. Quite right, Bilton, quite right: here you are. [He gives Bilton the box of matches]. Come, Stephen. Come, Charles, Bring Sarah. [He passes into the shed].

Bilton opens the box and deliberately drops the matches into the fire-bucket.

LOMAX. Oh! I say [*Bilton stolidly hands him the empty box*]. Infernal nonsense! Pure scientific ignorance! [*He goes in*].

SARAH. Am I all right, Bilton?

BILTON. Youll have to put on list slippers, miss: thats all. Weve got em inside. [*She goes in*].

STEPHEN [*very seriously to Cusins*] Dolly, old fellow, think. Think before you decide. Do you feel that you are a sufficiently practical man? It is a' huge undertaking: an enormous responsibility. All this mass of business will be Greek to you.

CUSINS. Oh, I think it will be much less difficult than Greek.

STEPHEN. Well, I just want to say this before I leave you to yourselves. Dont let anything I have said about right and wrong prejudice you against this great chance in life. I have satisfied myself that the business is one of the highest character. [*Emotionally*] I am very proud of my father. I— [*Unable to proceed, he presses Cusins' hand and goes hastily into the shed, followed by Bilton*].

   Barbara and Cusins, left alone together, look at one another silently.

CUSINS. Barbara: I am going to accept this offer.

BARBARA. I thought you would.

CUSINS. You understand, dont you, that I had to decide without consulting you. If I had thrown the burden of the choice on you, you would sooner or later have despised me for it.

BARBARA. Yes: I did not want you to sell your soul for me any more than for this inheritance.

CUSINS. It is not the sale of my soul that troubles me: I have sold it too often to care about that. I have sold it for a professorship. I have sold it for an income. I have sold it to escape being imprisoned for refusing to pay taxes for hangmen's ropes and unjust wars and things that I abhor. What is all human conduct but the daily and hourly sale of our souls? What I am now selling it for is neither money nor position nor comfort, but for reality and power.

BARBARA. You know that you will have no power, and that he has none.

CUSINS. I know. It is not for myself alone. I want to make power for the world.

BARBARA. I want to make power for the world too; but it must be spiritual power.

CUSINS. I think all power is spiritual: these cannons will not go off by themselves. I have tried to make spiritual power by teaching Greek. But the world can never be really touched by a dead language and a dead civilization. The people must have power; and the people cannot have Greek. Now the power that is made here can be wielded by all men.

BARBARA. Power to burn women's houses down and kill their sons and tear their husbands to pieces.

CUSINS. You cannot have power for good without having power for evil too. Even mother's milk nourishes murderers as well as heroes. This power which only tears men's bodies to pieces has never been so horribly abused as the intellectual power, the imaginative power, the poetic, religious power, the imaginative power, the poetic, religious power that can enslave men's souls. As a teacher of Greek I gave the rich man an intellecutal weapon against the poor man. I now want to give the poor man material weapons against the intellectual man. I want to arm him against the lawyers, the doctors, the priests, the literary men, the professors, the artists, and the politicians, who, once in authority, are more disastrous and tyrannical than all the fools, rascals, and impostors. I want a power simple enough for common men to use, yet strong enough to force the intellectual oligarchy to use its genius for the general good.

BARBARA. Is there no higher power than that [*pointing to the shell*]?

CUSINS. Yes; but that power can destroy the higher powers just as a tiger can destroy a man: therefore Man must master that power first. I admitted this when the Turks and Greeks were last at war. My best pupil went out to fight for Hellas. My parting gift to him was not a copy of Plato's Republic, but a revolver and a hundred Undershaft cartridges. The blood of every Turk he shot—if he shot any—is on my head as well as on Undershaft's. That act committed me to this place for ever. Your father's challenge has beaten me. Dare I make war on war? I dare. I must. I will. And now, is it all over between us?

BARBARA [*touched by his evident dread of her answer*] Silly baby Dolly! How could it be!

CUSINS [*overjoyed*] Then you—you—you— Oh for my drum! [*He flourishes imaginary drumsticks*].

BARBARA [*angered by his levity*] Take care, Dolly, take care. Oh, if only I could get away from you and from father and from it all! if I could have the wings of a dove and fly away to heaven!

CUSINS. And leave m e !

BARBARA. Yes, you, and all the other naughty mischievous children of men. But I cant. I was happy in the Salvation Army for a moment. I escaped from the world into a paradise of enthusiasm and prayer and soul saving; but the moment our money ran short, it all came back to Bodger: it was he who saved our people: he, and the Prince of Darkness, my papa. Undershaft and Bodger: their hands stretch everywhere: when we feed a starving fellow creature, it is with their bread, because there is no other bread; when we tend the sick, it is in the hospitals they endow; if we turn from the churches they build, we must kneel on the stones of the streets they pave. As long as that lasts, there is no getting away from them. Turning our backs on Bodger and Undershaft is turning our backs on life.

CUSINS. I thought you were determined to turn your back on the wicked side of life.

BARBARA. There is no wicked side: life is all one. And I never wanted to shirk my share in whatever evil must be endured, whether it be sin or suffering. I wish I could cure you of middle-class ideas, Dolly.

CUSINS [*gasping*] Middle cl—! A snub! A social snub to me! from the daughter of a foundling!

BARBARA. That is why I have no class, Dolly: I come straight out of the heart of the whole people. If I were middle-class I should turn my back on my father's business; and we should both live in an artistic drawing room, with you reading the reviews in one corner, and I in the other at the piano, playing Schumann: both very superior persons, and neither of us a bit of use. Sooner than that, I would sweep out these sheds, or be one of Bodger's barmaids. Do you know what would have happened if you had refused papa's offer?

CUSINS. I wonder!

BARBARA. I should have given you up and married the man who accepted it. After all, my dear old mother has more sense than any of you. I felt like her when I saw this place—felt that I must have it—that never, never, never could I let it go; only she thought it was the houses and the kitchen ranges and the linen and china, when it was really all the human souls to be saved: not weak souls in starved bodies, sobbing with gratitude for a scrap of bread and treacle, but fullfed, quarrelsome, snobbish, uppish creatures, all standing on their little rights and dignities, and thinking that my father ought to be greatly obliged to them for making so much money for him—and so he ought. That is where salvation is really wanted. My father shall never throw it in my teeth again that my converts were bribed with bread. [*She is transfigured*]. I have got rid of the bribe of bread. I have got rid of the bribe of heaven. Let God's work be done for its own sake: the work he had to create us to do because it cannot be done except by living men and women. When I die, let him be in my debt, not I in his; and let me forgive him as becomes a woman of my rank.

CUSINS. Then the way of life lies through the factory of death?

BARBARA. Yes, through the raising of hell to heaven and of man to God, through the unveiling of an eternal light in the Valley of The Shadow. [*Seizing him with both hands*] Oh, did you think my courage would never come back? did you believe that I was a deserter? that I, who have stood in the streets, and taken my people to my heart, and talked of the holiest and greatest things with them, could ever turn back and chatter foolishly to fashionable people about nothing in a drawing room? Never, never, never, never: Major Barbara will die with the colors. Oh! and I have my dear little Dolly boy still; and he has found me my place and my work. Glory Hallelujah! [*She kisses him*].

CUSINS. My dearest: consider my delicate health. I cannot stand as much happiness as you can.

BARBARA. Yes: it is not easy work being in love with me, is it? But it's good for you. [*She runs to the shed, and calls, childlike*] Mamma! Mamma! [*Bilton comes out of the shed, followed by Undershaft*]. I want Mamma.

UNDERSHAFT. She is taking off her list slippers, dear. [*He passes on to Cusins*]. Well? What does she say?

CUSINS. She has gone right up into the skies.

LADY BRITOMART [*coming from the shed and stopping on the steps, obstructing Sarah, who follows with Lomax. Barbara clutches like a baby at her mother's skirt*] Barbara: when will you learn to be independent and to act and think for yourself? I know as well as possible what that cry of "Mamma, Mamma," means. Always running to me!

SARAH [*touching Lady Britomart's ribs with her finger tips and imitating a bicycle horn*] Pip! pip!

LADY BRITOMART [*highly indignant*] How dare you say pip pip to me, Sarah? You are both very naughty children. What do you want, Barbara?

BARBARA. I want a house in the village to live in with Dolly. [*Dragging at the skirt*] Come and tell me which one to take.

UNDERSHAFT [*to Cusins*] Six o'clock tomorrow morning, Euripides.

THE END

Arms and the Man

A cold afternoon in November 1885. The battlefield of Slivnitza. Cannon thunder and smoke. Shells bursting. In the foreground a shell hole and a machine gun section. A company of Serbian troops, commanded by Bluntschli, a Swiss officer, are waiting to come into action, intent on their guns. He is a man of about 35, of middling stature and undistinguished appearance, with strong neck and shoulders, roundish obstinate looking head covered with short crisp bronze curls, clear quick eyes and good brows and mouth, hopelessly prosaic nose like that of a strong minded baby, trim soldierlike carriage and energetic manner, and with all his wits about him.

BLUNTSCHLI [*scanning through his field glasses*] What is that cavalry regiment doing there?

A couple of Austrian sublieutenants rise and use their glasses in the same direction.

FIRST SUBLIEUTENANT. It looks to me as if they were going to charge us, sir.

BLUNTSCHLI. Charge a battery of machine guns! They couldnt be such damned fools.

SECOND SUBLIEUTENANT. They a r e .

FIRST SUBLIEUTENANT. No mistake about it, sir. Those Bulgarian idiots are capable of anything.

SECOND SUBLIEUTENANT. They know no more about war than a cat knows of a holiday.

BLUNTSCHLI. Well, we shall just make holes in them, poor devils. Yes: theres no mistake: theyre coming for us. [*To the gunners*] Now, children: dont be afraid of the horses: dont move an inch: have your guns ready, and dont loose off until you can see the whites of the horses' eyes. Then let them have it. How are we off for ammunition?

A sergeant rushes in, with utter dismay in his countenance.

SERGEANT. Captain: theyve sent us the wrong belts. The guns wont work.

BLUNSTCHLI. Damnation! [*Peremptorily*] Run for it. Save himself who can. [*The gunners spring up and abandon their guns and rush away*].

FIRST SUBLIEUTENANT. They dont even know how to charge, the fools! Theyre galloping all the way and waving their silly swords.

SECOND SUBLIEUTENANT. Their horses will be tired before they reach us.

BLUNTSCHLI. No matter: they will be fresh enough to do for us. And my revolver isnt loaded, confound it.

FIRST SUBLIEUTENANT. Same here.

SECOND SUBLIEUTENANT. Same here.

BLUNTSCHLI. Nothing for it but a bunk. Off with you. That is an order.

The two lieutenants salute and run off. The cavalry charge sweeps down, with wild cheering and flourishing of sabres, Sergius Saranoff leading three yards in front. Bluntschli draws his sword and jumps into the shell hole.

Close-up. Bluntschli crouching in shell hole.

As before. The charge passes, cheering madly. Sounds of the fugitives being cut down. Bluntschli comes out of the shell hole, looks through his glasses after the rout and slaughter; then in the opposite direction at a body of Bulgarian foot who are following up the cavalry; shrugs his shoulders; sheathes his sword; and walks off to the right without hurrying himself in the least.

Change to:

Late evening. A road approaching a Bulgarian village. Masses of brambles, thistles, gorse, and weeds of all sorts border the roadway on the far side. Bulgarian infantry tramp along the road towards the village, singing a Bulgarian marching song, tired and dusty, but flushed with victory. Petkoff and Saranoff with them on horseback. The villagers rush out to meet them, cheering, throwing flowers (the girls showering them on Saranoff), handing cucumbers and apples, and kissing the soldiers who are natives of the village. The soldiers tramp on, keeping their formation as best they can. The villagers turn and go back into the village with them. The road is left deserted. The cheering and singing fade into the distance. From the apparently impenetrable thorn brake Bluntschli emerges cautiously, his uniform torn and his face and hands scratched and soiled by the thorns. His plight looks pretty desperate. He looks cautiously up and down the road.

An oldish peasant woman comes along, pulling a barrow full of loaves of bread. Bluntschli draws his revolver and hides until she is close to him, then springs out at her.

THE WOMAN [*recognizing his uniform*] Serbian! [*She begins screaming*].

BLUNTSCHLI [*covering her with the revolver*] Silence: not a word.

The woman gasps and throws up her hands, silent and terrified.

BLUNTSCHLI. Now listen, mother. I am not a Serb: I am a Swiss. I will not harm you; but I am hungry and you must sell me bread. I will pay for it: see! [*He holds up a silver coin as big as a half crown*]. The price of ten loaves. I take one.

The woman drops her hands and eyes the money greedily. He replaces his pistol in its case; takes a loaf from the barrow and throws the coin into it.

BLUNTSCHLI. Now off home with you; and say nothing. They will kill you if they find out that you have sold bread to an enemy. [*He hurries back into the brush, eating the loaf ravenously*].

The woman looks for the coin in the barrow; pockets it; trundles the barrow off towards the village as fast as she can. A distant burst of cheering accompanies her retreat.

Change to:

In the village. The square before the church. The church steps serve as a platform on which stand Petkoff, Saranoff, and the Mayor, a pudgy little man in red gown, chain of office, and three cornered hat. He is attended by a gigantic beadle, in whatever is the Bulgarian equivalent to a cocked hat and gold braided capes and trousers, carrying a mace on his shoulder, and a big bell in his disengaged hand.

Major Petkoff is a cheerful, excitable, insignificant, unpolished man of about 50, naturally unambitious except as to his income and his importance in local society, but just now greatly pleased with the military rank which the war has thrust on him as a man of consequence in his town.

Major Sergius Saranoff is a tall romantically handsome man, with the physical hardihood, the high spirit, and the susceptible imagination of an untamed mountaineer chieftain. But his remarkable personal distinction is of a characteristically civilized type. The ridges of his eyebrows, curving with an interrogative twist round the projections at the outer corners; his jealously observant eye; his nose, thin, keen, and apprehensive in spite of the pugnacious high bridge and large nostril; his assertive chin would not be out of place in a Parisian salon, shewing that the clever imaginative barbarian has an acute critical faculty which has been thrown into intense activity by the arrival of western civilization in the Balkans. The result is precisely what the advent of nineteenth century thought first produced in England: to wit, Byronism. By his brooding on the perpetual failure, not only of others, but of himself, to live up to his ideals; by his consequent cynical scorn for humanity; by his jejune credulity as to the absolute validity of his concepts and the unworthiness of the world in disregarding them; by his wincings and mockeries under the sting of the petty disillusions which every hour spent among men brings to his sensitive observation, he has acquired the half tragic, half ironic air, the mysterious moodiness, the suggestion of a strange and terrible history that has left nothing but undying remorse, by which Childe Harold fascinated the grandmothers of his English contemporaries.

The soldiers are drawn up along the foot of the steps between the speakers and the crowd, which is excited and very noisy.

THE BEADLE [*makes a fearful clamor with his bell, in stentorian tones*] Silence! Si-i-i-lensss! Silence for the Worshipful the Mayor.

The noise stops. All listen.

THE MAYOR. Fellow citizens. I have glorious news for you. A battle the like of which has never been fought in the history of the world has been fought at Slivnitza. [*Cheers from the crowd, which knows all about it but wants to hear speeches*].

THE BEADLE [*as before*] Silence! Silence! [*Clangs his bell*].

THE MAYOR. On that field Bulgaria has faced the invading hosts of our deadly enemies the Serbs. [*Cries of* Swine]. They were as the sands of the sea in number. The all devouring Austrian empire armed them, officered them, fed them, promised them victory. What had we to oppose these millions of ruthless foes? Two hundred men.

VOICE FROM THE CROWD. Two thousand.

THE BEADLE [*clanging*] Silence! Do you hear? Silence!

Tumult. The interrupter, kicked and hustled, has to fly for his life.

THE MAYOR. Two hundred men. A handful against a host. Yes, fellow citizens; but the two hundred were Bulgarians. [*Cheers*]. By whom were these Bulgarians led? Was it by those Russian generals who have come here to teach Bulgarians how to fight? No, fellow citizens: the cowardly Russian orders were defied. [*Cheers*]. We were led to a glorious victory by our fellow countryman Sergius Saranoff [*he pronounces the name with the stress on the second syllable: Sarahnoff*], who has not a drop of blood in his veins that is not true blue Bulgarian of the best. There he stands.

Tremendous cheering: the girls throw all the flowers they have left at Saranoff, who looks stern and irresponsive.

THE MAYOR [*at the top of his voice*] He will now address you.

THE BEADLE. Silence for the Right Honorable His Excellency Sergius Saranoff. [*Clanging*]. Silence, silence!

The tumult ceases as Saranoff steps forward. All listen eagerly.

SERGIUS. Mr Mayor: I am not a hero. [*Cries of* You are, *in which the girls join enthusiastically*]. I tell you I am not. There can be no single hero in a nation where all are heroes. [*Cheers suppressed by the beadle by a stroke of his bell*]. Why was I first in the charge that won the battle for us? I was no braver than the rest; but my horse is the fastest in Bulgaria: he cost me twenty thousand levas. [*Cheers and laughter*]. Cheer till you are hoarse: I will not accept a single cheer or flower that is not shared by every man that rode with me that day at Slivnitza. [*He steps back amid thunders of applause*].

THE BEADLE [*clanging*] Silence! silence for the Worshipful the Mayor!

THE MAYOR. I call on Commander Petkoff.

THE BEADLE. Silence for honorable and gallant Commander Petkoff.

PETKOFF [*stepping forward*] Citizens: we have won a battle; but the war is not over. I shall not sleep in my bed at home for six months yet: we have that much fighting still before us, and perhaps more. But however long it lasts you must keep a sharp lookout for Serbian runaways. I have just heard that one of your old women has been robbed within a hundred yards of the village by a scoundrel in Serbian uniform. You all know her: you buy your bread from her. She was on her way here with her basket of loaves peacefully and lawfully as she had a perfect right to do when a cowardly swine sprang from the bushes, flung her brutally to the ground, and trampled on her until she lost her senses. When she recovered the fellow was gone and her basket was empty: he had not left the poor woman a single crumb. Hunt that man down; and see that he gets what he deserves. He cannot be far off. You of the Home Guard: away with you.

With loud boos and execrations, the ablebodied men rush off and the meeting breaks up.

Change to:

Night. Full moon. A street in a small Bulgarian town. Only one of the houses has pretensions and has two storeys. One of its upper windows is lighted up, and has a balcony over the porch, which is a structure of trellis work covered with flowering creepers. There is a mounting block beside the door. Mountain tops, glittering with snow in the moonlight, are visible beyond the lowroofed houses opposite.

Bluntschli, a hunted fugitive, footsore, hungry, and utterly weary, steals in. He looks carefully about to satisfy himself that the town is asleep and no one in sight. He collapses on the mounting block, elbows on knees, head buried on his hands, dead beat, in a deplorable plight, bespattered with mud and blood and snow, his belt and the strap of his revolver-case keeping together the torn ruins of his blue tunic.

The lighted window is opened. He starts up and blots himself against the wall, watching the balcony. Raina appears in her nightdress, well covered by a long mantle of furs, and posts herself there, gazing at the snowy mountains, and looking distinctly operatic, like Elsa in Lohengrin.

Bluntschli stares at her.

Change to:

The balcony. Raina, intensely conscious of the romantic beauty of the night, and of the fact that her own youth and beauty are part of it, is gazing at the snowy Balkans.

Her reverie is interrupted by her mother, Catherine Petkoff, a woman over forty, imperiously energetic, with magnificent black hair and eyes, who might be a very splendid specimen of the wife of a mountain farmer, but is determined to be a Viennese lady, and to that end wears a fashionable tea gown on all occasions.

CATHERINE [*entering hastily, full of good news*] Raina! [*She pronounces it Raheena, with the stress on the ee; she goes to the bed, expecting to find Raina there*]. Why, where—? [*Raina looks into the room*].

Change to:

A lady's bedchamber. The interior of the room is not like anything to be seen in the west of Europe. It is half rich Bulgarian, half cheap Viennese. Above the head of the bed, which stands against a little wall cutting off the left hand corner of the room, is a painted wooden shrine, blue and gold, with an ivory image of Christ, and a light hanging before it in a pierced metal ball suspended by three chains. The principal seat, placed towards the other side of the room and opposite the window, is a Turkish ottoman. The counterpane and hangings of the bed, the window curtains, the little carpet, and all the ornamental textile fabrics in the room and oriental and gorgeous: the paper on the˘ walls is occidental and paltry. The washstand, against the wall on the side nearest the ottoman and window, consists of an enamelled iron basin with a pail beneath it in a painted metal frame, and a single towel on the rail at the side. The dressing table, between the bed and the window, is a common pine table, covered with a cloth of many colors, with an expensive toilet mirror on it. The door is on the side nearest the bed; and there is a chest of drawers between. This chest of drawers is also covered by a variegated native cloth; and on it there is a pile of paper backed novels, a box of chocolate creams, and a miniature easel with a large photograph of an extremely handsome officer, whose lofty bearing and magnetic glance can be felt even from the portrait. The room is lighted by a candle on the chest of drawers, and another on the dressing table with a box of matches beside it.

CATHERINE. Heavens, child! are you out in the night air instead of in your bed? Youll catch your death. Louka told me you were asleep.

RAINA [*dreamily*] I sent her away. I wanted to be alone. The stars are so beautiful! What is the matter?

CATHERINE. Such news! There has been a battle.

RAINA [*her eyes dilating*] Ah! [*She comes eagerly to Catherine*].

CATHERINE. A great battle of Slivnitza! A victory! And it was won by Sergius.

RAINA [*with a cry of delight*] Ah! [*They embrace rapturously*]. Oh, mother! [*Then, with a sudden anxiety*] Is father safe?

CATHERINE. Of course: he sends me the news. Sergius is the hero of the hour, the idol of the regiment.

RAINA. Tell me, tell me. How was it? [*Ecstatically*] Oh, mother! mother! mother! [*She pulls her mother down on the ottoman and they kiss one another frantically*].

CATHERINE [*with surging enthusiasm*] You cant guess how splendid it is. A cavalry charge! think of that! He defied our Russian commanders—acted without orders—led a charge on his own responsibility—headed it himself—was the first man to sweep through their guns. And you! you kept Sergius waiting a year before you would be betrothed to him. Oh, if you have a drop of Bulgarian blood in your veins, you will worship him when he comes back.

RAINA. What will he care for my poor little worship after the acclamations of a whole army of heroes? But no matter: I am so happy! so proud! [*She rises and walks about excitedly*]. It proves that all our ideas were real after all.

CATHERINE [*indignantly*] Our ideas real! What do you mean?

RAINA. When I buckled on Sergius's sword he looked so noble: it was treason to think of disillusion or humiliation or failure. And yet— [*She sits down again suddenly*]. Promise me youll never tell him.

CATHERINE. Dont ask me for promises until I know what I'm promising.

RAINA. Well, it came into my head just as he was holding me in his arms and looking into my eyes, that perhaps we only had our heroic ideas because we are so fond of reading Byron, and because we were so delighted with the opera that season at Bucharest. Real life is so seldom like that! indeed never, as far as I knew it them. [*laughing and snuggling against her mother*] Oh, to think that it was all true! that Sergius is just as splendid and noble as he looks! that the world is really a glorious world for women who can see its glory and men who can act its romance! What happiness! what unspeakable fulfilment!

They are interrupted by the entry of Louka, a handsome proud girl in a pretty Bulgarian peasant's dress with double apron, so defiant that her servility to Raina is almost insolent. She is afraid of Catherine, but even with her goes as far as she dares.

LOUKA. If you please, madam, all the windows are to be closed and the shutters made fast. They say there may be shooting in the streets. [*Raina and Catherine rise together, alarmed*]. The Serbs are being chased right back through the pass; and they say they may run into the town. Our cavalry will be after them; and our people will be ready for them, you may be sure, now theyre running away. [*She goes out on the balcony, and pulls the outside shutters to; then steps back into the room*].

RAINA. I wish our people were not so cruel. What glory is there in killing wretched fugitives?

CATHERINE [*businesslike, her housekeeping instincts aroused*] I must see that everything is made safe downstairs.

RAINA [*to Louka*] Leave the shutters so that I can just close them if I hear any noise.

CATHERINE [*authoritatively, turning on her way to the door*] Oh no, dear: you must keep them fastened. You would be sure to drop off to sleep and leave them open. Make them fast, Louka.

LOUKA. Yes, madam. [*She fastens them*].

RAINA. Dont be anxious about m e . The moment I hear a shot, I shall blow out the candles and roll myself up in bed with my ears well covered.

CATHERINE. Quite the wisest thing you can do, my love. Goodnight.

RAINA. Goodnight. [*Her emotion comes back for a moment*]. Wish me joy [*They kiss*]. This is the happiest night of my life—if only there are no figitives.

CATHERINE. Go to bed, dear; and dont think of them. [*She goes out*].

LOUKA [*secretly, to Raina*] If you would like the shutters open, just give them a push like this [*she pushes them: they open: she pulls them to again*]. One of them ought to be bolted at the bottom; but the bolt's gone.

RAINA [*with dignity, reproving her*] Thanks, Louka; but we must do what we are told. [*Louka makes a grimace*]. Goodnight.

LOUKA [*carelessly*] Goodnight. [*She goes out, swaggering*].

Raina, left alone, takes off her fur cloak and throws it on the ottoman. Then she goes to the chest of drawers, and adores the portrait there with feelings that are beyond all expression.

Interpolate here a view of the portrait the full size of the screen shewing Sergius in uniform (very splendid) either half length or equestrian, but anyhow recognizable by the audience as the man of the cavalry charge.

Raina does not kiss it or press it to her breast, or shew it any mark of bodily affection; but she takes it in her hands and elevates it, like a priestess.

RAINA [*looking up at the picture*] Oh, I shall never be unworthy of you any more, my soul's hero: never, never, never. [*She replaces it reverently, raises her eyes once more, thinking of the blessed reality, and murmurs*] My hero! my hero!

A distant shot breaks the quiet of the night. She starts, listening; and two more shots, much nearer, follow, startling her. Raina, at the sound of the shots, blows out her candle and jumps into bed.

Change to:

The street as before.

Bluntschli has returned to his seat on the mounting block; but he is less dejected, and is looking curiously up at the closed window. The shots startle him: he springs up, keenly alert, looking up and down the street. A mob of soldiers appear, "wild and drunk and furious" as Louka presently describes them, searching for imaginary fugitives in every corner, and firing recklessly at shadows. A couple of them see Bluntschli in the middle of the street and fire at him. He darts to the side of the portal farthest from them for cover. Peeping out, he sees that when they have reached the house they will catch him. He climbs the trellis and gets over into the balcony, where he crouches out of sight.

Change to:

Close-up of the balcony, with Bluntschli crouching and the noise of the search continuing.

Change back to Raina's darkened room, and she in bed.

The firing breaks out again: there is a startling fusillade quite close at hand. Whilst it is still echoing, the shutters disappear, pulled open from without; and for an instant the rectangle of snowy starlight flashes out with the figure of a man silhouetted in black upon it. The shutters close immediately; and the room is dark again. But the silence is now broken by the sound of panting. Then there is a scratch and the flame of a match is seen in the middle of the room.

RAINA [*crouching on the bed*] Who's there? [*The match is out instantly*]. Who's there? Who is that?

BLUNTSCHLI'S VOICE [*in the darkness, subduedly, but threateningly*] Sh-sh! Dont call out; or youll be shot. Be good; and no harm will happen to you. [*She is heard leaving her bed, and making for the door*]. Take care: it's no use trying to run away. [*Commandingly*] Strike a light and let me see you. Do you hear. [*Another moment of silence and darkness as she retreats to the chest of drawers. Then she lights a candle. In spite of his desperate predicament, Bluntschli has a sense of the humor of it, without, however, the least intention of trifling with it or throwing away a chance. Reckoning up what he can guess about Raina: her age, her social position, her character, and the extent to which she is frightened, he continues, more politely but still most determinedly*] Excuse my disturbing you; but you recognize my uniform? Serb! If I'm caught I shall be killed. [*Menacingly*] Do you understand t h a t ?

RAINA. Yes.

BLUNTSCHLI. Well, I dont intend to get killed if I can help it. [*Still more formidably*] Do you understand t h a t ? [*He locks the door quickly but quietly*]. RAINA [*disdainfully*] I suppose not. [*She draws herself up superbly, and looks him straight in the face, adding with cutting emphasis*] S o m e soldiers, I know, are a f r a i d to die.

BLUNTSCHLI [*with grim goodhumor, a prosaic reply to her heroics*] All of them, dear lady, all of them, believe me. It is our duty to live as long as we can. Now, if you raise an alarm—

RAINA [*cutting him short*] You will shoot me. How do you know that *I* am afraid to die?

BLUNTSCHLI [*cunningly*] Ah; but suppose I dont shoot you, what will happen them? A lot of your cavalry will burst into this pretty room of yours and slaughter me here like a pig; for I'll fight like a demon: they shant get m e into the street to amuse themselves with: I know what they are. Are you prepared to receive that sort of company in your present undress? [*Raina, suddenly conscious of her nightgown, instinctively shrinks, and gathers it more closely about her neck. He watches her, and adds, pitilessly*] Hardly presentable, eh? [*She turns to the ottoman. He raises his pistol instantly, and cries*] Stop! [*She stops*]. Where are you going?

RAINA [*with dignified patience*] Only to get my cloak.

BLUNSCHLI [*passing swiftly to the ottoman and snatching the cloak*] A good idea! I'll keep the cloak; and y o u l l take care that nobody comes in and sees you without it. This is a better weapon than the revolver. [*He throws the pistol down on the ottoman*].

RAINA [*revolted*] It is not the weapon of a gentleman!

BLUNTSCHLI. It's good enough for a man with only you to stand between him and death. [*As they look at one another for a moment, Raina hardly able to believe that even a Serbian officer can be so cynically and selfishly unchivalrous, they are startled by a sharp fusillade in the street*].

　Change to:

Downstairs. Clamor and disturbance. The pursuers in the street batter at the house door, shouting Open the door! Open the door! Wake up, will you?

NICOLA [*calling to them angrily*] This is Major Petkoff's house: you cant come in here!

　Change to:

Raina's bedroom as before.

LOUKA [*outside, knocking at the bedroom door*] My lady! My lady! get up quick and open the door. [*From below, a renewal of the clamor, and a torrent of blows on the door, end with a chain let down with a clank*].

BLUNTSCHLI [*the chill of imminent death hushes his voice*] Do you hear? If you are going to bring those blackguards in on me you shall receive them as you are.

　Change to:

Downstairs as before. A Bulgarian officer with three or four soldiers with their rifles at the ready come in looking for fugitives.

CATHERINE [*indignantly addressing the officer*] What does this mean, sir? Do you know where you are? [*The noise subsides suddenly*].

　Change to:

Raina's bedroom as before. The fugitive throws up his head with the gesture of a man who sees that it is all over with him, and drops the manner he has been assuming to intimidate Raina.

BLUNTSCHLI [*sincerely and kindly*] No use, dear: I'm done for. [*Flinging the cloak to her*] Quick! wrap yourself up: theyre coming.

RAINA. Oh, thank you. [*She wraps herself up with intense relief; then, anxiously*] What will you do?

BLUNTSCHLI [*grimly*] Keep out of the way. It wont last long. [*He draws his sabre and faces the door, waiting*].

RAINA [*impulsively*] I'll help you. I'll hide you. [*She drags him towards the window*]. Here! behind the curtains.

BLUNTSCHLI [*yielding to her*] Theres just half a chance, if you keep your head.

RAINA [*drawing the curtain before him*] Ssh!

BLUNTSCHLI [*putting out his head*] Remember: nine soldiers out of ten are born fools.

RAINA. Oh! [*She draws the curtain angrily before him*].

BLUNTSCHLI [*looking out at the other side*] If they find me, I promise you a fight: a devil of a fight.

She stamps at him. He disappears hastily. She takes off her cloak, and throws it across the foot of the bed. Then, with a sleepy, disturbed air, she opens the door. Louka enters excitedly.

LOUKA. One of those beasts of Serbs has been seen climbing up the waterpipe to your balcony. Our men want to search for him; and they are so wild and drunk and furious. [*She makes for the other side of the room to get as far from the door as possible*]. My lady says you are to dress at once, and to— [*She sees the revolver lying on the ottoman, and stops, petrified*].

Then a close-up of the revolver only. Then Louka smiling cunningly as she guesses.

RAINA [*as if annoyed at being disturbed*] They shall not search here. Why have they been let in?

CATHERINE [*coming in hastily*] Raina, darling: are you safe? Have you seen anyone or heard anything?

RAINA. I heard the shooting. Surely the soldiers will not dare come in here?

CATHERINE. I have found a Russian officer, thank Heaven: he knows Sergius. [*Speaking through the door to someone outside*] Sir: will you come in now. My daughter will receive you.

A young Russian officer, in Bulgarian uniform, enters, sword in hand.

OFFICER. [*with soft feline politeness and stiff military carriage*] Good evening, gracious lady. I am sorry to intrude; but there is a Serb hiding on the balcony. Will you and the gracious lady your mother please to withdraw whilst we search?

RAINA [*petulantly*] Nonsense, sir: you can see that there is no one on the balcony. [*She throws the shutters wide open and stands with her back to the curtain where the man is hidden, pointing to the moonlit balcony. A couple of shots are fired right under the window; and a bullet shatters the glass opposite Raina, who winks and gasps, but stands her ground; whilst Catherine screams, and the officer, with a cry of* Take care! *rushes to the balcony*].

THE OFFICER [*on the balcony, shouting savagely down to the street*] Cease firing there, you fools: do you hear? Cease firing, damn you! [*He glares down for a moment; then turns to Raina, trying to resume his polite manner*]. Could anyone have got in without your knowledge? Were you asleep?

RAINA. No: I have not been to bed.

THE OFFICER [*impatiently, coming back into the room*] Your neighbors have their heads so full of runaway Serbs that they see them everywhere. [*Politely*] Gracious lady: a thousand pardons. Goodnight. [*Military bow, which Raina returns coldly. Another to Catherine, who follows him out*].

Raina closes the shutters. She turns and sees Louka, who has been watching the scene curiously.

RAINA. Dont leave my mother, Louka, until the soldiers go away.

Louka glances at Raina, at the ottoman, at the curtain; then purses her lips secretively, laughs insolently, and goes out. Raina, highly offended by this demonstration, follows her to the door, and shuts it behind her with a slam, locking it violently. Bluntschli immediately steps out from behind the curtain, sheathing his sabre. Then dismissing the danger from his mind in a businesslike way, he comes affably to Raina.

BLUNTSCHLI. A narrow shave; but a miss is as good as a mile. Dear young lady: your servant to the death. I wish for your sake I had joined the Bulgarian army instead of the other one. I am not a native Serb.

RAINA [*haughtily*] No: you are one of the Austrians who set the Serbs on to rob us of our national liberty, and who officer their army for them. We hate them!

BLUNTSCHLI. Austrian! not I. Dont hate me, dear young lady. I am a Swiss, fighting merely as a professional soldier. I joined the Serbs because they came first on the road from Switzerland. Be generous: youve beaten us hollow.

RAINA. Have I not been generous?

BLUNSCHLI. Noble! Heroic! But I'm not saved yet. This particular rush will soon pass through; but the pursuit will go on all night by fits and starts. I must take my chance to get off in a quite interval. [*Pleasantly*] You dont mind my waiting just a minute or two, do you?

RAINA [*putting on her most genteel society manner*] Oh, not at all. Wont you sit down?

BLUNTSCHLI. Thanks. [*He sits on the foot of the bed*].

Raina walks with studied elegance to the ottoman and sits down. Unfortunately she sits on the pistol, and jumps up with a shriek. Bluntschli, all nerves, shies like a frightened horse to the other side of the room.

BLUNTSCHLI [*irritably*] Dont frighten me like that. What is it?

RAINA. Your revolver! It was staring that officer in the face all the time. What an escape!

BLUNTSCHLI [*vexed at being unnecessarily terrified*] Oh, is that all?

RAINA [*staring at him rather superciliously as she conceives a poorer and poorer opinion of him, and feels proportionately more and more at her ease*] I am sorry I frightened you. [*She takes up the pistol and hands it to him*]. Pray take it to protect yourself against me.

BLUNTSCHLI [*grinning wearily at the sarcasm as he takes the pistol*] No use, dear young lady: theres nothing in it. It's not loaded. [*He makes a grimace at it, and drops it disparagingly into his revolver case*].

RAINA. Load it by all means.

BLUNTSCHLI. Ive no ammunition. What use are cartridges in battle? I always carry chocolate instead; and I finished the last cake of that hours ago.

RAINA [*outraged in her most cherished ideals of manhood*] Chocolate! Do you stuff your pockets with sweets—like a schoolboy—even in the field?

BLUNTSCHLI [*hungrily*] I wish I had some now.

RAINA. Allow me. [*She sails away scornfully to the chest of drawers, and returns with the box of confectionery in her hand*]. I am sorry I have eaten them all except these. [*She offers him the box*].

BLUNTSCHLI [*ravenously*] Youre an angel! [*He gobbles the contents*]. Creams! Delicious! [*He looks anxiously to see whether there are any more. There are none; he can only scrape the box with his fingers and suck them. When that nourishment is exhausted he accepts the inevitable with pathetic goodhumor, and says, with grateful emotion*] Bless you, dear lady! You can always tell an old soldier by the inside of his holsters and cartridge boxes. The young ones carry pistols and cartridges: the old ones, grub. Thank you. [*He hands back the box. She snatches it contemptuously from him and throws it away. He shies again, as if she had meant to strike him*]. Ugh! Dont do things so suddenly, gracious lady. It's mean to revenge yourself because I frightened you just now.

RAINA [*loftily*] Frighten m e ! Do you know, sir, that though I am only a woman, I think I am at heart as brave as you.

BLUNTSCHLI. I should think so. You havnt been under fire for three days as I have. I can stand two days without shewing it much; but no man can stand three days: I'm as nervous as a mouse. [*He sits down on the ottoman, and takes his head in his hands*]. Would you like to see me cry?

RAINA [*alarmed*] No.

BLUNTSCHLI. If you would, all you have to do is to scold me just as if I were a little boy and you my nurse. If I were in camp now, they'd play all sorts of tricks on me.

RAINA [*a little moved*] I'm sorry. I wont scold you. [*Touched by the sympathy in her tone, he raises his head and looks gratefully at her: she immediately draws back and says stiffly*] You must excuse me: o u r soldiers are not like that. [*She moves away from the ottoman*].

BLUNTSCHLI. Oh yes they are. There are only two sorts of soldiers: old ones and young ones. I've served fourteen years: half of your fellows never smelt powder before. Why, how is it that youve just beaten us? Sheer ignorance of the art of war, nothing else. [*Indignantly*] I never saw anything so unprofessional.

RAINA [*ironically*] Oh! was it unprofessional to beat you?

BLUNTSCHLI. Well, come! is it professional to throw a regiment of cavalry on a battery of machine guns, with the dead certainty that if the guns go off not a horse or man will ever get within fifty yards of the fire? I couldnt believe my eyes when I saw it.

RAINA [*eagerly turning to him, as all her enthusiasm and her dreams of glory rush back on her*] Did you see the great cavalry charge? Oh, tell me about it. Describe it to me.

BLUNTSCHLI. You never saw a cavalry charge, did you?

RAINA. How could I?

BLUNTSCHLI. Well, it's a funny sight. It's like slinging a handful of peas against a window pane: first one comes; then two or three close behind him; and then all the rest in a lump.

RAINA. Yes, first One! the bravest of the brave!

BLUNTSCHLI [*prosaically*] Hm! you should see the poor devil pulling at his horse.

RAINA. Why should he pull at his horse?

BLUNTSCHLI [*impatient of so stupid a question*] It's running away with him, of course: do you suppose the fellow wants to get there before the others and be killed? Then they all come. You can tell the young ones by their wildness and their slashing. The old ones come bunched up under the number one guard: t h e y know that theyre mere projectiles, and that it's no use trying to fight. The wounds are mostly broken knees, from the horses cannoning together.

RAINA Ugh! But I dont believe the first man is a coward. I know he is a hero!

BLUNTSCHLI [*goodhumoredly*] Thats what youd have said if youd seen the first man in the charge today. He did it like an operatic tenor. A regular handsome fellow, with flashing eyes and lovely moustache, shouting his war-cry and charging like Don Quixote at the windmills. We did laugh. But when the sergeant ran up as white as a sheet, and told us theyd sent us the wrong ammunition, we laughed at the other side of our mouths. And there was Don Quixote, thinking he'd done the cleverest thing ever known, whereas he ought to be courtmartialled for it. Of all the fools ever let loose on a field of battle, that man must be the very maddest. He and his regiment simply committed suicide; only the pistol missed fire; thats all.

RAINA [*deeply wounded, but steadfastly loyal to her ideals*] Indeed! Would you know him again if you saw him?

BLUNTSCHLI. Shall I ever forget him!

She again goes to the chest of drawers. He watches her with a vague hope that she may have something more for him to eat. She takes the portrait from its stand and brings it to him.

RAINA. That is a photograph of the gentleman—the patriot and hero—to whom I am betrothed.

BLUNTSCHLI [*recognizing it with a shock*] I'm really very sorry. [*Looking at her*] Was it fair to lead me on? [*He looks at the portrait again*] Yes: thats Don Quixote: not a doubt of it. [*He stifles a laugh*].

RAINA [*quickly*] Why do you laugh?

BLUNTSCHLI [*apologetic, but still greatly tickled*] I didnt laugh, I assure you. At least I didnt mean to. But when I think of him charging the windmills and imagining he was doing the finest thing—[*He chokes with suppressed laughter*].

RAINA [*sternly*] Give me back the portrait, sir.

BLUNTSCHLI [*with sincere remorse*] Of course. Certainly. I'm really very sorry. [*He hands her the picture. She deliberately kisses it and looks him straight in the face before returning to the chest of drawers to replace it. He follows her, apologizing*]. Perhaps I'm quite wrong, you know: no doubt I am. Most likely he had got wind of the cartridge business somehow, and knew it was a safe job.

RAINA. That is to say, he was a pretender and a coward! You did not dare say that before.

BLUNTSCHLI [*with a comic gesture of despair*] It's no use, dear lady: I cant make you see it from the professional point of view. [*As he turns away to get back to the ottoman, a couple of distant shots threaten renewed trouble*].

RAINA [*sternly, as she sees him listening to the shots*] So much the better for you!

BLUNTSCHLI [*turning*] How?

RAINA. You are my enemy; and you are at my mercy. What would I do if I were a professional soldier?

BLUNTSCHLI. Ah, true, dear young lady: youre always right. I know how good youve been to me: to my last hour I shall remember those three chocolate creams.

366

It was unsoldierly; but it was angelic.

RAINA [*coldly*] Thank you. And now I will do a soldierly thing. You cannot stay here after what you have just said about my future husband; but I will go out on the balcony and see whether it is safe for you to climb down into the street. [*She turns to the window*].

BLUNTSCHLI [*changing countenance*] Down that waterpipe! Stop! Wait! I cant! I darent! The very thought of it makes me giddy. I came up it fast enough with death behind me. But to face it now in cold blood—! [*He sinks on the ottoman*]. It's no use: I give up: I'm beaten. Give the alarm. [*He drops his head on his hands in the deepest dejection*].

RAINA [*disarmed by pity*] Come: dont be disheartened. [*She stoops over him almost maternally: he shakes his head*]. Oh, you are a very poor soldier: a chocolate cream soldier! Come, cheer up! it takes less courage to climb down than to face capture: remember that.

BLUNTSCHLI [*dreamily, lulled by her voice*] No: capture only means death; and death is sleep: oh, sleep, sleep, sleep, undisturbed sleep! Climbing down the pipe means doing something—exerting myself—thinking! Death ten times over first.

RAINA [*softly and wonderingly, catching the rhythm of his weariness*] Are you as sleepy as that?

BLUNTSCHLI. Ive not had two hours undisturbed sleep since I joined. I havnt closed my eyes for forty-eight hours.

RAINA [*at her wit's end*] But what am I to do with you?

BLUNTSCHLI [*staggering up, roused by her desperation*] Of course. I must do something. [*He shakes himself; pulls himself together; and speaks with rallied vigor and courage*]. That pipe m u s t be got down: [*he hits himself on the chest*] do you hear that, you chocolate cream soldier? [*He turns to the window*].

RAINA [*anxiously*] But if you fall?

BLUNTSCHLI. I shall sleep as if the stones were a feather bed. Goodbye. [*He makes boldly for the window; and his hand is on the shutter when there is a terrible burst of firing in the street beneath*].

RAINA [*rushing to him*] Stop! [*She seizes him recklessly, and pulls him quite round*]. Theyll kill you.

BLUNTSCHLI [*coolly, but attentively*] Never mind: this sort of thing is all in my day's work. I'm bound to take my chance. [*Decisively*] Now do what I tell you. Put out the candle; so that they shant see the light when I open the shutters. And keep away from the window, whatever you do. If they see me theyre sure to have a shot at me.

RAINA [*clinging to him*] Theyre sure to see you: it's bright moonlight. I'll save you. Oh, how can you be so indifferent! You want me to save you, dont you?

BLUNTSCHLI. I am not indifferent, I assure you. But how is it to be done?

RAINA. Come away from the window. [*She takes him firmly back to the middle of the room. The moment she releases him he turns mechanically towards the window again. She seizes him and turns him back, exclaiming*] Please! [*He becomes motionless, like a hypnotized rabbit, his fatigue gaining fast on him. She releases him, and addresses him patronizingly*]. Now listen. You must trust to our hospitality. You do not yet know in whose house you are. I am a Petkoff.

BLUNTSCHLI. A pet what?

RAINA [*rather indignantly*] I mean that I belong to the family of the Petkoffs, the richest and best known in our country.

BLUNTSCHLI. Oh yes, of course. I beg your pardon. The Petkoffs, to be sure. How stupid of me!

RAINA. My father holds the highest command of any Bulgarian in our army. He is [*proudly*] a Major.

BLUNTSCHLI [*pretending to be deeply impressed*] A Major! Bless me! Think of that!

RAINA. Do you know what a library is?

BLUNTSCHLI. A library? A roomful of books?

RAINA. Yes. We have one, the only one in Bulgaria.

BLUNTSCHLI. Actually a real library! I should like to see that.

RAINA [*affectedly*] I tell you these things to shew you that you are not in the house of ignorant country folk who would kill you the moment they saw your Serbian uniform, but among civilized people. And if instead of threatening me with your pistol as you did you had simply thrown yourself as a fugitive on our hospitality, you would have been as safe as in your father's house.

BLUNTSCHLI. Quite sure?

RAINA [*turning her back on him in disgust*] Oh, it is useless to try to make y o u understand.

BLUNTSCHLI. Dont be angry: you see how awkward it would be for me if there was any mistake. My father is a very hospitable man: he keeps six hotels; but I couldnt trust him as far as that. What about y o u r father?

RAINA. He is away at Slivnitza fighting for his country. I answer for your safety. There is my hand in pledge of it. Will that reassure you? [*She offers him her hand*].

BLUNTSCHLI [*looking dubiously at his own hand*] Better not touch my hand, dear young lady. I must have a wash first.

RAINA [*touched*] That is very nice of you. I see that you are a gentleman.

BLUNTSCHLI [*puzzled*] Eh?

RAINA. You must not think I am surprised. Bulgarians of really good standing— people in o u r position—wash their hands nearly every day. So you see I can appreciate your delicacy. You may take my hand. [*She offers it again*].

BLUNTSCHLI [*kissing it with his hands behind his back*] Thanks, gracious young lady: I feel safe at last. And now would you mind breaking the news to your mother? I had better not stay here secretly longer than is necessary.

RAINA. If you will be so good as to keep perfectly still whilst I am away.

BLUNTSCHLI. Certainly. [*He sits down on the ottoman*].

Raina goes to the bed and wraps herself in the fur cloak. His eyes close. She goes to the door. Turning for a last look at him, she sees that he is dropping off to sleep.

RAINA [*at the door*] You are not going asleep, are you? [*He murmurs inarticurately: she runs to him and shakes him*]. Do you hear? Wake up: you are falling asleep.

BLUNTSCHLI. Eh? Falling aslee—? Oh no: not the least in the world: I was only thinking. It's all right: I'm wide awake.

RAINA [*severely*] Will you please stand up while I am away. [*He rises reluctantly*]. All the time, mind.

BLUNTSCHLI [*standing unsteadily*] Certainly. Certainly: you may depend on me.

Raina looks doubtfully at him. He smiles weakly. She goes reluctantly, turning again at the door, and almost catching him in the act of yawning. She goes out.

BLUNTSCHLI [*drowsily*] Sleep! sleep, sleep, sleep, slee— [*The words trail off into a murmur. He wakes again with a shock on the point of falling*]. Where am I? Thats what I want to know: where am I? Must keep awake. Nothing keeps me awake except danger: [*intently*] danger, danger, danger, dan— [*trailing off again: another shock*] Wheres danger? Mus' find it. [*He starts off vaguely round the room in search of it*]. What am I looking for? Sleep—danger—dont know. [*He stumbles against the bed*] Ah yes: now I know. All right now. I'm to go to bed, but not to sleep. Be sure not to sleep, because of danger. Not to lie down either, only sit down. [*He sits on the bed. A blissful expression comes into his face*]. Ah! [*With a happy sigh he sinks back at full length; lifts his boots onto the bed with a final effort; and falls fast asleep instantly*].

 Catherine comes in, followed by Raina.

RAINA [*looking at the ottoman*] He's gone! I left him here.

CATHERINE. Here! Then he must have climbed down from the—

RAINA [*seeing him*] Oh! [*She points*].

CATHERINE [*scandalized*] Well! [*She strides to the bed, Raina following until she is opposite her on the other side*]. He's fast asleep. The brute!

RAINA [*anxiously*] Sh!

CATHERINE [*shaking him*] Sir! [*Shaking him again, harder*] Sir!! [*Vehemently, shaking very hard*] Sir!!!

RAINA [*catching her arm*] Dont, mamma: the poor darling is worn out. Let him sleep.

CATHERINE [*letting him go, and turning amazed to Raina*] The poor darling! Raina!!!

RAINA. Well, he is quite harmless. And I can sleep in your room. He can have my bed for the night. He will be all right when he has had a good breakfast.

CATHERINE [*aghast*] A good breakfast! And what are we to do with him then, pray? Give him up to our soldiers?

RAINA. Never. They would kill him. We must not betray him: the guest is sacred. We must help him to escape.

CATHERINE. Dont be ridiculous, child. This isnt an opera: it's real life. How could he escape in that uniform?

RAINA. Oh, there are lots of father's old clothes in the blue closet. Father will never miss them.

CATHERINE. I never heard of such a thing. But I suppose you must have your way: now that I see the poor creature lying there helpless I dont feel I should like to see him murdered. But look at the mess he is making of your bed with his boots. His spurs will tear the sheets to pieces.

RAINA. Yes: we must pull them off. [*She seizes one of the boots and begins pulling it off*].

CATHERINE. Take care of the spurs. [*She sets to work on the other boot*].

 Bluntschli groans and snores protestingly but does not wake. The boots come off simultaneously; and the two ladies are left sitting on the floor, each hugging a military boot.

 Change to:

 Catherine's bedroom. There is a big double bed in which Catherine is fast asleep, and a little one in which Raina has slept. It is now empty. Raina enters in her dressing gown, with an old suit of clothes on her arm.

RAINA. Mother: get up, get up. It's nearly nine. [*She shakes the sleeper*].

CATHERINE [*rubbing her eyes*] Eh? What? What have you got there?

RAINA. Clothes for the man.

CATHERINE. What man?

RAINA. The man last night. Wake up, mother: youre half asleep still. The man that came in at my window.

CATHERINE [*sitting up*] We must get rid of him. Has he had his breakfast?

RAINA. I should think he has. He has eaten your breakfast and mine too on top of his own. I did not know that a man could be such a pig. His mouth was too full to speak to me.

CATHERINE. Where is he?

RAINA. In father's snuggery, undressing himself. Do you think these things will do [*shewing Catherine the clothes*]?

CATHERINE. Yes: just the thing. Your father is always asking for that old coat, and disgracing us by wearing it when we have visitors. I'll tell him the moths have eaten it and we have had to burn it.

RAINA. We shall have to burn the man's uniform, or bury it or something. I will take these to him. [*She goes out with the clothes, Catherine getting out of bed meanwhile and putting on her slippers*].

Change to:

Raina's bedroom, with the bed disordered as Bluntschki has left it.

Raina enters carrying the clothes, which she puts down on the bed while she goes to the chest of drawers, from which she takes out a packet of cabinet photographs and a red pencil. She picks out four of the photographs, and holds them up like a hand at cards, considering which to choose.

Close-up of the four photographs in her hand, shewing that they are portraits of herself in different poses.

As before. She selects one, and begins to write on it. The marks made by the pencil not being black enough, she puts it in her mouth and licks the lead. She resumes her writing.

Close-up of the selected pose, inscribed "Raina, to her Chocolate Cream Soldier: a Souvenir."

As before. She puts the inscribed photograph into the side pocket of the coat, smiling to herself complacently; gathers up the clothes; and goes out.

Change to:

The street with the house and porch as before, but in the early forenoon light. A Bulgarian postchaise (or diligence) is waiting at the porch.

Louka is watching from an upper window. The door opens; and Catherine and Raina come out and stand on the threshold.

Bluntschli comes out between them: a ridiculous spectacle in an old smoking cap and jacket, and Bulgarian civvies that do not fit him too well.

BLUNTSCHLI. [*with his characteristic crisp decision accentuated*] Gracious ladies: my eternal gratitude. Not a word about me. You would be shot for not giving me up. [*He jumps into the vehicle*]. Avanti! [*or its Bulgarian equivalent if we can discover it*].

The driver, startled by the command, which comes like a pistol shot, cracks his whip, which has a lash four feet long or thereabouts, and sets his horses off at full gallop.

The two women turn and stare at one another, completely taken aback.

Change to:

Close-up of Raina and Catherine in the doorway.

CATHERINE. The brute! Eternal gratitude indeed!

RAINA. Could we really be shot for saving a man's life?

CATHERINE. In wartime anybody can be shot for anything or nothing. He said it just to shut our mouths in case we wanted to give him away.

RAINA. What! Betray him! After all we did for him!

CATHERINE. Serbians are all like that: they think everybody as treacherous as themselves. [*She turns and goes in*].

RAINA [*following her*] He's not a Serb: he's a Swiss.

Change to:

A Council Chamber. Noon. A table with big inkstands at the ends and one in the middle. The plenipotentiaries of the conflicting States, including Petkoff and Saranoff (for Bulgaria) are seated round the table. Officials stand behind them. All look their glummest.

In the middle a white statue of Peace, ten feet high, spreads its wings over the scene. In its left hand is a wreath held out to the sitters. Its right hand is behind it, invisible.

The chief official has a sheet of vellum in his hand. In dead silence he places it before each plenipotentiary in turn. They sign, finishing with Petkoff and Sergius, who find writing their names a bit of a job.

THE CHIEF OFFICIAL [*gathering the signed document*] Your Excellencies will no doubt find it advisable to appear on the balcony and inform the people that the peace is concluded.

The plenipotentiaries rise, and follow the officials, almost scowling at one another. The other officials go out at the back, leaving the room empty.

A distant outburst of cheering announces that the crowd has heard the joyful news.

The statue turns slowly round and reveals its right hand held behind its back. The hand holds a revolver. The cheering continues.

Change to:

The garden of Major Petkoff's house. It is a fine spring morning: the garden looks fresh and pretty. Beyond the paling the tops of a couple of minarets can be seen, shewing that there is a valley there, with the little town in it. A few miles further the Balkan mountains rise and shut in the landscape. Looking towards them from within the garden, the side of the house is seen on the left, with a garden door reached by a little flight of steps. On the right the stable yard, with its gateway, encroaches on the garden. There are fruit bushes along the paling and house. A path runs by the house, and rises by two steps at the corner, where it turns out of sight. In the middle, a small table, with two bent wood chairs at it, is laid for breakfast with Turkish coffee pot, cups, rolls, etc.; but the cups have been used and the bread broken. There is a wooden garden seat against the wall on the right.

Louka, smoking a cigaret, is standing between the table and the house, turning her back with angry disdain on a man servant who is lecturing her. He is a middleaged man of cool temperament and low but clear and keen intelligence, with the complacency of the servant who values himself on his rank in servitude, and the impreturbability of the accurate calculator who has no illusions. He wears a white Bulgarian costume: jacket with embroidered border, sash, wide knickerbockers, and decorated gaiters. His head is shaved up to the crown, giving him a high Japanese forehead. His name is Nicola.

NICOLA. Be warned in time, Louka: mend your manners. I know the mistress. If she once suspects that you are defying her, out you go.

LOUKA. I do defy her. I will defy her. What do I care for her?

NICOLA. If you quarrel with the family, I never can marry you. It's the same as if you quarrelled with me!

LOUKA. You take her part against me, do you?

NICOLA [*sedately*] I shall always be dependent on the good will of the family. When I leave their service and start a shop in Sofia, their custom will be half my capital: their bad word would ruin me.

LOUKA. You have no spirit. I should like to catch them saying a word against me!

NICOLA [*pityingly*] I should have expected more sense from you, Louka. But youre young: youre young!

LOUKA. Yes; and you like me the better for it, dont you? But I know some family secrets they wouldnt care to have told, young as I am. Let them quarrel with me if they dare!

NICOLA. Do you think I know no secrets? I know things about the mistress that she wouldnt have the master know for a thousand levas. I know things about him that she wouldnt let him hear the last of for six months if I blabbed them to her. I know things about Raina that would break off her match with Sergius if—

LOUKA [*turning on him quickly*] How do you know? I never told you!

NICOLA [*opening his eyes cunningly*] So thats your little secret, is it? I thought it might be something like that. Well, you take my advice and be respectful; and make the mistress feel that no matter what you know or dont know, she can depend on you to hold your tongue and serve the family faithfully. Thats what they like; and thats how youll make most out of them.

LOUKA [*with searching scorn*] You have the soul of a servant, Nicola.

NICOLA [*complacently*] Yes: thats the secret of success in service.

A loud knocking with a whip handle on a wooden door is heard from the stable yard.

MALE VOICE OUTSIDE. Hollo! Hollo there! Nicola!

LOUKA. Master! Back from the war!

NICOLA [*quickly*] My word for it, Louka, the war's over. Off with you and get some fresh coffee. [*He runs out into the stable yard*].

LOUKA [*as she collects the coffee pot and cups on the tray, and carries it into the house*] Youll never put the soul of a servant into m e .

Major Petkoff comes from the stable yard, followed by Nicola.

PETKOFF [*pointing to the table with his whip*] Breakfast out here, eh?

NICOLA. Yes, sir. The mistress and Miss Raina have just gone in.

PETKOFF [*sitting down and taking a roll*] Go in and say Ive come; and get me some fresh coffee.

NICOLA. It's coming sir. [*He goes to the house door. Louka, with fresh coffee, a clean cup, and a brandy bottle on her tray, meets him*]. Have you told the mistress?

LOUKA. Yes: she's coming.

Nicola goes into the house. Louka brings the coffee to the table.

PETKOFF. Well: the Serbs havnt run away with you, have they?

LOUKA. No, sir.

PETKOFF. Thats right. Have you brought me some cognac?

LOUKA [*putting the bottle on the table*] Here, sir.

PETKOFF. T h a t s right. [*He pours some into his coffee*].

Catherine, who, having at this early hour made only a very perfunctory toilet, wears a Bulgarian apron over a once brilliant but now half worn-out dressing gown, and a colored handkerchief tied over her thick black hair, comes from the house with Turkish slippers on her bare feet, looking astonishingly handsome and stately under all the circumstances. Louka goes into the house.

CATHERINE. My dear Paul: what a surprise for us! [*She stoops over the back of his chair to kiss him*]. Have they brought you fresh coffee?

PETKOFF. Yes: Louka's been looking after me. The war's over. The treaty was signed three days ago at Bucharest; and the decree for our army to demobilize was issued yesterday.

CATHERINE [*springing erect, with flashing eyes*] Paul: have you let the Austrians force you to make peace?

PETKOFF [*submissively*] My dear: they didnt consult me. What could *I* do? [*She sits down and turns away from him*]. But of course we saw to it that the treaty was an honorable one. It declares peace—

CATHERINE [*outraged*] Peace!

PETKOFF [*appeasing her*] —but not friendly relations: remember that. They wanted to put that in; but I insisted on its being struck out. What more could I do?

CATHERINE. You could have annexed Serbia and made Prince Alexander Emperor of the Balkans. Thats what I would have done.

PETKOFF. I dont doubt it in the least, my dear. But I should have had to subdue the whole Austrian Empire first; and that would have kept me too long away from you. I missed you greatly.

CATHERINE [*relenting*] Ah! [*She stretches her hand affectionately across the table to squeeze his*].

PETKOFF. And how have you been, my dear?

CATHERINE. Oh, my usual sore throats: thats all.

PETKOFF [*with conviction*] That comes from washing your neck every day. Ive often told you so.

CATHERINE. Nonsense, Paul!

PETKOFF [*over his coffee and cigaret*] I dont believe in going too far with these modern customs. All this washing cant be good for the health: it's not natural. There was an Englishman at Phippopolis who used to wet himself all over with cold water every morning when he got up. Disgusting! It all comes from the English: their climate makes them so dirty that they have to be perpetually washing themselves. Look at my father! he never had a bath in his life; and he lived to be ninety-eight, the healthiest man in Bulgaria. I dont mind a good wash once a week to keep up my position; but once a day is carrying the thing to a ridiculous extreme.

CATHERINE. You are a barbarian at heart still, Paul. I hope you behaved yourself before all those Russian officers.

PETKOFF. I did my best. I took care to let them know that we have a library.

CATHERINE. Ah; but you didnt tell them that we have an electric bell in it? I have had one put up.

PETKOFF. Whats an electric bell?

CATHERINE. You touch a button; something tinkles in the kitchen; and then Nicola comes up.

PETKOFF. Why not shout for him?

CATHERINE. Civilized people never shout for their servants. Ive learnt that while you were away.

SERGIUS [*knocking at the stable gates*] Gate, Nicola!

PETKOFF. Theres Sergius. [*Shouting*] Hollo, Nicola!

CATHERINE. Oh, dont shout, Paul: it really isnt nice.

PETKOFF. Bosh! [*He shouts louder than before*]. Nicola!

NICOLA [*appearing at the house door*] Yes, sir.

PETKOFF. Are you deaf? Dont you hear Major Saranoff knocking? Bring him round this way.

NICOLA. Yes, major. [*He goes into the stable yard*].

PETKOFF. You must talk to him, my dear, until Raina takes him off our hands. He bores my life out about our not promoting him. Over m y head, if you please.

CATHERINE. He certainly ought to be promoted when he marries Raina. Besides, the country should insist on having at least one native general.

PETKOFF. Yes; so that he could throw away whole brigades instead of regiments. It's no use, my dear: he hasnt the slightest chance of promotion until we're quite sure that the peace will be a lasting one.

NICOLA [*at the gate, announcing*] Major Sergius Saranoff! [*He goes into the house and returns presently with a third chair, which he places at the table. He then withdraws*].

As Sergius enters from the stable gate, Catherine rises effusively to greet him. Petkoff is distinctly less disposed to make a fuss about him.

PETKOFF. Here already, Sergius! Glad to see you.

CATHERINE. My dear Sergius! [*She holds out both her hands*].

SERGIUS [*kissing them with a scrupulous gallantry*] My dear mother, if I may call you so.

PETKOFF [*drily*] Mother-in-law, Sergius: mother-in-law! Sit down; and have some coffee.

Sergius gets away from the table with a certain distaste for Petkoff's enjoyment of it, and posts himself with conscious dignity against the rail of the steps leading to the house.

CATHERINE. You look superb. The campaign has improved you, Sergius. Everybody here is mad about you. We were all wild with enthusiasm about that magnificent cavalry charge.

SERGIUS [*with grave irony*] Madam: it was the cradle and the grave of my military reputation.

CATHERINE. How so?

SERGIUS. I won the battle the wrong way when our worthy Russian generals were losing it the right way. In short, I upset their plans, and wounded their self-esteem. Two Cossack colonels had their regiments routed on the most correct principles of scientific warfare. Two major-generals got killed strictly according to military etiquette. The two colonels are now major-generals; and I am still a simple major.

CATHERINE. You shall not remain so, Sergius. The women are on your side; and they will see that justice is done to you.

SERGIUS. It is too late. I have only waited for the peace to send in my resignation.

PETKOFF [*dropping his cup in his amazement*] Your resignation!

CATHERINE. Oh, you must withdraw it!

SERGIUS [*with resolute measured emphasis, folding his arms*] I never withdraw.

PETKOFF [*vexed*] Now who could have supposed you were going to do such a thing?

SERGIUS [*with fire*] Everyone that knew me. But enough of myself and my affairs. How is Raina; and where is Raina?

RAINA [*suddenly coming round the corner of the house and standing at the top of the steps in the path*] Raina is here.

She makes a charming picture as they turn to look at her. She wears an underdress of pale green silk, draped with an overdress of thin ecru canvas embroidered with gold. She is crowned with a dainty eastern cap of gold tinsel. Sergius goes impulsively to meet her. Posing regally, she presents her hand: he drops chivalrously on one knee and kisses it.

PETKOFF [*aside to Catherine, beaming with parental pride*] Pretty, isnt it? She always appears at the right moment.

CATHERINE [*impatiently*] Yes: she listens for it. It is an abominable habit.

Sergius leads Raina forward with splendid gallantry. When they arrive at the table, she turns to him with a bend of the head: he bows; and thus they separate, he coming to his place, and she going behind her father's chair.

RAINA [*stooping and kissing her father*] Dear father! Welcome home!

PETKOFF [*patting her cheek*] My little pet girl. [*He kisses her. She goes to the chair left by Nicola for Sergius, and sits down*].

CATHERINE. And so youre no longer a soldier, Sergius.

SERGIUS. I am no longer a soldier. Soldiering, my dear madam, is the coward's art of attacking mercilessly when you are strong and keeping out of harm's way when you are weak. That is the whole secret of successful fighting. Get your enemy at a disadvantage and never, on any account, fight him on equal terms.

PETKOFF. They wouldnt let us make a fair stand-up fight of it. However, I suppose soldiering has to be a trade like any other trade.

SERGIUS. Precisely. But I have no ambition to shine as a tradesman; so I have taken the advice of that bagman of a captain that settled the exchange of prisoners with us at Pirot, and given it up.

PETKOFF. What! that Swiss fellow? Sergius: Ive often thought of that exchange since. He over-reached us about those horses.

SERGIUS. Of course he over-reached us. His father was a hotel and livery stable keeper; and he owed his first step to his knowledge of horse-dealing. [*With mock enthusiasm*] Ah, he was a soldier: every inch a soldier!

RAINA. Are there many Swiss officers in the Serbian Army?

PETKOFF. No. All Austrians, just as our officers were all Russians. This was the only Swiss I came across. I'll never trust a Swiss again.

RAINA. What was he like?

CATHERINE. Oh, Raina, what a silly question!

SERGIUS. He was like a commercial traveller in uniform. Bourgeois to his boots!

PETKOFF [*grinning*] Sergius: tell Catherine that queer story his friend told us about how he escaped after Slivnitza. You remember. About his being hid by two women.

SERGIUS [*with bitter irony*] Oh yes: quite a romance! He was serving in the very battery I so unprofessionally charged. Being a thorough soldier, he ran away like the rest of them, with our cavalry at his heels. To escape their sabres he climbed a waterpipe and made his way into the bedroom of a young Bulgarian lady. The young lady was enchanted by his persuasive commercial traveller's manners. She very modestly entertained him for an hour or so, and then called in her mother lest her conduct should appear unmaidenly. The old lady was equally fascinated; and the fugitive was sent on his way in the morning, disguised in an old coat belonging to the master of the house, who was away at the war.

RAINA [*rising with marked stateliness*] Your life in the camp has made you coarse, Sergius. I did not think you would have repeated such a story before me. [*She turns away coldly*].

CATHERINE [*also rising*] She is right, Sergius. If such women exist, w e should be spared the knowledge of them.

PETKOFF. Pooh! nonsense! what does it matter?

SERGIUS [*ashamed*] No, Petkoff: I was wrong. [*To Raina, with earnest humility*] I beg your pardon. I have behaved abominably. Forgive me, Raina. [*She bows reservedly*]. And you too, madam. [*Catherine bows graciously and sits down. He proceeds solemnly, again addressing Raina*]. The glimpses I have had of the seamy side of life during the last few months have made me cynical; but I should not have brought my cynicism here: least of all into your presence, Raina. I—[*Here, turning to the others, he is evidently going to begin a long speech when the Major interrupts him*].

PETKOFF. Stuff and nonsense, Sergius! Thats quite enough fuss about nothing: a soldier's daughter should be able to stand up without flinching to a little strong conversation. [*He rises*]. Come: it's time for us to get to business. We have to make up our minds how those three regiments are to get back to Philippopolis: theres no forage for them on the Sofia route. [*He goes towards the house*]. Come along. [*Sergius is about to follow him when Catherine rises and intervenes*].

CATHERINE. Oh, Paul, cant you spare Sergius for a few moments? Raina has hardly seen him yet. Perhaps I can help you to settle about the regiments.

SERGIUS [*protesting*] My dear madam, impossible: you—

CATHERINE [*stopping him playfully*] You stay here, my dear Sergius: theres no hurry. I have a word or two to say to Paul. [*Sergius instantly bows and steps back*]. Now, dear [*taking Petkoff's arm*]: come and see the electric bell.

PETKOFF. Oh, very well, very well.

They go into the house together affectionately. Sergius, left alone with Raina, looks anxiously at her, fearing that she is still offended. She smiles, and stretches out her arms to him.

SERGIUS [*hastening to her*] Am I forgiven?

RAINA [*placing her hands on his shoulders as she looks up at him with admiration and worship*] My hero! My king!

SERGIUS. My queen! [*He kisses her on the forehead*].

RAINA. How I have envied you, Sergius! You have been out in the world, on the field of battle, able to prove yourself there worthy of any woman in the world; whilst I have had to sit at home inactive—dreaming—useless—doing nothing that could give me the right to call myself worthy of any man.

SERGIUS. Dearest: all my deeds have been yours. You inspired me. I have gone through the war like a knight in a tournament with his lady looking down at him!

RAINA. And you have never been absent from my thoughts for a moment. [*Very solemnly*] Sergius: I think we two have found the higher love. When I think of you, I feel that I could never do a base deed, or think an ignoble thought.

SERGIUS. My lady and my saint! [*He clasps her reverently*].

RAINA [*returning his embrace*] My lord and my—[*Louka is heard singing within the house. They quickly release each other*]. I cant pretend to talk indifferently before her: my heart is too full. [*Louka comes from the house with her tray. She goes to the table, and begins to clear it, with her back turned to them*]. I will get my hat; and then we can go out until lunch time. Wouldnt you like that?

SERGIUS. Be quick. If you are away five minutes, it will seem five hours. [*Raina runs to the top of the steps, and turns there to exchange looks with him and wave him a kiss with both hands. He looks after her with emotion for a moment; then turns slowly away, his face radiant with the loftiest exaltation. The movement shifts his field of vision, into the corner of which there now comes the tail of Louka's double apron. His attention is arrested at once. He takes a stealthy look at her, and begins to twirl his moustache mischievously, with his left hand akimbo on his hip. Finally, striking the ground with his heels in something of a cavalry swagger, he strolls over to the other side of the table, opposite her, and says*] Louka: do you know what the higher love is?

LOUKA [*astonished*] No, sir.

SERGIUS. Very fatiguing thing to keep up for any length of time, Louka. One feels the need of some relief after it.

LOUKA [*innocently*] Perhaps you would like some coffee, sir? [*She stretches her hand across the table for the coffee pot*].

SERGIUS [*taking her hand*] Thank you, Louka.

LOUKA [*pretending to pull*] Oh, sir, you know I didnt mean that. I'm surprised at you!

SERGIUS [*coming clear of the table and drawing her with him*] I am surprised at myself, Louka. What would Sergius, the hero of Slivnitza, say if he saw me now? What would Sergius, the apostle of the higher love, say if he saw me now? What would the half dozen Sergiuses who keep popping in and out of this handsome figure of mine say if they caught us here? [*Letting go her hand and slipping his arm dexterously round her waist*] Do you consider my figure handsome, Louka?

LOUKA. Let me go, sir. I shall be disgraced. [*She struggles: he holds her hand inexorably*]. Oh, w i l l you let go?

SERGIUS [*looking straight into her eyes*] No.

LOUKA. Then stand back where we cant be seen. Have you no common sense?

SERGIUS. Ah! thats reasonable. [*He takes her into the stableyard gateway, where they are hidden from the house*].

LOUKA [*plaintively*] I may have been seen from the windows: Miss Raina is sure to be spying about after you.

SERGIUS [*stung: letting her go*] Take care, Louka. I may be worthless enough to betray the higher love; but do not you insult it.

LOUKA [*demurely*] Not for the world, sir, I'm sure. May I go on with my work, please, now?

SERGIUS [*again putting his arm round her*] You are a provoking little witch, Louka. If you were in love with me, would you spy out of windows on me?

LOUKA. Well, you see, sir, since you say you are half a dozen different gentlemen all at once, I should have a great deal to look after.

SERGIUS [*charmed*] Witty as well as pretty. [*He tries to kiss her*].

LOUKA [*avoiding him*] No: I dont want your kisses. Gentlefolk are all alike: you making love to me behind Miss Raina's back; and she doing the same behind yours.

SERGIUS [*recoiling a step*] Louka!

LOUKA. It shews how little you really care.

SERGIUS [*dropping his familiarity, and speaking with freezing politeness*] If our conversation is to continue, Louka, you will please remember that a gentleman does not discuss the conduct of the lady he is engaged to with her maid.

LOUKA. It's so hard to know what a gentleman considers right. I thought from your trying to kiss me that you had given up being so particular.

SERGIUS [*turning from her and striking his forehead as he comes back into the garden from the gateway*] Devil! devil!

LOUKA. Ha! ha! I expect one of the six of you is very like me, sir; though I a m only Miss Raina's maid. [*She goes back to her work at the table, taking no further notice of him*].

SERGIUS [*speaking to himself*] Which of the six is the real man? thats the question that torments me. One of them is a hero, another a buffoon, another a humbug, another perhaps a bit of a blackguard. [*He pauses, and looks furtively at Louka as he adds, with deep bitterness*] And one, at least, is a coward: jealous, like all cowards. [*He goes to the table*]. Louka.

LOUKA. Yes?

SERGIUS. Who is my rival?

LOUKA. You shall never get that out of me, for love or money.

SERGIUS. Why?

LOUKA. Never mind why. Besides, you would tell that I told you; and I should lose my place.

SERGIUS [*holding out his right hand in affirmation*] No! on the honor of a—[*He checks himself; and his hand drops, nerveless, as he concludes sardonically*]—of a man capable of behaving as I have been behaving for the last five minutes. Who is he?

LOUKA. I dont know. I never saw him. I only heard his voice through the door of her room.

SERGIUS. Damnation! How dare you?

LOUKA [*retreating*] Oh, I mean no harm: youve no right to take up my words like that. The mistress knows all about it. And I tell you that if that gentleman ever comes here again, Miss Raina will marry him, whether he likes it or not. I know the difference between the sort of manner you and she put on before one another and the real manner.

Sergius shivers as if she had stabbed him. Then, setting his face like iron, he strides grimly to her, and grips her above the elbows with both hands.

SERGIUS. Now listen you to me.

LOUKA [*wincing*] Not so tight: youre hurting me.

SERGIUS. That doesnt matter. You have stained my honor by making me a party to your eavesdropping. And you have betrayed your mistress.

LOUKA [*writhing*] Please—

SERGIUS. That shews that you are an abominable little clod of common clay, with the soul of a servant. [*He lets her go as if she were an unclean thing, and turns away, dusting his hands of her, to the bench by the wall, where he sits down with averted head, meditating gloomily*].

LOUKA [*whimpering angrily with her hands up her sleeves, feeling her bruised arms*] You know how to hurt with your tongue as well as with your hands. But I dont care, now Ive found out that whatever clay I'm made of, youre made of the same. As for her, she's a liar; and her fine airs are a cheat; and I'm worth six of her. [*She shakes the pain off hardily; tosses her head; and sets to work to put the things on the tray*].

He looks doubtfully at her. She finishes packing the tray, and laps the cloth over the edges, so as to carry all out together. As she stoops to lift it, he rises.

SERGIUS. Louka! [*She stops and looks defiantly at him*]. A gentleman has no right to hurt a woman under any circumstances. [*With profound humility, uncovering his head*] I beg your pardon.

LOUKA. That sort of apology may satisfy a lady. Of what use is it to a servant?

SERGIUS [*rudely crossed in his chivalry, throws it off with a bitter laugh, and says slightingly*] Oh! you wish to be paid for the hurt? [*He puts on his shako, and takes some money from his pocket*].

LOUKA [*her eyes filling with tears in spite of herself*] No: I want my hurt made well.

SERGIUS [*sobered by her tone*] How?

She rolls up her left sleeve; clasps her arm with the thumb and fingers of her right hand; and looks down at the bruise. Then she raises her head and looks straight at him. Finally, with a superb gesture, she presents her arm to be kissed. Amazed, he looks at her; at the arm; at her again; hesitates; and then, with shuddering intensity, exclaims Never! *and gets away as far as possible from her.*

Her arm drops. Without a word, and with unaffected dignity, she takes her tray, and is approaching the house when Raina returns, wearing a hat and jacket in the height of the Vienna fashion of the previous year, 1885. Louka makes way proudly for her, and then goes into the house.

RAINA. I'm ready. Whats the matter? [*Gaily*] Have you been flirting with Louka?

SERGIUS [*hastily*] No, no. How can you think such a thing?

RAINA [*ashamed of herself*] Forgive me, dear. I am so happy today.

He goes quickly to her, and kisses her hand remorsefully. Catherine comes out and calls to them from the top of the steps.

CATHERINE [*coming down to them*] I am sorry to disturb you, children; but Paul is distracted over those three regiments. He doesnt know how to send them to Philippopolis; and he objects to every suggestion of mine. You must go and help him, Sergius. He is in the library.

RAINA [*disappointed*] But we are just going out for a walk.

SERGIUS I shall not be long. Wait for me just five minutes. [*He runs up the steps to the door*].

RAINA [*following him to the foot of the steps and looking up at him with timid coquetry*] I shall go round and wait in full view of the library windows. If you are a moment longer than five minutes, I shall go in and fetch you, regiments or no regiments.

SERGIUS [*laughing*] Very well. [*He goes in*].

Raina watches him until he is out of her sight. Then, with a perceptible relaxation of manner, she begins to pace up and down the garden in a brown study.

CATHERINE. Imagine their meeting that Swiss and hearing the whole story! The very first thing your father asked for was the old coat we sent him off in. A nice mess you have got us into!

RAINA [*gazing thoughtfully at the gravel as she walks*] The little beast!

CATHERINE. Little beast! What little beast?

RAINA. To go and tell! Oh, if I had him here, I'd cram him with chocolate creams til he couldnt ever speak again!

CATHERINE. Dont talk such stuff. Tell me the truth, Raina. How long was he in your room before you came to me?

RAINA [whisking round and recommencing her march in the opposite direction] Oh, I forget.

CATHERINE. You cannot forget! Did he really climb up after the soldiers were gone; or was he there when that officer searched the room?

RAINA. No. Yes: I think he must have been there then.

CATHERINE. You t h i n k ! Oh, Raina! Raina! Will anything ever make you straightforward? If Sergius finds out, it will be all over between you.

RAINA [with cool impertinence] Oh, I know Sergius is your pet. I sometimes wish you could marry him instead of me. You would just suit him. You would pet him, and spoil him, and mother him to perfection.

CATHERINE [opening her eyes very widely indeed] Well, upon my word!

RAINA [capriciously: half to herself] I always feel a longing to do or say something dreadful to him—to shock his propriety—to scandalize the five senses out of him. [To Catherine, perversely] I dont care whether he finds out about the chocolate cream soldier or not. I half hope he may. [She again turns and strolls flippantly away up the path to the corner of the house].

CATHERINE. And what should I be able to say to your father, pray?

RAINA [over her shoulder, from the top of the two steps] Oh, poor father! As if h e could help himself! [She turns the corner and passes out of sight].

CATHERINE [looking after her, her fingers itching] Oh, if you were only ten years younger! [Louka comes from the house with a salver, which she carries hanging down by her side]. Well?

LOUKA. Theres a gentleman just called, madam. A Serbian officer.

CATHERINE [flaming] A Serb! And how dare he—[checking herself bitterly] Oh, I forgot. We are at peace now. I suppose we shall have them calling every day to pay their compliments. Well: if he is an officer why dont you tell your master? He is in the library with Major Saranoff. Why do you come to me?

LOUKA. But he asks for you, madam. He gave me this little ticket for you. [She takes a card out of her bosom; puts it on the salver; and offers it to Catherine].

CATHERINE [reading] "Captain Bluntschli"? Thats a German name.

LOUKA. Swiss, madam, I think.

CATHERINE [with a bound that makes Louka jump back] Swiss! What is he like?

LOUKA [timidly] He has a big carpet bag, madam.

CATHERINE. Oh Heavens! he's come to return the coat. Send him away. [Louka begins business of starting to go at each instruction and checking herself to hear the next]. Say we're not at home: ask him to leave his address and I'll write to him. Oh stop: that will never do. Wait! [She throws herself into a chair to think it out. Louka waits]. The master and Major Saranoff are busy in the library, arnt they?

LOUKA. Yes, madam.

CATHERINE [decisively] Bring the gentleman out here at once. [Peremptorily] And be very polite to him. Dont delay. Here [impatiently snatching the salver from her]: leave that here; and go straight back to him.

LOUKA. Yes, madam [going].

Catherine must be visible; but close-up ¼ length of Louka repeatedly starting to *go and turning as she is recalled.*

CATHERINE. Louka!

LOUKA [*stopping*] Yes, madam.

CATHERINE. Is the library door shut?

LOUKA. I think so, madam.

CATHERINE. If not, shut it as you pass through.

LOUKA. Yes, madam [*going*].

CATHERINE. Stop! [*Louka stops*]. He will have to go that way [*indicating the gate of the stableyard*]. Tell Nicola to bring his bag here after him. Dont forget.

LOUKA [*surprised*] His bag?

CATHERINE. Yes: here: as soon as possible. [*Vehemently*] Be quick! [*Louka runs into the house. Catherine snatches her apron off and throws it behind a bush. She then takes up the salver and uses it as a mirror, with the result that the handkerchief tied round her head follows the apron. A touch to her hair and a shake to her dressing gown make her presentable*]. Oh, how? how? h o w can a man be such a fool! Such a moment to select! [*Louka appears at the door of the house, announcing* Captain Bluntschli. *She stands aside at the top of the steps to let him pass before she goes in again. He is the man of the midnight adventure in Raina's room, clean, well brushed, smartly uniformed, and out of trouble, but still unmistakably the same man. The moment Louka's back is turned, Catherine swoops on him with impetuous, urgent, coaxing appeal*]. Captain Bluntschli: I am v e r y glad to see you; but you must leave this house at once. [*He raises his eyebrows*]. My husband has just returned with my future son-in-law; and they know nothing. If they did, the consequences would be terrible. If my husband discovers our secret, he will never forgive me; and my daughter's life will hardly be safe. Will you, like the chivalrous gentleman and soldier you are, leave at once before he finds you here?

BLUNTSCHLI [*disappointed, but philosophical*] At once, gracious lady. I only came to thank you and return the coat you lent me. If you will allow me to take it out of my bag and leave it with your servant as I pass out, I need detain you no further. [*He turns to go into the house*].

CATHERINE [*catching him by the sleeve*] Oh, you must not think of going back that way. [*Coaxing him across to the stable gates*] This is the shortest way out. Many thanks. So glad to have been of service to you. G o o d -bye.

BLUNTSCHLI. But my bag?

CATHERINE. It shall be sent on. You will leave me your address.

BLUNTSCHLI. True. Allow me. [*He takes out his card-case, and stops to write his address, keeping Catherine in an agony of impatience. As he hands her the card, Petkoff, hatless, rushes from the house in a fluster of hospitality, followed by Sergius*].

PETKOFF [*as he hurries down the steps*] My dear Captain Bluntschli—

CATHERINE. Oh Heavens! [*She sinks on the seat against the wall*].

PETKOFF [*too preoccupied to notice her as he shakes Bluntschli's hand heartily*] Those stupid people of mine thought I was out here, instead of in the—haw!—library [*he cannot mention the library without betraying how proud he is of it*]. Saranoff is with me: you remember him, dont you?

SERGIUS [*saluting humorously, and then offering his hand with great charm of manner*] Welcome, our friend the enemy!

PETKOFF. No longer the enemy, happily. [*Rather anxiously*] I hope youve called as a friend, and not about horses or prisoners.

CATHERINE. Oh, quite as a friend, Paul. I was just asking Captain Bluntschli to stay to lunch; but he declares he must go at once.

SERGIUS [*sardonically*] Impossible, Bluntschli. We want you here badly. We have to send on three cavalry regiments to Philippopolis; and we dont in the least know how to do it.

BLUNTSCHLI [*suddenly attentive and businesslike*] Philippopolis? The forage is the trouble, I suppose.

PETKOFF [*eagerly*] Yes: thats it. [*To Sergius*] He sees the whole thing at once.

BLUNTSCHLI. I think I can shew you how to manage that.

SERGIUS. Invaluable man! Come along! [*Towering over Bluntschli, he puts his hand on his shoulder and takes him to the steps, Petkoff following*].

Raina comes from the house as Bluntschli puts his foot on the first step.

RAINA. Oh! The chocolate cream solder!

Bluntschli stands rigid. Sergius, amazed, looks at Raina, then at Petkoff, who looks back at him and then at his wife.

CATHERINE [*with commanding presence of mind*] My dear Raina, dont you see that we have a guest here? Captain Bluntschli: one of our new Serbian friends.

Raina bows: Bluntschli bows.

RAINA. How silly of me! [*She comes down into the centre of the group, between Bluntschli and Petkoff*]. I made a beautiful ornament this morning for the ice pudding; and that stupid Nicola has just put down a pile of plates on it and spoilt it. [*To Bluntschli, winningly*] I hope you didnt think that y o u were the chocolate cream soldier, Captain Bluntschli.

BLUNTSCHLI [*laughing*] I assure you I did. [*Stealing a whimsical glance at her*] Your explanation was a relief.

PETKOFF [*suspiciously, to Raina*] And since when, pray, have y o u taken to cooking?

CATHERINE. Oh, whilst you were away. It is her latest fancy.

PETKOFF [*testily*] And has Nicola taken to drinking? He used to be careful enough. First he shews Captain Bluntschli out here when he knew quite well I was in the library; and then he goes downstairs and breaks Raina's chocolate soldier. He must—[*Nicola appears at the top of the steps with the bag. He descends; places it respectfully before Bluntschli; and waits for further orders. General amazement. Nicola, unconscious of the effect he is producing, looks perfectly satisfied with himself. When Petkoff recovers his power of speech, he breaks out at him with*] Are you mad, Nicola?

NICOLA [*taken aback*] Sir?

PETKOFF. What have you brought that for?

NICOLA. My lady's orders, major. Louka told me that—

CATHERINE [*interrupting him*] M y orders! Why should I order you to bring Captian Bluntschli's luggage out here? What are you thinking of, Nicola?

NICOLA [*after a moment's bewilderment, picking up the bag as he addresses Bluntschli with the very perfection of servile discretion*] I beg your pardon, captain, I am sure. [*To Catherine*] My fault, madam: I hope youll overlook it. [*He bows, and is going to the steps with the bag, when Petkoff addresses him angrily*].

PETKOFF. Youd better go and slam that bag, too, down on Miss Raina's ice pudding! [*This is too much for Nicola. The bag drops from his hand almost on his master's toes, eliciting a roar of*] Begone, you butter-fingered donkey.

NICOLA [*snatching up the bag, and escaping into the house*] Yes, major.

CATHERINE. Oh, never mind, Paul: dont be angry.

PETKOFF [*blustering*] Scoundrel! He's got out of hand while I was away. I'll teach him. Infernal blackguard! The sack next Saturday! I'll clear out the whole establishment—[*He is stifled by the caresses of his wife and daughter, who hang round his neck, petting him*].

CATHERINE | [*together*] | Now, now, now, it mustnt be angry. He meant no
RAINA | | Wow, wow, wow: not on your first day at home.
          | | Harm. Be good to please me, dear, Sh-sh-sh-sh!
          | | I'll make another ice pudding. Tch-ch-ch!

PETKOFF [*yielding*] Oh well, never mind. Come, Bluntschli: lets have no more nonsense about going away. You know very well youre not going back to Switzerland yet. Until you do go back youll stay with us.

RAINA. Oh, do, Captain Bluntschli.

PETKOFF [*to Catherine*] Now, Catherine: it's of you he's afraid. Press him; and he'll stay.

CATHERINE. Of course I shall be only too delighted if [*appealingly*] Captain Bluntschli really wishes to stay. He knows my wishes.

BLUNTSCHLI [*in his driest military manner*] I am at madam's orders.

   Nicola appears at the top of the steps.

NICOLA [*bowing formally*] Lunch is served. [*He remains with drooping head while they pass him*].

CATHERINE. Captain Bluntschli is staying to lunch, Nicola.

NICOLA. Yes, madam: his place is laid.

CATHERINE. Then let us go in.

   Catherine and Raina go into the house, the men following, and Bluntschli leading, Petkoff and Sergius mildly insisting on his precedence as guest.

   Change to:

   Interior. A spacious flagged kitchen. The table, with a meal set out for five persons, is piled with accessory foods: baskets of bread, melons, pickles, a cold ham, hors d'oeuvres of all sorts. At the back, two enormous vats. Everything indicates that Petkoff is a prosperous farmer in a country where everything is home made, big, rough, and plentiful. The fireplace has neither grate nor coals: it burns great logs and over it hangs a huge pot on a chain, a novelty in the shape of a gleaming tin roasting jack, and a pile of plates and dishes.

   Close-up: Louka takes three fat roast fowls from the jack, puts them on a dish, bastes them from the dripping pan, and hands them to Nicola, who places them on the table.

   The five guests enter in the order in which they have left the garden. Petkoff takes his seat before the fowls as head of the household. Catherine indicates that Bluntschli is to sit next Raina, Sergius taking the chair at her other hand. She herself sits next her husband.

PETKOFF [*taking up a huge carving knife and hone and shouting very unceremoniously*] For what we are about to receive may the Lord make us truly thankful. [*He sharps the knife noisily, as if it was a scythe, and cuts a fowl in halves at one stroke and puts one half on the top plate of the pile before him*]. Half a fowl to begin with, Bluntschli?

BLUNTSCHLI [*as Nicola places it before him*] Thank you.

LOUKA [*coming behind Bluntschli with a large black saucepan*] Vej?

BLUNTSCHLI [*helping himself from the saucepan*] Thank you.

LOUKA [*incredulously*] No sausages!!!

BLUNTSCHLI. Well, perhaps one small one [*he helps himself*].

PETKOFF. Raina: will you share a bird with Sergius or would you rather have a whole one?

RAINA [*vexed*] Oh, papa, you will make Captain Bluntschli think I am a boa constrictor. Half will be quite enough to begin with.

Petkoff carves accordingly. Nicola takes it to Raina. Then Louka mutely presents the saucepan, from which Raina takes a stupendous helping of miscellaneous vegetables. She adds three sausages.

Close-up of this incident, giving Bluntschli's stealthy look at the steaming plate. As before.

PETKOFF [*to Catherine*] Kit: you will split a bird with Sergius as usual, eh?

CATHERINE. Yes: I have no appetite today.

PETKOFF. Good! that leaves a whole one for me. [*He carves*].

Catherine and Sergius are served, Louka presenting the saucepan to each in silence and then replacing it at the fire. Petkoff dumps the remaining fowl on his own plate and sets to work with knife and fork.

Close-up of Raina pulling a leg off her half chicken with her fingers and gnawing it greedily, Bluntschli again noting this refinement in some dismay.

As before. All are busy eating.

PETKOFF. Nicola!

NICOLA. Yes, Major.

PETKOFF. Take the table out of the scullery and put it in the library.

NICOLA. Yes, Major.

PETKOFF. And take the pens and ink and paper off the desk in my office and put them on the table. We'll go up there when we've finished eating; and [*to Bluntschli*] you will shew us how to get those troops to Philippopolis, wont you?

BLUNTSCHLI. Yes: it wont be difficult. I know the route.

SERGIUS. You know everything, I think.

Change to:

The library after lunch. It is not much of a library. Its literary equipment consists of a single fixed shelf stocked with old paper covered novels, broken backed, coffee stained, torn and thumbed; and a couple of little hanging shelves with a few gift books on them: the rest of the wall space being occupied by trophies of war and the chase. But it is a most comfortable sitting room. A row of three large windows shews a mountain panorama, just now seen in one of its friendliest aspects in the mellowing afternoon light. In the corner next the right hand window a square earthenware stove, a perfect tower of glistening pottery, rises nearly to the ceiling and guarantees plenty of warmth. The ottoman is like that in Raina's room, and similarly placed; and the window seats are luxurious with decorated cushions. There is one object, however, hopelessly out of keeping with its surroundings. This is a small kitchen table, much the worse for wear, fitted as a writing table with an old canister full of pens, an eggcup filled with ink, and a deplorable scrap of heavily used pink blotting paper.

At the side of this table, which stands to the left of anyone facing the window, Bluntschli is hard at work with a couple of maps before him, writing orders. At the head of it sits Sergius, who is supposed to be also at work, but is actually gnawing the feather of a pen, and contemplating Bluntschli's quick, sure, businesslike progress with a mixture of envious irritation at his own incapacity and awestruck wonder at an ability which seems to him almost miraculous, though its prosaic character forbids him to esteem it. The Major is comfortably established on the ottoman, with a newspaper in his hand and the tube of his hookah within easy reach. Catherine sits at the stove, with her back to them, embroidering. Raina, reclining on the divan, is gazing in a daydream out at the Balkan landscape, with a neglected novel in her lap.

The door is one the same side as the stove, farther from the window. The button of the electric bell is at the opposite side, behind Bluntschli.

PETKOFF [*looking up from his paper to watch how they are getting on at the table*] Are you sure I cant help you in any way, Bluntschli?

BLUNTSCHLI [*without interrupting his writing or looking up*] Quite sure, thank you. Saranoff and I will manage it.

SERGIUS [*grimly*] Yes: we'll manage it. He finds out what to do; draws up the orders; and I sign em. Division of labor! [*Bluntschli passes him a paper*]. Another one? Thank you. [*He plants the paper squarely before him; sets his chair carefully parallel to it*].

Close-up of Sergius signing—arm on table, cheek on arm, tongue out convulsively following the difficult strokes of his pen.

SERGIUS. This hand is more accustomed to the sword than to the pen.

PETKOFF. It's very good of you, Bluntschli: it is indeed, to let yourself be put upon in this way. Now are you q u i t e sure I can do nothing?

CATHERINE [*in a low warning tone*] You can stop interrupting, Paul.

PETKOFF [*starting and looking round at her*] Eh? Oh! Quite right, my love: quite right. [*He takes his newspaper up again, but presently lets it drop*]. Ah, you havnt been campaigning, Catherine: you dont know how pleasant it is for us to sit here, after a good lunch, with nothing to do but enjoy ourselves. Theres only one thing I want to make me thoroughly comfortable.

CATHERINE. What is that?

PETKOFF. My old coat. I'm not at home in this one: I feel as if I were on parade.

CATHERINE. My dear Paul, how absurd you are about that old coat! It must be hanging in the blue closet where you left it.

PETKOFF. My dear Catherine, I tell you Ive looked there. Am I to believe my own eyes or not? [*Catherine rises and crosses the room to press the button of the electric bell*]. What are you shewing off that bell for? [*She looks at him majestically, and silently resumes her chair and her needlework*]. My dear: if you think the obstinacy of your sex can make a coat out of two old dressing gowns of Raina's, your waterproof, and my mackintosh, youre mistaken. Thats exactly what the blue closet contains at present.

Nicola presents himself.

CATHERINE. Nicola: go to the blue closet and bring your master's old coat here: the braided one he wears in the house.

NICOLA. Yes, madam [*He goes out*].

PETKOFF. Catherine.

CATHERINE. Yes, Paul.

PETKOFF. I bet you any piece of jewellery you like to order from Sofia against a week's housekeeping money that the coat isnt there.

CATHERINE. Done, Paul!

PETKOFF [*excited by the prospect of a gamble*] Come: heres an opportunity for some sport. Wholl bet on it? Bluntschli: I'll give you six to one.

BLUNTSCHLI [*imperturbably*] It would be robbing you, major. Madam is sure to be right. [*Without looking up, he passes another batch of papers to Sergius*].

SERGIUS [*also excited*] Bravo, Switzerland! Major: I bet my best charger against an Arab mare for Raina that Nicola finds the coat in the blue closet.

PETKOFF [*eagerly*] Your best char—

CATHERINE [*hastily interrupting him*] Dont be foolish, Paul. An Arabian mare will cost you 50,000 levas.

RAINA [*suddenly coming out of her picturesque revery*] Really, mother, if you are going to take the jewellery, I dont see why you should grudge me my Arab.

Nicola comes back with the coat, and brings it to Petkoff, who can hardly believe his eyes.

CATHERINE. Where was it, Nicola?

NICOLA. Hanging in the blue closet, madam.

PETKOFF. Well, I am d—

CATHERINE [*stopping him*] Paul!

PETKOFP. I could have sworn it wasnt there. Age is beginning to tell on me. I'm getting hallucinations. [*To Nicola*] Here: help me to change. Excuse me, Bluntschli. [*He begins changing coats, Nicola acting as valet*]. Remember: I didnt take that bet of yours, Sergius. Youd better give Raina that Arab steed yourself, since youve roused her expectations. Eh, Raina? [*He looks round at her; but she is again rapt in the landscape. With a little gush of parental affection and pride, he points her out to them, and says*] S h e ' s dreaming, as usual. [*The change is now complete. Nicola goes out with the discarded coat*]. Ah, now I feel at home at last. [*He sits down and takes his newspaper with a grunt of relief*].

BLUNTSCHLI [*to Sergius, handing a paper*] Thats the last order.

PETKOFF [*jumping up*] What! Finished?

BLUNTSCHLI. Finished.

PETKOFF [*with childlike envy*] Havnt you anything for me to sign?

BLUNTSCHLI. Not necessary. His signature will do.

PETKOPF [*inflating his chest and thumping it*] Ah well, I think weve done a thundering good day's work. Can I do anything more?

BLUNTSCHLI. You had better both see the fellows that are to take these.[*Sergius rises*] Pack them off at once; and shew them that Ive marked on the orders the time they should hand them in by. Tell them that if they stop to drink or tell stories—if theyre five minutes late, theyll have the skin taken off their backs.

SERGIUS [*stiffening indignantly*] I'll say so. [*He strides to the door*]. And if one of them is man enough to spit in my face for insulting him, I'll buy his discharge and give him a pension. [*He goes out*].

BLUNTSCHLI [*confidentially*] Just see that he talks to them properly, major, will you?

PETKOFF [*officiously*] Quite right, Bluntschli, quite right. I'll see to it. [*He goes to the door importantly, but hesitates on the threshold*]. By the bye, Catherine, you may as well come too. Theyll be far more frightened of you than of me.

CATHERINE [*putting down her embroidery*] I daresay I had better. You would only splutter at them. [*She goes out, Petkoff holding the door for her and following her*].

RAINA. You look ever so much nicer than when we last met. [*He looks up, surprised*]. What have you done to yourself?

BLUNTSCHLI. Washed; brushed; good night's sleep and breakfast. Thats all.

RAINA. Did you get back safely that morning?

BLUNTSCHLI. Quite, thanks.

RAINA. Were they angry with you for running away from Sergius's charge?

BLUNTSCHLI [*grinning*] No: they were glad; because theyd all just run away themselves.

RAINA [*going to the table, and leaning over it towards him*] It must have made a lovely story for them: all that about me and my room.

BLUNTSCHLI. Capital story. But I only told it to one of them: a particular friend.

RAINA. On whose discretion you could absolutely rely?

BLUNTSCHLI. Absolutely.

RAINA. Hm! He told it all to my father and Sergius the day you exchanged the prisoners. [*She turns away and strolls carelessly across to the other side of the room*].

BLUNTSCHLI [*deeply concerned, and half incredulous*] No! You dont mean that, do you?

RAINA [*turning, with sudden earnestness*] I do indeed. But they dont know that it was in this house you took refuge. If Sergius knew, he would challenge you and kill you in a duel.

BLUNTSCHLI. Bless me! then dont tell him.

RAINA. Can you not realize what it is to me to deceive him? I want to be quite perfect with Sergius: no meannesss, no smallness, no deceit. My relation to him is the one really beautiful and noble part of my life. I hope you can understand that.

BLUNTSCHLI [*sceptically*] You mean that you wouldnt like him to find out that the story about the ice pudding was a—a—a—You know.

RAINA [*wincing*] Ah, dont talk of it in that flippant way. I lied: I know it. But I did it to save your life. He would have killed you. That was the second time I ever uttered a falsehood. [*Bluntschli rises quickly and looks doubtfully and somewhat severely at her*]. Do you remember the first time?

BLUNTSCHLI. I! No. Was I present?

RAINA. Yes; and I told the officer who was searching for you that you were not present.

BLUNTSCHLI. True. I should have remembered it.

RAINA [*greatly encouraged*] Ah, it is natural that you should forget it first. It cost you nothing: it cost m e a lie! A lie!

She sits down on the ottoman, looking straight before her with her hands clasped round her knee. Bluntschli, quite touched, goes to the ottoman with a particularly reassuring and considerate air, and sits down beside her.

BLUNTSCHLI. My dear young lady, dont let this worry you. Remember: I'm a soldier. Now what are the two things that happen to a soldier so often that he comes to think nothing of them? One is hearing people tell lies [*Raina recoils; Bluntschli runs on crisply*]: the other is getting his life saved in all sorts of ways by all sorts of people.

RAINA. Oh, I see now exactly what you think of me! Y o u were not surprised to hear me lie. To you it was something I probably did every day! every hour!! [*Rising majestically*] T h a t is how men think of women. [*She paces the room tragically*].

BLUNTSCHLI [*dubiously*] Theres reason in everything. You said youd told only two lies in your whole life. Dear young lady: isnt that rather a short allowance?

387

I'm quite a straighforward man myself; but it wouldnt last me a whole morning.

RAINA [*staring haughtily at him*] Do you know, sir, that you are insulting me?

BLUNTSCHLI. I cant help it. When you strike that noble attitude and speak in that thrilling voice, I admire you; but I find it impossible to believe a single word you say.

RAINA [*superbly*] Captain Bluntschli!

BLUNTSCHLI [*unmoved*] Yes?

RAINA [*standing over him, as if she could not believe her senses*] Do you mean what you said just now? Do you k n o w what you said just now?

BLUNTSCHLI. I do.

RAINA [*gasping*] I! I!!!! [*She points to herself incredulously, meaning "I, Raina Petkoff tell lies!" He meets her gaze unflinchingly. She suddenly sits down beside him, and adds, with a complete change of manner from the heroic to a babyish familiarity*] How did you find me out?

BLUNTSCHLI [*promptly*] Instinct, dear young lady. Instinct, and experience of the world.

RAINA [*wonderingly*] Do you know, you are the first man I ever met who did not take me seriously?

BLUNTSCHLI. You mean, dont you, that I am the first man that has ever taken you quite seriously?

RAINA. Yes: I suppose I d o mean that. [*Cosily, quite at her ease with him*] How strange it is to be talked to in such a way! You know, Ive always gone on like that. I mean the noble attitude and the thrilling voice. [*They laugh together*]. I did it when I was a tiny child to my nurse. S h e believed in it. I do it before my parents. T h e y believe in it. I do it before Sergius. H e believes in it.

BLUNTSCHLI. Yes: he's a little in that line himself, isnt he?

RAINA [*startled*] Oh! Do you think so?

BLUNTSCHLI. You know him better than I do.

RAINA. I wonder—I w o n d e r is he? If I thought t h a t —! [*Discouraged*] Ah, well: what does it matter? I suppose now youve found me out, you despise me.

BLUNTSCHLI [*warmly, rising*] No, my dear young lady, no, no, no a thousand times. It's part of your youth: part of your charm. I'm like all the rest of them: your infatuated admirer.

RAINA [*pleased*] Really?

BLUNTSCHLI [*slapping his breast smartly with his hand, German fashion*] Hand aufs Herz! Really and truly.

RAINA [*very happy*] But what did you think of me for giving you my portrait?

BLUNTSCHLI [*astonished*] Your portrait! You never gave me your portrait.

RAINA [*quickly*] Do you mean to say you never got it?

BLUNTSCHLI. No. [*He sits down beside her, with renewed interest, and says, with some complacency*] When did you send it to me?

RAINA [*indignantly*] I did not send it to you. [*She turns her head away, and adds, reluctantly*] It was in the pocket of that coat.

BLUNTSCHLI [*pursing his lips and rounding his eyes*] Oh-o-oh! I never found it. It must be there still.

RAINA [*springing up*] There still! for my father to find the first time he puts his hand in his pocket! Oh, how could you be so stupid?

BLUNTSCHLI [*rising also*] It doesnt matter: it's only a photograph: how can he tell who it was intended for? Tell him he put it there himself.

RAINA [*bitterly*] Yes: that is so clever! isnt it? [*Distractedly*] Oh! what shall I do?

BLUNTSCHLI. Ah, I see. You wrote something on it. That was rash.

RAINA [*vexed almost to tears*] Oh, to have done such a thing for y o u , who care no more—except to laugh at me—oh! Are you sure nobody has touched it?

BLUNTSCHLI. Well, I cant be quite sure. You see, I couldnt carry it about with me all the time: one cant take much luggage on active service.

RAINA. What did you do with it?

BLUNTSCHLI. When I got through to Pirot I had to put it in safe keeping somehow. I thought of the railway cloak room; but thats the surest place to get looted in modern warfare. So I pawned it.

RAINA. P a w n e d it!!!

BLUNTSCHLI. I know it doesnt sound nice; but it was much the safest plan. I redeemed it the day before yesterday. Heaven only knows whether the pawnbroker cleared out the pockets or not.

RAINA [*furious: throwing the words right into his face*] You have a low shopkeeping mind. You think of things that would never come into a gentleman's head.

BLUNTSCHLI [*phlegmatically*] Thats the Swiss national character, dear lady. [*He returns to the table*].

RAINA. Oh, I wish I had never met you. [*She flounces away, and sits at the window fuming*].

Louka comes in with a heap of letters and telegrams on her salver, and crosses, with her bold free gait, to the table. Her left sleeve is looped up to the shoulder with a brooch, shewing her naked arm, with a broad gilt bracelet covering the bruise.

LOUKA [*to Bluntschli*] For you. [*She empties the salver with a fling on to the table*]. The messenger is waiting. [*She is determined not to be civil to an enemy, even if she must bring him his letters*].

BLUNTSCHLI [*to Raina*] Will you excuse me: the last postal delivery that reached me was three weeks ago. These are the subsequent accumulations. Four telegrams: a week old . [*He opens one*]. Oho! Bad news!

RAINA [*rising and advancing a little remorsefully*] Bad news?

BLUNTSCHLI. My father's dead. [*He looks at the telegram with his lips pursed, musing on the unexpected change in his arrangements. Louka crosses herself hastily. She should be in sight, to make her next comment more natural.*].

RAINA. Oh, how very sad!

BLUNTSCHLI. Yes: I shall have to start for home in an hour. He has left a lot of big hotels behind him to be looked after. [*He takes up a fat letter in a long blue envelope*]. Here's a whacking letter from the family solicitor. [*He pulls out the enclosures and glances over them*]. Great Heavens! Seventy! Two hundred! [*In a crescendo of dismay*] Four hundred! Four t h o u s a n d ! ! Nine thousand six hundred!!! What on earth am I to do with them all?

RAINA [*timidly*] Nine thousand hotels?

BLUNTSCHLI. Hotels! nonsense. If you only knew! Oh, it's too ridiculous! Excuse me: I must give my fellow orders about starting. [*He leaves the room hastily, with the documents in his hand*].

LOUKA [*knowing instinctively that she can annoy Raina by disparaging Bluntschli*] He has not much heart, that Swiss. He has not a word of grief for his poor father.

RAINA [*bitterly*] Grief! A man who has been doing nothing but killing people for years! What does he care? What does any soldier care? [*She goes to the door, restraining her tears with difficulty*].

LOUKA. Major Saranoff has been fighting too; and he has plenty of heart left. [*Raina, at the door, draws herself up haughtily and goes out*]. Aha! I thought you wouldnt get much feeling out of y o u r soldier. [*She is following Raina when Nicola enters with an armful of logs for the stove.*].

NICOLA [*grinning amorously at her*] Ive been trying all the afternoon to get a minute alone with you, my girl. [*His countenance changes as he notices her arm*]. Why, what fashion is that of wearing your sleeve, child?

LOUKA [*proudly*] My own fashion.

NICOLA. Indeed! If the mistress catches you, she'll talk to you. [*He puts the logs down, and seats himself comfortably on the ottoman*].

LOUKA. Is that any reason why y o u should take it on yourself to talk to me?

NICOLA. Come! dont be so contrairy with me. Ive some good news for you. [*She sits down beside him. He takes out some paper money. Louka, with an eager gleam in her eyes, tries to snatch it; but he shifts it quickly to his left hand, out of her reach*]. See! a twenty leva bill! Sergius gave me that, out of pure swagger. A fool and his money are soon parted. Theres ten levas more. The Swiss gave me that for backing up the mistress's and Raina's lies about him. H e ' s no fool, he isnt. The twenty will go to our savings; and you shall have the ten to spend if youll only talk to me so as to remind me I'm a human being. I get tired of being a servant occasionally.

LOUKA. Yes: sell your manhood for 30 levas, and buy me for 10! Keep your money. You were born to be a servant. I was not.

NICOLA [*daunted by her implacable disdain*] You have a great ambition in you, Louka. Remember: if any luck comes to you, it was I that made a woman of you.

LOUKA. You!

NICOLA. Yes, me. Who taught you to trim your nails, and keep your hands clean, and be dainty about yourself, like a fine Russian lady? M e : do you hear that? m e ! [*She tosses her head defiantly; and he turns away, adding, more coolly*] Ive often thought that if Raina were out of the way, and you just a little less of a fool and Sergius just a little more of one, you might come to be one of my grandest customers, instead of only being my wife and costing me money.

LOUKA. I believe you would rather be my servant than my husband. You would make more out of me. Oh, I know that soul of yours.

NICOLA [*going closer to her for greater emphasis*] Never you mind my soul; but just listen to my advice. If you want to be a lady, your present behavior to me wont do at all, unless when we're alone. It's too sharp and impudent; and impudence is a sort of familiarity: it shews affection for me. And dont you try being high and mighty with me, either. Youre like all country girls: you think its genteel to treat a servant the way I treat a stableboy. Thats only your ignorance; and dont you forget it. And dont be so ready to defy everybody. Act as if you expected to have your own way, not as if you expected to be ordered about. The way to get on as a lady is the same as the way to get on as a servant: youve got to know your place: thats the secret of it. And you may depend on me to know my place if you get promoted. Think over it, my girl. I'll stand by you: one servant should always stand by another.

LOUKA [*rising impatiently*] Oh, I must behave in my own way. You take all the courage out of me with your cold-blooded wisdom. Go and put those logs on the fire: thats the sort of thing y o u understand.

Before Nicola can retort, Sergius comes in. He checks himself a moment on seeing Louka; then goes to the stove. Nicola goes out sedately.

Louka, without looking at Sergius, pretends to arrange the papers on the table. He crosses slowly to her, and studies the arrangement of her sleeve reflectively.

SERGIUS. Let me see: is there a mark there? [*He turns up the bracelet and sees the bruise made by his grasp. She stands motionless, not looking at him: fascinated, but on her guard*]. Ffff! Does it hurt?

LOUKA. Yes.

SERGIUS. Shall I cure it?

LOUKA [*instantly withdrawing herself proudly, but still not looking at him*] No. You cannot cure it now.

SERGIUS [*masterfully*] Quite sure? [*He makes a movement as if to take her in his arms*].

LOUKA. Dont trifle with me, please. An officer should not trifle with a servant.

SERGIUS [*indicating the bruise with a merciless stroke of his forefinger*] That was no trifle, Louka.

LOUKA [*flinching; then looking at him for the first time*] Are you sorry?

SERGIUS [*with measured emphasis, folding his arms*] I am n e v e r sorry.

LOUKA [*wistfully*] I wish I could believe a man could be as unlike a woman as that. I wonder are you really a brave man?

SERGIUS [*unaffectedly, relaxing his attitude*] Yes: I am a brave man. My heart jumped like a woman's at the first shot; but in the charge I found that I was brave. Yes: that at least is real about me.

LOUKA. You dont know what true courage is.

SERGIUS [*ironically*] Indeed! I am willing to be instructed. [*He sits on the ottoman, sprawling magnificently*].

LOUKA. Look at me! how much am I allowed to have my own will? I have to get your room ready for you: to sweep and dust, to fetch and carry. But [*with subdued passion*] if I were Empress of Russia, above everyone in the world, then!! Ah then, though according to you I could shew no courage at all, you should see, you should see.

SERGIUS. What would you do, most noble Empress?

LOUKA. I would marry the man I loved, which no other queen in Europe has the courage to do. Would you dare as much if you loved me? No: if you felt the beginnings of love for me you would not let it grow. You would not dare: you would marry a rich man's daughter because you would be afraid of what other people would say of you.

SERGIUS [*bounding up*] You lie: it is not so, by all the stars! If I loved you, and I were the Czar himself, I would set you on the throne by my side. You know that I love another woman, a woman as high above you as heaven is above earth. And you are jealous of her.

LOUKA. I have no reason to be. She will never marry you now. The man I told you of has come back. She will marry the Swiss.

SERGIUS [*recoiling*] The Swiss!

LOUKA. A man worth ten of you. Then you can come to me; and I will refuse you. You are not good enough for me. [*She turns to the door*].

SERGIUS [*springing after her and catching her fiercely in his arms*] I will kill the

Swiss; and afterwards I will do as I please with you.

LOUKA [*in his arms, passive and steadfast*] The Swiss will kill you, perhaps. He has beaten you in love. He may beat you in war.

SERGIUS [*tormentedly*] Do you think I believe that she— s h e ! whose worst thoughts are higher than your best ones, is capable of trifling with another man behind my back?

LOUKA. Do you think s h e would believe the Swiss if he told her now that I am in your arms?

SERGIUS [*releasing her in despair*] Damnation! Oh, damnation! Mockery! mockery everywhere! everything I think is mocked by everything I do. [*He strikes himself frantically on the breast*]. Coward! liar! fool! Shall I kill myself like a man, or live and pretend to laugh at myself? [*She again turns to go*]. Louka! [*She stops near the door*]. Remember: you belong to me.

LOUKA [*turning*] What does that mean? An insult?

SERGIUS [*commandingly*] It means that you love me, and that I have had you here in my arms, and will perhaps have you there again. Whether that is an insult I neither know nor care: take it as you please. But [*vehemently*] I w i l l not be a coward and a trifler. If I choose to love you, I dare marry you, in spite of all Bulgaria. If these hands ever touch you again, they shall touch my affianced bride.

LOUKA. We shall see whether you dare keep your word. And take care. I will not wait long.

SERGIUS [*again folding his arms and standing motionless in the middle of the room*] Yes: we shall see. And you shall wait my pleasure.

   Bluntschli, much preoccupied, with his papers still in his hand, enters, leaving the door open for Louka to go out. He goes across to the table absently, sitting and putting down his papers. Sergius, without altering his resolute attitude, watches him steadily. Louka goes out, leaving the door open.

SERGIUS [*gravely, without moving*] Captain Bluntschli.

BLUNTSCHLI. Eh?

SERGIUS. You have deceived me. You are my rival. I brook no rivals. At six o'clock I shall be in the drilling-ground on the Klissoura road, alone, on horseback, with my sabre. Do you understand?

BLUNTSCHLI [*staring, but sitting quite at his ease*] Oh, thank you: thats a cavalry man's proposal. I'm in the artillery; and I have the choice of weapons. If I go, I shall take a machine gun. And there shall be no mistake about the cartridges this time.

SERGIUS [*flushing, but with deadly coldness*] Take care, sir. It is not our custom in Bulgaria to allow invitations of that kind to be trifled with.

BLUNTSCHLI [*warmly*] Pooh! dont talk to me about Bulgaria. You dont know what fighting is. But have it your own way. Bring your sabre along. I'll meet you.

SERGIUS [*fiercely delighted to find his opponent a man of spirit*] Well said, Switzer. Shall I lend you my best horse?

BLUNTSCHLI. No: damn your horse! thank you all the same, my dear fellow. [*Raina comes in, and hears the next sentence*]. I shall fight you on foot. Horseback's too dangerous: I dont want to kill you if I can help it.

RAINA [*hurrying forward anxiously*] I have heard what Captain Bluntschli said, Sergius. You are going to fight. Why? [*Sergius turns away in silence, and goes to the stove, where he stands watching her as she continues, to Bluntschli*] What about?

BLUNTSCHLI. I dont know: he hasnt told me. Better not interfere, dear young lady. No harm will be done: Ive often acted as sword instructor. He wont be able to touch me; and I'll not hurt him. It will save explanations. In an hour I shall be off home; and youll never see me or hear of me again. You and he will then make it up and live happily ever after.

RAINA [*turning away deeply hurt, almost with a sob in her voice*] I never said I wanted to see you again.

SERGIUS [*striding forward*] Ha! That is a confession.

RAINA [*haughtily*] What do you mean?

SERGIUS. You love that man!

RAINA [*scandalized*] Sergius!

SERGIUS. You allow him to make love to you behind my back, just as you treat me as your affianced husband behind his. Bluntschli: you knew our relations; and you deceived me. It is for that that I call you to account, not for having received favors *I* never enjoyed.

BLUNTSCHLI [*jumping up indignantly*] Stuff! Rubbish! I have received no favors. Why, the young lady doesnt even know whether I'm married or not.

RAINA [*forgetting herself*] Oh! [*Collapsing on the ottoman*] A r e you?

SERGIUS. You see the young lady's concern, Captain Bluntschli. Denial is useless. You have enjoyed the privilege of being received in her own room, late at night—

BLUNTSCHLI [*interrupting him pepperily*] Yes, you blockhead! she received me with a pistol at her head. Your cavalry were at my heels. I'd have blown out her brains if she'd uttered a cry.

SERGIUS [*taken aback*] Bluntschli! Raina: is this true?

RAINA [*rising in wrathful majesty*] Oh, how dare you, how dare you?

BLUNTSCHLI. Apologize, man: apologize. [*He resumes his seat at the table*].

SERGIUS [*with the old measured emphasis, folding his arms*] I n e v e r apologize!

RAINA [*passionately*] This is the doing of that friend of yours, Captain Bluntschli. It is he who is spreading this horrible story about me. [*She walks about excitedly*].

BLUNTSCHLI. No: he's dead. Burnt alive.

RAINA [*stopping, shocked*] Burnt alive!

BLUNTSCHLI. Shot in the hip in a woodyard. Couldnt drag himself out. Your fellows' shells set the timber on fire and burnt him, with half a dozen other poor devils in the same predicament.

RAINA. How horrible!

SERGIUS. And how ridiculous! Oh, war! war! the dream of patriots and heroes! A fraud, Bluntschli. A hollow sham, like love.

RAINA [*outraged*] Like love! You say that before me!

BLUNTSCHLI. Come, Saranoff: that matter is explained.

SERGIUS. A hollow sham, I say. Would you have come back here if nothing had passed between you except at the muzzle of your pistol? [*Enigmatically*] Raina is mistaken about your friend who was burnt. He was not my informant.

RAINA. Who then? [*Suddenly guessing the truth*] Ah, Louka! my maid! my servant! You were with her this morning all that time after—after—Oh, what sort of god is this I have been worshipping! [*He meets her gaze with sardonic enjoyment of her disenchantment. Angered all the more, she goes closer to him, and says, in a lower, intenser tone*] Do you know that I looked out of the window as I went upstairs, to have another sight of my hero; and I saw something I did not understand then. I know now that you were making love to her.

SERGIUS [*with grim humor*] You saw that?

RAINA. Only too well. [*She turns away, and throws herself on the divan under the centre window, quite overcome*].

SERGIUS [*cynically*] Raina: our romance is shattered. Life's a farce.

BLUNTSCHLI [*to Raina, whimsically*] You see: h e ' s found himself out now.

SERGIUS [*going to him*] Bluntschli: I have allowed you to call me a blockhead. You may now call me a coward as well. I refuse to fight you. Do you know why?

BLUNTSCHLI. No; but it doesnt matter. I didnt ask the reason when you cried on; and I dont ask the reason now that you cry off. I'm a professional soldier: I fight when I have to, and am very glad to get out of it when I havnt to. Youre only an amateur: you think fighting's an amusement.

SERGIUS [*sitting down at the table, nose to nose with him*] You shall hear the reason all the same, my professional. The reason is that it takes two men—real men—men of heart, blood and honor—to make a genuine combat. I could no more fight with you than I could make love to an ugly woman. Youve no magnetism: youre not a man: youre a machine.

BLUNTSCHLI [*apologetically*] Quite true, quite true. I always w a s that sort of chap. I'm very sorry. But now that youve found that life i s n t a farce, but something quite sensible and serious, what further obstacle is there to your happiness?

RAINA [*rising*] You are very solicitous about my happiness and his. Do you forget his new love—Louka? It is not you that he must fight now, but his rival, Nicola.

SERGIUS Rival!! [*bounding half across the room*].

RAINA. Dont you know that theyre engaged?

SERGIUS. Nicola! Nicola!!

RAINA [*sarcastically*] A shocking sacrifice, isnt it? Such beauty! such intellect! such modesty! wasted on a middleaged servant man. Really, Sergius, you cannot stand by and allow such a thing. It would be unworthy of your chivalry.

SERGIUS [*losing all self-control*] Viper! Viper! [*He rushes to and fro, raging*].

BLUNTSCHLI. Look here, Saranoff: youre getting the worst of this.

RAINA [*getting angrier*] Do you realize what he has done, Captain Bluntschli? He has set this girl as a spy on us; and her reward is that he makes love to her.

SERGIUS. False! Monstrous!

RAINA. Monstrous! [*Confronting him*] Do you deny that she told you about Captain Bluntschli being in my room?

SERGIUS. No; but—

RAINA [*interrupting*] Do you deny that you were making love to her when she told you?

SERGIUS. No; but I tell you—

RAINA [*cutting him short contemptuously*] It is unnecessary to tell us anything more. That is quite enough for us. [*She turns away from him and sweeps majestically back to the window*].

BLUNTSCHLI [*quietly, as Sergius, in an agony of mortification, sinks on the ottoman, clutching his averted head between his fists*] I told you you were getting the worst of it, Saranoff.

SERGIUS. Tiger cat!

RAINA [*running excitedly to Bluntschli*] You hear this man calling me names, Captian Bluntschli?

BLUNTSCHLI. What else can he do, dear lady? He must defend himself somehow. Come [*very persuasively*]: dont quarrel. What good does it do?

Raina, with a gasp, sits down on the ottoman, and after a vain effort to look vexedly at Bluntschli, falls a victim to her sense of humor, and actually leans back babyishly against the writhing shoulder of Sergius.

SERGIUS. Engaged to Nicola! Ha! ha! Ah well, Bluntschli, you are right to take this huge imposture of a world coolly.

RAINA [*quaintly to Bluntschli, with an intuitive guess at his state of mind*] I daresay you think us a couple of grown-up babies, dont you?

SERGIUS [*grinning savagely*] He does: he does. Swiss civilization nursetending Bulgarian barbarism, eh?

BLUNTSCHLI [*blushing*] Not at all, I assure you. I'm only very glad to get you two quieted. There! there! let's be pleasant and talk it over in a friendly way. Where is this other young lady?

RAINA. Listening at the door, probably.

SERGIUS [*shivering as if a bullet had struck him, and speaking with quiet but deep indignation*] I will prove that that, at least, is a calumny. [*He goes with dignity to the door and opens it. A yell of fury bursts from him as he looks out. He darts into the passage, and returns dragging in Louka, whom he flings violently against the table, exclaiming*] Judge her, Bluntschli. Y o u , the cool impartial man: judge the eavesdropper.

Louka stands her ground, proud and silent.

BLUNTSCHLI [*shaking his head*] I mustnt judge her. I once listened myself outside a tent when there was a mutiny brewing. It's all a question of the degree of provocation. My life was at stake.

LOUKA. My love was at stake. I am not ashamed.

RAINA [*contemptuously*] Your love! Your curiosity, you mean.

LOUKA [*facing her and her contempt with interest*] My love, stronger than anything y o u can feel, ever for your chocolate cream soldier.

SERGIUS [*with quick suspicion, to Louka*] What does that mean?

LOUKA [*fiercely*] It means—

SERGIUS [*interrupting her slightingly*] Oh, I remember: the ice pudding. paltry taunt, girl!

Major Petkoff enters, in his shirtsleeves.

PETKOFF. Excuse my shirtsleeves, gentlemen. Raina: somebody has been wearing that coat of mine: I'll swear it. Somebody with a differently shaped back. It's all burst open at the sleeve. Your mother is mending it. I wish she'd make haste: I shall catch cold. [*He looks more attentively at them*]. Is anything the matter?

RAINA. No. [*She sits down at the stove, with a tranquil air*].

SERGIUS. Oh no. [*He sits down at the end of the table, as at first*].

BLUNTSCHLI [*who is already seated*] Nothing. Nothing.

PETKOFF [*sitting down on the ottoman in his old place*] Thats all right. [*He notices Louka*]. Anything the matter, Louka?

LOUKA. No, sir.

PETKOFF [*genially*] T h a t s all right. [*He sneezes*] Go and ask your mistress for my coat, like a good girl, will you?

Nicola enters with the coat. Louka makes a pretence of having business in the room by taking the little table with the hookah away to the wall near the windows. RAINA [*rising quickly as she sees the coat on Nicola's arm*] Here it is, papa. Give it to me, Nicola; and do you put some more wood on the fire. [*She takes the coat, and brings it to the Major, who stands up to put it on. Nicola attends to the fire*]. PETKOFF [*to Raina, teasing her affectionately*] Aha! Going to be very good to poor old papa just for one day after his return from the wars, eh?

RAINA [*with solemn reproach*] Ah, how can you say that to me, father?

PETKOFF. Well, well, only a joke, little one. Come: give me a kiss. [*She kisses him*]. Now give me the coat.

RAINA. No: I am going to put it on for you. Turn your back. [*He turns his back and feels behind him with his arms for the sleeves. She dexterously takes the photograph from the pocket and throws it on the table before Bluntschli, who covers it with a sheet of paper under the very nose of Sergius, who looks on amazed, with his suspicions roused in the highest degree. She then helps Petkoff on with his coat*]. There, dear! N o w are you comfortable?

PETKOFF. Quite, little love. Thanks. [*He sits down; and Raina returns to her seat near the stove*]. Oh, by the bye, Ive found something funny. Whats the meaning of this? [*He puts his hand into the picked pocket*]. Eh? Hallo! [*He tries the other pocket*]. Well, I could have sworn—! [*Much puzzled, he tries the breast pocket*]. I wonder—[*trying the original pocket*]. Where can it—? [*He rises, exclaiming*] Your mother's taken it!.

RAINA [*very red*] Taken what?

PETKOFF. Your photograph, with the inscirption: "Raina, to her Chocolate Cream Soldier: a Souvenir." Now you know theres something more in this than meets the eye; and I'm going to find it out. [*Shouting*] Nicola!

NICOLA [*coming to him*] Sir!

PETKOFF. Did you spoil any pastry of Miss Raina's this morning?

NICOLA. You heard Miss Raina say that I did, sir.

PETKOFF. I know that, you idiot. Was it true?

NICOLA. I am sure Miss Raina is incapable of saying anything that is not true, sir.

PETKOFF. Are you? Then I'm not. [*Turning to the others*] Come: do you think I dont see it all? [*He goes to Sergius, and slaps him on the shoulder*]. Sergius: y o u r e the chocolate cream soldier, arnt you?

SERGIUS [*starting up*] I! A chocolate cream soldier! Certainly not.

PETKOFF. Not! [*He looks at them. They are all very serious and very conscious*]. Do you mean to tell me that Raina sends things like that to other men?

SERGIUS [*enigmatically*] The world is not such an innocent place as we used to think, Petkoff.

BLUNTSCHLI [*rising*] It's all right, Major. I'm the chocolate cream soldier. [*Petkoff and Sergius are equally astonished*]. The gracious young lady saved my life by giving me chocolate creams when I was starving: shall I ever forget their flavor! My late friend Stolz told you the story at Pirot. I was the fugitive.

PETKOFF. Y o u ! [*He gasps*]. Sergius: do you remember how those two women went on this morning when we mentioned it? [*Sergius smiles cynically. Petkoff confronts Raina severely*]. Y o u r e a nice young woman, arnt you?

RAINA [*bitterly*] Major Saranoff has changed his mind. And when I wrote that on the photograph, I did not know that Captain Bluntschli was married.

BLUNTSCHLI [*startled into vehement protest*] I'm n o t married.

RAINA [*with deep reproach*] You said you were.

BLUNTSCHLI. I did not. I positively did not. I never was married in my life.

PETKOFF [*exasperated*] Raina: will you kindly inform me, if I am not asking too much, which of these gentlemen you are engaged to?

RAINA. To neither of them. T h i s young lady [*introducing Louka, who faces them all proudly*] is the object of Major Saranoff's affections at present.

PETKOFF. Louka! Are you mad, Sergius? Why, this girl's engaged to Nicola.

NICOLA. I beg your pardon, sir. There is a mistake. Louka is not engaged to me.

PETKOFF. Not engaged to you, you scoundrel! Why, you had twenty-five levas from me on the day of your betrothal; and she had that gilt bracelet from Miss Raina.

NICOLA [*with cool unction*] We gave it out so, sir. But it was only to give Louka protection. She had a soul above her station; and I have been no more than her confidential servant. I intend, as you know, sir, to set up a shop later on in Sofia; and I look forward to her custom and recommendation should she marry into the nobility. [*He goes out with impressive discretion, leaving them all staring after him*].

PETKOFF [*breaking the silence*] Well, I a m —hm!

SERGIUS. This is either the finest heroism or the most crawling baseness. Which is it, Bluntschli?

BLUNTSCHILI. Never mind whether it's heroism or baseness. Nicola's the ablest man Ive met in Bulgaria. I'll make him manager of a hotel if he can speak French and German.

LOUKA [*suddenly breaking out at Sergius*] I have been insulted by everyone here. Y o u set them the example. You owe me an apology.

Sergius, like a repeating clock of which the spring has been touched, immediately begins to fold his arms.

BLUNTSCHLI [*before he can speak*] It's no use. He never apologizes.

LOUKA. Not to you, his equal and his enemy. To me, his poor servant, he will not refuse to apologize.

SERGIUS [*approvingly*] You are right. [*He bends his knee in his grandest manner*] Forgive me.

LOUKA [*timidly giving him her hand, which he kisses*] That touch makes me your affianced wife.

SERGIUS [*springing up*] Ah! I forgot that.

LOUKA [*coldly*] You can withdraw if you like.

SERGIUS. Withdraw! Never! You belong to me. [*He puts his arm about her*].

Catherine comes in and finds Louka in Sergius's arms, with all the rest gazing at them in bewildered astonishment.

CATHERINE. What does this mean?

Sergius releases Louka.

PETKOFF. Well, my dear, it appears that Sergius is going to marry Louka instead of Raina. [*She is about to break out indignantly at him: he stops her by exclaiming testily*] Dont blame m e . I v e nothing to do with it. [*He retreats to the stove*].

CATHERINE. Marry Louka! Sergius: you are bound by your word to us!

SERGIUS [*folding his arms*] Nothing binds me.

BLUNTSCHLI [*much pleased by this piece of common sense*] Saranoff: your hand. My congratulations. These heroics of yours have their practical side after all. [*To

Louka] Gracious young lady: the best wishes of a good Republican! [*He kisses her hand, to Raina's great disgust, and returns to his seat*].

CATHERINE. Louka: you have been telling stories.

LOUKA. I have done Raina no harm.

CATHERINE [*haughtily*] Raina!

Raina, equally indignant, almost snorts at the liberty.

LOUKA. I have a right to call her Raina: she calls me Louka. I told Major Saranoff she would never marry him if the Swiss gentleman came back.

BLUNTSCHLI. What nonsense! I assure you, my dear Major, my dear Madam, the gracious young lady simply saved my life, nothing else. She never cared two straws for me. Why, bless my heart and soul, look at the young lady and look at me. She, rich, young, beautiful, with her imagination full of fairy princes and noble natures and cavalry charges and goodness knows what! And I, a commonplace Swiss soldier who hardly knows what a decent life is after fifteen years of barracks and battles: a vagabond, a man who has spoiled all his chances in life through an incurably romantic disposition, a man—

SERGIUS [*starting as if a needle had pricked him and interrupting Bluntschli in incredulous amazement*] Excuse me, Bluntschli: w h a t did you say had spoiled your chances in life?

BLUNTSCHLI [*promptly*] An incurably romantic disposition. I ran away from home twice when I was a boy. I went into the army instead of into my father's business. I climbed the balcony of this house when a man of sense would have dived into the nearest cellar. I came sneaking back here to have another look at the young lady when any other man of my age would have sent the coat back—

PETKOFF. My coat!

BLUNTSCHLI.—yes: thats the coat I mean—would have sent it back and gone quietly home. Do you suppose I am the sort of fellow a young girl falls in love with? Why, look at our ages! I'm thirty-four: I dont suppose the young lady is much over seventeen. [*This estimate produces a marked sensation, all the rest turning and staring at one another. He proceeds innocently*] All that adventure which was life or death to me, was only a schoolgirl's game to her—chocolate creams and hide and seek. Heres the proof! [*He takes the photograph from the table*]. Now, I ask you, would a woman who took the affair seriously have sent me this and written on it "Raina, to her Chocolate Cream Soldier: a Souvenir"? [*He exhibits the photograph triumphantly, as if it settled the matter beyond all possibility of refutation*].

PETKOFF. Thats what I was looking for. How the deuce did it get there? [*He comes from the stove to look at it, and sits down on the ottoman*].

BLUNTSCHLI [*to Raina, complacently*] I have put everything right, I hope, gracious young lady.

RAINA [*going to the table to face him*] I quite agree with your account of yourself. You are a romantic idiot. [*Bluntschli is unspeakably taken aback*]. Next time, I hope you will know the difference between a schoolgirl of seventeen and a woman of twenty-three.

BLUNTSCHLI [*stupefied*] Twenty-three!

Raina snaps the photograph contemptuously from his hand; tears it up; throws the pieces in his face; and sweeps back to her former place.

SERGIUS [*with grim enjoyment of his rival's discomfiture*] Bluntschli: my one last belief is gone. Your sagacity is a fraud, like everything else. You have less sense than even I!

BLUNTSCHLI [*overwhelmed*] Twenty-three! Twenty-three!! [*He considers*]. Hm! [*Swiftly making up his mind and coming to his host*] In that case, Major Petkoff, I beg to propose formally to become a suitor for your daughter's hand, in place of Major Saranoff retired.

RAINA. You dare!

BLUNTSCHLI. If you were twenty-three when you said those things to me this afternoon, I shall take them seriously.

CATHERINE [*loftily polite*] I doubt, sir, whether you quite realize either my daughter's position or that of Major Sergius Saranoff, whose place you propose to take. The Petkoffs and the Saranoffs are known as the richest and most important families in the country. Our position is almost historical: we can go back for twenty years.

PETKOFF. Oh never mind that, Catherine. [*To Bluntschli*] We should be most happy, Bluntschli, if it were only a question of your position; but hang it, you know, Raina is accustomed to a very comfortable establishment. Sergius keeps twenty horses.

BLUNTSCHLI. But who wants twenty horses? We're not going to keep a circus.

CATHERINE [*severely*] My daughter, sir, is accustomed to a first-rate stable.

RAINA. Hush, mother: youre making me ridiculous.

BLUNTSCHLI. Oh well, if it comes to a question of an establishment, here goes! [*He darts impetuously to the table; seizes the papers in the blue envelope; and turns to Sergius*]. How many horses did you say?

SERGIUS. Twenty, noble Switzer.

BLUNTSCHLI. I have two hundred horses. [*They are amazed. Petkoff faints, so to speak*]. How many carriages?

SERGIUS. Three.

BLUNTSCHLI. I have seventy. [*Catherine faints, so to speak*]. Twenty-four of them will hold twelve inside, besides two on the box, without counting the driver and conductor. How many tablecloths have you?

SERGIUS. How the deuce do I know?

BLUNTSCHLI. Have you four thousand?

SERGIUS. No.

BLUNTSCHLI. I have. [*Louka faints, so to speak*]. I have nine thousand six hundred pairs of sheets and blankets, with two thousand four hundred eider-down quilts. I have ten thousand knives and forks, and the same quantity of dessert spoons. I have three hundred servants. I have six palatial establishments, besides two livery stables, a tea gardens, and a private house. I have four medals for distinguished services; I have the rank of an officer and the standing of a gentleman; and I have three native languages. [*Sergius faints, so to speak*]. Shew me any man in Bulgaria that can offer as much!

PETKOFF [*with childish awe*] Are you Emperor of Switzerland?

BLUNTSCHLI. My rank is the highest known in Switzerland: I am a free citizen.

CATHERINE. Then, Captain Bluntschli, since you are my daughter's choice, I shall not stand in the way. [*Petkoff is about to speak*]. That is Major Petkoff's feeling also.

PETKOFF. Oh, I shall be only too glad. Two hundred horses! Whew!

SERGIUS. What says the lady?

RAINA [*pretending to sulk*] The lady says that he can keep his tablecloths and his omnibuses. I am not here to be sold to the highest bidder. [*She turns her back on him*].

BLUNTSCHLI. I wont take that answer. I appealed to you as a fugitive, a beggar, and a starving man. You accepted me. You gave me your hand to kiss, your bed to sleep in, and your roof to shelter me.

RAINA. I did not give them to the Emperor of Switzerland.

BLUNTSCHLI. Thats just what I say. [*He catches her by the shoulders and turns her face-to-face with him*]. Now tell us whom you did give them to.

RAINA [*succumbing with a shy smile*] To my chocolate cream soldier.

BLUNTSCHLI [*with a boyish laugh of delight*] Thatll do. Thank you. [*He looks at his watch and suddenly becomes businesslike*]. Time's up, Major. Youve managed those regiments so well that youre sure to be asked to get rid of some of the infantry of the Timok division. Send them home by way of Lom Palanka. Saranoff: dont get married until I come back: I shall be here punctually at five in the evening on Tuesday fortnight. Gracious ladies [*his heels click*] good evening. [*He makes them a military bow, and goes*].

SERGIUS. What a man! Is he a man!

THE END

Cæsar and Cleopatra

An October night on the Syrian border of Egypt towards the end of the XXXIII Dynasty, in the year 706 by Roman computation, afterwards reckoned by Christian computation as 48 B.C. A great radiance of silver fire, the dawn of a moonlit night, is rising in the east. The stars and the cloudless sky are our own contemporaries, nineteen and a half centuries younger than we know them; but you would not guess that from their appearance. Below them are two notable drawbacks of civilization: a palace, and soldiers. The palace, an old, low, Syrian building of whitened mud, is not so ugly as Buckingham Palace; and the officers in the courtyard are more highly civilized than modern English officers. They are in two groups: one intent on the gambling of their captain Belzanor, a warrior of fifty, who, with his spear on the ground beside his knee, is stooping to throw dice with a sly-looking young Persian recruit; the other gathered about a guardsman who has just finished telling a naughty story (still current in English barracks) at which they are laughing uproariously. They are about a dozen in number, all highly aristocratic young Egyptian guardsmen, handsomely equipped with weapons and armor, very unEnglish in point of not being ashamed of and uncomfortable in their professional dress; on the contrary, rather ostentatiously and arrogantly warlike, as valuing themselves on their military caste.

Belzanor is a typical veteran, tough and wilful; prompt, capable and crafty where brute force will serve; helpless and boyish when it will not: an active sergeant, an incompetent general, a deplorable dictator. Would, if influentially connected, be employed in the two last capacities by a modern European State on the strength of his success in the first. Is rather to be pitied just now in view of the fact that Julius Cæsar is invading his country. Not knowing this, is intent on his game with the Persian, whom, as a foreigner, he considers quite capable of cheating him.

His subalterns are mostly handsome young fellows whose interest in the game and the story symbolize with tolerable completeness the main interests in life of which they are conscious. Their spears are leaning against the walls, or lying on the ground ready to their hands. The corner of the courtyard forms a triangle of which one side is the front of the palace, with a doorway, the other a wall with a gateway. The storytellers are on the palace side: the gamblers, on the gateway side. Close to the gateway, against the wall, is a stone block high enough to enable a Nubian sentinel, standing on it, to look over the wall. The yard is lighted by a torch stuck in the wall. As the laughter from the group round the storyteller dies away, the kneeling Persian, winning the throw, snatches up the stake from the ground.

BELZANOR. By Apis, Persian, thy gods are good to thee.

PERSIAN. Try yet again, O captain. Double or quits!

BELZANOR. No more. I am not in the vein.

THE SENTINAL [*poising his javelin as he peers over the wall*] Stand. Who goes there?

They all start, listening. A strange voice replies from without.

VOICE. The bearer of evil tidings.

BELZANOR [*calling to the sentry*] Pass him.

The sentinel grounds his javelin. Belzanor pockets the dice and picks up his spear. The guardsmen seize their spears and gather about the gate, leaving a way through for the new comer.

The owner of the voice, a fairhaired dandy, dressed in a different fashion from that affected by the guardsmen, but no less extravagently, comes through the gateway laughing. He is somewhat battlestained; and his left forearm, bandaged, comes through a torn sleeve. In his right hand he carries a Roman sword in its sheath. He swaggers down the courtyard, the Persian on his right, Belzanor on his left, and the guardsmen crowding down behind him.

BELZANOR. Who are thou that laughest in the House of Cleopatra the Queen, and in the teeth of Belzanor, the captain of her guard?

THE NEW COMER. I am Bel Affris, descended from the gods.

BELZANOR [*ceremoniously*] Hail, cousin!

ALL [*except the Persian*] Hail, cousin!

PERSIAN. All the Queen's guards are descended from the gods, save myself. I am Persian, and descended from many kings.

BEL AFFRIS [*to the guardsmen*] Hail, cousins! [*To the Persian, condescendingly*] Hail, mortal!

BELZANOR. You have been in battle, Bel Affris; and you are a soldier among soldiers. You will not let the Queen's women have the first of your tidings.

BEL AFFRIS. I have no tidings, except that we shall have our throats cut presently, women, soldiers, and all.

PERSIAN [*to Belzanor*] I told you so.

BELZANOR. Tell us what befell.

THE GUARDSMEN [*gathering eagerly round Bel Affris*] Ay: the tale of the battle.

BEL AFFRIS. Know then, that I am in the guard of the temple of Ra in Memphis. We went to Alexandria to inquire of King Ptolemy how we of Egypt should deal with the Roman Pompey, newly come to our shores after his defeat by Cæsar at Pharsalia.

BELZANOR. Cæsar defeated Pompey? Does Roman, then, fight Roman?

PERSIAN. Even as Egyptian fights Egyptian, and brother makes war on sister, here in your country. [*To Bel Affris*] What did you learn from the Queen's brother, Ptolemy, the Pretender?

BEL AFFRIS. We learnt that Cæsar is coming also in hot pursuit of his foe, and that Ptolemy has slain Pompey, whose severed head he holds in readiness to present to the conqueror. [*Sensation among the guardsmen*]. Nay, more: we found that Cæsar is already come; for we had not made half a day's journey on our way back when we came upon a city rabble flying from his legions.

BELZANOR. And ye, the temple guard! did ye not withstand these legions?

BEL AFFRIS. What man could, that we did. But this Cæsar throws a legion at you where you are weakest as he throws a stone from a catapult; and that legion is as a man with one head, a thousand arms, and no religion. I have fought against them; and I know.

BELZANOR [*derisively*] Were you frightened, cousin?

The guardsmen roar with laughter, their eyes sparkling at the wit of their captain.

BEL AFFRIS. No, cousin; but I was beaten.

The guardsmen, much damped, utter a growl of contemptuous disgust.

BELZANOR. Could you not die?

BEL AFFRIS. There was no time: all was over in a moment. There came the sound of a trumpet. Then saw we a moving wall of shields coming towards us. You know how the heart burns when you charge a fortified wall; but how if the fortified wall were to charge you?

PERSIAN. What did you do?

BEL AFFRIS. I said to myself: surely it is safer to stand than to lose my breath and be stabbed in the back; so I doubled my fist and smote a Roman on the sharpness of his jaw. He was but mortal after all: he lay down in a stupor; and I took his sword and laid it on. [*Drawing the sword*] Lo! a Roman sword with Roman blood on it!

THE GUARDSMEN [*approvingly*] Good! [*They take the sword and hand it round, examining it curiously*].

PERSIAN. And your men?

BEL AFFRIS. Fled. Scattered like sheep.

BELZANOR [*furiously*] The cowardly slaves! Leaving the descendants of the gods to be butchered.

BEL AFFRIS [*with acid coolness*] The descendants of the gods did not stay to be butchered, cousin. We escaped with our lives; and I am come to warn you that you must open your gates to Cæsar; for his advance guard is scarce an hour behind me; and not an Egyptian warrior is left standing between you and his legions.

THE SENTINEL. Woe, alas! [*He throws down his javelin and flies into the palace*].

BELZANOR. Nail him to the door, quick! [*The guardsmen rush for him with their spears; but he is too quick for them*]. Now this news will run through the palace like fire through stubble.

BEL AFFRIS. What shall we do to save the women from the Romans?

BELZANOR. Why not kill them?

PERSIAN. Because we should have to pay blood money. Better let the Romans kill them: it is cheaper.

BELZANOR [*awestruck at his brain power*] O subtle one! O serpent!

BEL AFFRIS. But your Queen?

BELZANOR. True: we must carry off Cleopatra. I will take her on the crupper of my horse.

PERSIAN. Listen to me, Belzanor. Cleopatra's brother Ptolemy is at war with her. Let us sell her to him secretly and then offer ourselves to Cæsar as volunteers to fight for the overthrow of her brother and the rescue of our Queen. He will listen to us if we come with her picture in our mouths. This Cæsar is a great lover of women: he makes them his friends and counsellors. He grows old now: he is past fifty and full of labors and battles. He is too old for the young women; and the old women are too wise to worship him. Cleopatra is not yet a woman: neither is she wise. But she already troubles men's wisdom.

BELZANOR. Ay: that is because she is descended from the river Nile and a black kitten of the sacred White Cat. What then?

PERSIAN. He will conquer and kill her brother, and reign in Egypt with Cleopatra for his Queen. And we shall be her guard.

GUARDSMEN. O subtlest of all the serpents! O admiration! O wisdom!

BEL AFFRIS. He will also have arrived before you have done talking, O word spinner.

BELZANOR. That is true. [*An affrighted uproar in the palace interrupts him*]. Quick: the flight has begun: guard the door. [*They rush to the door and form a cordon before it with their spears. A mob of women-servants and nurses surges out. Those in front recoil from the spears, screaming to those behind to keep back. Belzanor's voice dominates the disturbance as he shouts*] Back there. In again, unprofitable cattle. Send us out Ftatateeta, the Queen's chief nurse.

THE WOMEN [*calling into the palace*] Ftatateeta, Ftatateeta. Come, come. Speak to Belzanor.

A WOMAN. Oh, keep back. You are thrusting me on the spearheads.

A huge grim woman, her face covered with a network of tiny wrinkles, and her eyes old, large, and wise; sinewy handed, very tall, very strong; with the mouth of a bloodhound and the jaws of a bulldog, appears on the threshold. She is dressed like a person of consequence in the palace, and confronts the guardsmen insolently.

FTATATEETA. Make way for the Queen's chief nurse.

BELZANOR [*with grim humor*] Ftatateeta: daughter of a long-tongued, swivel-eyed chameleon, the Romans are at hand. [*A cry of terror from the women: they would fly but for the spears*].

FTATATEETA. Then fly and save yourselves, O cowardly ones, and leave us to shift for ourselves.

BELZANOR. Not until you have first done our bidding, O terror of manhood. Bring out Cleopatra the Queen to us; and then go whither you will.

FTATATEETA [*with a derisive laugh*] Now I know why the gods have taken her out of our hands. [*The guardsmen start and look at one another*]. The Queen has been missing since an hour past sundown.

BELZANOR [*furiously*] Hag!

THE WOMEN [*protesting officiously*] She speaks the truth, Belzanor.

BELZANOR. Search—quick—into the palace—search every corner.

The guards, led by Belzanor, shoulder their way into the palace through the flying crowd of women, who escape through the courtyard gate.

FTATATEETA [*screaming*] Sacrilege! Men in the Queen's chambers! Sa— [*her voice dies away as the Persian puts his knife to her throat*].

PERSIAN [*to Ftatateeta*] O mother of guile! You have hidden her to sell to Cæser or her brother.

BEL AFFRIS [*laying a hand on Ftatateeta's left shoulder*] Forbear her yet a moment, Persian. [*To Ftatateeta, very significantly*] Mother: your gods are asleep or away hunting; and the sword is at your throat. Bring us to where the Queen is hid, and you shall live.

FTATATEETA. As Osiris lives, I do not know. I told her she would be left alone here when the Romans came as a punishment for her disobedience. And now she is gone—run away—hidden.

BEL AFFRIS [*to the Persian*] May we believe this, O subtle one?

PERSIAN. You have made up this tale. [*Lifting his knife*] Taste death.

FTATATEETA. Not from thee, baby. [*She snatches his ankle from under him and*

*flies stooping along the palace wall, vanishing in the darkness within its precinct.
Bel Affris roars with laughter as the Persian tumbles. The guardsmen rush out of
the palace with Belzanor and a mob of fugitives, mostly carrying bundles].*
PERSIAN. Have you found Cleopatra?
BELZANOR. She is gone. We have searched every corner.
THE NUBIAN SENTINEL [*appearing at the door of the palace*] Woe! Alas! Fly,
fly!
BELZANOR. What is the matter now?
THE NUBIAN SENTINEL. The sacred white cat has been stolen.
ALL. Woe! woe! [*General panic. They all fly with cries of consternation. The torch
is thrown down and extinguished in the rush. The noise of the fugitives dies away.
Darkness and dead silence].*

   *The same darkness into which the Syrian palace vanished. The same silence.
Suspense. Then the blackness and stillness break softly into silver mist and strange
airs as the windswept harp of Memnon plays at the dawning of the moon. It rises
full over the desert; and a vast horizon comes into relief, broken by a huge shape
which soon reveals itself in the spreading radiance as a Sphinx pedestalled on the
sands. The light still clears, until the upraised eyes of the image are distinguished
looking straight forward and upward in infinite fearless vigil, and a mass of color
between its great paws defines itself as a heap of red poppies on which a girl lies
motionless, her silken vest heaving gently and regularly with the breathing of a
dreamless sleeper, and her braided hair glittering in a shaft of moonlight like a
bird's wing.*

   *Suddenly there comes from afar a vaguely fearful sound (it might be the bellow
of a Minotaur softened by great distance) and Memnon's music stops. Silence: then
a few faint high-ringing trumpet notes. Then silence again. Then a man comes from
the south with stealing steps, ravished by the mystery of the night, all wonder, and
halts, lost in contemplation, opposite the left flank of the Sphinx, whose bosom, with
its burden, is hidden from him by its massive shoulder.*
THE MAN. Hail, Sphinx: salutation from Julius Cæsar! I have wandered in
many lands, seeking the lost regions from which my birth into this world exiled
me, and the company of creatures such as I myself. I have found flocks and
pastures, men and cities, but no other Cæsar, no air native to me, no man kindred
to me, none who can do my day's deed, and think my night's thought. In the little
world yonder, Sphinx, my place is as high as yours in this great desert; only I
wander, and you sit still; I conquer, and you endure; I work and wonder, you
watch and wait; I look up and am dazzled, look down and am darkened, look
round and am puzzled, whilst your eyes never turn from looking out—out of the
world—to the lost region—the home from which we have strayed. Sphinx, you
and I, strangers to the race of men, are no strangers to one another: have I not
been conscious of you and of this place since I was born? Rome is a madman's
dream: this is my Reality. These starry lamps of yours I have seen from afar in
Gaul, in Britain, in Spain, in Thessaly, signalling great secrets to some eternal
sentinal below, whose post I never could find. And here at last is their sentinel—
an image of the constant and immortal part of my life, silent, full of thoughts,
along in the silver desert. Sphinx, Sphinx: my way hither was the way of destiny;
for I am he of whose genius you are the symbol: part brute, part woman, and part
god—nothing of man in me at all. Have I read your riddle, Sphinx?
THE GIRL [*who has wakened, and peeped cautiously from her nest to see who is*

speaking] Old gentleman.

CÆSAR [*starting violently, and clutching his sword*] Immortal gods!

THE GIRL. Old gentleman: dont run away.

CÆSAR [*stupefied*] "Old gentleman: dont run away"!!! This! to Julius Cæsar!

THE GIRL [*urgently*] Old gentleman.

CÆSAR. Sphinx: you presume on your centuries. I am younger than you, though your voice is but a girl's voice as yet.

THE GIRL. Climb up here, quickly; or the Romans will come and eat you.

CÆSAR [*running forward past the Sphinx's shoulder, and seeing her*] A child at its breast! a divine child!

THE GIRL. Come up quickly. You must get up at its side and creep round.

CÆSAR [*amazed*] Who are you?

THE GIRL. Cleopatra, Queen of Egypt.

CÆSAR. Queen of the Gypsies, you mean.

CLEOPATRA. You must not be disrespectful to me, or the Sphinx will let the Romans eat you. Come up. It is quite cosy here. ,

CÆSAR [*to himself*] What a dream! What a magnificent dream! Only let me not wake! [*He climbs to the Sphinx's flank, and presently reappears to her on the pedestal, stepping round to its right shoulder*].

CLEOPATRA. Take care. Thats right. Now sit down: you may have its other paw. [*She seats herself comfortably on its left paw*]. It is very powerful and will protect us; but [*shivering, and with plaintive loneliness*] it would not take any notice of me or keep me company. I am glad you have come: I was very lonely. Did you happen to see a white cat anywhere?

CÆSAR [*sitting slowly down on the right paw in extreme wonderment*] Have you lost one?

CLEOPATRA. Yes: the sacred white cat: is it not dreadful? I brought him here to sacrifice him to the Sphinx; but when we got a little way from the city a black cat called him, and he jumped out of my arms and ran away to it. Do you think that the black cat can have been my great-great-great-grandmother?

CÆSAR [*staring at her*] Your great-great-great-grandmother? Well, why not? Nothing would surprise me on this night of nights.

CLEOPATRA. I think it must have been. My great-grandmother's great-grandmother was a black kitten of the sacred white cat; and my blood is made with Nile water. That is why my hair is so wavy.

CÆSAR. What are you doing here at this time of night? Do you live here?

CLEOPATRA. Of course not: I am the Queen; and I shall live in the palace at Alexandria when I have killed my brother, who drove me out of it. When I am old enough I shall do just what I like. I shall be able to poison the slaves and see them wriggle, and pretend to Ftatateeta that she is going to be put into the fiery furnace.

CÆSAR. Hm! Meanwhile why are you not at home and in bed?

CLEOPATRA. Because the Romans are coming to eat us all. You are not at home and in bed either.

CÆSAR [*with conviction*] Yes I am. I live in a tent; and I am now in that tent, fast asleep and dreaming. Do you suppose that I believe you are real, you impossible little dream witch?

CLEOPATRA [*giggling and leaning trustfully towards him*] You are a funny old gentleman. I like you.

CÆSAR. Ah, that spoils the dream. Why dont you dream that I am young?

CLEOPATRA. I wish you were; only I think I should be more afraid of you. I like men, especially young men with round strong arms; but I am afraid of them. You are hundreds of years old; but you have a nice voice; and I like to have somebody to talk to, though I think you are a little mad. It is the moon that makes you talk to yourself in that silly way.

CÆSAR. What! you heard that, did you? I was saying my prayers to the great Sphinx.

CLEOPATRA. But this isnt the great Sphinx.

CÆSAR [*much disappointed, looking up at the statue*] What!

CLEOPATRA. This is only a dear little kitten of a Sphinx. Why, the great Sphinx is so big that it has a temple between its paws. This is my pet Sphinx. Tell me: do you think the Romans have any sorcerers who could take us away from the Sphinx by magic?

CÆSAR. Why? Are you afraid of the Romans?

CLEOPATRA [*very seriously*] Oh, they would eat us if they caught us. They are barbarians. Their chief is called Julius Cæsar. His father was a tiger and his mother a burning mountain; and his nose is like an elephant's trunk. [*Cæsar involuntarily rubs his nose*]. They all have long noses, and ivory tusks, and little tails, and seven arms with a hundred arrows in each; and they live on human flesh.

CÆSAR. Would you like me to shew you a real Roman?

CLEOPATRA [*terrified*] No. You are frightening me.

CÆSAR. No matter: this is only a dream—

CLEOPATRA [*excitedly*] It is not a dream: it is not a dream. See, see. [*She plucks a pin from her hair and jabs it repeatedly into his arm*].

CÆSAR. Ffff—Stop. [*Wrathfully*] How dare you?

CLEOPATRA [*abashed*] You said you were dreaming. [*Whimpering*] I only wanted to shew you—

CÆSAR [*gently*] Come, come: dont cry. A queen mustnt cry. [*He rubs his arm, wondering at the reality of the smart; the conviction that he is really awake forces itself on him*]. Cleopatra: can you see my face well?

CLEOPATRA. Yes. It is so white in the moonlight.

CÆSAR. Are you sure it is the moonlight that makes me look whiter than an Egyptian? [*Grimly*] Do you notice that I have a rather long nose?

CLEOPATRA [*recoiling, paralysed by a terrible suspicion*] Oh!

CÆSAR. It is a Roman nose, Cleopatra.

CLEOPATRA. Ah! [*With a piercing scream she springs up; darts round the left shoulder of the Sphinx; scrambles down to the sand; and falls on her knees in frantic supplication, shrieking*] Bite him in two, Sphinx: bite him in two. I meant to sacrifice the white cat—I did indeed—I [*Cæsar, who has slipped down from the pedestal, touches her on the shoulder*].

CÆSAR. Cleopatra: shall I teach you a way to prevent Cæsar from eating you?

CLEOPATRA [*clinging to him piteously*] Oh do, do, do. I will steal jewels and give them to you. I will make the river Nile water your lands twice a year.

CÆSAR. Peace, peace, my child. Your gods are afraid of the Romans: you see the Sphinx dare not bite me, nor prevent me carrying you off to Julius Cæsar.

CLEOPATRA [*in pleading murmurings*] You wont, you wont. You said you wouldnt.

CÆSAR. Cæsar never eats women.

CLEOPATRA [*springing up full of hope*] What!

CÆSAR [*impressively*] But he eats girls [*she relapses*] and cats. Now you are a silly little girl; and you are descended from the black kitten. You are both a girl and a cat.

CLEOPATRA [*trembling*] And will he eat m e ?

CÆSAR. Yes; unless you make him believe that you are a woman.

CLEOPATRA. Oh, you must get a sorcerer to make a woman of me. Are you a sorcerer?

CÆSAR. Perhaps. But it will take a long time; and this very night you must stand face to face with Cæsar in the palace of your fathers.

CLEOPATRA. No, no. I darent.

CÆSAR. Whatever dread may be in your soul—however terrible Cæsar may be to you—you must confront him as a brave woman and a great queen; and you must feel no fear. If your hand shakes: if you voice quavers; then—night and death! [*She moans*]. But if he thinks you worthy to rule, he will set you on the throne by his side and make you the real ruler of Egypt.

CLEOPATRA [*despairingly*] No: he will find me out: he will find me out.

CÆSAR [*rather mournfully*] He is easily deceived by women. Their eyes dazzle him.

CLEOPATRA [*hopefully*] Then we will cheat him. I will put on Ftatateeta's head-dress; and he will think me quite an old woman.

CÆSAR. If you do that he will eat you at one mouthful.

CLEOPATRA [*running after him and clinging to him*] Oh please, p l e a s e ! I will do whatever you tell me. I will be good. I will be your slave. [*Again the terrible bellowing note sounds across the desert, now closer at hand. It is the bucina, the Roman war trumpet*].

CÆSAR. Hark!

CLEOPATRA [*trembling*] What was that?

CÆSAR. Cæsar's voice.

CLEOPATRA [*pulling at his hand*] Let us run away. Come. Oh, come.

CÆSAR. You are safe with me until you stand on your throne to receive Cæsar. Now lead me thither.

CLEOPATRA [*only too glad to get away*] I will, I will. [*Again the bucina*]. Oh come, come, come: the gods are angry. Do you feel the earth shaking?

CÆSAR. It is the tread of Cæsar's legions.

CLEOPATRA [*drawing him away*] This way, quickly. And let us look for the white cat as we go. It is he that has turned you into a Roman.

CÆSAR. Incorrigible, oh, incorrigible! Away! [*He follows her, the bucina sounding louder as they steal across the desert*].

The moonlight wanes: the horizon again shews black against the sky, broken only by the fantastic silhouette of the Sphinx. The sky itself vanishes in darkness, from which there is no relief until the gleam of a distant torch falls on great Egyptian pillars supporting the roof of a majestic corridor. At the further end of this corridor a Nubian slave appears carrying the torch. Cæsar, still led by Cleopatra, follows him. They come down the corridor, Cæsar peering keenly about at the strange architecture, and at the pillar shadows between which, as the passing torch makes them hurry noiselessly backwards, figures of men with wings and hawk's heads, and vast black marble cats, seem to flit in and out of ambush. Further along, the wall turns a corner and makes a spacious transept in which Cæsar sees, on his right, a throne, and behind the throne a door. On each side of the throne is a slender pillar with a lamp on it.

CÆSAR. What place is this?

CLEOPATRA. This is where I sit on the throne when I am allowed to wear my crown and robes. [*The slave holds his torch to shew the throne*].

CÆSAR. Order the slave to light the lamps.

CLEOPATRA [*shyly*] Do you think I may?

CÆSAR. Of course. You are the Queen. [*She hesitates*]. Go on.

CLEOPATRA [*timidly, to the slave*] Light all the lamps.

FTATATEETA [*suddenly coming from behind the throne*] Stop. [*The slave stops. She turns sternly to Cleopatra, who quails like a naughty child*]. Who is this you have with you; and how dare you order the lamps to be lighted without my permission? [*Cleopatra is dumb with apprehension*].

CÆSAR. Who is she?

CLEOPATRA. Ftatateeta.

FTATATEETA [*arrogantly*] Chief nurse to—

CÆSAR [*cutting her short*] I speak to the Queen. Be silent. [*To Cleopatra*] Is this how your servants know their places? Send her away; [*to the slave*] do as the Queen has bidden. [*The slave lights the lamps. Meanwhile Cleopatra stands hesitating, afraid of Ftatateeta*]. You are the Queen: send her away.

CLEOPATRA [*cajoling*] Ftatateeta, dear: you must go away just for a little.

CÆSAR. You are not commanding her to go away: you are begging her. You are no Queen. You will be eaten. Farewell. [*He turns to go*].

CLEOPATRA [*clutching him*] No, no, no. Dont leave me.

CÆSAR. A Roman does not stay with queens who are afraid of their slaves.

CLEOPATRA. I am not afraid. Indeed I am not afraid.

FTATATEETA. We shall see who is afraid here. [*Menacingly*] Cleopatra—

CÆSAR. On your knees, woman: am I also a child that you dare trifle with me? [*He points to the floor at Cleopatra's feet. Ftatateeta, half cowed, half savage, hesitates. Caesar calls to the Nubian*] Slave. [*The Nubian comes to him*] Can you cut off a head? [*The Nubian nods and grins ecstacially, showing all his teeth. Cæsar takes his sword by the scabbard, ready to offer the hilt to the Nubian, and turns again to Ftatateeta, repeating his gesture*] Have you remembered yourself, mistress?

Ftatateeta, crushed, kneels before Cleopatra, who can hardly believe her eyes.

FTATATEETA [*hoarsely*] O Queen, forget not thy servant in the days of thy greatness.

CLEOPATRA [*blazing with excitement*] Go. Begone. Go away. [*Ftatateeta rises with stooped head, and moves backwards towards the door. Cleopatra watches her submission eagerly, almost clapping her hands, which are trembling. Suddenly she cries*] Give me something to beat her with. [*She snatches a snake-skin from the throne and dashes after Ftatateeta, whirling it like a scourge in the air. Cæsar makes a bound and manages to catch her and hold her while Ftatateeta escapes*].

CÆSAR. You scratch, kitten, do you?

CLEOPATRA [*breaking from him*] I w i l l beat somebody. I will beat h i m . [*She attacks the slave*]. There, there, there! [*The slave flies for his life up the corridor and vanishes. She throws the snake-skin away and jumps on the step of the throne with her arms waving, crying*] I am a real Queen at last—a real, real

411

Queen! Cleopatra the Queen! [*Cæsar shakes his head dubiously, the advantage of the change seeming open to question from the point of view of the general welfare of Egypt. She turns and looks at him exultantly. Then she jumps down from the steps, runs to him, and flings her arms round him rapturously, crying*] Oh, I love you for making me a Queen.

CÆSAR. But queens love only kings.

CLEOPATRA. I will make all the men I love kings. I will make you a king. I will have many young kings, with round, strong arms; and when I am tired of them I will whip them to death; but you shall always be my king: my nice, kind, wise, good old king.

CÆSAR. Oh, my wrinkles! You will be the most dangerous of all Cæsar's conquests.

CLEOPATRA [*appalled*] Cæsar! I forgot Cæsar. [*Anxiously*] You will tell him that I am a Queen, will you not?—a real Queen. Listen! [*stealthily coaxing him*]: let us run away and hide until Cæsar is gone.

CÆSAR. If you fear Cæsar, you are no true queen; and though you were to hide beneath a pyramid, he would go straight to it and lift it with one hand. And then—! [*he chops his teeth together*].

CLEOPATRA [*trembling*] Oh!

CÆSAR. Be afraid if you dare. [*The note of the bucina resounds again in the distance. She moans with fear. Cæsar exults in it, exclaiming*] Aha! Cæsar approaches the throne of Cleopatra. Come: take your place. [*He takes her hand and leads her to the throne. She is too downcast to speak*]. Ho, there, Teetatota. How do you call your slaves?

CLEOPATRA [*spiritlessly, as she sinks on the throne and cowers there, shaking*] Clap your hands.

He claps his hands. Ftatateeta returns.

CÆSAR. Bring the Queen's robes, and her crown, and her women; and prepare her.

CLEOPATRA [*eagerly—recovering herself a little*] Yes, the crown, Ftatateeta: I shall wear the crown.

FTATATEETA. For whom must the Queen put on her state?

CÆSAR. For a citizen of Rome. A king of kings, Totateeta.

CLEOPATRA [*stamping at her*] How dare you ask questions? Go and do as you are told. [*Ftatateeta goes out with a grim smile. Cleopatra goes on eagerly, to Cæsar*] Cæsar will know that I am a Queen, will he not? You must tell him.

CÆSAR. He will not ask me. He will know Cleopatra by her pride, her courage, her majesty, and her beauty. [*She looks very doubtful*] Are you trembling?

CLEOPATRA [*shivering with dread*] No, I—I—[*in a very sickly voice*] No.

Ftatateeta and three women come in with the regalia.

FTATATEETA. Of all the Queen's woman, these three alone are left. The rest are fled. [*They begin to deck Cleopatra, who submits, pale and motionless*].

CÆSAR. Good, good. Three are enough. Poor Cæsar generally has to dress himself.

FTATATEETA [*contemptuously*] The queen of Egypt is not a Roman barbarian. [*To Cleopatra*] Be brave, my nursling. Hold up your head before this stranger.

CÆSAR [*admiring Cleopatra, and placing the crown on her head*] Is it sweet or bitter to be a Queen, Cleopatra?

CLEOPATRA. Bitter.

CÆSAR. Cast out fear; and you will conquer Cæsar.

The Nubian comes running down the hall.

NUBIAN. The Romans are in the courtyard. [*He bolts through the door. With a shriek, the women fly after him. Ftatateeta's jaw expresses savage resolution: she does not budge. Cleopatra can hardly restrain herself from following them. Cæsar grips her wrist, and looks steadfastly at her. She stands like a martyr*].

CÆSAR. The Queen must face Cæsar alone. Answer "So be it."

CLEOPATRA [*white*] So be it.

CÆSAR [*releasing her*] Good.

A tramp and tumult of armed men is heard. Cleopatra's terror increases. The bucina sounds close at hand, followed by a formidable clangor of trumpets. This is too much for Cleopatra: she utters a cry and darts towards the door. Ftatateeta stops her ruthlessly.

FTATATEETA. You are my nursling. You have said "So be it"; and if you die for it, you must make the Queen's word good. [*She hands Cleopatra to Cæsar, who takes her back, almost beside herself with apprehension, to the throne*].

CÆSAR. Now, if you quail—! [*He seats himself on the throne*].

She stands on the step, all but unconscious, waiting for death. The Roman soldiers troop in tumultuously through the corridor, headed by their ensign with his eagle, and their bucinator, a burly fellow with his instrument coiled round his body, its brazen bell shaped like the head of a howling wolf. When they reach the transept, they stare in amazement at the throne; dress into ordered rank opposite; draw their swords and lift them in the air with a shout of Hail, Cæsar.

Dead silence. Cleopatra, stiff with terror, and staring at the soldiers for the arrival of Cæsar, sees no seven armed monster born of a tiger and a burning mountain. The saluting swords all point behind her. She turns and sees Cæsar sitting on the throne, his hitherto severe expression changed by a smile of extraordinary charm and kindliness. Fascinated and enlightened, she throws away her sceptre-staff and her head-dress (they are caught by Ftatateeta), and throws herself into Cæsar's lap, flinging her arms round his neck.

All the wood and brass in the orchestra let fly with every note in the chromatic scale fortissimo. Meanwhile the strings put on their mutes; and the screen goes black. The din is infernal; but it moderates as the instruments drop out one by one, the extreme discords first, then the 13ths, 11ths, 9ths down to the diminished 7ths, on which the muted strings join in with Schubertian sweetness, and modulate back to the nocturne of the sphinx in the desert. Simultaneously the blacked-out screen lightens into the desert scene with the moon in the east (the left side of the screen). The moon, accompanied by the nocturne music, passes across the screen to the west to indicate the passing of the night. The music is broken twice by a syncopated throb and flash of summer lightning. Towards the end of the transit the moon fades; the sky brightens into dawning sunlight; and the oboe cuts in with a pastoral descant. Tall straight lines of buildings appear with appropriate chords from the wind; and the scene dissolves into Cleopatra's bedchamber, and the music into a lullaby. Cleopatra is seen fast asleep in bed for long enough to let the audience take in the whole change.

The lullaby is interrupted by a brilliant reveille from the Roman military trumpets under the windows outside. This finishes the music. Cleopatra, rudely awakened, sits up with her knees under her chin, rubbing her eyes.

CLEOPATRA [*calling*] Ftatateeta! Ftatateeta!

413

Ftatateeta enters. She presents a figure different from that of the night before. She has not put on her official robe; and her powerful and handsome body is seen apparently naked except for a rich sash or sumptuous belt which serves also as an apron. [Really she is clad in skin tight silk of a deep bronze, with her face made up to match it. Her hair must not be woolly: she is an Egyptian slave, not an Ethiopian one: dark red brown but not black]. She carries bath towels on her arm. She comes to the foot of the bed. Her attitude is as commanding as ever.

CLEOPATRA. Oh, Ftatateeta, I have had such a wonderful dream. You will not believe it. How could I have thought of it all?

FTATATEETA. Get up, child. You must be bathed this morning.

CLEOPATRA [*dismayed*] No: I had my month's bath the day before yesterday.

FTATATEETA. In future you must have a bath every day.

CLEOPATRA. No, no: I should die of it.

FTATATEETA. You must. Your life is changed. You are still my child; but to all others you are now a grown woman and a queen; and you must begin by having a bath every day.

CLEOPATRA. Oh, why? Why? Why?

FTATATEETA. Your dream was not a dream. It happened. It was the will of Ra, the mightiest of our gods: we cannot gainsay him. Cæsar has come. He slept here last night.

CLEOPATRA. But that was what I dreamt: it cannot be true. What will be do with me?

FTATATEETA. Ask rather what you will do with him. My child: you have charmed him. You are safe: you are powerful. Fear nothing: I will guide you until you learn how to guide yourself.

CLEOPATRA. But the man in the dream was not the great and terrible Cæsar. He was only an elderly gentleman, lean and hungry looking, but quite kind.

FTATATEETA. He is a magician; and magicians can change their shapes as they please. Everything about him is magical. He would not sleep in the golden chamber: he chose a bare servant's room, saying it was more comfortable. For his breakfast he ate grains and drank warm barley water, like any slave, though the richest meats were placed before him. He rose early, as a servant rises: earlier than I. Yet everyone obeys him as if he were a god. I think he is a god in disguise; for he has changed your nature, has he not?

CLEOPATRA. Oh, yes he has. That is true, Ftatateeta. Yesterday I was afraid of you more than of anyone else on earth; and now I am not afraid of you at all. He made me a queen by his magic: that is true. Tell me what I must do to begin with if I really am a queen. If I am to be washed again so soon it must be a scented bath, Ftatateeta. Have you scented it?

FTATATEETA. No: he hates perfumes: and if you redden your lips he will not kiss them. He must indeed be a god; for only a god could be so unlike a man. Come, child: have your bath and get it over. Up with you. You will soon get used to it, and love it.

CLEOPATRA [*getting out of bed reluctantly*] Never. It is too dreadful. Where is he now?

FTATATEETA. Everywhere. I tell you he is a god. Ask the tax collectors. Ask the Jews. Ask the market women. He has summoned our General, Achillas, and all our great men, to meet him in the Council Chamber at eleven. Your brother Ptolemy is to be there.

CLEOPATRA. If that little beast is to be there I must be there too, or Cæsar will think he is the Pharaoh. Promise me that I shall be there, Ftatateeta.

FTATATEETA. You shall, my child, if I die for it.

CLEOPATRA. Where is Cæsar?

FTATATEETA. In the square telling his soldiers what to do, with his burly lieutenant Rufio, whom I fear more than I do Cæsar. I feel that he may be the death of me, and that Cæsar never will. He is not a god: he can kill.

CLEOPATRA. I will not let him: I am a queen now. Must I really have a bath?

FTATATEETA. You must, my child. Come.

Dissolve:

Noise outside: first the Roman trumpets: then the Alexandrian mob flying in terror, expressed by hurried music, culminating in the appearance on the screen of the street with the people running away in all directions, hiding where they can or crowding against the houses to leave the road clear for a column of Roman soldiers marching with a discipline which contrasts strongly with the disorder of the crowd. The Centurion, cudgel in hand, marches beside the files. The buglers and drummers are at the head of the column. Quick march. Meanwhile, the crowd as it flies shouts inarticulately while it is in motion, a few crying Fly, fly. The Romans, the Romans. Fly for your lives. Theyre coming, theyre coming. We shall be murdered. What are you running away for? Mind where you are going, will you? Its all right, theyll do you no harm. Stand, stand. Damn you for a parcel of fools. The Romans wont eat you. Theyre as civilized as you are. The children: save the children. Mother, mother. Father, father. This way, child: here, here.

CENTURION [*holding up his cudgel and marking time without advancing*] Halt. Mark time. [*To the band*] Sound the halt.

The buglers sound the halt while the column marks time. The drums then roll.

CENTURION. 'Tention!

The column stops marking time and becomes motionless. Dead silence.

CENTURION [*to the troops*] We wait here for our second in command under Cæsar, Rufio. This city is Alexandria: remember that: A-lex-andria, the Egyptian capital. Youve got to behave yourselves here. Be stiffish with the men; but you may fraternize with the women. [*A big laugh from the troops*] Silence! Silence, I tell you. [*A cavalry trumpet in the distance*] Thats Rufio. 'Tention! Half turn right. [*The troops turn to face across the street in profile. Rufio, on a mettlesome charger, arrives at a gallop and pulls up by the Centurion. Rufio is a burly, black bearded man of middle age, very blunt, prompt, and rough, with small clear eyes, and a plump nose and cheeks, which, however, like the rest of his flesh, are in ironhard condition*].

RUFIO. Centurion.

CENTURION. Sir? [*He stands at attention*].

RUFIO [*indicating the troops*] Do they know where we are?

CENTURION. Yessir. Alexandria, sir.

RUFIO. Well, you see that building [*pointing to the palace*]. That is the Council Chamber, part of the royal palace. Cæsar is in there. I'm going now to join him. Keep a platoon of picked men within call. They may be wanted. Picked men, you understand.

CENTURION. Yes, sir: I understand. How do we get in, sir? Where do we wait?

RUFIO. Take the lane to the left. Go in by the guardhouse gates. When the sentries challenge you "Who goes there?" reply "The Roman army of occupation" and march in, sentries or no sentries. There are steps up to the palace loggia: post yourselves there. If I call, up with you instantly and parade in the loggia in full view of the Council Chamber. You understand?

CENTURION. I understand, sir.

RUFIO [*looking round: he wants to dismount*] Where is my damned orderly?

CENTURION [*taking the bridle of the charger*] You were too quick for him, sir.

Rufio dismounts.

RUFIO. Remember: Cæsar will be in the Council Chamber. So will I. You will be at hand outside. Lose no time. [*He strides into the palace*].

The orderly arrives at a trot; and takes the charger from the Centurion.

CENTURION. 'Tention. Number three fall out. Number seven fall out. Number thirteen fall out. Fifteen and sixteen fall out.

A soldier falls out at each order and the Centurion's voice dies away as the scene fades out and changes to the Council Chamber.

A hall on the first floor of the Palace, ending in a loggia approached by two steps. Through the arches of the loggia the Mediterranean can be seen, bright in the morning sun. The clean lofty walls, painted with a procession of the Egyptian theocracy, presented in profile as flat ornament, and the absence of mirrors, sham perspectives, stuffy upholstery and textiles, make the place handsome, wholesome, simple and cool, or, as a rich English manufacturer would express it, poor, bare, ridiculous and unhomely. For Tottenham Court Road civilization is to this Egyptian civilization as glass bead and tattoo civilization is to Tottenham Court Road.

The young king Ptolemy Dionysus (aged ten) is at the top of the steps, on his way in through the loggia, led by his guardian Pothinus, who has him by the hand. The court is assembled to receive him. It is made up of men and women (some of the women being officials) of various complexions and races, mostly Egyptian; some of them, comparatively fair, from lower Egypt, some, much darker, from upper Egypt; with a few Greeks and Jews. Prominent in a group on Ptolemy's right hand is Theodotus, Ptolemy's tutor. Another group, on Ptolemy's left, is headed by Achillas, the general of Ptolemy's troops. Theodotus is a little old man, whose features are as cramped and wizened as his limbs, except his tall straight forehead, which occupies more space than all the rest of his face. He maintains an air of magpie keenness and profundity, listening to what the others says with the sarcastic vigilance of a philosopher listening to the exercises of his disciples. Achillas is a tall handsome man of thirty-five, with a fine black beard curled like the coat of a poodle. Apparently not a clever man, but distinguished and dignified. Pothinus is a vigorous man of fifty, a eunuch, passionate, energetic and quick witted, but of common mind and character; impatient and unable to control his temper. He has fine tawny hair, like fur. Ptolemy, the King, looks much older than an English boy of ten; but he has the childish air, the habit of being in leading strings, the mixture of impotence and petulance, the appearance of being excessively washed, combed and dressed by other hands, which is exhibited by court-bred princes of all ages.

All receive the King with reverences. He comes down the steps to a chair of state which stands a little to his right, the only seat in the hall. Taking his place before it, he looks nervously for instructions to Pothinus, who places himself at his left hand.

POTHINUS. The king of Egypt has a word to speak.

THEODOTUS [*in a squeak which he makes impressive by sheer self-*

opinionativeness] Peace for the King's word!

PTOLEMY [*without any vocal inflexions: he is evidently repeating a lesson*] Take notice of this all of you. I am the first-born son of Auletes the Flute Blower who was your King. My sister Berenice drove him from his throne and reigned in his stead but—but—[*he hesitates*]—

POTHINUS [*stealthily prompting*]—but the gods would not suffer—

PTOLEMY. Yes—the gods would not suffer—not suffer—[*He stops; then, crestfallen*] I forgot what the gods would not suffer.

POTHINUS [*suppressing his impatience with difficulty*] The King wished to say that the gods would not suffer the impiety of his sister to go unpunished.

PTOLEMY [*hastily*] Yes: I remember the rest of it. [*He resumes his monotone*]. Therefore the gods sent a stranger one Mark Antony a Roman captain of horsemen across the sands of the desert and he set my father again upon the throne. And now that my father is dead my sister Cleopatra would snatch the kingdom from me and reign in my place. But the gods would not suffer—

POTHINUS [*prompting*]—will not maintain—

PTOLEMY. Oh yes—will not maintain such iniquity. But with the help of the witch Ftatateeta she hath cast a spell on the Roman Julius Cæsar to make him uphold her false pretence to rule in Egypt. Take notice then that I will not suffer— that I will not suffer—[*pettishly, to Pothinus*] What is it that I will not suffer?

POTHINUS [*suddenly exploding with all the force and emphasis of political passion*] The King will not suffer a foreigner to take from him the throne of our Egypt. [*A shout of applause*]. Tell the King, Achillas, how many soldiers and horsemen follow the Roman?

ACHILLAS. But two Roman legions, O King. Three thousand soldiers and scarce a thousand horsemen.

The court breaks into derisive laughter; and a great chattering begins, amid which Rufio appears in the loggia.

RUFIO [*from the steps*] Peace, ho! [*The laughter and chatter cease abruptly*]. Cæsar approaches.

THEODOTUS [*with much presence of mind*] The King permits the Roman commander to enter!

Cæsar, plainly dressed, but wearing an oak wreath to conceal his baldness, enters from the loggia, attended by Britannus, his secretary, a Briton, about forty, tall, solemn, and already slightly bald, with a heavy, drooping, hazel-colored moustache trained so as to lose its ends in a pair of trim whiskers. He is carefully dressed in blue, with portfolio, inkhorn, and reed pen at his girdle. His serious air and sense of the importance of the business in hand is in marked contrast to the kindly interest of Cæsar, who looks at the scene, which is new to him, with the frank curiosity of a child, and then turns to the king's chair: Britannus and Rufio posting themselves near the steps at the other side.

CÆSAR [*looking at Pothinus and Ptolemy*] Which is the King? the man or the boy?

POTHINUS. I am Pothinus, the guardian of my lord the King.

CÆSAR [*patting Ptolemy kindly on the shoulder*] So you are the King. Dull work at your age, eh? [*To Pothinus*] Your servant, Pothinus. [*He turns away unconcernedly and comes slowly along the middle of the hall, looking from side to side at the courtiers until he reaches Achillas*]. And this gentleman?

THEODOTUS. Achillas, the King's general.

CÆSAR [*to Achillas, very friendly*] A general, eh? I am a general myself. But I began too old, too old. Health and many victories, Achillas!

ACHILLAS. As the gods will, Cæsar.

CÆSAR [*turning to Theodotus*] And you, sir, are—?

THEODOTUS. Theodotus, the King's tutor.

CÆSAR. You teach men how to be kings, Theodotus. That is very clever of you. [*Looking at the gods on the walls as he turns away from Theodotus and goes up again to Pothinus*] And this place?

POTHINUS. The council chamber of the chancellors of the King's treasury, Cæsar.

CÆSAR. Ah! that reminds me. I want some money.

POTHINUS. The King's treasury is poor, Cæsar.

CÆSAR. Yes: I notice that there is but one chair in it.

RUFIO [*shouting gruffly*] Bring a chair there, some of you, for Cæsar.

PTOLEMY [*rising shyly to offer his chair*] Cæsar—

CÆSAR [*kindly*] No, no, my boy: that is your chair of state. Sit down.

He makes Ptolemy sit down again. Meanwhile Rufio, looking about him, sees in the nearest corner an image of the god Ra, represented as a seated man with the head of a hawk. Before the image is a bronze tripod, about as large as a three-legged stool, with a stick of incense burning on it. Rufio, with Roman resourcefulness and indifference to foreign superstitions, promptly seizes the tripod; shakes off the incense; blows away the ash; and dumps it down behind Cæsar, nearly in the middle of the hall.

RUFIO. Sit on that, Cæsar.

A shiver runs through the court, followed by a hissing whisper of Sacrilege!

CÆSAR [*seating himself*] Now, Pothinus, to business. I am badly in want of money.

BRITANNUS [*disapproving of these informal expressions*] My master would say that there is a lawful debt due to Rome by Egypt, and that it is Cæsar's duty to his country to require immediate payment.

CÆSAR [*blandly*] Ah, I forgot. I have not made my companions known here. Pothinus: this is Britannus, my secretary. He is an islander from the western end of the world. [*Britannus bows stiffly*]. This gentleman is Rufio, my comrade in arms. [*Rufio nods*]. Pothinus: I want 1,600 talents.

The courtiers, appalled, murmur loudly, and Theodotus and Achillas appeal mutely to one another against so monstrous a demand.

POTHINUS [*aghast*] Impossible. There is not so much money in the King's treasury. We have been at strife here, because the King's sister Cleopatra falsely claims his throne. The King's taxes have not been collected for a whole year.

CÆSAR. Yes they have, Pothinus. My officers have been collecting them all morning. [*Renewed whisper and sensation, not without some stiffled laughter, among the courtiers*].

RUFIO [*bluntly*] You must pay, Pothinus. You are getting off cheaply enough.

POTHINUS [*bitterly*] Is it possible that Cæsar, the conqueror of the world, has time to occupy himself with such a trifle as our taxes?

CÆSAR. My friend: taxes are the chief business of a conqueror of the world. In return for your bounty, I will settle this dispute about the throne for you, if you will. You say the matter has been at issue for a year, Pothinus. May I have ten minutes at it?

POTHINUS. You will do your pleasure, doubtless.

CÆSAR. Good! But first, let us have Cleopatra here.

THEODOTUS. She is not in Alexandria: she is fled.

CÆSAR. I think not. [*To Rufio*] Call Totateeta.

RUFIO [*calling*] Ho there, Teetatota.

Ftatateeta enters the loggia, and stands arrogantly at the top of the steps.

FTATATEETA. Who pronounces the name of Ftatateeta, the Queen's chief nurse?

CÆSAR. Nobody can pronounce it, Tota, except yourself. Where is your mistress?

Cleopatra, who is hiding behind Ftatateeta, peeps out at them, laughing. Cæsar rises.

CÆSAR. Will the Queen favor us with her presence for a moment?

CLEOPATRA [*pushing Ftatateeta aside and standing haughtily on the brink of the steps*] Am I to behave like a Queen?

CÆSAR. Yes.

Cleopatra immediately comes down to the chair of state; seizes Ptolemy; drags him out of his seat; then takes his place in the chair. Ftatateeta withdraws.

PTOLEMY[*mortified, and struggling with his tears*] Cæsar: this is how she treats me always. If I am king why is she allowed to take everything from me?

CLEOPATRA. You are not to be King, you little cry-baby. You are to be eaten by the Romans.

CÆSAR [*touched by Ptolemy's distress*] Come here, my boy, and stand by me.

Ptolemy goes over to Cæsar, who, resuming his seat on the tripod, takes the boy's hand to encourage him. Cleopatra, furiously jealous, rises and glares at them.

CLEOPATRA [*with flaming cheeks*] Take your throne: I dont want it. [*She flings away from the chair, and approaches Ptolemy, who shrinks from her*]. Go this instant and sit down in your place.

CÆSAR. Go, Ptolemy. Always take a throne when it is offered to you.

Ptolemy slowly goes back to the throne, giving Cleopatra a wide berth, in evident fear of her hands. She takes his place beside Cæsar.

CÆSAR. Pothinus—

CLEOPATRA [*interrupting him*] Are you not going to speak to me?

CÆSAR. Be quiet. Open your mouth again before I give you leave; and you shall be eaten.

CLEOPATRA. I am not afraid. A queen must not be afraid. Eat my husband there, if you like: h e is afraid.

CÆSAR [*starting*] Your husband! What do you mean?

CLEOPATRA [*pointing to Ptolemy*] That little thing.

The two Romans and the Briton stare at one another in amazement.

THEODOTUS. Cæsar: you are a stranger here, and not conversant with our laws. The kings and queens of Egypt may not marry except with their own royal blood. Ptolemy and Cleopatra are born king and consort just as they are born brother and sister.

BRITANNUS [*shocked*] Cæsar: this is not proper.

THEODOTUS [*outraged*] How!

CÆSAR [*recovering his self-possession*] Pardon him, Theodotus: he is a barbarian, and thinks that the customs of his tribe and island are the laws of nature.

BRITANNUS. On the contrary, Cæsar, it is these Egyptians who are barbarians; and you do wrong to encourage them. I say it is a scandal.

CÆSAR. Scandal or not, my friend, it opens the gate of peace. [*Announcing*] Hear what I propose.

RUFIO. Hear Cæsar there.

CÆSAR. Ptolemy and Cleopatra shall reign jointly in Egypt.

BRITANNUS [*unconsciously anticipating a later statesman*] Peace with honor, Pothinus.

POTHINUS [*mutinously*] Cæsar: be honest. The money you demand is the price of our freedom. Take it; and leave us to settle our own affairs.

THE BOLDER COURTIERS [*encouraged by Pothinus's tone and Cæsar's quietness*] Yes, yes. Egypt for the Egyptians!

The conference now becomes an altercation, the Egyptians becoming more and more heated. Cæsar remains unruffled; but Rufio grows fiercer and doggeder, and Britannus haughtily indignant.

RUFIO [*contemptuously*] Egypt for the Egyptians! Do you forget that there is a Roman army of occupation here, left by Aulus Gabinius when he set up your toy king for you?

ACHILLAS [*suddenly asserting himself*] And now under m y command. *I* am the Roman general here, Cæsar.

CÆSAR [*tickled by the humor of the situation*] And also the Egyptian general, eh?

POTHINUS [*triumphantly*] That is so, Cæsar.

CÆSAR [*to Achillas*] So you can make war on the Egyptians in the name of Rome, and on the Romans—on m e , if necessary—in the name of Egypt?

ACHILLAS. That is so, Cæsar.

CÆSAR. And which side are you on at present, if I may presume to ask, general?

ACHILLAS. On the side of the right and of the gods.

CÆSAR. Hm! How many men have you?

ACHILLAS. That will appear when I take the field.

RUFIO [*truculently*] Are your men Romans? If not, it matters not how many there are.

POTHINUS. It is useless to try to bluff us, Rufio. Cæsar has been defeated before and may be defeated again.

ACHILLAS [*menacingly*] What can you do with 4,000 men?

THEODOTUS [*following up Achillas's speech with a raucous squeak*] And without money? Away with you.

ALL THE COURTIERS [*shouting fiercely and crowding towards Cæsar*] Away with you. Egypt for the Egyptians! Begone.

Rufio bites his beard, too angry to speak. Cæsar sits as comfortably as if he were at breakfast, and the cat were clamoring for a piece of Finnan-haddie.

CLEOPATRA. Why do you let them talk to you like that, Cæsar? Are you afraid?

CÆSAR. Why, my dear, what they say is quite true.

CLEOPATRA. But if you go away, I shall not be Queen.

CÆSAR. I shall not go away until you are Queen.

POTHINUS. Achillas: if you are not a fool, you will take that girl whilst she is under your hand.

RUFIO [*daring them*] Why not take Cæsar as well, Achillas?

POTHINUS [*retorting the defiance with interest*] Well said, Rufio. Why not?

RUFIO. Try, Achillas. [*Calling*] Guard there.

The loggia immediately fills with Cæsar's soldiers, who stand, sword in hand, at the top of the steps, waiting the word to charge from their centurion, who carries a cudgel. For a moment the Egyptians face them proudly: then they retire sullenly to their former places.

BRITANNUS. You are Cæsar's prisoners, all of you.

CÆSAR [*benevolently*] Oh no, no, no. By no means. Cæsar's guests, gentlemen.

CLEOPATRA. Wont you cut their heads off?

CÆSAR. What! Cut off your brother's head?

CLEOPATRA. Why not? He would cut off mine, if he got the chance. Wouldnt you, Ptolemy?

PTOLEMY [*pale and obstinate*] I would. I will, too, when I grow up.

Cleopatra is rent by a struggle between her newly-acquired dignity as a queen, and a strong impulse to put out her tongue at him. She takes no part in the scene which follows, but watches it with curiosity and wonder, fidgeting with the restlessness of a child, and sitting down on Cæsar's tripod when he rises.

POTHINUS. Cæsar: if you attempt to detain us—

RUFIO. He will succeed, Egyptian: make up your mind to that. We hold the palace, the beach, and the eastern harbor. The road to Rome is open; and you shall travel it if Cæesar chooses.

CÆSAR [*courteously*] I could do no less, Pothinus, to secure the retreat of my own soldiers. I am accountable for every life among them.

POTHINUS. I am the king's guardian: I refuse to stir. I stand on my right here. Where is your right?

CÆSAR. It is in Rufio's scabbard, Pothinus. I may not be able to keep it there if you wait too long.

Sensation.

POTHINUS [*bitterly*] And this is Roman justice!

THEODOTUS. But not Roman gratitude, I hope.

CÆSAR, Gratitude! Am I in your debt for any service, gentlemen?

THEODOTUS. Is Cæsar's life of so little account to him that he forgets that we have saved it?

CÆSAR. My life! Is that all?

THEODOTUS. Your life. Your laurels. Your future.

POTHINUS. I can call a witness to prove that but for us, the Roman army of occupation, led by the greatest soldier in the world, would now have Cæsar at its mercy. [*Calling through the loggia*] Ho, there, Lucius Septimius: come forth and testify before Cæsar.

CÆSAR [*shrinking*] No, no.

THEODOTUS. Yes, I say. Let the military tribune bear witness.

Lucius Septimius, a clean shaven, trim athlete of about 40, with symmetrical features, resolute mouth, and handsome, thin Roman nose, in the dress of a Roman officer, comes in through the loggia and confronts Cæsar, who hides his face with his robe for a moment; then, mastering himself, drops it, and confronts the tribune with dignity.

POTHINUS. Bear witness, Lucius Septimius. Cæsar came hither in pursuit of his foe. Did we shelter his foe?

LUCIUS. As Pompey's foot touched the Egyptian shore, his head fell by the stroke of my sword.

THEODOTUS [*with viperish relish*] Under the eyes of his wife and child! Remember that, Cæsar! They saw it from the ship he had just left.

LUCIUS. It is so. With this hand, that slew Pompey, I placed his head at the feet of Cæsar.

THEODOTUS. We have given you a full and sweet measure of vengeance.

CÆESAR [*with horror*] Vengeance! Vengeance!! Oh, if I could stoop to vengeance, what would I not exact from you as the price of this murdered man's blood? [*They shrink back, appalled and disconcerted*]. Was he not my son-in-law, my ancient friend, for 20 years the master of great Rome? Did not I, as a Roman, share his glory? Was the fate that forced us to fight for the mastery of the world, of our making? Am I Julius Cæsar, or am I a wild beast, that you fling to me the grey head of the old soldier, the laurelled conqueror, and then claim my gratitude for it! [*To Lucius Septimius*] Begone: you fill me with horror.

LUCIUS [*cold and undaunted*] Pshaw! You have seen severed heads before, Cæsar, and severed right hands too, I think; some thousands of them, after you vanquished the King of the Gauls. Did you spare him, with all your clemency? Was that vengeance?

CÆSAR. Would that it had been! Vengeance at least is human. No, I say: those severed right hands, and the brave King of the Gauls basely strangled in a vault beneath the Capitol were [*with shuddering satire*] a wise severity, a necessary protection to the commonwealth, a duty of statesmanship—follies and fictions ten times bloodier than honest vengeance! What a fool I was then! To think that men's lives should be at the mercy of such fools! [*Humbly*] Lucius Septimius, pardon me: why should the slayer of the King of the Gauls rebuke the slayer of Pompey? You are free to go, all here, in the palace.

RUFIO [*aghast at this clemency*] What! Achillas' army and all?

CÆSAR. Free, Rufio. [*To Lucius Septimus*] You are free to go with the rest. Or stay if you will: I will find a place for you in my service.

LUCIUS. The odds are against you, Cæsar, I go. [*He turns to go out through the loggia*]. Farewell. Come, Achillas, whilst there is yet time.

Cæsar, seeing that Rufio's temper threatens to get the worse of him, puts his hand on his shoulder and brings him down the hall out of harm's way, Britannus accompanying them and posting himself on Cæsar's right hand. This movement brings the three in a little group to the place occupied by Achillas, who moves haughtily away and joins Theodotus on the other side. Lucius Septimius goes out through the soldiers in the loggia. Pothinus, Theodotus and Achillas follow him with the courtiers, very mistrustful of the soldiers, who close up in their rear and go out after them, keeping them moving without much ceremony. The King is left in his chair, piteous, obstinate, with twitching face and fingers. During these movements Rufio maintains an energetic grumbling, as follows:

RUFIO [*as Lucius departs*] Do you suppose he would let us go if he had our heads in his hands?

CÆSAR. I have no right to suppose that his ways are any baser than mine.

RUFIO. Psha!

BRITANNUS. Cæsar: this is not good sense. Your duty to Rome demands that her enemies should be prevented from doing further mischief. [*Cæsar, whose delight in the moral eye-to-business of his British secretary is inexhaustible, smiles indulgently*].

RUFIO. It is no use talking to him, Britannus: you may save your breath to cool your porridge. But mark this, Cæsar. Clemency is very well for you; but what is it for your soldiers, who have to fight tomorrow the men you spared yesterday? You may give what orders you please; but I tell you that your next victory will be a massacre, thanks to your clemency. *I*, for one, will take no prisoners. I will kill my enemies in the field; and then you can preach as much clemency as you please: I shall never have to fight them again. And now, with your leave, I will see these gentry off the premises. [*He turns to go*].

CÆSAR [*turning also and seeing Ptolemy*] What! have they left the boy alone! Oh shame, shame!

RUFIO [*taking Ptolemy's hand and making him rise*] Come, your majesty!

PTOLEMY [*to Cæsar, drawing away his hand from Rufio*] Is he turning me out of my palace?

RUFIO [*grimly*] You are welcome to stay if you wish.

CÆSAR [*kindly*] Go, my boy. I will not harm you; but you will be safer away, among your friends. Here you are in the lion's mouth.

PTOLEMY [*turning to go*] It is not the lion I fear, but [*looking at Rufio*] the jackal. [*He goes out through the loggia*].

CÆSAR [*laughing approvingly*] Brave boy!

CLEOPATRA [*jealous of Cæsar's approbation, calling after Ptolemy*] Little silly. You think that very clever.

CÆSAR. Britannus: attend the King. Give him in charge to that Pothinus fellow. [*Britannus goes out after Ptolemy*].

RUFIO [*pointing to Cleopatra*] And this piece of goods? What is to be done with her? However, I suppose I may leave that to you. [*He goes out through the loggia*].

CLEOPATRA [*flushing suddenly and turning on Cæsar*] Did you mean me to go with the rest?

CÆSAR [*a little preoccupied, goes with a sigh to Ptolemy's chair, whilst she waits for his answer with red cheeks and clenched fists*] You are free to do just as you please, Cleopatra.

CLEOPATRA. Then you do not care whether I stay or not?

CÆSAR [*smiling*] Of course I had rather you stayed.

CLEOPATRA. Much, m u c h rather?

CÆSAR [*nodding*] Much, much rather.

CLEOPATRA. Then I consent to stay, because I am asked. But I do not want to, mind.

CÆSAR. That is quite understood. [*Calling*] Totateeta.

Ftatateeta, still seated, turns her eyes on him with a sinister expression, but does not move.

CLEOPATRA [*with a splutter of laughter*] Her name is not Totateeta: it is Ftatateeta. [*She claps her hands; Ftatateeta instantly comes to Cleopatra*].

CÆSAR [*stumbling over the name*] Tfatafeeta will forgive the erring tongue of a Roman. Tota: the Queen will hold her state here in Alexandria. Engage women to attend upon her; and do all that is needful.

FTATATEETA. Am I then the mistress of the Queen's household?

CLEOPATRA. [*sharply*] No: *I* am the mistress of the Queen's household. Go and do as you are told, or I will have you thrown into the Nile this very afternoon, to poison the poor crocodiles.

CÆSAR [*shocked*] Oh no, no.

CLEOPATRA. Oh yes, yes. You are very sentimental, Cæsar; but you are clever;

and if you do as I tell you, you will soon learn to govern.

Cæsar, quite dumbfounded by this impertinence, turns in his chair and stares at her.

Ftatateeta, smiling grimly, and shewing a splendid set of teeth, goes, leaving them alone together.

CÆSAR. Cleopatra: I really think I must eat you, after all.

CLEOPATRA [*kneeling beside him and looking at him with eager interest, half real, half affected to shew how intelligent she is*] You must not talk to me now as if I were a child.

CÆSAR. You have been growing up since the sphinx introduced us the other night; and you think you know more than I do already.

CLEOPATRA [*taken down, and anxious to justify herself*] No: that would be very silly of me: of course I know that. But—[*suddenly*] are you angry with me?

CÆSAR. No.

CLEOPATRA [*only half believing him*] Then why are you so thoughtful?

CÆSAR [*rising*] I have work to do, Cleopatra.

CLEOPATRA [*drawing back*] Work! [*Offended*] You are tired of talking to me.

CÆSAR [*sitting down again to appease her*] Well, well: another minute. But then—work!

CLEOPATRA. Work! what nonsense! You must remember that you are a king now: I have made you one. Kings dont work.

CÆSAR. Oh! Who told you that, little kitten? Eh?

CLEOPATRA. My father was King of Egypt; and he never worked.

CÆSAR. Well; he lost his throne; and how did he get it back again?

CLEOPATRA [*eagerly, her eyes lighting up*] I will tell you. A beautiful young man, with strong arms, came over the desert with many horsemen, and gave my father back his throne. [*Wistfully*] I was only twelve then. Oh, I wish he would come again, now that I am queen. I would make him my husband.

CÆSAR. It might be managed, perhaps; for it was I who sent that beautiful young man to help your father.

CLEOPATRA [*enraptured*] You know him!

CÆSAR [*nodding*] I do.

CLEOPATRA. Has he come with you? [*Cæsar shakes his head: she is cruelly disappointed*]. Oh, I wish he had, I wish he had. If only I were a little older; so that he might not think me a mere kitten, as you do! But perhaps that is because y o u are old. He is many m a n y years younger than you, is he not?

CÆSAR [*as if swallowing a pill*] He is somewhat younger.

CLEOPATRA. Would he be my husband, do you think, if I asked him?

CÆSAR. Very likely.

CLEOPATRA. But I should not like to ask him. Could you not persuade him to ask me—without knowing that I wanted him to?

CÆSAR [*touched by her innocence of the beautiful young man's character*] My poor child!

CLEOPATRA. Why do you say that as if you were sorry for me? Does he love anyone else?

CÆSAR. I am afraid so.

CLEOPATRA [*tearfully*] Then I shall not be his first love.

CÆSAR. Not quite the first. He is greatly admired by women.

CLEOPATRA. I wish I could be the first. But if he loves me, I will make him kill all the rest. Tell me: is he still beautiful? Do his strong round arms shine in the sun like marble?

CÆSAR. He is in excellent condition—considering how much he eats and drinks.

CLEOPATRA. Oh, you must not say common, earthly things about him; for I love him. He is a god. What is his name?

CÆSAR. His name is Mark Antony.

CLEOPATRA [*musically*] Mark Antony, Mark Antony, Mark Antony! What a beautiful name! [*She throws her arms round Cæsar's neck*]. Oh, how I love you for sending him to help my father! Did you love my father very much?

CÆSAR. No, my child; but your father, as you say, never worked. I always work. So you must run away for a little while and send my secretary to me.

CLEOPATRA [*coaxingly*] No: I want to stay and hear you talk about Mark Antony.

CÆSAR. But if I do not get to work, Pothinus and the rest of them will cut us off from the harbour; and then the way from Rome will be blocked.

CLEOPATRA. No matter: I dont want you to go back to Rome.

CÆSAR. But you want Mark Antony to come from it.

CLEOPATRA [*springing up*] Oh yes, yes, yes: I forgot. Go quickly and work, Cæsar; and keep the way over the sea open for my Mark Antony. [*She runs out, kissing her hand to Mark Antony across the sea*].

CÆSAR [*startled by the entry of a wounded Roman soldier, who confronts him from the upper step*] What now?

SOLDIER [*pointing to his bandaged head*] This, Cæsar; and two of my comrades killed in the market place.

CÆSAR [*quiet, but attending*] Ay. Why?

SOLDIER. There is an army come to Alexandria, calling itself the Roman army.

CÆSAR. The Roman army of occupation. Ay?

SOLDIER. Commanded by one Achillas.

CÆSAR. Well?

SOLDIER. The citizens rose against us when the army entered the gates. I was with two others in the market place when the news came. They set upon us. I cut my way out.

CÆSAR. Good. I am glad to see you alive. [*Rufio enters the loggia hastily, passing behind the soldier to look out through one of the arches at the quay beneath*]. Rufio: we are besieged.

RUFIO. What! Already?

Britannus runs in.

BRITANNUS. Cæsar—

CÆSAR [*anticipating him*] Yes: I know. [*To the soldier*] Comrade: give the word to turn out on the beach and stand by the boats. Get your wound attended to. Go with him, Britannus. [*They hurry out*]. Rufio: we have some ships in the west harbor. Burn them.

RUFIO [*staring*] Burn them!!

CÆSAR. Take every boat we have in the east harbor, and seize the Pharos—that island with the lighthouse. Leave half our men behind to hold the beach and the quay outside this palace: that is the way home.

RUFIO [*disapproving strongly*] Are we to give up the city?

CÆSAR. We have not got it, Rufio. This palace we have; and—what is that building next door?

425

RUFIO. The theatre.

CÆSAR. We will have that too: it commands the strand. For the rest, Egypt for the Egyptians!

RUFIO. Well, you know best, I suppose. Is that all?

CÆSAR. That is all. Are those ships burnt yet?

RUFIO. Be easy: I shall waste no more time. [*He runs out*].

BRITANNUS [*entering*] Cæsar: Pothinus demands speech of you.

CÆSAR. Where is he?

BRITANNUS. He waits without.

CÆSAR. Ho there! admit Pothinus.

BRITANNUS. In my opinion he needs a lesson. His manner is most insolent.

Pothinus appears in the loggia, and comes down the hall very haughtily to Cæsar's left hand.

CÆSAR. Well, Pothinus?

POTHINUS. I have brought you our ultimatum, Cæsar.

CSAR. Ultimatum! The door was open: you should have gone out through it before you declared war. You are my prisoner now. [*He goes to the chair and loosens his toga*].

POTHINUS [*scornfully*] I your prisoner! Do you know that you are in Alexandria, and that King Ptolemy, with an army outnumbering your little troop a hundred to one, is in possession of Alexandria?

CÆSAR [*unconcernedly taking off his toga and throwing it on the chair*] Well, my friend, get out if you can. And tell your friends not to kill any more Romans in the market place. Otherwise my soldiers, who do not share my celebrated clemency, will probably kill you. [*To Britannus*] Pass the word to the guard: Pothinus is now a prisoner. And fetch my armor. [*Britannus runs out, taking Pothinus with him. Rufio returns*].

RUFIO [*pointing from the loggia to a cloud of smoke drifting over the harbor*] See there!

CÆSAR. What, ablaze already! Impossible!

RUFIO. Yes, but it is not my doing: the Egyptians have saved me the trouble. They have captured the west harbor.

CÆSAR [*anxiously*] And the east harbor? The lighthouse, Rufio?

RUFIO [*with a sudden splutter of raging ill usage, coming down to Cæsar and scolding him*] Can I embark a legion in five minutes? The first cohort is already on the beach. We can do no more. If you want faster work, come and do it yourself.

CÆSAR [*soothing him*] Good, good. Patience, Rufio, patience.

RUFIO. Patience! Who is impatient here, you or I?

CÆSAR. Forgive me, Rufio; and [*anxiously*] hurry them as much as—

He is interrupted by an outcry as of an old man in the extremity of misfortune. It draws near rapidly; and Theodotus rushes in, tearing his hair, and squeaking the most lamentable exclamations. Rufio steps back to stare at him, amazed at his frantic condition.

THEODOTUS [*on the steps, with uplifted arms*] Horror unspeakable! Woe, alas! Help!

RUFIO. What now?

CÆSAR [*frowning*] Who is slain?

THEODOTUS. Slain! Oh worse that the death of ten thousand men! Loss irreparable to mankind!

RUFIO. What has happened, man?

THEODOTUS [*rushing down the hall between them*] The fire has spread from your ships. The first of the seven wonders of the world perishes. The library of Alexandria is in flames.

RUFIO. Psha! [*Quite relieved, he goes up to the loggia and watches the preparations of the troops on the beach*].

CÆSAR. Is that all?

THEODOTUS [*unable to believe his senses*] Cæsar: will you go down to posterity as a barbarous soldier too ignorant to know the value of books?

CÆSAR. Theodotus: I am an author myself; and I tell you it is better that the Egyptians should live their lives than dream them away with the help of books.

THEODOTUS [*kneeling, with genuine literary emotion: the passion of the pedant*] Cæsar: once in ten generations of men, the world gains an immortal book.

CÆSAR [*inflexible*] If it did not flatter mankind, the common executioner would burn it.

THEODOTUS. Without history, death will lay you beside your meanest soldier.

CÆSAR. Death will do that in any case. I ask no better grave.

THEODOTUS. What is burning there is the memory of mankind.

CÆSAR. A shameful memory. Let it burn.

THEODOTUS [*wildly*] Will you destroy the past?

CÆSAR. Ay, and build the future with its ruins. [*Theodotus, in despair, strikes himself on the temples with his fists*]. But harken, Theodotus, teacher of kings: you who valued Pompey's head no more than a shepherd values an onion. I cannot spare you a man or a bucket of water just now; but you shall pass freely out of the palace. Now, away with you to Achillas; and borrow his legions to put out the fire. [*He hurries him to the steps*].

THEODOTUS. Posterity will bless you, Cæsar.

CÆSAR. Will you stay to talk whilst the memory of mankind is burning? [*Calling through the loggia*] Ho there! Pass Theodotus out. [*To Theodotus*] Away with you.

THEODOTUS. I must save the library. [*He hurries out*].

RUFIO [*leaves the balcony and comes down into the hall*] Is this more clemency? Have you let him go?

CÆSAR [*chuckling*] I have let Theodotus go to save the library. We must respect literature, Rufio.

RUFIO [*raging*] Folly on folly's head!

CÆSAR. Besides, my friend: every Egyptian we imprison means imprisoning two Roman soldiers to guard him. Eh?

RUFIO. Agh! I might have know there was some fox's trick behind your fine talking. [*He gets away from Cæsar with an ill-humored shrug, and goes out*].

CÆSAR. Is Britannus asleep? I sent him for my armor an hour ago. [*Calling*] Britannicus, Britannicus!

Cleopatra runs in through the loggia with Cæsar's helmet and sword, snatched from Britannus, who follows her with a cuirass and greaves. They come down to Cæsar, she to his left hand, Britannus to his right.

CLEOPATRA. I am going to dress you, Cæsar. Sit down. [*He obeys*]. These Roman helmets are so becoming! [*She takes off his wreath*]. Oh! [*She bursts out laughing at him*].

CÆSAR. What are you laughing at?

CLEOPATRA. Youre bald [*beginning with a big B, and ending with a splutter*].

CÆSAR [*almost annoyed*] Cleopatra! [*He rises, for the convenience of Britannus, who puts the cuirass on him*].

CLEOPATRA. So that is why you wear the wreath—to hide it.

BRITANNUS. Peace, Egyptian: they are the bays of the conqueror. [*He buckles the cuirass*].

CLEOPATRA. Peace, thou: islander! [*To Cæsar*] You should rub your head with strong spirits of sugar, Cæsar. That will make it grow.

CÆSAR [*with a wry face*] Cleopatra: do you like to be reminded that you are very young?

CLEOPATRA [*pouting*] No.

CÆSAR [*sitting down again, and setting out his leg for Britannus, who kneels to put on his greaves*]. Neither do I like to be reminded that I am—middle aged.

CLEOPATRA [*puts the helmet on him*] Oh! How nice! You look only about 50 in it!

BRITANNUS [*looking up severely at Cleopatra*] You must not speak in this manner to Cæsar.

CLEOPATRA. Is it true that when Cæsar caught you on that island, you were painted all over blue?

BRITANNUS. Blue is the color worn by all Britons of good standing. In war we stain our bodies blue; so that though our enemies may strip us of our clothes and our lives, they cannot strip us of our respectability. [*He rises*].

CLEOPATRA [*with Cæsar's sword*] Let me hang this on. Now you look splendid. Have they made any statues of you in Rome?

CÆSAR. Yes, many statues.

CLEOPATRA. You must send for one and give it to me.

RUFIO [*coming back into the loggia, more impatient than ever*] Now Cæsar: have you done talking? The moment your foot is aboard the boats will race one another for the lighthouse.

CÆSAR [*drawing his sword and trying the edge*] Is this well set today, Britannicus? At Pharsalia it was as blunt as a barrel-hoop.

BRITANNUS. It will split one of the Egyptian's hairs today, Cæsar. I have set it myself.

CLEOPATRA [*suddenly throwing her arms in terror around Cæsar*] Oh, you are not really going into battle to be killed?

CÆSAR. No, Cleopatra. No man goes to battle to be killed.

CLEOPATRA. But they do get killed. My sister's husband was killed in battle. You must not go. Let him go [*pointing to Rufio. They all laugh at her*]. Oh please, please dont go. What will happen to me if you never come back?

CSAR [*gravely*] Are you afraid?

CLEOPATRA [*shrinking*] No.

CÆSAR [*with quiet authority*] Go to the balcony; and you shall see us take the Pharos. You must learn to look on battles. Go. [*She goes, downcast, and looks out from the balcony*]. That is well. Now, Rufio. March.

CLEOPATRA [*suddenly clapping her hands*] Oh, you will not be able to go!

CÆSAR. Why? What now?

CLEOPATRA. They are drying up the harbor with buckets—a multitude of soldiers—over there [*pointing out across the sea to her left*]—they are dipping up the water.

RUFIO [*hastening to look*] It is true. The Egyptian army! Crawling over the edge of the west harbor like locusts. [*With sudden anger he strides down to Cæsar*]. This is your accursed clemency, Cæsar. Theodotus has brought them.

CÆSAR [*delighted at his own cleverness*] I meant him to, Rufio. They have come to put out the fire. The library will keep them busy whilst we seize the lighthouse. Eh? [*He rushes out buoyantly through the loggia, followed by Britannus*].

RUFIO [*disgustedly*] More foxing! [*He rushes off. A shout from the soldiers announces the appearance of Cæsar below*].

CENTURION [*below*] All aboard. Give way there. [*Another shout*].

CLEOPATRA [*waving her scarf through the loggia arch*] Goodbye, dear Cæsar. Come back safe. Goodbye!

Dissolve to:

The edge of the quay in front of the palace, looking out west over the east harbor of Alexandria to Pharos island, just to the end of which, and connected with it by a narrow mole, is the famous lighthouse, a gigantic square tower of white marble diminishing in size storey by storey to the top, on which stands a cresset beacon. The island is joined to the main land by the Heptastadium, a great mole or causeway five miles long bounding the harbor on the south.

In the middle of the quay the Centurion joins a Roman sentinel, who stands on guard, pilum in hand. They look out to the lighthouse with strained attention, their left hands shading their eyes. The pilum is a stout wooden shaft $4\frac{1}{2}$ feet long, with an iron spit about three feet long fixed in it. They are so absorbed that they do not notice the approach from the north end of the quay of four Egyptian market porters carrying rolls of carpet, preceded by Ftatateeta and Appollodorus the Sicilian. Apollodorus is a dashing young man of about 24, handsome and debonair, dressed with deliberate æstheticism in the most delicate purples and dove greys, with ornaments of bronze, oxydized silver, and stones of jade and agate. His sword, designed as carefully as a medieval cross, has a blued blade shewing through an openwork scabbard of purple leather and filigree. The porters, conducted by Ftatateeta, pass along the quay behind the sentinel to the steps of the palace, where they put down their bales and squat on the ground. Apollodorus does not pass along with them: he halts, amused by the preoccupation of the Centurion and the sentinel.

APOLLODORUS [*calling to the sentinel*] Who goes there, eh?

They start violently and turn.

CENTURION. Whats this?

SENTINEL [*his pilum at the charge, revealing himself as a small, wiry, sandy-haired, conscientious young man with an elderly face*] Stand. Who are you?

APOLLODORUS. I am Apollodorus the Sicilian. My calling is to choose beautiful things for beautiful queens. [*Pointing to the carpets*] Carpets for the Queen's apartments in the palace.

CENTURION [*interrupting him*] The Queen! Yes, yes: [*to the sentinel*] pass him in. Pass all these bazaar people in to the Queen, with their goods. But mind you pass no one out that you have not passed in—not even the Queen herself. [*He turns and goes away*].

APOLLODORUS [*to the sentinel*] I have brought my caravan past three sentinels, all so busy staring at the lighthouse that not one of them challenged me. Is this Roman discipline?

SENTINEL. We are not here to watch the land but the sea. [*Looking at*

Ftatateeta] Who is this piece of Egyptian crockery?

FTATATEETA. Apollodorus: rebuke this Roman dog; and bid him bridle his tongue in the presence of Ftatateeta, the mistress of the Queen's household.

APOLLODORUS. My friend: this is a great lady, who stands high with Cæsar.

SENTINEL. So you are the carpet merchant?

APOLLODORUS [*hurt*] My friend: I am a patrician.

SENTINEL. A patrician! A patrician keeping a shop!

APOLLODORUS. I do not keep a shop. Mine is a temple of the arts. My motto is Art for Art's sake.

CLEOPATRA [*coming from the palace*] Ftatateeta, Ftatateeta.

FTATATEETA [*scandalized*] No, no. What are you dreaming of? There are men here. Oh that ever I was born!

CLEOPATRA [*running across the quay to Ftatateeta*] Ftatateeta: I have thought of something. I want a boat—at once.

FTATATEETA. A boat! No, no: you cannot. Apollodorus: speak to the Queen.

APOLLODORUS [*gallantly*] Beautiful Queen: I am Apollodorus the Sicilian, your servant, from the bazaar.

CLEOPATRA. I have no time for carpets today. Get me a boat.

FTATATEETA. You cannot go on the water except in the royal barge.

APOLLODORUS. Royalty, Ftatateeta, lies not in the barge but in the Queen. [*To Cleopatra*] The touch of your majesty's foot on the meanest boat in the harbor will make it royal.

CLEOPATRA. Apollodorus: you are my perfect knight; and I will always buy my carpets through you. [*Apollodorus bows joyously*].

APOLLODORUS. My oars shall be your majesty's wings. [*He turns to the harbor and calls seaward*]. Ho there, boatman! Pull in. Whither shall I row my Queen? [*An oar appears above the quay; and the boatman, a bullet-headed, vivacious, grinning fellow, burnt almost black by the sun, comes up a flight of steps from the water on the sentinel's right, oar in hand, and waits at the top*].

CLEOPATRA. To the lighthouse. Come. [*She makes for the steps*].

SENTINEL [*opposing her with his pilum at the charge*] Stand. You cannot pass.

CLEOPATRA [*flushing angrily*] How dare you? Do you know that I am the Queen?

SENTINEL. I have my orders. You cannot pass.

CLEOPATRA. Ftatateeta: strangle him.

SENTINEL [*alarmed—looking apprehensively at Ftatateeta, and brandishing his pilum*] Keep off, there. [*To Apollodorus*] Pass on to the palace and take the Queen with you.

APOLLODORUS. How if I do neither?

SENTINEL. Then I will drive this pilum through you.

APOLLODORUS. At your service, my friend. [*He draws his sword, and springs to his guard with unruffled grace*].

Cleopatra, half frightened, half delighted, takes refuge near the palace, where the porters are squatting among the bales. The boatman, alarmed, hurries down the steps out of harm's way, but stops, with his head just visible above the edge of the quay, to watch the fight.

APOLLODORUS [*To Cleopatra*] I shall not need help, lady. [*To the sentinel*] Shall it be sword against pilum, or sword against sword?

SENTINEL. Roman against Sicilian, curse you. Take that. [*He hurls his pilum at

Apollodorus, who drops expertly on one knee. The pilum passes whizzing over his head and falls harmless. Apollodorus, with a cry of triumph, springs up and attacks the sentinel, who draws his sword and defends himself, crying] Ho there, guard. Help! [*The sentinel is handicapped by his fear of an attack in the rear from Ftatateeta. His swordsmanship, which is of rough and ready sort, is heavily taxed, as he has occasionally to strike at her to keep her off between a blow and a guard with Apollodorus*].

FTATATEETA [*suddenly seizing the sentinel's arms from behind*] Thrust your knife into the dog's throat, Apollodorus. [*The chivalrous Apollodorus laughingly shakes his head; breaks ground away from the sentinel towards the palace; and lowers his point*].

SENTINEL [*struggling vainly*] Curse on you! Let me go. Help ho!

FTATATEETA [*lifting him from the ground*] Stab the little Roman reptile. Spit him on your sword.

A couple of Roman soldiers, with the Centurion, come running along the edge of the quay from the north end. They rescue their comrade, and throw off Ftatateeta, who is sent reeling away on the left hand of the sentinel.

CENTURION. What is this? Make your report, soldier.

SENTINEL. This old woman is dangerous: she is as strong as three men.

FTATATEETA. Centurion: he would have slain the Queen.

SENTINEL [*bluntly*] I would, sooner than let her pass.

CENTURION [*turning to Cleopatra*] Cleopatra: I am loth to offend you; but without Cæsar's express order we dare not let you pass beyond the Roman lines.

APOLLODORUS. Well, Centurion; and has not the lighthouse been within the Roman lines since Cæsar landed there?

CLEOPATRA. Yes, yes. Answer that, if you can.

CENTURION. Cleopatra, I must abide by my orders, and not by the subtleties of this Sicilian. You must withdraw into the palace and examine your carpets there.

CLEOPATRA [*pouting*] I will not: I am the Queen. Cæsar does not speak to me as you do. Have Cæsar's centurions changed manner with his scullions?

CENTURION [*sulkily*] I do my duty. That is enough for me.

APOLLODORUS. Majesty: when a stupid man is doing something he is ashamed of, he always declares that it is his duty.

CENTURION [*to Apollodorus*] As for you, Apollodorus, you may thank the gods that you are not nailed to the palace door with a pilum for your meddling. Is the woman [*referring to Ftatateeta*] your wife?

APOLLODORUS [*horrified*] No, no! [*Correcting himself politely*] Not that the lady is not a striking figure in her own way. But [*emphatically*] she is not my wife.

FTATATEETA [*to the Centurion*] Roman: I am Ftatateeta, the mistress—

CENTURION. Keep your hands off our men, mistress; or I will have you pitched into the harbor, though you were as strong as ten men.

FTATATEETA [*malignantly*] We shall see whom Isis loves best: her servant Ftatateeta or a dog of a Roman.

APOLLODORUS [*to Cleopatra*] Hear my counsel, star of the east. Let me go to Cæsar with a message from you, and a present; and before the sun has stooped half way to the arms of the sea, I will bring you back Cæsar's order of release.

CENTURION [*sneering at him*] And you will sell the Queen the present, no doubt.

APOLLODORUS. Centurion: the Queen shall have from me, without payment,

431

the richest of these carpets for her present to Cæsar.

CLEOPATRA [*exultantly, to the Centurion*] Now you see what an ignorant common creature you are!

CENTURION [*curtly*] Well, a fool and his wares are soon parted. [*He turns to his men*]. Two more men to this post here; and see that no one leaves the palace but this man and his merchandise. If he draws his sword again inside the lines, kill him.

He goes out, leaving two auxiliary sentinels with the other.

Apollodorus takes out his purse, jingling the coins in it, as he goes to the sentinels.

SENTINEL [*very sulky*] Get about your business.

FIRST AUXILIARY. You ought to know better. Off with you.

SECOND AUXILIARY [*looking longingly at the purse—this sentinel is a hooknosed man, unlike his comrade, who is squab faced*] Do not tantalize a poor man.

APOLLODORUS [*to Cleopatra*] Pearl of Queens: the centurion is at hand; and the Roman soldier is incorruptible when his officer is looking. I must carry your word to Cæsar.

CLEOPATRA [*who has been meditating among the carpets*] Are these carpets very heavy?

APOLLODORUS. It matters not how heavy. There are plenty of porters.

CLEOPATRA. How do they put the carpets into boats? Do they throw them down?

APOLLODORUS. Not into small boats, majesty. It would sink them.

CLEOPATRA. Not into that man's boat, for instance? [*pointing to the boatman*].

APOLLODORUS. No. Too small.

CLEOPATRA. But you can take a carpet to Cæsar in it if I send one?

APOLLODORUS. Assuredly.

CLEOPATRA. And you will have it carried gently down the steps and take great care of it? Great, g r e a t care?

APOLLODORUS. More than of my own body.

CLEOPATRA. Good. Come, Ftatateeta. [*Ftatateeta comes to her. Apollodorus offers to squire them into the palace*]. No, Apollodorus, you must not come. I will choose a carpet for myself. You must wait here. [*She runs into the palace*].

APOLLODORUS [*to the porters*] Follow this lady [*indicating Ftatateeta*] and obey her.

The porters rise and take up their bales.

FTATATEETA [*addressing the porters as if they were vermin*] This way. And take your shoes off before you put your feet on those stairs.

She goes in, followed by the porters with the carpets. Meanwhile Apollodorus goes to the edge of the quay and looks out over the harbor. The sentinels keep their eyes on him malignantly.

APOLLODORUS. Listen: were you set here to watch me, or to watch the Egyptians?

SENTINEL. We know our duty.

APOLLODORUS. Then why dont you do it? There is something going on over there [*pointing southwestward to the mole*]. See there. The Egyptians are moving. They are going to recapture the Pharos. They will attack by sea and land along the great mole. Stir yourselves: the hunt is up. [*A clangor of trumpets from several points along the quay*].

Dissolve to:

The Pharos.

Rufio, the morning's fighting done, sits munching dates on a faggot of brushwood outside the door of the lighthouse, which towers gigantic to the clouds on his left. His helmet, full of dates, is between his knees; and a leathern bottle of wine is by his side. Behind him the great stone pedestal of the lighthouse is shut in from the open sea by a low stone parapet, with a couple of steps in the middle to the broad coping. A huge chain with a hook hangs down from the lighthouse crane above his head. Faggots like the one he sits on lie beneath it ready to be drawn up to feed the beacon.

Cæsar is standing on the step at the parapet looking out anxiously, evidently ill at ease.

CÆSAR [*coming away from the parapet, shivering and out of sorts*] Rufio: this has been a mad expedition. We shall be beaten. I wish I knew how our men are getting on with that barricade across the great mole.

RUFIO [*angrily*] Must I leave my food and go starving to bring you a report?

CÆSAR [*soothing him nervously*] No, Rufio, no. Eat, my son, eat. [*He takes another turn, Rufio chewing dates meanwhile*]. The Egyptians cannot be such fools as not to storm the barricade and swoop down on us here before it is finished. It is the first time I have ever run an avoidable risk. I should not have come to Egypt.

RUFIO. An hour ago you were all for victory.

CÆSAR [*apologetically*] Yes: I was a fool—rash, Rufio—boyish.

RUFIO. Boyish? Not a bit of it. Here [*offering him a handful of dates*].

CÆSAR. What are these for?

RUFIO. To eat. Thats whats the matter with you. When a man comes to your age, he runs down before his midday meal. Eat and drink; and then have another look at our chances.

CÆSAR [*taking the dates*] My age! [*He shakes his head and bites a date*]. Yes, Rufio: I am an old man—worn out now—true, quite true. [*He gives way to melancholy contemplation, and eats another date*]. Achillas is still in his prime: Ptolemy is a boy. [*He eats another date, and plucks up a little*]. Well, every dog has had his day; and I have had mine: I cannot complain. [*With sudden cheerfulness*] These dates are not bad, Rufio.

Dissolve to:

The edge of the quay in front of the palace, looking toward the Pharos. The small, wiry young sentinel stands guard. Four porters come from the palace carrying a carpet, followed by Ftatateeta.

SENTINEL [*handling his pilum apprehensively*] You again! [*The porters stop*]. Keep your distance. Come within a yard of me, you old crocodile, and I will give you this [*the pilum*] in your jaws.

FTATATEETA. Peace, Roman fellow: you are now single-handed. Apollodorus: this carpet is Cleopatra's present to Cæsar. It has rolled up in it ten precious goblets of the thinnest Iberian crystal, and a hundred eggs of the sacred blue pigeon. On your honor, let not one of them be broken.

APOLLODORUS. On my head be it! [*To the porters*] Into the boat with them carefully.

FIRST PORTER. Those eggs of which the lady speaks must weigh more than a pound apiece. [*Looking down at the boat*] This boat is too small for such a load.

BOATMAN [*excitedly rushing up the steps*] Oh thou injurious porter! Oh thou unnatural son of a she-camel! [*To Apollodorus*] My boat, sir, hath often carried five men. Shall it not carry your lordship and a bale of pigeon's eggs? [*To the porter*] Thou mangey dromedary, the gods shall punish thee for this envious wickedness.

FIRST PORTER [*stolidly*] I cannot quit this bale now to beat these; but another day I will lie in wait for thee.

APOLLODORUS [*going between them*] Peace there.

FTATATEETA [*anxiously*] In the name of the gods, Apollodorus, run no risks with that bale.

APOLLODORUS. Fear not, thou venerable grotesque: I guess its great worth. [*To the porters*] Down with it, and gently; or ye shall eat nothing but stick for ten days.

The boatman goes down the steps, followed by the porters with the bale: Ftatateeta and Apollodorus watching from the edge.

APOLLODORUS. Gently, my sons, my children—[*with sudden alarm*] gently, ye dogs. Lay it level in the stern—so—tis well.

FTATATEETA [*screaming down at one of the porters*] Do not step on it, do not step on it. Oh thou brute beast!

FIRST PORTER [*ascending*] Be not excited, mistress: all is well.

FTATATEETA [*panting*] Oh, thou hast given my heart a turn! [*She clutches her side, gasping*].

The four porters have now come up and are waiting at the stairhead to be paid.

APOLLODORUS. Here, ye hungry ones. [*He gives money to the first porter, who holds it in his hand to shew to the others. They crowd greedily to see how much it is, quite prepared, after the Eastern fashion, to protest to heaven against their patron's stinginess. But his liberality overpowers them*].

FIRST PORTER. O bounteous prince!

SECOND PORTER. O lord of the bazaar!

THIRD PORTER. O favored of the gods!

FOURTH PORTER. O father to all the porters of the market.

SENTINEL [*enviously, threatening them fiercely with his pilum*] Hence, dogs: off. Out of this. [*They fly before him northward along the quay*].

APOLLODORUS. Farewell, Ftatateeta. I shall be at the lighthouse before the Egyptians. [*He descends the steps*]. Give me the oars, O son of a snail. [*He takes the oars and gives money to the boatman, who remains behind*].

FTATATEETA. The gods speed thee!

The sentry returns from chasing the porters and looks down at the boat, standing near the stairhead lest Ftatateeta should attempt to escape.

APOLLODORUS [*as the boat moves off*] Farewell, valiant pilum pitcher.

SENTINEL. Farewell, shopkeeper.

APOLLODORUS. Ha, ha! Push, thou brave boatsman, push. Soho-o-o-o! [*He begins to sing in barcarolle measure to the rhythm of the oars*].

> My heart, my heart, spread out thy wings:
> Shake off thy heavy load of love—

[*In the distance*]

> My heart, my heart, be whole and free:
> Love is thine only enemy.

Dissolve to:

The Pharos. Britannus comes out of the lighthouse door, greatly excited, with a leathern bag. He calls to Cæsar.

BRITANNUS [*triumphantly*] Our brave mariners have captured a treasure. [*He throws the bag down at Cæsar's feet*]. Our enemies are delivered into our hands.

CÆSAR. In that bag?

BRITANNUS. Wait till you hear, Cæsar. This bag contains all the letters which have passed between our enemies.

CÆSAR. Well?

BRITANNUS [*impatient of Cæsar's slowness to grasp the situation*] Well, we shall now know who your foes are. The name of every man who has plotted against you since you crossed the Rubicon may be in these papers, for all we know.

CÆSAR. Put them in the fire.

BRITANNUS. Put them—[*he gasps*]!!!!

CÆSAR. In the fire. Would you have me waste the next three years of my life condemning men who will be my friends when I have proved that my friendship is worth more than that of my enemies?

BRITANNUS. But your honor—the honor of Rome—

CÆSAR. I do not make human sacrifices to my honor, as your Druids do. Since you will not burn these, at least I can drown them. [*He picks up the bag and throws it over the parapet into the sea*].

BRITANNUS. Cæsar: this is mere eccentricity. Are traitors to be allowed to go free for the sake of a paradox?

RUFIO [*rising*] Cæsar: when the islander has finished preaching, call me again. [*He goes into the lighthouse*].

BRITANNUS [*with genuine feeling*] O Cæsar, my great master, if I could but persuade you to regard life seriously, as men do in my country!

CÆSAR. Do they truly do so, Britannus?

BRITANNUS. Have you not been there? Have you not seen them? What Briton speaks as you do in your moments of levity? What Briton neglects to attend the services at the sacred grove? What Briton wears clothes of many colors as you do, instead of plain blue, as all solid, well esteemed men should? These are moral questions with us.

CÆSAR. Well, well, my friend: some day I shall settle down and have a blue toga, perhaps. Meanwhile, I must get on as best I can in my flippant Roman way.

Apollodorus climbs up a ladder onto the parapet.

BRITANNUS [*turning quickly, and challenging the stranger with official haughtiness*] What is this? Who are you? How did you come here?

APOLLODORUS. Calm yourself, my friend: I am not going to eat you. [*Rufio appears at the lighthouse door*]. Hail, great Caesar! I am Apollodorus the Sicilian, an artist.

BRITANNUS. An artist! Why have they admitted this vagabond?

CÆSAR. Peace, man. Apollodorus is a famous patrician amateur.

BRITANNUS [*disconcerted*] I crave the gentleman's pardon. [*To Cæsar*] I understood him to say that he was a professional.

CÆSAR. Welcome, Apollodorus. What is your business?

APOLLODORUS. First, to deliver to you a present from the Queen of Queens.

CÆSAR. Who is that?

APOLLODORUS. Cleopatra of Egypt.

CÆSAR [*taking him into his confidence in his most winning manner*] Apollodorus:

435

this is no time for playing with presents. Pray you, go back to the Queen, and tell her that if all goes well I shall return to the palace this evening.

APOLLODORUS. Cæsar: I cannot return. As I approached the lighthouse, some fool threw a great leathern bag into the sea. It broke the nose of my boat; and I had hardly time to get myself and my charge to the shore before the poor little cockleshell sank.

CÆSAR. I am sorry, Apollodorus. The fool shall be rebuked. Well, well: what have you brought me? The Queen will be hurt if I do not look at it.

RUFIO. Have we time to waste on this trumpery? The Queen is only a child.

CÆSAR. Just so: that is why we must not disappoint her.

APOLLODORUS. Cæsar: it is a Persian carpet—a beauty! And in it are—so I am told—pigeons' eggs and crystal goblets and fragile precious things. I dare not for my head have it carried up that narrow ladder from the causeway.

RUFIO. Swing it up by the crane, then.

APOLLODORUS. The crane! Cæsar: I have sworn to tender this bale of carpet as I tender my own life.

CÆSAR [cheerfully] Then let them swing you up at the same time; if the chain breaks, you and the pigeons' eggs will perish together. [He goes to the chain and looks up along it, examing it curiously].

APOLLODORUS [to Britannus] Is Cæsar serious?

BRITANNUS. His manner is frivolous because he is an Italian; but he means what he says.

APOLLODORUS. Serious or not, he spake well. Give me a squad of soldiers to work the crane.

BRITANNUS. One elderly Tyrian works the crane; and his son, a well conducted youth of 14.

APOLLOOORUS [looking at the chain] What! An old man and a boy work that! Twenty men, you mean.

BRITANNUS. Two only, I assure you. They have counterweights, and a machine with boiling water which I do not understand: it is not of British design. Leave the crane to me. Go and await the descent of the chain.

APOLLODORUS. Good. You will presently see me there [turning to them all and pointing with an eloquent gesture to the sky above the parapet] rising like the sun with my treasure.

He goes back the way he came. Britannus goes into the lighthouse.

RUFIO [ill-humoredly] Are you really going to wait here for this foolery, Cæsar?

CÆSAR [backing away from the crane as it gives signs of working] Why not?

RUFIO. The Egyptians will let you know why not if they have the sense to make a rush from the shore end of the mole before our barricade is finished. And here we are waiting like children to see a carpet full of pigeons' eggs.

The chain rattles, and is drawn up high enough to clear the parapet. It then swings round out of sight behind the lighthouse.

CÆSAR. Fear not, my son Rufio. When the first Egyptian takes his first step along the mole, the alarm will sound; and we two will reach the barricade from our end before the Egyptians—we two, Rufio: I, the old man, and you, his biggest boy. And the old man will be there first. So peace; and give me some more dates.

APOLLODORUS [from the causeway below] Soho, haul away. So-ho-o-o-o! [The chain is drawn up and comes round again from behind the lighthouse. Apollodorus *is swinging in the air with his bale of carpet at the end of it. He breaks into song as he soars above the parapet]*

    Aloft, aloft, behold the blue
    That never shone in woman's eyes.

Easy there: stop her. [*He ceases to rise*]. Further round! [*The chain comes forward above the platform*].

RUFIO [*calling up*] Lower away there. [*The chain and its load begin to descend*].

APOLLODORUS [*calling up*] Gently—slowly—mind the eggs.

RUFIO [*calling up*] Easy there—slowly—slowly.

 Apollodorus and the bale are deposited safely on the flags in the middle of the platform. Rufio and Cæsar help Apollodorus to cast off the chain from the bale.

RUFIO. Haul up.

 The chain rises clear of their heads with a rattle. Britannus comes from the lighthouse and helps them to uncord the carpet.

APOLLODORUS [*when the cords are loose*] Stand off, my friends: let Cæsar see. [*He throws the carpet open*].

RUFIO. Nothing but a heap of shawls. Where are the pigeons' eggs?

APOLLODORUS. Approach, Cæsar; and search for them among the shawls.

RUFIO [*drawing his sword*] Ha, treachery! Keep back, Cæsar: I saw the shawl move: there is something alive there.

BRITANNUS [*drawing his sword*] It is a serpent.

APOLLODORUS. Dares Cæsar thrust his hand into the sack where the serpent moves?

RUFIO [*turning on him*] Treacherous dog—

CÆSAR. Peace. Put up your swords. Apollodorus: your serpent seems to breathe very regularly. [*He thrusts his hand under the shawls and draws out a bare arm*]. This is a pretty little snake.

RUFIO [*drawing out the other arm*] Let us have the rest of you.

 They pull Cleopatra up by the wrists into a sitting position. Britannus, scandalized, sheathes his sword with a drive of protest.

CLEOPATRA [*gasping*] Oh, I'm smothered. Oh, Cæsar, a man stood on me in the boat; and a great sack of something fell upon me out of the sky; and then the boat sank; and then I was swung up into the air and bumped down.

CÆSAR [*petting her as she rises and takes refuge on his breast*] Well, never mind: here you are safe and sound at last.

RUFIO. Ay; and now that she is here, what are we to do with her?

BRITANNUS. She cannot stay here, Cæsar, without the companionship of some matron.

CLEOPATRA [*jealously, to Cæsar, who is obviously perplexed*] Arnt you glad to see me?

CÆSAR. Yes, yes; I am very glad. But Rufio is very angry; and Britannus is shocked.

CLEOPATRA [*contemptuously*] You can have their heads cut off, can you not?

CÆSAR. They would not be so useful with their heads cut off as they are now, my sea bird.

RUFIO [*to Cleopatra*] We shall have to go away presently and cut some of your Egyptians' heads off. How will you like being left here with the chance of being captured by that little brother of yours if we are beaten?

CLEOPATRA. But you mustnt leave me alone. Cæsar: you will not leave me alone, will you?

RUFIO. What! not when the trumpet sounds and all our lives depend on Cæsar's being at the barricade before the Egyptians? Eh?

CLEOPATRA. Let them lose their lives: they are only soldiers.

CÆSAR [*gravely*] Cleopatra: when that trumpet sounds, we must take every man his life in his hand, and throw it in the face of Death. And of my soldiers who have trusted me there is not one whose hand I shall not hold more sacred than your head. [*Cleopatra is overwhelmed. Her eyes fill with tears*]. Apollodorus: you must take her back to the palace.

APOLLODORUS. Am I a dolphin, Cæsar, to cross the seas with young ladies on my back? My boat is sunk: all yours are either at the barricade or have returned to the city. [*He goes back to the parapet*].

CLEOPATRA [*struggling with her tears*] It does not matter. I will not go back. Nobody cares for me.

CÆSAR. Cleopatra—

CLEOPATRA. You want me to be killed.

CÆSAR [*still more gravely*] My poor child: your life matters little here to anyone but yourself. [*She gives way altogether at this, casting herself down on the faggots weeping. Suddenly a great tumult is heard in the distance, bucinas and trumpets sounding through a storm of shouting. Britannus rushes to the parapet and looks along the mole. Cæsar and Rufio turn to one another with quick intelligence*].

CÆSAR. Come, Rufio.

CLEOPATRA [*scrambling to her knees and clinging to him*] No no. Do not leave me, Cæsar. [*He snatches his skirt from her clutch*]. Oh!

BRITANNUS [*from the parapet*] Cæsar: we are cut off. The Egyptians have landed from the west harbor between us and the barricade!!!

CÆSAR [*ruthfully*] Rufio, Rufio: my men at the barricade are between the sea party and the shore party. I have murdered them.

RUFIO. Ay: that comes of fooling with this girl here.

APOLLODORUS [*coming up quickly from the parapet*] Cæsar.

CÆSAR. We must defend ourselves here.

APOLLODORUS. I have thrown the ladder into the sea. They cannot get in without it.

RUFIO. Ay; and we cannot get out.

APOLLODORUS. Not get out! Why not? You have ships in the east harbor.

BRITANNUS [*hopefully, at the parapet*] The galleys are standing in towards us already. [*Cæsar quickly joins Britannus at the parapet*].

RUFIO [*to Apollodorus, impatiently*] And by what road are we to walk to the galleys, pray?

APOLLODORUS [*with gay, defiant rhetoric*] By the road that leads everywhere— the diamond path of the sun and moon. [*He throws away his cloak and cap, and binds his sword on his back*]. How far off is the nearest galley?

BRITANNUS. Fifty fathom.

CÆSAR. No, no: nearly quarter of a mile, Apollodorus.

APOLLODORUS. Good. Defend yourselves here until I send you a boat from that galley.

RUFIO. Have you wings, perhaps?

APOLLODORUS. Water wings, soldier. Behold!

He runs up the steps between Cæsar and Britannus to the coping of the parapet;

springs into the air; and plunges head foremost into the sea.

CÆSAR [*like a schoolboy —wildly excited*] Bravo, bravo! [*Throwing off his cloak*] By Jupiter, I will do that too.

RUFIO [*seizing him*] You are mad. You shall not.

CÆSAR. Why not? Can I not swim as well as he?

RUFIO [*frantic*] Can an old fool dive and swim like a young one?

CÆSAR [*breaking loose from Rufio*] Old!!!

BRITANNUS [*shocked*] Rufio: you forget yourself.

CÆSAR. I will race you to the galley for a week's pay, father Rufio.

CLEOPATRA. But me! me!! me!!! what is to become of me?

CÆSAR. I will carry you on my back to the galley like a dolphin. Rufio: when you see me rise to the surface, throw her in.

CLEOPATRA. No, no, NO. I shall be drowned.

CÆSAR. And then in with you after her, both of you.

BRITANNUS. Cæsar: I am a man and a Briton, not a fish. I must have a boat. I cannot swim.

CLEOPATRA. Neither can I.

CÆSAR [*to Britannus*] Stay here, then alone, until I recapture the lighthouse: I will not forget you. Now, Rufio.

RUFIO. You have made up your mind to this folly?

CÆSAR. The Egyptians have made it up for me. And mind where you jump: I do not want to get you in the small of my back as I come up. [*He runs up the steps and stands on the coping*].

BRITANNUS [*anxiously*] One last word, Cæsar. Do not let yourself be seen in the fashionable part of Alexandria until you have changed your clothes.

CÆSAR [*calling over the sea*] Ho, Apollodorus: [*he points skyward and quotes the barcarolle*]

        The white upon the blue above—

APOLLODORUS [*swimming in the distance*]

        Is purple on the green below—

CÆSAR[*exultant*] Aha! [*He plunges into the sea*].

CLEOPATRA [*running excitedly to the steps*] Oh, let me see. He will be drowned [*Rufio seizes her*]—Ah—ah—ah—ah! [*He pitches her screaming into the sea. Rufio and Britannus roar with laughter*].

RUFIO [*looking down after her*] He has got her. [*To Britannus*] Hold the fort, Briton. Cæsar will not forget you. [*He springs off*].

BRITANNUS [*watching them as they swim*] Hip, hip, hip, hurrah!

* *The lighthouse passes out of sight and leaves the sky, which darkens into night. The new moon appears in the east and crosses waxing and waning five times to appropriate music: a tune with five variations. When it rises for the fifth time it is on the desert with the old musician and the harp girl travelling through it: she on a handsome Bactrian camel, half caged in red curtains: he on a well caparisoned ass. The harp is part of the luggage on the camel.*

MUSICIAN. Woa! [*He pulls up the ass and stops the camel*]. Listen to me, you. We are approaching Alexandria, where you are to play for the Queen. If you play your best, I may become the Queen's teacher. If you play badly—if you miss a

---

* Against his better judgment, says Shaw, he wrote an alternative transition scene. See Appendix I for this scene, which is set in a barber's shop.

note—the Queen's nurse, Ftatateeta, a terrible woman, will have you flogged until your flesh is cut to ribbons. But remember: the real ruler of Egypt now is the Roman conqueror, Julius Cæsar. He has been King in Alexandria for five months. He is a mighty sorcerer: when he and his soldiers should have died of thirst he dug wells in the sea sand, and by his magic made the salt water fresh and sweet. He may be present when you play. If so, kiss his feet, and play as you have never played before. Do not speak: let them hear nothing from you but music: leave the talking to me. Now onward: we shall be there by noon.

They travel on.

Dissolve to:

A boudoir in the Alexandrian palace. Cleopatra is passing the afternoon among a bevy of her ladies, listening to the slave girl who is playing the harp in the middle of the room. The harpist's master, the old magician, with a consciously keen and pretentious expression is squatting on the floor, watching her performance. Except the harp player all are seated: Cleopatra in a chair opposite the door on the other side of the room; the rest on the ground. Cleopatra's ladies are all young, the most conspicuous being Charmian and Iras, her favorites. Charmian is a hatchet faced, terra cotta colored little goblin, swift in her movements, and neatly finished at the hands and feet. Iras is a plump, goodnatured creature, rather fatuous, with a profusion of red hair, and a tendency to giggle on the slightest provocation.

The ladies laugh.

CLEOPATRA [*frowning*] You laugh; but take care, take care. I will find out some day how to make myself served as Cæsar is served.

CHARMIAN. Old hooknose! [*They laugh again*].

CLEOPATRA [*revolted*] Silence, Charmian: do not be a silly little Egyptian fool. Do you know why I allow you all to chatter impertinently just as you please, instead of treating you as Ftatateeta would treat you if she were Queen?

CHARMIAN. Because you try to imitate Cæsar in everything; and he lets everybody say what they please to him.

CLEOPATRA. No; but because I asked him one day why he did so; and he said "Let your women talk; and you will learn something from them." What have I to learn from them? I said. "What they a r e," said he; and oh! you should have seen his eyes as he said it. You would have curled up, you shallow things. [*They laugh. She turns fiercely on Iras*]. At whom are you laughing—at me or at Cæsar?

IRAS. At Cæsar.

CLEOPATRA. If you were not a fool, you would laugh at me; and if you were not a coward you would not be afraid to tell me so.

IRAS [*as she reluctantly rises*] Heigho! I wish Cæsar were back in Rome.

CLEOPATRA [*threateningly*] It will be a bad day for you all when he goes. Oh, if I were not ashamed to let him see that I am as cruel at heart as my father, I would make you repent that speech! Why do you wish him away?

CHARMIAN. He makes you so terribly prosy and serious and learned and philosophical. It is worse than being religious, at our ages. [*The ladies laugh*].

CLEOPATRA. Cease that endless cackling, will you. Hold your tongues.

CHARMIAN [*with mock resignation*] Well, well: we must try to live up to Cæsar.

They laugh again. Cleopatra rages silently. Ftatateeta enters with Pothinus, who halts on the threshold.

FTATATEETA [*at the door*] Pothinus craves the ear of the—

CLEOPATRA. I suppose he has offered you a bribe to admit him to my presence.

FTATATEETA [*protesting*] Now by my father's gods—

CLEOPATRA [*cutting her short despotically*] Have I not told you not to deny things? You all sell audiences with me, as if I saw whom you please, and not whom I please. Go take the bribe; and bring in Pothinus. [*Ftatateeta is about to reply*]. Dont answer me. Go.

   Ftatateeta goes to the threshold. Pothinus approaches Cleopatra, who deliberately speaks to the old musician rather than to him.

CLEOPATRA. I want to learn to play the harp with my own hands. Cæsar loves music. Can you teach me?

MUSICIAN. Assuredly I and no one else can teach the queen. All the other teachers are quacks: I have exposed them repeatedly.

CLEOPATRA. Good: you shall teach me. How long will it take?

MUSICIAN. Not very long: only four years. Your Majesty must first become proficient in the philosophy of Pythagoras.

CLEOPATRA. Has she [*indicating the slave*] become proficient in the philosophy of Pythagoras?

MUSICIAN. Oh, she is but a slave. She learns as a dog learns.

CLEOPATRA. Well, then, I will learn as a dog learns; for she plays better than you. You shall give me a lesson every day for a fortnight. [*The musician hastily scrambles to his feet and bows profoundly*]. After that, whenever I strike a false note you shall be flogged; and if I strike so many that there is not time to flog you, you shall be thrown into the Nile to feed the crocodiles. [*To Ftatateeta*] Give the girl a piece of gold; and send them away.

MUSICIAN [*much taken aback*] But true art will not be thus forced.

FTATATEETA [*pushing him out*] What is this? Answering the Queen, forsooth. Out with you. [*The girl follows with her harp, amid the laughter of the ladies*].

CLEOPATRA. Well, Pothinus: what is the latest news from your rebel friends?

POTHINUS [*haughtily*] I am no friend of rebellion. And a prisoner does not receive news.

CLEOPATRA. You are no more a prisoner than I am—than Cæsar is. These five months we have been besieged in this palace by my subjects. You are allowed to walk on the beach among the soldiers. Can I go further myself, or can Cæsar?

POTHINUS. You are but a child, Cleopatra, and do not understand these matters.

   The ladies laugh. Cleopatra looks inscrutably at him.

CHARMIAN. I see you do not know the latest news, Pothinus.

POTHINUS. What is that?

CHARMTAN. That Cleopatra is no longer a child. Shall I tell you how to grow much older, and much, m u c h wiser in one day?

POTHINUS. I should prefer to grow wiser without growing older.

CHARMIAN. Well, go up to the top of the lighthouse; and get somebody to take you by the hair and throw you into the sea. [*The ladies laugh*].

CLEOPATRA. She is right, Pothinus: you will come to the shore with much conceit washed out of you. [*The ladies laugh. Cleopatra rises impatiently*]. Begone, all of you. I will speak with Pothinus alone. [*They run out laughing*]. What are you waiting for?

FTATATEETA. It is not meet that the Queen remain alone with—

CLEOPATRA [*interrupting her*] Ftatateeta: must I sacrifice you to your father's gods to teach you that *I* am Queen of Egypt, and not you?

FTATATEETA [*indignantly*] You are like the rest of them. You want to be what these Romans call a New Woman. [*She goes out, banging the door*].

CLEOPATRA [*sitting down again*] Now, Pothinus: why did you bribe Ftatateeta to bring you hither?

POTHINUS [*studying her gravely*] Cleopatra: what they tell me is true. You are changed.

CLEOPATRA. Do you speak with Cæsar every day for six months: and you will be changed.

POTHINUS. It is the common talk that you are infatuated with this old man?

CLEOPATRA. Infatuated? What does that mean? Made foolish, is it not? Oh no: I wish I were.

POTHINUS. You wish you were made foolish! How so?

CLEOPATRA. When I was foolish, I did what I liked. Now that Cæsar has made me wise, it is no use my liking or disliking: I do what must be done, and have no time to attend to myself. That is not happiness; but it is greatness. If Cæsar were gone, I think I could govern the Egyptians; for what Cæsar is to me, I am to the fools around me.

POTHINUS [*looking hard at her*] Cleopatra: this may be the vanity of youth.

CLEOPATRA. No, no: it is not that I am so clever, but that the others are so stupid.

POTHINUS [*musingly*] Truly, that is the great secret.

CLEOPATRA. Well, now tell me what you came to say?

POTHINUS [*embarrassed*] I! Nothing.

CLEOPATRA. Nothing!

POTHINUS. At least—to beg for my liberty: that is all.

CLEOPATRA. For that you would have knelt to Cæsar. No, Pothinus: you came with some plan that depended on Cleopatra being a little nursery kitten. Now that Cleopatra is a Queen, the plan is upset.

POTHINUS [*bowing his head submissively*] It is so.

CLEOPATRA [*exultant*] Aha!

POTHINUS [*raising his eyes keenly to hers*] Is Cleopatra then indeed a Queen, and no longer Cæsar's prisoner and slave?

CLEOPATRA. Pothinus: we are all Cæsar's slaves—all we in this land of Egypt—whether we will or no. And she who is wise enough to know this will reign when Cæsar departs.

POTHINUS. You harp on Cæsar's departure.

CLEOPATRA. What if I do?

POTHINUS. Does he not love you?

CLEOPATRA. Love me! Pothinus: Cæsar loves no one. Who are those we love. Only those whom we do not hate: all people are strangers and enemies to us except those we love. But it is not so with Cæsar. He has no hatred in him: he makes friends with everyone as he does with dogs and children. His kindness to me is a wonder: neither mother, father, nor nurse have ever taken so much care for me, or thrown open their thoughts to me so freely.

POTHINUS. Well: is not this love?

CLEOPATRA. What! when he will do as much for the first girl he meets on his way back to Rome? Ask his slave, Britannus: he has been just as good to him. Nay, ask his very horse! His kindness is not for anything in me: it is in his own nature.

POTHINUS. But how can you be sure that he does not love you as men love women?

CLEOPATRA. Because I cannot make him jealous. I have tried.

POTHINUS. Hm! Perhaps I should have asked, then, do you love h i m ?

CLEOPATRA. Can one love a god? Besides, I love another Roman—no god, but a man—one who can love and hate—one whom I can hurt and who would hurt me.

POTHINUS. Does Cæsar know this?

CLEOPATRA. Yes.

POTHINUS. And he is not angry?

CLEOPATRA. He promises to send him to Egypt to please me!

POTHINUS. I do not understand this man.

CLEOPATRA [*with superb contempt*] You understand Cæsar! How could you? [*Proudly*] I do—by instinct.

POTHINUS [*deferentially, after a moment's thought*] Your Majesty caused me to be admitted today. What message has the Queen for me?

CLEOPATRA. This. You think that by making my brother king, you will rule in Egypt because you are his guardian and he is a little silly.

POTHINUS. The Queen is pleased to say so.

CLEOPATRA. The Queen is pleased to say this also. That Cæsar will eat up you, and Achillas, and my brother, as a cat eats up mice; and that he will put on this land of Egypt as a shepherd puts on his garment. And when he has done that, he will return to Rome, and leave Cleopatra here as his viceroy.

POTHINUS [*breaking out wrathfully*] That he shall never do. We have a thousand men to his ten; and we will drive him and his beggarly legions into the sea.

CLEOPATRA [*with scorn, getting up to go*] You rant like any common fellow.

POTHINUS. Cleopatra—

CLEOPATRA. Enough, enough: Cæsar has spoiled me for talking to weak things like you. [*She goes out*].

POTHINUS. Let me go forth from this hateful place. [*He begins to leave when Ftatateeta enters and stops him*].

FTATATEETA. What angers you?

POTHINUS. The curse of all the gods of Egypt be upon her! She sold her country to the Roman, that she may buy it back from him with her kisses.

FTATATEETA. Fool: did she not tell you that she would have Cæsar gone?

POTHINUS. You listened?

FTATATEETA. I took care that some honest woman should be at hand whilst you were with her.

POTHINUS. Mark this, mistress. You thought, before Cæsar came, that Egypt should presently be ruled by you and your crew in the name of Cleopatra. I set myself against it—

FTATATEETA [*interrupting him —wrangling*] Ay; that it might be ruled by you and y o u r crew in the name of Ptolemy.

POTHINUS. Better me, or even you, than a woman with a Roman heart; and that is what Cleopatra is now become. Whilst I live, she shall never rule. So guide yourself accordingly. I know to whom I must go now.

Dissolve:

It is drawing on to dinner time. The table is laid on the roof of the palace; and thither Rufio is now climbing, ushered by a majestic palace official, wand of office in hand, and followed by Pothinus and a guard.

RUFIO. Wait here.

After several stairs Rufio and the official emerge into a massive colonnade on the roof. Light curtains are drawn between the columns on the north and east to soften the westering sun. The official leads Rufio to one of these shaded sections.

THE OFFICIAL [*bowing*] The Roman commander will await Cæsar here.

The slave sets down the stool near the southernmost column, and slips out through the curtains.

RUFIO [*sitting down, a little blown*] Pouf! That was a climb. How high have we come?

THE OFFICIAL. We are on the palace roof, O Beloved of Victory!

RUFIO. Good! the Beloved of Victory has no more stairs to get up.

A second official enters from the opposite end, walking backwards.

THE SECOND OFFICIAL. Cæsar approaches.

Cæsar, fresh from the bath, clad in a new tunic of purple silk, comes in, beaming and festive, followed by two slaves carrying a light couch, which is hardly more than an elaborately designed bench. They place it near the northernmost of the two curtained columns. When this is done they slip out through the curtains; and the two officials, formally bowing, follow them. Rufio rises to receive Cæsar.

CÆSAR [*coming over to him*] Why, Rufio! [*Surveying his dress with an air of admiring astonishment*] A new baldrick! A new golden pommel to your sword! And you have had your hair cut! But not your beard—? impossible! [*He sniffs at Rufio's beard*]. Yes, perfumed, by Jupiter Olympus!

RUFIO [*growling*] Well: is it to please myself?

CÆSAR [*affectionately*] No, my son Rufio, but to please me—to celebrate my birthday.

RUFIO [*contemptuously*] Your birthday! You always have a birthday when there is a pretty girl to be flattered or an ambassador to be conciliated. We had seven of them in ten months last year.

CÆSAR [*contritely*] It is true, Rufio! I shall never break myself of these petty deceits.

RUFIO. Have you noticed that I am before my time?

CÆSAR. Aha! I thought that meant something. What is it?

The curtains are drawn, revealing the roof garden with a banqueting table set across in the middle for four persons, one at each end, and two side by side. One side is blocked with golden wine vessels and basins. A gorgeous major-domo is superintending the laying of the table by a staff of slaves. The colonnade goes round the garden at both sides to the further end, where a gap in it, like a great gateway, leaves the view open to the sky beyond the western edge of the roof, except in the middle, where a life size image of Ra, seated on a huge plinth, towers up, with hawk head and crown of asp and disk. His altar, which stands at his feet, is a single white stone. Cæsar sits down on the bench left by the two slaves.

RUFIO [*sitting down on a stool*] Pothinus wants to speak to you. I advise you to see him: there is some plotting going on here among the women.

CÆSAR. Who is Pothinus?

RUFIO. The little King's leader, whom you kept prisoner.

CÆSAR [*annoyed*] Has he not escaped?

RUFIO. No.

CÆSAR [*rising imperiously*] Why not? Have I not told you always to let prisoners escape unless there are special orders to the contrary? Are there not enough mouths to be fed without him?

RUFIO. Yes; and if you would have a little sense and let me cut his throat, you would save his rations. Anyhow he wont escape. He prefers to stay and spy on us.

CÆSAR [*resuming his seat, argued down*] Hm! And you want me to see him?

RUFIO [*obstinately*] I dont want anything. I daresay you will do what you like. Dont put it on me.

CÆSAR [*with an air of doing it expressly to indulge Rufio*] Well, well: let us have him.

RUFIO [*calling*] Ho there, guard! Release your man and send him up. [*To Cæsar*] Who is to dine with us—besides Cleopatra?

CÆSAR. Apollodorus the Sicilian.

RUFIO. That popinjay!

CÆSAR. Come! the popinjay is an amusing dog—tells a story; sings a song; and saves us the trouble of flattering the Queen.

RUFIO. Well, he can swim a bit and fence a bit: he might be worse, if he only knew how to hold his tongue.

CÆSAR. The gods forbid he should ever learn!

Pothinus enters and stops mistrustfully between the two, looking from one to the other.

CÆSAR [*graciously*] Ah, Pothinus! You are welcome. And what is the news this afternoon?

POTHINUS. Cæsar: I come to warn you of a danger, and to make you an offer.

CÆSAR. Never mind the danger. Make the offer.

RUFIO. Never mind the offer. Whats the danger?

POTHINUS. Cæsar: you think that Cleopatra is devoted to you.

CÆSAR [*gravely*] My friend: I already know what I think. Come to your offer.

POTHINUS. I will deal plainly. I know not by what strange gods you have been enabled to defend a palace and a few yards of beach against a city and an army. But we know now that your gods are irresistible, and that you are a worker of miracles. I no longer threaten you—

RUFIO [*sarcastically*] Very handsome of you, indeed.

POTHINUS. So be it: you are the master.

CÆSAR [*gently urging him to come to the point*] Yes, yes, my friend. But what then?

RUFIO. Spit it out, man. What have you to say?

POTHINUS. I have to say that you have a traitress in your camp. Cleopatra—

THE MAJOR-DOMO [*at the table, announcing*] The Queen! [*Cæsar and Rufio rise*].

RUFIO [*aside to Pothinus*] You should have spat it out sooner, you fool. Now it is too late.

Cleopatra, in gorgeous raiment, enters in state through the gap in the colonnade, and comes down past the image of Ra and past the table to Cæsar. Her retinue, headed by Ftatateeta, joins the staff at the table. Cæsar gives Cleopatra his seat, which she takes.

CLEOPATRA [*quickly, seeing Pothinus*] What is he doing here?

CÆSAR [*seating himself beside her, in the most amiable of tempers*] Just going to tell me something about you. You shall hear it. Proceed, Pothinus.

POTHINUS [*disconcerted*] Cæsar—[*he stammers*]

CÆSAR. Well, out with it.

POTHINUS. What I have to say is for your ear, not for the Queen's.

CLEOPATRA [*with subdued ferocity*] There are means of making you speak. Take care.

POTHINUS [*defiantly*] Cæsar does not employ those means.

CÆSAR. My friend: when a man has anything to tell in this world, the difficulty is not to make him tell it, but to prevent him from telling it too often. Let me celebrate my birthday by setting you free. Farewell: we shall not meet again.

CLEOPATRA [*angrily*] Cæsar: this mercy is foolish.

POTHINUS [*to Cæsar*] Will you not give me a private audience? Your life may depend on it. [*Cæsar rises loftily*].

RUFIO [*calls as before*] Ho there, guard! Pass the prisoner out. He is released. [*To Pothinus*] Now off with you. You have lost your chance.

POTHINUS [*his temper overcoming his prudence*] I w i l l speak.

CÆSAR [*to Cleopatra*] You see. Torture would not have wrung a word from him.

POTHINUS. Cæsar: you have taught Cleopatra the arts by which the Romans govern the world.

CÆSAR. Alas! they cannot even govern themselves. What then?

POTHINUS. What then? Are you so besotted with her beauty that you do not see that she is impatient to reign in Egypt alone, and that her heart is set on your departure?

CLEOPATRA [*rising*] Liar!

CÆSAR [*shocked*] What! Protestations! Contradictions!

CLEOPATRA [*ashamed, but trembling with suppressed rage*] No. I do not deign to contradict. Let him talk. [*She sits down again*].

POTHINUS. From her own lips I have heard it. You are to be her catspaw: you are to tear the crown from her brother's head and set it on her own, delivering us all into her hand—delivering yourself also. And then Cæsar can return to Rome, or depart through the gate of death, which is nearer and surer.

CÆSAR [*calmly*] Well, my friend; and is not this very natural?

POTHINUS [*astonished*] Natural! Then you do not resent treachery?

CÆSAR. Resent! O thou foolish Egyptian, what have I to do with resentment? Do I resent the wind when it chills me, or the night when it makes me stumble in darkness? Shall I resent youth when it turns from age? To tell me such a story as this is but to tell me that the sun will rise tomorrow.

CLEOPATRA [*unable to contain herself*] But it is false—false. I swear it.

CÆSAR. It is true, though you swore it a thousand times, and believed all you swore. [*She is convulsed with emotion. To screen her, he rises and takes Pothinus to Rufio, saying*] Come, Rufio: let us see Pothinus past the guard. I have a word to say to him. [*Aside to them*] We must give the Queen a moment to recover herself. [*He takes Pothinus and Rufio out with him, conversing with them meanwhile*]. Tell your friends, Pothinus, that they must not think I am opposed to a reasonable settlement of the country's affairs—[*They pass out of hearing*].

CLEOPATRA [*in a stifled whisper*] Ftateeta, Ftatateeta.

FTATATEETA [*hurrying to her from the table and petting her*] Peace, child: be comforted—

CLEOPATRA [*interrupting her*] Can they hear us?

FTATATEETA. No, dear heart, no.

CLEOPATRA. Listen to me. If he leaves the Palace alive, never see my face again.

FTATATEETA. He? Poth—

CLEOPATRA [*striking her on the mouth*] Strike his life out as I strike his name

446

from your lips. Dash him down from the wall. Break him on the stones. Kill, kill, kill him.

FTATATEETA [*shewing all her teeth*] The dog shall perish.

CLEOPATRA. Fail in this, and you go out from before me for ever.

FTATATEETA [*resolutely*] So be it. You shall not see my face until his eyes are darkened.

Cæsar comes back, with Apollodorus, exquisitely dressed, and Rufio.

CLEOPATRA [*to Ftatateeta*] Come soon—soon. [*Ftatateeta turns her meaning eyes for a moment on her mistress; then goes grimly away past Ra and out. Cleopatra runs like a gazelle to Cæsar*]. So you have come back to me, Cæsar. [*Caressingly*] I thought you were angry. Welcome, Apollodorus. [*She gives him her hand to kiss, with her other arm about Cæsar*].

APOLLODORUS. Cleopatra grows more womanly beautiful from week to week.

CLEOPATRA. Truth, Apollodorus?

APOLLODORUS. Far, far short of the truth! Friend Rufio threw a pearl into the sea: Cæsar fished up a diamond.

CÆSAR. Cæsar fished up a touch of rheumatism, my friend. Come: to dinner! to dinner! [*They move towards the table*].

CLEOPATRA [*skipping like a young fawn*] Yes, to dinner. I have ordered s u c h a dinner for you, Cæsar!

CÆSAR. Ay? What are we to have?

CLEOPATRA. Peacock's brains.

CÆSAR [*as if his mouth watered*] Peacock's brains, Apollodorus!

APOLLODORUS. Not for me. I prefer nightingales' tongues. [*He goes to one of the two covers set side by side*].

CLEOPATRA. Roast boar, Rufio!

RUFIO [*gluttonously*] Good! [*He goes to the seat next Apollodorus, on his left*].

CÆSAR [*looking at his seat, which is at the end of the table, to Ra's left hand*] What has become of my leathern cushion?

CLEOPATRA [*at the opposite end*] I have got new ones for you.

THE MAJOR-DOMO. These cushions, Cæsar, are of Maltese gauze, stuffed with rose leaves.

CÆSAR. Rose leaves! Am I a caterpillar? [*He throws the cushions away and seats himself on the leather mattress underneath*].

CLEOPATRA. What a shame! My new cushions!

THE MAJOR-DOMO [*at Cæsar's elbow*] What shall we serve to whet Cæsar's appetite?

CÆSAR. What have you got?

THE MAJOR-DOMO. Sea hedgehogs, black and white sea acorns, sea nettles, beccaficoes, purple shellfish—

CÆSAR. Any oysters?

THE MAJOR-DOMO. Assuredly.

CÆSAR. British oysters?

THE MAJOR-DOMO [*assenting*] British oysters, Cæsar.

CÆSAR. Oysters, then. [*The Major-Domo signs to a slave at each order; and the slave goes out to execute it*]. I have been in Britain—that western land of romance—the last piece of earth on the edge of the ocean that surrounds the world. I went there in search of its famous pearls. The British pearl was a fable; but in searching for it I found the British oyster.

APOLLODORUS. All posterity will bless you for it. [*To the Major-Domo*] Sea hedgehogs for me.

RUFIO. Is there nothing solid to begin with?

THE MAJOR-DOMO. Fieldfares with asparagus—

CLEOPATRA [*interrupting*] Fattened fowls! have some fattened fowls, Rufio.

RUFIO. Ay, that will do.

CLEOPATRA [*greedily*] Fieldfares for me.

THE MAJOR-DOMO. Cæsar will deign to choose his wine? Sicilian, Lesbian, Chian—

RUFIO [*contemptuously*] All Greek.

APOLLODORUS. Who would drink Roman wine when he could get Greek. Try the Lesbian, Cæsar.

CÆSAR. Bring me my barley water.

RUFIO [*with intense disgust*] Ugh! Bring me my Falernian. [*The Falernian is presently brought to him*].

CLEOPATRA [*pouting*] It is waste of time giving you dinners, Cæsar. My scullions would not condescend to your diet.

CÆSAR [*relenting*] Well, well: let us try the Lesbian. [*The Major-Domo fills Cæsar's goblet; then Cleopatra's and Apollodorus's*]. But when I return to Rome, I will make laws against these extravagances. I will even get the laws carried out.

CLEOPATRA [*coaxingly*] Never mind. Today you are to be like other people: idle, luxurious, and kind. [*She stretches her hand to him along the table*].

CÆSAR. Well, for once I will sacrifice my comfort—[*kissing her hand*] there! [*He takes a draught of wine*]. Now are you satisfied?

CLEOPATRA. And you no longer believe that I long for your departure for Rome?

CÆSAR. I no longer believe anything. My brains are asleep. Besides, who knows whether I shall return to Rome?

RUFIO [*alarmed*] Eh? What?

CÆSAR. One year of Rome is like another, except that I grow older.

APOLLODORUS. It is no better here in Egypt. The old men, when they are tired of life, say "We have seen everything except the source of the Nile."

CÆSAR [*his imagination catching fire*] And why not see that? Cleopatra: will you come with me and track the flood to its cradle in the heart of the regions of mystery? Shall I make you a new kingdom, and build you a holy city there in the great unknown?

CLEOPATRA [*rapturously*] Yes, yes. You shall.

RUFIO. Ay: now he will conquer Africa with two legions before we come to the roast boar.

APOLLODORUS. No scoffing. This is a noble scheme: in it Cæsar is no longer merely the conquering soldier, but the creative poet-artist. Let us name the holy city, and consecrate it with Lesbian wine.

CÆSAR. Cleopatra shall name it herself.

CLEOPATRA. It shall be called Cæsar's Gift to his Beloved.

APOLLODORUS. No, no. Something vaster than that—something universal, like the starry firmament.

CÆSAR [*prosaically*] Why not simply The Cradle of the Nile?

CLEOPATRA. No: the Nile is my ancestor; and he is a god. Oh! I have thought of something. The Nile shall name it himself. Let us call upon him. [*To the Major-*

Domo] Send for him. [*The three men stare at one another; but the Major-Domo goes out as if he had received the most matter-of-fact order*]. [*To the retinue*] Away with you all.

The retinue withdraws, making obeisance.

A priest enters, carrying a miniature sphinx with a tiny tripod before it. A morsel of incense is smoking in the tripod. The priest comes to the table and places the image in the middle of it. The light begins to change to the magenta purple of the Egyptian sunset, as if the god had brought a strange colored shadow with him. The three men are determined not to be impressed; but they feel curious in spite of themselves.

CLEOPATRA [*to the priest*] Go. I am a priestess, and have power to take your charge from you. [*The priest makes a reverence and goes*].

CÆSAR. What hocus-pocus is this?

CLEOPATRA. It is not hocus-pocus. To do it properly, we should kill something to please him; but perhaps he will answer Cæsar without that if we spill some wine to him.

APOLLODORUS [*turning his head to look up over his shoulder at Ra*] Why not appeal to our hawkheaded friend here?

CLEOPATRA [*nervously*] Sh! He will hear you and be angry.

RUFIO [*phlegmatically*] The source of the Nile is out of his district, I expect.

CLEOPATRA. Now let us call on the Nile all together. You must say with me "Send us thy voice, Father Nile."

ALL FOUR [*holding their glasses together before the idol*] Send us thy voice, Father Nile.

The death cry of a man in mortal terror and agony answers them. Appalled, the men set down their glasses, and listen. Silence. The purple deepens in the sky. Cæsar, glancing at Cleopatra, catches her pouring out her wine before the god, with gleaming eyes, and mute assurances of gratitude and worship. Apollodorus springs up and runs to the edge of the roof to peer down and listen.

CÆSAR [*looking piercingly at Cleopatra*] What was that?

CLEOPATRA [*petulantly*] Nothing. They are beating some slave.

CÆSAR. Nothing.

RUFIO. A man with a knife in him, I'll swear.

CÆSAR [*rising*] A murder!

APOLLODORUS [*at the back, waving his hand for silence*] S-sh! Silence. Did you hear that?

CÆSAR. Another cry?

APOLLODORUS [*returning to the table*] No, a thud. Something fell on the beach, I think.

RUFIO [*grimly, as he rises*] Something with bones in it, eh?

CÆSAR [*shuddering*] Hush, hush, Rufio. [*He leaves the table and returns to the colonnade: Rufio following at his left elbow, and Apollodorus at the other side*].

CLEOPATRA [*still in her place at the table*] Will you leave me, Cæsar? Apollodorus: are you going?

APOLLODORUS. Faith, dearest Queen, my appetite is gone.

CÆSAR. Go down to the courtyard, Apollodorus; and find out what has happened.

Apollodorus nods and goes out, making for the staircase by which Rufio ascended.

CLEOPATRA. Your soldiers have killed somebody, perhaps. What does it matter?

The murmur of a crowd rises from the beach below. Cæsar and Rufio look at one another.

CÆSAR. This must be seen to. [*He is about to follow Apollodorus when Rufio stops him with a hand on his arm as Ftatateeta comes back by the far end of the roof, with dragging steps, a drowsy satiety in her eyes and in the corners of the bloodhound lips*].

CÆSAR. Is she drunk?

RUFIO. Not with wine.

FTATATEETA. The Queen looks again on the face of her servant.

RUFIO [*in a low tone*] There is some mischief between these two.

Cleopatra looks at her for a moment with an exultant reflection of her murderous expression. Then she flings her arms round her; kisses her repeatedly and savagely; and tears off her jewels and heaps them on her. The two men turn from the spectacle to look at one another. Ftatateeta drags herself sleepily to the altar; kneels before Ra; and remains there in prayer. Cæsar goes to Cleopatra, Rufio following.

CÆSAR [*with searching earnestness*] Cleopatra: what has happened?

CLEOPATRA [*in mortal dread of him, but with her utmost cajolery*] Nothing, dearest Cæsar. [*With sickly sweetness, her voice almost failing*] Nothing. I am innocent. [*She approaches him affectionately*]. Dear Cæsar: are you angry with me? Why do you look at me so? I have been here with you all the time. How can I know what has happened?

CÆSAR [*reflectively*] That is true.

CLEOPATRA [*greatly relieved, trying to caress him*] Of course it is true. [*He does not respond to the caress*]. You know it is true, Rufio.

The murmur without suddenly swells to a roar and subsides.

RUFIO. I shall know presently. Remember, Cæsar, your bodyguard is within call. [*He goes*].

Cleopatra, presuming upon Cæsar's submission to Rufio, leaves the table and sits down on the bench in the colonnade.

CLEOPATRA. Why do you allow Rufio to treat you so? You should teach him his place.

CÆSAR. Teach him to be my enemy, and to hide his thoughts from me as you are now hiding yours?

CLEOPATRA [*her fears returning*] Why do you say that, Cæsar? Indeed, indeed, I am not hiding anything. You are wrong to treat me like this. [*She stifles a sob*]. I am only a child; and you turn into stone because you think some one has been killed. I cannot bear it. [*She purposely breaks down and weeps. He looks at her with profound sadness and complete coldness. She looks up to see what effect she is producing. Seeing that he is unmoved, she sits up, pretending to struggle with her emotion and to put it bravely away*]. But there: I know you hate tears: you shall not be troubled with them. I know you are not angry, but only sad; only I am so silly, I cannot help being hurt when you speak coldly. Of course you are quite right: it is dreadful to think of anyone being killed or even hurt; and I hope nothing really serious has—[*her voice dies away under his contemptuous penetration*].

CÆSAR. What has frightened you into this? What have you done? [*A trumpet sounds on the beach below*]. Aha! that sounds like the answer.

CLEOPATRA [*sinking back trembling on the bench and covering her face with her hands*] I have not betrayed you, Cæsar: I swear it.

CÆSAR. I know that. I have not trusted you. [*He turns from her, and is about to go out when Apollodorus and Britannus drag in Lucius Septimius to him. Rufio follows*].

RUFIO. The town has gone mad, I think. They are for tearing the palace down and driving us into the sea straight away. We laid hold of this renegade in clearing them out of the courtyard.

CÆSAR. Release him. [*They let go his arms*]. What has offended the citizens, Lucius Septimius?

LUCIUS. What did you expect, Cæsar? Pothinus was a favorite of theirs.

CÆSAR. What has happened to Pothinus? I set him free, here, not half an hour ago. Did they not pass him out?

LUCIUS. Ay, through the gallery arch sixty feet above ground, with three inches of steel in his ribs. He is as dead as Pompey. We are quits now, as to killing—you and I.

CÆSAR [*shocked*] Assassinated!—our prisoner, our guest! [*He turns reproachfully on Rufio*] Rufio—

RUFIO [*emphatically —anticipating the question*] Whoever did it was a wise man and a friend of yours [*Cleopatra is greatly emboldened*]; but none of u s had a hand in it. So it is no use to frown at me. [*Cæsar turns and looks at Cleopatra*].

CLEOPATRA [*violently —rising*] He was slain by order of the Queen of Egypt. I am not Julius Cæsar the dreamer, who allows every slave to insult him. Rufio said I did well: now the others shall judge me too. [*She turns to the others*]. This Pothinus sought to make me conspire with him to betray Cæsar. I refused; and he cursed me and came privily to Cæsar to accuse me of his own treachery. He insulted me—me, the Queen! to my face. Cæsar would not avenge me: he spoke him fair and set him free. Was I right to avenge myself? Speak, Lucius.

LUCIUS. I do not gainsay it. But you will get little thanks from Cæsar for it.

CLEOPATRA. Speak, Apollodorus. Was I wrong?

APOLLODORUS. I have only one word of blame, most beautiful. You should have called upon me, your knight; and in a fair duel I should have slain the slanderer.

CLEOPATRA [*passionately*] I will be judged by your very slave, Cæsar. Britannus: speak. Was I wrong?

BRITANNUS. Were treachery, falsehood, and disloyalty left unpunished, society must become like an arena full of wild beasts, tearing one another to pieces. Cæsar is in the wrong.

CÆSAR [*with quiet bitterness*] And so the verdict is against me, it seems.

CLEOPATRA [*vehemently*] Listen to me, Cæsar. If one man in all Alexandria can be found to say that I did wrong, I swear to have myself crucified on the door of the palace by my own slaves.

CÆSAR. If one man in all the world can be found, now or forever, to k n o w that you did wrong, that man will have either to conquer the world as I have, or be crucified by it. [*The uproar in the streets again reaches them*]. Do you hear? These knockers at your gate are also believers in vengeance and in stabbing. You have slain their leader: it is right that they shall slay you. And then in the name of that right [*he emphasizes the word with great scorn*] shall I not slay them for murdering their Queen, and be slain in my turn by their countrymen as the invader of their fatherland? And so, to the end of history, murder shall breed murder, always in the name of right and honor and peace, until the gods are tired of blood and create a race that can understand. [*Fierce uproar. Cleopatra becomes white with terror. Loftily, Cæsar wraps himself up in an impenetrable dignity*]. Let the Queen of Egypt now give her orders for vengeance, and take her measures for defence; for she has renounced Cæsar. [*He turns to go*].

CLEOPATRA [*terrified, running to him and falling on her knees*] You will not desert me Cæsar. You will defend the palace.

CÆSAR. You have taken the powers of life and death upon you. I am only a dreamer.

CLEOPATRA. But they will kill me.

CÆSAR. And why not?

CLEPATRA. In pity—

CÆSAR. Pity! What! has it come to this so suddenly, that nothing can save you now but pity? Did it save Pothinus?

She rises, wringing her hands, and goes back to the bench in despair. Apollodorus shews his sympathy with her by quietly posting himself behind the bench. The sky has by this time become the most vivid purple, and soon begins to change to a glowing pale orange, against which the colonnade and the great image shew darklier and darklier.

RUFIO. Cæsar: enough of preaching. The enemy is at the gate.

CÆSAR [*turning on him and giving way to his wrath*] Ay; and what has held him baffled at the gate all these months? Was it my folly, as you deem it, or your wisdom? In this Egyptian Red Sea of blood, whose hand has held all your heads above the waves? [*Turning on Cleopatra*] And yet, when Cæsar says to such an one, "Friend, go free," you, clinging for your little life to my sword, dare steal out and stab him in the back? [*To Lucius Septimius*] Is it any magic of mine, think you, that has kept your army and this whole city at bay for so long? Yesterday, what quarrel had they with me that they should risk their lives against me? But today we have flung them down their hero, murdered; and now every man of them is set upon clearing out this nest of assassins—for such we are and no more. And you, soldiers and gentlemen, and honest servants as you forget that you are, applaud this assassination, and say "Cæsar is in the wrong." By the gods, I am tempted to open my hand and let you all sink into the flood.

RUFIO [*desperately*] Will you desert us because we are a parcel of fools? I mean no harm by killing: I do it as a dog kills a cat, by instinct. We are all dogs at your heels; but we have served you faithfully.

CÆSAR [*relenting*] Alas, Rufio, my son, my son: as dogs we are like to perish now in the streets.

APOLLODORUS [*at his post behind Cleopatra's seat*] Cæsar: what you say has an Olympian ring in it: it must be right; for it is fine art. But I am still on the side of Cleopatra. If we must die, she shall not want the devotion of a man's heart nor the strength of a man's arm.

CLEOPATRA [*sobbing*] But I dont want to die.

CASAR [*sadly*] Oh, ignoble, ignoble!

LUCIUS [*coming forward between Cæsar and Cleopatra*] Hearken to me, Cæsar. It may be ignoble; but I also mean to live as long as I can.

CÆSAR. Well, my friend, you are likely to outlive Cæsar. Take courage, then;

and sharpen your sword. Pompey's head has fallen. Cæsar's head is ripe.

APOLLODORUS. Does Cæsar despair?

CÆSAR [*with infinite pride*] He who has never hoped can never despair. Cæsar, in good or bad fortune, looks his fate in the face.

LUCIUS. Look it in the face, then; and it will smile as it always has on Cæsar.

CÆSAR [*with involuntary haughtiness*] Do you presume to encourage me?

LUCIUS. I offer you my services. I will change sides if you will have me.

CÆSAR [*suddenly coming down to earth again, and looking sharply at him, divining that there is something behind the offer*] What! At this point?

LUCIUS [*firmly*] At this point.

RUFIO. Do you suppose Cæsar is mad, to trust you?

LUCIUS. I do not ask him to trust me until he is victorious. I ask for my life, and for a command in Cæsar's army. And since Cæsar is a fair dealer, I will pay in advance.

CÆSAR. Pay! How?

LUCIUS. With a piece of good news for you.

Cæsar divines the news in a flash.

RUFIO. What news?

CÆSAR [*with an elate and buoyant energy which makes Cleopatra sit up and stare*] What news! What news, did you say, my son Rufio? The relief has arrived: what other news remains for us? Is it not so, Lucius Septimius? Mithridates of Pergamos is on the march.

LUCIUS. He has taken Pelusium.

CÆSAR [*delighted*] Lucius Septimius: you are henceforth my officer. Rufio: the Egyptians must have sent every soldier from the city to prevent Mithridates crossing the Nile. There is nothing in the streets now but mob—mob!

LUCIUS. It is so. Mithridates is marching by the great road to Memphis to cross above the Delta. Achillas will fight him there.

CÆSAR [*all audacity*] Achillas shall fight Cæsar there. See, Rufio. [*He runs to the table; snatches a napkin; and draws a plan on it with his finger dipped in wine, whilst Rufio and Lucius Septimius crowd about him to watch, all looking closely, for the light is now almost gone*]. Here is the palace [*pointing to his plan*]: here is the theatre. You [*to Rufio*] take twenty men and pretend to go by that street [*pointing it out*]; and whilst they are stoning you, out go the cohorts by this and this. My streets are right, are they, Lucius?

LUCIUS. Ay, that is the fig market—

CÆSAR [*too much excited to listen to him*] I saw them the day we arrived. Good! [*He throws the napkin on the table, and comes down again into the colonnade*]. Away, Britannus: tell Petronius that within an hour half our forces must take ship for the western lake. See to my horse and armor. [*Britannus runs out*] With the rest, *I* shall march round the lake and up the Nile to meet Mithridates. Away, Lucius; and give the word. [*Lucius hurries out after Britannus*]. Apollodorus: lend me your sword and your right arm for this campaign.

APOLLODORUS. Ay, and my heart and life to boot.

CÆSAR [*grasping his hand*] I accept both. [*Mighty handshake*]. Are you ready?

APOLLODORUS. Ready for Art—the Art of War. [*He rushes out after Lucius, totally forgetting Cleopatra*].

RUFIO. Come! this is something like business.

CÆSAR [*buoyantly*] Is it not, my only son? You understand about the streets, Rufio?

453

RUFIO. Ay, I think I do. I will get through them, at all events.

The bucina sounds busily in the courtyard beneath.

CÆSAR. Come, then: we must talk to the troops and hearten them. You down to the beach: I to the courtyard. [*He makes for the staircase*].

CLEOPATRA [*rising from her seat, where she has been quite neglected all this time, and stretching out her hands timidly to him*] Cæsar.

CÆSAR [*turning*] Eh?

CLEOPATRA. Have you forgotten me?

CÆSAR [*indulgently*] I am busy now, my child, busy. When I return your affairs shall be settled. Farewell; and be good and patient.

He goes, preoccupied and quite indifferent. She stands with clenched fists, in speechless rage and humiliation.

RUFIO. That game is played and lost, Cleopatra. The woman always gets the worst of it.

CLEOPATRA [*haughtily*] Go. Follow your master.

RUFIO [*in her ear, with rough familiarity*] A word first. Tell your executioner that if Pothinus had been properly killed—i n t h e t h r o a t —he would not have called out. Your man bungled his work.

CLEOPATRA [*enigmatically*] How do you know it was a man?

RUFIO [*startled, and puzzled*] It was not you: you were with us when it happened. [*She turns her back scornfully on him. It is now a magnificent moonlit night. Ftatateeta is seen in the light of the moon and stars, again in prayer before the white altar-stone of Ra. Rufio starts; closes the curtains again softly; and says in a low voice to Cleopatra*] Was it she? with her own hand?

CLEOPATRA [*threateningly*] Whoever it was, let my enemies beware of her. Look to it, Rufio, you who dare make the Queen of Egypt a fool before Cæsar.

RUFIO [*looking grimly at her*] I will look to it, Cleopatra. [*He nods in confirmation of the promise, and slips out through the curtains, loosening his sword in its sheath as he goes*].

ROMAN SOLDIERS [*in the courtyard below*] Hail, Cæsar! Hail, hail!

Cleopatra listens. The bucina sounds again, followed by several trumpets.

CLEOPATRA [*wringing her hands and calling*] Ftatateeta. Ftatateeta. It is dark; and I am alone. Come to me. [*Silence*] Ftatateeta. [*Louder*] Ftatateeta. [*Silence. In a panic she snatches the cord and pulls the curtain apart*].

Ftatateeta is lying dead on the altar of Ra, with her throat cut. Her blood deluges the white stone.

Dissolve to:

High noon. Festival and military pageant on the esplanade before the palace. In the east harbor Cæsar's galley, so gorgeously decorated that it seems to be rigged with flowers, is alongside the quay, close to the steps Apollodorus descended when he embarked with the carpet. A Roman guard is posted there in charge of a gangway, whence a red floorcloth is laid down the middle of the esplanade, turning off to the north opposite the central gate in the palace front, which shuts in the esplanade on the south side. The broad steps of the gate, crowded with Cleopatra's ladies, all in their gayest attire, are like a flower garden. The façade is lined by her guard, officered by the same gallants to whom Bel Afris announced the coming of Cæsar six months before in the old palace on the Syrian border. The north side is lined by Roman soldiers, with the townsfolk on tiptoe behind them, peering over their heads at the cleared esplanade, in which the officers stroll about, chatting.

Among these are Belzanor and the Persian; also the centurion, vinewood cudgel in hand, battle worn, thick-booted, and much outshone, both socially and decoratively, by the Egyptian officers.

Apollodorus makes his way through the townsfolk.

PERSIAN. Any fresh news from the war, Apollodorus?

APOLLODORUS. The little King Ptolemy was drowned. Cæsar attacked them from three sides at once and swept them into the Nile. Ptolemy's barge sank.

BELZANOR. A marvellous man, this Cæsar! Will he come soon, think you?

APOLLODORUS. He was settling the Jewish question when I left.

A flourish of trumpets from the north, and commotion among the townsfolk, announces the approach of Cæsar.

PERSIAN. He has made short work of them. Here he comes.

The soldiers stand at attention, and dress their lines. Cæsar arrives in state with Rufio: Britannus following. The soldiers receive him with enthusiastic shouting.

CÆSAR. I see my ship awaits me. The hour of Cæsar's farewell to Egypt has arrived. And now, Rufio, what remains to be done before I go?

RUFIO [*at his left hand*] You have not yet appointed a Roman governor for this province.

CÆSAR [*looking whimsically at him, but speaking with perfect gravity*] What say you to Mithridates of Pergamos?

RUFIO. Why, that you will want him elsewhere.

CÆSAR. Indeed! Well, what say you to yourself?

RUFIO [*incredulously*] I! I a governor! What are you dreaming of? Do you not know that I am only the son of a freedman?

CÆSAR [*affectionately*] Has not Cæsar called you his son? [*Calling to the whole assembly*] Peace awhile there; and hear me.

THE ROMAN SOLDIERS. Hear Cæsar.

CÆSAR. Hear the service, quality, rank and name of the Roman governor. By service, Cæsar's shield; by quality, Cæsar's friend; by rank, a Roman soldier. [*The Roman soldiers give a triumphant shout*]. By name, Rufio. [*They shout again*].

RUFIO [*kissing Cæsar's hand*] Ay: I am Cæsar's shield; but of what use shall I be when I am no longer on Cæsar's arm? [*He becomes husky, and turns away to recover himself*].

CÆSAR. Where is that British Islander of mine?

BRITANNUS [*coming forward on Cæsar's right hand*] Here, Cæsar.

CÆSAR. Who bade you, pray, thrust yourself into the battle of the Delta, uttering the barbarous cries of your native land, and affirming yourself a match for any four of the Egyptians, to whom you applied unseemly epithets?

BRITANNUS. Cæsar: I ask you to excuse the language that escaped me in the heat of the moment.

CÆSAR. And how did you, who cannot swim, cross the canal with us when we stormed the camp?

BRITANNUS. Cæsar: I clung to the tail of your horse.

CÆSAR. These are not the deeds of a slave, Britannicus, but of a free man.

BRITANNUS. Cæsar: I was born free.

CÆSAR. But they call you Cæsar's slave.

BRITANNUS. Only as Cæsar's slave have I found real freedom.

CÆSAR [*moved*] Well said. Ungrateful that I am, I was about to set you free; but now I will not part from you for a million talents. [*He claps him friendly on the shoulder. Britannus, gratified, but a trifle shamefaced, takes his hand and kisses it sheepishly*].

BELZANOR [*to the Persian*] This Roman knows how to make men serve him.

PERSIAN. Ay: men too humble to become dangerous rivals to him.

BELZANOR. O subtle one! O cynic!

CÆSAR [*seeing Apollodorus in the Egyptian corner, and calling to him*] Apollodorus: I leave the art of Egypt in your charge. Remember: Rome loves art and will encourage it.

APOLLODORUS. I understand, Cæsar. Rome will produce no art itself; but it will buy up and take away whatever the other nations produce.

CÆSAR. What! Rome produce no art! Is peace not an art? is war not an art? is government not an art? is civilization not an art? All these we give you in exchange for a few ornaments. You will have the best of the bargain. [*Turning to Rufio*] And now, what else have I to do before I embark? [*Trying to recollect*] There is something I cannot remember: what can it be? Well, well: it must remain undone: we must not waste this favorable wind. Farewell, Rufio.

RUFIO. Cæsar: I am loth to let you go to Rome without your shield. There are too many daggers there.

CÆSAR. It matters not: I shall finish my life's work on my way back; and then I shall have lived long enough. Besides: I have always disliked the idea of dying: I had rather be killed. Farewell.

RUFIO [*with a sigh, raising his hands and giving Cæsar up as incorrigible*] Farewell. [*They shake hands*].

CÆSAR [*waving his hand to Apollodorus*] Farewell, Apollodorus, and my friends, all of you. Aboard!

The gangway is run out from the quay to the ship. As Cæsar moves towards it, Cleopatra, cold and tragic, cunningly dressed in black, without ornaments or decoration of any kind, and thus making a striking figure among the brilliantly dressed bevy of ladies as she passes through it, comes from the palace and stands on the steps. Cæsar does not see her until she speaks.

CLEOPATRA. Has Cleopatra no part in this leavetaking?

CÆSAR [*enlightened*] Ah, I k n e w there was something. [*To Rufio*] How could you let me forget her, Rufio? [*Hastening to her*] Had I gone without seeing you, I should never have forgiven myself. [*He takes her hands, and brings her into the middle of the esplanade. She submits stonily*]. Is this mourning for me?

CLEOPATRA. No.

CÆSAR [*remorsefully*] Ah, that was thoughtless of me! It is for your brother.

CLEOPATRA. No.

CÆSAR. For whom, then?

CLEOPATRA. Ask the Roman governor whom you have left us.

CÆSAR. Rufio?

CLEOPATRA. Yes: Rufio. [*She points at him with deadly scorn*]. He who is to rule here in Cæsar's name, in Cæsar's way, according to Cæsar's boasted laws of life.

CÆSAR [*dubiously*] He is to rule as he can, Cleopatra. He has taken the work upon him, and will do it in his own way.

CLEOPATRA. Not in your way, then? Without punishment. Without revenge. Without judgment.

CÆSAR [*approvingly*] Ay: that is the right way, the great way, the only possible way in the end. [*To Rufio*] Believe it, Rufio, if you can.

RUFIO. Why, I believe it, Cæsar. But look you. Cleopatra had a tigress that killed men at her bidding. I thought she might bid it kill you some day. I might have punished it. I might have revenged Pothinus on it.

CÆSAR [*interjects*] Pothinus!

RUFIO [*continuing*] I might have judged it. But I put all these follies behind me; and, without malice, only cut its throat. And that is why Cleopatra comes to you in mourning.

CLEOPATRA [*vehemently*] He has shed the blood of my servant Ftatateeta. On your head be it as upon his, Cæsar, if you hold him free of it.

CÆSAR [*energetically*] On my head be it, then; for it was well done. Rufio. This was natural slaying: I feel no horror at it.

Rufio, satisfied, nods at Cleopatra, mutely inviting her to mark that.

CLEOPATRA [*pettish and childish in her impotence*] No: not when a Roman slays an Egyptian. All the world will now see how unjust and corrupt Cæsar is.

CÆSAR [*taking her hands coaxingly*] Come: do not be angry with me. I am sorry for that poor Totateeta. [*She laughs in spite of herself*]. Aha! you are laughing. Does that mean reconciliation?

CLEOPATRA [*angry with herself for laughing*] No, no, NO!! But it is so ridiculous to hear you call her Totateeta.

CÆSAR. What! As much a child as ever, Cleopatra! Have I not made a woman of you after all?

CLEOPATRA. Oh, it is you who are a great baby: you make me seem silly because you will not behave seriously. But you have treated me badly; and I do not forgive you.

CÆSAR. Bid me farewell.

CLEOPATRA. I will not.

CÆSAR [*coaxing*] I will send you a beautiful present from Rome.

CLEOPATRA [*proudly*] Beauty from Rome to Egypt indeed! What can Rome give me that Egypt cannot give me?

APOLLODORUS. That is true, Cæsar. If the present is to be really beautiful, I shall have to buy it for you in Alexandria.

CÆSAR. You are forgetting the treasures for which Rome is most famous, my friend. You cannot buy them in Alexandria.

APOLLODORUS. What are they, Cæsar?

CÆSAR. Her sons. Come, Cleopatra: forgive me and bid me farewell; and I will send you a man, Roman from head to heel and Roman of the noblest; not old and ripe for the knife; not hiding a bald head under his conqueror's laurels; not stooped with the weight of the world on his shoulders; but brisk and fresh, strong and young, hoping in the morning, fighting in the day, and revelling in the evening. Will you take such an one in exchange for Cæsar?

CLEOPATRA [*palpitating*] His name, his name?

CÆSAR. Shall it be Mark Antony? [*She throws herself into his arms*].

RUFIO. You are a bad hand at a bargain, mistress, if you will swop Cæsar for Antony.

CÆSAR. So now you are satisfied.

CLEOPATRA. You will not forget.

CÆSAR. I will not forget. Farewell: I do not think we shall meet again. Farewell. [*He kisses her on the forehead. She is much affected and begins to sniff. He embarks*].

457

THE ROMAN SOLDIERS [*as he sets his foot on the gangway*] Hail, Cæsar; and farewell!

He reaches the ship and returns Rufio's wave of the hand.

APOLLODORUS [*to Cleopatra*] No tears, dearest Queen: they stab your servant to the heart. He will return some day.

CLEOPATRA. I hope not. But I cant help crying, all the same. [*She waves her handkerchief to Cæsar; and the ship begins to move*].

THE ROMAN SOLDIERS [*drawing their swords and raising them in the air*] Hail, Cæsar!

A Note on the Texts

Since the screenplays in this volume are collected here for the first time, and since most of them are previously unpublished in whole, in part, or in this form, some comment about their texts is in order. Before discussing each particular screenplay, let me treat general matters. Initially, I should try to answer the question, 'Why didn't Shaw publish them himself?'

Actually, he published two, *Pygmalion* and *Major Barbara*, though he did not do so in the form of screenplays. Rather, they were 'screen versions', which combined new film sequences with uncut and unaltered acts of the stage plays. In the case of *Pygmalion*, he did not publish all the new sequences; in that of *Major Barbara*, he published more than were filmed.

Without explanation by Shaw, one must infer his reasons. Perhaps because he did not want stage directors to cut the texts of his plays along the lines of his cuts for a different medium, he did not reveal such cuts. Possibly because he did not wish new film sequences added to stage productions, he published only those unlikely to find their way onto the stage, such as Liza Doolittle's bath and the Undershaft family's tour of the factory.

One reason he did not undertake a 'screen version' of *Cæsar and Cleopatra* may have been his age. He was ninety when the movie was released in America, perhaps too weak to undertake the job. Possibly too, since he wrote little new material for this film, the screenplay would consist of authored or authorized cuts and rearrangements of sequences he did not want to appear authorized for stage productions of this long play.

What of the other screenplays? Again I must guess. After he wrote *Saint Joan* and *Arms and the Man*, few months passed when he or a producer was not trying to arrange their production. Since he wanted them filmed, he directed his energies toward that end rather than toward publication. Whereas the G.B.S. of the 1890s was a new dramatist in search of a public, Shaw of the 1930s and 1940s, by then a Nobel Prize winner, was more than established, he was institutionalized. For *The Devil's Disciple*, an additional reason may be incompleteness. Shaw's film sequences reach only the beginning of the play's first act.

Like his stage plays, Shaw's holograph drafts of his screenplays run straight across the page. For *Saint Joan* and *Pygmalion*, these drafts refer to cut, marginally annotated editions of the plays. When typists transcribed the manuscripts and marked play texts, their pages employed the standard, technical format used in the studio: audio, including dialogue, on the right side of the page; video on the left. Partly because Shaw himself composed the screenplays without an invisible vertical line down the middle of the page, I have followed his practice.

Another reason was to make the screenplays more accessible to, that is, more readable for, the non-technician. This practice also conforms to the practice of other screenplay editors during the last few years.

To help the screenplay reader visualize the characters in action, as Shaw helped the stage-play reader, I have restored character and set descriptions when these do not affect the cinematic adaptation and have repositioned the former when the screen version introduces a character earlier than the stage version does. However, I have cut those parts of the set descriptions that relate to the proscenium arch stage.

In some screenplays or film sequences, Shaw numbers the scenes and refers to these numerals when he returns to the same setting or camera shot. In others, he does not do so. For consistency and readability, I have chosen the second option throughout. A technician preparing a shooting schedule would find it helpful to read, for example, that Scene 43 of the first version of *Saint Joan* is 'Same as Scene 38'. However, a series of such references would no doubt frustrate a non-technician. Instead of forcing the latter to flip back pages again and again to discover where he is, I have briefly repeated the direction he would find once he got to, say, Scene 38.

The reader may have noticed the reference to the *first* version of *Saint Joan*. Usually, more than one version exists for these screenplays. To determine selection, I have—except where unavoidable, contradictory, or contrary to Shavian custom—attempted to use objective rather than subjective aesthetic criteria. For these exceptions, I explain editorial decisions. Where external evidence does not exist, 'Which passages represent Shaw's latest thoughts on the matter?' was my key question, rather than 'Which do I regard as the better or best version?' With the exceptions, the problem is usually an interpolation, deletion, or change by hands other than the author's—standard practice in movie making. Where external sources or internal matter provide strong reasons for believing one of these to have been the case, the addition or change is rejected in favour of a Shavian text. But I have not assumed that a trite sequence is not by Shaw, who like Homer occasionally nodded. If Shaw omits a passage or character whose absence I regret, I call attention to the omission in the introduction, but I do not restore it.

Silently, I have made a few changes and restorations. I have revised to conform to Shaw's idiosyncratic punctuation and spelling. For emphasis, he employs s p a c e s rather than *italics*. In words like *you'll* and *don't*, he removes the apostrophes; he spells *show* and *haven't*, *shew* and *havnt*; he changes the British spelling of words like *vigour* and *realise* to the American *vigor* and *realize*. Where he is inconsistent, the reason is sometimes obvious (the retention of apostrophes in *he'll* and *I'll*) but not always (*Ive* has no apostrophe, *I'm* does). I have quietly corrected typographical errors and where Shaw slips—characters who rise after cut dialogue that contains stage directions to sit or kneel, a pronoun that follows the deletion of a passage with the noun to which it refers—I have without announcement put him on his feet again.

Saint Joan

In preparing the text of the *Saint Joan* screenplay, I have perused five sources: (1) Shaw's holograph manuscript (dated 15 Oct. 1934 on the title page, 13 Nov. 1934 on the final page), which contains new film sequences plus transitions between them and the play, with numerals and page references keyed to a cut and similarly numbered edition of the play (HRC)*; (2) the edition just referred to (London: Constable, 1931), with a notation on the title page, 'Cut for Scenario Nov. 1934 GBS' (Shaw's Corner, Ayot St Lawrence); (3) a collation of the first two sources, marked 'St Joan Proposed Film Scenario', with an invisible line down the centre of each page, the video portion to the left, the audio to the right (BL 50634); (4) the same text as the last source, inscribed 'Miss Elizabeth [sic] Bergner's copy, from G. Bernard Shaw 30th Nov. 1934,' with holograph cuts, additions, and changes neither in Shaw's nor Bergner's hand but probably that of her husband, the film's proposed director, Paul Czinner (privately owned by Mr and Mrs Charles Sharp); (5) another version of the *Saint Joan* screenplay, with neither title page nor date, marked by the Catholic Action censor (BL 50634).

Nos. (3) and (4), the first version, are obviously by Shaw since except for typographical errors they correspond exactly to a combination of Nos. (1) and (2). No. (5), the revised version, is also by Shaw, though another hand or hands appear to have tinkered with it here and there. As for determination of Shaw's authorship, the chief source is Shaw himself. In a letter to Gabriel Pascal (8 Oct. 1940), he declares himself uncertain whether *he* did not spoil *Saint Joan* for Czinner and Bergner by having broken up the tent scene (VP). In this revised version, but not in the first version, the tent scene is broken by cuts to and from Charles's coronation. In neither Shaw's published comments on the censor's cuts and changes nor his own holograph notes on them (BL 50633), moreover, does he give the slightest indication that the revised screenplay is not his. In addition, the censor's marginal comments indicate that this is the Shavian work that Elisabeth Bergner says Father Cyril Martindale took to Rome (see Introduction).

On the basis of internal evidence, too, No. (5) seems a revision of Nos. (3) and (4). To begin with, if No. (5) were written earlier, it is improbable that Shaw would have laboriously rewritten in longhand scenes that are the same as those that had been typed, or that he would have employed as basic text upon which to ring variations the earlier, published play to which the holograph text alludes. Another reason is that seven passages which the Catholic censor marked with disapprobation are not in the other version. Since Shaw consistently refused to submit to such censorship, it is difficult to believe he would have cut any of these passages.

Further evidence also suggests No. (5) is the revised version. The others contain long sections of stage directions, taken verbatim from the play, which do not always distinguish between a proscenium arch stage and a motion picture screen; the revised version polishes for cinema those directions it retains. Shaw did not simply approve director Czinner's proposed cuts, additions, and changes marked in No. (4). Not only does No. (5) ignore many of them, it restores passages that Shaw himself, in the earlier version, had cut from the play. In addition, it corrects errors that had slipped into the first version. In deleting the entire Poulengey scene from the first version, Shaw cut the introduction of Joan of Arc by name. The revised version restores it and also Cauchon's explanation, deleted from the first version, as to why Joan is a heretic rather than a witch. Through cuts, the revised version corrects Shavian errors in the play: whereas Joan tells Robert de Baudricourt she needs only three men, for instance, she then names four;

* For list of abbreviations, see pp. 154–55.

461

although Warwick and the Executioner had met previously, the earl asks who he is. The revision also removes a new film sequence from the earlier version, between Stogumber and the Cardinal of Winchester (see Appendix B), which though funny recapitulates what the audience has seen.

On a few occasions I have restored cuts and deleted additions by others, most obviously the censor. I have assumed that ungrammatical additions or changes are not Shaw's and have reverted to the earlier screenplay. Restorations include two passages whose omission Shaw violently objected to elsewhere. When I visited Elisabeth Bergner on 6 Jan. 1976, she let me see briefly but did not permit me to take notes on her copy of the play which contained Max Reinhardt's cuts and Shaw's ironic or angry marginal comments. Afterward, I noted two deletions I remembered; the 'Blethers' and 'I call that muck' speeches; beside them were intemperate Shavian denunciations to the effect that to drop those aspects of Joan's character that were rough, lower-class, and unladylike is idiotic. Czinner's cuts in No. (4) include both speeches.

I have also restored three passages whose illogical deletions derive from Czinner's marks on No. (4): Baudricourt's definition of the word *goddam* (its omission makes Joan's use of the word seem an uncharacteristic obscenity), the Archbishop's and Joan's explanation of why she recognizes Bluebeard (without them, her selection of the Dauphin may seem truly miraculous and therefore out of harmony with the other apparent miracles), the trifle that motivates Cauchon's insistence that the Court should not waste time on trifles.

Because some additions or changes in the revised screenplay contradict Shaw's statements or customary practice, they may be the work of the director or his scenario transcriber. In these instances, I have reverted to the first screenplay. In Charles's presence, Bluebeard laughs unrestrainedly at him, though an earlier direction, retained in the revised screenplay, indicates his desire to make himself agreeable. One very brief battle scene, apparently brought in for variety, is uncharacteristic of Shaw, since it interrupts rather than intensifies the dramatic continuity and shows 'no details'. Interrupting important dialogue later, the camera suddenly cuts to another room with unfamiliar faces of the people who listen, the kind of distraction of which Shaw frequently disapproved. The opening of the revised screenplay gives the dates 1429–1431, which cover, though the screenplay nowhere says so, the entire action of the play. Since a later screen title, the Epilogue, gives a specific year, which is common Shavian practice when he pinpoints a dramatic present, I have returned to the earlier screenplay, with the specific year of the opening action, 1429.

On the basis of internal logic, I have made a small restoration from the earlier screenplay. Joan's last speech at the end of what corresponds to Scene V of the play, the final speech of that scene in the revised screenplay, is reduced to a single, despairing sentence which thereby changes the dramatic point of the scene's end. I have restored portions of that speech to harmonize with the end of that scene in the play and first screenplay: Joan's verbal and emotional victory in counterpoint to her failure to persuade her erstwhile friends.

Pygmalion
For the text of *Pygmalion*, I have examined four sources: (1) Shaw's holograph manuscript (dated 1 Oct. 1934, but lined out, at the foot of the last page), which contains new film sequences plus transitions between them and the play, with

numerals and page references keyed to a cut and similarly numbered edition of the play (BL 50628); (2) the edition just mentioned (London: Constable, 1927), with Shaw's holograph note on p. 105, 'The scenario begins with 7 pages of the pencilled MS' and changes of dialogue indicated in the margins (Shaw's Corner, Ayot St Lawrence); (3) *Pygmalion a Scenario*, a typed manuscript, inscribed by Shaw 'to Floryan Sobienowski for translation into Polish', dated 1 March 1938 (HRC); (4) the Bodley Head edition of the text of the play, revised by Shaw for the Standard Edition, which contains film sequences.

Nos. (1) and (2) constitute the 1934 screenplay. No. (3) is basically the same, with some additions, deletions, and typographical errors. Its chief differences are an expanded film sequence at the reception where Liza wins Higgins's bet and a different final scene. No. (4) is the uncut text of the play with some but not all film sequences interpolated. It includes a new film scene Shaw wrote after the 1938 manuscript had been typed, a phonetics lesson between Higgins and Liza. It fails to include the new final scene but ends as the stage play does. An example of its patchwork quality is the fact that it prints the indoor ambassadorial reception scene composed in 1938 for the movie but retains the 1912 reference in Act IV to Liza's triumph at a garden party.

For the text in this volume, I have followed the most recently revised film sequences (No. 4) except where the earlier wording of film directions makes their cinematic nature clearer. Replacing this text's last scene is Shaw's new final scene for the film (No. 3). Scenes carried over from the play are cut, as Shaw indicated in 1934 and 1938, and dialogue revised, partly to bridge deleted passages, as he revised it then. Appendix D contains the film sequence replaced by the phonetics lesson; Appendix E, the earlier ballroom scene; and Appendix F, the earlier last scene.

The Devil's Disciple

The sources of the film sequences of *The Devil's Disciple* are: (1) a typescript of the dialogue scenes between George III and Lord North, and between Lord Germain and his Secretary, with holograph changes by Shaw (BL 50643); (2) a typescript that incorporates these changes and also contains sequences preceding those scenes, with holograph changes by Shaw, plus screen directions following them (ibid.); (3) the dialogue scenes printed from Marjorie Deans's copy, signed by Shaw (DC, Appendix B). Apart from a single phrase ('from Quebec'), whose omission from the typescripts is probably a typographical error, the differences among these versions are insignificant. The basic text here is No. (2), with the phrase in No. (3).

Following the final screen direction of the second typescript is a phrase, 'From the play instructions:' with nothing after the colon. I have not only not succeeded in locating the edition of the play to which Shaw refers, I do not know whether he refers to a specific, marked edition.

Major Barbara

The chief problems in establishing a text of *Major Barbara* are, paradoxically, that no text exists and that several exist.

Whereas Shaw actually composed screenplays of *Saint Joan* and *Pygmalion*, that is, he wrote film sequences and bridges, keyed to a printed text of the play whose dialogue he cut and revised for the new medium, he did not do so for

Major Barbara. By the time he prepared a film version of this play, he had found a movie maker whose artistic judgment he trusted, whose desire for fidelity to his plays, he felt, was greater than that of anyone else he was likely to encounter, and who had sufficient technical and managerial skills to do the job: Gabriel Pascal. For *Major Barbara*, and for his screenplays after *Major Barbara*, Shaw wrote new film sequences and discussed with Pascal deletions and rearrangements of passages from the play text. Since they often held such discussions in person, records do not usually exist.

Because Pascal sometimes acted contrary to Shaw's wishes—Bill Walker's return, discussed in the introduction, is a prime example in the *Major Barbara* film—shooting scripts are not entirely reliable guides. Nor, for reasons discussed below, is the so-called 'screen version' Shaw prepared in 1944 after he wrote the movie sequences (1939–40) and Pascal made the film (1940). On the other hand, says Marjorie Deans, Scenario Editor of *Major Barbara*, Shaw authorized internal cuts. Unless specific evidence turns up or something illogical points to the contrary, she believes, it is safe to assume that Shaw authorized all cuts and changes (IMD).

In practical terms, several screen versions exist. None in authoritative. All are authorized to a greater or lesser extent, all reliable to a greater or lesser extent. Each is different from the others in major features: the prologue, the encounter between Bill Walker and Todger Fairmile, and everything that follows the play's second act. Let me first discuss the sources, then the text I have prepared from them.

(1) The Penguin Books 'screen version', as Shaw calls it in a prefatory note (published 1945), obviously represents his final treatment. Although it is a 'screen version', it resembles less a screenplay than it does a Reading Edition, as distinct from an Acting Edition. In the Penguin edition, probably in order to retain the most complete features of the play version and the most complete of the film version, Shaw included if not everything, then as close to everything as he could. The result is a scissors-and-paste job that intercuts film sequences with stage sequences. Thus, after a prologue written for the movie, comes the entire first act of the play with only a single cut: a change in the stage direction that sets the play in January 1906 (the film is set in vaguely modern times, with no specific date). Except for the removal of less than two pages of Act II (restored to a later film sequence) and a new scene that depicts Bill Walker's struggle with Todger Fairmile (to replace his description of it), Act II is unchanged. The result is inconsistency. While the screen version is set in modern times and the third act updates several references, notably the law under which Cusins is technically a bastard, the first two acts contain such play holdovers as a request Lady Britomart made to Gladstone; a stage direction which describes Cusins upon his entrance in Act I, though a screen direction described him at the start of the prologue; and Mrs Baines's account of a recent riot, in 1886. Indicative of the illogical and patchwork nature of this 'screen version' is that Barbara's superior is called 'Mrs Baines' in the sequence taken directly from Act II of the play, but 'The General' in Shaw's new film sequence at the great Salvation Army meeting. In the play's only major alteration for this edition, Shaw thoroughly rearranged the scenes that comprise Act III and interlaced them, often uncut and unchanged, with new film sequences.

(2) *Major Barbara* Second Rehearsal Script, 15 April 1940 (courtesy David

Tree) is a shooting script with a prologue that considerably abbreviates Shaw's and an ending in which Bill Walker returns. Those portions of the script that correspond to Acts I and II of the play contain many internal cuts. The sequence of episodes following Act II differs from that in No. (1), as does a good deal of dialogue. (3) Shooting script of *Major Barbara*, undated and without title page (BL 50617), contains Shaw's prologue, with some changes and cuts, and the return of Bill Walker at the end. Its internal cuts in Acts I and II are the same as No. (2). The sequence of episodes that follows Act II differs from Nos. (1) and (2), as does some dialogue. Many pages have holograph changes by Shaw, apparently in preparation for publication. Following the shooting script is an arrangement of the choral song Shaw wrote to Rossini's music. Since two phrases do not conform to the published verses in No. (1), I infer that the arranger worked from an earlier text.

(4) Typescripts with holograph corrections by Shaw, shorthand pages with holograph and typed passages by Shaw (ibid.) of: a list of cuts in Act III, Scene 2; a similar list for preface and play; fragments of the film prologue, dated 1940; the Bill Walker-Todger Fairmile scene, the Salvation Army meeting hall scene, and the scene in Undershaft's flat. (5) An insert for the film: the announcement of the Rossini-Shaw performance (HRC).

(6) Correspondence after Pascal began shooting: a letter from Shaw to Pascal, 28 July 1940, with additional dialogue for Undershaft in order to convey more completely Barbara's reassurance that Bill Walker's soul is not lost (photostatic copy, WHEB); a letter from Shaw to Pascal, 25 Sept. 1940 (VP), with advice to cut a passage after Undershaft's 'I can buy the Salvation Army' and a transition line in place of the deletion. (7) Evidence indicates certain scenes in Nos. (2) and (3) are not by Shaw: Bill Walker's return at the end (see introduction); a Chinaman bringing laundry to Jenny Hill and Bill Walker meeting a woman on a rubbish heap (IMD). In a letter to Pascal, 28 June 1940 (photostatic copy, WHEB), Shaw argues that the first act must remain in one set, with no changes to the nursery, and begin with two people, then pile up more and more, until it ends with Stephen alone, which suggests that the changes of locale in Nos. (2) and (3) are not by Shaw. A rehearsal note, Shaw to Pascal, 12 Sept. 1940 (VP), declares that Morrison should not be self-possessed but knocked to pieces by the unexpected reappearance of Undershaft—a suggestion that the filmed sequence where Morrison with great self-possession brings Undershaft his glass of hot lemon and ginger, which the butler remembers he always took at a certain hour, is not by Shaw. Buttressing both evidence and suggestions is the fact that Shaw included none of these sequences or passages in No. (1).

Further complicating all that has been discussed is a letter, 11 Jan. 1944, in which Shaw tells Marjorie Deans that in preparing the Penguin 'screen version' he would not stick to the movie but might restore some cuts and cut some restorations (MD).

The text in this edition keeps all of the new Shavian film sequences in No. (1), which is the latest state in which Shaw left them. From No. (1) I have cut passages of scenes that correspond to Acts I and II in accordance with the cuts in Nos. (2) and (3), which are identical, but have restored those few passages which Pascal restored in his own print of the film (BFI). To bring Act II in line with the new film sequence that shows the great meeting, I have changed references to 'Mrs Baines' to 'The General'. I have obeyed Shaw's directives in No. (6) on the additional dialogue and cut passage, and have acted on the evidence in No. (7). One might legitimately ask why Shaw did not incorporate the directives of No. (6) in the Penguin text. Possibly, he did not keep a carbon copy of his letters to Pascal and four years later he forgot about these matters. Since the play text is easily available, the reader interested in discovering how the screenplay would otherwise read can easily compare these passages with those in the play. I have already indicated where the latter occurs. The former, additional dialogue for Undershaft, goes before Barbara's line, 'Oh, you are right', in Act III, Scene 1.

The scenes after Act II present the major editorial problem. Because Nos. (1), (2), and (3) differ from each other, the alternatives were to select one, to combine the best features of all, and to infer what cuts Shaw might have permitted in No. (1). Frankly, I believe that cuts are warranted in No. (1) and that several features of Nos. (2) and (3) are more attractive than No. (1). Yet despite the temptation of the second and third alternatives, as well as their invigorating challenge to editorial ingenuity, they involve too many subjective criteria to be viable. Accordingly, for the scenes after Act II, I have with one exception followed Shaw's text in No. (1). Whatever its deficiencies, it is authentically Shavian throughout. The exception is the correction of an error: Lady Britomart did not tell Stephen about the Undershaft tradition 'last night' but the night before that. Apropos, another corrected error in No. (1) is the place where Lady Britomart receives Undershaft, not the boudoir but the library, where it is in the play and where a later film reference in No. (1) says it was.

Arms and the Man

The basic text of Shaw's new film sequences for *Arms and the Man* is (1) a typescript with holograph corrections by Shaw (BL 50643). It contains scenes that precede the play's first act, an exterior scene that interrupts Raina's adoration of Sergius's portrait early in that act, and scenes that bridge Acts I and II, and II and III. In this text, I have made only minor, stylistic changes. I have compared it with (2) a typed copy (MD) and (3) a version of No. (2) published in DC, Appendix D. With only unimportant stylistic changes, they are the same as No. (1), except that No. (3) errs in incorporating as part of the scenes that precede Act I the short sequence that interrupts it.

Into No. (1), I have incorporated (4) two screen directions in Shaw's hand (HRC): a close-up of Sergius's portrait and a single-sentence description of Bulgarian soldiers in search of the fugitive. (5) I have taken the opportunity to correct two Shavian errors noted but forgotten by Shaw when he prepared and revised the play for publication. On 16 April 1894, he asked Alma Murray, who played Raina in the first production, directed by him, to inform Bluntschli that in Act III ' "In the morning" should be "In an hour"', as he has already received the telegram' (*Collected Letters 1874–1897*, p. 423). In his holograph marginal corrections and changes of Cecil Lewis's draft shooting script of the 1932 production (BC), he corrected a passage wherein Louka tells Catherine that Bluntschli does not know who she is: 'A slip of mine. Raina has told him that she is a Petkoff and that her father is a major.' (6) Despite the temptation, I have not corrected Bluntschli's boast near the end of the comedy that as a Swiss he has three native languages. Technically, he has four: German, French, Italian, and Romansch. Since only one per cent or so of the Swiss speak Romansch, the point is academic: appropriate to note here but not to alter the text of the play. I have resisted another temptation as well. The last new edition of the play printed in Shaw's lifetime, *The Complete Plays of Bernard Shaw* (London: Odhams Press, 1950), changes the final punctuation mark from an exclamation point to a question mark. Although this alteration seems to me to make more sense of the words that precede it, I have let the exclamation point stand, as it does in the last edition Shaw himself authorized. For the record, however, I note my preference here.

(7) As for cuts and changes within the scenes that correspond to the play's three acts, I have been unable to locate any indication of Shaw's wishes in 1941. Since he customarily accepted and himself suggested alterations, there is no reason to believe that he would have changed this practice for *Arms and the Man*. I have therefore, with three exceptions, cut those passages either suggested by Shaw in his holograph marginal notes on or authorized by him in Cecil Lewis's 1932 scenario. I have not incorporated cuts that result from Lewis's changes of locale, have restored cuts restored in the sound track of the film, and have restored a cut that was an obvious slip: Bluntschli's Act I explanation to Raina why he considers Sergius a fool. Without it, she might think his mockery of her betrothed a matter of sour grapes. Those curious as to the nature of the deletions can easily satisfy their curiosity by examining the text of the play, which is easily available in uncut form. (8) Finally, I have added to scenes from the play several camera and character directions or descriptions made by Shaw in 1932, but only when these do not alter or interrupt the dialogue or action.

Cæsar and Cleopatra

As he did with *Major Barbara*, according to Pascal's Scenario Editor Marjorie Deans and Shaw's secretary Blanche Patch (see Introduction), Shaw composed new film sequences, changed dialogue, approved and suggested cuts and transpositions in the text of the play. He neither wrote a scenario, as he had for *Saint Joan* and *Pygmalion*, nor prepared a published 'screen version', as he did of *Pygmalion* and *Major Barbara*. As Shaw put it in his inscription to Pascal on a copy of a shooting script he had Pascal deposit at the United States Library of Congress, a script containing the cuts, new dialogue, and other alterations just alluded to, 'The words are mine: the pictures are yours.'

One of the basic sources of this *Cæsar and Cleopatra* screenplay consists of (1) typescripts, with holograph corrections by Shaw, of a transition and new scene between Cleopatra and Ftatateeta, after Act I, dated 15 March 1944; a scene immediately after this new scene, with Roman soldiers, a Centurion, and Rufio, with a transition to Act II, dated 24 July 1945; a transition scene with a musician and harp girl, between Acts III and IV, dated 24 July 1945; and a barber's shop scene, dated 8 August 1945, which provides the same transition as the musician and harp girl scene (BL 50610). I have compared these sequences with (2) typed transcriptions of them plus a transcription of Shaw's screen direction (which I have seen nowhere else) that precedes the barber's shop scene (MD) and (3) printed versions of the barber's shop scene (complete, except for the beginning screen direction) and excerpts from the others (in MS and DC). With the exception noted, the typescripts and printed texts have only insignificant differences from No. (1), which is my basic text. Except for changing 'O.P.' (opposite prompter's side of the stage), which Shaw no doubt typed through force of habit, to '*the left side of the screen*', my only revisions have been, as before, stylistic. I have placed all but one of the new film sequences where Shaw's typescript indicates he wanted them; in contrast, Pascal interpolated the first into the middle of Act II, where Deans erroneously says Shaw wanted it (see Introduction). The exception is the barber's shop scene, which Pascal did not film and which Shaw says he wrote against his better judgment (see Introduction). Preceded by the screen direction mentioned in No. (2), it is in Appendix I.

I have examined four shooting scripts, each labelled 'Final Shooting Script', all but two of them different from each other. In all, passages from the Syrian Palace prologue are interpolated into a transition scene outside the palace at Alexandria before Act II. (4) The earliest of these final scripts, 10 March 1944 (Department of Rare Books, Cornell University Library), contains none of Shaw's new scenes and omits the Syrian Palace prologue. Later final shooting scripts cut some of its passages and restore some of its cuts. (5) The shooting script dated 1 June 1944 (LC) contains only the first of Shaw's new transition scenes, but transposed as I have indicated. It too omits the Syrian Palace prologue. (6) Although dated 4 June 1944, the copy at the Library of Congress which contains the Shavian inscription I have quoted, is the same as No. (5). (7) For several reasons, the shooting script at HRC, dated 1 June 1944, is more authoritative than the others. Its title page is marked in what may be Marjorie Deans's hand, 'KEY COPY'. Unlike the others, it begins with an abridged version of the Syrian Palace prologue, which on 30 Dec. 1944 (see Introduction) Shaw demanded be included in the film. Those passages from this prologue duplicated in the later transition scene are crossed out in the later scene. The first page of the scenes that follow the Syrian Palace prologue bears the words 'CORRECTED COPY.' Because of the restoration of the prologue, the corrections may have been made at Shaw's prompting. Regardless, the subsequent pages contain restorations of passages from the play, plus some holograph cuts, mostly in Marjorie Deans's hand.

Accordingly, my text of Shaw's *Cæsar and Cleopatra* screenplay consists essentially of Nos. (1) and (7). In addition, I have (8) made the two changes demanded by Shaw in correspondence with Vivien Leigh and Claude Rains (see Introduction). Where Nos. (1) and (7) conflict in the placement of a new film sequence, or where the latter abridges or otherwise alters it, I follow No. (1), which is unquestionably Shaw's. Where the sequence of other scenes in No. (7) differs from that of the play, I follow with one exception the cinematic version in No. (7), since as Deans says and as his own demand about the Syrian Palace prologue reveals, Shaw would have made his wishes known had he disapproved. The exception is the interpolation of some half dozen speeches, not crossed out, of three characters in the prologue into a transition that precedes the Council Chamber scene. Shaw's scene with the Centurion, his troops, and Rufio was composed a year after the shooting script's interpolated scene. At its start, in No. (1), Shaw indicated it is 'to follow Cleopatra being bathed by Ftatateeta.' It concludes with a cross-fade into the Council Chamber. Clearly, Shaw designed it as a transition scene to replace the interpolated sequence, and I have followed this design.

Where changes are directorial rather than authorial—an assignment of a speech to a different character when it is not, as in *Pygmalion*, necessitated by a deleted passage, or the substitution of two for three of Cleopatra's serving women—I have reverted to Shaw's usage in his play. Since the text of this screenplay is by Shaw, I have on a few occasions restored brief transitional speeches or stage directions from the play when the shooting script substitutes in their place what, in the phrase Shaw uses in his inscription of No. (6), are obviously Pascal's pictures. Where the actual film restores passages cut from the shooting script, I restore them too. I have taken the opportunity to correct an obvious inconsistency. Although Shaw's stage direction (not in the screenplay) indicates by specific dates a lapse of five months between the Pharos scene and the scene in Cleopatra's chamber, and while the Musician (in a new film sequence) mentions a period of five months, Shaw slips (in both play and screenplay) by having Cleopatra say they have been there six months. The slip is corrected. As author or authorizer, Shaw himself remedies an error in the play. To clear the stage of Pothinus in Act II, he has Cæsar set him free to help Theodotus. In Act IV, however, Pothinus reappears, a prisoner. All shooting scripts correct the slip. Instead of setting Pothinus free, Cæsar has him removed in custody. This screenplay conforms to the correction.

Finally, there is what has become the inevitable question when Pascal films a Shaw play, the end. Whereas Shaw concludes *Cæsar and Cleopatra* with a rousing cry of 'Hail. Caesar!' by the Roman soldiers as his ship begins to move, Pascal's shooting scripts substitute Cleopatra, a gleam in her eyes, saying, 'Mark Antony' under her breath. Since the 'CORRECTED COPY' (No. [7]) crosses out this line, perhaps at Shaw's prompting, I have taken advantage of the correction to restore Shaw's own, final line and to treat Cleopatra's look in the film (she does not speak the words aloud) as one of the pictures that are Pascal's rather than Shaw's.

APPENDIX A

Credits of Motion Pictures Based on Screenplays
by or with Screenplays Supervised by Bernard Shaw.

Cathedral Scene from Saint Joan (British)

CAST:	JOAN	Sybil Thorndike
PRODUCER:		Vivian Van Dam for The DeForest Phonofilm Company
DIRECTOR:		Widgey Newman
DIALOGUE:		Bernard Shaw
First Showing:		July or August 1927 (London)

How He Lied to Her Husband (British)

CAST:	He	Robert Harris
	She	Vera Lennox
	Her Husband	Edmund Gwenn
PRODUCER:		John Maxwell for British International Pictures
ADAPTATION	AND	
DIRECTION:		Cecil Lewis
DIALOGUE:		Bernard Shaw
SCENARIO:		Frank Launder
PHOTOGRAPHY:		John J. Cox
EDITOR:		S. Simmonds
COSTUMES AND SETTINGS:		Gladys Calthrop
First Showing:		12 January 1931 (London)

Arms and the Man (British)

CAST:	Bluntschli	Barry Jones
	Sergius	Maurice Colbourne
	Raina	Anne Grey
	Louka	Angela Baddeley
	Petkoff	Frederick Lloyd
	Catherine	Margaret Scudamore
	Nicola	Wallace Evenett
	Plechanoff	Charles Morton

PRODUCER: John Maxwell for British International Pictures
SCENARIO AND DIRECTION: Cecil Lewis
WRITER AND ADAPTER: Bernard Shaw
PHOTOGRAPHY: Jack Cox, James Wilson, Brian Langley
EDITORS: Walter Stokvis, C. H. Frend
SOUND: Alec Murray
ART DIRECTION: John Mead
ASSISTANT DIRECTOR: Douglas Murray
First Showings: 4 August 1932 (Malvern Festival)* 24 September 1932 (London)

Pygmalion (German)

CAST:
Liza Doolittle. . . . . Jeny Jugo
Henry Higgins . . . . Gustaf Gründgens
Colonel Pickering . . . . Anton Edthofer
Alfred Doolittle. . . . . Eugen Klöpfer
Mrs Higgins . . . . Hedwig Bleibtreu
Mrs Pearce . . . . Käthe Haack
Mrs Hill . . . . Olga Limburg
Clara Hill . . . . Karin Evans
Freddy Hill . . . . Vivigenz Eickstedt
Betsy . . . . Erika Glässner
Jonny . . . . Hans Richter

PRODUCER: Eberhard Klagemann for Klagemann Film der Tobis-Rota
DIRECTOR: Erich Engel
SCREENPLAY: Heinrich Oberländer, Walter Wassermann
FROM PLAY BY: Bernard Shaw
MUSIC: Theo Mackeben
PHOTOGRAPHY: Bruno Mondi
EDITOR: René Matain
SETTINGS: Emil Hasler, Arthur Schwarz
HEAD OF PRODUCTION TEAM: Gustav Rathje, Erich Frisch
ASSISTANT DIRECTOR: Rudolf Schaad
First Showing: 2 September 1935 (Berlin)

Pygmalion (Dutch)

CAST:
Liza Doolittle. . . . . Lily Bouwmeester
Henry Higgins . . . . Johan de Meester
Colonel Pickering . . . . Eduard Verkade
Mrs Higgins . . . . Emma Morel
Alfred Doolittle. . . . . Mathieu van Eysden

* An invitation to the World Première indicates 3 August at midnight (BC). I follow Costello in interpreting 4 August—in the early hours—as date of showing (DC, p. 154).

And:	Wim Kan
	Sara Heyblom
	Nel Oosthout
	Elly van Steklenburg
	Taus Sigma
PRODUCER:	Rudolph Meyer for Filmex Cinetone of Amsterdam
DIRECTOR:	Ludwig Berger
PHOTOGRAPHY:	Akos Farkas
SOUND:	T. J. Citroen
SETTINGS:	A. H. Wegerif
MAKE-UP:	D. H. Michels
MUSIC:	Masc Tak
First Showing:	March 1937 (Amsterdam)

Pygmalion (British)

CAST:

Henry Higgins	Leslie Howard
Liza Doolittle	Wendy Hiller
Alfred Doolittle	Wilfrid Lawson
Mrs Higgins	Marie Lohr
Colonel Pickering	Scott Sunderland
Mrs Pearce	Jean Cadell
Freddy Eynsford-Hill	David Tree
Mrs Eynsford-Hill	Everley Gregg
Clara Eynsford-Hill	Leueen MacGrath
Count Aristid Karpathy	Esme Percy
Ambassadress	Violet Vanbrugh
Vicar	O. B. Clarence
First Bystander	Wally Patch
Second Bystander	H. F. Maltby
Third Bystander	George Mozart
Sarcastic Bystander	Ivor Barnard
Ysabel	Iris Hoey
Perfide	Viola Tree
Duchess	Irene Brown
A Grand Old Lady	Kate Cutler
Her Son	Leo Genn
A Lady	Kathleen Nesbitt*
First Constable	Cecil Trouncer
Second Constable	Stephen Murray
Taxi Driver	Frank Atkinson
Parlormaid	Eileen Beldon
Hairdresser	Anthony Quayle

PRODUCER:	Gabriel Pascal
DIRECTORS:	Anthony Asquith, Leslie Howard
SCREENPLAY AND DIALOGUE:	Bernard Shaw

* As it appears on the credits, rather than the now-usual Cathleen.

ADAPTERS: W. P. Lipscomb, Cecil Lewis, Ian Dalrymple
SET DESIGNER: Laurence Irving
DRESS DESIGNER: Professor L. Czettell
EXECUTED BY: Worth and Schiaparelli
PHOTOGRAPHY: Harry Stradling
CAMERA: Jack Hildyard
EDITOR: David Lean
MUSIC: Arthur Honegger
ADDITIONAL COMPOSITION: Dr William Axt
CONDUCTOR: Louis Levy
ART DIRECTOR: John Bryan
ASSISTANT DIRECTOR: Teddy Baird
RECORDIST: Alex Fisher
PRODUCTION MANAGER: Phil G. Samuel
First Showings: 6 October 1938 (London)
                         7 December 1938 (New York; distributed in the United States by Loew's, Inc.)

Major Barbara (British)
    CAST: Major Barbara................. Wendy Hiller
               Adolphus Cusins .... Rex Harrison
               Undershaft .... Robert Morley
               Bill Walker.................. Robert Newton
               The General .... Sybil Thorndike
               Snobby Price................. Emlyn Williams
               Lady Britomart............... Marie Lohr
               Sarah Undershaft .... Penelope Dudley Ward
               Stephen Undershaft .... Walter Hudd
               Charles Lomax .... David Tree
               Jenny Hill................... Deborah Kerr
               Peter Shirley................. Donald Calthrop
               Rummy Mitchens.............. Marie Ault
               Todger Fairmile .... Torin Thatcher
               Mog Habbijam .... Cathleen Cordell
               Morrison.................... Miles Malleson
               James .... Felix Aylmer
               Policeman................... Stanley Holloway
               Ling........................ S. I. Hsiung
               Mrs Price .... Kathleen Harrison
               A Girl...................... Mary Morris
               Pettigrew................... O. B. Clarence
               Bilton...................... Charles Victor
    PRODUCER AND DIRECTOR: Gabriel Pascal
    SCENARIO AND DIALOGUE: Bernard Shaw
    COSTUMES: Cecil Beaton
    ART DIRECTORS: Vincent Korda, John Bryan
    ASSISTANTS IN DIRECTION: Harold French, David Lean

ASSISTANT IN PRODUCTION: Stanley Haynes
CAMERAMEN: Ronald Neame, Jack Hildyard
FILM EDITOR: Charles Frend
MONTAGE: David Lean
DIALOGUE SUPERVISOR: Harold French
SOUND: Martin Paggi
MUSIC: William Walton
CONDUCTOR: Muir Mathieson
SCENARIO EDITOR: Marjorie Deans
First Showings: 7 April 1941 (London)
13 May 1941 (New York: distributed in the United States by United Artists)

Cæsar and Cleopatra (British)

CAST:

Cæsar	Claude Rains
Cleopatra	Vivien Leigh
Apollodorus	Stewart Granger
Ftatateeta	Flora Robson
Pothinus	Francis L. Sullivan
Rufio	Basil Sydney
Britannus	Cecil Parker
Lucius Septimius	Raymond Lovell
Achillas	Anthony Eustrel
Theodotus	Ernest Thesiger
Ptolemy	Anthony Harvey
Belzanor	Stanley Holloway
Persian	Alan Wheatley
Bel Affris	Leo Genn
Iras	Renee Asherson
Charmian	Olga Edwardes
Musician	O. B. Clarence
Centurian	Michael Rennie
Major-Domo	Esme Percy
Wounded Centurion	James McKechnie
Sentinel	John Bryning
Boatman	Anthony Holles
First Porter	Charles Victor
Second Porter	Ronald Shiner
First Sentinel	John Laurie
Second Sentinel	Charles Rolfe
Nubian Slave	Robert Adams
Lady Attendant	Harda Swanhilde
First Nobleman	Felix Aylmer
Second Nobleman	Ivor Barnard
First Guardsman	Valentine Dyall
Second Guardsman	Charles Deane
High Priest	Gibb McLaughlin
Harp Girl	Jean Simmons

PRODUCER: Gabriel Pascal for The Rank Organisation

DIRECTOR: Gabriel Pascal

SCENARIO AND DIALOGUE: Bernard Shaw

COSTUMES AND SETTINGS: Oliver Messel

PHOTOGRAPHY: Frederick Young, Jack Hildyard, Robert Krasker, Jack Cardiff (photographed in Technicolour)

ART DIRECTOR: John Bryan

MUSIC: Georges Auric

CONDUCTOR: Muir Mathieson

FILM EDITOR: Frederick Wilson

SCRIPT EDITOR: Marjorie Deans

GENERAL PRODUCTION MANAGER: Tom White

PRODUCTION ASSISTANTS: Bluey Hill, Brian Desmond Hurst

First Showings: 13 December 1945 (London)
5 September 1946 (New York; distributed in the United States by United Artists)

APPENDIX B

The Cardinal of Winchester and de Stogumber (*Saint Joan*).

In Shaw's first version of his *Saint Joan* screenplay, following the moonlit scene wherein D'Alençon finds Joan kneeling in prayer at the top of the tower, is a new film sequence wherein De Stogumber, Keeper of the Private Seal to the Cardinal of Winchester, visits the Cardinal. In his revised version, Shaw replaces this scene with Joan's victory procession through Orleans (above, p. 199). Below is the discarded scene.

In the palace of the Cardinal of Winchester. XIII century architecture, in Rouen. The Cardinal, uncle to King Henry VI of England, is elderly and too fat. He is seated at breakfast, eating, and eating too much. Serving men in waiting in sumptuous liveries.

De Stogumber, a bullnecked English chaplain of 50, rushes in distractedly, with papers in his hand.

THE CHAPLAIN. My lord, my lord, bad news, terrible news.

THE CARDINAL. Oh dear! Why do you bring me bad news at breakfast? I shall really have to get another secretary. You are so hotheaded! so thoughtless! so inconsiderate! And you know how easy it is to upset my digestion.

THE CHAPLAIN. My lord, this is not a time to think of breakfast.

THE CARDINAL [*yelling*] What!!!

THE CHAPLAIN. My lord, you m u s t give your mind to this. Orleans has fallen.

THE CARDINAL. Oh dear! dear! That comes of our commanders never being on speaking terms. No team work. Dear! dear! I told them so. *I* told them so.

THE CHAPLAIN. My lord, you did not tell them that the sorceries of the abominable witch from Lorraine would open the flaming pit of hell beneath their feet and swallow up Sir William Glasdale and all his men.

THE CARDINAL. Oh dear! dear! dear! I never liked Glasdale. But you may have some masses said for him.

THE CHAPLAIN. But that is not all, my lord. The witch is taking Charles to Rheims to crown him there.

476

THE CARDINAL. Well, why do they let her? There are plenty of troops to stop her. What is John Talbot doing?

THE CHAPLAIN. My lord, Sir John Talbot is defeated and taken prisoner.

THE CARDINAL. Oh dear! He wont like that.

THE CHAPLAIN. But do listen, my lord. There has been battle after battle, at Jargeau, at Meung, at Beaugency, at Patay. The witch has won them all. Our own troops, my lord, our Englishmen who used to put the enemy to flight by the mere sound of their British cheers, are cowed and paralyzed at sight by the witch's white banner. When they drive arrows through her throat the archers drop dead, and she rides on unharmed. Will not your lordship take the field and exorcise the devils that protect her and fight for her? It is not a task for sinful soldiers but for holy Churchmen.

THE CARDINAL. What! A cardinal stoop to exorcise a peasant girl! You forget my rank, Messire de Stogumber. Get some bishop to do it. Choose one of lowly birth. And now will you let me finish my breakfast before it is quite spoilt?

THE CHAPLAIN. Is a breakfast spoilt a worse calamity than all France lost?

THE CARDINAL. France can wait half an hour. My breakfast cannot.

THE CHAPLAIN. May I go to the Earl of Warwick about it?

THE CARDINAL. Yes, yes, yes. He's just the man to worry about such things. Off with you. Goodbye, goodbye.

The chaplain rushes out.

THE CARDINAL. Now my omelette is spoilt, I suppose.

THE BUTLER. Oh no, my lord. When you are delayed the cook begins a fresh one every half minute. [*To the others*] The omelette there!

The omelette is brought in and set before the Cardinal.

THE CARDINAL. Ah! Good. Good. Good. [*He falls to*].

APPENDIX C

Spoken Preface to American Audiences of *Pygmalion*

Filmed in 1938, printed in *The New York Times*, 11 Dec. 1938, reprinted in Vol. 5 of the Bodley Head edition of Shaw's plays, and revised to conform to Shaw's idiosyncratic punctuation.

Oh, my American friends, how do you do? Now, since I've got you all here, might I make a little speech? Right! I will. Do you mind if I sit down? I am very old.

Now, it's a delightful thing to sit here, and to think that although at this moment I'm sitting in London, I can talk in this way to an American audience. Oh—stop a minute—I quite forgot to tell you who I am. I am the author of the film that you are going to see, but I'm also Bernard Shaw.

Mind you, t h e Bernard Shaw. Your newspapers are so full of me that you must have heard about me. Now you've seen the animal. I hope you like it.

You know, Ive suffered a great deal from America in this matter of motion pictures. For years past youve been trying to teach me how to make a film. And I'm going to show you really how it should be done.

One thing that youve never dreamed of doing is—when you want to know how to make a film—send for the author. Youll never send for the author. Youll send for an electrician when the light goes wrong. Youll send for a photographic expert when the camera goes wrong. But when the play goes wrong, you send for anybody who happens to be about. Of course, I know it's not your fault. Youre not in this business. Well, thats the sort of thing that theyve been giving me in America, and the result is—my plays have not been filmed.

And, then, the American newspapers say that I dont want to have my plays screened and that Ive always refused to have them made. Ive never refused to have them filmed. I can do a great deal more with them on the screen than I can do on the stage. So dont you believe anything that you hear or read in the newspapers about me and about the film business. I know all about the motion picture business and I'm going to teach you—I mean, of course, the gentlemen who make the films— but I'm going to teach them what really a film should be like.

My friend, Mr Gabriel Pascal, who has made this production, has tried the extraordinary experiment of putting a play on the screen just as the author wrote it and as he wanted it produced.

If you agree with me when you see this film of mine—if you enjoy it, very well. Youll show it in the usual way by coming to see it—each of you—about twenty times. And then, if you do that, there will be other films. I'm thinking of doing an American play that I once wrote called "The Devil's Disciple." Probably another play of mine, "Cæsar and Cleopatra," you may see that on the film. But the really good thing about it is that when you have seen these on the screen— and if you like them—all the American films will become much more like my films. And that will be a splendid thing for America, and it wont be such a bad thing for me. Although, as you know, I'm pretty near the oldest writer here, and I shant have much enjoyment of them.

Youll have to make up your mind that youll lose me presently, and then, Heaven only knows what will become of America. I have to educate all the nations. I have to educate England. Several of the Continental nations require a little education, but America most of all. And I shall die before Ive educated America properly. But I'm making a beginning.

Now I think it's time for me to get out of the way. I was asked to say something to you. I'm always glad to say something to you. I was asked to say something very agreeable to you. Ive done my best. Thats my aged idea of an agreeable speech. But, I'm quite friendly. I think youve always heard that about me; at any rate, it's been written—you ought to.

APPENDIX D

Entr'acte Between Laboratory Scene and Drawing Room Scene,
1934 Screenplay of *Pygmalion*

In his 1934 scenario for *Pygmalion*, and again in 1938, before he composed a phonetics lesson between Higgins and Liza, Shaw suggested this scene to bridge what corresponds to Acts II and III of the play.

A woodland with a lake and distant hills. October, November, December, January and February, impersonated by dancers, pursue each other across the scene. After December an old man, the Old Year, is followed by a child, the New Year. The dresses of the dancers change with the seasons. The landscape also changes, shewing the fall of the leaf in October, the freezing of the lake and the snow in December and January, and the approach of Spring in February. No dialogue. Music (not jazz).

This can be omitted: it is only a suggestion; but it would mark the break in the play, and would be a relief to the string of interiors. There is more fresh air in it than in the stale device of exhibiting a calendar with Father Time tearing off the months.

APPENDIX E

Ballroom Scene, 1934 Screenplay of *Pygmalion*.

Ambassador's quarters in London. In the street before the hall door, which has aw awning and a carpet across the sidewalk to the kerb. It is after dark. A grand reception is in progress. A small crowd is lined up to see the guests arrive.

A Rolls-Royce car drives up. Pickering, in evening dress, with medals and orders, alights, and hands out Liza in opera cloak, brilliant evening dress, diamonds, fan, flowers, and all accessories. Higgins follows. The car drives off, leaving the view of the carpet and awning unobstructed. The three go up the steps and into the house, the door opening for them as they approach.

The Colonel's style is perfect. Higgins, bringing up the rear, is elephantine and sulky.

First flight of grand staircase within the building. Liveried man servant at foot, announcing. Another on the landing above, announcing.

The three guests arrive. Liza goes up.

Colonel Pickering whispers to the servant before following her with Higgins.

FIRST SERVANT. Miss Doolittle. Colonel Pickering. Professor Higgins.

SECOND SERVANT [*as Liza passes him*] Miss Doolittle. Colonel Pickering. Professor Higgins.

The second flight. The landing at the top is occupied by the Ambassador and his wife, en grand tenue, *receiving in front of a crowd of chattering guests. Nothing of their greeting civilities or the responses thereto can be distinguished in the din of conversation.*

Liza is received and greeted. She gets through the ordeal gracefully and passes into the crowd. Pickering, evidently persona grata *with the Ambassador's wife, shakes hands warmly with her, and is introducing Higgins when the shot fades out.*

APPENDIX F

Ending, 1934 Screenplay of *Pygmalion*.

HIGGINS. Goodbye, mother. [*He is about to kiss her, when he recollects something*]. Oh, by the way, Eliza, order a ham and a Stilton cheese, will you? And buy me a pair of reindeer gloves, number eights, and a tie to match that new suit of mine. You can choose the color. [*His cheerful, careless, vigorous voice shews that he is incorrigible*].

LIZA [*disdainfully*] Buy them yourself. [*She sweeps out*].

MRS HIGGINS. I'm afraid youve spoiled that girl, Henry. But never mind, dear: I'll buy you the tie and gloves.

HIGGINS [*sunnily*] Oh, dont bother. She'll buy em all right enough. Goodbye.

They kiss. Mrs Higgins runs out. Higgins, left alone, rattles his cash in his pocket; chuckles; and disports himself in a highly self-satisfied manner, and goes out through the window to the balcony.

Higgins on the balcony smiling benevolently down to the party beneath.

Chelsea Embankment. Mrs Higgins's limousine standing opposite her door. Doolittle holds the car door open in a courtly manner for Mrs Higgins, who gets in. He gets in himself, leaving Liza on the pavement.

Freddy appears.

LIZA. Here he is, Mrs Higgins. May he come?

MRS HIGGINS. Certainly, dear. Room for four.

Liza kisses Freddy.

The balcony.

Higgins's smile changes to an expression of fury.

He shakes his fist at the kissing couple below.

The Embankment.

Liza cocks a snook prettily at Higgins, and gets into the car.

Freddy takes off his hat to Higgins in the Chaplin manner and follows Liza into the car.

The car drives off. Wedding march.

482

APPENDIX G

Spoken Preface to American Audiences of *Major Barbara*.

Filmed in 1940 and printed in various books and periodicals—including Vol. 3 of the Bodley Head edition of Shaw's plays, Mander and Mitchenson's *Theatrical Companion to Shaw*, *Variety* (21 May 1941), and *The Cleveland Plain Dealer* (25 May 1941)—this text is from the first mentioned work, revised to conform to Shaw's idiosyncratic punctuation.

Citizens of the United States of America, the whole 130 millions of you, I am sending you my old plays, just as you are sending us your old destroyers. Our government has very kindly thrown in a few naval bases as well; it makes the bargain perhaps more welcome to you. Now, the German humorist, I think his name is Dr Goebbels, he has got a great deal of fun out of that. He tells us—or rather he tells the rest of the world—that England has sold her colonies for scrap iron. Well, why shouldnt we? We are in very great need of scrap iron. We are collecting iron from door to door. Our women are bringing out their old saucepans; our men are bringing out their old bicycles, and you, with equal devotion, are bringing out your old destroyers. Well, a very good bargain for us. Every one of those destroyers will be worth much more to us than their weight in bicycles and saucepans.

And now, what about our colonies? Our colonies are always much the better when we have plenty of Americans visiting them. You see, in America you have all the gold in the world. We have to barter things for want of that gold, and accordingly, when we see Americans coming along with gold to spend, when we think of our colonies with American garrisons in them, we are delighted.

If you had only known, we would have given you those naval bases—Dr Goebbels calls them colonies, but let us be correct and call them naval bases—you could have had those naval bases for nothing but your friendship. Absolutely nothing. We should have been only too glad to have you. In fact, if you would like a few more, say in the Isle of Wight or the Isle of Man, or on the West Coast of Ireland, well, we shall be only too glad to welcome you. Delightedly!

Now, here I am in an English county, one of the counties that we call the home counties. I am within forty minutes' drive of the center of London, and at any

483

moment a bomb may crash through this roof and blow me to atoms, because the German bombers are in the skies. Now, please understand, I cant absolutely promise you such a delightful finish to this news item. Still, it may happen, so dont give up hope—yet. If it does happen, well, it will not matter very much to me. As you see, I am in my eighty-fifth year. I have shot my bolt, I have done my work. War or no war, my number is up. But if my films are still being shewn in America, my soul will go marching on, and that will satisfy me.

When I was a little boy, a child, just taught to read, I saw in the newspaper every day a column headed The Civil War in America. That is one of my first recollections. When I grew up they told me that that war in America had abolished black slavery, so that job having been done, I determined to devote my life as far as I could to the abolition of white slavery. That is just as much in your interest as it is in my interest or that of England. I hope you will have a hand in that abolition as you had a hand in the last abolition.

And I dont think I need detain you any longer. Look after my plays and look after my films. They are all devoted to the abolition of that sort of slavery. And I should like to imagine that when my mere bodily stuff is gone, I should like to imagine that you are still working with me, with my soul—in your old phrase—at that particular job. That is all I have got to say. And so, farewell!

APPENDIX H

Handwritten Preface to British Audiences of *Major Barbara*.

Filmed in 1940, printed in Vol. 3 of the Bodley Head edition of Shaw's plays and Costello's *The Serpent's Eye: Shaw and the Cinema*, this text is from Shaw's handwriting, seen on the screen.

Friend
     What you are about to see is not an idle tale of people who never existed and things that could never have happened. It is a PARABLE.
     Do not be alarmed: you will not be bored by it. It is, I hope, both true and inspired. Some of the people in it are real people whom I have met and talked to. One of the others may be YOU.
     There will be a bit of you in all of them. We are all members one of another. If you do not enjoy every word of it we shall both be equally disappointed.
     Well, friend: have I ever disappointed you? Have I not been
                         always your faithful servant
                         Bernard Shaw

APPENDIX I

The Barber's Shop Scene (*Cæsar and Cleopatra*).

At Gabriel Pascal's request, Shaw wrote this scene to replace another film sequence, in which an old musician and his harpist approach Alexandria (above, p. 439). Each one provides a transition between the scenes that correspond to the play's end of Act III and beginning of Act IV. Because Basil Sydney, who played Rufio, was no longer available when Shaw completed the scene, Pascal did not film it. Shaw was pleased. 'This sequence is quite unnecessary', he wrote on the first page of the typescript, and he told Pascal he composed the scene against his better judgment.

(NOTE: There must be no camera tricks in the change: nothing u n n a t u r a l. The fading out of the lighthouse and the sea may be slow and accompanied by music or distant shouting, but the barber's shop must appear instantaneously, fully lighted, with a clash of the full orchestra, cymbals fortissimo, quite frankly, without any attempt to make the change gradual. The atmosphere must be cleared with a bang for a fresh start. The suggested tricks with a basin and sponge appearing first are quite damnable: they would give away the illusion of reality and change the play into an exhibition of camera conjuring.)

A barber's shop in Alexandria. The barber is operating on a customer wrapped in the usual surplice. He has almost finished with him, and is holding two bronze mirrors (looking glasses have not yet been invented) so that the customer can see the back of his head.

BARBER. How is that, Excellency? [*Putting aside the mirrors*] Brilliantine?

CUSTOMER. Yes: plenty of it. But not the perfumed sort.

BARBER [*applying the wash and brushing it in*] I understand, Excellency. A royal major-domo must be neutral. If you have the same scent as a courtier he thinks you have stolen it from him.

CUSTOMER. True. I meet nobody but courtiers: you meet all sorts. These Romans now. What do you make of them?

BARBER. To a barber, Excellency, all men are alike. Romans, Greeks, Egyptians, Jews wear the same robe in my chair and say the same things. Fair or dark, the same scissors cuts them all. What can you say of any man but that he is a man?

CUSTOMER. But these Romans are barbarians: they burnt our library, one of

486

the seven wonders of the world. They are magicians: they dig wells in the salt sand and draw fresh water from them. Their biggest and heaviest men swim like dolphins and carry the Queen on their backs.

BARBER. That might be the Queen's magic. She rides on Cæsar's back now, on land as on the sea. She has made him king here these five months.

CUSTOMER. Do not believe it. He has made her Queen.

BARBER. One good turn deserves another. But I know nothing about women: I am not a lady's hairdresser.

CUSTOMER. And all Romans are alike to you?

BARBER. All men are alike to me.

CUSTOMER. You would not say that if you knew Cæsar and his henchman Rufio.

BARBER. Ah, I forgot Rufio. You are right, Excellency: no other man alive has such whiskers. My one professional ambition is to shave them off and make him look like a human being.

Rufio strides in.

Rufio. You are engaged. How soon will you be free?

BARBER. Your Worship's name was the last word in our mouths. Three minutes, general: not a moment more.

CUSTOMER. Dont you recognize me in this gown?

RUFIO. What! The royal major-domo! I crave your pardon: I have seen you only in your court splendor.

CUSTOMER [*to the barber*] Finish up quickly. Do not keep the general waiting.

RUFIO. Take it easy: I am in no hurry.

CUSTOMER. You are a busy man, general: always in a hurry. [*To the barber, rising*] There: thats enough. [*He throws off his gown and stands in his breeches and singlet until the barber fetches his official coat and arrays him in his courtly magnificence*].

Rufio throws himself into the vacated chair.

RUFIO. Now you look like yourself, major. [*The barber approaches him with the surplice*]. No gown for me. Take it away.

BARBER. But, general, the cut hair will be all over your clothes.

RUFIO. Cut a single hair and I will cut your thumbs off. Let my head alone. Attend to my whiskers.

BARBER [*terribly disappointed*] But am I not to cut them off?

RUFIO. No. Your Queen says they remind her of a lousy bird's nest. I have to banquet with her this afternoon. Make them look glossy and smell nice.

CUSTOMER. I must take my leave, general. I also have to be on duty at the banquet. Au revoir.

RUFIO [*offhandedly*] Good afternoon.

The customer goes out, giving a coin to the barber as he passes.

BARBER [*half voice*] A thousand thanks, Excellency. [*He bows the customer out, and returns to the chair*]. Nobody in Alexandria under sixty lets hair grow on his face, general. Can I not persuade you to have them off?

RUFIO. Have them off! What should I look like without them? My authority is in them. I should look like that bumptious noodle who has just left us. Do as I tell you; and look sharp about it.

The barber, with a sigh, resigns himself to his task.

The scene fades out.